KU-536-290

000000722691

1914

Also by Paul Ham

Hiroshima Nagasaki
Sandakan

PAUL HAM

1914

THE YEAR
THE WORLD ENDED

Doubleday

LONDON · TORONTO · SYDNEY · AUCKLAND · JOHANNESBURG

TRANSWORLD PUBLISHERS
61–63 Uxbridge Road, London W5 5SA
A Random House Group Company
www.transworldbooks.co.uk

First published in Australia
in 2013 by William Heinemann

First published in Great Britain
in 2014 by Doubleday
an imprint of Transworld Publishers

Copyright © Paul Ham 2013

Paul Ham has asserted his right under the Copyright, Designs
and Patents Act 1988 to be identified as the author of this work.

A CIP catalogue record for this book
is available from the British Library.

ISBNs 9780857522368

This book is sold subject to the condition that it shall not,
by way of trade or otherwise, be lent, resold, hired out,
or otherwise circulated without the publisher's prior
consent in any form of binding or cover other than that
in which it is published and without a similar condition,
including this condition, being imposed on the
subsequent purchaser.

Every effort has been made to acknowledge and contact the copyright holders for
permission to reproduce material contained in this book. Any copyright holders who
have been inadvertently omitted from acknowledgements and credits should contact
the publisher and omissions will be rectified in subsequent editions.

'Dulce et Decorum Est' by Wilfred Owen is reproduced from *Wilfred Owen: The War Poems*
by kind permission of the publisher, Chatto & Windus, and editor, Jon Stallworthy.

Original maps: Arthur Banks; restyled by Alicia Freile, apart from Europe 1914, Balkan 1911
and Balkans 1914 by Alicia Freile, Tango Media. Maps by Arthur Banks from *A Military Atlas
of the First World War*, published by Leo Cooper/Pen and Sword Books

Addresses for Random House Group Ltd companies outside the UK
can be found at: www.randomhouse.co.uk
The Random House Group Ltd Reg. No. 954009

The Random House Group Limited supports the Forest Stewardship Council® (FSC®),
the leading international forest-certification organisation. Our books carrying the FSC label
are printed on FSC®-certified paper. FSC is the only forest-certification scheme supported
by the leading environmental organisations, including Greenpeace. Our paper procurement
policy can be found at www.randomhouse.co.uk/environment

Typeset in 10.5/15 pt Baskerville
Printed and bound in Great Britain by
Clays Ltd, Bungay, Suffolk

2 4 6 8 10 9 7 5 3 1

MIX
Paper from
responsible sources
FSC® C016897

To the unknown soldier

DUDLEY LIBRARIES	
000000722691	
Askews & Holts	26-May-2014
	£25.00
LYE	

Contents

Contents

Original maps courtesy of Arthur Banks and restyled by Alicia Freile, apart from Europe 1914, Balkans 1911 and Balkans 1914 by Alicia Freile.

0	100	200	300	400

Miles

0	200	400	600	800

KM

Archangel

Petrograd

TONIA

VONIA

Riga

NIA

RUSSIA

Moscow

Smolensk

Minsk

UKRAINE

Rostov

ROUMANIA

Bucharest

Black Sea

BULGARIA

ofia

Constantinople

Adrianople

TURKEY

ka

E

Athens

CYPRUS

CRETE

Allied Powers

Neutral Powers

Central Powers

Principal Rail Lines

EUROPE
1914

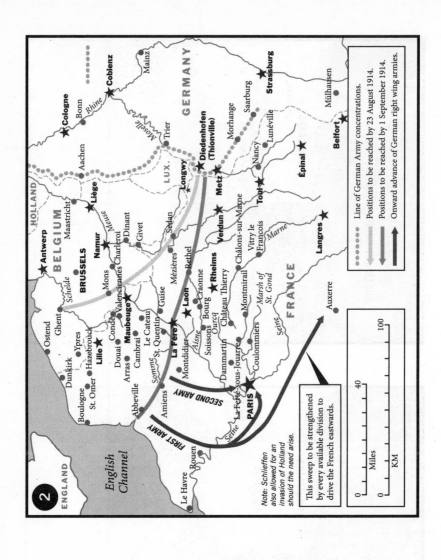

SCHLIEFFEN PLAN –
FRANCE

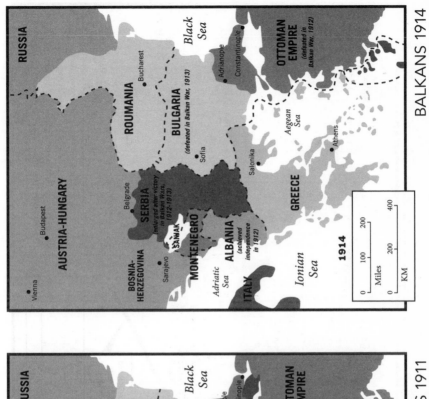

BALKANS 1914

OTTOMAN EMPIRE
(defeated in Balkan War, 1912)

Black Sea

RUSSIA

ROUMANIA

Bucharest

BULGARIA
(defeated in Balkan War, 1913)

Adrianople

Constantinople

Sofia

Aegean Sea

Salonika

Athens

AUSTRIA-HUNGARY

Vienna

Budapest

Belgrade

SERBIA
(enlarged after victory in Balkan Wars, 1912-1913)

SANJAK

BOSNIA-HERZEGOVINA

Sarajevo

MONTENEGRO

ALBANIA
(achieved independence in 1912)

Adriatic Sea

GREECE

ITALY

Ionian Sea

1914

Miles
0   100   200   400

KM
0   200   400

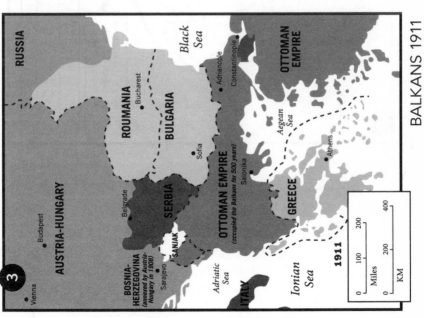

BALKANS 1911

RUSSIA

Black Sea

ROUMANIA

Bucharest

BULGARIA

Sofia

Adrianople

Constantinople

Aegean Sea

OTTOMAN EMPIRE

Salonika

Athens

AUSTRIA-HUNGARY

Vienna

Budapest

Belgrade

SERBIA

SANJAK

BOSNIA-HERZEGOVINA
(annexed by Austria-Hungary in 1908)

Sarajevo

OTTOMAN EMPIRE
(occupied the Balkans for 500 years)

Adriatic Sea

GREECE

ITALY

Ionian Sea

1911

Miles
0   100   200   400

KM
0   200   400

3

GERMAN ATTACKS ON BELGIUM
AND THE FRENCH FRONTIERS

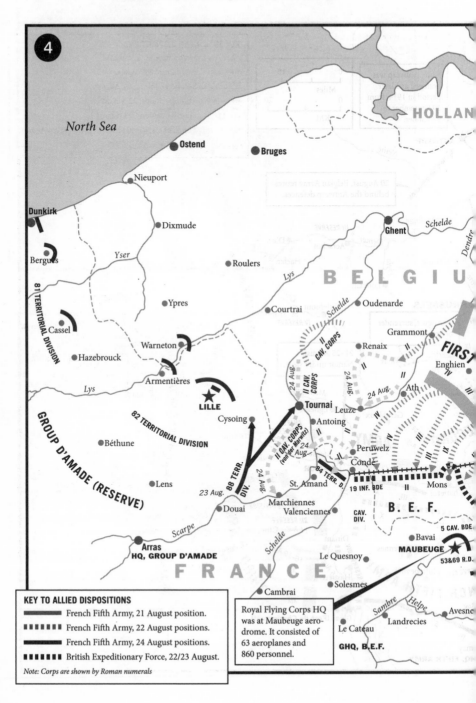

4

North Sea

HOLLAN

Ostend

Bruges

Nieuport

Dunkirk

Dixmude

Ghent

Schelde

Bergues

Yser

Roulers

Lys

B E L G I U

Cassel

Ypres

Courtrai

Schelde

Oudenarde

81 TERRITORIAL DIVISION

Hazebrouck

Warneton

Grammont

Renaix

FIRST

Armentières

Lys

II CAV. CORPS

Enghien

LILLE

82 TERRITORIAL DIVISION

Cysoing

II CAV. CORPS

24 Aug.

24 Aug.

24 Aug.

Ath

Béthune

GROUP D'AMADE (RESERVE)

Tournai

Leuze

Antoing

II CAV CORPS (von der Marwitz)

24 Aug.

Peruwelz

Condé

Lens

88 TERR. DIV.

23 Aug.

24 Aug.

St. Amand

84 TERR. D.

19 INF. BDE

II

Mons

Douai

Marchiennes
Valenciennes

CAV.
DIV.

B. E. F.

Scarpe

Schelde

Bavai

5 CAV. BDE

Arras
HQ, GROUP D'AMADE

Le Quesnoy

MAUBEUGE

53&69 R.D.

F R A N C E

Cambrai

Solesmes

Sambre

Helpe

Avesne

Landrecies

Le Cateau

GHQ, B.E.F.

KEY TO ALLIED DISPOSITIONS

▬▬▬ French Fifth Army, 21 August position.

▪▪▪▪▪▪ French Fifth Army, 22 August positions.

━━━ French Fifth Army, 24 August positions.

▪▪▪▪▪▪ British Expeditionary Force, 22/23 August.

Note: Corps are shown by Roman numerals

Royal Flying Corps HQ
was at Maubeuge aero-
drome. It consisted of
63 aeroplanes and
860 personnel.

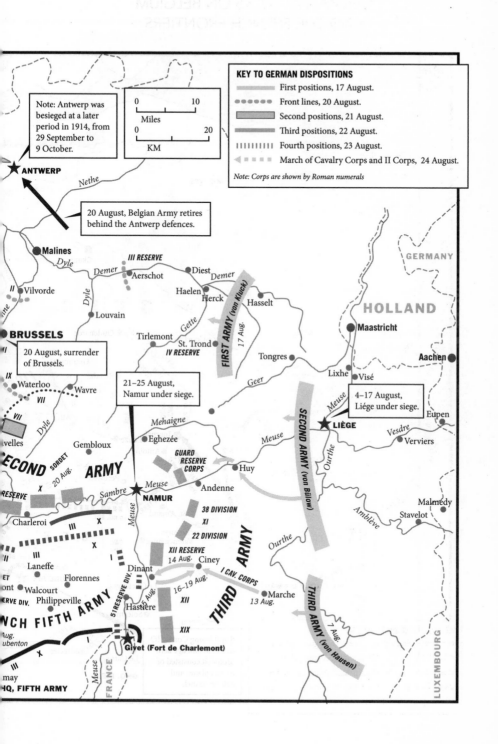

KEY TO GERMAN DISPOSITIONS

First positions, 17 August.
Front lines, 20 August.
Second positions, 21 August.
Third positions, 22 August.
Fourth positions, 23 August.
March of Cavalry Corps and II Corps, 24 August.

Note: Corps are shown by Roman numerals

Note: Antwerp was besieged at a later period in 1914, from 29 September to 9 October.

0   10
Miles
0   20
KM

ANTWERP

Nethe

20 August, Belgian Army retires behind the Antwerp defences.

Malines

Dyle

III RESERVE

Demer   Aerschot   Diest   *Demer*

Haelen   Herck

Hasselt

GERMANY

II   Vilvorde

Dyle

Louvain

FIRST ARMY (von Kluck)

17 Aug.

HOLLAND

BRUSSELS

Tirlemont   St. Trond
IV RESERVE

Tongres

Maastricht

20 August, surrender of Brussels.

Gette

Geer

Lixhe   Visé

Aachen

IX

Waterloo   Wavre

VII

21–25 August, Namur under siege.

Mehaigne

Eghezée

4–17 August, Liége under siege.

VII

Dyle

Gembloux

SECOND ARMY (von Bülow)

Meuse

LIÈGE

Vesdre

Verviers

Meuse

Ourthe

Eupen

velles

GUARD RESERVE CORPS

Huy

ECOND   SORDET   ARMY

20 Aug.

Andenne

Malmédy

Stavelot

X

RESERVE

Sambre   *Meuse*

NAMUR

Amblève

Charleroi

III   X

38 DIVISION
XI

Meuse

22 DIVISION

Ourthe

III

Laneffe

XII RESERVE
14 Aug.   Ciney

THIRD ARMY

ET

ont   Walcourt

Florennes

Dinant

I CAV. CORPS

ERVE DIV.   Philippeville

I

16–19 Aug.

Marche
13 Aug.

THIRD ARMY (von Hausen)

7 Aug.

5 Aug.

XII

NCH FIFTH ARMY

5 RESERVE DIV.

Hastière

XIX

Aug.

ubenton

X

I

Givet (Fort de Charlemont)

Meuse

III

may

HQ, FIFTH ARMY

FRANCE

LUXEMBOURG

THE RETREAT

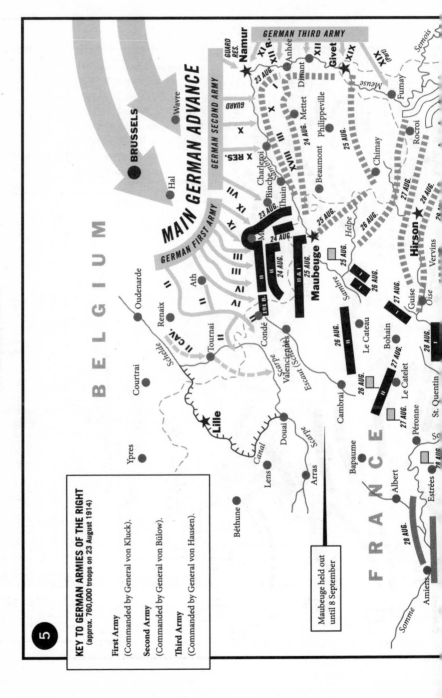

KEY TO GERMAN ARMIES OF THE RIGHT
(approx. 760,000 troops on 23 August 1914)

First Army
(Commanded by General von Kluck).

Second Army
(Commanded by General von Bülow).

Third Army
(Commanded by General von Hausen).

5

MAIN GERMAN ADVANCE

GERMAN FIRST ARMY

GERMAN SECOND ARMY

GERMAN THIRD ARMY

Maubeuge held out
until 8 September

BELGIUM

FRANCE

BRUSSELS

Namur

Givet

Hirson

Lille

Maubeuge

Hal
Wavre
Oudenarde
Courtrai
Renaix
Ypres
Ath
Tournai
Condé
Valenciennes
Douai
Lens
Arras
Bapaume
Albert
Cambrai
Le Cateau
Bohain
Le Catelet
Péronne
St. Quentin
Guise
Vervins
Roctoi
Chimay
Beaumont
Philippeville
Mettet
Dinant
Anhée
Fumay
Estrées
Amiens
Béthune

Charleroi
Binche
Thuin

GUARD RES.
XII R.
XI
XII
XIX
XIX (part)
GUARD
X
X RES.
VII
XI
IX
III
III
IV
IV
II
II
I CAV.
II CAV.

23 AUG.
24 AUG.
25 AUG.
26 AUG.
27 AUG.
28 AUG.
1918!
I & I
II & I

Scheldt
Scarpe
Escaut (Scheldt)
Canal
Scarpe
Somme
Sambre
Helpe
Oise
Meuse
Semois

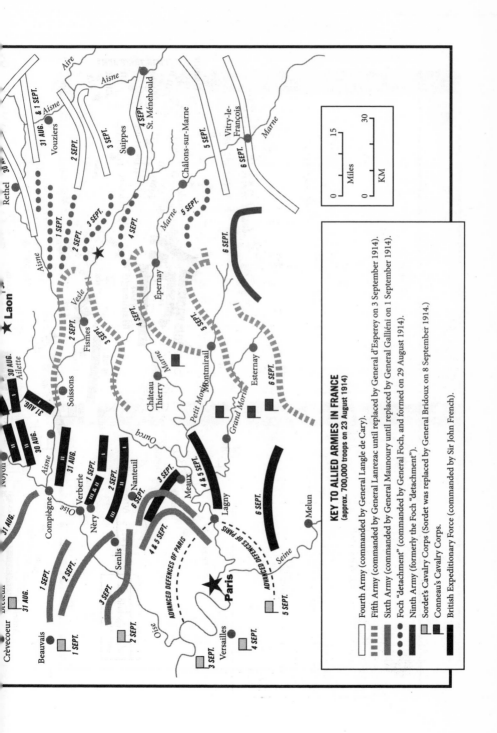

KEY TO ALLIED ARMIES IN FRANCE
(approx. 700,000 troops on 23 August 1914)

Fourth Army (commanded by General Langle de Cary).

Fifth Army (commanded by General Lanrezac until replaced by General d'Esperey on 3 September 1914).

Sixth Army (commanded by General Maunoury until replaced by General Galliéni on 1 September 1914).

Foch "detachment" (commanded by General Foch, and formed on 29 August 1914).

Ninth Army (formerly the Foch "detachment").

Sordet's Cavalry Corps (Sordet was replaced by General Bridoux on 8 September 1914.)

Conneau's Cavalry Corps.

British Expeditionary Force (commanded by Sir John French).

THE MIRACLE OF THE MARNE

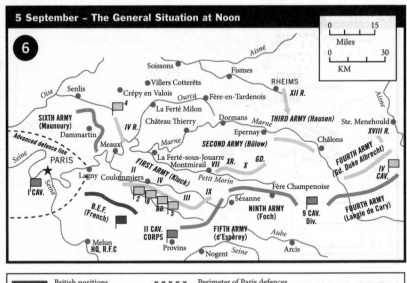

5 September – The General Situation at Noon

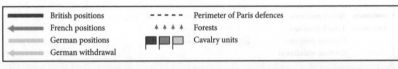

British positions

French positions

German positions

German withdrawal

Perimeter of Paris defences

Forests

Cavalry units

6 September – Withdrawal of the German First Army's Right Wing

7 September – Withdrawal of the German First Army's Left Wing

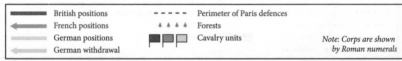

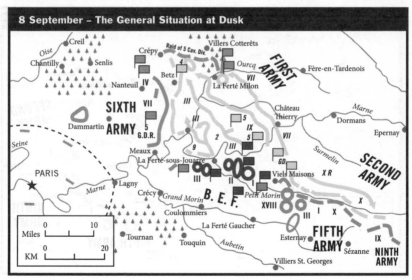

8 September – The General Situation at Dusk

THE BATTLE OF TANNENBERG

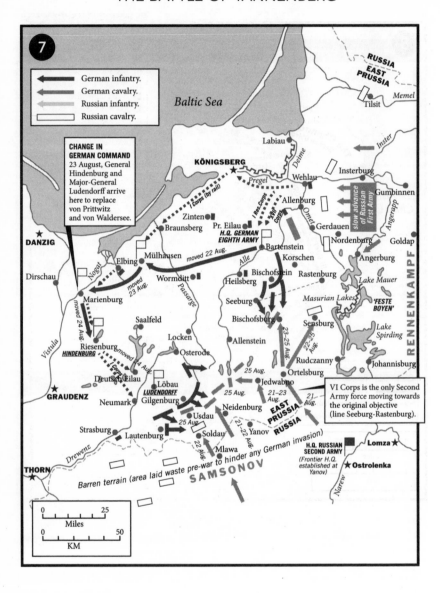

7

German infantry.
German cavalry.
Russian infantry.
Russian cavalry.

Baltic Sea

RUSSIA
EAST
PRUSSIA

Memel

Tilsit

CHANGE IN GERMAN COMMAND
23 August, General Hindenburg and Major-General Ludendorff arrive here to replace von Prittwitz and von Waldersee.

Labiau

KÖNIGSBERG

Wehlau   Insterburg

Inster

Pregel   Allenburg   Gumbinnen

I Corps (by rail)   I Res.Corps   Gerdauen

Deime

XVII Corps

Zinten   Pr. Eilau
Braunsberg   **H.Q. GERMAN EIGHTH ARMY**

Omet

Nordenburg   Goldap

slow advance of Russian First Army

Angerapp

★ DANZIG

Elbing   Mülhausen   *moved 22 Aug.*   Bartenstein
Korschen   Angerburg

Nogat   *moved 23 Aug.*   Wormditt   *Alle*   Bischofstein   Rastenburg
Heilsberg

Dirschau

Vistula

Marienburg

Saalfeld

Riesenburg *moved 24 Aug.*
HINDENBURG

Deutsch Eilau

★ GRAUDENZ   Neumark   Gilgenburg

Löbau
LUDENDORFF

Passarge

Seeburg

Bischofsburg

Locken
Osterode   Allenstein

Lake Mauer

Masurian Lakes

'FESTE BOYEN'

Sensburg   *Lake Spirding*

23–25 Aug.   *22–23 Aug.*
Rudczanny   Johannisburg

25 Aug.   Ortelsburg
Jedwabno

RENNENKAMPF

Strasburg   Lautenburg

Usdau
25 Aug.   Soldau

Neidenburg   *25 Aug.*   *21–23 Aug.*   *21 Aug.*
EAST PRUSSIA   *21–22 Aug.*   Yanov   RUSSIA

VI Corps is the only Second Army force moving towards the original objective (line Seeburg-Rastenburg).

22 Aug.   Mlawa
to hinder any German invasion   **H.Q. RUSSIAN SECOND ARMY**
(Frontier H.Q. established at Yanov)

Lomza ★

★ Ostrolenka

THORN ★   *Drewenz*   Barren terrain (area laid waste pre-war   **SAMSONOV**

Narew

0   25
Miles
0   50
KM

THE RACE TO THE SEA

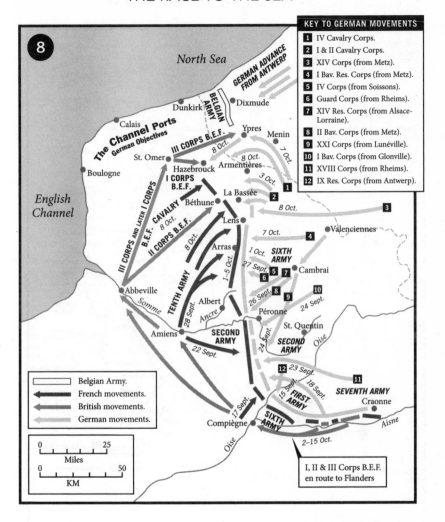

KEY TO GERMAN MOVEMENTS

1. IV Cavalry Corps.
2. I & II Cavalry Corps.
3. XIV Corps (from Metz).
4. I Bav. Res. Corps (from Metz).
5. IV Corps (from Soissons).
6. Guard Corps (from Rheims).
7. XIV Res. Corps (from Alsace-Lorraine).
8. II Bav. Corps (from Metz).
9. XXI Corps (from Lunéville).
10. I Bav. Corps (from Glonville).
11. XVIII Corps (from Rheims).
12. IX Res. Corps (from Antwerp).

North Sea

GERMAN ADVANCE FROM ANTWERP

Dunkirk   Dixmude
Calais
BELGIAN ARMY
The Channel Ports
German Objectives   Ypres   Menin
III CORPS B.E.F.
St. Omer   8 Oct.
Boulogne   Hazebrouck   Armentières   8 Oct.
English Channel   **I CORPS B.E.F.**   3 Oct.   **1**
III CORPS AND LATER I CORPS   La Bassée   **2**
B.E.F. CAVALRY   8 Oct.   Béthune   8 Oct.   **3**
II CORPS B.E.F.   8 Oct.   Lens
8 Oct.   7 Oct.   **4**   Valenciennes
Arras   1 Oct.   **SIXTH ARMY**
Abbeville   1–5 Oct.   27 Sept.   **5 7**   Cambrai
Somme   28 Sept.   **6**
TENTH ARMY   Albert   26 Sept.   **8 9**   **10**
Ancre   24 Sept.
Amiens   Péronne   St. Quentin
SECOND ARMY   24 Sept.   **SECOND ARMY**   Oise
22 Sept.   24 Sept.
12 23 Sept.   **11**
15 Sept.   18 Sept.   **SEVENTH ARMY**
FIRST ARMY   Craonne
17 Sept.   **SIXTH ARMY**
Compiègne   Aisne
Oise   2–15 Oct.

I, II & III Corps B.E.F. en route to Flanders

☐ Belgian Army.
◀ French movements.
◀ British movements.
◀ German movements.

0 ————— 25
Miles
0 ————— 50
KM

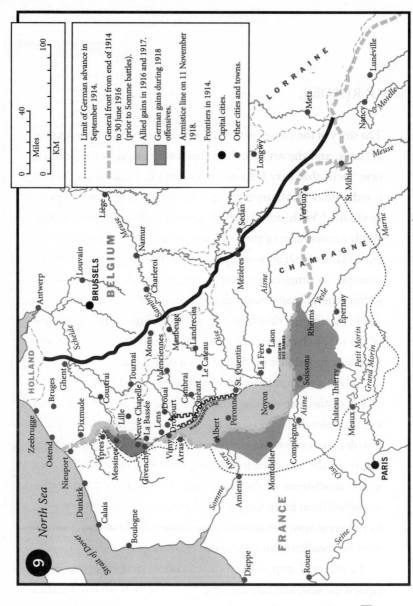

THE WESTERN
FRONT,
1914–1918

9

North Sea

Strait of Dover

HOLLAND

BELGIUM

FRANCE

BRUSSELS

PARIS

LORRAINE

CHAMPAGNE

HINDENBURG LINE

CHEMIN DES DAMES

Antwerp
Zeebrugge
Ostend
Nieuport
Dunkirk
Calais
Boulogne
Dieppe
Rouen
Bruges
Ghent
Courtrai
Dixmude
Ypres
Messines
Givenchy
Lille
Neuve Chapelle
La Bassée
Lens
Douai
Vimy
Drocourt
Arras
Cambrai
Quéant
Albert
Péronne
St. Quentin
Le Cateau
Landrecies
Maubeuge
Mons
Valenciennes
Tournai
Amiens
Montdidier
Noyon
Compiègne
Soissons
Château Thierry
Meaux
Rheims
Épernay
Laon
La Fère
Mézières
Sedan
Charleroi
Namur
Liège
Louvain
Verdun
St. Mihiel
Longwy
Metz
Nancy
Lunéville

North Sea
Somme
Ancre
Oise
Seine
Aisne
Aisne
Vesle
Petit Morin
Grand Morin
Marne
Meuse
Oise
Schelde
Sambre
Meuse
Moselle

Miles
0   40   100
0   100
KM

.... Limit of German advance in
        September 1914.

━ ━ ━ General front from end of 1914
        to 30 June 1916 (prior to Somme battles).

▢   Allied gains in 1916 and 1917.

▨   German gains during 1918
        offensives.

━━━   Armistice line on 11 November
        1918.

· · · · Frontiers in 1914.

●   Capital cities.

•   Other cities and towns.

DEAR READER,

The story of the causes of the Great War has been told thousands of times, and the archives have been ransacked in the hunt for new 'facts' that may help us understand it. Perhaps the subject is exhausted? Perhaps there are no new themes, facts, heroes or villains? Yet history is never complete, and, daringly, on this 100th anniversary of the outbreak of the First World War, this book takes a fresh approach, in several modest ways. It aims, for example, to simplify the story, to make the labyrinth accessible to the general reader without compromising the integrity of the whole. At times, it simply offers a portrait of the thinking of some of the main characters, to show how this reflected a pervasive feeling or mood that made war more or less likely.

1914 is a straightforward narrative history that exhumes the causes of the war through the accumulation of events, actions and attitudes that led to it. In this way, it sets that fateful year in a broader context, taking the reader on a journey that necessarily begins in the last decades of the nineteenth century and ends in the maelstrom of the twentieth. The year 1914 cannot be wrenched from its anchorage in time and examined in isolation. In the same way, the terms 'conservative', 'liberal' and 'radical' must be considered in their proper situations.

In places, I step outside the narrative and reflect on what caused the war, and how it ended the world as its contemporaries knew it. For example, was the war an act of God or a necessary Darwinian struggle, both of which the human hand was helpless to avert, as many leaders later claimed? How did the experiences of the rulers (monarchs, politicians, diplomats in the salons of power) compare with those of the ruled (ordinary men and women) who fought the battles?

Throughout, I rely on the primary archives of the main participant countries, as well as the classic texts. I owe a particular debt to the greatest writers on the subject, including Luigi Albertini, Niall Ferguson, Fritz Fischer, Martin Gilbert, John Keegan, John Keiger, Paul Kennedy, Bernadotte Schmitt, Zara Steiner, David Stevenson, Hew Strachan, Barbara Tuchman and Samuel R. Williamson. And I freely draw on new and less obvious sources, to set the scene for an avoidable nightmare that would determine the direction of the twentieth century.

Yours sincerely,

Paul Ham, Paris

PRELUDE

THE LONG SHADOW OF SUMMER, 1914

THE EUROPEAN SUMMER OF 1914 WAS WARMER and drier than usual. The leisured classes took tea in their sunrooms, went punting on the rivers, and attended their customary balls and parties. 'One lolled outside on a folding canvas chaise . . . One read outdoors, went on picnics, had tea served from a white wicker table under the trees,' writes the critic Paul Fussell, with that peculiarly American fondness for upper-class English social rites.[1] The poor waited on the rich, worked in the fields, mines and sweatshops, or begged. And they were kept below stairs, as usual.

The 'Gilded Age' continues to be resurrected in the twenty-first century, in popular screenplays, novels and films. The first episodes of the television series *Downton Abbey* and *Parade's End* drew millions of viewers, enchanted by the aristocratic world of pre-war Oxbridge, winged collars and formal dress at dinner. In those tranquil days, it seemed everyone was able to quote something from the classics. Perhaps the English officer *was* the most literate young man ever to don a uniform? Many would read Shakespeare, the romantic poets and the Bible in the trenches. Many wrote poems, dared, as the French novelist Louis-Ferdinand Céline would write, 'to compose

quatrains in an abbatoir'.[2] 'Literature dominated the war from beginning to end,' Fussell claims.[3]

Reminiscences of that July so often lapse into 'mawkish and
maudlin' sentiments about a 'sun-dappled and cultured civilisation',
warns the historian Hew Strachan.[4] And no doubt contemporary
films and novels tend to draw on the experiences, or social types, of
a few enlightened spirits of that lost era. A recurring character, for
example, is the gallant young poet Siegfried Sassoon, Marlborough
and Cambridge-educated. That summer, we glimpse him fresh back
from fox hunting and about to play a game of county cricket, a 'nice'
unquestioning youth of good family, an 'athlete and dreamer',[5] and
unrecognisable as the broken man three years later, old before his
time, who would declare through his shell shock a 'splendid war on
the war'.[6] And here is Sassoon's fellow officer, Wilfred Owen, whom
we find teaching English to French boys in a village in Bordeaux
before the war, conceiving sweet poems with none of the rest-
less agony of the disturbed soldier who would write 'Anthem for
Doomed Youth' (before he himself would die on the Western Front).
Another is the writer Robert Graves, similarly young and brilliant,
and a stranger to the bitter old curmudgeon who would flay in the
flintiest prose the politicians whose gift to his generation was the first
day of the Somme (in *Goodbye to All That*).

Yet the name the English-speaking world romantically attaches
to the Great War is that of the poet Rupert Brooke. The author
of 'The Soldier' was 'the handsomest young man in England',
said Yeats, 'a golden warrior', who was said to express the soul of
England.[7] Almost inevitably, he was Cambridge educated and a public-school dandy of the first order. 'Oh my darling are you doing too
much?' Brooke wrote to an actor friend. 'You looked so like a tired
child last night at Drury Lane. If you knew how difficult it was for
me not to take you in my arms, with Queen Alexandria and George
Bernard Shaw . . . all looking on.'[8] Brooke's death, in 1915, seemed to
inter the spirit of the age, in the eyes of his Bloomsbury contemporaries and, most recently, in Alan Hollinghurst's novel *The Stranger's*

Child, whose main character is modelled on him. Less well known is the pathos of Brooke's demise: he never saw combat and died of an infected mosquito bite on his way to Gallipoli.

These are the characters whose 'types' are so often used in the English-speaking world to evoke all that would perish in the Great War. That their battered lives should be deployed to symbolise a 'lost generation' is hardly their fault. Yet it skews the picture. Millions of ordinary young men, with no literary pretensions or public-school vowels – British, French, German, Russian, Serbian, Austro-Hungarian, Indian, African, Australian, Canadian, Irish, New Zealanders – were similarly scarred and lie forgotten in 'some corner of a foreign field'[9] or remembered only by their families, in village services, their remains buried in a distant graveyard, their letters gathering dust in library archives.

Others would survive the war and achieve immortality of a different kind. Céline, born Louis Ferdinand Auguste Destouches and decorated for bravery in 1914, would become a French novelist (author of *Journey to the End of the Night*, regarded as one of the finest novels of the twentieth century), an anti-semite and alleged Nazi collaborator during the Second World War, redeemed by the brilliance of his prose and his care for the poor. James Chadwick, interned in Germany in 1914, where he had been studying physics at the Technical University of Berlin, would earn the Nobel Prize for Physics for his discovery of the neutron, critical to the construction of the atomic bomb used on Hiroshima. Fellow physicist Erwin Schrödinger, who served as an officer in the Austrian Fortress Artillery during the war, would pioneer the wave theory of quantum mechanics and formulate the paradoxical mind experiment known as Schrödinger's Cat. And, of course, the failed artist Adolf Hitler, who volunteered for the German infantry in 1914 and earned the Iron Cross for bravery, would rise to lead Germany to ignominious ruin in another world war 30 years later.

—

The tranquillity of those days disguised an extreme peril. Few realised that a meeting of Austro-Hungarian ministers had effectively
declared war on Serbia on 7 July 1914, three weeks before the outbreak of hostilities (see Chapter 25). And some cities were far from
peaceful. Huge rallies filled Berlin, Vienna and Belgrade. The warm
July weather and the strange sense of something in the air drew
people out of their homes. In the aftermath of Franz Ferdinand's
assassination, on 28 June 1914, lynch mobs prowled the streets of
Vienna and Budapest. Thousands clamoured for war against their
perceived enemies, be they Slav, Teuton, Latin or Anglo-Saxon –
'race' was a much bigger factor in the war than we suppose. When
war was declared, in early August, there was open euphoria, weeping and embracing, old friends shaking hands. Adolf Hitler fell to
his knees and 'thanked heaven from an overflowing heart that it
had granted me the good fortune to be alive at such a time'.[10] It is
even claimed that those balmy days hastened the leaders' decision to declare war, by enabling mass outdoor protests in favour of
hostilities.[11]

Were European leaders so impressionable? Were the people and
the press – Britain's all-powerful 'public opinion' – really willing
war? Had public opinion compelled the German, French, Russian
and British Governments to declare war? It seems unlikely. A few
thousand extreme nationalists, the jingo minority and a complicit
media made a big noise but were hardly representative of the mainstream. The warmongering on display in Berlin, Belgrade, Vienna
and Paris did not reflect the general mood in Europe. Most French,
British, Russian and German people did not want war, but they
were powerless to stop it. 'Militarism was far from being the domi-
nant force in European politics on the eve of the Great War,' concludes Niall Ferguson. 'On the contrary, it was in political decline
. . . The evidence is unequivocal: Europeans were not marching to
war, but turning their backs on militarism.'[12] The July protests were
unrepresentative of the feelings of millions of quiet, unasked mothers and fathers, wives and sisters, who dreaded the loss of their

sons, brothers and husbands in a coming conflagration.

—

Europe's rulers and political leaders knew something most of their people did not: a war was coming. A few powerful, old, aristocratic men brought war on the world behind closed doors, free from the scrutiny of a fully enfranchised public or an uncensored press. They later claimed they were 'shocked' by it and unable to prevent it. Yet, three weeks before Germany invaded France, the German chancellor Theobald von Bethmann-Hollweg could say that he 'expects that a war, whatever its outcome, will result in the uprooting of everything that exists'.[13] He played a central role in its outcome, yet later claimed, as did other leaders, that he was helpless to stop it. Yet such premonitions of armageddon filled the minds of Europe's rulers years before 1914.

For most ordinary people, those premonitions began a few weeks before the declaration of war, in July 1914. Years later, they would look back on those summer days through the lens of a global conflict of unspeakable horror, loss and waste. And the contrast was unbearable. Understandably, they longed for that blissful peace, engraved in their minds as warm and sunbathed, as if idealising the weather would somehow suspend in aspic, if never quite retrieve, the 'eminently pastoral' pre-war world.[14]

A hundred years on, we dare to call it innocence. Or we presume, in our dreadful knowingness, to call it madness, or callous indifference, at a time when the greatest war machines and largest land armies were mobilising to destroy their world. But that is to project the opening blows of the bloodiest century back on a stranger, simpler time, before the guns of August blew it apart forever. The simple truth is that most people, as always, did not know what was going to happen next.

Part 1

THE TYRANNY OF THE PAST, 1870–1900s

1

NIJINSKY'S FAUN

*The extraordinary thing was the way in which everyone took it
for granted that this oozing, bulging wealth of the English upper
and upper-middle classes would last forever, and was part of
the order of things . . . Before the war the worship of money was
entirely unreflecting and untroubled by any pang of conscience. The
goodness of money was as unmistakable as the goodness of health
or beauty, and a glittering car, a title, or a horde of servants was
mixed up in people's minds with the idea of actual moral virtue.*
George Orwell, 'Such, Such Were the Joys'

Only by understanding the past may we free ourselves from its
tyranny.

—

They were a louche, happy tribe, the Edwardian rich. They satiated
themselves in the literature, art and finery of everything that went
by the name of 'modern' during that period known to posterity
as La Belle Époque, La Fin de Siècle and the Gilded Age. Artists,
musicians and revolutionaries were thought to have flourished in
what nobody knew would be the last years of a relatively peaceful

1

era, between the Franco-Prussian War of 1870–71 and the summer of 1914. For many, it was a time of great prosperity and an efflorescence of artistic and scientific talent redounding to the genius of the cultural heart of the civilised world: Paris. And it was a time of upheaval. 'The world has changed less since the time of Jesus Christ than it has in the last thirty years,' wrote the young French poet Charles Péguy in 1913.[1] (He would soon die on the Western Front.)

Some things had not changed: chiefly, the way most men and women *thought*. For most people, the conservative triumvirate of God, King and Country remained firmly in place in the 1890s and 1900s. The decadent values of the Belle Époque had not overturned half a century of Victorian values. In the 1900s, old-fashioned conservatism, and respect for tradition, were making strident returns, mainly among the young. In European schools and universities, French and German students were reacting against the dilettantism and indulgence of their parents' Bohemian generation, and rallying to the standards of the old world: patriotic, Christian and authoritarian.[2]

The conservative mainstream stoutly resisted democratic reforms such as votes for women, better working conditions, social welfare and universal healthcare. In this sense, the radicalism on display had barely impinged on the actual polity of the pre-war world. By the turn of the century, Australia and New Zealand were the only Western countries to have extended the vote to women, and Germany under Bismarck was the only European country to have introduced a recognisable welfare state and universal male suffrage. The essential conflict of the era, observed George Orwell, 'was between the tradition of 19th century asceticism and the actual existing luxury and snobbery of the pre-1914 age'.[3]

Victorian values did not simply disappear with the passing of Queen Victoria. She died in 1901, in the arms of her beloved grandson, Kaiser Wilhelm II of Germany. Her death touched all of Europe, for Victoria was the royal matriarch of three empires, closely linked through royal blood: Britain, Germany and Russia. Tsar

Nicholas II, Kaiser Wilhelm II and King Edward VII were cousins. The reign of Edward, Victoria's dissolute son, lent a decadent veneer to an era that clung to her train long after her death. When she died, many shared the feelings of the novelist Henry James:

> I mourn the safe, motherly old middle class queen who held the nation warm under the folds of her big, hideous, Scotch-plaid shawl . . . I felt her death far more than I should have expected. She was a sustaining symbol and the wild waters are upon us now.[4]

Or they felt as George Orwell did. Looking back on his pre-war childhood, he wrote in 1947:

> There never was, in the history of the world, a time when the sheer vulgar fatness of wealth, without any kind of aristocratic elegance to redeem it, was so obtrusive as in those years before 1914. It was the age when crazy millionaires in curly top-hats and lavender waistcoats gave champagne parties in rococo house boats on the Thames, the age of diabolo and hobble skirts, the age of the 'knut' in his grey bowler and cutaway coat, the age of *The Merry Widow*, Saki's novels, *Peter Pan* and *Where the Rainbow Ends*, the age when people talked about chocs and cigs and ripping and topping and heavenly, when they went for divvy weekends at Brighton and had scrumptious teas at the Troc. From the whole decade before 1914 there seems to breathe forth a smell of the more vulgar, un-grown-up kind of luxury, a smell of brilliantine and *creme-de-menthe* and soft-centred chocolates – an atmosphere, as it were, of eating everlasting strawberry ices on green lawns to the tune of the Eton boating song. The extraordinary thing was the way in which everyone took it for granted that this oozing, bulging wealth of the English upper and upper-middle classes would last forever, and was part of the order of things . . . Before the war the worship of money was

entirely unreflecting and untroubled by any pang of conscience. The goodness of money was as unmistakable as the goodness of health or beauty, and a glittering car, a title, or a horde of servants was mixed up in people's minds with the idea of actual moral virtue.[5]

Behind this social gossamer were the iron laws of laissez-faire economics, which prevailed through to 1914 and were worshipped as if they existed in an objective reality beyond the reach of mankind's ability to amend them. Those blessed by unfettered capitalism – the rich – were good, successful and somehow wholesome. All who were damned by it – the poor – were dirty, sinful and somehow deserving of their plight. A family may prosper one moment and be ruined the next. Charity remained the chief form of welfare. Government intervention was frowned upon, and deemed helpless before the 'natural law' of the invisible hand: trade cycles, price fluctuations and unemployment. If the apostles of the Gladstonian era were right *in principle* – that a free market engendered individual liberty and a higher standard of living more efficaciously than any other economic 'system' – the practice required moderation and amendment, for an unrestrained free market plainly had not delivered the services needed to sustain a civilised society. The gospels of complete market freedom, which perversely gave rise to its opposite – crushing monopoly and government favouritism – went virtually unchallenged before 1914, and were not fundamentally altered until 1930.[6]

—

Henry James's wild waters of modernism were thought to have threatened the conservative values underlying the nineteenth century's asceticism and idolatry of money. We do not use the term 'conservative' here in a narrow, party political sense. We mean the forces of *preservation* of the existing economic and social system. The radical ideals of the *fin de siècle* – sensual, liberal, democratic – were supposed to have transformed the world, a world the artists and writers readily absorbed and reflected. In the visual arts, the 'impressionists' were said to have broken down reactionary ways of seeing, and challenged the very foundation of a squalid and unjust reality . . . at least, to the few who were looking. On 29 April 1874, six artists – Pissarro, Monet, Sisley, Renoir, Degas and Guillaumin – held 'L'exposition du boulevard des Capucines: Les impressionnistes', the first major exhibition of the new movement. It appeared three years after the end of the Franco-Prussian War, which devastated France's impression of itself as a great power. The six artists had signed a petition refusing to show their work at the official Paris salon.

The establishment scorned or were simply indifferent to the show, revealing a glimpse of the true spirit of the age. The critic Jules Castagnary sneered:

> The common view [of these artists] as a collective force within our disintegrating age is their determination not to aim for perfection . . . Once the impression is captured, they declare their role finished. Starting from idealization, they will arrive at that degree of unbridled romanticism where nature has become a mere excuse for dreaming, and where the imagination has become powerless to formulate anything except personal subjective fantasies, with no echo in general reason, because they are without control or any possible verification in reality.[7]

Another critic, Albert Wolff, merely scoffed, 'They take canvas, paint and brushes, fling something at random and hope for the best . . .'[8]

This majority verdict barely changed in the ensuing years. In the decade before 1914, relatively few people gave a damn what Picasso painted, or whether he painted at all. You'd be hard-pressed to find an auction room full of business tycoons cuddling up to a Gauguin or a Pissarro. Van Gogh committed suicide, penniless and mad. Rigid conservative opinion did not turn doe-eyed at the sight of Matisse's *Le bonheur de vivre* (1905) and surrender to the Fauvist vision. The symbolists, the Nabi, the cubists, the futurists were fringe dwellers, their exhibitions barely noticed. Taut, old-world convention would not understand Cézanne's 'way of seeing', or fathom his purpose – to conjure the *nature* of things in paint – until decades after his death (in 1906).

The faintly ridiculous traditional artist William Bouguereau received a better reception, in the sense of a higher price, in the late 1890s and early 1900s. His paintings of 'ample buttocks on angelic maidens' were still hugely popular to mainstream, conservative taste in America and Europe.[9] He died in 1905, one of many artists for whom 'the visible world existed', concluded a perceptive obituary.[10]

—

Modernist literature, too, was similarly ignored, or pilloried, before the war. Politicians censored or banned books deemed 'subversive'. Writers were outlawed or prosecuted if they dared to criticise the government. The establishment attacked the great French writer Émile Zola for his article *J'Accuse*, which appeared on the front page of *L'Aurore* on 13 January 1898. His powerful defence of the Jewish officer Alfred Dreyfus, who had been unjustly imprisoned, divided French society between the Dreyfusard socialist/republican groups and the anti-Dreyfusard conservative establishment, who believed that the reputation of the army, 'the defender of the security and greatness of France . . . immune from criticism', had been gravely sullied.[11] For defending an innocent man, Zola was found guilty of libel and fled to England to avoid prison.

Whether the French novelist Proust found the time he'd lost did not interest most people, and his pre-war classic, *In Search of Lost Time*, which he started in 1905, was not fully published until after the war. If Proust had discovered 'a new conception of time', of the unlived memory, the transformative power of his masterpiece seems clear only in hindsight. At the time, the great majority of people seemed to be looking forward, not backward. Doomed by the same reactionary forces, but for different reasons, was the brilliant Irish playwright and wit Oscar Wilde, who personified the *fin de siècle*.

Sentenced to years of hard labour for sodomy, he died in 1900 at the age of 46, broken on the wheel of English hypocrisy and intolerance.

Modern dance similarly enraged or upset the reactionary guardians of public morality. The British and German Governments sought to outlaw the tango and the turkey trot, then sweeping the music halls and clubs of London, Paris and Berlin. The Kaiser forbade German officers from dancing the new steps.[12] Isadora Duncan's beautiful Dionysian movements were condemned as pornographic. Then along came Nijinsky's faun. Diaghilev and Nijinsky represented the highest form of artistic expression in dance. For this, many forgave or ignored their alleged bisexuality. But Debussy's ballet *L'Apres-midi d'un faune*, staged by Diaghilev's Ballets Russes in Paris in 1912, and choreographed and danced by Nijinsky, caused outrage when it opened.

Bacchic impressions the great dancer had seen on a Grecian vase in the Louvre had inspired his conception of the ballet. It disgusted the old guard, for whom the little satyr posed a threat to public morality. Gaston Calmette, editor of the conservative newspaper *Le Figaro*, spiked a favourable review of the ballet and informed his readers that it 'was neither a pretty pastoral nor a work of profound meaning. We are shown a lecherous faun, whose movements are filthy and bestial in their eroticism, and whose gestures are as crude as they are indecent.'[13] The scandal acquired a political dimension. *Le Figaro* was accused of attacking the Ballets Russes because the paper opposed the military alliance between France and Russia. The ballet 'represented an opening to smear all things Russian'.[14] The Russian ambassador became involved, French politicians signed petitions and the French president and prime minister set up a commission of inquiry. The ballet's alleged obscenity drew the Paris police to the second night. The faun seems emblematic now of a last little prance of beauty, slightly pathetic in the context, perhaps, before the curtain came down on the Belle Époque.

—

In sum, society's great reactionary midriff – the white-collar bour-geoisie and the conservative working class – largely ignored, or rub-bished, the progressive forces in their midst. If they thought about it at all, the establishment regarded modernism as frivolous and deca-dent, and not the prophecy of a world on the verge of fragmentation. The Belle Époque, in their eyes, appealed merely to aristocratic dan-dies, bohemian perverts and political radicals (socialists, anarchists, etc.). If reality *was* fragmenting, as the artists and writers suggested, if truth and perception *were* the same thing, and the perceiver existed in a realm of impressions, fleeting, sensual and unkempt, if tradi-tional certainties *were* giving way to forces of democratic upheaval and the splintering of political autocracy, who was looking?

To the conservatives who noticed, the modernist 'impression' of a world on the brink of collapse and rebirth was plainly nonsense. In their eyes, the world manifestly *was not breaking up*. Their world was hardening into a steel block, a skyscraper, a dreadnought, an assem-bly line. Their images were forged in a smelter (rather like Adolf von Menzel's 1875 painting *The Forge*). Their future envisaged the rise of nation states and global empires, and the preservation of order, class and hierarchy.

In this sense, littering the late nineteenth and early twentieth centuries with bohemian influences that supposedly captured a pop-ular mood is profoundly misleading. The great lights of modernity dazzle with hindsight but shone on precious few at the time. The pre-war artists articulated a new consciousness that eluded the old order. Not until years later, after a world war had devastated Europe, would the bourgeoisie concede the point in the only way they knew how: by putting a price tag on the sublime and appropriating it as their own. In 1870–1914, however, the democratic ideals of a more humane and tolerant world, expressed in art and literature, were to be throttled, ignored or postponed.

—

The war would blow it all away. Old world, patriarchal forces would smash apart the Belle Époque, an incidental casualty of a war fought to preserve God, King and Country. If radical ideas had disturbed the moral order a little too much, then their party was over. The irritated conservative rump had lost patience with the tawdry course of fashionable civilisation. The Old Certainties would not be mocked and trampled underfoot. Europe's monarchies and the hierarchical systems they symbolised must be fought for, preserved, avenged.

That is not to suggest the provocations of a few bohemians drove the world to war. Rather, that the revolutionary political forces of social reform, which underlay these artistic movements, threatened to overturn the established systems. In a perverse kind of way, Nijinsky's 'disgusting faun' and all it represented added to the chorus of voices prophesying war. One can readily imagine the enraged forces of reaction training their cannons, symbolically at least, on the dancer's 'filth'. The governments and ruling elites of the reactionary states of Germany, Austria-Hungary and Russia, and, to a lesser extent, the relatively liberal France and Britain, had this psychology in common: revolted by the dilettantism of the times, but genuinely afraid of the social reforms behind it, they ennobled the rush to arms as a moral response to a revolutionary era. The tired expression 'What we need is a good war' was common enough: 'a good war' that would sustain the conservative certainties – or, in the view of the Italian futurists and fringe groups, a 'cleansing war' that would do away with everything old and start anew.

Yet surely, as every schoolchild knows, the Great War was fought over tangible issues such as colonies, economic hegemony, nationalism, Alsace-Lorraine, Franz Ferdinand's death and naval supremacy? The list of 'rational' causes and triggers seems inexhaustible. And they all have validity, as we shall see. Yet, taken together, or alone, these 'causes' do not seem to get us closer to understanding why millions of young men had to die, over four years of slaughter.

In this light, Germany, Austria-Hungary and Russia were fighting to protect their royal dynasties and autocratic systems of government. If that meant war, as a socially binding, preservative force, then so be it. The prevailing order would never surrender its privileges without a fight. The world as they knew it was under serious political and social threat. The war offered a grand opportunity to ignore proper domestic reforms and bind the people against a common foe. This varied in degree and direction. Russia's Tsarist regime, sitting on a cauldron of revolutionary pressures, welcomed the war as a way of unifying the country and suppressing dissent. Austria-Hungary's old empire was falling apart, and hastened the outbreak of war in order to restore its power and self-respect. Germany demanded a global empire to buttress its rising European power.

The Central and East European regimes were answerable to a kaiser, emperor or tsar and the systems they represented. When Germany declared war, it was the Kaiser *in person* who was at war, as the spiritual embodiment of the nation. The German, Austro-Hungarian and Russian Governments repeatedly defended the war as the only way to save the prevailing system and defend the monarch. France, if sharing the least responsibility for the war, nonetheless unleashed a wave of vengeful patriotism in the 1900s, which tended in that direction. Only Asquith's Liberal Party made a serious attempt at social reform before 1914, then postponed most of it until after the war and succumbed to conservative demands. It is worth stressing that the people most responsible for driving the world to war tended to be the political elite in alliance with the press, not the financiers and businessmen, or 'capitalists', most of whom consistently opposed it. None wished to see the destruction of their markets and the source of capital.

In this sense, the champions of liberalism and social reform were powerless to resist the rush to arms. They temporarily surrendered their principles, as we shall see. The liberal, democratic values they espoused, expressed in art and literature and progressive politics, were saplings in the path of a hurricane. If liberals 'applauded novelty at random simply to show their contempt for the people in the boxes', as Jean Cocteau observed, they ignored a terrible truth.[15] It was the privileged few up in the boxes, not the Social Democrats in the stalls, who would plunge the world into chaos. The eminent, bewhiskered men in plumed hats, their chests heavy with medals, the top-hatted, white-tied elite, with their bejewelled wives at their sides peering down their lorgnettes on the rabble below . . . *they* would decide how and when Europe descended into hell. And in time these pied pipers of the apocalypse – kings, reactionary politicians, generals and media bosses – would send millions of their nation's students, shopkeepers, workers and sons of the landed gentry to the trenches without giving a fig for Zola, cubism or Nijinsky's faun. And millions would follow.

2

THE RISE OF THE MACHINES

Is War Now Impossible?
The title of Ivan Stanislavovich Bloch's 1898 book

———————————

MORE DISTRACTING FOR the millions of people drawn to the cities in search of jobs and pleasure were the great inventions and new consumer goods that spilt off the factory lines: tinned soup, for example. The French poet Péguy was right in this sense: the man-made world had radically changed in the past 30 years. A society of mass urbanisation rose around him, the last stages of the industrialisation of the West. It was a world of stifling conformity, extremes of wealth and poverty, and rapid mechanisation. The vast machines, electric lights and steel cathedrals outdid the church's traditional power to hold the mind in unblinking awe. The enormous structures and roaring engines and twinkling lights of what was known as the Machine Age reached their height between 1880 and 1920. The great industrial fairs, the discoveries of science, the rise of secular temples, the freedom of the automobile, cruiseliner and aircraft: these were the opiates of the people at the turn of the nineteenth century.

The Eiffel Tower (completed in 1889), the tallest man-made structure on earth, seen by millions of visitors to world fairs, was the most sensational example of the marriage of modern engineering and architectural grandeur. 'And in its height,' wrote the art critic Robert Hughes, 'its structural daring, its then-radical use of industrial materials for the commemorative purposes of the State, it summed up what the ruling classes of Europe conceived the promise of technology to be: Faust's contract, the promise of unlimited power over the world and its wealth.'[1]

If the ideals of the Belle Époque suggested the possibility of a humane, compassionate society, the great chugging sound of industrialisation conjured a more utilitarian, impersonal world. No doubt, it was a more comfortable and healthier one for many people, yet its direction was far from secure. One thing was certain: never had the man-made landscape changed so rapidly. From the end of the Franco-Prussian War (1871) to the beginning of the First World War, the civilised nations witnessed, in awestruck wonder, the inventions of: the phonograph (1877), the first synthetic fibre (1883), the Maxim machine gun (1885), the Kodak box camera, the Tesla electric motor (1888), cordite (1889), the Diesel engine (1892), the Ford automobile (1893), the cinematograph (1894), Roentgen's X-rays, Marconi's radio telephony and the Lumière movie camera (1895), radium, sound recording and the Wright brothers' powered flight (1903), and, in 1909, the first flight across the English Channel, by the Frenchman Louis Blériot.

In 1900, at the greatest of the industrial expos, L'Exposition Universelle in Paris, Rudolf Diesel demonstrated, to general astonishment, an engine that ran on peanut oil. The Paris Expo, which ran from April to November, celebrated the triumphs of Western progress and technology. Electrification brought light and movement to the world. Since 1850, electric tramways had spread through German and American cities, thanks to the pioneering work of Siemens and Edison; tramways would not appear on British streets until the turn of the century, an omen of the empire's relative decline. Indeed, British innovation petered out in the latter years of the nineteenth century, yielding to the success of German and

American inventors. During the 50 years before the outbreak of war, British engineers produced only two inventions of note: the Parsons Turbine, the source of electrical generation, and the Dunlop pneumatic tyre.[2]

These were the manifestations of the Machine Age, which produced the tools for the entertainment, movement and massacre of crowds. The machines were lauded, obsessed over, and not viewed, in the popular mind, with suspicion or dismay. William Blake's warning of 'dark satanic mills' belonged to the early Industrial Revolution and had lost much of its potency. The Machine Age had many apologists, who idealised the process of mechanisation as liberating: to them, machines were not seen as instruments of oppression or the tools of capitalists. They would raise people above the common drudgery of routine, create endless hours of leisure and free humanity to do the edifying work for which we were so obviously designed. Hughes wrote:

> In the past the machine had been represented and caricatured as an ogre, a behemoth, or – due to ready analogy between furnaces, steam, smoke and Hell – as Satan himself. But by 1889 its 'otherness' had waned, and the World's Fair audience tended to think of the machine as unqualifiedly good, strong, stupid, and obedient. They thought of it as a giant slave, an untiring steel Negro, controlled by reason in a world of infinite resources.[3]

And they were a source of great entertainment. The automobile and aircraft – the machine at its most glamorous – drew on a deeper well of adulation, a fetishistic need for the latest technology, not unlike the rush for mobile gadgets in our time, the difference being that these were very expensive toys initially only available to the rich. In 1896, the German engineer Karl Benz designed and patented the first internal-combustion flat engine, called a *boxermotor*. Benz's company became the world's largest automobile manufacturer, producing 572 units in 1899. Messrs Rolls and Royce soon followed.

Automobile (and soon air) travel represented more than a triumph over the tyranny of distance. For those who were able to afford it, a motor car asserted their brassy independence and ascendancy over the troglodyte world. By 1911, automobile and air races transfixed the public imagination. Mass production would soon bring cars to a mass audience: in 1913, the first assembly-line models rolling off the Ford production line.

—

The pace and sheer congestion of discovery in the 30 years before 1914 utterly changed the human landscape. The impossible became probable, and dreams expectations. Great entrepreneurial forces harnessed the new technology. The 'first-mover advantage'[4] gained by rapid adoption of technology spurred the German and American economies in the decades before 1914. At the turn of the century, Great Britain remained the richest country in Europe; but Germany and America were rapidly catching up (rather like China's race with America in the 21st century). Between 1893 and 1913, British exports of manufactured goods more than doubled; Germany's trebled; and America achieved a five-fold increase. During the same period, British production of coal, pig iron and steel rose by 75, 50 and 131 per cent respectively; in Germany, the increase was 159, 287 and 522 per cent; and in the United States, 210, 337 and 715 per cent.[5] Britain's humiliation was some way off, but already the world's largest commercial empire relied on 'invisible earnings'. Nothing to do with new machines or manufacturing, these were chiefly the interest and dividends on investments drawn from Britain's vast multinational portfolio, which, until 1914, balanced the nation's trade deficit.[6]

—

Arms manufacturers were in the van of technological innovation. If rearmament was one of the drivers of the Machine Age, the reverse was also true: new kinds of weapons hastened militarism. Trains, planes, automobiles, cannons and machine guns would unleash seemingly endless opportunities for people to kill and maim each other. Wireless telegraphy would transform military intelligence. Indeed, in the field of warfare, the technological advances were most rapid, and lethal.

Artillery presented humankind with the most efficient method of slaughtering itself. Before long-range bombers and nuclear weapons were conceived, huge cannons were invented that could rain shells containing shrapnel (and later, gas) onto the heads of armies. Germany showed the way in the development of artillery and by 1914 had built the most powerful guns on earth. These meant that battles would be fought over greater and more precise ranges, above the heads of the infantry, who would surge forward beneath the raining bombs in a wave, or 'front' – the term was first used in the 1900s to describe the advance of huge lines of troops.

The British Lee-Enfield .303 rifle, with a maximum range of 2.7 kilometres, and the recoilless machine gun ensured an unprecedented number of them would die, or suffer dreadful wounds. The new machine guns could fire 400 rounds a minute. By 1900, military planners had glimpsed the strategic, if not the moral, consequences of the recoil-operated Maxim machine gun, which would mow down advancing lines of men like a threshing machine. Smokeless gunpowder ensured the firers were undetectable. Hand grenades, mortars, the new French 75-millimetre quick-firing field guns and the hideous prospect of poisonous gas would send the casualties soaring. Governments would place the first few hundred orders for primitive aircraft in the year before the war, and Zeppelins or airships soon became a familiar sight in the sky. At sea, the ironclad steamship, the turbine-propelled destroyer, torpedoes, mines, submarines and the ultimate battleship of the day, the dreadnought, transformed naval warfare.

To the generals and admirals, the new technology conjured the vision of a war so terrible it would surely be over in months. Nobody had experienced such a war. Old soldiers could remember short, sharp colonial clashes of horse and sabre, the limited firepower of cannon, and the range of musketry (140 metres), where engagements were decided in a few days, on battlefields misted over with the smoke of powder. Such were the characteristics of the African colonial wars, the Napoleonic Wars and the American Civil War. Those involved horrendous loss of life: more than 600,000 Americans died in the Civil War between 1861 and 1865. Yet scarcely anyone in the 1890s apprehended four years of chronic bloodshed leading to tens of millions of dead and wounded in wars fought on several fronts across Europe and in distant colonies. No army had applied the new tactics required by such concentrated force.

—

The human factor in the military could not keep up with the pace of technological change. Whatever the differences between the Prussian, French, Russian and British Armies, they shared this characteristic in the late 1890s: none had fired their new weapons in anger, and none knew exactly how to deploy and supply such vast forces. The Prussian Army was the most advanced, having had the recent, salutary experience of defeating the French in 1870–71. At the other extreme, the English Army was woefully ill-prepared to fight a continental war. All officers were still mounted, tended to excel at polo (until it was banned in officer training colleges in 1894 because it encouraged bankruptcy) and hailed from Eton, Harrow or Winchester, and then, by extension, Sandhurst and the Camberley Staff College. Not that these institutions prescribed inadequacy or feebleness; rather, they conformed to a system that refused to reform itself or admit outside, expert opinion. As a social institution, the British Army was a success; as a fighting machine, it was largely 'a sham'.[7] Inefficient, with inadequate training, it produced officers utterly unable to deploy a division or supply an army. They knew all about the romanticism and the grandeur of past battles, and nothing about the shock of modern artillery.

The Royal Navy, at least until 1900, tended to be similarly

past-thinking and inadequate to the challenge of the new machines at its disposal. From 1884, when the *Pall Mall Gazette* published Jacky Fisher's pamphlet 'What is the Truth about the Navy?', to his jolting question almost 20 years later, 'How many of our Admirals have minds?', the British Admiralty tacked waywardly close to irrelevance in a future sea war to be fought by ironclad steamships. 'A drowsy, inefficient, moth-eaten organism' manned by men trained to sail ships in a peaceful world is how one critic damned it.[8] In fairness, the Royal Navy had not been called upon to fire a cannon against a great power since 1855.

—

The shock of the Boer War, the Russo-Japanese War and several colonial disputes transformed this picture of British military ossification, through bloody trial and error. War plans in the 1900s envisaged battle on a completely different scale, fought by a different kind of infantryman, dressed not in bright colours, plumes and red coats, on horseback or bearing sabres, but camouflaged in dirt grey or khaki, helmeted, and armed with a swiftly reloadable rifle. New technologies had to be absorbed into the conception of a new kind of warfare, of hitherto unimaginable deadliness.

Had the military elites deigned to listen to warnings of the future nature of combat, they may have reformed their forces earlier. As early as 1898, it was all laid out in a book of remarkable prescience and horrifying vision, *Is War Now Impossible?*, written by the Russian banker and self-taught military analyst Ivan Stanislavovich Bloch. Bloch's work grasped precisely what the future held, in tactical, strategic and political terms:[9]

- New arms technology (better rifles and machine guns)
  made bayonet and cavalry charges obsolete. The next war
  would be a prolonged fight between entrenched forces,
  in which entrenched men would enjoy a fourfold advantage over infantry advancing across open ground, Bloch

calculated. This message fell on deaf British ears 18 years before the first day of the Somme.

- The belligerents would settle the resulting stalemate by committing armies numbering in the millions, spread across an enormous battlefront, locked in a chronic conflict that would take years to resolve. At the time, commanders failed to digest these truths. Not until November 1912 would Helmuth von Moltke, the chief of the German General Staff, attempt to disabuse the German High Command of their 'short war illusion'.[10] It would be a very long war, he warned. Lord Kitchener was 'already predicting a war of three years in 1909'.[11] But Bloch's view left little impression on the architect of Germany's original war plan, Count Alfred von Schlieffen, who anticipated a swift, short war of several months (see Chapter 10). On 5 August 1914 – the day after Britain declared war on Germany – Kitchener told the council of war that Britain should raise an army of a million men; the French, German and Russian Armies already calculated in terms of millions of men.

- Colossal casualties could be expected, with a huge social cost. The war would become a duel of industrial might, of total economic attrition. It would unleash financial havoc and revolution, and would risk famine, disease and the 'break-up of the whole social organization'.

Bloch tried to distribute his vast thesis at the Hague Peace Conference in 1899. Nobody paid much attention. France, Britain and Russia wouldn't heed his warnings until they encountered exactly the kind of war he described, in August 1914. Bloch wrote with exasperation to a British magazine in 1901:

Having busied myself for over fourteen years with the study of war . . . I am astonished to find that the remarkable evolution

which is rapidly turning the sword into a ploughshare has passed
almost unnoticed even by the professional watchmen who are
paid to keep a sharp look-out . . . What I could not foresee was
the stubbornness which [the military class] not only recoiled
from taking action but set itself to twist and distort the facts.
Patriotism is highly respectable, but it is dangerous to identify
it with the interests of a class. The steadfastness with which the
military caste clings to the memory of a state of things which
has already died is pathetic and honourable. Unfortunately it is
also costly and dangerous. Therefore I venture now to appeal to
the British masses, whose vital interests are at stake and whose
verdict must be final.[12]

Others warned of the human cost of fully mechanised war. A desperate vision weighed on poor Charles Masterman, the Liberal politician and author of the best-selling *The Condition of England* (1909).
Masterman saw the Machine Age as a great illusion. Machines did
not make us any safer, he wrote, but rather heralded our oblivion:

> [O]f all illusions of the opening twentieth century, perhaps the
> most remarkable is that of security. Already gigantic and novel
> forces of mechanical invention . . . are exhibiting a society in the
> beginnings of change . . . With Europe facing an international
> discontent amongst its industrial peoples, the nations, as an
> armed camp [are] heaping up instruments of destruction . . .
> A few years back men loved to anticipate an age of innocence
> and gold . . . Today the critic of a less sanguine outlook openly
> proclaims that modern civilization carries within itself the seeds
> of its own destruction.[13]

Masterman himself would grow sceptical of this vision. Appointed
head of the British War Propaganda Bureau in 1914, his job would
be to portray the enemy in the worst possible light, rally the British
to the cause of war and urge the Americans, and their gigantic forces

of mechanical invention, to join the fight on the British and French side.

3

A GERMAN PLACE IN THE SUN

If Germany is to become a colonizing power,
all I say is 'God Speed her!'
Prime Minister William Gladstone, 1884

IN 1899, AN EYEWITNESS returned from the 'Dark Continent' with a grim message for mankind: the colonial adventure had not brought light to darkness; it had not civilised 'the savages'. Belgium's activities in Africa were nothing more than the most brutal form of exploitation. The scramble for ivory in Belgium's Congo Free State was barbaric and un-Christian, the methods of the coloniser cruel beyond imagining. That was a central theme of Joseph Conrad's novel *Heart of Darkness*.

Many read the novel as a moral allegory, not a bloody fact. Yet 'the horror, the horror' – the last words of the corrupt ivory trader 'Mistah Kurtz' – was real and happening. Lots of people may know what Germany did to the Belgians in the First World War, but who, today, knows what Belgium previously did to the Congolese? Nearly eight million of Congo's 16 million native inhabitants would die between 1885 and 1908, casualties of Belgium's 'indiscriminate war', starved, denied medical care and worked to death, the direct consequence of the colonialists' plan to subdue and enslave the native people.

Belgium was one of the first imperialists to plunder Africa. The colonial race there, soon to be a source of great antagonism between Germany, Britain and France, began two decades before Conrad conceived *Heart of Darkness*. It proceeded between 1870 and 1914 at astonishing speed, and led to the complete sequestration of the continent.

At the century's end, every English schoolboy had beheld a map of the world swathed in pink or red, signifying the empire on which the sun never set. In 1900, the Englishman's burden extended to every corner of the planet. London held dominion over more than 450 million people, then a fifth of the earth's population, living in colonies or territories covering 33,700,000 square kilometres, from the Rift Valley to the Australian outback, Hong Kong to Bombay, and Capetown to Cairo, connected by a global telegraph line, inaugurated in 1902, called the All Red Line. The British were determined to preserve and expand this empire, and defend it to the death. Any challenge to English supremacy provoked an extreme response at home, among the public and in the press. At this time, the empire not only delivered great, if declining, wealth; it secured a host of intangibles: undreamt of power, huge prestige and international political leverage.

It is churlish to claim the British Empire brought no benefits, and at independence the more enlightened colonies adopted the democratic and judicial system of Westminster, along with the quotidian delights of football and cricket. This was not the case with the French Empire, whose subjected peoples kept very little recognisably French – with the exception, in places, of the language, street names and cuisine. Regardless of whether the imperial legacy was brioche or cricket whites, pith helmets or Christ, the imperial powers had one chief goal: to strip their colonies of resources, usually done under the pretence of civilising them (France's *mission civilisatrice*). The British Raj may have seemed less malignant in India than the French in West Africa or Indochina but were just as indifferent to the suffering that proceeded under their occupation. Queen Victoria, crowned the Empress of India, reigned over the worst famines in the country's pre-war history: some 15 million Indians died in successive famines in the late nineteenth century, partly due to the inaction and laissez-faire attitude of the East India Company and English poobahs.

If they claimed to rule the world, the British and French periodically disburdened themselves of responsibility for what happened to the people of the world. Indeed, colonial excesses in Asia and Africa moved liberal Europeans to question the moral, if not the economic, legacy of their 300-year quest for global domination. Even the proud British imperialist Winston Churchill would concede, with magnificent understatement, in 1913, at the height of England's dispute with Germany over the size of their navies: 'We have got all we want in territory, and our claim to be left in unmolested enjoyment of vast and splendid possessions, mainly acquired by violence, largely maintained by force, often seems less reasonable to others than to us.'[1]

—

In the late 1870s, the European powers turned the machinery of conquest onto the world's last unexploited continent, rich in minerals, diamonds, gold, ivory and oil, and blessed with vast tracts of arable land and a huge store of cheap labour: Africa. The slave trade was over; the previous two centuries had witnessed millions of African men and women captured, corralled, manacled and sold to estates in the Americas, European colonies and plantations in the Caribbean. Yet the abolition of the sale of human life did little to hinder the effective enslavement of the African people at home, in the mines of central and southern Africa, the plantations of the Gold Coast and the ivory belt of the Congo, where they were compelled to work in appalling conditions. Yes, there were treaties and missionaries, protectorates and power-sharing arrangements, but the aim, and effect, was oppression and wholesale resource theft. They called it the 'Scramble for Africa'.

In the rush, France and Britain vied for control of most of Africa; Italy cast a hungry eye on Abyssinia (Ethiopia and Eritrea); and King Leopold of Belgium oversaw the rape of Belgian Congo. Portugal and Spain claimed parts of west and north Africa. Germany belatedly sought a stake. Together, they bartered and occupied, swapped and dealt, in land and peoples, rivers and mountains, and superimposed new names and borders on the traditional map of this richly diffuse society, utterly ignorant or careless of the ethnic or tribal groups that underlay their new economic zones. Tribes and their lands 'became little more than pieces on a chessboard', writes Martin Meredith in his epic history of Africa since independence. 'By the time the Scramble was over, some 10,000 African polities had been amalgamated into forty European colonies and protectorates.'[2]

England and France grabbed the lion's share. To French fury, Britain occupied Egypt in 1882 (and would declare it a protectorate in 1914), and consolidated its grip on the colonies of South Africa. Having defeated the Zulus in 1879, the English forces subdued the Dutch colonists in the first Boer War of 1881 and utterly defeated them in the second, fought essentially over control of Witwatersrand gold fields, yielding in 1902 complete dominion over Transvaal, Cape Colony, Natal and the Orange Free State, and infuriating Germany, which coveted a slice of the continent. Nor was it ever as simple as Germany against the old rulers of the world. If the Prussians were the new pretenders to empire, then Italy and Portugal also had a hand in the scramble.

By the turn of the century, Britain controlled almost 30 per cent of Africa's population, spread across Egypt, Sudan, Nigeria, South Africa and states then known as British Somaliland, British East Africa, Rhodesia, British Gold Coast and many other smaller protectorates and colonies. Nigeria alone yielded 15 million new British subjects, more than in the whole of French West Africa or the entire German African stake.

France snared more territory (3.75 million square miles, mostly desert, compared with Britain's far richer two million square miles), in what it named French West Africa (including Mauritania, Senegal, Guinea, Ivory Coast and others), French Equatorial Africa (Gabon, French Congo and Chad), French North Africa (Algeria, Tunisia, Morocco) and French East Africa (Madagascar, Coromoros and other Indian Ocean islands, and French Somaliland). In the last two decades of the nineteenth century, this headlong colony grab added nearly a fifth of the land area of the globe to Europe's colonial possessions.[3]

At what cost? The greatest authority is Thomas Pakenham's monumental study *The Scramble for Africa*:

> Suddenly, in half a generation, the Scramble gave Europe the whole continent: including 30 new colonies and protectorates, 10 million square miles of new territory and 110 million dazed new subjects . . . Africa was sliced up like a cake, and the pieces swallowed by five rival nations . . . By the end of the century, the passions generated by the Scramble had helped to poison the political climate in Europe, brought Britain to the brink of war with France, and precipitated a struggle with the Boers, the costliest, longest and bloodiest war since 1815 . . .[4]

———

Conspicuous by its near-absence from the beginning of the scramble was Germany. Near the end of the nineteenth century, it held a fraction of Africa and scraps of the Pacific but ached for more. In the 1880s, Germany was a young nation in a great hurry. 'Germany's claim to world power,' writes Fritz Fischer, 'was based on her consciousness of being a "young", growing and rising nation.'[5] Germany needed to expand rapidly abroad to feed her growth at home: 'Germany was developing more and more into a highly industrialised exporting country, and the problem of finding markets and raw materials to support her population was growing increasingly urgent.'[6] Greater wealth across all classes, international business interests and a growing reliance on imports made Germany determined to join the scramble for the colonies. The contrast between her rising economic power in Europe and lack of an empire was a source of chronic and acute frustration in Berlin.

To understand why Germany found itself in this state, one has only to delve into the meaning of what it meant to be 'German' in the last two decades of the nineteenth century. The region that became known as Germany comprised, until 1871, a confederation of 'states', a loosely associated jumble of kingdoms, duchies or principalities created by the Congress of Vienna in 1815. They joined together as the North German Confederation after the Austro-Prussian War of 1866, which left Austria weakened and excluded. The dividing lines on the map reflected local loyalties in, for example, Saxony, Bavaria, Hanover and the most powerful member state, the Kingdom of Prussia.

Under the firm stewardship of Count Otto von Bismarck, the principalities were brought together, often violently, as a collective nationality, to form the first German 'Reich', with its capital, Berlin, in the Prussian heartland. Prussia had hitherto been thought of as 'an army in control of a state' rather than the other way around; now, it was set to grow into a much bigger army, still hugely influential over a unified state in the thrall of Bismarck, the 'Iron Chancellor'. The new Germany declared its official unification into a single administrative and political entity on 18 January 1871.

The Prussian victory over France in the war of 1870–71 imbued the new nation with the confidence to set its sights on foreign conquest. For the second time that century, Prussian arms had defeated the French. While France quickly recovered from its humiliation, the victory gave the new Germany an immense boost, financially and psychologically, and consolidated the nation's unification. Germany was determined to position itself in the front rank of European powers, wisely investing in home-grown manufacturing industries and building its economy.

The unification of Germany was Bismarck's towering achievement. A pervasive feature of the new nation state was the citizens' rich conception of themselves as 'German', in the sense of sharing a national – and racial – identity. This seems obvious now; back then, the birth of a German identity was a novel concept, and paradoxically an ancient one, which looked beyond the rise of Prussia in the aftermath of the Napoleonic years to the Romantic and Neoclassical ideals, philosophy, artistic and religious achievements of the sixteenth to eighteenth centuries, and further back, to the Holy Roman Empire, the pagan myths and ancient tribes. It all converged in a modern, palpable German identity.

The German people were conscious of their country as a strong, resourceful and, above all, militarily powerful nation whose creation declared to Europe and the world the arrival of an economic and cultural force. The creation of Germany and the people's conscious pride in it were mutually reinforcing, and a fervent patriotism, utterly loyal to the Fatherland, resulted. By extension, and with varying intensity in the coming years, this new sensibility excluded non-Germans, or non-Teutonic breeds, to use the racially charged language of the era. Slavs and Jews were explicitly lesser breeds. In this sense, the creation of Germany went far beyond diplomatic wrangling, small wars and lines drawn on a map; it expressed a *racial* force, the emergence of a new consciousness, a full-blown 'German' consciousness.

The British, French and Russian Governments witnessed this process with awe and apprehension. The drawing together of the reins of 'Deutschland' was the single most arresting political and economic fact in Europe during the last 20 years of the nineteenth century.

—

The German Reich naturally clamoured for a slice of the global cake, and was determined to build a colonial empire in under-exploited Africa, in defiance of the French and British imperialists already rooted there. If three powers – Britain, France and Russia, and their satellites and dominions – effectively 'owned' the planet's then-known resources and were determined to expand their colonies,

Germany refused to accept relegation and hankered for a place in the tropical sun.

Bismarck was initially opposed to the creation of a German colonial empire and focused his powers on building German power in Europe. The chief goal of his concept of 'revolutionary nationalism' (*Realpolitik*) was to carve out Germany's pre-eminence in Europe, while at the same time preserving the balance of power to assure continental peace. The Bismarckian system of large alliances bound by common economic interests helped to preserve the peace in Europe until 1912. And yet, it also, paradoxically, created great power blocs that evolved into hostile camps under leaders who replaced his policy of balance with one that strove to dominate.

Bismarck realised the importance of German involvement in the scramble, which was intensely popular in Germany. Failure to win a colonial empire threatened the very prestige of the new German nation. He belatedly judged that the people would vote for a German place in the sun. In the early 1880s, with the support of Germany's National Liberal and Free Conservative parties, whose votes he needed, and in league with a zealously supportive press, Bismarck suddenly reversed his long-standing opposition to imperialism and agitated for the proliferation of German power abroad.

His chief purpose was to relieve the economic malaise at home. Germany's rapid industrialisation had led to massive over-production and unemployment, and a search for foreign markets for German exports. The fruits of German imperialism were so far miserably few, but the perception that Germany wanted an empire to rival that of Britain and France set the new policy on a collision course with Berlin's European rivals.

Powerful commercial interests helped to persuade Bismarck to accelerate the policy: industrialists needed new export markets. In 1884, German chambers of commerce, financiers and corporations together urged the government to join the scramble and secure overseas markets. 'Yes,' answered Friedrich Fabri firmly, to his celebrated treatise of 1879, 'Does Germany Need Colonies?'[7] The avowed white supremacist Heinrich von Trietschke, a German history professor, gave a racial justification: 'For, as the aim of human culture,' he lectured, 'will be the aristocracy of the white race over the whole earth, the importance of a nation will ultimately depend upon what share it has in the domination of the transatlantic world . . . We wish and ought to take our share in the domination of the world by the white race. We have still an infinite deal to learn from England in this connection . . .'[8]

These forces were brought together under a pressure group of German imperialists, the *Kolonialverein*, founded in 1882. Within three years it had 10,000 members, and 42,000 by 1914.[9] They tended to envy the British Empire, yet delusions of grandeur as well as plain economic opportunism persuaded Germany to join the race for colonies. '[T]he best card in the government's hand at present,' observed Friedrich von Holstein, an influential German statesman, 'is definitely a harsh move against England. One can hardly believe *how* popular it is in the business world.'[10] A 'harsh move' did not mean war. It meant a belligerent economic gesture, a land grab, a brusque insistence on access to British markets. Military intervention was not then proposed.

Bismarck's new colonial policy hoped to deliver these prizes. In 1884, Germany accelerated her imperial ambitions, on a wave of public support. Bismarck's gut feel proved correct: that year's elections plumbed a well of popularity 'in awakening latent anglophobia and desire for colonies among the German people'.[11] To this end, Bismarck played a gradualist policy, in the game of high diplomacy at which the German chancellor excelled. He set in train the diplomatic manoeuvres that would steadily prise open German colonies in Africa and the Pacific, starting with New Guinea and soon to include protectorates over East Africa (now Rwanda, Burundi and mainland Tanzania and Zanzibar), Togoland (Togo and part of Ghana), German Cameroon (Cameroon and part of Nigeria) and German South West Africa (Namibia). These represented a small slice of the cake by British and French standards, but it was a start.

Colonial rivalry between Germany, Britain and France did not lead to war. Germany was simply not strong enough to trouble British and French colonial aims. Before 1914, Germany never posed a serious threat to the British Empire. Britain was by far the supreme power in terms of foreign assets and financial wealth, as Niall Ferguson shows.[12] Germany, while outstripping Britain in terms of its share of world manufacturing between 1880 and 1913, had nothing to compare with Britain's foreign investments and international financial clout. Britain's overseas assets rose tenfold, in absolute terms, from £370 million in 1860 to £3.9 billion in 1913. In that year, France's foreign assets were less than half, and Germany's about a quarter, of those of Britain, which accounted for about 44 per cent of total foreign investment.[13]

In fact, confident of her pre-eminence, Britain initially welcomed Germany's arrival on the colonial scene. Here was a fellow protestant, Anglo-Saxon power, whose Kaiser had blood ties with the King, and who seemed a natural ally in Britain's struggle against her Latinate/Catholic and Slavic/Orthodox colonial rivals. For one thing, German competition might help to undermine the high tariffs in which France routinely cocooned her colonies. And Germany's rapid industrialisation brought extra capital that would help to finance colonial expansion, expand trade for all and, it was felt, generally increase British wealth.

The British prime minister William Gladstone conveyed these feelings in a speech to the House of Commons in 1884: 'If Germany is to become a colonizing power, all I say is "God Speed her!" She becomes our ally and partner in the execution of the great purposes of Providence for the advantage of mankind.'[14] At the time, he meant it. Germanophiles in the British ruling classes tended to see the Germans as kinsmen, racially compatible and likely allies during these clashes over great tracts of global real estate. The English upper orders had historic blood links with the German aristocracy, and the two countries seemed obvious bedfellows, notwithstanding the fact that families are often the most ferocious war zones.

Yet at the extremities of the world, in the mid-1880s, small British 'blocking actions' had disrupted German efforts to annex territory. Australia and New Zealand respectively renewed their claims on New Guinea and Samoa, and the British consulates in east and southern Africa annexed territory in anticipation of German hegemony. '[I]t is easy to see why Bismarck could accuse London of systematic *Deutschfeindlichkeit* [Germanophobia]' writes Kennedy, 'and also easy to understand why, from 1883 onwards, he was weighing up the various possible counter-measures.'[15] These tensions were soon defused. Britain would overrule local objections and accept German claims on Papua New Guinea, Fiji and parts of East Africa, mere trinkets in the world's colonial treasury.

Not that it mattered much, in relative terms, to Britain. In the 1880s, Whitehall had vastly bigger fish to fry, such as negotiating French, Russian and American colonial disputes over Egypt, Afghanistan and the Bering Strait, respectively. The prospect of appeasing or denying the aspirations of upstart imperialists such as Germany were of little immediate importance. Whitehall's eyes were 'not upon Kilimanjaro or Apia, but upon Kabul and Khartoum, and still more upon St Petersburg, Berlin and Toulon'.[16]

—

A sense of being ignored, of not winning a seat at the top table, angered Berlin. Scraps of territory failed to appease Germany's resurgent ambitions, and the indifference or quiet containment with which Britain and France treated this imperial pretender infuriated Bismarck and his government. But Germany was its own worst enemy. It was a young nation, with a naive grasp of global diplomacy. In the colonial stakes, Berlin refused to play the game, or learn how to cheat. Bismarck, later regarded as Germany's finest statesman, failed to engage profitably with British foreign policy and tended to explode in a rage at what he saw as British obstructionism over Africa.

In the late 1880s and 1890s, frustrated at the slow progress, Germany adopted a strategy of sowing division between its colonial rivals, attempting to set Britain against France and both against Russia. Berlin would convey the impression of being a cooperative participant, looking for friends, not enemies, in the race for colonies – meanwhile seeking to undermine the existing world order to its sole benefit.

Germany's sub-Machiavellian strategy largely backfired, galvanising intense anti-British feeling in Germany and anti-German feeling in Britain and France. In the late 1890s, Whitehall brusquely declined Germany's proposals for an Anglo-German alliance. Germany's dream of a 'colonial marriage' with Britain was based on a simplistic assumption: her natural kinship with the English. Indeed, at least until the end of the nineteenth century, France and Russia – and not Germany – were seen as Britain's most likely enemies in a future war, over rival claims to Egypt, West Africa, Afghanistan and other tracts of the planet.

In a wider sense, the relationships between the European powers were ever changing in a kaleidoscopic rush for world power. Throughout the last decade of the nineteenth century, flashpoints, treaties, attempted treaties and loose alliances confounded any settled notion of political allegiance. Everything was in flux, up for grabs, power relations were as ephemeral as ever, and the truism that governments have no friends, only interests, was never more forcefully on display. Britain and France were old hands in this game, of course. The new Germany sought to fix deals and tie things down, failing to grasp the fluidity of this friendless world.

At one point, in the 1880s, France and Germany were firmly aligned against Britain on the question of who would control Egypt. At another point, in the 1890s, Germany and Britain reached colonial settlements that excluded, and outraged, France. And, throughout the decade, Russia and England were viewed as the most obvious foes. The long-anticipated Anglo-Russian war almost erupted on 21 February 1884 when Russian troops stationed at the Zulficar Pass threatened not only Afghanistan but also, to London's horror, India. The Crimean War of 1853–56 was still fresh in the memories of old soldiers.

For now, Germany brooded – on the fact of being the fastest-growing industrial power in Europe with the weakest claim to an empire. It was this very weakness that made the country so volatile and so dangerous: her burgeoning power at home stood in stark contrast to her impotence abroad, creating a curious diplomatic psychology. Berlin demanded a seat at the high table, based on Germany's rising strength in Europe, but lacked the imperial prestige to propel and consolidate it.

As a result, Germany was, by turns, impetuous and timid, bullying and insecure, boisterous and moody. It was insufferable that she should be excluded from Europe's imperial club, ignored or demeaned by her most obvious ally, England, and recent enemy, France. It was intolerable that Russia and France should speak of an alliance, with the obvious intent of squeezing the fledgling Reich. Such was Berlin's prevailing perception of the world in the last years of the nineteenth century.

4

SERBIAN VENDETTAS

Whoever will not fight at Kosovo,
may nothing grow that his hand sows
Serbian epic poem

WHILE THE GREAT POWERS ARGUED over the spoils of empire, a new source of conflict arose in a corner of Europe that the gentlemen of Whitehall and the Quai d'Orsay tended to regard as of little consequence: a backward outpost of religious and ethnic strife, a commingling of goatherds, pig farmers, addled aristocrats, fuming revolutionaries and family madness – and the cultural fault line, as it happened, where the Islamic met the Christian world in Europe. It was the Balkan Peninsula, which had been ruled by the Ottoman Turks for more than 500 years.

The gradual removal of the Turks, the explosion of religious and racial hatred, and the sponsorship of local states by great power blocs in a series of small wars: such were the forces that convulsed the Balkans in the late nineteenth and early twentieth centuries and shaped the battle lines of Europe. Here, between 1880 and 1914, three vast power blocs, divided by religion and ethnicity, would crash into each other and wage a vicious fight for supremacy. Embedded in the Balkan mess were three racial rivals: Turk/Muslim; Teutonic/ Protestant-Catholic; Slav/Orthodox. What were its causes? Why did these forces converge on the peninsula?

Luigi Albertini, still regarded as the greatest historian of the causes of the First World War, who interviewed many of the political leaders of the time, offers a starting point to understanding the Balkan mess: Russia's ancient mission to liberate the Slavs and Greeks from Turkish occupation. 'Eight wars at least,' Albertini reminds us, '[Russia] had waged on the Turks either to take their territory or to help Orthodox Slavs and Greeks to throw off the Turkish yoke.'[1] Setting aside St Petersburg's pro-Slav rhetoric, Russia's goals were self-interested: to seize the Dardanelles Straits and the Black Sea from Turkish control and ensure a direct naval passage to the Mediterranean. This was Russia's ancient dream, and most of its actions in the Balkans must be seen through this lens.

Yet it would be foolish to understate Russia's intangible bonds, of race and religion, to the Balkans. These were strongly felt, even if they often served as a convenient mask to Russian imperialism. The Slavic states of Serbia, Bulgaria and Bosnia-Herzegovina shared Russia's racial and religious blend. Orthodox Christianity was the faith of a majority of Russians, Serbs, Bulgarians, Greeks, Montenegrins and Macedonians.

In the late nineteenth century, Russia thought it was about to realise its dream and rid the Balkans of its old Muslim adversary. Yet the liberation of Slavic culture from the grip of Islamicised Turkey would not be fully complete until 1913, and would never result in the creation of a new, unified Slavic kingdom. Instead, Turkey's retreat, like that of the Soviet Union in the 1990s, threatened anarchy and revolution, and drew deep into the Balkan storm another old imperial power: Austria-Hungary (see Chapter 5).

—

For thousands of years, Serbs, or the inhabitants of *Sklavinia* ('Slav lands'), existed at the heart of that peninsula and were periodically torn apart like a rag in the claws of brawling animals. No country, with the modern exception of Poland, has seen its livelihood, hopes and dreams so thoroughly and repeatedly crushed in the pincers of empires. The endless struggle, the violence and atrocities inflicted on and by its people spawned a nation of rare stoicism and cold-blooded resilience. The little country survived the upheavals of the Roman, Byzantine, Mediaeval Christian and Ottoman Empires like a cork on stormy seas, tossed hither and thither yet never losing sight of itself as a single entity – now a Celtic tribe, now a Christian principality, a Slavic people, a European nation.

Indeed, Serbia has traditionally held the strongest claim to being the leading Slavic power in the Balkans, despite its size and small population, by virtue of a long and dogged history of violent struggle for legitimacy. Heavily Romanised – 17 Roman emperors were born in Serbia, including the first Christian emperor, Constantine the Great – Serbia fell into the Byzantine half of the empire at its split, in AD 395. This was providential for Serbian identity: the pull away from the east began immediately. The Serbian Slav lands were initially independent and self-governing, and in the ninth century the Serbian Principality 'stretched over the greater part of Dalmatia'.[2]

Under the Nemanjić dynasty of the late middle ages, Serbia grew to a position of dominance in the Balkan region. In 1196, Stefan Nemanja, the father of the dynasty, chose the church of Constantinople over the Church of Rome. His son Rastko (Saint Sava) 'consolidated the religious identification of the Serbs with Orthodoxy', writes Tim Judah, a specialist on Serbia.[3] Dušan the Great, emperor of the Serbs and Greeks, expanded Serbian territory to incorporate most of the Balkans, including Greece. In 1346, Greater Serbia achieved the height of its power.

The Ottoman Empire, noting the strategic value of the Balkan Peninsula in the Mediterranean and the Dardanelles, soon invaded. The Turks wore down Serbian resistance, culminating in the Battle of Kosovo, which fell to the Ottomans on 28 June 1389, commemorated in Serbia as St Vitus' Day. Kosovo, the home of the Serbian soul and the symbolic heartland of the country, submitted to Ottoman rule, but not without an epic struggle immortalised in Serbian verse. The curse, or vendetta-mindedness, is ever-present:

> Whoever will not fight at Kosovo,
> may nothing grow that his hand sows,
> neither the white wheat in his field
> nor the vine of the grapes on his mountain.[4]

Facts of the Battle of Kosovo are scarce. What remains in the Serbian memory is a perception of what happened, or what should have happened, as Judah shows in his penetrating analysis of the 'Kosovo Cycle': the 'Last Supper' of the Serbian knights before battle; their heroic slaughter of the Sultan; the betrayal of the Serb leaders by their own 'Judas'; and the death of the Serbian hero Lazar, who chose self-sacrifice over submission. His choice was inscribed in the national psyche: Serbia would always choose a Christ-like martyrdom over slavery.

After the loss of Kosovo, Serbia fought on, defending Christendom for decades before surrendering most of the country to the Turks in 1455, two years after the fall of Constantinople. For the next 70 years, Belgrade alone resisted the besieging Ottomans, and fell in 1521. The whole country was now a vassal of Turkey. However, while the Turks swept away the Serbian state, the Orthodox Church held fast in the Serbian mind, as Judah stresses:

> The church canonized many of the Nemanjic monarchs, and they became immortalized . . . This meant that for hundreds of years the churchgoing Serbian peasant saw before him images of Christ, the apostles, *and* the holy Serbian kings of the lost golden age. In other words, the resurrection was not just a spiritual affair; Serbia itself would one day be raised from the dead.[5]

The resurrection of Serbia, like the second coming of Christ, would end the cycle of the nation's struggle. The story is so fundamental to Serbian history that it has embedded in the national psyche a sense of its people as chronic victims of the world and, like the Jews, a chosen or 'heavenly people'.[6]

———

Over the following centuries, Austria and Russia many times tried, and failed, to throw the Ottomans out of Serbia. It took Serbian resolve to achieve this, in two bloody uprisings, the first between 1804 and 1813 and the second in 1815, after which the people won their autonomy, and eventually full independence from Turkey, in 1835. The formal recognition of the independent nation of Serbia would await the Congress of Vienna in 1878.

Ever-present at Serbia's side on the long road to independence was the looming shadow of fellow Orthodox Russia. St Petersburg's diplomatic support, for example, played a decisive role in imposing Article 8 of the Treaty of Bucharest in 1812, under which:

> The Turkish government recognized Obrenovich as the chief knez of Serbia, regularized the amount of taxes due to Turkish landowners (spahis) by Serb peasants, and granted the Serbs themselves the right to collect the obligations. In Belgrade, a People's Chancellery was created – the highest administrative and judicial institution, in which the district (nakhi) knezy had the right to take part.[7]

Without mother Russia, Serbia would never have found a foothold in the greater world. Friedrich Engels and Karl Marx were in no doubt about Serbia's critical dependence on the military, material and diplomatic support of Russia. 'When the Serb revolution erupted in 1804,' Engels wrote, 'Russia immediately took the insurgent "raija" under its protection, supported them in two wars, and in two treaties guaranteed the independence of their country in regard to internal affairs.'[8]

—

Serbia's bloody history seemed to inject a strain of defiance into the very veins of the independent nation, whose great historic rallying points were acts of violence and resistance. Its heroes were men of war and revolts, notably Karađorđe, the leader of the first uprising against Turkey and founder of the independent state. Nominated insurgent leader in 1802, this giant of a man led 9000 men and two cannons to victory over the Turks at Mišar on 14 August 1806, against forces four times the size. 'He was a peasant of gigantic stature,' writes Albertini, 'devoid of all culture but endowed with a sort of military genius, astute, violent and despotic, capable of every crime to the point of murdering his own father and brother, the latter having gained great prestige among his comrades.'[9]

Saddled with this besieged provenance, Serbia nursed deep grievances against real and imagined enemies. The tradition of finding scapegoats evolved into a cultural centrepiece, a kind of chronic vendetta-mindedness – regardless, at times, of the validity of the source of the animosity. The Serbian nation clung to these ancient nostrums rather like an old and ailing family, blaming others for its benighted lot. In times of economic misery, Serbia needed, thirsted for, scapegoats. And nothing, it seemed – neither reason nor reward – would change the chemistry of Serbia's sense of victimhood. A defiant legend arose on Serbia's Pannonian Plain and Carpathian Mountains and valley of the Danube, one baptised in the blood of its ancestors, cruelled by the wanton seizure of its lands, and determined never again to accept subjugation.

In this light, the Slavic nation has largely defined itself according to its enemy at any given point in time, be they Turks, Austro-Hungarians, Germans, Muslims, non-Slavs, NATO – indeed, any outsider that dared to intervene in its affairs. There is some truth in this, of course: Serbia, rather like Vietnam and Poland, had been a subjected and threatened nation. Unlike those countries, Serbia appears to thrive on finding enemies to defy, rather than to nurture an inner domestic peace. The scapegoat has always been alive and well in Serbian politics, despite the emergence of the restraining voice of a small, if highly educated, middle class. This is perhaps understandable in a country that, in the 1900s, had no claim to economic or military power and had barely emerged from its agrarian state. And yet, Serbia has a singular claim on European affections: no nation other than Greece had defied the Islamic invader for so long and so well, nourishing the broader Serbian narrative as the martyred defender of European civilisation.

Distant colonial conflicts seemed unlikely to spark a European war. They tended to be resolved through negotiation. The remoteness of such events – in Africa, the Far East, India – insulated the powers from confrontation at home. A war at home was more likely to break out over a hotly contested region where the great powers abutted each other and immediate interests were at stake. The Balkan Peninsula was such a place. Here, racial hatred between Teuton and Slav overlaid and exacerbated the political tension between Austria-Hungary (along with her more powerful ally, Germany) and the de facto Slavic states of Serbia and Bulgaria, which cleaved for their protection to the Orthodox mother ship, Russia.

If this delineation along racial lines seems crude, it accurately reflects the thinking of the time. The role of race cannot be understated in an era of fervent social Darwinism. For decades, the Balkans had enacted in microcosm the racial hatreds at great-power level. In consequence, the Balkan states were likely, indeed expected, periodically to blow a head gasket over racial and religious differences, and threaten a major confrontation by dragging their powerful sponsors into the local mess.

Such a convulsion occurred in 1885–88 – another 'Bulgarian crisis' – when a little local rebellion (Eastern Rumelia sought to reunite with Bulgaria in violation of the Treaty of Berlin of 1878) almost put Germany and Russia on a war footing. Bismarck, in a speech to the Reichstag in February 1888, made a resonant observation, which, if we replace 'Bulgaria' with 'Serbia', acquires a dark, prophetic note:

'Bulgaria, the little country between the Danube and the Balkans, is far from being an object of adequate importance for which to plunge Europe from Moscow to the Pyrenees, and from the North Sea to Palermo, into a war whose issue no man can foresee. At the end of the conflict we should scarcely know why we fought.'[10]

5

ENTER AUSTRIA-HUNGARY

*No other family has endured so long or left so deep
a mark on Europe: the Habsburgs were the greatest
dynasty of modern Europe, and the history of central
Europe revolves around them, not they around it.*
A. J. P. Taylor in *The Habsburg Monarchy, 1809–1918*

AUSTRIA-HUNGARY, THE DUAL MONARCHY formed in
January 1867 at the signing of the *Ausgleich* ('Equalisation'), closely
watched the gradual eviction of the Ottoman Turks from parts of the
Balkan Peninsula. The emperor Franz Joseph, the deeply conservative
old head of the House of Habsburg, ruled over this odd conglomera-
tion of fag ends thrown up by the tremors of history – a dozen or so
ethnic groups, all of whom hankered for rights and representation. It
had nine official languages and five religions. 'The Habsburg lands
were not bound together either by geography or by nationality,' writes
A. J. P. Taylor.[1] They had been called the 'Lands of the Holy Roman
Empire' but lost the imperial designation in 1740–45, and then 'the
lands of the valley of the Danube' or simply the 'lands of the House of
Habsburg'. The Good Soldier Švejk's confusion over which nation he
was supposed to be fighting for in the world war is the funniest expression of Austria-Hungary's identity crisis.

43

Nobody really understood the region's true provenance, because the Habsburg family, and not borders, race or religion, tended to bind it all together. The Habsburgs were landlords, not rulers, and they oversaw a collection of entailed estates, not a nation. 'No other family,' writes Taylor, 'has endured so long or left so deep a mark on Europe: the Habsburgs were the greatest dynasty of modern Europe, and the history of central Europe revolves around them, not they around it.'[2] The Habsburg princes personified the region, by turns benevolent, greedy, incompetent, weak – making them prime targets for disgruntled 'tenants' who inhabited their vassal states or annexed protectorates.

Imperial power, through the Austrian and Magyar elites, kept this cauldron of nobles and peasants at a simmer; common enemies bound them together. The Habsburgs played off the constituent parts in a constant game of divide and conquer. The Ottoman Turks had traditionally been the biggest threat to Habsburg rule. And, with the partial eviction of Turkey, Vienna cast a covetous eye over the recrudescent Slavs to the south. Emperor Franz Joseph and his fiercely anti-Slav court were determined to lay claim to the Balkan territory vacated by the Turks, and, with German support, freeze Russia out of the peninsula.

—

In this pursuit, Austria-Hungary in the 1870s proceeded to deny the Slavic states any hope of unifying along the lines that Russia and Serbia so desired. Vienna won the support of the new Germany in this enterprise, who shared the view of the Slavic people as a lesser breed. This went deeper than mere discrimination: underneath the diplomatic veneer, ancient racial hatreds re-emerged, nourished by newly united Germany's presumption of racial supremacy in an age of social Darwinism. The Slavs were an inferior people, in German eyes, who had no right to exist in the front rank of nations.

In practice, this meant the steady subjection of the Slavic world to Teutonic rule. The Habsburgs made this project clear the moment they entered the negotiations at the Congress of Berlin. They aimed to subdue the Serbs (something the Ottomans proved unable to do); block the expansionist hopes of their old foe, Russia; and control the Balkans. In essence, Austria-Hungary's immediate interests reflected its long-term policy, which Germany shared.

In response to these pressures, the Congress of Berlin delivered no more than what Austria-Hungary asked for: the right to occupy and administer Bosnia and Herzegovina. If this was seen as the thin end of a bigger Viennese wedge, the Russians did not object. Why? On the face of it, they settled for the lesser evil: they preferred Austrian rule to the Turkish, at least in the short term. A truer reason why the Russians didn't object is that, by occupying Bosnia, Austria-Hungary had opened itself up to a kind of reverse colonisation. Slavic influence was now free to flow into the Habsburg embrace and work its lethal ministry. In a sense, the Bosnian Serbs had found an opening to the Austrian tent.

———

Serbia was denied any voice in these negotiations. As parts of the Balkans slipped by increments under Vienna's control, Serbia's protests were ignored. The Serbian delegates to the Congress were not invited to the sessions that determined Austria's right to occupy Bosnia. It appeased Belgrade, for now, to receive as recompense a few provinces that were earlier earmarked for Bulgaria. Yet the whole episode demonstrated how the great powers intended to treat the Balkans: as a cake to be sliced up and handed out, with little recourse to, or consultation with, the people who lived there. In so doing, the powers had gravely underestimated Belgrade's wounded pride. For now, no doubt, Vienna had won a great diplomatic victory, acquiring the right to occupy a chunk of Balkan territory without war.

Indeed, Austria-Hungary was the only participant who emerged satisfied from the negotiations. The Treaty of Berlin that resulted left a 'disastrous heritage of discontent', according to Albertini. He goes on:

Turkey had lost half her European territory; Bulgaria received only half of what was assigned to her by the Treaty of San Stefano; Serbia had been done out of Bosnia-Herzegovina . . . Russia had seen the fruits of her victory vanish, while Austria had won two large Slav provinces without sacrifice.[3]

Serbia would not be appeased for long. Russia had ceded Bosnia without a word of dissent. When the Serbian delegation complained to the Russian party, the latter replied that the situation was 'temporary' and 'within fifteen years at the latest we shall be forced to fight Austria'.[4] 'Vain consolation,' replied the Serbs. The Russian prophecy reflected a general feeling, which insinuated itself into the river of Slavic consciousness: some kind of conflict with Austria-Hungary seemed inevitable. The Tsar himself contributed to the sense of a gradual decoupling of Russia and Germany/Austria-Hungary in a letter to Bismarck on 15 August 1879, in which he accused the chancellor of siding with Vienna and forgetting Russia's neutrality during the Franco-Prussian War. The outcome, he wrote, might 'turn out disastrous for both countries'.[5]

———

Bismarck had no need of the Tsar's letter to persuade him to change his resistance to military coalitions. Clearly, some sort of alliance against Russia was needed, especially as rumours were arriving of St Petersburg's designs on a similar 'defensive' alliance with Paris or Rome. In September, Bismarck went to Vienna to persuade the Austro-Hungarian foreign minister, Gyula Andrássy, who needed little persuading, despite the initial reluctance of Franz Joseph. On 7 October 1879, Germany and Austria-Hungary signed the treaty that created the Dual Alliance, pledging that each would come to the other's aid if attacked. It was explicitly a *defensive* treaty. Russia was the implied aggressor but nowhere mentioned – in fact, the Russian threat was deliberately played down, in deference to Kaiser Wilhelm I's fear that the treaty might catalyse the marriage of Russia and France.

The Dual Alliance was the first great European power bloc to emerge in the last decade of the nineteenth century after the German and Italian unifications. Rigid, stubborn, seemingly unbreakable, this was the pact that bound the Germanic world, and it would last until the end of the First World War. In 1882, a new pact was negotiated with Italy, which enfolded Rome into a three-way alliance (which did little to cheer Bismarck, who saw Italy as weak and uncommitted). The result, known as the Triple Alliance, was signed on 20 May 1882 in strictest secrecy. Though defensive, the alliance prescribed the creation of a military power in the heart of Europe. Its purpose was to secure the central powers against Russia, whose rapidly growing population presented the greatest threat to German and Austro-Hungarian security.

The first few articles went to the heart of the matter:

ARTICLE 1. The High Contracting Parties [Germany, Austria-Hungary and Italy] . . . will enter into no alliance or engagement directed against any one of their States . . .

ARTICLE 3. If one, or two, of the High Contracting Parties, without direct provocation on their part, should chance to be attacked and to be engaged in a war with two or more Great Powers non-signatory to the present Treaty, the *casus foederis* [the case for enacting the alliance] will arise simultaneously for all the High Contracting Parties.

ARTICLE 4. In case a Great Power non-signatory to the present Treaty should threaten the security of the states of one of the High Contracting Parties, and the threatened Party should find itself forced on that account to make war against it, the two others bind themselves to observe towards their Ally a benevolent neutrality. Each of them reserves to itself, in this case, the right to take part in the war, if it should see fit, to make common cause with its Ally.

ARTICLE 5. If the peace of any of the High Contracting Parties should chance to be threatened under the circumstances foreseen by the preceding Articles, the High Contracting Parties shall take counsel together in ample time as to the military measures to be taken with a view to eventual cooperation. They engage henceforward, in all cases of common participation in a war, to conclude neither armistice, nor peace, nor treaty, except by common agreement among themselves.

ARTICLE 6. The High Contracting Parties mutually promise secrecy as to the contents and existence of the present Treaty.[6]

In short, each party would defend the other if one were the target of an 'unprovoked' attack. Technically, neither Austria nor Italy would be obliged to defend Germany in a war that Germany had provoked. But how was 'provocation' to be defined or decided? Warfare is invariably the result of mutual tensions and provocations, on all sides.

The terms of the treaty quickly leaked to Europe's embassies. If the defensive nature of the alliance had the aim of reassuring Europe, it failed. France and Russia were outraged at the secret alliance, and a series of provocative amendments intensified their feelings – a side deal with Spain, for example, excluding it from entering into any treaty that may threaten the interests of the signatories. Indeed, news of the Triple Alliance soon hastened the creation of a similar bloc between Russia and France.

A war between members of the Alliance and Britain was unthinkable at this stage. In fact, an additional provision stated that the treaty 'cannot in any case be regarded as being directed against England'.[7] Britain was in no sense an implied enemy by its exclusion (the same could not be said for Russia and France). In fact, Berlin hoped that Britain might be persuaded to join the Alliance. Negotiations never advanced, partly because it was feared Francophile sympathisers in the London Cabinet would inform

France of the Alliance's existence. But, more generally, Britain refused to enter any continental alliances, a policy of 'wait and see' that it upheld – to the anger and frustration of Germany, Russia and France – until the declaration of war in August 1914.

6

THE KAISER'S WORLD

Weltpolitik would be 'a sort of Napeolonic
supremacy . . . in the peaceful sense'.
Kaiser Wilhelm II, on Germany's 'world policy'

SLOWLY, THE POLES OF EUROPE were aligning. In a very real sense, Germany and Austria-Hungary were *conscious* of their likely enemies in a future war. The biggest and most threatening lay directly to the east. As early as the spring of 1888, Germany regarded war with Russia as probable, if not inevitable, and the German General Staff discussed a preventive strike to thwart Russia's emerging military power. To this argument, Bismarck was firmly opposed, and he clung to his core purpose, of maintaining the balance of power in Europe.

Bismarck proceeded on his course of peace with cold disregard for anyone in his path; the high political end was what mattered. He drew on charm, deceit, violence and sheer, indomitable will – any card that stacked his hand and got the desired result. But, above all, his method involved accurately second-guessing the rest of the field. '[I]t suited Bismarck's peculiar genius for politics to maintain in his head multiple possible moves by adversaries,' concludes Jonathan

Steinberg (whose harsh biography of Bismarck presents his subject as having few other qualities). 'He was and remained to the end master of the finely tuned game of diplomacy . . . He could outplay and outsmart the smartest people in other states . . .'[1]

The idea of a German pre-emptive strike did not impress this proud Prussian nobleman, whose foreign policy, if it meant anything, meant keeping the peace even as Germany expanded in Europe and abroad. It was just this sort of paradox – of seizing power *peacefully* – that appealed to and challenged Bismarck's famous definition of politics as 'the art of the possible'.

He took up this theme in his great speech to the Reichstag on 6 February 1888. It was a plea for peace wrapped in the German flag, delivered three days after he published the text of the hitherto secret Dual Alliance with Austria. That revelation delighted the German people but received the darkest reading in Russia, which instantly identified itself as the target. Bismarck therefore stressed his belief in a defensive war, but clothed his peaceful intent in the language of violence. His speech thus roused intense patriotic feeling, by appealing to the German identity as a race apart and identifying the very source of German insecurity and future paranoia, which was the country's geographical position, squeezed between France and Russia:

> When I say that it is our duty to endeavour to be ready at all times and for all emergencies, I imply that we must make greater exertions than other people for the same purpose, because of our geographical position. We are situated in the heart of Europe, and have at least three fronts open to an attack. France has only her eastern, and Russia only her western frontier where they may be attacked. God has placed us where we are prevented, thanks to our neighbours, from growing lazy and dull. He has placed by our side the most warlike and restless of all nations, the French, and He has permitted warlike inclinations to grow strong in Russia, where formerly they existed to a lesser degree.

Thus we are given the spur, so to speak, from both sides, and are compelled to exertions which we should perhaps not be making otherwise. The pikes in the European carp-pond are keeping us from being carps by making us feel their teeth on both sides . . .

If we Germans wish to wage a war with the full effect of our national strength, it must be a war which satisfies all who take part in it, all who sacrifice anything for it, in short the whole nation. It must be a national war, a war carried on with the enthusiasm of 1870, when we were foully attacked. A war into which we are not borne by the will of the people will be waged, to be sure, if it has been declared by the constituted authorities who deemed it necessary; it will even be waged pluckily, and possibly victoriously, after we have once smelled fire and tasted blood, but it will lack from the beginning the nerve and enthusiasm of a war in which we are attacked. In such a one the whole of Germany from Memel to the Alpine Lakes will flare up like a powder mine; it will be bristling with guns, and no enemy will dare to engage this *furor teutonicus* which develops when we are attacked.

I am, therefore, not in favor of any kind of an aggressive war, and if war could result only from our attack – somebody must kindle a fire, we shall not kindle it. Neither the consciousness of our strength, which I have described, nor our confidence in our treaties, will prevent us from continuing our former endeavours to preserve peace. In this we do not permit ourselves to be influenced by annoyances or dislikes. The threats and insults, and the challenges, which have been made have, no doubt, excited also with us a feeling of irritation, which does not easily happen with Germans, for they are less prone to national hatred than any other nation. We Germans fear God, and naught else in the world! It is this fear of God which makes us love and cherish peace. If in spite of this anybody breaks the peace, he will discover that the ardent patriotism of 1813, which called to the standards the entire population of Prussia – weak, small, and drained to the marrow as it then was – has today become the common property of the whole German nation. Attack the German nation anywhere, and you will find it armed to a man, and every man with the firm belief in his heart: God will be with us.[2]

These last words brought thunderous applause and the Reichstag deputies cheering to their feet.

———

After Bismarck's fall, in 1890, his successors abandoned this policy of restraint. In the months before his dismissal, the chancellor cut a lonely figure, his voice marginalised, his peers distant or contemptuous. He had lost his royal sponsor. With the death of the nonagenarian Kaiser Wilhelm I on 9 March 1888, and then the death of his seriously ill son Frederick III – emperor for three months – the crown passed to Wilhelm II, son of Frederick, and the direct grandson of Victoria and Albert.

The new emperor, aged 29, was unpredictable, irascible and of unsound mind. His closest courtiers considered him infantile or mad, according to Hermann Lutz, a German civil servant who wrote *Die europäische politik un der Julikrise 1914* (1930) (European Policy and the July Crisis) for the Reichstag Commission investigating the causes of the war.[3] The Kaiser's 'flamboyance, his aggressive speeches, his public image and dress, his quick wit and capacity to create slogans, the exaggeration of his uniforms and bellicosity' gave the explosive growth of the German Empire between the 1890s and the First World War its 'Wilhelmine' character, claims Steinberg.[4] It is doubtful that a man as limited as the new Kaiser could embody so much; the explosive growth would have proceeded without him. But certainly his impulsiveness, mood swings and streak of cruelty had a startling early influence on the new government.

Wiser politicians later tried to control and muzzle this unruly monarch, whose grossly offensive remarks upset many state dinners. Ultimately, Wilhelm proved ineffectual and timid. During the war years, his generals would ignore him. But, for now, the Kaiser ruled in the full flood of impetuous youth, intimidating anyone who disagreed with him and commanding considerable popularity. Perhaps his strained machismo stemmed from a childhood disability resulting from a breech birth that left him with a withered left arm, 15 centimetres shorter than his right, which inhibited his ability to play sport or serve in the forces. He learnt to disguise the crippled limb by holding the hilt of a sword or cane 'to give the effect of a useful limb posed at a dignified angle'.[5]

Old man Bismarck, used to a long leash under Wilhelm I, soon found working for the new Kaiser intolerable. He confided to a friend in October 1892:

In the last few months before my dismissal, the question constantly occupied my mind in sleepless night whether I could endure things any longer under him [Kaiser Wilhelm II]. Love for my country told me: 'You must not go, you are the only one who can still serve as a counterpoise to his will.' But on the other hand I knew the Monarch's mental state which opened up in my mind prospects of the most lamentable complications . . . the Kaiser himself put an end to my inward struggle by intimating that he no longer wanted me.[6]

—

The end of Bismarck brought a profound change in German policy. Until now, Bismarck, for all his 'blood and iron' speeches, his Prussian bombast, had pursued a softly softly approach, shrewd, gradualist and, above all, peaceable. And it had worked, to a point. The one thing he sought to avoid was a European war, the bloody scale of which he alone, among the higher ranks of the Prussian ruling class, seemed to comprehend.

One of Wilhelm II's first acts would bring that nightmare closer.

The Kaiser refused to renew the secret Reinsurance Treaty with Russia, on the advice of his new chancellor, Leo von Caprivi, and other ministers opposed to Bismarck. The treaty had been a central plank of the Bismarckian world since 1887. It obliged Germany and Russia to remain neutral in the event of the other's entry into a war. The sticking point was that it committed Germany to stand by and watch if Russia was to occupy the Dardanelles – an event the new regime vowed to forbid. The net effect was to sever a last tendon in the fragile relationship between Germany and Russia. In tandem, the Kaiser spoke forcefully in favour of a preventive war against Russia, despite Bismarck's firm counsel against such a course (not that many took Wilhelm's bellicose utterances seriously; he would talk up war one day and peace the next).

At a stroke, the Bismarckian vision and his great 'juggling act' that held Europe in his thrall was overthrown. In the 1890s, Germany embarked on a 'new course', the Kaiser's famous 'world policy', or *Weltpolitik*, defined as little more than a brazen bid for global power based on the notion of Germany's self-appointed destiny as the ultimate ruler of the world. This grand delusion arose out of Germany's conception of itself as the usurper of the British Empire. The Kaiser's ministers, chiefly Holstein, once a Bismarck protégé, and his new chancellor, Bülow, now set about dismantling every plank of Bismarck's legacy in pursuit of *Weltpolitik*.

Germany considered itself *entitled* to an empire, rather like a spoilt child. The Kaiser rejoiced in the dream of 'a sort of Napolonic supremacy . . . in the peaceful sense'.[7] 'The question,' Bülow said, 'is not whether we want to colonise or not, but that we must colonise.'[8] In other words, 'to say that Germany should cease her Weltpolitik was rather like a father telling his son: "If only you would not grow, you troublesome youth, then I would not need to buy you longer trousers!" We can't do anything other than carry out Weltpolitik.'[9] Social Darwinists such as Admiral Alfred von Tirpitz went further: to him, Germany's global dominance was inevitable, as 'irresistible as a natural law'.[10]

—

The race for colonies created the brief Anglo-German 'colonial marriage' between Berlin and London in 1890. It engendered high hopes of a lasting friendship and even of the admission of Britain into the Triple Alliance. Those great expectations made the rupture all the more complete when the marriage failed. A colonial agreement in East Africa, under which Germany would acquire Heligoland in exchange for concessions to British interests in East Africa and Zanzibar, consummated the relationship. The deal, though relatively minor, marked the high point of Anglo-German cooperation over the spoils of Africa. Kennedy writes:

> It was the nearest equivalent, in both its range and its purpose,
> to the Anglo-French settlement of 1904: yet, whereas the latter
> marked the beginning of an entente which was to grow ever
> firmer as the years progressed, the Heligoland-Zanzibar treaty
> was to be followed within a short space of time by mutual
> disillusionment and distrust.[11]

The treaty led nowhere; the friendship soured. There were fleeting expressions of goodwill ('Germany, our natural ally', *The Times* unconvincingly reported). But Britain's policy of splendid isolation intensified under Gladstone's new Liberal government of 1892. To Germany, Britain was dealing in the scraps of empire. It dawned on Berlin that the idea of Britain forming some sort of quadruple alliance with Germany, Italy and Austria-Hungary was fantasy. Within a few years, the relationship degenerated, and extreme, mutual antagonism set Germany's world policy on a dangerous course.

In the mid-1890s, Germany launched a new race for colonies – with or without Britain – spurred by the formation in 1891 of the Pan-German League, an extreme ultra-nationalist political organisation. The league pursued not only the proliferation of German interests in Europe and abroad but also the transcendence of Germany as something racially and culturally superior. Its rapidly growing membership took for granted the supremacy of the German people over what were viewed as inferior 'races', chiefly the Slavs, Jews and Latins. For them, social Darwinism meant the active propagation of the Teutonic people and the preservation of the purity of German blood.

The British Empire presented an insufferable geographical hindrance to the expression of Pan-German superiority. The Kaiser would often express his fury at English duplicity and arrogance. He revealed his colours in explosive style during a little argument over South Africa, on 29 December 1895, which plunged Anglo-German relations to their worst for the decade. It was triggered by the 'Kruger Telegram', sent by the Kaiser to congratulate Stephanus Johannes Kruger, president of the Transvaal Republic, for repelling an attack by 600 British soldiers under the command of Leander Starr Jameson. 'I express to you my sincere congratulations,' the Kaiser told his Dutch friends, 'that you and your people, without appealing to the help of friendly powers, have succeeded by your energetic action against the armed bands which invaded your country . . .'[12]

The Kaiser's cable, not least the belittling term 'armed bands', outraged British diplomatic circles and the press, and revealed the new and disturbing face of German *Weltpolitik*: aggressively expansionist and willing to contest Britain's presumptive rights to the world. In Berlin's eyes, it offered the satisfaction of witnessing the haughty vulnerability of the English, easily provoked from their imperial heights. The incident carried serious consequences and policy implications. Admiral Georg von Müller, an adviser to the Kaiser up to and during the Great War, formalised these in a famous memo of 1896. It stated that Germany aimed to dismantle 'England's world domination so as to lay free the necessary colonial possessions for the central European states who need to expand'.[13] It did not, however, threaten war, although the possibility of an Anglo-German war was discussed formally for the first time.

—

Weltpolitik had a pervasive influence on the nation's mentality. The German people experienced a dawning consciousness that their time had come. There was a palpable awareness of this zeitgeist, and euphoria in Prussian officer clubs, academic circles, the military, the Reichstag and the beer halls. German intellectuals, writers and economists readily promoted Germany's destiny, as though it was somehow racially or divinely ordained that Germany should acquire a 'fitting share of the world power which human nature and higher Providence assign to the civilised peoples'.[14] The philosopher Max Weber, and his colleagues in the Liberal imperialist group and the Pan-German movement, lent intellectual ballast to the new policy. The unification of Germany would be looked upon as a 'youthful folly' if it was not the 'starting point' of Germany's world expansion, Weber declared in his Inaugural Lecture to Freiburg University in 1895.[15]

Would pursuing these delusions of grandeur make war inevitable? Germany's chancellor Bülow (and later Bethmann-Hollweg) was careful not to use warlike language. He hoped, like Bismarck, that Germany's empire could be achieved peacefully. Even the Kaiser was careful to add peace-riders to his bellicose remarks. Others were persuaded that if Germany failed to fulfil its 'destiny', war would inevitably follow. They were usually intellectuals, journalists or dangerous militarists (see Chapter 14), who made warlike noises in the wings but had no direct hold on policy. The historian Hans Delbruck declared in 1899, for example:

> We want to be a World Power and pursue colonial policy in the grand manner . . . Here there can be no step backward. The entire future of our people among the great nations depends on it. We can pursue this policy with England or without England. With England means in peace; against England means – through war.[16]

That did not mean war was inevitable, contrary to those who

believed that German hegemony led to unavoidable conflict. Most colonial flare-ups had hitherto been contained, or resolved through negotiation, such as over Portugal, Samoa, West Africa, and many other examples. The Berlin–Baghdad Railway involved, for a time, an English investment consortium. The crisis over the Kruger Telegram faded. Even the Boer War, though it exacerbated Anglo-German tensions, did not lead to threats of war. If war came to Europe, it seemed less likely to be fought over colonies with every passing year. In fact, between 1898 and 1901, at the very height of the Boer War, the British Government sought an alliance with Germany in reaction to a French colonial threat – and was rebuffed! Such was the fluidity of political relations in trying to reconcile global with continental tensions.

—

By 1900, Germany seemed to be realising its economic, if not imperial, destiny. In the 30 years since unification, the nation had enjoyed the most enviable economic record in the world, exceeded only by America. A huge investment in home industries made Germany the most powerful manufacturing base in Europe. One reason was the thriving local marketplace, driven by sheer force of numbers. Germany's population had risen from 41 million in 1871 to 56 million by 1900; whereas the numbers of French and Britons had barely budged in that period, with 38 million each at the turn of the century. The new masses converged on the cities in the industrial heartlands, looking for jobs – leading to rapid German industrialisation, especially in the great mining and manufacturing regions of the Ruhr Valley, Lorraine, Saxony and Silesia.

Germany's state-sponsored policy of 'neo-mercantilism' made industry flourish: textile production rose tenfold between 1878 and 1905. Coal, iron and steel output accelerated since 1871 'with a rapidity unparalleled elsewhere in Europe', concludes Fritz Fischer.[17] In that time, coal production rose by eight times, while England's mines merely doubled theirs. Only America outstripped German coal output in the first decade of the twentieth century. In the quarter-century before 1912, German iron and steel output easily outdid her European rivals. Raw iron-ore production rocketed from four million tonnes in 1887 to 15.5 million tonnes in 1912, up 387 per cent, compared with America's 368.5 per cent and Britain's mere 30.6 per cent. The rate of growth of German steel production led the world, rising in the period by 1335 per cent, from 0.9 million tonnes in 1886 to 13.6 million tonnes. Imports and exports soared, rising about 240 per cent and 185 per cent respectively, over the two decades before 1912, with Germany easily the greatest importer in Europe, and Britain and France growing at less than half the German rate.

That reflected Germany's huge demand for imported commodities, from Latin America and other foreign markets, to fuel expansion, a growth spurt comparable with China's a century later. At the end of the nineteenth century, Germany's foreign trade was growing at more than double the rate of Britain and France. German banks played a critical role in financing overseas developments, seizing business from British merchant banks. As Fritz Fischer shows in his exhaustive analysis, the four great German banks financed, through overseas subsidiaries, the Otavi Mining and Railway Company in south-west Africa, the Baghdad Railway in Asia Minor, the Shantung Railroad and Mining Company in China, the Tientsin-Puckow Railway and other major railroads, as well as oil enterprises in Roumania (as it was spelt at the time) and Iraq[18] – all projects that Britain, France or Russia would traditionally have won.

Such astonishing growth, the seizing of overseas contracts, the massive movement of goods and people, the general thrust into global markets, drove the need to build a vast merchant marine, replacing Germany's old sailing vessels of the 1880s with a modern fleet of steamships. In tandem rose the perception that Germany must acquire a new navy that would not only protect her overseas interests and merchant fleet but also challenge Britain's sea supremacy. Germany's foreign interests needed protection, and Berlin had always eyed Britain's command of the seas with a mixture of envy and alarm. It gave a pretext to build a navy that would at least intimidate, if not actually threaten, England's. Here was an ironclad case that *Weltpolitik* meant more than simply dreams of a bigger place in the sun (see Chapter 3).

The designs for a German navy paralleled the development of German ports – built to handle the massive turnover of merchant and military shipping, which grew by 300 per cent in the 25 years to 1912, small by British standards but surpassing continental growth rates. In this light, Germany would *impose* friendship on Britain through mutual recognition of strength. 'A German navy would,' states Fischer, 'force Britain to regard Germany as an equal, a desirable ally and a friend, and thus become a symbol of Germany's claim to world power'[19] – the operative word being 'force'.

Towards the end of the century, Germany was thus gradually disabused of the idea of a colonial alliance with Britain. Britain's indifference to, or failure to engage with, Germany's nascent foreign policy infuriated Berlin. For the most part, British trade priorities were deaf to the economic benefits of such an alliance. Berlin strove to punch above its weight but had no colonial fat. In any case, responding to Germany was hardly a priority in Whitehall. Talk of better relations fell foul of political pressures, media opposition and the burgeoning naval arms race with Germany. Britain's colonial dealings with France, Russia and America were of far greater importance, and tended to sideline the 'German problem'.

And that is the real reason why London refused to strike an alliance with Berlin. German *weakness*, and not, as is commonly supposed, German strength, destroyed the prospect of an alliance with Britain. London saw little of value in it. 'It was, after all, the British who killed off the alliance idea, as much as the Germans,' explains Niall Ferguson. 'And they did so not because Germany began to pose a threat to Britain but, on the contrary, because they realized she did *not* pose a threat' (Ferguson's emphasis).[20] In this light, it is easier to see why, when Germany's emerging financial and military strength *did* start to worry Britain, France and Russia in the 1900s, they drew together into a three-way entente, the better to preserve their empires . . . and leave Germany in the cold.

7

THE FRANCO-RUSSIAN VICE

If France is attacked by Germany . . . Russia shall
employ all her available forces to attack Germany. If
Russia is attacked by Germany . . . France shall employ
all her available forces to attack Germany.
Article I of the Franco-Russian Alliance

ALSACE AND LORRAINE: how often would schoolchildren hear
them cited as causes of the Great War? But how important were they?
The harsh terms Germany imposed on France after the Prussian victory of 1871 alerted Europe to the presence of a rapacious military
aristocracy in their midst, given to the plunder and confiscation of its
neighbours' territory – similar, in fact, to Napoleon 80 years earlier.

The Prussian settlement at the Treaty of Frankfurt infuriated the French people (as the Treaty of Versailles would Germany,
in 1918). Especially humiliating was the loss of the eastern border
provinces of Alsace and Lorraine, annexed to the unified German
Reich. Bismarck himself opposed the annexation but was overruled
by General Helmuth von Moltke the Elder and his generals, with
the support of Emperor Wilhelm I. The chancellor rightly observed
that France 'would be forever hostile'[1] towards Germany for carrying

off two French provinces and forcibly 'Germanicising' their inhabitants. Even British Prime Minister William Gladstone in isolationist England condemned the act as a 'violent laceration'.[2]

France's loss of Alsace and Lorraine had serious military consequences. Germany now enjoyed a defensive 'buffer' and an offensive 'jump-off' point in any new war with France. Memories of the Napoleonic Wars were never far away. And the provinces delivered resources to feed Germany's insatiable appetite. Lorraine's chief appeal were vast reserves of iron ore, the production of which had quadrupled in the previous decade and was about to accelerate further with the discovery of a new method of smelting. This flowed into Germany's steel foundries and raised the galling prospect of French mines fuelling a future German war against France.

The emotional and political consequences were acutely felt in the provinces, at least initially. If some Alsatians spoke a German dialect, 'they remained firm in their allegiance to France, and the Germans never succeeded in assimilating them'.[3] On the other hand, the Treaty of Frankfurt gave Alsatians and Lorrainers until 1 October 1872 to decide whether to move to France or remain in their homes and submit to German nationality. By 1876, about 100,000, or just five per cent of the residents of Alsace-Lorraine, had chosen to emigrate and retain their French nationality.[4] Most preferred to keep their homes, understandably; and most of these new 'Germans' rejected their status. In the 1880s, the 15 deputies the provinces sent to the Reichstag consistently opposed the annexation and refused to accept their new nationality. They were known as protester deputies (*députés protestataires*), who resisted the annexation with the motion, 'May it please the Reichstag to decide that the populations of Alsace-Lorraine that were annexed, without having been consulted, to the Germanic Empire by the treaty of Frankfurt have to come out particularly against this annexation.'[5]

—

Feelings in France about Alsace and Lorraine tended to ebb and flow, depending on the political and economic climate. Politicians routinely called for their return to incite patriotic fervour. This was not always a political ploy. Some politicians – chiefly those who had been forced to leave their homes, in order to retain their French nationality – were deeply committed to the provinces' reclamation.

In the decade after the Prussian War, France's reparations were swiftly paid, and the country made an astonishing economic recovery – a testament to the self-confidence and economic strength of the French nation. By the late 1870s, there was fresh talk of reclaiming Alsace and Lorraine. It was indeed galling to France and Britain that Germany should continue to control the provinces. London was 'shocked' at this wanton desecration of French sovereignty – a standard Britain did not apply, of course, to its imperial conquests.[6]

The popular cry for the provinces' return faded in the 1880s. If most French people still desired it, few were willing to fight *la revanche* – a new war of reconquest – to recover them. In fact, France and Germany enjoyed several years of détente (1878–85). The Republican victory at the French elections of 1877 had demolished the chances of a monarchist restoration, delighting Bismarck, whose fear of *la revanche*, which had obsessed him in his final years in power, now thoroughly receded.

Indeed, in the 1880s, Bismarck actually encouraged French colonial expansion in order to turn Paris's attention from the 'lost provinces'. This formed the cornerstone of the détente. 'I hope to reach the point when you will forgive Sedan as you have forgiven Waterloo,' Bismarck declared. 'Renounce the Rhine and I will help you secure everywhere else the satisfactions you require.'[7] Bismarck honoured his word, backing French expansion in the 1880s into Tunisia, Morocco, West Africa, Egypt, Madagascar and Tonkin.

In the 1890s, many French people grew weary of talk of *la revanche*. Closer economic and cultural ties with Germany all but removed the issue from French policy. 'In this last decade of the nineteenth century,' writes the historian John Keiger, 'it was clear that the Alsace-Lorraine myth was in sharp decline and that virtually nobody in France recommended war to return the provinces to France. Some still wished for the peaceful return sometime in the future, but true *revanche* was dead.'[8]

France and Germany became important trading partners, despite periodic French protests of an 'economic Sedan' after German incursions on French markets. By 1890, Germany was France's third biggest supplier and fourth biggest buyer.[9] Nor were French feelings towards Germany altogether hostile. French intellectuals admired and connected with their German counterparts. Wagner's music and German philosophers, from Kant to Nietzsche, seduced the French cultural elite.

Even in Alsace-Lorraine, the picture was mixed. If many Alsace-Lorrainers dreamt of their provinces' return to France at some point, a substantial minority were content with their new parents, consoled by the economic security offered by the burgeoning German state. A minority of Alsace and Lorraine's 15 deputies elected to the Reichstag supported the province's autonomy in the late 1890s. One former Alsatian, Count Paul de Leusse, entertained, a century ahead of his time, the idea of a Franco-German internal market, as proposed in his essay 'Peace by a Franco-German Customs Union'.

Indeed, the era of détente gradually entered the phase of rapprochement and even talk of a Franco-German alliance, as Keiger's study shows. 'With such an alliance France would at one blow regain her standing,' remarked a former French war minister, General Jean-Baptise Campenon. 'France and Germany united would rule the world.' While the two governments of Jules Ferry applauded the new relationship, he stopped short of talk of such an alliance. The French public would tolerate only 'occasional collaboration' with Germany.[10]

—

The radical and conservative ends of French politics were having none of this. They found repugnant the pro-German policy of Ferry's government. French conservatives never abandoned their pursuit of the provinces, culminating in the famous exchange in 1882 between

Ferry and extreme patriot Paul Déroulède, founder of *Ligue des Patriotes*, who, in reply to Ferry's claim, 'You will end by making me think you prefer Alsace-Lorraine to France,' uttered his famous line, 'I have lost two sisters and you offer me twenty chambermaids.'[11]

But the left made the sharpest attack on French dalliances with Germany. The future premier Georges Clemenceau, getting into his stride as a young political animal, accused Ferry's administration of high treason. The wound was terminal. Ferry lost the 1885 elections, hastening the end of détente and the beginning of a new era of tense Franco-German coexistence punctuated by periodic blasts of French nationalism that almost brought the two countries to blows (for example, the aggressive stance of the new war minister General Boulanger, and the Schnäbele customs affair, where German police arrested a senior French customs official on the German border).

Yet, as the century rounded out, and the European order settled back into a state of peaceful balance, Alsace-Lorraine lost importance again, slipping further into the German orbit. Germans now accounted for 40 per cent of the population of Strasbourg and more than half of Metz. Intermarriage spread, and the once fierce French identity became blurred and Germanicised in the coal-rich provinces. By 1900, Alsace and Lorraine hardly threatened a dinner-party argument, far less to drive the two nations to war. As the German ambassador to Paris reported in 1898, most Frenchmen were starting 'to forget Alsace Lorraine'.[12]

That would change once more in the mid-1900s, as new nationalistic forces rallied again for the return of the lost provinces. Two brilliant young French men, who despised the perpetrators of Sedan and the mutilators of French pride, breathed life into the revanchist case: Lorraine-born intellectual Raymond Poincaré, whose family lost their home in the annexation; and Ferdinand Foch, who witnessed German humiliation of French soldiers at Alsace as a young officer in the Prussian War. Poincaré would become French president in 1913, and Foch the saviour of Paris, as commander of the French 9th Army at the Battle of the Marne in 1914 (see Chapter 43).

—

In 1897, Franco-German relations degenerated into a sort of cold war, which persisted right up to the declaration of actual war in 1914. That year, the French Government revealed the existence of a secret military convention, signed on 17 August 1892, between France and Russia. Conceived as another 'defensive' treaty in response to the Triple Alliance, its existence and its clauses were kept so secret that 'few French ministers even knew of their details until the First World War'.[13]

Germany perceived clearly enough the strategic understanding that bound the powers on her east and west borders. Russia aimed to dominate the Balkans through its Serbian protégé; and France sought the return of Alsace and Lorraine. In both cases, Germany was the ultimate obstacle.

Russia's broader strategic interests lay in containing German power. Another German defeat of France would free the Teutonic world to throw everything they had at the east. France, for its part, refused to countenance the existence of a powerful Germany, newly unified, across its border. In this light, it was hard not to see Russia and France as the opposing jaws of a Franco-Russian vice.

Even so, the Tsar was initially hesitant about an alliance with France. His autocratic regime regarded the French Third Republic with suspicion. His deep distrust of the German-led power bloc sandwiched between them overrode his concerns, and the two powers swiftly found common ground in a policy of German containment. Of course, Russia and France were already old accomplices. In finance and diplomacy, they were closely bound. Since 1888, Russia had raised cheap loans on the French Bourse to finance arms purchases, the two nations shared military training operations, and the Russian aristocracy were enamoured of French culture (a compliment France tended not to return). This friendship chaperoned the negotiations. The Kaiser's refusal to renew the Reinsurance Treaty with Russia proved the last straw, and St

Petersburg eagerly sought a formal alliance with Paris.

—

The Franco-Russian Alliance, signed on 7 August 1892, announced the end of the signatories' military isolation through the creation of a highly provocative defensive pact. It went much further than Berlin's treaties with Vienna and Rome; it formally identified Germany, Austria and Italy as the enemies, thus deepening the fissure that spread across central Europe. It was brutally simple: Russia and France would defend each other if attacked. It explicitly identified German or German-sponsored aggression as the threat. At a darker level, the Franco-Russian pact seemed to anticipate, in its casual presumption of a violent world, total war in Europe. The Alliance reads:

> France and Russia, being animated by a common desire to preserve peace, and having no other object than to meet the necessities of a defensive war provoked by an attack of the forces of the Triple Alliance against either of them, have agreed upon the following provisions:
>
> 1. If France is attacked by Germany [or Italy/Austria-Hungary, supported by Germany] Russia shall employ all her available forces to attack Germany. If Russia is attacked by Germany . . . France shall employ all her available forces to attack Germany.
>
> 2. In case the forces of the Triple Alliance . . . should be mobilized, France and Russia, at the first news of this event . . . shall mobilize immediately and simultaneously [transfer] the whole of their forces as far as possible to their frontiers.
>
> 3. The available forces to be employed against Germany shall be, on the part of France, 1,300,000 men, on the part of Russia, 700,000 or 800,000 men. These forces shall engage to the full

with such speed that Germany will have to fight simultaneously on the East and on the West.

4. The General Staffs of the Armies of the two countries shall cooperate with each other at all times . . . They shall communicate with each other, while there is still peace, all information relative to the armies of the Triple Alliance which is already in their possession or shall come into their possession . . .

5. France and Russia shall not conclude peace separately.

6. The present Convention shall have the same duration as the Triple Alliance.

7. All the clauses enumerated above shall be kept absolutely secret.[14]

This agreement would persist in this form, more or less, up until 1914, when it would soon be rendered obsolete by the huge forces that were thrown against the signatories.

A critical moment in the negotiations was the discussion of what 'mobilisation' meant. The Russian generals were explicit. Mobilisation, said General Nikolai Obruchev, 'cannot now be regarded as a peaceful act; on the contrary, it is now the most decisive act of war; ie would be inseparable from an *aggression*'. His counterpart, Raoul de Boisdeffre, concurred:

Mobilisation is declaration of war. To mobilise is to oblige one's neighbour to do the same . . . to allow a million men to mobilise on one's frontiers without at once doing the same oneself is to forfeit all possibility of following suit, is to put oneself in the position of an individual with a pistol in his pocket who allows his neighbour to point a weapon at his head without reaching for his own.

Tsar Alexander III agreed: 'That is how I too understand it.'[15]

In 1914, the Russians would insist on a different definition of mobilisation. Moving a million men to Germany's border would not, under the new meaning, necessarily lead to war. How could Germany, or any power, be expected to believe this, given the understanding of mobilisation that prevailed up until 1914? Mobilising soldiers, in the Prussian mind, was inseparable from sending them into battle. The Russian Duma hardly clarified the issue when, in 1912, it tried to divide the process into several parts, with a period called 'preparation for war' in advance of partial or full mobilisation. The Germans would fail to see the distinction.

8

THE WILD CARD

The English never came back to us. They
went instead to our enemies.
Erich Brandenburg, German historian

THE WILD CARD WAS BRITAIN. Nobody could foresee how British isolationism would end; and, if it did, with whom the British Empire would dally in Europe. For the most part, England looked on, safe in her island redoubt, cut off by sea and a self-imposed policy of splendid isolation. But the British, too, would soon have to choose. As London watched and waited, another colonial fracas arose between France and Britain in a distant part of Africa. Its repercussions would realign London's loyalties in Europe and bring the British in from the cold.

Freed by her Russian military pact, France embarked with renewed confidence on the colonial race, plunging into the scramble for Africa with fresh vigour. This policy, led by French foreign minister Gabriel Hanotaux, set Paris on a collision course with London over long-held claims to East Africa and, in particular, Egypt and the Upper Nile. The confrontation, at Fashoda in the Sudan valley, brought the two powers to the brink of war.

The Fashoda Crisis climaxed in September 1898 with the meeting of British and French forces at the isolated South Sudan fort, the point at which Britain's Cairo–Capetown and France's Dakar–Somaliland axes intersected. The French forces, having endured an epic 14-month trek across Africa from Brazzaville, outnumbered the British; the British outgunned the French. They both sought control of the Upper Nile, Egypt's water source, vital for crop irrigation – and ultimately Egypt itself. Since 1882, British forces had occupied much of Egypt, a colonial claim the legality of which France refused to accept.

In the event, no shots were fired at Fashoda, but the confrontation inflamed chauvinism at home, where the well-informed French and British press railed against what they saw as the other nation's aggression. Neither empire was prepared to make concessions on power sharing in Egypt. Yet the British clearly had the upper hand: they already occupied most of the country and felt entitled to speak for Alexandria. In occupying the source of the Nile, British forces were acting in 'Egyptian interests', London claimed. If not all Egyptians were persuaded, the more astute Frenchmen, seasoned old imperialists, accepted it. Théophile Delcassé, the new French foreign minister, saw the futility of a land war in a remote part of Africa against a rival power who controlled the sea. The dispute was resolved in Britain's favour. On 3 November 1898, the French accepted Britain's free hand in Egypt and quietly withdrew their troops.

—

The Fashoda Crisis had strange and profound repercussions. In the short term, the clash embittered French and British relations, and drove both powers cynically to seek rapprochement with Germany, the sad wallflower who had been overlooked at the dance. All of a sudden, France was taken with the idea of befriending Germany, in support of its colonial ambitions. But, as Keiger shows, the issue kicked into the light of day France's curious double life. On the one hand, Paris courted Berlin, to arrest British ambitions abroad; on the other, Paris turned to St Petersburg, to contain German expansion at home. France couldn't do both, and received no German support in its clash with the English in Africa. French colonial and continental aspirations were politically unsustainable.

London, too, offered to put Germany at the top of its dance card. Before Fashoda erupted, London had been wooing Germany about a colonial agreement as a wedge against France's aggressive claims on Egypt, the Upper Nile and other parts of Africa. Fashoda accelerated those efforts. On three occasions, in 1898, 1899 and 1901, Joseph Chamberlain, secretary of state for the colonies in Salisbury's coalition government (and father of the future appeaser, Neville), pressed unsuccessfully for an Anglo-German alliance. In all three cases, Germany rejected British overtures.

Chamberlain was convinced Britain's future lay with the Germans. In his famous speech in Leicester on 30 November 1899, he aligned German and British interests, and even went so far as to call for a 'New Triple Alliance' of Britain, Germany and the USA – 'the Teutonic race and the two great trans-Atlantic branches of the Anglo-Saxon race' – whose purpose would be to check French and Russian power.[1]

The idea briefly enthralled the future foreign secretary Edward Grey, who envisaged a union between 'the greatest fleet in the world' and 'the greatest army in the world'.[2] Yet, if the Kaiser liked the idea, the German public and press did not. Neither the British nor the German press had forgotten or forgiven past grievances (such as the Kruger Telegram). For his reckless use of the word 'alliance', Chamberlain received a blistering attack in *The Times*. The German papers flayed the idea to death. Under such a sustained attack, Chancellor Bernhard von Bülow rejected any thought of an Anglo-German rapprochement and abandoned his undertaking to offer Chamberlain a reply.

Instead, barely a fortnight later, Bülow stood before the Reichstag to defend the Second Navy Bill. He pointedly made no reference to

Chamberlain's offer of an alliance and unwisely described Britain as a declining nation, jealous of Germany. He declared, in a direct challenge to British sea supremacy, that Germany must have a navy strong enough to deter any power: 'In the coming century Germany will be either the hammer or the anvil.'[3]

In such moments, doors are closed, never to re-open. Chamberlain, a self-made businessman whose word was his bond, abandoned his faith in a German alliance. 'I will say no more here about the way Bülow has treated me,' he wrote to a friend on 28 December 1899, 'but in any case I think we must drop all further negotiations on the subject of the alliance . . .'[4]

—

In the longer run, then, the Fashoda Crisis forced upon Britain and France the recognition of where their true interests lay: oddly, with each other. Both powers commanded vast tracts of foreign territory; both wished to protect them. Germany had rejected their entreaties. They resolved instead upon a new course of give and take, of mutual accommodation, just as they had done at Fashoda, and this formed a template for dealing with future colonial disputes.

Indeed, if France's 'Fashoda complex' led at times to fury at the English, it would prove fortifying. The two old sparring partners coexisted rather like circles on a Venn diagram: overlapping in some places, where they squabbled and fought; separate and pristine in others, where they held out the hand of friendship. In this light, the repercussions of Fashoda would greatly benefit Anglo-French relations. Their self-interest, the preservation of their empires, relied on cooperation and coexistence, and that recognition drew these unnatural bedfellows together. As we shall see, the signing of the Entente Cordiale, in 1904, may be traced directly to the imperial accommodation that followed Fashoda. The Entente would complete the alignment of great-power relationships that divided Europe and nourished Germany's gnawing self-perception of being gradually surrounded.

—

Bülow and the Kaiser were playing a longer game, which led them into the wilderness. They persisted with the idea that London would continue 'coming [to us] as we expected they would', Wilhelm assured his chancellor in January 1901. 'Your Majesty is quite right,' Bülow replied, 'in feeling that it is the English who must make advances to us.'[5] He enumerated all the reasons why Britain needed a strong partner like Germany in order to 'maintain their world empire . . . against so many adversaries.' He dismissed the prospect – threatened by Chamberlain – that Britain may decide to abandon its isolation and join hands with France or Russia. 'The threat of an English agreement with [Russia or France],' Bülow wrote, 'is only a threatening apparition to scare us, which the English have been using for years.' These exchanges reveal how far the Kaiser and Bülow misunderstood British resolution.

On 22 January 1901, Queen Victoria passed away in the arms of her German grandson. Any future hope of an Anglo-German alliance died with her. The new King, Edward VII, held Wilhelm in contempt and favoured an anti-German policy designed to isolate his nephew's kingdom. Neither Britain nor Germany was inclined to continue muted talks about a 'defensive pact', then in progress. They came to an abrupt halt.

The elderly prime minister Lord Salisbury moved finally to reject a military alliance with Germany or any other power, because British government was answerable to the electorate in the event of war, not a foreign regime. 'If the government,' he declared, in a famous memo of 29 May 1901, 'promised to declare war for an object which did not commend itself to public opinion, the promise would be repudiated, and the Government would be turned out.'[6] No statement better defined the difference between the British and German polities. With it, the prospect of a German alliance came fully to an end, and the British turned their backs, never to return.

The German historian Erich Brandenburg wrote, in a masterful summary:

> In trying . . . to escape the danger of being exploited by England and then left in the lurch, our political leaders conjured the far greater peril of driving our natural allies into the arms of our opponents and leaving ourselves isolated. Yet they constantly cherished the conviction that they had acted wisely because England must and would eventually return. . . . The English never came back to us. They went instead to our enemies.[7]

Part 2

WILFUL
BLINDNESS
AND BLINKERED
VISION, 1900–1914

9

RUNAWAY WAR

*[O]ne of the most sensitive strategic blows that France
has dealt to us since the war of 1870–71.*
Helmuth von Moltke the Younger, chief of the German
General Staff, on the French railway loan to Russia

OF ALL THE PRESSING CONCERNS of the German regime,
the need to defend the Fatherland exercised the most important
brains. Sandwiched between France, their erstwhile enemy, to the
west, and the vast Russian Empire to the east, the German people
had, since unification, felt an encroaching, irreducible sense of being
surrounded. In time, this manifested itself as a sort of national claus-
trophobia. Whether their neighbours were hostile or not, the very
perception of unfriendliness was enough to focus Germany's leaders
on the prospect of war. The people easily imagined it; Bismarck had
made the threat palpably clear in his speeches.

In the 1900s, Germany did not plan to conquer Europe. Her
Weltpolitik conceived of a colonial empire. That distinction is vital
to any understanding of Germany's relationship with her European
neighbours. Before 1914, Germany felt threatened in Europe;
Germany did not believe it posed a threat to Europe. That is why

Berlin and the Prussian generals construed a 'defensive' war against Russia: to assure Germany's future existence between two unfriendly neighbours. They readily foresaw the day the Russian hordes would come tearing down from the east; and France, it was felt, hankered for revenge ever since the Prussian victory. National survival, not territorial gain, was the objective of a German preventive war. And so the Germans made plans.

'Armies make plans' is how John Keegan opens his great history of the First World War.[1] His point is that armies map operations and scenarios in advance. In a broader sense, they plan for war: they train and equip men, develop transport systems, study the terrain, devise operations and strategy, and stockpile weapons. This is an obvious part of any country's self-defence. Yet the very fact that Keegan feels compelled to state it is a salutary reminder that wars don't just happen; wars are decided, usually by small groups of elderly, powerful men, and not by God or Darwin or some sort of 'ism', such as nationalism or patriotism.

Implicit in the decision to go to war is the freedom to decide not to. War planners have – or ought to have – the power to reverse their plans, to amend or tear up their designs, and postpone or avert war altogether, should circumstances change. The act of planning a war does not make it inevitable or necessary. Plans are as good as the human agency in their creation: ambitious, flawed, improvable, unworkable, stupid, brilliant and probably all of these things. The one thing they should not be is irreversible.

Far from being a great shock to the rulers of civilisation, the war that erupted in August 1914 was widely expected, rigorously rehearsed, immensely resourced and meticulously planned. Nobody then realised it would turn into a global war lasting four years and condemn to death or scar for life millions of young men. Most people, in power and on the streets, thought it would be over in a few short months. But plan it they did, in different ways, and to varying degrees of detail, in Germany, France, Britain and Russia.

The plans were drawn up in the strictest secrecy, shared only with the innermost military circles of the major powers. The lives of millions were in the play of a few old men, with little or no accountability to parliaments. Nor, as Keegan points out, did any of the belligerent nations have an integrated national security policy, which drew together government departments, the armed forces and the intelligence services.[1]

Britain was, at least in part, an exception to this picture of covert military planners operating with little or no civilian restraint. There, politicians, commanders and civil servants served on a Committee of Imperial Defence (CID). In other words, a dialogue ran between the commanders of the British Army, which dominated the CID, and the country's elected representatives.[2]

Compare the British example of civilian–military dialogue to the near-Byzantine situation in Germany, where war planning belonged exclusively to the Great General Staff – a situation resulting from the decision by the Kaiser and army chiefs in 1889 to remove the German Parliament and the War Ministry from any involvement in war planning. This meant, in effect, that Germany's army officers had extraordinary powers over when – and indeed whether – their country went to war, with little if any accountability to the parliament or politicians. Bethmann-Hollweg, the chancellor from 1909, was not even aware of Germany's general war plan until 1912. Nor was the fledgling German Navy kept abreast of the plan's development, in a nation where the Prussian Army held the upper hand (the direct opposite of the situation in Britain). '[T]he navy's admirals were fed crumbs,' remarks Keegan.[3]

—

Crucial to every plan in Europe was the railway. The railroad accommodated the generals' grandest ambitions. This transformative invention of the nineteenth century changed the way future armies would be deployed and supplied. Railways greatly reduced the time between the order to 'mobilise' – i.e. to move an army to the front – and the actual attack. By the 1900s, the European rail networks were able to deliver millions of troops to distant battlegrounds within days.

Mobilisation, in this light, involved the cooperation of the whole nation. The scale of the logistical exercise was staggering, according to planners' calculations. To mobilise the German Army would require, by 1914, 20,800 trains, moving 2,070,000 men, 118,000 horses (each eating ten times as much as one man) and 400,000 tonnes of materiel. France would require 10,000 trains, and Britain 1000 trains to mobilise their armies, according to the historian David Stevenson.[4] This mobilisation stage would deliver armies to their depots, from where they would be entrained to the railheads near the frontier zones – 'concentration'. Here, the troops would disembark and march the remaining distance to the front lines.

Faster trains and better networks offered both a great opportunity and an awesome threat: the opportunity to send armies direct to the front line on an enemy's border, and the threat that the enemy's train system would get there first. Deciding to send off the first train was comparable, in a way, to pushing the nuclear button in our time. Both triggered war – the former within days, the latter almost instantly. The railway system had thus set the conditions for a logistical race across Europe. The winner would be the country able to deliver the maximum number of men to the front lines as quickly as possible. Once the trains were on their way, they would be difficult – though not technically impossible – to stop (see Chapter 34), since their departure would provoke the departure of the enemy's trains down the opposing lines.

A. J. P. Taylor famously claimed that the rail timetables 'imposed' war on the statesmen of Europe.[5] He meant the new rail timetable thrust an 'inadvertent' war on governments who were helpless to stop 'runaway trains'. These 'runaway trains', packed with troops, hurtling towards the front lines made war inevitable – so long as the trains ran on time. Common sense suggests this is nonsense; yet there was a terrible truth in the metaphor.

Who had the power to send, or stop, the trains? Nominally, the War Offices of the governments. In practice, however, the generals would play the decisive role. At least until 1911, the British War Office, exceptionally, had had little influence over the construction and management of the British rail network, which was largely run by private companies. Under the 1871 Regulation of the Forces Act, the government awarded itself the power to commandeer the railways at mobilisation, and the War Railway Council gave the rail companies the information they required to 'begin timetabling'. But, right up to 1914, there was little or no liaison between the armed forces and the railway companies. As usual, the British muddled through until they found the right man for the job, in the formidable Sir Henry Wilson, the War Office's director of military operations from 1910, who persuaded the prime minister Herbert Asquith to speed up rail deployments. Britain's network soon grew into the densest in Europe.

French, German and Russian railways were partly nationalised in the 1900s. The French Government owned the rail bed, operated the network and owned one of the six railway companies. Bismarck nationalised most German railways after 1879, to coordinate them with military demands, as did Austria-Hungary between 1892 and 1905. Tsarist Russia had nationalised most of its railways by 1914, a motive being the poor performance of private rail operators in the war with Turkey in 1877–78.

Germany set the norm for military control of the rail systems in Europe. Under the 1871 Constitution, the generals effectively had a 'standing right' to 'supervise railway building, equipment and operations in the interests of national defence'.[6] The Imperial Railway Office oversaw the drafting of mobilisation schedules, which were annually revised and kept locked in iron cabinets for printing and distribution when the moment arrived. Helmuth von Moltke, chief of the General Staff from 1906, inherited a solid understanding of the railways' importance from his predecessors, Helmuth von Moltke the Elder (who held the position from 1857 to 1888) and Alfred von Schlieffen (1891–1905). Moltke exhorted his countrymen to build more railways, not fortresses. The French general Derrecagaix similarly wrote in 1885 that the country's first priority must be 'to cover its territory with a network of railways which will ensure the most rapid possible concentration'.[7]

———

The imperative of getting as many men to the front as quickly as possible spurred a race to build the best and most flexible rail networks. Between 1870 and 1914, European track length tripled, from 105,000 to 290,000 kilometres. Steel rails replaced iron, and double-tracked lines rapidly replaced single-tracked ones. By 1914, only 27 per cent of Russia's train lines were double-tracked, compared with 38 per cent of German lines, 43 per cent of French and 56 per cent of British.[8] These may seem boring statistics, but consider what they meant: at least twice the number of trains, carrying twice the number of soldiers, bearing down on a distant front line, there to be disgorged and sent straight into battle. In Russia, 14 trains a day rattled along a single-tracked line, and 32 along a double. The proliferation of railway networks in the late 1800s was, then, an arms race, as lethal in its intent as the ballistic-missile race in our own time.

In the 1900s, the race was well and truly on. France and Germany rushed to construct more lines running to their common border. In 1870, the Germans had nine lines to the border and the French four. By 1886, France had 12 and Germany still nine; and, by 1913, France had 16 and Germany 13. By 1914, each French line could deliver three army corps (80,000–135,000 men) to a station behind the deployment area, where the troops would detrain and march to the front.[9]

Throughout the 1900s, the French and German Armies were constantly testing and improving their rail networks in line with their war plans. In 1911, Joseph Joffre, newly appointed chief of the French General Staff, ordered a complete revision of the French war plan. The new 'Plan XVII' cut the time taken to concentrate his forces at the front lines to two days and allowed him to shift the detraining point of each army corps 'forwards, backwards, and even sideways, along the transverse lines'.[10] German and Russian planners were similarly investigating how railways would allow the fast and flexible mobilisation of their forces.

———

The most ominous developments were in Russia. Until 1908, its immense rail network was in poor shape: its tracks rusting and broken, its trains old and badly maintained. Then, as the country's economy recovered from the loss to Japan, the Russian Government started to regenerate the network. By 1910, it had laid ten new links to the German border. In 1912, it decided to invest in a massive new network: 900 kilometres of new track were laid that year. That was just the start. Russia's General Staff aimed to achieve two goals: to mobilise the millions of men living in the interior of Russia's vast land mass; and to slash the time between the start of mobilisation and a putative invasion of Germany. The goal was to deliver more than a million men to combat positions on the 15th day or earlier after mobilisation.

A second Franco-Russian loan, of 2.5 billion French francs, agreed in December 1913, gave the Russian war minister Vladimir Sukhomlinov the money he needed to lay a further 5330 kilometres of strategic lines over four years, between 1914 and 1918, extending deep into the country. The huge project would place Russia in a position to annihilate not only Germany but all of continental Europe. That prospect horrified the German Government. Helmuth von Moltke the Younger described the French rail loan as 'one of the most sensitive strategic blows that France has dealt to us since the war of 1870–71'. The convergence of the Russian and French railway systems on the German borders would create 'a decisive turning point to Germany's disadvantage'.[11]

By 1914, then, the tentacles of the French, German and Russian railway systems were literally plugged into the common borders, ready to disgorge millions of soldiers along a huge front. In this light, the new railway networks, as David Stevenson shows, were not only a precondition for a European war; they contributed to German plans to fight a preventive war at a future point – that is, to strike sooner rather than allow Russia the time to build an unconquerable, highly mobile army. The planet had never experienced a war on such a scale, the planning for which devolved upon a man of singular authority in the Prussian hierarchy armed with a chilling vision for humanity.

10

SCHLIEFFEN'S APOCALYPSE

An endeavor is afoot to bring all these powers together for a
concentrated attack on the Central Powers. At the given moment,
the drawbridges are to be let down, the doors are to be opened
and the million-strong armies let loose, ravaging and destroying,
across the Vosges, the Meuse, the Niemen, the Bug and even
the Isonzo and the Tyrolean Alps. The danger seems gigantic.
Count Alfred von Schlieffen, author of the Schlieffen
Plan, on the German terror of encirclement

A WAR PLAN THAT REFLECTS GLORY on those for whom the
plan is intended and aggrandises the victory implicit in its design
carries a curious potency. It sits in the mind, and on the desk, gathering a strange potential energy. It reconciles divergent or hostile opinions. It transports the commanders, who fondly imagine the realisation of its dormant power. The plan thus acquires a legitimacy and
strength in its own right. By laying the spectacle of the mobilisation
of millions of men and thousands of machines on the page, the war
planners had somehow prefigured their own triumphant destiny.
By drawing together the dreams and careers that depended on it for
their fulfilment, such a plan may even be said to prescribe, and in a

sense *foretell*, the very outcome for which it was drafted. It becomes, in certain fervid, warlike minds, a self-fulfilling prophecy.

By 1905, Germany had conceived of such a plan. They called it the Schlieffen Plan, the production of Count Alfred von Schlieffen, a severe and unyielding Prussian general who had served as chief of the German Great General Staff since 1891 and was now nearing retirement. The plan took him eight years to develop, from 1897 to 1905, and was annually updated thereafter. Schlieffen, and the small group of senior officers under his command, continually tested, probed and revised his great work. They laboured in secret, with no accountability to the German Government, who did not in fact know the extent of their work until 1912. Civilian meddlers were unwelcome in the inner sanctum of Prussian military power.

The whole concept remained more or less intact until 1914 – with several critical modifications. The Schlieffen Plan described a vast two-front war, in which the bulk of Germany's forces would mobilise first against France, and defeat her within the extraordinary deadline of 42 days. The army would then regroup and turn its full strength on Russia. The success of Schlieffen's plan hinged on three critical factors: the slower mobilisation rate of the Russians; the free passage of German troops through Belgium; and the efficient running of the German railways, in order to supply the troops. To this day, controversy surrounds the plan: did it prescribe a 'defensive' or an 'offensive' war? Or a 'preventive' war? Was the plan simply an army fund-raiser? Was it even a 'plan', or rather a grand scenario? Could the 1905 version be applied to the world of 1914?

—

To find the answers, it's worth knowing a little about its architect. Born in 1833 to an old Prussian family, Schlieffen first studied law and showed little interest in the military until he was selected as an officer cadet after completing his year of compulsory military service. Thus began a 53-year career in the Prussian Army, during which Schlieffen served as a staff officer in the Austro-Prussian War

(1866) and led a small force in one of the most exacting campaigns of the Franco-Prussian War (1870–71). These were brief interruptions to a long career as a desk-bound topographical expert, staff officer and theoretician.

Schlieffen lived and breathed the strategic planning of the German Army. 'He was a man without hobbies,' Keegan concludes. He found relaxation in reading military history to his daughters.[1] He was not a politician's soldier and had no need to be one at a time when the Prussian generals tended to overrule the politicians. He had no truck with drawn-out diplomacy and little patience with the political process. He thought of war – as did many Prussian generals – as the noblest solution to his country's problems. He thought in grand visions and big pictures, and furnished them down to the finest details. Central to his thinking, as he approached retirement, was a near-obsessive belief in the primacy of force. The overwhelming power of the Prussian Army would answer the great issues facing Germany. Might, in this unholy scenario, was indubitably right.

Berlin saw in him the perfect man to draw up a military solution to Germany's fears of gradual encirclement. Germany's military leaders warned Kaiser Wilhelm II that hostile powers were gradually squeezing the Fatherland. In response, the Kaiser and the Prussian General Staff turned to Schlieffen's vast conception of war fought on the eastern and western fronts. It was a grand recipe for a sudden, gigantic charge out of the besieged German fortress.

—

The Schlieffen Plan would serve as a kind of covenant: all future military strategies would fall into lock step with the ideas of the German General Staff's longest serving and most respected chief. It was, in short, the only plan they had. Schlieffen's staff had examined the German strategic problem from every angle. Their final production drew up the dates by which daily advances should be completed, the towns or cities to be taken by certain times, the likely body count of the battles, and, of course, the train timetables: how many men, how much matériel, could be entrained to certain marshalling points at certain times.

By late 1905, Schlieffen had compressed his very big and very aggressive ideas into a realisable design for war. The Germans clung to their claim that this would be a defensive war right up until the guns of 1914. This plea lost credibility on two counts: first, every one of the great powers claimed to be preparing to fight a 'defensive war', thus depriving the phrase of any meaning; second, Schlieffen's conception was surely the most offensive 'defensive war' ever laid out on a map of Europe. The most ingenious way out of this semantic trap was to call it a 'preventive war': i.e. to prevent the rise of a future, unbeatable Russia by destroying the Russian forces now. In other words, to launch a war according to a hypothesis based on the assumption that Russia would mount a massive invasion of Germany within a few years – probably in 1917, when Russia's combat-ready army was scheduled to reach two million.

Schlieffen envisaged a stunning opening blow that would deliver complete victory in a short war. How would this be achieved? A small German and Austro-Hungarian force (nine per cent of the total) would temporarily hold the Russian advance on the eastern front, while the bulk of the German Army (91 per cent) would crash across the French border and destroy the French forces via a vast circling motion through Belgium. And then, Germany would hurl her remaining military might on the eastern front and destroy the Slavic armies. It was an 'all or nothing' gambit that critically depended on defeating France within the first few weeks of battle – that is, before the Russians were able effectively to mobilise their enormous population. In this light, one understands the vital importance of mobilising before, or faster than, the enemy – a lesson France learnt during the Franco-Prussian War. Mobilisation by any one of the belligerent powers would force the others to enact panic-stricken mobilisation orders, with the result that huge, unstoppable forces would be set in motion.

To fight and win on two fronts required of Germany an

astonishing feat of arms. 'The total battle as well as its parts,' Schlieffen later wrote (1909), 'the separated as well as the contiguous battles, will be played out on fields and across areas that dwarf the theatres of earlier martial acts.'[2] Schlieffen compared this great act to Hannibal's victorious campaign at Cannae:

> A battle of annihilation can be carried out today according to the same plan devised by Hannibal in long forgotten times. The enemy front is not the goal of the principal attack. The mass of the troops and the reserves should not be concentrated against the enemy front; the essential is that the flanks be crushed. The wings should not be sought at the advanced points of the front but rather along the entire depth and extension of the enemy formation. The annihilation is completed through an attack against the enemy's rear . . . To bring about a decisive and annihilating victory requires an attack against the front and against one or both flanks . . .[3]

—

Schlieffen's plan gathered, like iron filings to a magnet, a solid following of senior German commanders, who saw in the grandeur of his vision the deliverance of Germany. The plan's illustrious author added to the near mystique. 'The effect,' warns Keegan, 'exerted by paper plans on the unfolding of events must never be exaggerated. Plans do not determine outcomes.'[4]

Of course, the Schlieffen Plan did not determine or precipitate the war of 1914; men did. The question is: to what extent were those men – chiefly Helmuth von Moltke and the General Staff – contained by Schlieffen's vision? Certainly, Schlieffen had an immense influence on German commanders, who tended to act in the thrall of his mind-boggling vision. His ideas offered a palliative to the 'siege mentality' that gradually possessed the Kaiser and Moltke, and senior members of the General Staff. Keegan concludes:

The 'Schlieffen Plan' was the most important government
document written in any country in the first decade of the
twentieth century; it might be argued that it was to prove the
most important official document of the last hundred years,
for what it caused to ensue on the field of battle, the hopes it
inspired, the hopes it dashed, were to have consequences that
persist to this day.[5]

———

If cracks appeared in his masterwork, Schlieffen was confident that
none had escaped his owl-like scrutiny. In fact, they were not errors
of detail but rather flaws in the very conception; a disease in the
trunk rather than the leaves. But to admit that would be to admit
failure, and failure was inconceivable to a man of Schlieffen's temperament. Schlieffen was a stubborn, supremely self-assured man, for
whom there were only 'contingencies' that must be met. What would
happen if the English fought on France's side? Schlieffen answered
that the Germans would then 'defeat the English and continue the
operations against the French'.[6] Would enough troops be available?
Schlieffen recommended the raising of eight new army corps, to be
deployed on the right wing. How would so many troops be trans-
portable to the front line? By train to the railhead on the border
and then by road, thereafter marching 12 miles (19 kilometres) a
day. Would the Belgians simply stand aside and watch the German
steamroller pass through? Schlieffen simply assumed they would.

Critical to the concept was the kind of war Schlieffen prescribed: a swift German triumph reminiscent of the stunning
Prussian victory over France in 1871. Schlieffen ruled out a long
war of attrition, which Germany could not afford: 'A strategy of
attrition will not do if the maintenance of millions costs billions.'[7]
To avoid that costly mistake, the troops would be pressed to complete the conquest of France within a strict timetable, calculated
down to the day: 'It is therefore essential to accelerate the advance
of the German right wing as much as possible.'[8]

The reason for the vast circling motion through Belgium lay on the French border with Alsace and Lorraine, in the form of a line of huge fortifications, from Verdun to Belfort, erected after the Franco-Prussian War. Somehow, these fortifications had to be breached. German artillery lacked the firepower to destroy the French forts in the time required to penetrate the French interior, conquer Paris and regroup to attack the Russians in the east. Schlieffen's answer was to avoid the forts altogether, by invading through Belgium, via the towns of Liège and Namur. He reached this conclusion as early as 1897, when he privately mused that Germany 'must not shrink from violating the neutrality of Belgium and Luxembourg'.[9]

So Belgium would act as the free corridor into the heart of France; Belgium would fast track the offensive. The lack of resistance would compensate for the lengthier route. Nobody believed Belgium would dare oppose the German juggernaut; the plan's very success turned on it. Under this scenario, virtually the entire German Army would violate Belgian neutrality, supposedly guaranteed by France, Britain and Prussia under the Treaty of London 1839, in the largest mass movement of troops ever sent to defeat a rival nation. Belgium would serve as 'a sort of funnel through which German armies could pass, then flood out beyond the French armies and encircle them', writes A. J. P. Taylor.[10] It is worth reminding ourselves that this was the plan for a preventive war, of self-defence.

Schlieffen first openly named Belgium as the corridor for the invasion of France in his Great Memorandum of December 1905, which would apply (with revisions) in 1914 (see Map 2). It envisaged the bulk of the German Army – some 700,000 troops – wheeling across southern Belgium to reach the French border within 22 days. Within ten days of that, the invaders would surround Paris from the west, and then drive eastward, to meet up with the German left wing. The remains of the French Army would then be crushed within this 'great semi-circular pincer, 400 miles [645 kilometres] in circumference, the jaws separated by 200 miles [320 kilometres]'.[11] Within 42 days, the war on the western front would be over, and

Germany free to turn her forces on Russia.

Schlieffen's plan, if properly resourced, he believed, would be the saviour of Germany. Yet Schlieffen, his staff and their successors made a series of terrible blunders, as we shall see: they misjudged Belgium's resolve; misunderstood the English; gravely underestimated Russia's speed of mobilisation; and miscalculated the impediment of narrow roads to such a monstrous gathering of arms and men. If the Schlieffen Plan 'dreamed of a whirlwind; the calculations warned of a dying thunderstorm'.[12]

—

In retirement, in 1909, until his death in 1913, Schlieffen continued to obsess over his plan, entertaining new scenarios and outcomes. He was prone in his dotage to view war in the abstract, as a vast operation on a map or board, disembodied from the bloody clash of life and limb that his ink marks represented. And he fretted deeply over the encirclement problem, keeping the theme alive in retirement, in his essay, 'Der Krieg in der Gegenwart' ('The War in the Present', January 1909). Bülow had first used the term 'encirclement' in the Reichstag in November 1906. Since then, the popular press had seized on the slogan, and a consensus accepted 'encirclement as a fact'.[13] Under this thesis, France was thirsting for revenge for the loss of Alsace and Lorraine; Britain, envious of Berlin's economic miracle, was determined to crush Germany's nascent empire; and the Russian Slav bore a congenital hatred of the Teutonic people. Since the Franco-Russian military agreement, such themes were never far from the Kaiser's mind.

Schlieffen, at the age of 80, wrote:

An endeavor is afoot to bring all these powers together for a concentrated attack on the Central Powers [Germany, Austria-Hungary, Italy]. At the given moment, the drawbridges are to be let down, the doors are to be opened and the million-strong armies let loose, ravaging and destroying, across the Vosges, the Meuse, the Niemen, the Bug and even the Isonzo and the Tyrolean Alps. The danger seems gigantic.[14]

On 2 January 1912, the Kaiser read this lurid description of German encirclement to his generals and concluded, 'Bravo.'[15] General Helmuth von Moltke the Younger, Schlieffen's successor, warmly praised it, and General Karl von Einem, the minister of war, saw no reason not to publish and disseminate it.

11

ENGLAND COMES IN FROM THE COLD

Yes, [the Kaiser] loves to get himself talked about. The agreements we have negotiated apart from him, without his permission and without his help, have stupefied him; they have produced in him a sense of isolation, hence his agitation and ill-humour.

King Edward VII on the Kaiser's response to the Entente Cordiale

---

IN THE FIRST FEW YEARS OF THE NEW CENTURY, Great Britain abandoned her long policy of splendid isolation and sought new relations with the continental powers. London's aim was to protect its empire by indulging, and seeking the indulgence of, the established imperialists, France and Russia. A secondary concern was to silence the curious blasts of *Weltpolitik* issuing from central Europe. London had no choice other than to come in from the cold. With her colonies under threat, the lonely old imperialist needed new friends in a chilling world. British re-engagement with Europe was born of necessity: to find a peaceful way of protecting the empire.

The European powers did not initially welcome this old

prizefighter stepping back into the ring. France and Britain had scarcely known quiescent relations in their long, bloody history. Nobody had forgotten Waterloo. And after Crimea, in 1856, and a series of colonial collisions in the Far East, Russia and Britain were hardly friends. If anything, Britain and Germany were natural partners. The pair had fought Napoleon together and shared the Protestant faith. They were racially similar insofar as being neither Latin nor Slav. Yet their attempts to forge an alliance had collapsed. Britain's break from its 'natural' friendship with Germany was a long, wrenching process, like severing links with an outcast member of the family. 'So many props and ties had successively to be demolished,' wrote Edward Grey, the future foreign secretary. 'British suspicions of Russia in Asia, the historic antagonism to France, memories of Blenheim, of Minden and of Waterloo, the continued disputes with France in Egypt and the Colonial sphere, the intimate business connections between Germany and England, the relationships between the Royal families.'[1]

Britain stepped into the European cauldron strengthened by her alliance with Japan, signed on 30 January 1902. This set a framework for British continental diplomacy: a peaceful means of preserving the empire through mutual recognition, not bullets. The signatories to the Anglo-Japanese Alliance recognised each other's claims on Chinese and Korean territory respectively (neither asked China or Korea if they cared to be occupied), and agreed to remain neutral if the other was attacked. With this Asian success, Britain embarked on a determined re-engagement with the two European powers who were most likely to threaten her global interests: France and Russia.

—

Germany in the early 1900s looked out on a different world, distorted by the Kaiser's solipsistic rants and the confused direction of *Weltpolitik*. Germany wanted an empire but scarcely understood how to get one. As time passed, and the world clearly had not transitioned into Germany's possession, the term *Weltpolitik* lost any meaning it might have had. The policy's architect, Chancellor von Bülow, never produced a defining policy statement. 'We are supposed to be pursuing *Weltpolitik*,' General Alfred von Waldersee wrote in his diary in January 1900. 'If only I knew what that was supposed to be.'[2]

Germany seemed to define itself by what it was not and probably never would be. It was not a friend of France or Russia. It was not global power. This outlook nourished a debilitating psychology of the perennial underdog. If France and Britain became new friends, then, *ipso facto*, in the Kaiser's mind, their friendship was anti-German, regardless of whether the signatories bore Germany ill will. This siege mentality steadily intensified and prompted in June 1902 Berlin's renewal of the Triple Alliance with Austria-Hungary and Italy. This aggravated the process of division that had created it in the first place and nudged France and Britain further into each other's embrace. It was not with a care for Germany, however, that King Edward VII sailed for Paris in 1903 and initiated Britain's famous rapprochement with France.

—

The King's visit to Paris on 1 May 1903 has been seen, in hindsight, as the most important royal sojourn of the twentieth century, in light of what it did for European relations. His reception began uncharitably, with scattered cries at the Bois de Boulogne station of '*Vive les Boers*' and '*Vive Fashoda*'. If the Fashoda Crisis brought France and Britain to the brink of war, though, memories were short, and these unpleasant reminders did little to impede the royal charm offensive. The King put on a marvellous show of goodwill and all-round Francophilia, seducing his hosts faster and with greater effect than a career diplomat might have done.

'The friendship and admiration,' the King told his hosts, 'which we all feel for the French nation and their glorious traditions may, in the near future, develop into a sentiment of the warmest affection and attachment between the peoples of the two countries. The achievement of this aim is my constant desire.' He repeated these sentiments the following day at a state banquet held in his honour at the Élysée Palace; and again, more emphatically, at a reciprocal banquet in London on 6 July 1903, for then French president Loubet, when the King expressed his 'ardent wish that the rapprochement between the two countries may be lasting'.[3]

The King's wishes were met. The silken path of Edwardian diplomacy weaved its royal magic. Both countries worked at finding common ground, in an agreement designed to preserve and fortify their colonial wealth. The result was the Entente Cordiale, signed on 8 April 1904. It marked the consummation of a relationship of peaceful coexistence that had lasted since the Napoleonic Wars and formalised a new era of Anglo-French friendship that the powers had rarely known over a millennium of almost chronic conflict, intrigue, invasion and counter-invasion.

The Entente Cordiale was not a treaty or an alliance in any legal sense. A formal alliance with France would have driven the Germans to desperation and possibly destroyed Asquith's Liberal Party, as Bernadotte Schmitt explains.[4] It was rather an understanding, literally a 'cordial agreement', under which the signatories recognised each other's claims to disputed colonies. For example, France conceded British power over Egypt, and Britain, in exchange, ceded France's sole claim to Morocco. On the face of it, the Entente Cordiale seemed merely a settlement over a ragbag of colonies. However, it formalised what was tacitly understood, in disputes over Fashoda, and in Newfoundland and Siam (Thailand). As such, the agreement inaugurated a period of happy accommodation, in the interests of imperial expansion, rarely seen in the nations' histories.

Strictly speaking, the Entente was not an anti-German pact – 'at least not from Whitehall's perspective', writes Christopher Clark, 'but one that was intended to mute colonial tensions with France'.[5] Nor was the Entente militarily binding. It committed neither power to defend the other in the event of war. That left the British position in limbo if Germany was to invade France again, as many feared. Neither neutral nor committed to France, Britain remained on the

fence, casting a hostage to fortune that would torture their relationship up until August 1914.

The spirit of the Entente would, however, evolve into a quasi-military obligation, at least in the mind of the future French president
Raymond Poincaré. For him, the Entente would protect France 'by
virtue of which England has declared herself ready to come to the aid
of France in the event of an attack by Germany', as he later explained
to the Russian foreign minister Sazonov.[6] The British were far from
decided on this. The Foreign Office seemed to regard the Entente as
little more than a state of mind, a verbal understanding, so long as it
secured English assets from French meddling.

—

Through German eyes, however, the Entente Cordiale was a deal
riddled with sinister intent. This was not about Britain and France
tossing up over a few colonies. To Berlin, it sent the clearest message of Britain's future allegiance in Europe. It answered one of the
great questions of the late nineteenth century: who would Britain
support in the event of a European war? And the answer shocked
Berlin. Leading conservatives believed Germany had every reason to
fear encirclement by the old imperial powers.

Chancellor Bülow put a brave face on the development. He
rejected the accusation that his policy had condemned Germany
to isolation, and affected to welcome 'the elimination of the causes
of friction between France and Britain'.[7] He tried to reassure the
Reichstag that Germany's commercial interests in Morocco ('the
essential point of the agreement') would not be damaged.

If Bülow pretended to welcome the Anglo-French announcement, the Cordiale stunned the Kaiser, who vented his anger in a
series of half-crazed speeches, one of which, at Karlsruhe, went so far
as to hail the victories over France of 1870–71. The Kaiser's bellicosity was not lost on the British royal family. King Edward VII visited
Kiel on 25 June 1904 to reassure his fuming nephew that the Anglo-
French accord meant no harm.

On his return more than a fortnight later, the King told Paul Cambon, French ambassador to London, that he found Wilhelm's court 'much perturbed at our intimate relations'. He went on, 'I reassured them, reminding them that England and France has [sic] many joint and parallel interests . . . their good understanding was an added guarantee of European peace.'[8]

In reply, Cambon directed the King's attention to the 'true cause of the nervousness which seems to have afflicted Wilhelm':

> for several months [the Kaiser] never would believe in the possibility of an Anglo-French accord; he continued to speculate on the misunderstanding between our two countries as he did on all the germs of discord that exist between the Powers; he had sought to get himself regarded as the supreme arbiter of Europe, the defender and the guarantor of the general peace; in a word, he expected to play the leading role everywhere. And he sees with bitterness Your Majesty taking this role from him.[9]

To which Edward replied, 'Yes, [the Kaiser] loves to get himself talked about. The agreements we have negotiated apart from him, without his permission and without his help, have stupefied him; they have produced in him a sense of isolation, hence his agitation and ill-humour.'[10]

Germany responded with deepening alarm, embarking on a series of doomed attempts at establishing new relationships with the powers. Over and again, Germany failed. It failed, in 1905, to forge a Russo-German alliance, the stillborn Treaty of Bjorko, which the Kaiser unilaterally amended by limiting its application to Europe and not Asia. Wilhelm's tilt at diplomacy rendered the treaty incompatible with the Triple Alliance. How could it apply if France and Germany went to war, as the Tsar patiently declared (after it had been signed)? The Tsar's declaration effectively annulled the treaty.

The whole experience drew attention to the Kaiser's weak grip on reality. The historian Albertini exclaimed:

To such a man was entrusted so great a part in the destinies of the world! Those who served him – Bülow at their head – many times asked themselves whether he was of sound mind, and whether he should not be put under restraint, but they never dared to do this. They dared not, because, whether brilliant or dull-witted, they all, with the exception of Bismarck, were courtiers before they were statesmen.[11]

—

The Kaiser soon displayed his impulsive, histrionic nature in spectacular style. The Entente Cordiale sparked a fierce dispute between Germany and France over the latter's claim to Morocco. Receiving Britain's nod to the territory, Paris moved swiftly to consolidate the French possession, sending a diplomatic mission in January 1905. This infuriated the Germans, not because Berlin had a special claim on Morocco (it hadn't), but because the French foreign minister, Théophile Delcassé, had failed to alert Germany to France's occupation of Morocco – a political courtesy that Paris had been in the habit of making. 'In opting to freeze the Germans out,' Christopher Clark writes, 'Delcassé built an entirely unnecessary element of provocation into his North African policy . . .'[12] Delcassé's colleagues were astonished at this wanton provocation and implored him, at the very least, to negotiate with Berlin. But the foreign minister refused to have anything to do with the Germans, whom he dismissed as 'repugnant' and 'swindlers'[13] – a position even Eugène Étienne, the leader of the French Colonial Party, thought imprudent.

Germany surveyed these events with growing resentment, and on 31 March 1905, three months after the French landed and demanded control of the Moroccan Army from the local authorities, the Kaiser himself made a spectacular visit to Tangier. To a rousing welcome, Wilhelm staked Germany's economic claims to the colony and then abruptly departed. His visit lasted two hours. Those two hours infuriated the French – who were obliged to recognise Germany's interests in Morocco, if any, under previously accepted conventions. The fracas led to Delcassé's dismissal. The Germans, briefly triumphant, insisted that the dispute be resolved at an international conference.

The Algeciras Conference was a resounding disaster for Germany. The French prepared well and got the support of the other European powers. The Russians rallied to their ally, and the British were similarly keen to see France retain what London had approved under the Entente Cordiale. In the event, Morocco received semi-independence, at the cost of French control of key institutions, including the 'independent' police force and a controlling stake in the Banque d'État, which gave France effective control of the country's economic development.

The result was another German humiliation. 'The uselessness of the Triple Alliance was revealed for all to see,' writes Clark. 'The German policymakers had bungled.'[14] The failure was especially acute for the Kaiser, who had conceived his sabre-rattling mission to Morocco as a way of freezing Britain out of North Africa, part of Wilhelm's madder agenda of organising a continental coalition against the English, whose power he distrusted. It all came back to the mysterious *Weltpolitik*, in which Wilhelm was 'anxious to be both Admiral of the Atlantic and King of Jerusalem'.[15] The failure at Algeciras relegated Germany to the sidelines of the great game of imperial power and emboldened Britain to seek a firmer relationship with Russia, who then menaced her Far Eastern colonies.

—

Over the next two years, a deeper shock awaited Germany, with the gradual drawing in of England to the Franco-Russian sphere in what would become, in 1907, a three-way accord, known to the world as the Triple Entente. London and St Petersburg seduced each other to join this extraordinary pact between past enemies. Russia came to the table in a ragged state. Severely weakened by her loss to Japan in the war of 1904–05 and the revolution of 1905, Russia sought any opportunity to improve her relations in Europe and to stave off the

Teutonic menace. For its part, London grabbed the chance to lend a hand to a stricken power, in exchange for Russia abandoning any claims on Britain's Far Eastern assets.

The Anglo-Russian agreement saved Britain the immense cost of having to defend the Indian Empire from Russian incursions. According to Kitchener, the cost of defending India from the 'menacing advance of Russia' would be '£20m plus an annual charge of another £1.5m'.[16] The bill disturbed the Liberal government that won power in 1905, and the new foreign secretary Edward Grey was determined to bring Russia into the tent, to neutralise through peaceful persuasion the Russian threat to the Asian extremities of the British Empire.

And he succeeded. Grey and the Foreign Office removed St Petersburg's interest in China, India and Persia, secured Russian recognition of Afghanistan as a British sphere of influence and thwarted any prospect of a Russo-German alliance. Clause 3, incidentally, demonstrated the global reach of the European powers: 'an agreement on Tibet recognising its territorial integrity and independence under the suzerainty of China'.[17] Thus were destinies sealed, of tiny countries in far-off places, of which the occupiers knew little.

—

The Anglo-Russian deal led inevitably to the loose alignment of the three powers known as the Triple Entente. For the first time in history, imperial Britain stood as one with France and Russia, in peaceful accommodation. Hitherto, Russia and England seemed destined to be chronic foes; now, they glad-handed each other in the flush of self-interested friendship. Britain's Franco-Russian allies regarded their new friend with barely disguised delight, and fondly imagined a time when Britain would join them in a three-way, fully fledged military alliance. For his part, Edward VII embraced this historic milestone, which brought England warmly in from the cold on the side of France and Russia.

The tripartite understanding, however, horrified the German

nationalists, who felt more deeply spurned and more entrenched than ever before. The Kaiser worked himself into a lather of spluttering rage that this could happen. He thought it astonishing, impossible, that England would nuzzle up to Russia, its arch-foe in Asia. If neither the Entente Cordiale nor the Anglo-Russian Convention were conceived as explicitly anti-German, the three powers well knew the effect the agreements would have on German thinking. By the very act of excluding Germany, they fed the incipient paranoia of the German regime. To them, preserving their empires and ensuring their security in Europe were worth the price.

And so Europe had evolved within a decade into two great power blocs: the Triple Entente and the Triple Alliance. For a time, they had a deterrent effect. To paraphrase Churchill, they 'stood side by side, not face to face'. The Triple Entente was 'peaceful' and meaning no harm, historians claim.[18] The trouble is, Germany manifestly did not view the Triple Entente as friendly or peaceful. How could it? The three-way relationship brought together the greatest empires on earth, beside which Germany, Austria-Hungary and Italy were economically shaky and politically jejune.

In fact, the Triple Entente realised the worst fears of Bismarck, who had written on 27 May 1885 that an Anglo-Franco-Russian agreement 'would provide the basis for a coalition against us more dangerous than any other she might have to face'.[19] The three powers had fulfilled his prophecy, and the ghostly voice of the gruff old Prussian returned to haunt his nemesis. The Triple Entente acted upon the Kaiser like a great vice, exacerbating to an unbearable degree Berlin's acute sense of friendlessness. True, Berlin had friends in Vienna and Budapest, but Italy wavered under the gravitational pull of the Entente and looked like abandoning the central powers.

It is easy to dismiss Berlin's fears at this time as the paranoia of a closed, highly sensitive, authoritarian state. Yet clearly there was some justification in Germany's concern. Perhaps some in the British Foreign Office – not least Eyre Crowe, the most influential Germanophobe – were right in casting Germany as a ferocious predator. Or perhaps other truths prevailed beyond their knee-jerk anti-German view of the Prussian ascendancy. They might, for example, have tried to appreciate the external provocations that beset Germany at this time. Within the space of three years, Berlin had found itself facing: to the east, the teeming populace of Russia, then able to field unknown millions of troops; to the west, a revanchist, proud and increasingly vengeful France; and to the north, the lord of the seas and the possessor of the greatest empire the world has known, Great Britain – and all this at a time when Italy was showing every sign of jumping ship. Italy, supposedly Germany's ally, supported France over Morocco! Seen through German eyes, then, the Franco-Russo-British friendship immeasurably aggravated the nation's sense of being hemmed in between hostile powers, to the point where senior Prussian military figures now urged a preventive war in order to break free from what they saw as a stifling and intolerable encirclement.

12

ENGLISH GERMANOPHOBIA

*Germany is deliberately following a policy which is
essentially opposed to vital British interests, and that an
armed conflict cannot in the long run be averted.*
Eyre Crowe Memo, the British Foreign Office, 1907

TO SOME ENGLISH OFFICIALS, Britain's re-engagement
with Europe arose out of a perception that a hostile and economically powerful Germany would one day threaten the colonial jewels.
Nowhere was that perception more forcefully put than in the
words of a German-born senior clerk at the Foreign Office, Sir Eyre
Alexander Barby Wichart Crowe. Crowe was not an anti-German
extremist like the journalists Leo Maxse, editor of the conservative
National Review, James Louis Garvin, editor of *The Observer*, and
John St Loe Strachey, editor of *The Spectator*, who made German-
bashing a full-time occupation.[1] Nor did he share the hatred of
Germany routinely peddled in the popular press, chiefly the *Pall
Mall Gazette*, *Daily Mail* and *Morning Post*. Coherent, historically
based and highly articulate, Crowe's argument against Germany disturbed the pro-German members of Asquith's Cabinet.

Crowe was born in Leipzig in 1864, to Britain's well-connected commercial attaché in Berlin, Sir Joseph Archer Crowe, and his German wife, Asta von Barby. Sir Joseph's friendships with German royalty and prominent German Liberals in the 1860s 'made him probably the best informed Englishman of all upon the German political scene'.[2] His connections with German business and Reichstag deputies conferred upon him a keen understanding of the deeper political trends in German society, and it was this characteristic that would find a striking expression in his son.[3] In 1903, Eyre Crowe married his widowed German cousin, Clema, whose uncle, Henning von Holtzendorff, was destined to become chief of the German Navy General Staff and notorious for his 1916 memo to the Kaiser urging unrestricted submarine warfare against Britain. The war would literally be all in the family.

Eyre Crowe first came to England in 1882, aged 17, when he sat the Foreign Office service examination. While not fluent in English, his intellectual brilliance overcame his linguistic shortcomings, and he won a place. His adopted country did not look kindly on this German-born subject. However much he demonstrated his loyalty to England, Crowe could never quite escape his Teutonic taint or tame his accent. His provenance at a time of rising anti-German feeling provoked hostility in certain political circles and, of course, the British press. He cared little for these jingoistic spasms about his German birth. Wasn't Queen Victoria herself the Kaiser's grandmother? Were not many members of the British aristocracy linked to German ruling families?

The Foreign Office would have seemed even less hospitable than the nation: a world of old public schoolboys, virtually all of whom went to Eton, Winchester or Harrow, and Oxford or Cambridge. Being an outsider in this intimidating company did not seem to impede Crowe's initial rise. Indeed, his understanding of Germany probably assisted his promotion to senior clerk in the Western Department – an influential posting in which he worked under Edward Grey, the new foreign secretary. Yet he would never fulfil his ambitions, and therein lay one source of his provocative and at times insubordinate temperament.

An unusually influential civil servant, Crowe cloaked himself in the Union Jack and became a staunch defender of the British realm. His full-throated patriotism possibly overcompensated for his half-German origins. The obverse emotion was an unhealthily suspicion verging on paranoia of anything German. In Crowe's mind, all that endangered British security must be sourced to Germany. He identified the German Navy as the biggest threat to Britain's survival (a prediction that would prove unfounded). Of course, he was not a default anti-German. His conclusions were drawn from a close reading of Prussian history. Germany, he declared, consciously aimed 'at the establishment of a German hegemony at first in Europe, and eventually in the world'.[4] To Crowe's way of thinking, this was the logical extension of Germany's history of aggression.

—

If Crowe was right – if Germany actually planned to overwhelm Europe as a prelude to world conquest – then surely Britain should have been very worried? On the contrary, the majority of the British Cabinet was pro-German in 1907, and displayed a cheerful insouciance towards Berlin's colonial expansion, a vestige of the free-trade 'old liberalism' that Prime Minister Henry Campbell-Bannerman had inherited from Gladstone. Crowe arrogantly viewed these men, not least the chancellor David Lloyd George, then the most powerful pro-German member of the Cabinet, as foolish and misguided. He knew better.

Campbell-Bannerman's brand of liberalism was fading. Prominent members of his Cabinet, including Asquith (who would succeed Campbell-Bannerman in 1908, when he retired due to ill health), Lloyd George, Grey and Churchill, dared to speak of social reform, of a welfare state, of economic intervention. They looked out on a resentful, envious world anxious to dismantle Britain's cherished empire. Dividing them was the question of Germany: did Berlin's ambitions pose the chief threat to British interests? For Crowe, the answer was a resounding yes, and he made it his mission to compel the new Foreign Office to act.

In this capacity, Crowe acted as a sort of unofficial spokesman, or lightning rod, for the anti-German hawks who dominated the Foreign Office. He articulated what senior officials thought but were reluctant to state. Their ranks included: William Tyrrell, Edward Grey's private secretary (1907–15), the classic gentleman public servant, urbane, witty and charming, friendly with Crowe, whose views he shared until he had a change of mind in 1912; Sir Cecil Spring-Rice, who would become the British ambassador to the United States (1912–18) and had a well-known reputation for paranoia towards Germany; Sir Horace Rumbold, a career diplomat and 'an ancient critic of Prusso-German expansionism',[5] who deeply distrusted Germany; Charles Hardinge, permanent undersecretary (1905–10), a brilliant career diplomat and future Indian Viceroy, and very concerned about German expansionism; Francis Bertie, ambassador to France, where he played a key part in strengthening the Entente; and Sir Arthur Nicolson, British ambassador to Russia (1906–10), a strenuously anti-German diplomat who believed in forging full defensive alliances with Russia and France against Germany.[6] These officials did not call themselves 'anti-German', or anything so crassly undiplomatic; they preferred to see themselves as 'pro-British', to distinguish themselves from the more pungent Germanophobes in parliament.

One of Crowe's most willing listeners, at least from 1907, was his departmental chief, Sir Edward Grey, who had become foreign secretary in 1905, the year of the Moroccan Crisis. 'Before he even entered the Foreign Office, Grey identified Germany as the enemy. That conviction never altered . . .'[7] Grey shared Crowe's belief in the nature of the German threat: 'the Foreign Secretary not only assumed that Germany was prepared to challenge Britain's position but that she had the potential to fulfil her dangerous intention'.[8] With Grey's approval, Crowe carved out a reputation as the most strident anti-German voice in Whitehall, the 'arch anti-appeaser'[9] who developed, in his memos, an 'unfortunate habit of indicating to the Foreign Secretary and his colleagues in the Cabinet that they were not only ill-informed but weak and silly'.[10]

While Crowe's detractors regarded him as the 'evil spirit' of the Foreign Office's Germanophobes,[11] he was seen, for a time, as the most authoritative anti-German official in the department. His words articulated, and partly shaped, the changing direction of Britain's pre-war policy towards Germany. And while Grey rejected Crowe's assumption that war with Germany was probably inevitable, the foreign secretary keenly circulated his adviser's blunt observations – blunt, some believed, to the point of warmongering.

—

Even his closest colleagues were unprepared for the inflammatory tone of Crowe's innocuously titled 'Memorandum on the Present State of British Relations with France and Germany', which he presented to the Foreign Office in January 1907 in advance of the Second Hague Peace Conference (June to October 1907). The 20-page memo, requested by Grey, reads with Crowe's familiar polemical voice, reminiscent of a 'Boy's Own' morality tale, notes Christopher Clark, in which the bully is always Germany.[12] The memo is much more than a hectoring history lesson or teenage adventure story about Germany's dark designs. Implicit in Crowe's vision was a call to arms, to save Europe from German conquest.

Essentially, the memo is a tract warning of the political and military consequences of Germany's spectacular rise to power. It arose out of Crowe's fervently held belief that England must contain German pretensions to great-power status. He had in mind the threat posed by Germany's ever-expanding fleet to Britain's sea supremacy. At the time of its dispatch, Crowe's words exerted great influence on senior members of the government, notably Grey, who annotated the memo with words of 'warm approval'[13] and had it circulated to senior colleagues. It thus deserves deeper scrutiny, for if any document in England constituted a premonition of war, it was Eyre Crowe's incendiary memorandum.

The memorandum's core assumption was that a unified Germany, rather like France under Napoleon, believed it had an inalienable right to the status and possessions of a world power, the equal of Britain and France. These ambitions, Crowe warned, would inevitably set Berlin on the path of economic and military conflict with Britain.

He opens with a neat outline of the grand coalitions in Europe. He rejects the idea that the Entente was hostile to Germany. Nor was the Franco-Russian Alliance 'conceived in a spirit of bellicose aggression' against Germany. Similarly, he finds nothing inherently hostile to German interests in the Cordiale, which innocently aimed to accommodate French and British colonies. All these were peaceful, unthreatening moves, in Crowe's view. He sees no merit in the claim that the Entente was a consequence of France rushing to embrace England after Russia's severe weakening in the war with Japan and the 1905 revolution.

In disqualifying the hostile reaction in Germany to these great allegiances, Crowe was wilfully deceiving himself. He overlooked one of the obvious causes of the rising tension between the rival powers right up to July 1914: Germany *perceived* these relationships to be threatening and was therefore determined to challenge or dismantle them. The perception of events is vital to understanding why Europe went to war. The signatories to the Franco-Russian Alliance were committed to defending the other if attacked. This seemed peaceful. Yet provocation is difficult to prove, as countless books about the war attest. Who provoked or 'started' the Great War? There is still no consensus. Nonetheless, to Crowe and the anti-Germans in the Foreign Office, Germany was and always would be the sole provocateur.

'[T]he Emperor's government,' Crowe wrote, 'was determined to resort to any measures likely to bring about the dissolution of a fresh political combination, which it was felt [would] ultimately prove another stumbling block in the way of German supremacy, as the Franco-Russian alliance had previously been regarded.'[14]

Germany enacted the spirit of this policy at the Algeciras Conference, Crowe claims. The German delegates felt confident that France would yield to threats and withdraw from Morocco. Yet Germany underestimated the resolve of Britain in refusing to tolerate the humiliation of France. The two colonial 'superpowers' closed ranks against the German 'bully' (regardless of the fact that Germany was within her legal rights to question France's occupation).

As Crowe wrote:

> Herr von Holstein, and on his persuasion, Prince Bülow, practically staked their reputation on the prophecy that no British government sufficiently bullied and frightened would stand by France, who had for centuries been England's ubiquitous opponent, and was still the ally of Russia, England's 'hereditary foe'.[15]

The German delegates secretly pressed upon the British representatives the folly of supporting France, 'and painted in attractive colours a policy of co-operation with Germany for France's overthrow'.[16] German faith in this 'prophecy' was profoundly misplaced; Britain held firm and did not go over to Germany, and Holstein was sacked after the policy that Bülow had pressed upon him failed.

The Moroccan Crisis introduced a new spark in the Anglo-French marriage, Crowe suggests. Where the Cordiale had originally been just that – a 'cordial agreement' – a new factor entered the equation, 'an element of common resistance to outside dictation and aggression, a unity of special interests tending to develop into active co-operation against a third power'.[17]

Having named the bully – the 'third power' being, of course, Germany – Crowe really gets into his stride. He subjects his readers – Grey and senior members of the Foreign Office – to a long history of Prussian aggression: the seizure of Silesia, the partitions of Poland, the annexation of Hanover and Schleswig-Holstein, culminating in the 'reconquest' of Alsace and Lorraine in 1871. Crowe concedes that 'other countries have made their conquests, many of them much larger and more bloody' – one shrinks from the thought that he may be referring to his adopted country – but Prussia's stamp of conquest was different, in his eyes. In seeing British colonial wars, occupations and annexations as natural and desirable, Crowe exhibits a 'comic tendency', Christopher Clark wryly observes. Germany's colonial ambitions, on the other hand, are self-evidently baleful and malign:

> whereas British hegemony was welcomed and enjoyed by all and envied and feared by none on account of its political liberality and the freedom of its commerce, the vociferations of the Kaiser and the pan-German press showed that German hegemony would amount to a 'political dictatorship' that would be 'the wreckage of the liberties of Europe'.[18]

Crowe goes further. The German Empire was designed to aggrandise the state of greater Germany in the name of the Teutonic *race*: 'In [Germany] the preservation of national rights and the realization of national ideas rest absolutely on the readiness of every citizen in the last resort to stake himself and his State on their assertion and vindication.'[19] The spirit of Prussia had passed into the new Germany through 'blood and iron'. But the new Germany 'must have Colonies' to command a place in the sun and a seat at the councils of Europe. Crowe completes his history lesson with a dark warning that Germany's colonial ambitions would lead inevitably to a poisonous growth, rather like a cancer, and then war:

> A healthy and powerful State like Germany, with its 60 million inhabitants, must expand, it cannot stand still, it must have territories to which its overflowing population can emigrate without giving up its nationality . . . When it is objected that the world is now actually parcelled out among independent States, and that territory for colonization cannot be had except

by taking it from the rightful possessor, the reply again is: 'We cannot enter into such considerations. Necessity has no law. The world belongs to the strong. A vigorous nation cannot allow its growth to be hampered by blind adherence to the status quo . . .!'[20]

If we strip away Crowe's sub-Darwinian theme – his reference to 'necessity' predates Bethmann-Hollweg's use of the term in his speech defending the invasion of Belgium – we are left with his central idea: that Berlin's future actions could be adduced simply by extrapolating Germany's past – i.e. aggression begets aggression, and there could be no deviation from this iron law. In Crowe's view, Germany's history of predation condemned the country to continue on that course, to use the aggression necessary to acquire power. If Crowe was to apply this simplistic extrapolation to France and Britain, starting from, say, the occupation of India or the French Revolution, would those countries stand similarly charged? Crowe doesn't say. He is convinced, however, of the presence in Europe of a new, violent regime that will stop at nothing to conquer its neighbours.

Crowe's final warning is devastating to British hopes of survival. The object of his inquiry 'was to ascertain whether there is any real and natural ground for opposition between England and Germany'. He answers that:

such opposition has, in fact, existed in an ample measure for a long period, but that it has been caused by an entirely one-sided aggressiveness, and that on the part of England the most conciliatory disposition has been coupled with never-failing readiness to purchase the resumption of friendly relations by concession and concession.

The evidence he uses to indict Germany's 'entirely one-sided aggressiveness' is not compelling: a few disputes over African colonies, a spat over China and bad blood in the German press (the feeling was mutual in the British press). It is true that Bülow rejected British entreaties to build stronger relations in 1898–1902. This does not, however, lead to the conclusion of a 'tradition' of 'extreme hostility between Germany and Britain'. On many occasions in the past 20 years, Germany and Britain had been on good terms.

Crowe goes much further, however. Germany's antagonism towards Britain was so deeply rooted, he contends, that only Britain's complete surrender would satisfy the Prussian leadership. In short:

> Germany is deliberately following a policy which is essentially opposed to vital British interests, and that an armed conflict cannot in the long run be averted, except by England either sacrificing those interests, with the result that she would lose her position as an independent Great Power, or making herself too strong to give Germany the chance of succeeding in a war.

Crowe claims to have presented conclusive 'evidence' that Berlin was 'consciously aiming at the establishment of a German hegemony, at first in Europe, and eventually the world'.[21]

Having asserted that Germany and Britain were heading for an 'inevitable war', Crowe proceeds to damage his case – such as it is – by admitting two great flaws in his argument. The first is that if Germany really planned to conquer Europe, why would Berlin make enemies of its neighbours and put them on a war footing? Surely Germany would keep England 'in good humour until the moment arrived for striking the blow fatal to her power'.[22] Setting aside the possibility that enemies do not always pretend to be friends as a prelude to war, his idea falls flat on several counts. First, England, France and Russia were not on a war footing in 1907; far from it. Nor was Germany trying to put the two countries on a war footing. The secret Schlieffen Plan was a military scenario to be enacted only if Germany was threatened. Germany's naval build-up did not lead inevitably to war. The reason for German belligerence related to the recently formed Triple Entente. Indeed, at no time before July 1914 did the German *Government* show any sign that it wanted war with its European neighbours. In this light, Crowe's whole thesis – that the German Government sought war with France, Britain and Russia – seems based merely on an extrapolation of Prussian history.

His second self-diagnosed error is more serious, and threatens the whole edifice of his argument. He wonders, near the end of his memo, whether he had, after all, misread Germany's intentions and methods and that perhaps 'the great German design is in reality no more than the expression of a vague, confused and unpractical statesmanship, not fully realizing its own drift'.[23] In entertaining this possibility, Crowe concedes the exception of the Bismarck era; i.e. Bismarck's policies were focused and coherent, while those of the present regime were a misguided mess. Indeed, the Kaiser's *Weltpolitik* answered precisely to the latter description. In recognising this, Crowe's trenchancy loses its power, and what seemed like a damning indictment of Germany's Napoleonic plan becomes more like a sandbag emptying of sand.

—

The memo provoked, and still provokes, deep division. At the time, the Foreign Office's most strident critic was Thomas Sanderson, who rejected Crowe's simplistic portrayal of German history as 'an unchecked record of black deeds'.[24] Since then, however, historians have tended to come down on Crowe's side. Fritz Fischer's *Germany's Aims in the First World War* is the most controversial meditation on the idea that Germany sought to conquer Europe and the world. Yet his book is confined to Germany's aims *during the war*, i.e. after the war began, when all nations were fighting for their lives; it finds no persuasive evidence that Germany intended global *conquest* – through force of arms – before the war began. *Weltpolitik* certainly meant acquiring colonies, after the French and British example, but not the conquest of Europe. Imanuel Geiss, Fischer's student, describes Crowe's memo as 'the most intelligent and precise analysis of German Weltpolitik' and 'long considered in Germany as a major factor contributing to war'.[25] Albertini calls the memo 'admirable'.[26] To Paul Kennedy (*The Rise of the Anglo-German Antagonism*), it represented the 'Official Mind' of the British Government and was 'generally regarded as the classic statement of London's pre-war policy of moving against Germany in order to preserve the balance of power'.[27] Others are not persuaded. Niall Ferguson (*The Pity of War*) questions the whole notion that Germany aimed to fight a Napoleonic War of conquest in Europe – Britain's 'Napoleon neurosis', he calls it – rejects the idea that Germany's *pre-war* aims implied global hegemony and tends to dismiss Crowe as a tiresome Germanophobe.[28]

One thing was clear: the popular British outcry against Germany in the press and among the British public tended to reflect Crowe's ideas, even if they weren't expressed in the public-school accents and Oxbridge prose of the Foreign Office. The British press had agreed, more or less, with Crowe's sentiments since the late 1890s. In fact, at its most hysterical, anti-German feeling suggested that England planned to attack Germany, rather than the other way around.

In the 1890s, for example, a respectable magazine called *The Saturday Review*, numbering Oscar Wilde and Lord Salisbury among its contributors, published a series of anti-German articles under the theme '*Germania est delenda*' (Germany must be destroyed). 'Our chief rival,' ran one piece ('Our True Foreign Policy'), 'in trade and commerce today is not France but Germany. In case of a war with Germany, we should stand to win much and lose nothing . . .'[29] Another item suggested, 'The biological view of foreign policy is plain. First, federate our colonies and prevent geographical isolation turning the Anglo-Saxon race against itself. Second, be ready to fight Germany, as *Germania est delenda* . . .'[30]

The same themes pervaded newspapers, journals, books and cartoons right up until 1914, as Niall Ferguson's extensive survey shows.[31] Novels portraying a German invasion were best-sellers. They ranged from penny dreadfuls such as William Le Queux's *The Invasion of 1910* to Saki's more highbrow *When William Came:*

A Story of London Under the Hohenzollerns. German publishers, of course, knocked out the same fantasies about annihilating wars between England and Germany. The press in both nations were reliably on hand to fan anti-German or anti-British feelings to an unnecessary degree, because, when asked 'What sells a newspaper?', one of Lord Northcliffe's editors answered for everyone (then and now): 'War.'[32]

The press and commentators held much more sway back then. 'The extraordinary point,' writes Ferguson, 'is how seriously the scaremongers' allegations were taken by senior British officials and ministers.'[33] These officials solemnly drew up terrifying scenarios of Germany striking at the heart of the empire. Hardinge, Crowe and Grey all accepted that 'the Germans studied and are studying the question of invasion' of Britain.[34] On the contrary, German planners were studying how best to defend Germany. All of this sheds a different light on Crowe's memo, which may be read as an erudite version of an anti-German tirade launched in any British pub. At a darker level, Crowe mirrored the paranoia felt in Germany towards her real and imagined enemies.

We may console ourselves with the thought that not everyone fell into lock step with the war prophets. Satirists and cartoonists flourished, in both countries. In 1907, a German joker produced a world map on which the British Empire is reduced to Iceland and Germany has the rest. The finest rebuttal to the hysteria was *The Swoop! Or How Clarence Saved England: A Tale of the Great Invasion* (1909), by the great comic writer P. G. Wodehouse, which presents England being overrun not only by Germany but also by the Russians, the Chinese, the Swiss, Morocco, the 'Mad Mullah' and Monaco. The German invasion, in this line-up, excites less interest than a country cricket match:

SURREY DOING BADLY
German Army Lands in England

. . . with the news stuck between the cricket scores and the horse-racing results:

> Surrey 147 for 8. A German army landed in Essex this afternoon.
> Loamshire Handicap: Spring Chicken, 1; Salome, 2; Yip-i-addy,
> 3. Seven ran.[35]

13

MEANWHILE, IN BOSNIA-HERZEGOVINA

*Of course we shall do nothing against the annexation! But I am
deeply offended in my feelings as an ally not to have been admitted
into [the] secret! . . . I am last in all Europe to know anything!*
The Kaiser, on being told of the annexation of Bosnia-
Herzegovina to Austria-Hungary in 1908

IN 1908, A SECRET TURKISH SOCIETY was agitating to
regain control of Balkan territory lost to Austria-Hungary. Popularly
known as the Young Turks, the society's members were organised
under the innocuously named Committee of Union and Progress, an
umbrella group of Turkish intellectuals, students and military cadets
modelled on the revolutionary Italian underground movement the
Carbonari. The Young Turks' uprising, co-led by the future war
leader Enver Pasha, spread like a vine into the Turk-dominated areas
of the Balkans, chiefly Macedonia, raising a revolutionary standard
against the decrepit leadership of the ailing Ottoman Empire. The
movement's nationalist agenda was ambitious: to supplant the old
order in Turkey, no less, and replace it with an elected parliament
determined to reclaim full Turkish control over the territories of

Bulgaria and the provinces of Bosnia-Herzegovina.

The recent history of the disputed territories was, as everything in the Balkans, complex. It can be boiled down to a struggle between three groups, each of whom sought to dominate the peninsula for their own political and strategic ends. These were the Slavic states, led by Serbia and sponsored by Russia, who dreamt of creating an enlarged Slav kingdom; the Austro-Hungarian Empire, who sought to divide and conquer the Balkans to deny Slavic and Turkish ambitions; and the old Ottoman Empire, who hoped to retain a powerful Muslim presence in Europe and control the Dardenelles (denying Russia access to the Mediterranean). The Young Turks injected a fierce secular force for Turkish democracy into this three-way struggle. Another wild card was Serbia. Where Vienna, St Petersburg and Turkey laid political and strategic claims on the Balkan territories, Serbia's interests were essentially nationalistic, hence unpredictable and passionate.

—

Negotiating a path between these discordant claims would prove highly perilous. The whole struggle turned on the fate of a little outpost of the Ottoman Empire that everyone with an interest in the region claimed as theirs: the province of Bosnia-Herzegovina. For more than 400 years, Bosnia-Herzegovina was one of the furthermost western provinces of the Ottoman Empire, the Sultan's Muslim-dominated footprint in the heart of Europe. Bounded by Croatia, Serbia and Montenegro (see Map 3), with its capital in Sarajevo, Bosnia-Herzegovina was a land of peasants and herdsmen, of green, undulating hills, landlocked except for a narrow, strategically critical 26-kilometre strip of Adriatic coastline. Whoever controlled it had access to the Mediterranean, which was especially appealing to landlocked Serbia.

A microcosm of Balkan ethnicity, Bosnia-Herzegovina was home to Turks, Serbs, Croats and a range of smaller groups and their respective religious complexions. They seemed to inhabit a crazy multi-patched quilt, tossed about on the vicissitudes of destiny and wrenched at the seams where East met West and Christian met Muslim. These groups vied for political and economic influence, and were periodically convulsed by wars of religion and race. In time, Slav-speaking Muslims grew to dominate as a result of the rupture in the Christian Church between the Orthodox and Catholic faiths.

The Orthodox Bosnian Serbs, the second-largest ethnic group in the province, developed a fierce tribalism and saw themselves as part of a greater Serbian state, backed by Russia. The importance of Bosnia-Herzegovina to Serbia cannot be overstated. If Kosovo was the soul of Serbia, then Bosnia-Herzegovina was the future garden of pan-Slavism, fulfilling the Serb dream of a unified kingdom. 'It is the sensitive spot of all political minded Serbs, the centre around which revolve their aspirations and their hopes,' wrote Kallay in 1870.[1] The heroes of Serbian folklore found their provenance here; Serbian poets were given to composing poems in Bosnian dialects. The province represented a sort of mythical expansion of the Serbian homeland, and the sight of Austrian troops garrisoning Sarajevo deeply affronted Serbian pride.

The Bosnian Serbs carried the torch for these dreams of independence. Probably the province's most distinctive minority, they never accepted Vienna's occupation of their country. Their resistance received a powerful boost when Serbia installed a virulently anti-Austrian regime after the 1903 coup (see Chapter 24).

Most Bosnia-Herzegovinians tended to share these feelings towards Vienna. Yet the alternative – life under Belgrade – hardly appealed to those who did not share an ethnic or religious kinship with Serbia. They simply wanted to be left alone, to go about their business in peace. The sad truth is nobody in Bosnia-Herzegovina could escape their country's violent past, which periodically returned to torment them, often with devastating results. And what of the role of Russia, Serbia's ultimate overlord? If the Bosnian Serbs saw a clear future free of the clutches of Vienna, their links with Belgrade were, ultimately and inextricably, connected to the supreme Slavic sponsor in Eastern Europe.

—

In 1880, Bosnia-Herzegovina contained 500,000 Orthodox Christians, 200,000 Catholics and 450,000 Muslims. Most were Slavs, yet with divided ethnic and religious loyalties. Somehow, they were to be unified, according to Belgrade's vision of an enlarged Slavic state. Between 1857 and 1870, the Pan-Slav Movement – which predated the Pan-German movement – entrusted to Russia 'the task of liberating and uniting all Slavs in one vast confederation'.[2] The history of the Balkan struggle may be traced to this Slavic longing for union, a struggle sponsored by Russia through her chief protégé, Serbia.

The dream seemed close to reality in 1878. From 13 June to 13 July that year, the great powers met at the Congress of Berlin, convened to stabilise the Balkans after Russia's victory over the Turks in the wars of 1877–78. After the deposition of Sultan Murad V in 1876, his weakened successor, Sultan Abdülhamid II, had proved unable to control his Slavic vassals, and the delegates gathered in Berlin to determine the new order in the peninsula. Bismarck hosted the proceedings – a fitting recognition of his rising influence in Europe – and leaders of Britain, France, Germany, Austria-Hungary, Italy, Russia and the Ottoman Empire attended. With a surprising lack of rancour, they managed to thrash out the Treaty of Berlin – the name itself an emphatic reminder of Germany's ascendancy in European affairs – which formally recognised the 'independence' of the de facto principalities of Serbia, Montenegro and Bulgaria from Ottoman rule.

This was the beginning of the end of Turkey's half-millennial reign in the Balkans. In fact, the treaty went further, in seeming to address Slavic demands. It revised the earlier Treaty of San Stefano, signed on 3 March that year, which created an autonomous Bulgaria, effectively liberating that principality from 500 years of

Ottoman rule (and celebrated in Bulgaria today as Liberation Day). Although the Turks still retained control over Macedonia and parts of Bulgaria, the twilight of their empire in Europe had arrived.

One empire's retreat invited another to advance. In Habsburg eyes, something had to be done to control these unruly Bosnia-Herzegovinians. The great powers stepped in. The Congress of Berlin granted Austria-Hungary the right to occupy and subdue the rebellious province – nominally still under Ottoman suzerainty – and Vienna swiftly sent troops to garrison the Bosnia-Herzegovinian towns. This blow to Ottoman pride was the price of failing to curb Bosnian unrest. For its part, Serbia deeply resented the decision, which killed its hopes of incorporating the province into an enlarged Slavic state, under the control of Belgrade. The apparent victor, Austria-Hungary, little realised that it had grabbed hold of the colonial equivalent of a porcupine: bristling with spines and likely to flare up at any moment.

The Congress of Berlin also created an enlarged Slavic Principality of Bulgaria (under the Treaty of San Stefano) and then, in the same year (under the Treaty of Berlin), reversed this decision and broke up Bulgaria into three separate provinces (one of which was Macedonia) before handing them back to Turkish control.

The whole effect of these measures was to curb Ottoman and Russian ambitions in the Balkans, splinter Serb hopes of an enlarged Slavic kingdom and empower Vienna. Critically, in 1881, Austria obtained from Russia and Germany a mandate to annex Bosnia-Herzegovina at a time of its choosing. The Russian position changed in 1897, when new tsar Nicholas II refused to accept the deal. Henceforth, Russia would resist any Austrian attempt to annex the province, a hostage to fortune that would return to haunt the Balkans with terrific consequences.

———

In the 1900s, then, the Austrians and the Young Turks cast their hungry eyes over the spoils of the Ottoman Empire's weakening grip in the Balkans. Since 1902, when they first formed an opposition in exile, in Paris, the Young Turks were determined to replace the crepuscular Ottoman autocracy, under Sultan Abdul Hamid II, with democratic, secular government, and to reclaim Macedonia, Bosnia-Herzegovina and parts of Bulgaria for Constantinople. But first they had to supplant the Sultan's regime, and this is what drove their revolution throughout the 1900s.

The ambitions of the Young Turks horrified Viennese officials, for whom a resurgent Turkey threatened their plan to control the Balkans. Equally disturbing was the prospect of a Russian-sponsored Greater Serbia. In 1908, those fears stirred Austria-Hungary to act – to fill the power vacuum in the Balkans and thus deny the dream of a Turkish return *or* the establishment of a Russian-sponsored Slavic realm.

It was natural, then, for Austria-Hungary to covet the little province where Vienna already had troops. The annexation of Bosnia-Herzegovina would serve as a prelude to the full subjugation of the Slavic territories. For Vienna, this was a case of 'now or never', because the original deal conferring the right to annex the province was due to expire in 1908. The great unknown was Russia: would it tolerate Bosnia's spiriting away to Viennese control? Perhaps St Petersburg might do so, in return for Austro-Hungarian recognition of the free passage of Russian warships through the Bosphorus and the Dardenelles – 'the Straits' (without changing the existing arrangements that compelled Turkey to close the Straits to all other powers). To some Russians, especially in the Tsar's court, exclusive access to the Mediterranean at the cost of shuffling off to Austria a tiny patch of the Balkans seemed a bargain. And so, in 1908, with this carrot in mind, Austria-Hungary set in train a plan to annex Bosnia-Herzegovina. The ensuing crisis would demonstrate to all Europe why the Balkans were likely to become the furnace of war.

—

The diplomatic struggle involved a clash of two of the cleverest, most egocentric and personally flawed statesmen in Europe: Count Alois Lexa von Aehrenthal, the Austrian foreign minister, and his Russian counterpart, Alexander Izvolsky. Both were highly accomplished men experienced in the unscrupulous arts of diplomacy. Aehrenthal, born in 1854 to a family of wealthy Jewish grain merchants, was 'a mixture of pretension and subtlety, of force and ruse, of realism and cynicism: his readiness to cheat, to circumvent, to outwit hid a harsh and ruthless will', observes a biographer.[3] Clever, cool and patient, he was endowed with an outward calm that belied 'a lively and dominating imagination more passionate than clear-sighted', notes Albertini.[4]

Izvolsky was a gifted if dangerously ambitious Russian Orthodox nobleman prone to rash and unpredictable decisions. 'Izvolsky,' observed a colleague, 'is undoubtedly highly cultured and intelligent but unfortunately his excessive irritability and his pride do him much harm. An attack in a newspaper article causes him a sleepless night.'[5]

Both men were eager to play the great game of European power politics. They saw the destiny of nations as a series of high-powered chess moves, over which they had personal control: a wrong move could dislocate whole peoples; a right one might empower them. Neither man wanted war, but both were intrinsically involved in the events leading to the Great War. The author Alexander Kerensky suggested 'Europe on the Road to the Great War' as the subtitle to Izvolsky's personal correspondence, so intimately was the Russian diplomat involved in the machinations that took the world to 1914.[6]

Aehrenthal, thwarted in his hopes of rehabilitating the *Dreikaiserbund*, the association of the two emperors that had once underwritten the relationship between Austria-Hungary and Russia, set his sights on restoring the battered prestige of the old Habsburg Empire through a bold intervention in the Balkan Peninsula. Mindful that Vienna had asserted the right to annex the provinces 'at whatever moment she shall deem opportune', he now meant to fulfil that plan.[7] His grander ambition was to draw the Croats (and other non-Serbian Slavs) into an enlarged tripartite empire made up of Austria, Hungary and the Southern Slavs. His purpose was to isolate Serbia, as 'the severed limb of a vast, Croat-dominated South Slav entity within the [Austro-Hungarian] Empire'.[8]

—

Between October 1907 and September 1908, Aehrenthal struck a series of concessions that would smooth the path to full annexation of Bosnia-Herzegovina and transform the European order. He needed Russian acquiescence in the plan. His opening gambit was shrewd, in that he gave away the Sanjak (an Ottoman administrative unit) of Novibazar, a strip of territory in present-day Montenegro, which the Austrian troops then occupied. Apparently, it contained little military value. His intentions were ostensibly to appease the rival powers, especially Turkey and Russia, by renouncing Austria-Hungary's claim to the Sanjak. This seemed a valuable card to yield, since Austria retained the right to occupy the Sanjak under the Treaty of Berlin. However, on 27 January 1908, Aehrenthal temporarily stalled his plan with a rider: he had received a concession from the Sultan to construct a railroad through the Sanjak, to Mitrovitsa, on the Serbian border.

This amendment enraged Izvolsky (and Belgrade), who saw the proposed railway line as 'a bomb thrown between his feet'[9] – a military tactic designed to funnel Austrian troops to the frontier of Serbia, threatening Russia's Slavic cousin. Would Austria-Hungary thus serve as Germany's Trojan Horse into the Slavic realm? The Russian state-controlled press reacted with predictable violence, claiming that German domination of the Balkans would result; a few editors even speculated about war.

Izvolsky chose not to challenge the railway openly. Instead, he expressed himself willing, as Vienna had hoped, to acquiesce in the annexation of Bosnia-Herzegovina in exchange for Austrian recognition of Russia's most coveted goal: naval control of the Turkish Straits. The gift of Bosnia-Herzegovina, which Austria already occupied, seemed a small price to pay for such a grand prize, Izvolsky reasoned.

Izvolsky approached his rival with this deal in mind, sponsored by the Tsar himself. Of course, Russia's acceptance of it risked infuriating Serbia, so Izvolsky pledged Aehrenthal to secrecy, hoping to hide Russia's complicity from its Serbian friends, who plainly did *not* want Austria to annex the provinces. Izvolsky thus handed Aehrenthal a devastating weapon: the threat to expose the Russian's secret involvement in the gift of Bosnia-Herzegovina to Vienna.

Izvolsky made his offer to Aehrenthal on 2 July 1908: '[I]n view of the extreme importance to our two countries of seeing the [future of Bosnia-Herzegovina] settled in accordance with their mutual interests, the Imperial Government would be prepared to enter into the discussion of them in a friendly spirit of reciprocity'.[10]

In such innocuous tones are whole states brought down and folded into hostile realms. Aehrenthal saw his chance and struck. Feigning a studied nonchalance at the Russian 'compromise', he saw immediately that Izvolsky had made a dreadful blunder by hastily offering up Bosnia-Herzegovina. Izvolsky had thus betrayed the urgency of Russia's naval ambitions and played all St Petersburg's cards at once. The Austrian foreign minister resolved on a course that would make a dupe of his Russian adversary, and pitch Austria-Hungary's relations with the Slavic world into open and chronic conflict.

—

Aehrenthal moved quickly to consolidate his chance. During July 1908, the Young Turkish revolution was gathering steam and spreading through Macedonia, proclaiming an end to the autocratic Turkish reign of the past 30 years and a return to the liberal constitution of 1876. The Young Turks hoped soon to realise their gains in the Balkans. So too Aehrenthal, who meant to press ahead with the annexation as soon as possible. The stick of the Turkish revolt and the carrot of Russia's secret offer proved irresistible.

Aehrenthal, of course, declined to share this new expedient with Izvolsky, who persisted under the delusion that a secret deal, of great benefit to Russia, was within reach. The two foreign ministers resumed their negotiations at Schloss Buchlau on 16 September, where, over two six-hour marathon sessions, they thrashed out the terms of an 'agreement', the central point of which was Russia's consent to the annexation of Bosnia-Herzegovina by Austria-Hungary.

In exchange for what? In one of the strangest denouements in European diplomatic history, Russia failed to conclude its side of the bargain, such as it was, in writing; only a few desultory memos trailed the discussion, and these failed to nail the terms. In the following weeks, both sides sought to redefine what they thought they had agreed. Aehrenthal claimed that the Russian delegation had agreed that in any future negotiations over the Straits 'there could be no more word of Bosnia-Herzegovina' (i.e. no public link between the annexation and Russian naval access to the Mediterranean). This inhibited any reference to the provinces in Russia's claim on the Straits – and would prevent Izvolsky 'from putting the annexation and the Straits questions on the same plane, ie would leave him – as in fact it did – with his hands empty'.[11] For his part, Izvolsky stated that he presumed the annexation plan would be submitted for further discussion at a future meeting on 8 October.

Vienna went ahead with annexation two days earlier. Having sown a paper trail of letters to the embassies of Europe, alluding to the imminent event but declining to give a precise date, Aehrenthal smoothed acceptance of the announcement, by Emperor Franz Joseph, on 6 October 1908, of the formal annexation of Bosnia-Herzegovina. A day earlier, the King of Bulgaria declared his nation formally independent. Both events contravened the Treaty of Berlin, and drew the sharpest reactions from Russia, France and Serbia, who were furious to see the Bosnian and Herzegovinian provinces fall under complete Austro-Hungarian control. Russia was utterly humiliated. The annexation was directly responsible for the later tensions that sparked the Austro-Serbian War.

As the annexation worked its way through the diplomatic diges-
tive tract, it became clear that Vienna had called Europe's bluff
and won. The reason lay with Germany, the one power in whose
gift Austria-Hungary's audacious diplomatic moves swam or sank.
Berlin's support for the annexation established a pattern in its relationship with Vienna. From now on, Germany tended to rubber-
stamp any Austrian action or declaration that curbed Serbia's ambitions – and, by extension, Russia's. The linkages were not lost on the
members of the Triple Entente, who were, as ever, finely attuned to
Berlin's response to any breach of the peace in central Europe.

The annexation revealed something else about Germany: the
extent of the marginalisation of the Kaiser. Wilhelm had been
informed of Austria's actions, he sulkily claimed, via a Turkish
source a day before, and not by his own government. 'Of course we
shall do nothing against the annexation!' he wrote. 'But I am deeply
offended in my feelings as an ally not to have been admitted into His
Majesty's secret! . . . I am last in all Europe to know anything!'[12]

—

The repercussions were bitter and chronic. An empire had forcibly
digested a sovereign state, in Russian eyes. Yet Izvolsky had informed
none of his colleagues in St Petersburg of his secret dealings and tacit
acceptance of the annexation. When they heard of his complicity,
through his letter of 2 July, the news shocked the St Petersburg government. The highly respected prime minister Pyotr Stolypin threatened to resign if German-backed Austria was allowed to proceed
with the annexation. The Russians insisted on an international conference to validate the terms of the 1878 treaty.

After initial foot-dragging, Germany came to Austria-Hungary's
aid, and, using a 'veiled threat of war', writes the historian James
Joll, 'forced the Russian government to give way and to acquiesce
in the Austrian action'. According to Joll, 'The crisis showed how
easily the rivalry between Russia and Austria in the Balkans could
become of European concern.'[13] For the first time, Germany revealed

its loyalties in military terms. The Kaiser declared rather stupidly that he stood by the Austrians 'in shining armour'; while Helmuth von Moltke, German chief of staff, told his counterpart in Austria, General Franz Conrad von Hötzendorf, 'The moment Russia mobilises, Germany will also mobilise.'[14]

France and England sympathised with the Serbs and mildly opposed the annexation, but nobody contemplated force. Clemenceau's reaction was perhaps the harshest. For him, the annexation was 'a serious infringement of contractual obligations and an offence against public morality which would constitute a precedent, if allowed to pass'.[15]

In London, Foreign Secretary Edward Grey, on hearing the news via Hardinge, who had received private notification from Aehrenthal on 3 October, promptly urged Vienna to rethink this grave breach of international protocols laid down in the Treaty of London of 1871, which stipulated that no power may renege on its pledges in relation to neighbouring states without the consent of the signatories. Vienna ignored this endearingly English respect for 'international law'.

King Edward echoed the mood in a glacial meeting with the Austrian ambassador on 9 October. At the same time, Izvolsky was received in London with all the pomp and circumstance thought necessary to reassure a humiliated member of the Triple Entente. In a few days, the fault lines of Europe had hardened into an unbridgeable divide.

Yet, nobody moved to resist Vienna's action. Beyond the snorts of indignation, more words were spent attacking it than actions were taken to resist it. Cooler heads in St Petersburg, Paris and London scraped around for a silver lining. What about compensation for Serbia? Or concessions from Vienna? Why had the Austro-Hungarians not offered Belgrade a scrap of Bosnia-Herzegovina, to placate them? Aehrenthal had dismissed Izvolsky's proposal of the partition of Bosnia at their Buchlau meeting, and now saw no point in revisiting negotiations, which he claimed had been thoroughly settled. Nobody, of course, consulted the Bosnia-Herzegovinians about who they would prefer to rule them.

A proposed conference to decide the issue foundered on confusion over the agenda and German opposition. Berlin did not wish to be seen as a conciliator between Vienna and the Triple Entente. In any case, Russia encountered all kinds of complications in divining the Turkish position on the issue of naval access through the Dardanelles, the secret quid pro quo that the disgraced Izvolsky had hoped to secure. Without Turkish assent, the St Petersburg government risked hoisting Russia on another petard.

—

Serbia and Russia reacted most vehemently to the loss of Bosnia-Herzegovina (ironically, in the latter's case, given Izvolsky's secret sell-out). Belgrade ordered the mobilisation of 120,000 men and put the nation on emergency alert. On 17 October, the Serbian foreign minister Milovanović left on a protest tour of European capitals. Only the threat of Austrian military action persuaded Serbia to abandon its stand and issue a statement of acceptance, pledging to be a good neighbour. Yet the whole issue deeply rankled.

The historian Ninčić writes:

> there was a feeling that irreparable harm had been done, that
> we were on the eve of a national disaster, and that Austria-
> Hungary, the implacable enemy of Serbia and the Serb race,
> was preparing to destroy every symptom of resistance in a
> people who wanted to live independent and free.[16]

Elsewhere, he claimed the annexation crisis contained 'all the elements that were to recur in 1914 and were the direct cause of the Great War'.[17]

The Austrian offence reached the heart of the Serbian Government and its intelligence apparatus. On 8 October 1908, just two days after Austria annexed Bosnia, Serbian ministers, officials and generals held a meeting at City Hall in Belgrade. Their purpose was to establish a semi-secret society to be called *Narodna Odbrana* (National Defence), which would serve as the organising body for pan-Slavism in the Balkans. More specifically, as Michael Shackelford writes, it aimed 'to recruit and train partisans for a possible war between Serbia and Austria', to combat the Austrian presence in the Balkans through propaganda, espionage and sabotage.[18] Satellite groups were to be set up in Bosnia-Herzegovina, Slovenia and Istria.

Within a year, *Narodna Odbrana* had been so successful in raising pan-Slav awareness that Vienna compelled the Serbian Government to put a stop to the agitation. With Russia reluctant at this point to support Serbia's 'anti-Austrian insurrection', Belgrade was grudgingly forced to comply. *Narodna Odbrana* henceforth 'concentrated on education and propaganda within Serbia, trying to fashion itself as a cultural organization'.[19] A deadlier pan-Slavic organisation called *Ujedinjenje ili Smrt* (Unification or Death) soon replaced it.

The most ominous consequences of the Bosnia-Herzegovinian crisis were human, all too human, and rested in the hearts and minds of the Russian leadership. St Petersburg had been humiliated in the eyes of the world and would soon turn this emotional response into political and military action, as Hew Strachan shows. The annexation, in Russian eyes, was evidence of Austria's ambition to expand in the Balkans and might 'eventually take the Dual Monarchy to the gates of Constantinople and to a landward domination of the Straits . . .'[20] The Russian Government even appropriated funds for rearmament. Henceforth its whole foreign policy would press for the creation of an anti-Austrian polity in central and south-eastern Europe. To this end, relations between Russia and Serbia hardened into a seemingly unbreakable Slavic bloc.

14

TEUTONS – AND AN ITALIAN – UNDER SIEGE

Full of the zest of battle the army awaits the tasks to which it is
called. We go into battle with the consciousness that on us depends
the future of our Empire. If we return victorious, we shall not only
have conquered a foreign land: we shall have won back Austrian
self-respect, given new life to the Imperial idea . . . Our blood
throbs in our veins, we strain at the leash. Sire! Give us the signal!
Article on the front page of the Austrian military journal
Danzer's Armee-Zeitung, 7 January 1909

IT WAS A MERE VIENNESE NEWSPAPER ARTICLE, but its
authority, bellicosity and tendency to blame every European power
except Germany for Austria-Hungary's divided state revealed the
frightened psychology of a regime whose military chiefs considered
war the only means of preserving the self-esteem and continuity of
the Habsburg dynasty. The article, 'The Eve of War', caused serious
alarm throughout Europe. Published on 7 January 1909 in *Danzer's
Armee-Zeitung*, the journal of the Austro-Hungarian armed forces,
it reflected the views of the High Command and had the seal of

approval of Conrad von Hötzendorf, the gruff, heavily moustachioed Austro-Hungarian chief of staff.

Consistent with his belief in social Darwinism – which boiled down to a belief in war as the test of the fittest race – Conrad understood conflict as the necessary expression of 'the inexorable struggle for existence'. War, in this sense, was a replacement for, rather than an extension of, politics.[1] His views scarcely differed from that of the average, educated staff officer in the Austro-Hungarian Army, for whom war would decide who would inherit the earth.[2] Conrad explained:

> [T]he recognition of the struggle for existence as the basic principle of all events on this earth is the only real and rational basis for policy-making . . . Whoever remains blind to the mounting danger, or whoever recognizes it but remains too indolent to arm himself, and is too undecided to deliver the blow at the proper moment, deserves his fate.[3]

Keen to put his theory into practice, Conrad consistently urged the Austro-Hungarian Government to invade and subdue Serbia. Only force of arms would assure the future security of the Dual Monarchy.

—

In a fascinating parallel, Conrad applied a similar strategy in his private life. Denuded of conventional morality and any sense of discretion, he invaded the domestic peace of a woman half his age, the 28-year-old Gina von Reininghaus, mother of six and wife of the wealthy businessman Hans von Reininghaus. Gina was a tall Italian beauty, with dark, flowing hair. Conrad was an intense, charismatic man with a slight, wiry build and a handlebar moustache. They met at a dinner party on 20 January 1907, and Conrad was transfixed. He never let go of the idea that she would one day be his wife. He paid her constant, unsolicited attention and proposed often. He wrote daily, relentlessly; he poured out his sorrows in his

personal 'Diary of My Woes', a trove of mawkish, self-pitying ver-
biage, most of it unsent, redolent of a much younger man's sudden
discovery of sexual passion. She drove him 'to achieve great things',
he wrote. Conrad would rise – he fantasised, in one unsent letter –
during the Bosnian crisis to the status of a triumphant commander
and return to Vienna in glory, whereupon he would 'throw all caution to the winds and make Gina his wife'.[4] While she seemed flattered, if perhaps bewildered, by this incessant attention, Conrad was
troubled to find that he could not prevail upon her to leave her husband and children for a man of 54 who seemed unable to control his
infatuation.

Conrad's biographer amusingly compares the Austrian's obsession with Napoleon's pursuit of Josephine. Like Napoleon, 'Conrad's
belief in the cult of the offensive on the battlefield was reflected in
his quest for Gina. His "attacks" were relentless, with no rational
consideration of the chances of success and no concern for the "casualties", moral or emotional.'[5] In total, Conrad sent or wrote 3000 letters to Gina between 1907 and 1915. They probably became lovers
in 1908, or earlier – with her husband's apparent compliance. We
would otherwise ignore the private life of the love-stricken Austrian
chief of staff were it not for the fact that his obsession affected his
mental stability and the discharge of his duties. His obsessive relationship impinged on Conrad's moods, exciting his wayward temper
and emboldening him to great deeds, etc., not all of them sound.

—

Conrad and Gina had thoroughly consummated their love affair at
the time of the appearance of 'The Eve of War' in *Danzer's Armee-
Zietung* (a journal which he occasionally contributed to and avidly
read), a few months after the Bosnian annexation. The article, which
Conrad had approved, was timed for maximum impact in the wake
of the Triple Entente's outrage and Russia's deep humiliation over
Austria-Hungary's annexation.

While Austria triumphed in that diplomatic confrontation, 'The

Eve of War' portrays the country as the wounded party, rather like Conrad himself in his diary of woes. Indeed, it is difficult not to hear the defiant voice of Conrad the Conqueror in the article's blood-curdling tones. This underdog mentality, shared by the Prussian nobility, looked out on a friendless world. They already considered Italy, a nominal ally, whose relations with Germany and Austria were cooling, an arch-enemy. Italy had just suffered the terrible earthquake at Messina, yet Conrad's scribes saw this as an opportunity to kick the Italian dog while it was down (one shudders to think how the Italian-born Gina responded to this insensitivity).

Yet 'The Eve of War' cannot be dismissed as another warmonger's screed. It was a call to arms, to prosecute a preventive war against the enemies of Austria-Hungary and Germany. It was clearly written for Berlin and the Kaiser, and the old Habsburg emperor Franz Joseph. Blind to the consequences of their actions, the authors reveal an official mindset incapable of perceiving other nations' viewpoints, only potential enemies. If their defiant wail of an empire under siege had little direct influence on specific policy, it served as a bellwether of the mood in the upper echelons of the Austro-Hungarian imperial forces, the loudest shout in the rising chorus of voices prophesying war. For all these reasons, 'The Eve of War' deserves an extended hearing:

The hour has struck. War is inevitable.

Never was a war more just. And never yet was our confidence in a victorious issue more firmly grounded.

We are being driven into war: Russia drives us. Italy drives us. Serbia and Montenegro drive us, and Turkey drives us.

Russia drives us: . . . Russia today is ready for a war of offence; so for the time being she recognizes the Austrian claim to Bosnia (Russia regards as only a secondary consideration the fact that long ago by numerous treaties and promises she pledged herself to the recognition of the annexation); but, says Izvolsky, Russia is preparing to fulfill in time her historic mission in the Balkans and will in the meanwhile use all means to promote a league of all the Balkan states against Austria-Hungary . . . either [we must] strike at once while Russia is still suffering from the after-effects of her recent war [with Japan] and her revolution [1905] at home, or withhold our blow until she has gathered strength again and by diplomatic wiles sets Roumania and Bulgaria against us, leaving us entirely isolated.

Italy drives us: for if officially we still see Italy on our side, this is only in order that she may later the more effectually spring all her mines against us. Gnashing her teeth, Italy feigns to be a loyal ally only because she knows herself not yet to be ready. But with giant strides she is repairing the neglect of two decades. Are we to wait until Italy sees the favourable moment for the war against us?

[After referring to more than 100,000 people who perished in the Messina earthquake:] . . . As human beings we are moved to the most profound and sincere sympathy by the terrible events of 28 December [1908]. But politics is a ruthless trade and we must regard the Messina earthquake as a favourable factor in our calculations. Five years ago we were simple-minded enough to show consideration for Russian misfortunes in the Far East and to let slip the chance of bringing about a definite solution in the Balkans satisfying to our views. The thanks for our chivalrous spirit were not long in coming: Russia today stands in the ranks of our foes! We are cured of such chivalry and shall not hesitate, even in these days of national mourning, to speak a decisive word to Italy.

Serbia drives us: The Serbian prime minister's speech needs no further commentary. A jaw like his asks for the answering fist and any officer of the Imperial and Royal Army would be ashamed of the sword he wears, if the state he serves submitted to such provocation without protest.

Turkey drives us: Our representatives in Constantinople are treated with scorn and derision. Our prestige there is down to a mere remnant. The boycott against us is nothing else than a never-ending underhand war. Turkey is now in the hands of a clique of traitors, bribed with English money and working for the interests of England; Turkey, too, is in a transition stage which now renders her less able to undertake action and will probably continue to be so, and it will not be our fault if we are obliged to take advantage of this internal crisis.

If our power were as organized, as unchallenged, and as impressive as that of the German Empire, we could lightly dispense with an ultimatum and wait for things to take their course, standing at ease. But because our prestige in foreign eyes is undermined, because we are thought to be weaker than we are, because we are measurelessly underrated, we cannot for that very reason do otherwise than invoke the *ultima ratio* of nations, seizing the favourable occasion, and in the first place replying to Serbian provocation with the sword as forcefully and emphatically as our self-respect and interest demand.

On the speed and success of this first move will depend whether or not it will end the military operations of this fateful year.

We have formally taken possession of Bosnia which has long been ours. Under the stress of circumstances we shall now lay hand on Serbia and, by our protection, give that sorely-tried land the chance of beginning a new life under our protectorate . . .

Full of the zest of battle the army awaits the tasks to which it is called. We go into battle with the consciousness that on us depends the future of our Empire. If we return victorious, we shall not only have conquered a foreign land: we shall have won back Austrian self-respect, given new life to the Imperial idea and vanquished not only the foreign enemy but the enemy in our midst.

Our blood throbs in our veins, we strain at the leash. Sire! Give us the signal![6]

Here, then, was the authentic voice of Austro-Hungarian military paranoia, issuing from the top echelons of its armed forces. It revealed a state of mind that would prevail in July 1914. If we are to comprehend it, we must invert our modern assumption of war as the last resort after the failure of diplomacy and acquaint ourselves with the mentality that war was inevitable, necessary, *desirable*. According to this rationale, it would be a proving ground for the fittest in the ultimate Darwinian struggle, out of which a perfect race of blonde Nietzschean supermen (and superwomen) would emerge, who, after restoring the prestige of the Habsburg royal family, would go on to dominate the earth. Conrad's tirade concludes with the unedifying spectacle of Vienna, the thief of Bosnia-Herzegovina, casting herself as a cornered dog, 'straining at the leash' to conquer Greater Serbia in order to restore 'Austrian self-respect'. If the article betrayed Conrad's raging libido and crisis of masculinity, it certainly enjoyed the resounding approbation of the Kaiser.

—

Indeed, Germany smiled on her Austrian ally with the concern of a bemused parent trying to rein in a wayward adolescent. Berlin was troubled and suspicious. No doubt, Austria-Hungary would fight with Germany, her staunch ally, if war came, but *against whom* would the old empire fight if it came to blows? Would Vienna and Budapest restrict their armies to Serbia and Italy, the wait-and-see wallflower whose nominal allegiance to the Triple Alliance fooled nobody? (Aehrenthal himself had expressed his concerns over Italy in a letter to Bülow on 8 December 1908, recommending that Conrad and Moltke 'examine the hypothesis of Italian neutrality'.)[7] Or would Austria-Hungary rally to fight Germany's most feared enemy – Russia – and help hold off the Muscovite hordes, should they come? Germany sat and studied its Teutonic cousins, and wondered.

In this light, the German Government's cast of mind in 1909 is hard to assess, given the ideas, perceptions and sentiments on display. These ranged from the hysteria and inconsistency of the Kaiser to the relative sobriety and moderate outlook of the new chancellor, Theobald von Bethmann-Hollweg; from the Prussian military's belief in a preventive war to the accommodation and compromise of the liberals and socialists. A common denominator binding these extremes was Germany's strange national solipsism, a sort of collective self-referential narrative in which the Reich was the cause or catalyst of other nations' alliances and friendships. Relationships between Russia, France and Britain were always conceived *in spite of* Germany. The troubling thing was, as 1908 fell into the critical years of 1909–14, the German narrative had substance: Germany had become the point of contention around which the European powers revolved.

—

To his credit, Bethmann-Hollweg tried to arrest Germany's slide into isolation and besiegement, and solder together a new relationship with Britain. This goal would prove elusive, not least because Bethmann-Hollweg failed to understand the English (as we shall see). Let us try to understand him. Of all the details of Chancellor Bethmann-Hollweg's life that interest us, one is critical to appreciating his actions leading up to the declaration of war in 1914: he had never served in the armed forces. He was not a soldier. And that rankled with the Prussian generals nominally under his command – yet very vocal in their advice. Their pressure intimidated him and explained why his grip on power would unravel in the coming crisis. Bethmann-Hollweg was, in spirit, an intellectual, from a family of prominent Prussian lawyers and civil servants. He spoke several languages and read the Greek and Roman classics in the original. Whether these qualities prepared him for statesmanship was not a question in an age that valued a classical education over the skills of diplomacy and negotiation.

As a young man, Bethmann-Hollweg enjoyed the cloistered world of Schulpforta, the elite boarding school where he rejected 'the personal demands of militarism' and fashioned himself as a lone thinker, 'the philosopher from Hohenfinow'[8] (his birthplace, in Brandenburg), a sort of Goethian hero. 'Refusing to join a fraternity, he lived in his own imagination, preferring the world of ideas and ideals to prosaic reality,' wrote one biographer.[9] If so, he kept his head, and went on to be the school head prefect, excel at his law exams and gain a reputation in society as a great host of shooting parties: 'all in all, [he] exemplified most admirably Bismarck's epigram that Prussia produces excellent Privy Councillors and routine ministers, but no statesmen'.[10]

Bethmann-Hollweg's yearning to fulfil his 'uncommon aspirations' outstripped his talents and personality, and he became an extremely driven autodidact. His failure at formal scholarship and literary expression, for example, propelled him to over-achieve in other spheres of life and to seek the transitory consolations of power. 'He assumed a character,' writes Jarausch, 'both cold and fervent, cynical and idealistic, conservative and reformist.' At 23, he was, at once, 'astonishingly old and personally naïve, and was ready to concretize his "hazy ideas about the future"'.[11] Politics accommodated this contrarian, curiously unformed character better than any other pursuit and, in the absence of appealing alternatives, Bethmann-Hollweg pragmatically set forth to dedicate his life to the service of the state.

He rose through the political ranks of nationalist conservatives to become, in 1907, imperial state secretary for the interior. In 1909, he succeeded Bülow as chancellor on the latter's resignation. Once in power, he immediately focused his efforts on Britain. Somehow, the British had to be 'befriended' again. That would prove tricky because Germany, having rejected British invitations to form an alliance in 1898–1902, had played a critical role in driving London to sign the Entente Cordiale with Paris. Seeing this error, Bethmann-Hollweg sought to lure London back into the German embrace and away from the Franco-Russian Alliance. The Triple Entente 'beleaguered' Germany, Bethmann-Hollweg wrote.[12]

For this reason, Bethmann-Hollweg's first act as chancellor, in 1909, was to place the German alliance with Austria-Hungary on a 'defensive' war footing, which had been forced upon him, he claimed, by the formation of the Triple Entente. Germany had not provoked its encirclement, according to Bethmann-Hollweg's interpretation. For him, the Germans were a peace-loving people who looked out on a rampant and aggressive world that was slowly closing in. The 'official policy' of France, Russia and Britain was to limit Germany's economic ascendancy, he claimed, and curb the Pan-German movement.

—

The mind on display in Bethmann-Hollweg's memoir (which he wrote in 1919–20, before he died that year) is a literary engine of self-exculpation and evasion, winnowing out a version of history that presents Germany as the perennially misunderstood victim. The author does, however, portray the besieged mood of Berlin in 1909 and blames the rise of Pan-Germanism squarely on the Triple Entente:

> I cannot assert too emphatically that these efflorescences of Pan-Germanism were to no small extent the effect of the passionate explosions of Chauvinism in the countries of the Entente. But this chauvinism, unlike that of Germany, had its source in the official Policy of these [Entente] powers . . . But if we for our part were guilty of an excessive national exuberance, yet the cry from the other camp that rang in the ears of a listening world – *Germania delenda* ['Germany must be destroyed'] – came from the soberest commercial calculation. No doubt that made it all the more effective.[13]

In the pantheon of Germany's enemies, according to Bethmann-Hollweg, the French were a people of 'war-like ambition' who, increasingly under the influence of Poincaré, had no interest in rapprochement or autonomy, only the return of Alsace-Lorraine.[14]

The English were scheming and perfidious, whose Liberal policies were conceived to contain Germany's naval ambitions and would, if pursued, 'increasingly imperil the peace of the world'.[15] And the Russians were the most dangerous and cantankerous liars, who repeatedly deceived Germany over its deepening involvement in successive Balkan crises.

The truth or otherwise of these assertions is not the point. In the war of perceptions, what mattered was that Germany's leaders sternly believed in this cemented state of a world controlled by their European rivals, whose sinister project was to limit the frontiers of German 'living space' (*Lebensraum*), even as they gorged on the fruits of empire in Asia and Africa. And Bethmann-Hollweg was of the moderate tendency.

No doubt, there were more moderating influences in the Reichstag – the Social Democrats, the Liberals – who sought to contain the rabid German press and the outrageous utterances of the Kaiser. The trouble is these voices of restraint were rarely heard outside Germany, and not at all where they mattered, in Britain and France.

—

The Kaiser, on the other hand, made himself absurdly visible. Wilhelm had the unfortunate habit of openly defending, as if someone might snatch it away, his glorious place in the German firmament. 'The Foreign Office?' he declared on one occasion. 'Why, I am the Foreign Office!'[16] In a letter to his uncle (before Edward became king), he wrote, 'I am the sole master of German policy . . . and my country must follow me wherever I go.' If a dwindling number of German politicians shared this view, it was no doubt true that the Kaiser stood at the apex of the German Government and armed forces. As the commander-in-chief and head of state, his personality had a pervasive influence on decision-making – at least until 1908, when the generals and politicians wearied of his reckless ideas and wayward tongue, and sought to muzzle and marginalise him.

Wilhelm identified himself with the 'German spirit' to the point where the two concepts became, in his mind, indistinguishable. He unburdened himself of an endless series of speeches, comments, interviews and margin notes in official correspondence, on all state matters that took his passing fancy. His curiously adolescent eruptions, which belched forth from pen and mouth throughout his 30-year reign, were usually made public and reported in the foreign media. If these were not so inflammatory and dangerously misunderstood, they deserved merely scorn or laughter. Yet this was, after all, the sovereign of all Germany, not 'an infatuated schoolboy', as one American official dismissed him after reading an ingratiating letter from the Kaiser to the President. Wilhelm symbolised immense power.

As such, the world felt inclined to listen – even as his ministers blanched at the sound – to the Kaiser's thoughts. Throughout the 1900s, he proposed alliances with virtually every major power on earth, in a frantic stampede towards realising his cherished *Weltpolitik*. At various points in his maddening reign, he called for military alliances with France, Russia, Britain, USA, China, Japan and the Triple Entente, against a litany of others. One week, he would take a liking to Russia, the next to Britain, and then France. He talked tough in theory; in practice, he shunned conflict. The one thing that seemed to silence his outbursts was the risk of plunging Germany into actual war; he tended to flee, or give in, at the first whiff of real and present danger.

Two extraordinary examples of the Kaiser on the verbal warpath, cited by the historian Christopher Clark, give a sense of his buffoonish behaviour. As a guest at a dinner hosted by the US Embassy in Berlin on 4 April 1906, Wilhelm sallied forth – presumably, in jest – on the theme of German overpopulation; it had grown from 40 million to 60 million since his accession. To ease the pressure on food supply, Germany needed extra living space. Would not France, large portions of which seemed to be under-populated and backward, agree to withdraw her border westward to accommodate the burgeoning German Empire? At a gala dinner in January 1904, to celebrate his birthday, he confided in an astonished King Leopold of Belgium that, if Brussels were to stand with Germany in a future war with France, the Belgians would receive new territory taken from the French and Leopold would be crowned king of old Burgundy. Leopold replied that his ministers would reject such a fanciful plan, at which Wilhelm retorted that he could not respect a monarch who felt beholden to parliament, 'rather than to the Lord God'. If that were Belgium's position, Wilhelm continued, Germany would be obliged to 'proceed on purely strategic principles' – i.e. to invade and occupy Belgium. Deeply disturbed by these comments, Leopold reportedly put his helmet on back to front after dinner.[17] This indecent proposal, concludes Clark, 'was not conceived as an offensive venture, but as part of a German response to a French attack'.[18] It was not so much the breach of Belgian neutrality that appalled everyone (that had been examined in full behind closed doors) but the fact that the Kaiser felt it appropriate to discuss the matter at a state banquet with the Belgian king.

The Kaiser's most damaging indiscretion was the outlandish interview he gave London's *Daily Telegraph* on 28 October 1908. 'You English,' Wilhelm famously began, 'are mad, mad, mad as March hares. What has come over you that you are so completely given over to suspicions quite unworthy of a great nation?'[19] He went on to admit German hostility to Britain, talked up the German naval threat and revealed state secrets. The interview severely embarrassed Germany, alienated Britain, France and Russia, and led to calls for the Kaiser's abdication. He lapsed into depression and never fully recovered from the humiliation, losing much of the influence he had previously exercised in domestic and foreign policy, according to one biographer.[20] Bülow ultimately lost his job over the disastrous interview and poured out his bitterness in his memoirs:

> All the warnings, all the dismal prophecies of the man [Wilhelm] had dismissed from office, Prince Bismarck, returned to the

public mind. A dark foreboding ran through many Germans that such . . . stupid, even puerile speech and action on the part of the Supreme Head of State could lead only to one thing – catastrophe.[21]

The Kaiser was, it seems, a scatterbrained buffoon hobbled by a delusional image of his place in the world and borne down by a chronic sense of being Europe's punching bag. Clark writes:

> [Wilhelm's] rhetorical menaces were always associated with imagined scenarios in which Germany was the *attacked* party. . . . It was one of this Kaiser's many peculiarities that he was completely unable to calibrate his behaviour to the contexts in which his high office obliged him to operate. Too often he spoke not like a monarch, but like an over-excited teenager giving free rein to his current preoccupations. He was an extreme exemplar of that Edwardian social category, the club bore who is forever explaining some pet project to the man in the next chair.[22]

—

If he was easy to caricature, his ministers were careful not to dismiss him. He enjoyed great, if sporadic, popularity. For this reason, his ministers moved to contain, and control, their errant ruler, and Wilhelm's idiotic musings held little sway over German public policy. His recklessness did, however, influence the German leadership indirectly, by tending to concentrate executive policymaking power within a small coterie of supremely self-assured men, who wielded an overtly expansionist stick. In managing or countermanding the Kaiser's excesses, the German Government also found itself easy prey for the military chiefs, who had exploited their relationship with their commander-in-chief and tended to use the imperial nod to further their own schemes.

Among the more strident examples was the shadowy Friedrich von Holstein, director of the political department of the German

Foreign Office, who determined foreign policy in the 1890s, won the colony of Samoa for Germany, and was highly influential during the Moroccan crisis of 1905, when he hoped, and failed, to rip apart the Anglo-French Détente. Perhaps his greatest bequest to the German Government, on his death in 1909, was his consistent example of how to 'manage' the Kaiser. Bethmann-Hollweg was a close student of the problem and would prove adept at curbing Wilhelm's enthusiasms, squirrelling him off on holiday at critical moments.

As time passed, the Kaiser sang in his chains, and was consulted chiefly as protocol dictated and not because he was thought to offer coherent advice or leadership. In this light, he was hardly the war-hungry monster of English and French textbooks but rather a bemedalled poseur dressed in colourful costumes. He was a kindly, pacific soul, according to Bethmann-Hollweg, whose intentions 'were really entirely peaceable', and his portrayal as a tyrant 'lusting for war, world-power and carnage' was an 'odious caricature' of a fundamentally decent, God-fearing man.[23] Many who read the stream of warlike noises gushing from the Kaiser disagreed with this assessment. It was true, however, that Wilhelm shrank from violence when the threat confronted him, and was prone to hide beneath his plumed hat and sue for peace.

15

A GUNBOAT TO AGADIR

*But if a situation were to be forced upon us in which peace could
only be preserved by the surrender of the great and beneficent
position Britain has won by centuries of heroism and achievement,
by allowing Britain to be treated where her interests were vitally
affected as if she were of no account in the Cabinet of nations,
then I say emphatically that peace at that price would be a
humiliation intolerable for a great country like ours to endure.*
Chancellor David Lloyd George's Mansion House speech, 1911

DIPLOMATIC DISPUTES RAPIDLY ESCALATED into
European threats of war in this climate of wilful blindness, paranoia and distrust. On 1 July 1911, a decrepit German gunboat, the
Panther, weighed anchor off the Moroccan Atlantic port city of
Agadir. The clapped-out vessel, due for the scrapyard two years earlier, threatened no one. Yet such was the climate of paranoia and suspicion in Europe that its very presence almost sparked a continental
war.

Manned by nine officers and 121 men, the vessel had been sent
ostensibly to protect German life and property during a Moroccan
rebellion against the sultan Abdelhafid, then besieged in his castle

in Fez. The *Panther*'s more accurate role was to intimidate and prise African colonial concessions out of France. One thing was clear to the government in Berlin: the *Panther*, or, rather, the German power it represented, had no interest whatsoever in securing further advantages in Morocco, which formed no part of German foreign policy at the time.

Germany, on the contrary, was demonstrating its displeasure at France's military intervention in Morocco, a flagrant breach of the Treaty of Algeciras signed after the First Moroccan Crisis, which the Kaiser had so spectacularly attended (see Chapter 11). The *Panther*'s crude intervention was also designed to arouse domestic approval at home. 'Bethmann-Hollweg and Kiderlen [the imperial state secretary for foreign affairs, Alfred von Kiderlen-Wachter] needed a diplomatic triumph,' write Steiner and Neilson, 'they hoped that this demonstration of "Weltpolitik" and a French retreat would lead to an upsurge of imperial sentiment which would strengthen their domestic position.'[1] The gunboat was merely a provocation, sent to challenge the cosy colonial prerogatives of the Entente Cordiale. Bethmann-Hollweg wrote:

> [Germany] could not let pass in silence a forward move [by French troops] of so arbitrary a character which had in no way been provoked by us . . . [T]he dispatch of the *Panther* was no more than a notification that France would not be allowed to ignore our desire for a thorough discussion, forced upon us by the dilatory procedure of the Cabinet at Paris.[2]

France and Britain thought otherwise: in the *Panther*, they perceived a German plan to intervene militarily in Morocco and possibly occupy the port of Agadir. That perception led to a dangerous escalation, fanned by the usual media hysteria, which brought France and Germany to the brink of war, and prompted the British Cabinet to warn the German ambassador of a Royal Naval intervention to protect British interests in the region.

—

Bethmann-Hollweg was right, in this case. France was the agent provocateur in Morocco in 1911. In April that year, hawkish members of the French Foreign Ministry persuaded the Quai D'Orsay to dispatch a flying column of French troops to put down the Moroccan rebellion. Their true purpose, however, was the effective seizure of Morocco, as a prelude to its complete digestion into the French Empire. The trouble was the French troop presence in Morocco broke the spirit and the letter of the Franco-German accord of 1909 and the Act of Algeciras, signed with Germany in 1906, which had settled, if temporarily, what now became known as the First Moroccan Crisis and excluded France from further colonial seizures in the region. Those breaches handed Germany a bargaining chip, with which it could prise out of France fresh claims to territory in the Congo and West Africa. Thus arose the term 'gunboat diplomacy'.

The *Panther* triggered a second Moroccan crisis. The little gunboat acted as a powerful animus on the members of the Triple Entente, not least the Germanophobes in the French and British foreign ministries, who, incensed at Berlin's intrusion, launched a ferocious press campaign that all but declared war on Germany. The French press offensive was the handiwork of Maurice Herbette, chef du cabinet at the French Foreign Ministry, whose compliant editors routinely jumped at his order. Herbette and his colleagues, determined to undermine any French attempt to accommodate German interests, recruited the new foreign minister Justin de Selves, one in a succession of mediocre French foreign ministers. A willing accomplice to the Herbette faction, de Selves urged the government to send cruisers to Agadir – a move vetoed by the prime minister, Joseph Caillaux. The result was a government split between de Selves and the hawks, who favoured military action, and Caillaux and the moderates, who favoured negotiation. Caillaux, observes Christopher Clark, became so exasperated by Herbette's repeated moves to sabotage any conciliatory effort that he summoned the recalcitrant minister and, snapping his pencil, said, 'I will break you like this pencil.'[3]

Caillaux's moderate stance eventually prevailed, and Germany agreed to a compensatory package in exchange for recognising complete French dominion over Morocco. But the deal only succeeded because Caillaux negotiated with the German Government through the French ambassador in Berlin, Jules Cambon, and adroitly bypassed the usual channels of communication at the Quai D'Orsay. As Clark says, 'The result was that by the beginning of August, Caillaux had secretly accepted a compensation deal with Berlin to which his foreign minister Justin de Selves remained adamantly opposed.'[4]

Further misunderstandings and special interests threatened to dislodge the agreement; not least the shrieking headlines of the German press, which weighed into the debate utterly out of tune with its own government's policy. 'West Morocco to Germany!' hardly chimed with the aims of the minister responsible, Kiderlen-Wachter, nor the Kaiser, for that matter, neither of whom had any interest in claiming a slice of Moroccan territory. Kiderlen hoped instead to use French military intervention in Morocco to secure incremental gains elsewhere, chiefly French Congo.

—

The British Government's reaction to the events in Morocco ranged from concerned to incandescent – another example of the strange, trigger-happy atmosphere in which the slightest whiff of German meddling in British colonial affairs unleashed a storm of condemnation and warmongering. In the minds of some Cabinet members, the *Panther* conjured the outrageous prospect of a German naval base on the Atlantic. The Admiralty drew up to its full height and condemned the German incursion. If Germany intended, by this act, to land at Agadir, then Britain would feel compelled to send warships to defend her interests there.

A shrewder view held that Germany acted not in the interests of territorial gain but in order to disrupt the Triple Entente. The Eyre Crowe faction – if the British Germanophobes may be so described – feared that a Franco-German agreement over Morocco would tilt the balance of power in Europe and undermine the Entente. They urged the foreign minister Edward Grey to issue a formal warning to the German ambassador. The German intervention was 'a trial of strength, if anything', Crowe wrote. 'Concession means not loss of interests or loss of prestige. It means defeat, with all its inevitable consequences.'[5] This was sheer bombast. Germany had sent the *Panther* to protest at France's military occupation of Morocco, in clear breach of its treaty obligations, as Bethmann-Hollweg later wrote:

> those Powers [who] accused Germany of disturbing the peace of the world . . . must nevertheless have known well that if we had intended a military menace of France we should have chosen a very different method from the mooring of a small gunboat in the Port of Agadir.[6]

On the contrary, Crowe, Bertie (Sir Francis Bertie, the British ambassador in Paris), Nicolson (Sir Arthur Nicolson, permanent undersecretary at the Foreign Office and a former ambassador to St Petersburg) and other anti-German voices called for a British show of strength and urged Grey to send a gunboat to rival the *Panther*, if necessary. Nicolson reported that he was suspicious of German intentions, that Kiderlen-Wachter hoped to see negotiations fail and that 'the situation remained very grave'.[7]

Cooler heads prevailed, at first. The Cabinet meeting on 4 July took a lenient line, asking Germany to consult with London about any settlement in Morocco. In a telegram to Berlin, Grey demanded the withdrawal of the *Panther* and requested, not unreasonably, an explanation as to German intentions in Agadir. 'We decided,' Churchill put it in a letter to his wife on 5 July 1911, 'to use pretty plain language to Germany and to tell her that if she thinks

Morocco can be divided up without John Bull, she is jolly well mis-taken.'[8] Again, this was sheer fantasy: the *Panther* had no intention of threatening British interests.

Two days later, in a speech to parliament, Grey insisted again that Germany clarify its intentions. Berlin, resentful and sulky, failed to respond. Bethmann-Hollweg did not think Germany owed London an explanation for its foreign policy. Britain, after all, was not in the habit of answering peremptory demands from foreign powers for 'explanations'. In any case, the Moroccan affair, reasoned Berlin, was between Germany and France.

Concerns in London rose. How dare these Germans show such effrontery to the British Empire! British hackles were up. The anti-German voices in the Foreign Office raised the temperature. Sir Arthur Nicolson warned on 18 July that the Germans intended to convert Agadir into a fortress within striking distance of the Canary Islands and hence pose a threat to British interests.

Up until about mid-July, Grey had wisely ignored the provoca-tions of his anti-German colleagues and tolerated German gains in the Congo in return for a French hold on Morocco. The hawks, however, would now allow *no* German compensation for France's daylight robbery. On the 16th, Germany overreached itself and demanded *all* of French Congo, in response to which the British Foreign Office 'rose in great alarm'.[9] Grey was forced to adopt sterner measures. He proposed an international conference – a favourite tactic of Grey's, when forced to choose – on Morocco, but postponed the decision, leaving the Cabinet deeply divided.

By 21 July, Germany had still not responded to Grey's request for an explanation, first issued 17 days ago. Angry at Berlin's imper-tinence, and under pressure from the rising anti-German voices in his department, Grey warned the German ambassador Paul Wolff Metternich that Britain 'would recognize no settlement in Morocco in which we had not a voice'.[10] Something had to give, and it was in these tense circumstances that the chancellor Lloyd George, hitherto the most powerful anti-imperialist in Cabinet and a voice of tolerance towards Germany, rose to give his annual speech at the Mansion House.

—

The British people were unaccustomed to hearing chauvinistic outbursts from this leftist Cabinet dove. As a 'radical' member of Asquith's Liberal government, Welsh-born David Lloyd George had been pro-Boer during the Boer War and stridently opposed to the government's policy in South Africa. He supported social reform, pensions for the elderly and national insurance. Considered a fine orator, he possessed great political acumen and a finely attuned elasticity of mind. With this background, he might have counselled caution over Morocco, or even urged Britain's partial disengagement from her deepening European entanglements.

Instead, Lloyd George delivered a mighty blow for Britain, a demonstration of British sabre rattling such as the world's greatest imperial power had not seen or heard since the Crimea or Waterloo. His speech had the full approval of Asquith and Grey, who partly composed it, and, while he mentioned no foreign power by name, his words, the nation assumed, were intended for Berlin. A war between Britain and Germany, Lloyd George suggested, was highly probable unless Germany ceased to threaten Britain's vital foreign interests. He had in mind, it seemed, Germany's recent challenge to British naval supremacy, pathetically symbolised by the *Panther*:

> Personally, I am a sincere advocate of all means which would lead to the settlement of international disputes by methods such as those which civilization has so successfully set up for the adjustment of differences between individuals . . .
>
> But I am also bound to say this – that I believe it is essential in the highest interests, not merely of this country, but of the world, that Britain should at all hazards maintain her place and her prestige amongst the Great Powers of the world.
>
> Her potent influence has many a time been in the past,

and may yet be in the future, invaluable to the cause of human liberty. It has more than once in the past redeemed Continental nations, who are sometimes too apt to forget that service, from overwhelming disaster and even from national extinction.

I would make great sacrifices to preserve peace. I conceive that nothing would justify a disturbance of international good will except questions of the greatest national moment. But if a situation were to be forced upon us in which peace could only be preserved by the surrender of the great and beneficent position Britain has won by centuries of heroism and achievement, by allowing Britain to be treated where her interests were vitally affected as if she were of no account in the Cabinet of nations, then I say emphatically that peace at that price would be a humiliation intolerable for a great country like ours to endure.[11]

The speech, published in full in *The Times*, made international news. The British people rallied to their chancellor's revived spirit of nationalism. The speech revealed an uncharacteristic bellicosity in the speaker and announced to the world his allegiance with the anti-German members of Asquith's Cabinet, of whom the leading figure was Grey, championed by his hawkish colleagues Nicolson, Crowe, Bertie and others. Lloyd George's pronouncement received the greatest plaudits from Brigadier General Henry Wilson, the influential director of operations (see Chapter 17). The chancellor had abruptly thrown in his towel with the hardliners, for whom Germany was the nation's biggest threat.

—

The German reaction was one of shock and dismay. True, Berlin had failed to answer Britain's inquiries. But did this warrant in reply a virtual threat of war, in a major public speech by the British chancellor? At their first meeting three days after the speech, on the 24th, Metternich told Grey that Germany had no claims on Morocco and sought only compensation from France for the French incursions in breach of the Algeciras Treaty. Berlin still expected and hoped for a slab of French Congo.

Mollified, Grey sought permission to quote Metternich's remarks in parliament. But, at a subsequent stormy meeting, Metternich refused and repeated his demand that, if no satisfactory compensation was received from France, Germany would be compelled to resort to armed intervention in Morocco – *against France*. Grey interpreted this as a direct threat to the British Navy and warned Churchill, 'The Fleet might be attacked at any moment.'[12] Grey had misinterpreted the German diplomat: Berlin hardly meant to challenge the British Navy over a colonial squabble with France in Morocco.

Lloyd George's speech thus came at a perilous time. Bethmann-Hollweg condemned it as causing 'a violent excitement' in Germany: 'England therein laid claims to that very world-empire that we were later to be hypocritically accused of aspiring to.'[13] It provoked a flurry of later interpretations, the most radical being A. J. P. Taylor's claim that Lloyd George intended the speech as a riposte to the French, not the Germans, for upsetting the world order. That interpretation contradicted the reflections of Grey, Churchill and Asquith, who correctly saw the speech as a direct warning to Germany.

Whether Lloyd George's speech was a *proportionate* response to German aggression is another matter. Had Germany, by its actions in Agadir, seriously 'challenged the strength of the Anglo-French Entente'?[14] Had it posed a threat to Britain's maritime supremacy? Any reasonable assessment must conclude that Germany had not. But Grey acted in receipt of warnings of Germany's claims on Morocco – a goal not shared in Berlin. He swallowed a complete misreading of German intentions, not only from Nicolson but also in a letter from Bertie, Britain's ambassador to France, sent in July. Germany, according to Bertie, sought nothing less than a naval fortress on the Atlantic, against which Grey had been poised to deploy British warships.

—

The Asquith government failed to see the Agadir Crisis for what it was: an overreaction by Germany to France's perfidy in sending troops to Fez without consulting their co-signatory in the Algeciras Treaty. Grey might have reasoned that Germany, thus armed, could not possibly have occupied Agadir. Were Germany's actions in Morocco 'a direct threat to the premier navy in the world', as the historian Hew Strachan claims?[15] German bellicosity seems rather to have been a residual gasp of frustration at being thrown the table scraps of the African scramble. Nobody seemed to comprehend the depth of Berlin's dismay at France's impetuous dispatch of troops to Agadir, a clear act of aggression that breached international law (such as it was) and received nothing like the volleys of anger thrown at the German gunboat. Instead, London focused on the narrow issue and used it as a pretext for Lloyd George's strange war cry.

That an easily containable dispute could provoke the three powers to the brink of military action should have sent loud warning signals throughout the embassies of Europe – warnings of the utter failure of existing diplomatic channels to arrest the process of military escalation. 'There is something very odd about the Agadir crisis,' concluded Christopher Clark. 'It was allowed to escalate to the point where it seemed that a Western-European war was imminent, yet the positions advanced by the opposing parties were not irreconcilable and eventually provided the basis for an enduring settlement.'[16]

The Agadir Crisis was actuated by misplaced impressions, wilful blindness and colonial greed. An illegal French intrusion on Morocco lit the tinder; Germany foolishly heated it, by sending a gunboat; the British, French and German newspapers bellowed the kindling; and British and French Governments threatened to send their armies or navies to douse the flames. Anti-German extremists in Britain and France, ignorant of the details, foamed for vengeance. London radicals subjected parliament to a campaign to oust Grey, whom they deemed too moderate, and who was forced to defend his Moroccan policy in a speech in November 1911. Then it fizzled out.

Indeed, it need not have happened at all. Unknown to most

people – including the press – the French and German leaders (Caillaux and Bethmann-Hollweg) were working calmly behind the scenes to reach a negotiated, peaceful deal. In the end, France and Germany achieved an abiding settlement, in the Treaty of Fez, signed on 30 March 1912, in which Germany recognised Morocco as a French protectorate and France ceded part of French Congo to Germany. The settlement of the Agadir Crisis threatened nobody, neither the Entente, nor the Cordiale, and least of all the British Navy. The only losers were the Sultan (who abdicated), and the people of Morocco and Middle Congo, who were treated merely as colonial trophies of negotiations in distant, wood-panelled rooms. Despite a peaceful settlement, the dispute disinterred the most warlike tendencies and gave voice to wrong-headed European chauvinism, 'full of passionate intensity'.[17]

16

FRIEDRICH VON BERNHARDI'S FITTEST

Without war, inferior or decaying races would easily choke the growth of healthy budding elements, and a universal decadence would follow . . . Since almost every part of the globe is inhabited, new territory must, as a rule, be obtained at the cost of its possessors – that is today, by conquest, which thus becomes a law of necessity.
Germany and the Next War, General Friedrich von Bernhardi, 1911

WRITING IN THE SHADOW OF AGADIR was a German general who, undistracted by the possibility of peaceful human coexistence, understood warfare as a Darwinian imperative and hence inevitable. Men must fight wars to survive, he wrote. War was not only a duty; it was a biological necessity. The most senior German and Austro-Hungarian military circles accepted Bernhardi's interpretation of the human condition.

In the mind of General Friedrich Adolf Julius von Bernhardi, human beings behaved in the grip of the same rules of survival that governed beasts: war was 'sanctioned by the findings of Darwin'. Man must decide between expansionism or certain death, 'world power or decline'. The code of the survival of the fittest did not mean General Bernhardi thought that humans who fought for their survival were bestial. On the contrary, war was a noble aspiration, a duty – indeed, a 'divine business' – that overrode the arts of political persuasion, the power of reason and the compass of tolerance.

Bernhardi, on the other hand, had no truck with diplomacy, restraint, tolerance, treaties, détentes and negotiation, which he regarded as weaknesses. He glorified the ruthless expression of power by the sword. He wrote *Germany and the Next War* (the second volume of *On War Today*) partly in response to Agadir, during which he could 'scarcely disguise his impatience and alarm over the government's lack of determination' to punish France, according to one introduction to his book.[1] A point implicit in his treatise is that Germany should have crushed the French at Agadir – a course that would have triggered a European war.

Bernhardi was no crank. He was a military historian of great influence whose ideas represented a broad swathe of opinion among the German ruling class. The most respected German military writer of his time, he enjoyed great prestige in Prussian officers' circles. In short, he demands to be taken seriously, as a powerful representative of the military outlook and culture of his time. His prophecies, of a general world war, were chillingly accurate. Yet the general was not a policymaker, nor did he reflect the precise position of the German General Staff, or indeed the mass of German people. Outside the Prussian elite, his greatest influence lay abroad, especially in Britain, where his book was a runaway best-seller and ran to nine editions between 1911 and 1914, chiefly because it seemed to confirm England's worst fears of German aggression.

Bernhardi offered thousands of British readers the portrait of a mind at the heart of the Prussian military machine and the Pan-German movement, the vehemence of whose beliefs suggested an ascendancy of the military clique over Berlin's civilian leadership. Bernhardi's screed was thus extremely dangerous. It infected foreign minds against Germany while failing to represent the true policy of the nation's comparatively moderate civilian rulers, such as Bethmann-Hollweg. Once again, in the sad descent of humanity to the worst war it had known, inflamed perceptions overrode the calm assessment of the truth.

—

Though born of Estonian-German parents in St Petersburg in 1849, Bernhardi's provenance was that of a classic Prussian aristocrat. He fought in the Franco-Prussian War, at the end of which he was reputed to have been the first German to ride under the Arc de Triomphe. Between 1898 and 1901, he served as chief of the war historical section of the General Staff, and thereafter rose through the ranks to become, in 1907, the commanding general of the Seventh Army Corps. Heavily bewhiskered, even by the standards of the day, he retired in 1909 and settled down to write (he would later emerge from retirement to lead a division in the Great War).

When it appeared in 1911, Bernhardi's book *Germany and the Next War* caused a sensation throughout Europe and provoked extreme disquiet in the Triple Entente. He aimed his greatest hostility at England, against whom victory in a naval war was contingent, he insisted, upon Germany prevailing in a European land war. He called for an offensive first strike as the best means of defence. His work confirmed everything that Britain, France and Russia feared about an aggressive, expansionist Germany. 'He preached the necessity of war with an urgency bordering on panic,' concluded one introduction.[2] He lamented the 'pacifists' in Germany, but the term loses any coherent meaning in the presence of the general's opinions, because he regarded war as a natural and permanent condition of the human race, in which 'peace' and 'pacifism' were unnatural aberrations. He wrote in a trenchant, persuasive prose style, demonstrating that a skilled author may evince any idea, no matter how unsettling, mad or plain wrong.

A digest of Bernhardi's central ideas, as he expressed them, reveals the thinking in the innermost echelons of the Prussian military.[3] The pursuit of peace was 'poisonous', he declared. Germany had a 'right to make war'. He goes on:

> [The] desire for peace has rendered most civilized nations anaemic, and marks a decay of spirit and political courage such as has often been shown by a race of Epigoni . . .
>
> Without war, inferior or decaying races would easily choke the growth of healthy budding elements, and a universal decadence would follow . . . Strong, healthy, and flourishing nations increase in numbers. . . Since almost every part of the globe is inhabited, new territory must, as a rule, be obtained at the cost of its possessors – that is today, by conquest, which thus becomes a law of necessity. The right of conquest is universally acknowledged . . .
>
> We must rouse in our people the unanimous wish for power . . . together with the determination to sacrifice on the altar of patriotism, not only life and property, but also private views and preferences in the interests of the common welfare. Then alone shall we discharge our great duties of the future, grow into a World Power, and stamp a great part of humanity with the impress of the German spirit. If, on the contrary, we persist in that dissipation of energy which now marks our political life . . . we shall be dishonourably beaten; that days of disaster await us in the future, and that once again, as in the days of our former degradation, the poet's lament will be heard:
>
> O Germany, thy oaks still stand
> But thou art fallen, glorious land![4]

———

German nationalists and militarists warmly received *Germany and the Next War*, but the book's greatest sales were in England, where it rallied the anti-German faction. It ran to five editions in Germany in the first year and sold thousands of copies abroad. Most English reactions to Bernhardi's book assumed the general had expressed

German policy. He had not. There is no evidence that in 1911–12 Germany was planning a world war to crush its European rivals. If those goals existed, they were not officially expressed until September 1914, *after* the war began.[5] Bernhardi did, however, attempt a crude definition of *Weltpolitik*: 'world power or decline'. Indeed, implicit in his theory was the concept of the *Stufenplan*: the idea, shared by the elder Moltke, that Germany must conquer Europe before the world. Bernhardi envisaged, writes the historian Holger Herwig, 'a long, life-and-death struggle between Germany and Austria-Hungary on the one side and France, Britain and Russia on the other'.

Of the many English reviews of Bernhardi's work, *The Literary Digest* offered a fairly typical example. 'Never has the policy of Berlin been proclaimed so clearly and so fearlessly,' its 4 May 1912 number states. 'The General's book gives a candid expression of the view that his country must fight its way to predominance regardless of the rights and interests of other people . . . "Might is right," he thinks, and this can be decided only by war.'[5]

Lord Esher, a respected historian, Liberal politician and considered one of England's foremost military authorities (he was offered, but declined, the position of war secretary), wrote a most eloquent condemnation of Bernhardi upon reading his book in 1912:

> It is hardly conceivable that after 2,000 years of Christian teaching, and in the midst of a people from whom have sprung some of the loftiest thinkers and some of the greatest scientific benefactors of the human race, such opinions could find expression. They emanate, too, from a soldier hitherto held in the highest respect by all who have studied war as an odious possibility, not as an end desirable in itself. No one could have supposed that such ideas so crude and juvenile could have survived the awakening process of recent times.[6]

17

BRIGADIER GENERAL SIR HENRY WILSON'S PLAN

[A] war between Germany on the one hand and
France and England on the other, with Russia of course
playing her part, might, I think, end in the defeat
of Germany provided three things are done.

Brigadier General Sir Henry Wilson, British director of military
operations, to the Committee of Imperial Defence, 23 August 1911

THE SHARP SPUR OF THE TWO MOROCCAN CRISES
accelerated war plans in Britain and France. From 1905, British and
French strategists began jointly to anticipate a war with Germany as
their biggest and likeliest threat, and adjusted their whole outlook in
readiness (in early 1906, these talks briefly involved the chief of the
Belgian General Staff).

In 1906, the powerful Esher Committee, chaired by Lord Esher,
had the job of implementing military reforms under the guidance of
the war secretary Richard Haldane. They drew up a basic outline for
an Expeditionary Force of 156,000 men but avoided any discussion
of how and where it would be deployed. In those days, India was

still considered a battlefield. Europe, for political reasons, could not be named as a future theatre, 'as no government could admit that it contemplated sending an army into Europe'.[1] These reforms met vehement resistance from the 'navalists' and the Cabinet 'radicals' and led to the formation of an 'invasion inquiry' in 1907. This failed to reconcile the fiercely divergent views between the War Office, which envisaged a European land war, and the Admiralty, which contemplated vast sea battles in which the army was insignificant.

The French were particularly anxious to secure a British military commitment to the continent. A European land war was high in the mind of Clemenceau, the then French prime minister (1906–09). On several occasions, in Paris and London, his officials appealed for a firm British commitment but were rebuffed. Grey unhelpfully warned them that they would have to depend on the Russians. Hardinge feebly told a French delegation in May 1908 that 'at the best our army can never have more than a moral effect on the Continent, since we could never send an expedition of more than 150,000 men, while continental armies are counted by millions'.[2] The reasons were chiefly that Britain had not yet introduced conscription and had a vast empire to guard – excuses that hardly reassured France, which persistently pressed Britain to adopt conscription.

In French minds, Albion had earned its reputation for perfidy, as Sir Francis Bertie, the English ambassador in Paris, warned. 'The French,' he wrote, 'have an instinctive dread of Germany and an hereditary distrust of England, and with these characteristics they are easily led to believe that they may be deserted by England and fallen upon by Germany.'[3] His assessment accurately described France's psychology in the 1900s and explained why Paul Cambon, the French ambassador in London, persistently tried to convert the Entente Cordiale into a full military alliance. His efforts foundered on the rocks of British division and French suspicion, to the point where the Entente seemed 'to be dependent upon the personalities and the whims of the British government'.[4] While the anti-German members of the Foreign Office favoured a military alliance with

France, the Asquith government repeatedly showed its lack of faith in the idea. Grey's sporadic dalliances with Germany, and efforts to create a new friendship with Berlin in tandem with the Entente, hardly reassured France.

Two events transformed this picture of English foot-dragging and French distrust, and gave Anglo-French military preparations a forceful new direction: the shock of the Agadir Crisis, which forced both governments to 'reconsider every aspect of the Entente relationship'[5]; and the appointment of a 'rabid Francophile' as the chief architect of British plans for a European land war, should it come.

—

Brigadier General Sir Henry Wilson, appointed director of military operations (DMO) in 1910, was a one-man propaganda unit for the Anglo-French entente, and quickly became 'more influential than any single Foreign Office official', conclude the historians Steiner and Neilson.[6] By disposition and intellect a Conservative, Wilson liked to call himself 'Irish' and went on to become an Ulster Unionist politician after the war. He was born in County Longford, Ireland, and educated at Marlborough, the result being a curious Anglo-Irish concoction: charming, urbane, fiercely argumentative and, at times, more English than the English. Wilson formed a network of close confidants and – unusually for a British officer – embraced the French Embassy and his French counterparts. Quite simply, he loved France. Unlike Grey, who could speak no French, Wilson was fluent. His favourite summer recreation was cycling around north-eastern France, his tall, lanky frame wobbling through the fields, his mind never far from imagining the tumult of the massed advance of the German Army through Belgium; or, when colleagues compelled Wilson to abandon this (correct) prediction, a direct invasion of French territory below the River Meuse. Like Crowe's, Nicolson's and Bertie's, his mind was settled: Germany was the arch-aggressor who must be contained at all costs.

Wilson went further. He meant to extract a firm British

commitment to the defence of France. In this pursuit, he defied the profile of the 'Official Mind' of the British Government, supposedly moderate, aloof and impartial[7] – and certainly not willing, as Grey told parliament in November 1911, to 'make secret engagements which commit Parliament to obligations of war'.[8] Wilson's prejudices, like Crowe's, conformed to a refined version of a *Times* leader: anti-German, pro-France and resigned to the inevitability of war with Germany. For this eventuality, he set his mind to planning. Wilson was a meticulous planner and brilliant strategist – a human calculator of train timetables, horse requirements and the litany of needs of a modern army – who correctly foresaw the direction of a conceivable German invasion.

———

As DMO, Wilson spent the spring of 1911 finessing his plans for the mobilisation of the British Expeditionary Force. His office incubated war plans in glorious isolation, separated from the prying civilian eyes of the government. Wilson acted, at times, as his own agent, fomenting military allegiances without the knowledge of his nominal superiors. He had little time for Grey's aloofness and dithering, and often expressed his acute frustration with the foreign secretary. Sometimes, this manifested itself in a contemptuous reassignment of responsibilities to himself. It was extraordinary, for example, that Wilson should decide not to inform the Foreign Office of the DMO's plan for joint military action with France should the Agadir Crisis lead to war.

On 20 July – the day before Lloyd George's Mansion House speech – Wilson went to Paris to talk about plans for joint mobilisation. He and his French counterpart, General Auguste Dubail, both transfixed by the *Panther* off the Moroccan coast, outlined a proposal for landing 150,000 British troops at Rouen and Le Havre. They named no commander; they left the question of the conditions that would trigger British deployment unresolved. Wilson lacked the authority to make such commitments. Yet he came home with a signed agreement for a joint Anglo-French military operation, which even fixed the British zone of occupation, in the Arras-Cambrai-St Quentin region. 'The signed accord,' noted Steiner and Neilson, 'came close to a military alliance and was far more detailed than parallel Franco-Russian or German-Austrian arrangements.'[9]

It was an astonishing manifestation of Wilson's role as Anglo-French military liaison. Grey had *not* committed Britain to the defence of France in the event of a German invasion. Wilson had overstepped the remit of his duties. The Foreign Office and the Cabinet were left in the dark about the details. Yet Wilson's secret Anglo-French agreement gradually acquired the status of an unofficial, joint war plan within the Entente Cordiale. It framed an outcome that seemed likelier with every passing hour in which it sat, unchallenged, in the minds of the few commanders and politicians in the loop. Crucially, it initiated the process of leading the commanders of the French armed forces – and, in time, the officials at the Quai d'Orsay – to believe they could rely on British military support.

How Wilson, then a brigadier general and senior government official, was able to shape events in this manner is a question rooted in personalities rather than official power structures. His personal jottings portray an intellectually arrogant man who tended to ridicule anyone who opposed his schemes. His rapier swipes were chiefly directed at his superiors, several of whom he considered daft or ineffectual. After a meeting with Sir William Nicholson, chief of the Imperial General Staff, Wilson wrote, 'The Chief talked absolute rubbish, disclosing an even greater ignorance of the problem than I had credited him with. He did not even know where the Sambre was.' Wilson reserved his most pungent criticism for Grey, who continued to refuse to offer military ballast to the Entente. After emerging deeply despondent from a meeting on 9 August 1911, where Grey, Haldane and even Crowe failed to meet Wilson's hopes of a solid commitment to France, the general described the foreign secretary as 'an ignorant, vain and weak man, quite unfit to be the foreign minister of any country larger than Portugal. A man who knew nothing of policy and strategy going hand in hand.'[10]

Implicit here was Wilson's definition of himself as a man who knew a great deal about aligning policy and military strategy, and his intellectual self-confidence shines through his war plans. A century later, his extraordinary prescience lays a cold finger on the spine: 'It is of course possible that the Germans may seize Liège in the first few days of mobilization, and then by stretching to the north give themselves sufficient elbow room to allow of their vast numbers being deployed . . .'[11]

—

Wilson soon had a chance to present his ideas. The Agadir Crisis prompted an extraordinary meeting of the Committee of Imperial Defence (CID), on 23 August 1911. Wilson hoped the all-day meeting, urgently called by Asquith over dinner with Grey and Haldane two days earlier, would deliver part of what he wanted: official approval of his war strategy. It relieved him to find that dovish – 'radical' – members of Cabinet would not be invited to the meeting, including Lewis Harcourt, secretary of state for the colonies, who later fumed that the meeting was 'arranged some time ago for a date when it was supposed that we should all be out of London . . . to decide on where and how British troops could be landed to assist a French Army on the Meuse!!!',[12] and Lord Esher, who later described the meeting as 'a packed Defence Committee' and 'a small junta of Cabinet ministers'.[13] Present were: Prime Minister Asquith (in the chair); Chancellor David Lloyd George; Foreign Secretary Sir Edward Grey; Winston Churchill, secretary of state for the Home Department; Reginald McKenna, first lord of the Admiralty; Sir Arthur Wilson, first sea lord of the Admiralty; A. E. Bethell, director of naval intelligence; Viscount Haldane, secretary of state for war; Field Marshal Sir William Nicholson, chief of the Imperial General Staff; Brigadier General Henry Wilson, director of military operations; General Sir John French, inspector general of the forces; Rear

Admiral Sir Charles Ottley (secretary); and Major General Sir A. J. Murray, director of military training.

The day was a success, at least for Wilson. He came well prepared. His detailed examination of 'a war between Germany and France' calculated that within nine days of mobilisation Germany would deploy a force of 39 divisions on the frontier between Aix-la-Chapelle and Altkirch. He conveyed a terrifying picture of the scale of the likely conflict: 'By the evening of the 13th day of Mobilization the German forces in this theatre will have increased from 39 to 57 divisions, while the French forces will have risen from 34 to 63 divisions.'[14] That is to say, about one million German troops against 1.1 million French, assuming about 17,500 troops per division.[15] At one point, Asquith asked how big a British force would have to be to intervene effectively in Europe. Wilson replied that 'five infantry divisions would have almost as great a moral effect as six, and that four would be better than none'[16] – in sum, a little more than 100,000 men.

Grilled by Churchill and General French on the detail, Wilson dismissed the possibility that the Germans would smash through the Maubeuge–Lille gap. Yet odd blanks in Wilson's knowledge were revealed. He admitted that he did not know France's contingency plans, if this were to occur, and seemed unaware of the latest assessment of the French Plan XVI.

Wilson's war plans, masterfully presented if only partially divulged, received official sanction and he was encouraged to continue planning for a continental war. The minutes concluded:

the Committee have examined the plans of the General Staff, and are of opinion that, in the initial stages of a war between France and Germany, in which the Government decided to assist France, the plan to which preference is given by the General Staff [i.e. Wilson's] is a valuable one, and the General Staff should accordingly work out all the necessary details . . . [O]n the second hypothesis that the United Kingdom becomes the active ally of France . . . we should mobilise and dispatch the whole of our available regular army of six divisions and a cavalry division immediately upon the outbreak of war, mobilising upon the same day as the French and Germans.[17]

The key word here is 'hypothesis'. The British Government would not clarify until the very eve of war whether it would come to France's aid if Germany invaded.

———

The CID meeting failed in two important ways. First, it exposed the incompetence of the much-vaunted Royal Navy, which had earlier refused to offer assurances that the Expeditionary Force could be transported safely across the Channel. Sir Arthur Wilson, Fisher's successor as first sea lord and an 'abrasive, inarticulate, and autocratic' admiral,[18] reinforced this impression of weakness at the meeting. The navy, he said, could spare no extra men, officers or ships to assist the army's Channel crossing, as it would be fully stretched blockading Germany and destroying the German fleet in the North Sea. He offered a weak rider to this dire outlook, notes the minutes: 'The Channel would, however, be covered by the main operations, and provided the French protected the transports within their own harbours, the Admiralty could give the required guarantee as to the safety of the expedition.'[19] This was far from convincing, given the fact that the French fleet would be wholly occupied in the Mediterranean.

Second, the secret meeting provoked deeper divisions in Cabinet. The government doves were furious when they heard they'd been frozen out of a critical meeting on war policy. A backbench revolt ensued. The radicals demanded that Henry Wilson be dismissed and that the government publicly state that only Cabinet should decide matters of grave military policy. Grey and Asquith were forced to defend their actions. Grey dissembled. 'There may be reasons,' he told parliament on 27 November, 'why a Government should make secret arrangements of that kind if they are not things of first-rate importance.'[20] This defied any sensible logic. If a discussion of military plans for a continental war was not 'a thing of first-rate importance', what was it? On the contrary, the CID meeting was, as Steiner and Neilson write, 'the only time before 1914 that the two services rehearsed their respective strategies and . . . actually discussed the plans for a British intervention in France in some detail'.[21]

In sum, the CID meeting revealed deep-rooted problems at the Admiralty (prompting Asquith later to replace McKenna with Churchill), made the case for British intervention in a land war in Europe and endorsed Henry Wilson's argument that:

> a war between Germany on the one hand and France and England on the other, with Russia of course playing her part, might, I think, end in the defeat of Germany provided three things are done:
>
> First – Our mobilization *must* be ordered same day as France.
>
> Second – The whole 6 divisions . . . *must* be sent [to France]
>
> . . .
>
> Third – Arrangements *must* be made to enable the expeditionary force to maintain its effective [*sic*] throughout the war, and if possible other formations from home, from India or from the dominions [chiefly Australia, Canada and South Africa] should be brought to the theatre of operations as rapidly as possible.[22]

18

FRENCH VENGEANCE

*[T]he Germans were quite determined to make us feel the
weight of their victory. By their violence and brutality, without
even the smallest pretext, they showed us that they considered
it as giving them the right to do whatever they pleased.*
Marshal Ferdinand Foch, recalling the end of the Franco-Prussian War

RAYMOND POINCARÉ WAS A POLITICIAN of great intelligence and incorruptibility who served as French foreign minister,
prime minister (five times, starting with the ministry of 1912–13)
and French president (1913–20). He felt a high-blown pride in
his country, a kind of visceral patriotism that seems unique to the
French people, untouched by the cynicism and self-parody of the
English, or the sporadic, deadening loss of self-confidence of the
Germans. He was born in 1860, in Lorraine. It is impossible to say
how the course of French history may have changed had he been
born in, say, Nice, but no doubt his birthplace profoundly shaped his
outlook on the world. During the Franco-Prussian War, his family
suffered the indignity of being bundled out of their home and evacuated to Dieppe, and then forced to return to live under German
occupation – an experience the future French leader never forgot and

for which he never forgave the Germans. His rosebud would be their Waterloo.

Poincaré wrote as a young man:

> Disgusting soldiers are in the house. One paints a skull and crossbones on our sideboard, the other spits, like a Cossack, in our stew. At every moment we see ourselves watched. We know our words are weighed, our gestures noted . . . How wonderful was that day when the bells pealed out to announce that the last soldier had left Town, that day when all the flags flew from joyful houses.[1]

A brilliant student, with a Sisyphean capacity for hard work, Poincaré progressed through the French legal system to the Bar and then entered politics, earning his first ministerial portfolio, Education and Culture, at the age of 33. He combined the artistic and mathematical gifts of a latter-day Renaissance man (his cousin was the great French mathematician Henri Poincaré). He excelled as minister for finance in 1894 and again in 1906. In 1909, he adorned his cap with a new feather: election to the Académie française, in recognition of his literary gifts. His cautious political sensibility wove a moderate course through the Dreyfus Affair, and he emerged largely unscathed from the debacle. But his inability to take decisive action marked him down as a political fence-sitter, especially in the violent debates accompanying the extreme anti-clerical policies of the Waldeck-Rousseau government, which he initially supported. Radicals scorned, even as they grew to admire, this calm and efficient man whose energies were wasted, according to the leading radical of the day, Clemenceau, in 'stating the advantage of what is good and bad rather than what could be'.[2]

If, like Hamlet, Poincaré analysed every side of the argument before deciding how to act, unlike Hamlet he was more likely to abstain than act at all. He made an 'art', Clemenceau wrote, of balancing the ledger of his ideas and policies, and weighing up the credit against the debit side, rather like an accountant balances the books. Even his closest friends were exasperated by his indecisiveness. 'Civil courage,' wrote his friend Alexander Millerand, 'was never the characteristic of Poincaré . . . he had to a degree which I have rarely seen, a phobia of responsibility.'[3]

At times, he spun like a weathervane in the direction of the media's arguments for or against his policy decisions. To Paul Cambon, he simply lacked 'guts', but on other occasions could be 'Napoleonic'. All this led the historian John Keiger to conclude, in a masterful study, that Poincaré was marked with 'a certain self-doubt, his greatest weakness, which led him to agonise for long periods when making crucial political judgments, preferring as often as not to stay as close as possible to the *status quo*'.[4]

Poincaré was the kind of leader who drew power to himself, not because he had megalomaniacal tendencies but because he lacked faith in those to whom he was obliged to delegate. He was, as a result, immensely overworked. He spent a great deal of time reforming the Foreign Ministry and denuding it of power. Henceforth, *he* would command the Foreign Ministry, not the wilful bureaucrats at the Quai d'Orsay who had hitherto behaved as a separate entity, aloof and independent of the government. Poincaré brought them down to earth with a thud. He treated career diplomats with the same measured detachment and pointedly not the deference to which they had been accustomed. *He* would make the critical foreign policy decisions, relegating the supercilious elites at the Quai to the new and wholly unfamiliar status of subordinates. His tremendous workload did not faze him; he relished the tasks he set for himself and gradually took complete control of the direction of foreign policy.

———

On one point, Poincaré's mind was firmly made up, and closed to qualification or compromise: he distrusted Germany to the marrow of his bones. This was deeply personal, harking back to the humiliation of 1871 – a trait he shared with many leading Frenchmen of his day. His overriding priority was to maintain the Triple Entente as France's deterrent against Germany. That meant maintaining, not destabilising – even to France's benefit – the balance of power in Europe.

As foreign minister, he immersed himself in the legal distinctions between the two huge power blocs, and showed unusual decisiveness in keeping the spirit and letter of the agreements that created the Triple Alliance and Triple Entente distinct and separate. This was best exemplified in his reluctance to woo Italy out of the Triple Alliance and into the Entente; he considered Italy untrustworthy and fickle. He sidelined the Italophiles in the diplomatic service, chiefly the powerful French ambassador in Rome, Camille Barrère, who had worked tirelessly to draw the Italians into the Franco-Russian tent.

If his instincts were correct with regard to Italy, Poincaré wholly misjudged the case of Germany. In late 1911 and early 1912, Berlin adopted a policy of détente with France. Bethmann-Hollweg played down Agadir and appealed through the French ambassador in Berlin, Jules Cambon (Paul's brother) for a radical new direction in Franco-German relations . . . towards friendship! At the very least, Berlin sought an easing of the tensions between the two countries that had threatened war over Morocco. Understandably, Germany felt the French had misunderstood its intentions in Agadir.

Jules Cambon rallied to the German initiative and harnessed it, urging Poincaré to embrace the spirit of rapprochement with Berlin. Diplomatic channels and editors' desks buzzed with talk of a complete transformation of Franco-German relations; even Alsace and Lorraine would be promised full autonomy, if not restoration to France, 'if French policy moved over to the German side', according to the German undersecretary of state.[5] This was further than Germany had been willing to go since the 'lost provinces' fell into Prussian hands after the 1870–71 war. An impressed Cambon awaited instructions from Paris as to how to respond to these overtures.

They fell on deaf ears. Poincaré, the old Lorrainer, saw the German entreaties as nothing more than a devious attempt to drive a wedge between France and her established allies, Britain and Russia. This view had some substance, but Poincaré offered not a civil word, not a single olive leaf, to Germany's approach. Instead, he ordered the termination of all talks with Germany, saying:

> In listening to propositions like those, we would fall out with England, and with Russia, we would lose all the benefits of a policy that France has been following for many years, we would obtain for Alsace only illusory satisfactions and we would find ourselves the following day only isolated, diminished and disqualified.[6]

To which Jules Cambon wondered: would Britain and Russia so severely punish France for talking with Germany? Would they go so far as to 'isolate and disqualify' France from the Entente? Surely, better relations between France and Germany were critical to avoiding a European war? So thought Cambon, who believed France should pursue a rapprochement with Germany while the window remained open. He foresaw a dark future if Paris slammed it shut: 'By blocking up too many outlets of a boiler does one not cause it to explode?'[7]

Blind to this risk, Poincaré refused to entertain the possibility of *any* talks with Germany. His anti-German instincts drove him to suspect Berlin of deceit, of laying traps, which was, in this case, unfounded. Bethmann-Hollweg sought a genuine détente with France, and the Kaiser himself hoped for some kind of peaceful coexistence. These sentiments failed to penetrate the fog of Germanophobia that enshrouded the Quai d'Orsay and stalled France's relations with Berlin long after the Agadir Crisis had melted in the haze. Bethmann-Hollweg recalled that the usually gregarious and positive ambassador Jules Cambon 'visibly changed' after Poincaré took charge. Bethmann-Hollweg wrote:

I had no more of procedure by personal contact. And when the Ambassador visited me after one of his frequent trips to Paris, while he remained amiable as ever, he would become monosyllabic in spite of an epigrammatic and exquisite French wit whenever the conversation turned upon public opinion in France. Everything was avoided that could suggest that the Poincaré Ministry was guided by the same spirit of reconciliation that he had always been prepared to proclaim when the previous Cabinet was in office.[8]

In a conventional world, it might have fallen to Paris, one would think, to initiate friendlier relations with Germany, rather than the other way around, given that France had provoked Agadir. Yet such speculation of human civility had no place in a world in which Germany was seen as the ascendant aggressor. A desperate irony lay in the fact that Germany, for a brief period in late 1911 and early 1912, was trying to form peaceful relationships with its European neighbours at a time when everyone had persuaded themselves that all Berlin wanted was war. Cambon's pressure cooker was looking more explosive day by day.

—

Meanwhile, the resurgence of a highly combustible strain of French nationalism thwarted any hope of rapprochement. Poincaré's deference to public opinion exacerbated this outcome. His fierce French pride and Lorrainer's defiance stoked the flames, and, unwittingly or not, his presidency unleashed a new and dangerous tendency in France in the early twentieth century: the forces of rampant chauvinism, baying for the restitution of French 'honour'. It little mattered that the lost provinces of Alsace and Lorraine, if French in spirit, were enjoying great economic benefits on board the German locomotive; indeed, most Lorrainers and Alsatians preferred the status quo to another war, which they knew would destroy their homes again. Many were not interested in the strident calls for their 'liberation'. Intermarriage was rife, and a second generation of Franco-German children was growing up there. But that hardly stemmed the revanchist forces in France.

Jules Cambon was, in a sense, a victim of these forces. Throughout 1912, he continually pressed Poincaré to take a more positive attitude to Germany. After the Italian defeat of Turkey, he seized his chance and proposed a Franco-German mediation of the peace, which Poincaré instantly knocked on the head, as he did any proposal that did not involve Russia and Britain. It reflected Poincaré's wishful elevation of the Entente Cordiale to something approaching an alliance – which Britain refused to contemplate, as Henry Wilson had angrily discovered. Grey would repeatedly decline to reassure France of British support in the event of a German invasion. So here was Poincaré closing the door on Germany's appeals for better relations, in deference to London's sensitivities, even as the British Government refused to offer France any hope of military backing.

—

If he was, in some ways, Poincaré's bête noire, Georges Clemenceau shared his political rival's pursuit of a single idea in foreign policy: to rid France of the German threat forever. To this cause (among many), he devoted his life. A son of the Vendée in west-central France, Clemenceau seemed endowed with the region's stubborn strain of rebelliousness. The *département* on the Atlantic coast was the scene of terrible bloodshed during the wars of religion. Between 1793 and 1796, a bloody peasant revolt against the ruling classes claimed almost a quarter of a million lives there. Clemenceau lived and breathed the Vendean 'type': radical, suspicious, stubborn, independent. No wonder, then, that this precociously clever medical student felt a kinship with fellow radicals, notably Thaddeus Stephens, the great American anti-slavery campaigner.

Yet, as his political antenna matured, Clemenceau's belief in democracy and social justice clashed with the scientific principles he studied at medical school, chiefly Charles Darwin's theory of natural selection. Like most intelligent men of his age, he assumed the law of the survival of the fittest could apply to human relationships in the present day. The survival of the Teutonic, Slav or Latin 'race' relied, like the survival of the blacks, on their fitness of character, their strength of mind, their willingness to fight. Character was destiny, he wrote: 'In this ruthless struggle for existence carried on by human society, those who are weaker physically, intellectually, or morally must in the end yield to the stronger.'[9] Unlike Bernhardi or Conrad, he did not intend by this that the weaker should lay down their arms and submit. He meant they should fight on and on until 'right' prevailed; there must be no compromise in this battle for truth and justice.

Where Poincaré so often sought excuses not to act, Clemenceau relished the fight and, in the words of the historian Geoffrey Bruun:

> plunged into each new fray with a sense of escape from indecision and fought each issue with the narrow, belligerent fury of a peasant defending his fields . . . To Clemenceau ideas were weapons, thought was a form of action, action was life, and life was conflict.[10]

The failure of his marriage, after seven years, to the American Mary Plummer, with whom he had three children, engendered in this fiery young man a deep sense of isolation, a kind of detachment from his fellow human beings. Yet he never succumbed to cynicism. Clemenceau was always attuned to the 'still, sad music of humanity',[11] to the lot of the destitute, and how and why he must help them.

The Franco-Prussian War exerted a cathartic effect on the young doctor, transforming him into a radical republican, and gave his political ideology a fixed and uncompromising direction. He became a sort of self-willed engine of political ideas, which revolved around the central vision of a strong and free France, rid of the German curse. His mind was always tilting at what *could be*, not at what was. Only a vibrant French republic could withstand the slings and arrows of its bellicose neighbour; only a powerful France led not by sclerotic royalist or religious institutions but by republicans of unyielding vision and action would deliver the nation.

In such thoughts, he set off, divorced, isolated and angry, to pursue a political and journalistic career of unswerving conviction, first as the mayor of Montmartre during the bloody Paris Commune – 'it forced upon me a sound appreciation of the stupidity of public life to find myself between two parties, both of which desired my death'[12] – then as a radical republican, searing polemicist (on every social issue that vexed him, culminating in his evisceration of the lies and injustice of the Dreyfus case), Cabinet minister and finally into the lap of the nation as prime minister, the man they dubbed the 'Tiger', and leader of the French at war.

Yet, as he progressed through the ministerial ranks, this wily old fighter grew more practical, less blinkered by ideology. As premier in 1907, he moved to empower the armed forces and entrench the Entente Cordiale. His motives were consistent with his earliest fears of German imperialism. Clemenceau was alarmed at the relative strength of the German Army. In 1907, France spent 27 per cent of the national budget on defence, compared with Germany's 37 per cent, according to the estimates of *The Statesman's Yearbook*.[13] By 1909, Germany would be able to mobilise 1,700,000 combat-ready soldiers, compared with France's 1,300,000. These estimates would prove to be exaggerations. Nevertheless, they exerted a powerful impetus on French policy. Bound by tight budgets and government inertia, Clemenceau had little room to move to address this parlous situation; so he acted within his limitations, to solidify France's foreign relations, chiefly with Russia and Britain, and to strengthen the existing army.

To that end, he overrode the anti-religious ethos of his radical colleagues to promote a devout Catholic and conservative to command the prestigious École de Guerre, France's premier officer training college. General Ferdinand Foch, an artilleryman immersed in the tactics and strategies of 'modern warfare', thus took control of the training of the future officers of the French Army. Foch would prove, along with Kitchener, one of the few commanders who foresaw the scale and nature of the coming conflict, for which he was now charged with preparing the French soldier.

—

Beyond the immediate demands that pressed on Foch were the deeper, more mysterious animators of action. Like Poincaré and Clemenceau, Foch lived in the shadow of the humiliation of Sedan, the memory of which had been scored into his mind. Back then, he had enlisted as a young man, but the war ended before he could participate. Instead, he was made to see what defeat meant. Resuming his studies as a young maths student in Metz, he shared quarters with German troops of the 37th Pomeranian Regiment and witnessed other units passing triumphantly through town. '[T]he Germans were quite determined to make us feel the weight of their victory', Foch later wrote. 'By their violence and brutality, without even the smallest pretext, they showed us that they considered it as giving them the right to do whatever they pleased.'[14]

As their forces occupied Alsace and Lorraine, the Germans inflicted further indignities on the French people. Foch witnessed a parade of German commanders, princes and officials enter Nancy, where he was then living:

> Each arrival was greeted by the same noisy outbursts of enthusiasm, the same military parades and ceremonies, in honour of generals who had led the German armies to victory or of statesmen who, in spite of the unanimous protests of the populations concerned, had torn Alsace and Lorraine from France.[15]

No wonder, then, that the restoration of French honour was one of Foch's driving motives. Another was vengeance. 'The disastrous war from which we had just emerged,' he later wrote, of the

Franco-Prussian War, 'imposed upon all of us, and especially upon the youth of the nation, the sacred task of building up our country, now dismembered and constantly menaced with complete destruction.'[16]

He joined the artillery, known as the 'little hats', a field of warfare in a state of great innovation. He inherited his training officer's opinion that firepower had become, since 1870, the dominating factor in battle, 'to such a degree that the advance of any body of troops not possessing an unquestionable superiority of fire would be paralysed'.[17] And so, along with thousands of young officers, Foch worked to reinvent the French Army from scratch for a future war with Germany, which he thought, along with his men, to be inevitable.

The future Marshal Foch was prone, however, to let his hatred of Germany infect his better judgement. In dark moments, he imagined a world completely overrun by Germans, who would spread like a virus to occupy every nation on the planet, against whom 'no government, above all no democratic government, would have dared to take effective measures of protection, lest it incur the ultimate disaster of domination by its own population'.[18] Foch warned, 'By 1914 all Germany had become completely Prussified and every German held that might makes right.'[19] Had the war of 1914 not been fought, he wrote, 'the world would have found itself Germanized and humanity in shackles'.[20] Clemenceau and Poincaré would not have used such impolitic language but shared the general's guiding animus: vengeance was theirs.

19

SEA SUPREMACY

I have no desire for a good relationship with England at the sacrifice of the increase of Germany's navy . . . The [Navy] law [of 1908] shall be carried into execution to the last detail; whether this suits the British or not is no matter! If they want war, they can begin it, we do not fear it!

Kaiser Wilhelm II, on the German naval race with Britain

BETWEEN 1897 AND 1912, Germany and Britain engaged in a ruinously expensive naval arms race to build a fleet capable of dominating the world through unassailable command of the sea. The pursuit of sea supremacy, if not a direct cause of the war, was a powerful impetus towards it. The naval race stirred the brew of mutual suspicion, distrust and paranoia that led to war. 'So far as contemporary opinion was concerned, it was the naval question above everything else which exacerbated Anglo-German relations,' concludes Paul Kennedy.[1]

In the 1900s, Britain easily occupied the role of the greatest sea power. One cannot overstate the revered place of the Royal Navy in the British psyche: victorious at Trafalgar, victorious over the Spanish Armada, synonymous with Nelson, Anson, Hawke,

Raleigh, Drake, the conqueror of the world, the guardian of the empire . . . the accolades were inexhaustible. The Admiralty's power reached its apogee in the first decade of the twentieth century. Britain's 'absolute supremacy' at sea acquired a kind of self-evident legitimacy: having the greatest empire somehow entitled Britain to dominance of the oceans. In this spirit, Churchill declared the fleet 'a necessity' on which Britain's very existence depended. He dismissed Germany's navy as a 'luxury', the aim of which was simply 'expansion'.[2] Given that Britain planned to blockade Germany and starve it into submission at the outbreak of hostilities, it is hard to disagree with Ferguson that Churchill was, in this instance, speaking 'tremendous humbug'.[3]

So the prospect of a rival on the high seas was more than a conventional military threat; it provoked a deep emotional reaction in Britain. Germany's naval ambitions, it was feared, would challenge the very existence of the empire. Yet Germany would never actually threaten British sea supremacy, despite the monomaniacal ambitions of the German Admiralty. Britain won the naval arms race well before 1914, and was quite capable of blockading German ports and controlling the North Sea lanes when war broke out. What tested Anglo-German relations to the limit of tolerance was the violent psychology that accompanied the naval race, rather than its actual outcome.

The usual misperceptions, media hysteria and plain untruths bedevilled the story. It was grossly inflammatory to claim, as the British did well into the 1900s, that the Prussian General Staff intended the wholesale invasion of the British Isles (that idea had been soundly scotched in 1898 as unworkable). Nor did a strong German Navy automatically mean war with Britain, despite the ridiculous claims of the British press. Without a powerful navy to protect it, Germany's merchant shipping, so vital to her booming overseas trade, sank or sailed entirely at the pleasure of the British Admiralty. In that sense, a stronger German Navy could be construed as a perfectly legitimate, defensive measure, especially given the ease with which British ships could blockade German ports. For their part, the Germans argued that their nation needed a navy as powerful as Britain's solely to protect its merchant shipping. Yet such half-truths infuriated Eyre Crowe:

> it is quite ridiculous to believe that we are taken in by the pretence of the necessities of 'defending German commerce' etc. as the reason for a bigger fleet. Commerce is defended in one way and one way only: namely the destruction of the opponent's naval force . . .[4]

Violence was not the only way of protecting sea commerce, of course, but Crowe tended to disallow peaceful alternatives where Germans were concerned.

—

To understand how the naval war developed, scroll back a little in time. In the last years of the nineteenth century, the Kaiser developed an obsession with the idea that Germany needed a new navy, partly through his familial envy of Britain's and partly through reading Rear Admiral Alfred Thayer Mahan's highly influential *The Influence of Sea Power on History*, which persuaded him that more battleships were vital to Germany's imperial ambitions. In this enterprise, the Kaiser found a naval ally who articulated his obsession: Grand Admiral Alfred von Tirpitz.

Sporting a long, forked beard, reminiscent perhaps of King Neptune, Tirpitz was not only a highly ranked sailor; he was also a wily, independent-minded political fixer. His rough rise to the Admiralty received a smoothing agent in 1887 when he struck up a friendship with Wilhelm (who would become Kaiser the following year). Wilhelm shared and encouraged Tirpitz's hubristic vision of German naval supremacy over Britannia. This meeting of minds accelerated Tirpitz's advancement, first to chief of the Naval Staff in 1892, then rear admiral in 1895, and finally state secretary of the

Imperial Naval Office in 1896. Tirpitz entered the Reichstag in 1897 determined to use his new-found political clout to realise the Kaiser's dream of becoming the world's premier maritime power.

On 6 December 1897, Tirpitz revealed his naval ambitions to the Reichstag: a program to create a battle-fleet capable of challenging Britain's hitherto unrivalled naval dominance. Two navy bills, in 1898 and 1900, followed, supplemented by further bills in 1906, 1908 and 1912. Together, they formed the legislative basis for the Tirpitz Plan, which aimed to raise more than 400 million marks to create a fleet of 60 capital ships, positioned between Heligoland and the English Channel.

The new fleet would thus present a direct threat to Britain's command of the North Sea. By revealing his vision, Tirpitz placed Berlin on a political collision course with London even before construction began – signalling the start of an arms race of unprecedented scale and cost. The Tirpitz Plan had more disturbing implications to monitors of German foreign policy in Whitehall. It was the most obvious symbol yet seen of Germany's complete abandonment of the Bismarckian principle of peaceful coexistence and its replacement with *Weltpolitik*. For the first time, the presumption that Britannia ruled the waves would be sorely tested.

Tirpitz forcefully argued in the Reichstag that, without a new fleet, Germany would realise neither its imperial ambition nor the 'semi-hegemony' it sought to impose on Europe. For Tirpitz, only a massive shipbuilding enterprise would 'propel the Reich into the position of a superpower' by 1920–21. Of the four great powers to emerge in the coming century – Russia, Britain, America and Germany – Britain still had the mightiest fleet. The new German Navy aimed not only to challenge British sea power and defend the Reich but also to secure an overseas empire (according to the definitive analysis of the Tirpitz Plan by Volker R. Berghahn).[5] In Tirpitz's uncompromising mind, the fleet was 'an absolute necessary for Germany, without which she will encounter ruin'.[6] Germany must bet everything on the single card of 'navalism', he assured the Kaiser, in order to fulfil her vast global ambitions. The fleet would take the form, in Paul Kennedy's description, 'of a sharp knife, held gleaming and ready only a few inches away from the jugular vein of Germany's most likely enemy' – Britain.[7]

In a frightening echo of Schlieffen, Tirpitz foresaw Germany striking a single massive blow, to British naval might, in the sea off Heligoland. There would be no compromise, no half-measures, in this maritime *Götterdämmerung* (twilight of the gods, or end of days): it was either a case of a 'decisive battle on the high sea' or 'inactivity, that is, moral self-destruction'.[8] His aim was to create such a formidable threat that Britain would refuse to engage in a sea battle, not because the latter feared losing but because the loss of capital ships would damage London's ability to protect her empire. Thus ran Tirpitz's thinking, which the Kaiser shared. In this sense, the new German Navy would be a lethal military *and* political weapon, serving as a deadly deterrent, rather like the nuclear arsenals of the Cold War. A powerful rival navy, Tirpitz told the Kaiser, would drain Britain of 'every inclination to attack us and as a result concede to Your Majesty such a measure of naval influence and enable Your Majesty to carry out a great overseas policy'.[9]

Not everyone agreed with the admiral's diagnosis. When Tirpitz presented his final plan to the scrutiny of the Reichstag in 1898, August Bebel, a revolutionary socialist and one of the founders of the German Social Democratic Party, condemned it as Anglophobic madness. To imagine a German fleet could take on the Royal Navy, Bebel argued, was insanity, and anyone saying it belonged in the madhouse.[10] Unimpressed by this defeatist talk, the deputies reached the opposite conclusion. On 26 March 1898, Tirpitz's first bill passed by a majority of 212 to 139. His second bill, which would double the number of battleships, from 19 to 38, and planned the completion of the second-largest fleet in the world by 1920, passed two years later.

Ecstatic relief in the Kaiser's circle greeted the success. At last, Germany would take her rightful place on the high seas. The triumph drove the formation of the Navy League, whose purpose was to promote Germany's claim to world-power status. Membership rose from 78,000 in 1898, to 600,000 in 1901, to 1.1 million in 1914. For his part, Tirpitz was elevated to the front rank of government ministers and won a seat on the Prussian Ministry of State. For a few years, he enjoyed immense influence in government and at court, with the unqualified support of the Kaiser, the Foreign Office and, for a time, the chancellor. Until the mid-1900s, he commanded 'the centre stage of German politics'.[11]

—

Yet Tirpitz's belief in the primacy of the navy found a powerful opponent: the German Army, who were neither pleased nor persuaded by the case for so much money going to ships. The Prussian generals looked to Schlieffen and Bernhardi to put the case that the nation relied more on the army than on the navy for its survival. 'I have examined the probable conditions of the next naval war in some detail,' Bernhardi ominously declared in *The Next War*. He continued:

> [W]e cannot count on an ultimate victory at sea unless we are victorious on land. If an Anglo-French Army invaded North Germany through Holland, and threatened our coast defenses in the rear, it would soon paralyze our defense by sea. The same argument applies to the eastern theatre. If Russian armies advance victoriously along the Baltic and cooperate with a combined fleet of our opponents, any continuation of the naval war would be rendered futile by the operations of the enemy on land.

Only by making Germany 'absolutely safe' on land could it pursue a successful sea policy, Bernhardi argued:

> So long as Rome was threatened by Hannibal in Italy there

could be no possible idea of empire. She did not begin her triumphal progress in history until she was thoroughly secure in her own country.[12]

As his vision started to fray under the scrutiny of the Prussian generals, Tirpitz's faith in his naval program bloomed into a dangerous obsession, overwhelming his judgement and draining him of credibility. The admiral pursued his new navy without reason or restraint, rather like a monomaniacal fisherman fixed on reeling in some huge, elusive prey.

—

The Tirpitz Plan, in fact, foundered at the moment of its conception. It was ruinously expensive, strategically ill planned and deeply provocative. Most Reichstag deputies were blind to these hard truths because they tended, with a few brave exceptions, to back the Kaiser's wishes in the early years of his reign. Yet the instant the British Admiralty, under the redoubtable Sir John Fisher, got wind of the plan, London responded with a massive naval build-up of its own. 'Our only probable enemy is Germany,' Fisher told the Prince of Wales. 'Germany keeps her whole fleet always concentrated within a few hours of England. We must therefore keep a fleet twice as powerful . . . always concentrated within a few hours of Germany.'[13]

The spearhead of British naval development was the new dreadnought class of battleship. The first, launched in February 1906, was equipped with steam turbine propulsion and an unprecedented number of heavy-calibre guns. The dreadnought transformed the nature of sea war. Henceforth, all capital ships would have to measure up to the new standard. Germany was the first to upgrade, producing three dreadnoughts in 1907, and four in 1908 and 1909. The dreadnought race with Britain climaxed in 1910 and 1911, when Germany produced four dreadnoughts to Britain's five. In the critical year 1908, to the horrified British Admiralty, Germany briefly seemed to be speeding up its naval production, within reach of Britain's lead. Lord Fisher dismissed this possibility, warning against the 'Hysteria Germanicus'. Yet even he was forced to concede that Britain would have to expand its program.[14]

In October that year, the Kaiser gave his notorious interview to *The Daily Telegraph*. His views on the German Navy added immeasurably to the hysteria:

> But, you will say, what of the German navy? Surely, that is a menace to England! Against whom but England are my squadrons being prepared? If England is not in the minds of those Germans who are bent on creating a powerful fleet, why is Germany asked to consent to such new and heavy burdens of taxation? My answer is clear. Germany is a young and growing empire. She has a worldwide commerce which is rapidly expanding . . . Germany must have a powerful fleet to protect that commerce and her manifold interests in even the most distant seas. She expects those interests to go on growing, and she must be able to champion them manfully in any quarter of the globe. Her horizons stretch far away.[15]

So did the Kaiser's imagination. He and his admirals had rejected repeated British offers to limit naval spending, as an affront to German dignity. In a footnote to the text of a conversation between Grey and the German ambassador on 14 July 1908, in which they discussed a naval agreement, Wilhelm had scrawled:

> I have no desire for a good relationship with England at the sacrifice of the increase of Germany's navy . . . The [Navy] law [of 1908] shall be carried into execution to the last detail; whether this suits the British or not is no matter! If they want war, they can begin it, we do not fear it![16]

Wiser German heads knew they were beaten as early as November

1908. German reason made a brief cameo in an anonymous article published in *Marine-Rundschau*:

> Britain could only be defeated by a power that seized permanent command of the British sea . . . Boxed in between France and Russia, Germany has to maintain the greatest army in the world . . . It is obviously beyond the capacity of the German economy to support at the same time a fleet which could outgrow the British.[17]

Mindful of this, in 1909 the then chancellor Bülow proposed a bilateral 'slowing down' of naval construction. He presented the idea at a meeting in Berlin on 3 June, attended by Tirpitz, Moltke, Bethmann-Hollweg and Metternich (the German ambassador to London). Germany would build three instead of four ships a year if Britain offered something 'concrete' in return. Tirpitz shrewdly agreed but suggested that they 'wait quietly' for Britain to make the first move. That effectively scotched the idea. Bülow soon resigned, and the Kaiser ignored his former chancellor's warning of the great gravity of the situation.

Bülow's successor Bethmann-Hollweg continued to entertain the idea of a naval deal with Britain. In his mind evolved a bizarre trade-off: he dared to link a German offer to restrict its shipbuilding to a British commitment to neutrality. The offer arose during the British war secretary Viscount Haldane's mission to Berlin from 8 to 12 February 1912 – an attempt to smooth friction over the naval arms race. Bethmann-Hollweg offered to limit the size of Germany's fleet to three capital ships a year if Britain agreed to remain neutral in the event of a European war.

Plainly, Britain was unable to fulfil this outrageous and insulting proposal, given its obligations to the Triple Entente. Haldane wanted a political deal that would contain the naval race, not a commitment to neutrality in some future war. The implications perplexed him. According to Bethmann-Hollweg, Haldane 'showed that he was apparently really afraid that we would break loose against France if we were sure of the neutrality of England'.[18] The chancellor amended the offer to make it more palatable: would England maintain 'benevolent neutrality' to Germany 'should a war be forced on Germany'?

Grey adamantly refused. Britain could not enter into any agreements with Germany that 'should imperil existing friendships with other powers'.[19] To do so, write Steiner and Neilson, would have meant 'abandoning the whole system of ententes which had been so carefully nurtured during the past six years'.[20] Bethmann-Hollweg had indeed underestimated 'the binding force of England's engagements' with France and Russia, as he admitted.[21] In German eyes, Britain's true European allegiances, in the event of war, were quickly revealing themselves. The Haldane mission failed to extract any German naval concessions. No political accommodation would ensue. The Foreign Office considered the naval talks a 'diplomatic disaster' that would antagonise the French and Russians and achieve nothing.[22] 'It would be a political mistake of the first magnitude,' wrote Crowe, ever ready to up the ante, 'to allow the German government to squeeze concessions out of us and leave them quite free to pursue the policy of carefully preparing their inevitable war against us.'[23]

—

So the naval race ran on, and petered out, for lack of money. At the Kaiser's so-called 'war council' of December 1912, Moltke argued for an early preventive war but Tirpitz requested another 18 months' grace because the German Navy was not yet ready. It would never be. The German Naval Law of 1912 proposed a further 33 German battleships and battlecruisers, which would, if built, outnumber the Royal Navy in home waters. London responded with plans to build ten super-dreadnoughts in the 1912 and 1913 budgets. Germany, in the end, could afford to build half that number; hard cash had decided the future of the naval race. Both sides were eager to end the hugely expensive adventure and curb the rate of shipbuilding. The naval race concluded, with Britain retaining her supremacy.

At what price? The costs were staggering, in both financial and political terms. And Germany did present an awesome naval power, if not a complete rival. By 1913, the Tirpitz Plan had endowed Germany with the second-largest navy in the world, albeit 40 per cent smaller than the Royal Navy. It contained 17 modern dreadnoughts, five battlecruisers, 25 cruisers, 20 pre-dreadnought battleships as well as over 40 submarines. The British were sufficiently impressed to seek French help. The alternative was a prohibitively expensive shipbuilding plan at a time of huge social welfare demands on the budget. Winston Churchill, who became first lord of the Admiralty in 1912, pursued a new course, under which the French Navy would assume responsibility for the Mediterranean – an issue raised at the CID meeting in August 1911 – while the British would protect the north coast of France. In short, all Tirpitz's efforts had come to this: a greatly expanded and deadlier British naval presence, concentrated entirely on the North Sea and the English Channel.

—

By the end of 1913, Britain's new naval partnership with France had turned the Entente Cordiale into a quasi-military relationship – and even anticipated talks of Anglo-Russian naval cooperation. The British Navy was stronger than ever, outnumbering German dreadnoughts by 20 to 13, battlecruisers nine to six, with more than double the number of pre-dreadnought battleships. Germany had lost the naval race and faced renewed hostility from all sides. This dire situation drew a splutter of outrage from the usual quarters, chiefly the Kaiser, who reprised all the old arguments that triggered the naval race in the first place: of dastardly England refusing to share the high seas with any other power.

This painful process was not lost on several powerful German leaders – chiefly Bülow, Bethmann-Hollweg and Moltke – who had noted the monstrous folly of the Tirpitz Plan but had been powerless to act against it. In their eyes, the enlarged German battle-fleet 'simply worsened Germany's position and consequently was disliked by all who believed that, not Britain, but Russia and France were their country's real foes'.[24]

The Tirpitz Plan collapsed on its own contradictions and forced upon Germany a terrible choice. Would Berlin continue to pursue the policy of global hegemony, or *Weltpolitik*, championed by the Kaiser and Tirpitz, in which sea power was crucial? Or would it abandon overseas expansion in favour of the home-grown policy favoured by Chancellor Bethmann-Hollweg, which viewed France and Russia as Germany's arch-enemies and aimed at dividing the Triple Entente by re-engaging with Britain? The second course relied on a huge land army and could not be pursued while Germany challenged British sea supremacy. Berlin could not simultaneously threaten and befriend the English. Ignoring these arguments, the increasingly isolated Tirpitz clung to his program until well after the outbreak of war – and never realised his goal. The huge Prussian-led army, as Schlieffen and Bernhardi had argued, henceforth assumed central importance in German military strategy.

20

CRISES IN THE BALKANS

*[W]ar was inevitable, and that the sooner
it came the better for Germany.*
Von Moltke, chief of the German General Staff, to
the Kaiser's 'war council', 8 December 1912

THE BALKAN PENINSULA was the proxy battlefield on which
the great game of European power would now be tested. This little
cluster of agrarian communities, scarcely raised out of subsistence,
acted as though they were fully independent nations, convinced that
whatever action they took, however much blood they spilt, or lives
they destroyed, in pursuit of more territory, or a longer border, or
access to the sea, their struggle would redound to their valour and
prestige in the eyes of the world. It would not. They violently coveted
their neighbours' land and treasure, and echoed, in pathetic microcosm, the bloody scramble at great-power level.

At tactical level, they were forces unto themselves. 'The ambitious peoples of the Balkans,' grumbled Bethmann-Hollweg, 'were
not such tame tools in the hands of the mighty as to let them at a
word cut down their national aims or curb their racial hate.'[1] At strategic level, they were compelled to act, more or less, in the sway of

an occupying force, either the Ottoman Empire or the European powers. Occasionally, at rare moments in history when an incumbent overlord was thrown out (the Turks in 1912) or abandoned them (the Soviet Union in the 1990s), they were shocked to find themselves genuinely free, and, rather than try to settle their differences and enjoy the fruits of peace, they exerted their will with terrible force, bloodshed and consequences for Europe. That is what happened during the two Balkan Wars of 1912–13 (and during the break-up of Yugoslavia in the 1990s). These two wars, more than any other event, created the conditions that led to the outbreak of world war in 1914.

Why the great powers lassoed their future to a peninsula of farms and goatherds, of little economic or colonial use, is one of the most vexing questions of the story of 1914. The answers lie in a web of alliances, strategic expedience, historic vendettas and racial hatred. For it was a miserable truth that, once Russia and Austria-Hungary had bound themselves irrevocably to the Balkans, their respective allies, to a greater or lesser degree, were drawn into the region's orbit. There were blood ties and racial differences, of 'blonde' versus 'Slav', as the popular German press would report; and the Balkans had great strategic value as the gateway from the Black Sea to the Mediterranean.

Even so, the European powers were not enthusiastic cheerleaders on the sidelines of the Balkan Wars. Britain was strongly opposed to linking her interests to any war in the Balkans. France was initially opposed. Germany awaited Austro-Hungarian action before giving its approval. Even Russia wavered in its support for the Slavic states against the Ottomans and then Austro-Hungarians, when larger interests intervened. But none could deny that their relationships within the European power blocs were inextricably linked with their Balkan protégés. A Russian war with Austria-Hungary, for example, through its sponsorship of Serbian aggression, implied French involvement (under the Franco-Russian Alliance), in opposition to Austria-Hungary, who would in turn appeal for German help (under the Triple Alliance). If this sequence sounds unstoppable

– like a machine that had got a life of its own – it demonstrates how the links in the chain made a European war, sprung from hatred in the Balkans, easier to discern.

At a simple level, the Balkan Wars were two vicious little campaigns triggered by Italy's conquest of Turkish interests in Africa from September 1911 to October 1912. The so-called Libyan war – Italy's capture of the Ottoman provinces of Tripolitania, Cyrenaica and Fezzan led to the creation of modern Libya – gave a powerful impetus to discontent in the Balkans. The ease with which the Italian forces, not renowned for their martial skill, conquered Turkish interests in Africa encouraged Serbia and Bulgaria to do the same in the Balkans. They joined forces and strove to eject the weakened Turks once and for all from the peninsula. Their dream, as always, was a free Slavic state. At a higher level, the wars left a power vacuum in the peninsula that had explosive consequences for the relationship between the European powers. The wars' immediate repercussions were: the defeat and final expulsion of the Turks from the Balkans after centuries of occupation; the rearrangement of the region's borders to nobody's satisfaction, chiefly Bulgaria; the creation of an independent state of Albania, to Serbia's fury; and the emergence of an enlarged Serbian state, Russia's only remaining Balkan ally, which, in need of a new enemy, held Austria-Hungary in the sights of its vendetta-minded 'foreign policy'.

—

The origins of the First Balkan War may be traced to Austria-Hungary's annexation of Bosnia-Herzegovina. That event, as we've seen, deeply humiliated Russia and outraged Serbia. The Russian official responsible, former foreign minister Alexander Izvolsky, was subsequently sacked and dispatched to Paris, as Russian ambassador. There, he brooded deep on revenge. His replacement was the weak-willed, impressionable Sergei Sazonov, whose chief sin in the eyes of St Petersburg's fiercely pro-Slavic elements was a moderate line in the Balkans. In practice, however, Sazonov deferred to the authority of Izvolsky, who, from his Parisienne redoubt, persisted in hatching plans to retaliate against Austria-Hungary and humiliate his opposite number in Vienna, Aehrenthal. Izvolsky decided on a course that would have bloody consequences: to promote an alliance of the Balkan nations, which would supposedly form a Slavic super-state powerful enough to eject the hated Ottomans from the penin-sula, and be capable of acting as a buffer to Austro-Hungarian (and German) expansion. A 'pure' Slavic stronghold would secure Russian access to the Mediterranean and dominance of the region, and sal-vage Izvolsky's battered reputation.

The man St Petersburg sent to Belgrade to enact this ambi-tious plan was a rabidly pro-Slav diplomat called Nicholas Hartwig. Hartwig nursed an abiding hatred of Austria-Hungary and an unhealthy affection for everything Serb. Some thought him 'more Serbian than the Serbs', and he became a sort of cult figure in the Serb capital, as the approving eyes and ears of benevolent mother Russia. He developed an intimate friendship with the Serb prime minister, Nikola Pašić. In time, Hartwig often overdid his remit to St Petersburg, and he frequently exaggerated Russia's sympathy for the Serbian and Slav cause. He felt he acted both for official Russia and as an unofficial ambassador for the Pan-Slav Movement. He often pursued a pro-Serb agenda at odds with the milder line of his nominal boss, Sazonov, and presumed to speak for the militantly pro-Serbian Russian court and the Tsar himself.

Hartwig wasted no time in facilitating a pan-Balkan dialogue and was instrumental in creating a system of alliances between Serbia and Bulgaria, and Greece and Montenegro, negotiated in early 1912 and known as the Balkan League. These were plainly military agreements; they prescribed nothing short of offensive war. The Serbo-Bulgarian Alliance, for example, signed in March, com-mitted the signatories to fight to protect each other from foreign attack. But the agreement also obliged them to go to war if a foreign power sought to annex or occupy *any part* of the Balkan territories then under Turkish rule. That was a Pandora's box. A precondition to armed intervention, contained in a secret annex, was that Russia's consent must be sought if the situation warranted it – if, for example, Austria was to invade Albania. 'Should an agreement be reached as to military action,' the annex stated, 'Russia shall be informed, and should it raise no objection the allies shall thereupon proceed with the proposed military operations. It is understood that both parties bind themselves to accept as a final frontier such line as H.M. the Tsar may think good to lay down.'[2] Those two sentences revealed the secret role of Russia as the chief puppeteer of her Slavic protégés.

The Germans were deeply suspicious, even if they were unaware of the secret clause. 'We see the hand of Russia throughout,' wrote Bethmann-Hollweg later. 'The ultimate decision of all disputes [in the Balkans] was reserved to the Tsar. He would have the last word in partitions of territory after the war.'[3]

In Sazonov, however, Russia had appointed an inadequate and foolish puppet-master. The new foreign minister (Izvolsky retained a strong influence on foreign policy from Paris) was a feeble operator, inadequate to the task. Hartwig made it his business to undermine or ignore him. Sazonov, according to Baron Taube, a permanent official of the Russian Foreign Ministry, was 'sickly by nature, finely sensitive . . . soft and vague, unceasingly variable in his impressions and "intuitions", refractory to all sustained effort of thought, incapable of pursuing a train of reasoning to its logical conclusion'.[4] If others' assessments were less uncharitable, nobody seems to have had much confidence in the man appointed to guide Russian foreign policy through a period of mounting crises. 'Did Sazonov,' wonders Albertini, 'realize the bearing of [the Balkan] treaties, which could not fail, in the near future, to lead to a war that might spread to the rest of Europe? Certain it is that the new minister was no match for the events that were soon to take place.'[5]

—

The great powers were painfully aware of the Balkan League as a tinderbox at the heart of Europe. To varying degrees, they sought to restrain its more incendiary elements. When Poincaré visited Moscow in August 1912, Sazonov showed him the text of the Serbo-Bulgarian Alliance. It was 'an agreement for war', the then French prime minister brusquely observed.[6] He advised Paris to expect a Slav war against Turkey and Austria, giving Russia effective control over Bulgaria and Serbia. Sazonov admitted this. Serbia and Bulgaria, he said, 'could not mobilise without his consent'.[7]

Even before the Italians completed their defeat of Turkey in Africa, the Balkan Slavs stirred. The spark that lit the fuse was a bloody uprising against the Turks in Albania during the summer of 1912. Privately aghast at the prospect of an independent Albanian state, yet publicly supportive of the uprising, Serbia, Bulgaria and Montenegro seized the chance to mobilise against Turkish forces in the whole peninsula (in accordance with the Serbo-Bulgarian Treaty). Vienna viewed these developments with rising alarm: the Turks had hitherto acted as a brake on Slavic irredentism in the Balkans. Now, a Serbo-Bulgarian military alliance, were it victorious over the Turks, would directly challenge Austro-Hungarian power.

The Russian foreign minister Sazonov belatedly sensed the terrible risk of this local war spreading to engulf Russia, should Vienna enter the conflict against the Balkan League. He had no evidence to suggest this would happen, only his instincts. Austria-Hungary had not drawn up any plans to intervene in the Balkans in 1912–13, contrary to a popular fiction. Perceptions were so often decoupled from reality in the years before 1914.

Appalled at the prospect of a European war, Sazonov and Izvolsky, like two Russian Frankensteins, tried to rein in the Balkan monster they had created. In talks in Paris on 20 September 1912 and in statements to the press and French officials, the two men outraged Russia's Slavic friends by saying that it would be preferable if Turkey *defeated* the Balkan League (which they had had a direct hand in creating!), should a full-scale war erupt, because 'a big Serbo-Russian success would lead to Austrian intervention'.[8]

Russia's extraordinary backpedalling drew condemnation: the

Serbs were outraged and Hartwig acutely embarrassed. Others were sickened at the way the Russian diplomats had apparently provoked war and then sought peace. Sazonov attracted particular scorn. The French ambassador in Constantinople wrote on 27 September:

> He thoughtlessly unchains the tempest, then, all of a sudden, scared of his action, he throws up his plans, reins in the appetites which he himself has whetted, abruptly brings to a halt the little states that he himself has set in motion, and thus creates a general state of disorder and nervous over-excitement in . . . the Balkans, out of which Heaven knows what may emerge. In less than a year he has turned the Balkan peninsula topsy-turvy.[9]

—

By then, it was too late. The strings to Russia's Balkan puppets had snapped, and they were unleashed with a life of their own. In October, Montenegro, followed by Serbia, Bulgaria and Greece, declared war on Turkey. King Peter I of Serbia issued a statement to his people:

> The Turkish governments showed no interest in their duties towards their citizens and turned a deaf ear to all complaints and suggestions. Things got so far out of hand that no one was satisfied with the situation in Turkey in Europe. It became unbearable for the Serbs . . . By the grace of God, I have therefore ordered my brave army to join in the Holy War to free our brethren and to ensure a better future.[10]

Hard-line Slavs sought more than the destruction of Turkey-in-Europe. Once the Ottoman devil had been thrown out, they would turn on Austria-Hungary as their ultimate prey. In this sense, the First Balkan War was the prelude to a far more provocative gamble. And so, emboldened by the prospect of a historic Slav resurgence, between October and December 1912 the Balkan League launched a series of ferocious attacks on the Ottoman Turks. In terms of manpower per capita, these were devastating battles that implied huge losses to the little belligerents. Their rapidly growing populations, 'without any accompanying industrialization to soak up the available labour, had permitted the Balkan states to form huge peasant armies'.[11] Bulgaria fielded almost 600,000 men, out of a population of just 4.3 million; Serbia mobilised 255,000 out of a population of 2.9 million. They fought a 335,000-strong Turkish force, across three theatres, in the Sanjak, Thrace and Macedonia.

The Balkan League won a stunning victory. Within three months, they achieved what no European power had done in centuries: vanquished the Turkish armies in Europe. By December 1912, most of the Turks were driven out, save for a few resistant pockets. The Ottomans sustained about 330,000 casualties – dead, wounded or captured – almost their entire force; the Balkan League suffered 108,000 casualties. By December 1912, the First Balkan War was effectively over. The spectacular defeat of Turkey was a grave blow to Germany and Austria-Hungary, who had lost the chief obstacle to Russia in the Black Sea and to Britain in Egypt and Persia.[12]

London convened a peace conference. The resulting Treaty of London ceded all captured Ottoman territory to the Balkan League and declared Albania an independent state. The 'agreement' antagonised the participants, chiefly Bulgaria – who had given most and lost more in the war than its allies. The division of spoils, the new borders – chiefly in Macedonia – handed an unacceptable portion of territory to Serbia. As a result, Bulgaria refused to accept the treaty. And so a new war, between Serbia and Bulgaria, impended. Indeed, Bulgaria had started to transfer her forces west before the ink was dry on the London treaty.

—

The First Balkan War sent a grim warning to London, Berlin, Paris and St Petersburg that another Balkan confrontation could spark a major European conflict. A question arising out of the First Balkan

War was this: why did Austria-Hungary not challenge the emergence of a powerful Slavic alliance to the south and seek to curb its violent ambitions when it had the chance? The popular fiction is that Germany vetoed any Austro-Hungarian intervention. The truth was otherwise. Germany was prepared to support Austrian military action in the Balkans but relied on Austria's willingness to take the initiative and thrash out a plan. This Vienna failed to do. The reason may be found in the vacillating performance of Count Leopold Berchtold, the new Austrian foreign minister who failed to fill the boots of his formidable predecessor, Aehrenthal. Berchtold was a wealthy aristocrat, owner of a racing stable, who was said never to miss a horse race regardless of his political duties. Resplendently dressed, tall and urbane, 'wavering in his decisions and of unfathomable ignorance', he treated his foreign ministerial role as a subordinate interest, 'of less importance to him than clothes or the Turf', according to Heinrich Kanner.[13]

At a notorious meeting with Bethmann-Hollweg in Buchlau in September 1912, Berchtold revealed his complete ignorance of, and careless attitude towards, the grave events on Austria's doorstep. Despite Germany's tacit support, Austria failed to act. Berchtold had, at times during the struggle, persuaded himself that Turkey would defeat the Balkan alliance – another reason for him to do nothing. The Russians even assured him that they would not intervene, if Austria, for example, was compelled to resist a Serbian invasion of neighbouring Sanjak.[14] Yet Berchtold still did nothing – not through noble restraint but through ignorance and indecision. He failed to see that Russia had offered Austria a rare opportunity to curb Serbian expansion without fear of intercession by the Russian bear.

On one issue, Austria-Hungary drew the line on Serb aspirations: on no account would Serbia have access to a port on the Adriatic Sea. Belgrade coveted a seaport in the Mediterranean and eyed the Albanian port of Scutari. This would be firmly denied it, Vienna decided. Berchtold insisted on the 'creation' of Albania explicitly to deny Serbia a Mediterranean port.[15] He personally rebuffed, in the coarsest possible way, Serbian premier Pašić's peaceful offer to come to Vienna to discuss these issues, including a possible Serbian corridor to the sea. Instead, Austria-Hungary drew up an ultimatum – a haunting precedent for Vienna's far more dreadful ultimatum to Serbia of 1914 – on 18 October 1913, forcing Serbian forces to withdraw from Albania, which would be granted 'independence'.

The Serbs and Montenegrins reluctantly acquiesced and withdrew – under pressure from Russia and France. Whatever their allegiances, the Entente powers knew the gift of a seaport to Serbia was the bone that would make the Triple Alliance bark. Yet, to appease Serbia's denial of a port, Russia forced Vienna to make humiliating concessions to the Balkan state. For this, the Viennese government earned open ridicule; even the emperor was not beyond reproach. Berchtold was roundly execrated as a lamentable fool who had wagered the monarchy's prestige on a fight over Albania – 'that poverty stricken grazing ground for goats', as Conrad von Hötzendorf, chief of the Austrian General Staff, described it.[16] It is worth reminding ourselves that Conrad never ceased banging the drum for an immediate, bloody suppression of Serbia and the Slavic union, the threat of which, if not checked, would 'penetrate to the very marrow of Germany'.[17]

All of this signalled an irrecoverable loss of prestige for Austria-Hungary and the Habsburgs, and exposed their weaknesses. Perhaps, by doing nothing, the Austro-Hungarians had unwittingly averted the likelihood of a European war. And yet, Vienna and Budapest were shown to be feeble-minded, indecisive, wounded and in a precipitous frame of mind. The crepuscular shadow of the humiliated empire was not an edifying sight.

The corollary was a surge in Slav spirits. To say their victories over the Turks had gone to their heads understates the effusion of self-confidence that swept the Balkan League, especially Serbia. A spineless Austria-Hungary gave them an additional boost and even prompted talk of the return of Bosnia-Herzegovina to the Slavic fold.

—

The reaction of the European powers gave an ominous dimension to the story – not through what they did or said but, rather, in how they *perceived* these events: wrongly, as it happened. The First Balkan War raised fears that Russia would join the Balkan League in a battle against Austria-Hungary/Germany (a hypothesis). If so, would France join Russia in the fight (a hypothesis based on a hypothesis)? Not according to the letter of the Franco-Russian Alliance, which obliged the signatories to *defend* each other only *if attacked*. That plainly did not entail French intervention on Russia's side in a Balkan conflict. However, Poincaré's abrasive nationalism and support for Russia opened the door to a more aggressive interpretation of the Franco-Russian Alliance. Would German intervention in the Balkans trigger a *casus foederis*, i.e. a situation that enacted the treaty and obliged France to intervene? Yes, Poincaré seemed to imply, in a letter to Izvolsky, the contents of which he duly cabled to St Petersburg on 17 November 1912. Izvolsky concluded from this, in reply, that, 'If Russia goes to war, France too will go to war.' Poincaré later confirmed the substance of this intelligence, arguing only that Izvolsky's cable was 'too general'.[18] In other words, St Petersburg was perilously close to arguing that any German involvement in the Balkan conflict would trigger the Franco-Russian Alliance! This blurred the terms of the treaty and pitched the relationship into extremely dangerous waters, which Poincaré did nothing to ease.

Indeed, the First Balkan Crisis seemed to unleash French antagonism, which grew louder when Poincaré became president of the French Republic on 17 January 1913. In fact, the new president assured St Petersburg that France would make every diplomatic effort to back Russia's position in the Balkans. That is what Izvolsky concluded from fresh discussions with the president and his new foreign minister, Jonnart, at the Élysée Palace on 30 January 1913. In an extraordinary cable to St Petersburg, Izvolsky described the new understanding between France and Russia:

In present circumstances, as a result of the network of existing alliances and *ententes*, any unilateral manifestation by any Power in the field of Balkan affairs may very quickly lead to a general European war. The French Government perfectly understands and recognizes the special position of the Russian Government which has to reckon with national feeling and with our powerful traditions. Hence, the French Government does not in the least dream of depriving Russia of her freedom of action nor does it mean to cast doubt upon the moral obligations incumbent upon her in regard to the Balkan states. Therefore Russia can count, not only on the armed co-operation of France in the case provided for in the Franco-Russian agreement, but *on her most vigorous and effective diplomatic assistance in all the enterprises of the Russian government on behalf of those [Slav] States.* [My emphasis.][19]

In short, the deepening of France's commitment to Russia led St Petersburg to feel that it could count on French diplomatic and military backing for *any* action against Austria-Hungary/Germany over the Balkans. The perception, as much as the substance, of these events mattered in the embassies and governments of Europe. The ricocheting action of their alliances took firm shape – at least on paper – in the direction of a European war.

Germany, like Russia and France, moved to reassure its own protégé in the region. Alarmed by a pan-Slav threat to Austria-Hungary, Berlin baldly declared that it would fight to defend its ally. On 2 December 1912, Bethmann-Hollweg told the Reichstag that it would go to war for Austria-Hungary, if threatened. Three days later, Germany, Austria-Hungary and Italy (fearing Serbian access to the Adriatic) renewed the Triple Alliance in the face of the Slavic menace.

And then, on 8 December, the Kaiser, in explosive mood, convened a 'war council', as the historian Fritz Fischer labelled the famous meeting in the Berlin *Schloss* of Moltke, Tirpitz, August von Heeringen (chief of the Naval Staff) and Georg Alexander von

Müller (chief of the Kaiser's naval cabinet). Wilhelm had summoned the meeting in direct response to British war secretary Haldane's passing remark to the German ambassador in London that Britain would come to France's aid 'if a Russo-Austrian war led to a German attack on France'.[20] Those few words aroused Germany's worst fears and provoked the Kaiser's '*Gotterdammerung* mentality'.[21] 'If Russia supports the Serbs . . . then war would be unavoidable for us too,' he said.[22] In that event, he dreamt, in a daunting imaginative leap, that Bulgarian, Turkish and Roumanian forces would join the Triple Alliance, freeing Austro-Hungarian forces to hold off Russia while Germany dealt with France. An excitable Moltke welcomed this astonishing scenario. To him, 'war was inevitable, and that the sooner it came the better for Germany'.[23]

Though members of the Naval Staff dominated the Kaiser's war council, Tirpitz marginalised himself by revealing that his much-vaunted new navy wouldn't be ready in time for this great clash of arms (see Chapter 21). That was the 'death knell' of the Tirpitz Plan, writes Herwig.[24] In short, the war council neither declared war on anyone nor set a date for war. It ended with a single resolution: to launch a press campaign to prepare the German people for war with Russia. 'The outcome,' Müller concluded, 'was thus apparently zero.'[25]

Not exactly. The war council had unintended effects, of terrifying portent. By terminating any faith in the Tirpitz Plan, the meeting rededicated Germany to its continental army. As Bethmann-Hollweg said with relief a fortnight later, 'Because of the navy we have neglected the army and our "naval policy" has created enemies around us.' The army would now be brought up to full strength: 'We cannot afford to leave out any recruit who can wear a helmet.' The Kaiser faithfully relayed this message in his New Year's address: 'The navy will surrender to the army the major portion of the available funds.'[26] The largest single call-up during peacetime took place on 5 March 1913, of 4000 officers and 117,000 men, with the goal of raising an army of 750,000.

And what of England? Grey made clear that public opinion would not support British intervention in a faraway conflict of little consequence to British interests. The government seemed to withdraw into semi-isolation during the First Balkan War. That, at least, was London's outward stance. Surreptitiously, London played an active, incremental hand. Britain threatened to abandon, for example, its policy of restraining Russia and France (see Haldane's remark above). Grey supported Russia every step of the way over Albania and the Scutari issue but stood firm against Russia's determination to occupy Adrianople, which Turkey recaptured from the Bulgarians during the Second Balkan War. Indeed, it was the Second Balkan War that dragged England off the fence once and for all, and into the European melee.

—

And so, once again . . . In June 1913, Bulgaria declared war on Serbia over the spoils of the previous conflict, triggering the Second Balkan War. Hundreds of thousands of young men were again subjected to terror, dismemberment, capture or death, in the name of a line on a map. Bulgaria fielded about 570,000 men against more than one million Serbian, Greek, Montenegrin, Turkish and Roumanian troops. The Serbs spearheaded the offensive and prevailed over the Bulgarians. Sofia fell in July 1913. We need not delve into the ghastly details of these battles; their repercussions for European peace concern us.

The reactions of Austria-Hungary were again pivotal. This time, they backed Bulgaria as a tool with which to conquer the Serbs, and threatened to enter the war. Berchtold revealed the dual monarchy's motives in a telegram on 4 July 1913: 'a decisive Serbian victory would not only mean a considerable moral and material reinforcement of our traditionally hostile neighbour but would result in a spread of the Pan-Serbian idea and propaganda'. Austria-Hungary must intervene to prevent such an outcome. He warned, however, that Vienna's intervention, 'only an act of natural self-defence', might cause Russia 'to give up the passive role of an onlooker and thus involve the Triplice [Triple Alliance] and Roumania [then an Austro-Hungarian ally] in a war with Russia which would carry with it all the dangers and consequences of a major European conflagration'.[27]

For these reasons, Berlin and Rome restrained them. Bitterly for the Austro-Hungarians, Germany refused to give its assent to any intervention in the second Balkan stoush – a stance that infuriated Berchtold, who this time round gave the appearance of being will-ing to act. Regardless of whether he was or not, the key issue is that Germany had intervened to stop Vienna from fighting on Bulgaria's side. In a year's time, in July 1914, Berlin would do the reverse and wave on the Austrian juggernaut. The lines between the powers – Germany and Austria-Hungary, Russia and Serbia, France and Russia – had hardened beyond rupture. The only uncertain position was Britain's.

—

The spoils were divided at the Treaties of Bucharest and Constantinople. Once again, the Balkans were carved up. Communities, villages and towns awoke to find themselves living within new borders, with new flags, without any recourse to their feelings on the matter. Bulgaria lost most of the ground it gained in the First Balkan War. Serbia, Montenegro and Greece were the outright winners: whole regions suddenly found themselves part of Serbia or Greece. Greece increased her territory by 68 per cent. Serbia almost doubled in size, and her population rose from 2.9 mil-lion to 4.5 million. Yet the Serbs lost any hope of an outlet to the Adriatic Sea: Albania's independence and borders were officially confirmed. Grey hosted a conference in London in the summer of 1913 that consolidated these results and somehow managed to pacify most of the participants. In so doing, Grey revealed 'talents which I confess I did not think he possessed', observed Nicolson.[28]

Belgrade was the least able to complain. The most far-reach-ing result of the Second Balkan War was the rise of the pan-Slavic

Serbian state. Its victory over Bulgaria anointed Serbia as the most powerful nation in the Balkans, confident, expansive and keen to avenge the loss of Bosnia-Herzegovina to her new arch-enemy, Austria-Hungary. Meanwhile, Russia's greatest friend and ally rejoiced in the prospect of a pan-Slavic future for the Balkan Peninsula.

—

Archduke Franz Ferdinand, the next in line to the Austro-Hungarian throne, took an intriguing view of these events. Insofar as anyone listened to him, the nephew of the emperor Franz Joseph seemed anxious for peace with the Slavic world and tolerated a southern Slav union. It was a bitter irony of his sad life that the archduke actually sought peace between Serbia and Russia, and even hoped for a return of the alliance of the three emperors (of Germany, Austria-Hungary and Russia).

The archduke's liberal, somewhat quixotic stance won him few political allies at home and placed him in the crosshairs of extremists abroad, in both the Triple Alliance and the Slavic world. As 1914 approached, the Balkans had become no place for tolerant or moderate men, especially those first in line to the Austro-Hungarian throne.

The Balkan Wars had entrenched the powers of Europe and delineated the belligerents and their allies. The great power blocs confronted each other, no longer side by side but face to face. Contrary to the popular notion that 1914 shocked the world, the politicians, commanders and monarchs in the salons of power now spoke of war as inevitable. Europe's rulers referred to it in cables, speeches and letters with frightening regularity. They sounded resigned to it.

21

ARMED FOR 'INEVITABLE WAR'

It cannot be stressed enough that German planners dealt not so much in the day-to-day evaluations as in grand designs, whose sweep often encompassed the lives of a generation or two. The strengths and weaknesses of potential enemies were taken into account only after inflexible blueprints had been drafted.

Holger Herwig, historian

STRIKING BY ITS ABSENCE was any serious effort to restrain the European powers through negotiation, to arrest the process set in motion by the confusion, misunderstandings, paranoia and basic lack of goodwill between the foreign ministries of Austria-Hungary, Russia, Germany, France and Britain. It was as if, weary after years of rising tension, European leaders curiously relished the prospect of a military solution; as though, having exhausted the diplomatic channels, they had no other choice than to bow to the war cries of a powerful press and sheer paranoia. One thing was clear: the governments failed adequately to understand one another. They failed to apprehend or wilfully ignored the forces that would, left unchecked, lead to catastrophe.

If this is easy to say in hindsight, it was just as easy to say at the time. The ministers and commanders knew, more or less, what was happening. They had traced the web of alliances. The domino effect of the Balkan Wars was now plain for all to see. The generals repeatedly alluded to the 'inevitability' of war. Having created the parlous state of Europe, the powers routinely thought of war as 'imminent' and 'coming'.

Curiously, they all identified the *effect* but failed or refused to identify its *causes*. Listen to German secretary of state Gottlieb von Jagow, for example, who referred to 'the coming world war' in a top-secret military-estimates meeting in the Reichstag in April 1913. Or General Franz Gustav von Wandel, of the Prussian War Office, who warned, in 1911, 'that we are surrounded by our enemies, that a conflagration with them can scarcely be avoided, and that in the process we will be fighting for our world policy'.[1] There were countless similar references, in Paris, London, St Petersburg and Vienna. These men, and many others, were resigned to war and made little concerted effort to restrain the process, or to understand their supposed enemies. The crushing weight of fatalism wore down their energies and intellects. 'We all live under a dull pressure,' wrote Moltke in 1905, 'which kills the joy of achievement, and almost never can we begin something without hearing the inner voice say: "What for? It is in vain!"'[2]

Volatile, passionate, or self-righteous men such as Conrad, Moltke, Crowe, Hartwig, Berchtold and Bethmann-Hollweg hastened the march to oblivion. They spoke openly, resignedly and at times impatiently of a coming war. Moltke alternated between keenly advocating war and appearing horrified at the prospect. Despair gripped him on the eve of hostilities, which he described as 'the mutual tearing to pieces by Europe's civilized nations'.[3] This was the man who had strongly urged Germany to go to war at the Kaiser's conference on 8 December 1912. Bethmann-Hollweg displayed a similar helplessness interspersed with defiance. 'Gravely distressed' by Germany's relative weakness, he wrote that 'one must have a good deal of trust in God and count on the Russian revolution

as an ally in order to be able to sleep at all'.[4] His only consolation was
God and the Bolsheviks? None of the men in power seemed alive to
the possibility that *he* might act to prevent war. Conrad had no time
for what he contemptuously dismissed as peace talks. Other senior
officials, at different times, and with less vehemence, would scorn
attempts at mediation. Only Grey, in fairness, consistently held a
candle for the possibilities of a mediated peace, and then did much
to kill the process by failing to state Britain's position.

—

The main political actors so often placed their faith in incendiary
communiqués, plain untruths and blinkered or prejudiced arguments (witness the fracas over Morocco, and the Balkans). Or they
obfuscated and dithered, faded from view at crucial times or paid
less attention than such complex events demanded of them. Sheer
laziness, unintelligence and inability to concentrate were common-
place. Berchtold seemed to find the whole process a tedious distraction from his beloved horses. Grey rarely missed a chance to flee
the tension of London and resume trout fishing. Conrad's passionate love affair with a married woman obviously impaired his judgement. In 1914, as we shall see, the leaders of the French and German
Governments would be holidaying on the eve of hostilities.

Understanding and, dare we say, empathy between the great
powers was noticeably absent. No doubt, their channels of communication were weak, and telegraphs were delayed, or often
crossed. A babel of voices spoke in code, in different languages.
That hardly excused the awful silence at the top table. Nobody proposed a summit to discuss the European crisis. The Algeciras and
Balkan conferences stuck to a narrow remit. There was not a single
pan-European conference between the Agadir Crisis and the eve of
1914 to debate the awful direction of the world. True, there were
treaties and cables. Ambassadors came and went. And Germany
rejected Grey's valiant efforts at arranging a conference in the wake
of Agadir. The British foreign secretary's impressive attempt to calm

tensions and find a settlement to the Second Balkan War might have cranked up the process of broader conciliation. Yet nobody in a position of power proposed a meeting of minds to restrain, or at least discuss, the terrible trajectory of Europe, which they all knew was heading for disaster.

—

That did not mean, of course, that governments or the people wanted war. Militarism, in the sense of a popular longing for hostilities, was a myth, as Niall Ferguson has persuasively argued. Nor was it economically desirable: free trade relied on peace to function. While arms makers would temporarily enjoy rising sales during war, the capitalist system clearly did not prescribe or imply the destruction of markets and whole economies, contrary to the assertions of socialists who argued that war feathered the nests of pirate capitalists and would lead to millions of workers killing each other to enrich their bosses. (In fact, at the declaration of war, the trade unions and socialist movements throughout Europe postponed their political struggle to fight for their countries.)

The bankers 'were appalled at the prospect' of war, writes Ferguson, 'not least because war threatened to bankrupt most if not all of the major acceptance houses engaged in financing international trade'.[5] No doubt, monopolistic arms-makers – such as the manufacturers of the new machine gun, Vickers and Maxim-Nordenfelt, and the German shipbuilders – aggressively sought markets for their weapons. It did not follow that they wanted a world war, which would destroy their clients' economies. 'Inconveniently for Marxist theory,' concludes Ferguson, 'there is scarcely any evidence that these interests made businessmen *want* a major European war.'[6]

—

Meanwhile, disdainful of their meddling civilian politicians, German and Russian military commanders were impatient for the order to strike, to take command. They spoke for vast forces and huge arsenals. The stockpiling of weapons and the building of armies gathered a furious momentum in 1912–14, hastened by the fear of Germany's temptation to charge out of the fortress. Soldiers bristled in the ranks. New recruits longed for glory on the battlefield. Conscripts and reservists flowed into the system, captured by the extension of national service in France (to three years) and Germany. Throughout Europe, the mainstream press peddled this militarist line. The 'inevitability' of a great battle seemed to insinuate itself into public consciousness. The idea of war as a horrific calamity to be avoided at all costs had little purchase on these deliberations. War was seen as likely, even necessary, and certainly not the last resort.

Politicians never seriously tried to control their generals, and curb the huge build-up of arms and men, which obviously exacerbated tensions and led historian A. J. P. Taylor to conclude that the belligerents were 'entrapped by the ingenuity of their preparations'.[7] He meant their railway systems and war plans, chiefly the Schlieffen Plan and France's Plan XVII. By extension, he also meant the arsenals, technology and armies on which these war plans depended. The premeditated German encirclement of north-west France, for example, could not have proceeded without the huge new Krupp guns, which were capable of blasting holes in Belgium's fortresses (see Chapter 40).

A sort of collective denial failed to confront obvious flaws in these plans. When Germany abandoned the race for sea supremacy, through the lack of cash, she found herself preparing for a vast land war without a navy capable of challenging Britain's. That made German ports vulnerable to blockade and the German people to starvation. Berlin's military planners turned instead to building their ground forces, which they believed would decide the war. In 1912–14, Berlin prepared to fight a preventive war on two huge fronts without a navy capable of defending its North Sea ports.

To proceed with the Schlieffen Plan in such circumstances would appear senseless folly to any reasonable mind. But the Germans in power were not reasonable. As early as 1908, a young German captain discerned the core of the issue that eluded, or failed to persuade, his superiors in 1914:

> The thought that there is a Power on earth always in a position to annihilate any other navy, and therefore to cut off the country in question from the sea, is a cause for anxiety . . . [O]nly when our fleet is so far developed that it can successfully prevent any blockade can we breathe freely and say that our sea power is equal to our needs.[8]

The German Navy never would be.

—

Could Germany win a battle on land, through a massive counter-boost in their land armies and arsenals? As the world entered 1914, the size of the Triple Alliance's standing armies fell short of the combined might of the Triple Entente. Germany and Austria-Hungary, which most Britons supposed were armed to the teeth, had less than half the number of men in uniform as France and Russia.

Germany responded to the crisis by enforcing universal national service, as recommended by General Erich Ludendorff, a rising star in the Prussian firmament and disciple of Schlieffen, in his 'Great Memorandum' of December 1912. This raised the call-up rate from 52 to 82 per cent – an increase of 300,000 recruits over two years, producing a peacetime German Army of 748,000 men. Adding Austro-Hungarian forces gave a combined total of 1,242,000 in 1913. That was about half the combined strength of the Franco-Russian Army, of 2,170,000 men. Another 116,000 extra Frenchmen conscripted under the new three-year military service were added in 1914.[9]

Nor would Ludendorff's reforms drastically change the picture at the outbreak of war. In mid-1914, Germany and Austria-Hungary would field a wartime force of 3.45 million men, facing a combined Serb, French, Russian and Belgian force of 5.6 million (Britain would supply, initially, 120,000–150,000). The Entente armies contained 218 infantry divisions, to Germany's and Austria-Hungary's 137; and 49 cavalry divisions to the latter's 22. In short, the Entente forces were overwhelmingly more powerful, in terms of sheer numbers, than Germany and Austria-Hungary, the supposed chief aggressors in Europe. France was by far the most militarised nation, with 2.29 per cent of the population serving in the army or navy, compared with Germany's 1.33 per cent and Britain's 1.17 per cent.[10]

These numbers tell only part of the story. Russia's *potential strength*, for example, was what truly disturbed German policymakers: how many Russians would be in uniform in several years? Should Berlin launch a preventive war while the Russians remained vulnerable? The fear of a German first strike hastened the transformation of the Russian Army. Since 1906, it had been able to deploy 1.5 million men, twice that of Germany and 300,000 more than Germany and Austria combined.[11] Yet Russia aimed, with French money, to build a standing army of two million (which it would almost attain in 1917). France's huge investment in Russian railroads further focused German planners on a preventive war.[12]

Yet critical to total manpower were the reserves a nation could draw on for immediate mobilisation. Germany had 760,000 trained reservists in 1913, doubling its peacetime standing army to the size of Russia's. France, however, had just 87,000 reservists immediately available, bringing its total force to a little over 900,000.[13] This put Germany's numerical inferiority in a very different light and encouraged Berlin to stick to an amended version of the Schlieffen Plan.

—

The planning continued. Preparations were made in partial darkness, or in a realm divorced from reality and then wishfully imposed upon it. European intelligence gathering was in its infancy. Wilful blindness to their shortcomings let dangerous ideas bloom. Faith in God, élan and cultural or racial superiority replaced serious attention to weakness and deficiency. German intelligence relied on a press-cutting service. Officers scrutinised the daily papers, in France (such as *L'Écho de Paris*, *Le Gaulois*, *L'Humanité*, *Le Matin* and *Le Temps*), Britain (such as *The Daily News*, *Daily Chronicle*, *The Times* and *The Nation*) and Russia (such as *Birzhevye vedomosti*, *Petersburskii kurier* and *Rech*); and compared the military and service journals of the three countries (for example, in France, *Armée et Démocratie*, *Armée Moderne*, *France Militaire*, *Revue Militaire Generale* and *Journal des Sciences Militaires*), paying special attention to articles by incumbent generals.[14]

This had obvious flaws. Governments routinely planted false stories in the press to deceive their enemies. The British Navy, for instance, leaked news that it would arm the *Invincible* with 9.2-inch guns, which the credulous German Admiralty duly matched; in fact, the *Invincible* received 12-inch guns. Yet Germany's crude cross-referencing delivered, in parts, a surprisingly accurate result, according to a study by the historian Herwig.[15] Berlin knew of the first Anglo-French Army staff talks in 1905, and the joint manoeuvres of the French and Russian armies in the autumn of 1911 (via *Le Matin*).[16] In 1913, the Prussian General Staff were able to discover the size of the French, Russian and Belgian armies, the conversion of the great Russian fortresses of Novo, Georgievsk, Grodno and Kovno into troop-marshalling centres, and the disturbing fact that a double-tracked Trans-Siberian railway would be completed by 1914, 'allowing the Tsar to shuttle nearly six Siberian divisions to the German-Austro-Hungarian front'.[17]

Yet German planners were dead wrong about Russian mobilisation rates, concluding that Russia's first-line troops would be at the front within five days of the order to mobilise, and second-line troops within eight days. In fact, it would take between 15 and 21 days for the Russian Army fully to mobilise in August 1914. The error would hasten the outbreak of war, by provoking Germany to rush to arms at the first sign of Russia's 'partial mobilisation'.

Nor did allies share much information. Deep suspicions divided supposed friends. Sir Henry Wilson, England's most senior

Francophile, admitted he knew nothing of the revised French plan. The Prussian General Staff were similarly in the dark about Austria-Hungary's readiness for war, and so took to spying on their main ally. Their findings, in early 1914, were deeply discouraging. They judged the Habsburg forces, numbering 27,000 officers and 442,000 men, to be well below German standards of intelligence and education; the infantry ill-prepared for modern warfare; and their training and weaponry with 'much to be desired'. In fact, these findings were over-optimistic. Germany prophetically concluded that Conrad's forces, facing the combined strength of Russia and Serbia, 'would be unable to offer much succour to German troops in East Prussia'.[18]

French intelligence was utterly inadequate and near fatally underestimated the German threat. France's High Command misjudged the strength and direction of the coming German offensive and 'quite wrongly based French strategy on an early victory'.[19] France's renewed self-confidence seemed to compensate for her military unreadiness, and mysteriously propelled the idea that pure élan would cut through Germany's ironclad ranks.

—

The great question that troubled all governments and military commanders was which war plan would succeed, at a time when new weapons and huge armies prescribed very different combat conditions? The French Army was hobbled by a flawed strategy, branded 'mad' by Niall Ferguson. This was Joffre's Plan XVII, agreed in May 1913. It fell prey to the 'cult of the offensive' – that a sudden, fast-moving offensive would win the war.[20] It envisaged a cavalry and bayonet charge into the maw of German cannon, delivering up the lost provinces of Alsace and Lorraine in a sudden lunge, as dashing as it was doomed (see Chapter 41). Up to the eve of war, Joffre believed in a swift and assured French victory, despite repeated, chilling reminders of France's inferiority in arms.[21] In fact, French commanders were well aware, months before the outbreak of hostilities,

of the datedness of their heavy artillery and inadequacy of their siege
and fortress guns.[22]

In Germany, Schlieffen's projections of a six-week victory over
the French had given way to estimates from the high command of
a long and tedious struggle. Ludendorff and Moltke warned instead
that Germany would have to fight:

> numerous hard lengthy battles until we force down *one* of our
> enemies . . . we will have to win in several theatres in the West
> and East . . . The need for much ammunition for a long period
> of time will become absolutely necessary.[23]

The aged general Schlieffen had anticipated neither the manpower
shortage nor the transformation of Russian power. Russia's new railroads and huge expansion of its army under the 'Great Program' of
1914 threw German planners into disarray: should they attack now,
to thwart the rise of the giant to the east? '[I]t is easy to understand
now,' Sir Henry Wilson noted early in the year, 'why Germany is
nervous about the future and why she may think that it is a case of
"now or never".'[24] Germany could only hope to win a war on two
fronts if its reserves were rapidly called up and made combat-ready.
That left a very brief window of opportunity.

In anticipation of these problems, in 1913 the Schlieffen Plan
received major surgery under the knife of Moltke, who would concentrate Germany's forces on France and rely more on the weak
Habsburg forces to hold the Russians in the east. Moltke's amendment contained a critical flaw: the German right flank's great
encirclement of northern France – Schlieffen's centrepiece – would
sweep through Belgium in a much weakened form, on the assumption that Belgium's six divisions, dismissed as 'chocolate soldiers',
would offer no resistance.[25] Moltke argued that more units were
needed in the centre, to meet the expected French invasion of
Lorraine. These adjustments reflected Germany's painful awareness of the limits on its manpower. Its main army, half of whom

(760,000) were reservists, faced an apparently insurmountable task.

Whether Moltke's revisions ruined the execution of Schlieffen's plan is impossible to say. The original was already fatally flawed and drew on assumptions that imperilled its execution, chiefly its inflexible timetable and impossible demands on the troops. The problem went much deeper. The blind acceptance of the Schlieffen Plan questioned the sanity, or their claim on common sense, of Prussia's military leaders. The military historian Holger Herwig concluded:

> Germany's leaders based their grand strategies . . . upon certain inflexible ideological convictions and military principles. One needs above all to understand and appreciate that strange composite of historical determinism, racism, and autism which constituted the *mentalité* of Wilhelmian Germany. It cannot be stressed enough that German planners dealt not so much in the day-to-day evaluations as in grand designs, whose sweep often encompassed the lives of a generation or two. The strengths and weaknesses of potential enemies were taken into account only after inflexible blueprints had been drafted.[26]

Whether or not the Prussian leaders were conscious of those considerations, nothing swayed them from their commitment to Schlieffen's basic concept: of a vast two-front battle precipitated by a great wheeling attack through Belgium and north-eastern France. In short, the Schlieffen Plan was, as Hew Strachan concludes, the 'definitive statement'[27] on German thinking and the closest thing to the military equivalent of a prescription for war. Schlieffen died on 4 January 1913, 19 months before the outbreak of war. On his deathbed, he seemed to anticipate the cause of the failure of his plan. His last words were said to have been, 'Remember: keep the right wing very strong.'[28]

Part 2

Part 3

1914 – IN THE SALONS OF POWER

22

A BETTER YEAR?

What we need right now is a war, but I am afraid Franz
Joseph and little Nicholas won't do us the favor.
Vladimir Ilyich Lenin, in a letter to Maxim Gorky in 1913

THE YEAR 1914 OPENED WITH the promise of better things. Surely, the Balkan outrages were behind us, people hoped. Surely, the world seemed a more settled, happier place. So some dared to think. A snapshot of Europe at the time suggests a sense of relief and the anticipation of a prosperous year ahead. The year boded well. Relations between the great powers – especially Britain and Germany – were less tense, notwithstanding the Balkan mess and four political assassinations, including King George of Greece and Hussein Nazim Pasha, commander of the Turkish Army.[1]

The felicitous mood was especially strong in Germany and Russia, which enjoyed booming economies. Britain was in a state of relative economic decline, but most of the country hardly noticed and looked forward to many years of imperial prosperity. Nobody knew, of course, that 1914 would be the year the party ended in Europe. Looking back, the period 1870–1913 would be seen as an economic golden age in European history, in terms of exports and economic growth, exceeded in the twentieth century only by the period 1950–73.[2]

From its commanding heights, Britain's relative decline was already discernible. Unknown to most British people, but detectable to the Treasury, the boom in international investment seemed to be plateauing. Between 1870 and 1913, Britain exported more capital overseas, to finance the empire, than at any other time. By the end of 1913, Britain's overseas assets totalled £4 billion, most of it invested in African mines, South American railways and infrastructure, Asian manufacturing – virtually everywhere Britain had a colony.

At home, the British had had a difficult year, experiencing a new record in industrial strikes and trade disputes. The nation mourned Captain Robert Scott and four of his comrades who had died during their expedition to the South Pole. The all-male parliament voted down votes for women, to the fury of the suffragette movement. The militant women's activist Emily Davison fell or threw herself under the King's horse at the Epsom Derby. Home Rule for Ireland divided both the House of Commons and House of Lords.

The only dull note to the frivolities of high society seemed the new King George V, an abstemious, dutiful man who frowned on the dissipated age, unlike his rakish father, Edward VII, who died in 1910. Notwithstanding his 'uninspiring' character, as he described himself, George was something of an enlightened monarch, instrumental in creating a more politically self-confident country. A year after his coronation, the House of Commons, the elected lower house, won executive power over the unelected House of Lords, through the Parliament Act of 1911. The new King assisted the bill's passage, which reinforced the link between parliament and the people. There was a happy irony in the first cousin of the autocratic Kaiser Wilhelm II and Tsar Nicholas II (with whom George bore a striking resemblance) furthering British democracy. Yet his awkward provenance as the reigning 'German' King of England, Scotland, Wales and Ireland, the patriarch of the House of

Saxe-Coburg and Gotha, unsettled the British people – and in 1917, in deference to extreme anti-German sentiment in Britain, George V would rename his family the House of Windsor.

—

Germany looked forward to another 'festive year'.[3] The Kaiser was more popular than ever, given to carousing with his people in the Tiergarten dressed in the black and white uniform of the Death's Head Hussars, astride a huge white thoroughbred. The previous year had been a big one for Wilhelm. Hoping to invigorate the hollow displays of rote celebration that usually attended his birthday, he had decided to merge the 100th anniversary of Prussia's victory over Napoleon with the silver anniversary of his reign.[4] He thus identified himself personally with the crushing of the French under Napoleon. The union of the two events inspired in many people a kind of 'war mentality' (*Kriegsmentalitat*), which would manifest itself more powerfully in August 1914.[5] The Kaiser's exuberant reassertion of his authority – after the fiasco of the *Daily Telegraph* episode – led to another clanger, in November 1913, when he told King Albert, the Belgian king, during a visit to Berlin that war with France was inevitable. That went down badly with King Albert, but the German people were spared the grisly details. In fact, throughout 1913 and 1914, state propagandists worked hard to remake Wilhelm as a popular ruler – a *Volkskaiser*. They aimed to equate the monarchy with the people. It seemed to be working. To a delighted reception, Wilhelm cast himself as another Frederick the Great, leading a holy crusade of his people against 'those who dare encroach upon her!' (i.e. the French).[6]

This chimed with expectations of another year of glowing economic success. Germany had the most advanced industries in Europe, rapidly growing cities and huge ambitions. German mines and factories now outpaced Britain's in the production of pig iron, iron ore and steel. The names Opel, Benz, Diesel and Krupp were ranked among the world's largest corporations.

The only blot on the rosier outlook seemed to be Russia – always Russia, in German eyes – whose resurgent economic success and huge army darkened Germany's eastern frontier. 'As a soldier,' the Kaiser wrote in late 1913, 'I feel from all the information received, not the slightest doubt that Russia is systematically preparing for war against us and I shape my policy accordingly.' He carried those sentiments into 1914. His government found a reason to be cheerful: relations with Britain had greatly improved, as Chancellor Bethmann-Hollweg told the Reichstag in December 1913. Bethmann-Hollweg held out hopes 'of a permanent rapprochement between nations of the same stock'.[7] He pointedly did not mean the Slavs.

—

The Russians, as 1913 folded into 1914, looked out on a world enshrouded in winter darkness, ice and wind. The austerity of the Tsar's regime added to the gloom. Nicholas had gone one further than his cousin Wilhelm and banned the tango *and* the two-step. The elite seemed not to notice. St Petersburg's aristocracy danced away the season, to the waltz and quadrille, the jingle of sleigh bells in their ears as they arrived at rose balls and fancy-dress parties, which often degenerated into midnight visits to the gypsy colony on the edge of the city. They patronised the best salons, such as the fashionable palace of Princess Olga Orlov, wife of Prince Vladimir Orlov, head of the Tsar's military cabinet. The Tsarina did not partake; she had excluded herself from society, and fell steadily under the influence of Rasputin, the dissolute 'monk' and self-declared faith-healer whose ministrations, she believed, eased the torments of her son, Alexei, a haemophiliac.

The Russian economy was strong. The stockmarket surged. Rampant speculation by a few very rich investors (such as the 'Big Three of St Petersburg'), drew thousands to the bourse in the hope of amassing great wealth. In a 1913 census, 40,000 Russian people described themselves as 'stock market speculators'.[8] 'The provinces joined in the gambling orgies of the capital,' wrote the Grand Duke

Alexander, the Tsar's brother-in-law and a more sentient aristocrat. He continued:

> The haughty leaders of society included stockbrokers in their visiting lists. The aristocratic officers of the Imperial Guards, though unable to distinguish stocks from bonds, began to discuss the imminent rise in the prices on 'broad' steel . . . Fashionable hostesses acquired a habit of featuring the presence of 'that marvellous genius from Odessa who has made a terrific killing in tobacco'. The holy men of the church subscribed to the financial publications, and the velvet-upholstered carriages of the archbishops were often observed in the neighbourhood of the Stock Exchange.[9]

The volatility continued well into 1914.

The Duma, the weak Russian Parliament created after the 1905 revolution, struggled to accommodate Russia's political extremes. On one side, dominating the house, was the Tsarist right wing. At the other extreme, a few Bolsheviks danced to the tune of their exiled leader Vladimir Ilyich Lenin, whose impassioned speeches, copied and circulated, called for the violent overthrow of Tsarism and its replacement with a dictatorship of the proletariat. Lenin longed for a war with Germany, because he believed it would help destroy the Russian ruling class and facilitate the rise of Bolshevism. He would be proved chillingly accurate. 'A war between Austria and Russia would be a very useful thing for the revolution,' he wrote to Maxim Gorky in January 1913, 'but it's not very probable that [Austro-Hungarian emperor] Franz-Josef and [Tsar] Nicky will give us this pleasure.'[10]

In the rural areas, the Duma's policies had attempted to improve the lot of the peasants. Between 1906 and 1914, the State Peasant Land Bank had resold more than 20 million acres of their former landlords' property to the serfs. But the process of agricultural reform was grindingly slow. A growl of discord issued from the towns and cities: Russian cities were among the poorest in Europe. Moscow's population density per housing unit was twice that of Western European cities, with a death rate nearly twice as high.

Meanwhile, work had begun on a vast network of Russian strategic railways, financed by a huge loan from the French Government and deemed crucial in the likelihood of hostilities with Germany. Warmongering was endemic among the militarists and pan-Slavs who dominated the Tsar's court. They rejoiced at the prospect of war, as recorded in the Imperial Russian Army newspaper in the last week of 1913, to Germany's dismay: 'We all know we are preparing for a war in the West. Not only the troops, but the whole nation must accustom itself to the idea that we arm ourselves for a war of annihilation against the Germans . . .' The commanders of the Russian Army, though short of guns, shells, boots and uniforms, declared, 'We are ready.'[11]

—

The French seemed to be in a chronic state of defiance, in politics, military affairs, diplomacy and fashion. In politics, Poincaré defied the radicals and became president (in 1913), earning the opprobrium of Georges Clemenceau, who believed the new government's shrill chauvinism made war with Germany inevitable. The socialist leader Jean Jaurès went much further, issuing defiant appeals to workers to desert the factories, to ignore any call to colours and to refuse to fight for capitalist leaders, should they precipitate war.

Poincaré's priorities were national defence and the preservation of the Triple Entente. He continued to refuse on any grounds to countenance a rapprochement with Germany. He replaced the respected ambassador to Russia, Georges Louis, who had consistently advised Paris against joining Russia in a Balkan war, with the florid, impulsive, strident anti-German Maurice Paléologue. Poincaré's speeches consistently appealed to 'a strong France' and a 'great France', which drove the nation, as Clemenceau feared, to an outpouring of jingoistic sentiment not seen since 1870.

In the military, Joffre defied the warnings that his version of War Plan XVII – which pivoted on a great, glittering French charge into the German lines in Alsace and Lorraine – relied on outdated weaponry and was likely to lead to disaster. The conception of the French offensive lay at the heart of French strategy and gathered great momentum. A stage play called *Alsace* gave new hope to revanchists.

More duels were fought in Paris in 1913 than in any other European capital, mostly between readers and journalists who had offended them. The trend continued in 1914. An unusual rise in cases of *crimes passionnels* – the murder of unfaithful lovers – led to a new law recognising crimes of passion, which would be famously applied in the Caillaux case (see Chapter 26). The start of 1914 saw great festivities in Paris, where the tango, condemned by the clergy as 'a disgusting dance of low origin', proliferated.

—

Underlying the sanguine mood were deep currents of hatred and premonitions of disaster. In the spring of 1914, President Woodrow Wilson had sent his chief adviser, Colonel E. M. House, to evaluate the state of affairs in Europe. House reported to the president:

> The situation is extraordinary. It is militarism run stark mad. Unless someone acting for you can bring about a different understanding, there is some day to be an awful cataclysm. No one in Europe can do it. There is too much hatred, too many jealousies. Whenever England consents, France and Russia will close in on Germany and Austria . . .[12]

Except that he had misread the likely aggressor. In 1914, France had no intention of starting a European war. Russia and Germany, on the other hand, eyed each other with the deepest unease. Nobody knew what Britain would do.

23

EDWARD GREY'S MÉNAGE À QUATRE

*[A] convention between Russia and England . . . concerns
the active co-operations of their naval fighting forces,
should warlike operations, agreed upon by Russia and
England, take place with the participation of France.*
Letter from Sazonov, Russian foreign minister, to his
ambassador on 13–26 May 1914, proposing secret naval
cooperation between London and St Petersburg

EDWARD GREY, the British foreign secretary, seemed to haunt
Whitehall like a wraith. On the face of it, Grey was a well-bred,
upright, decent character within the mould of the Edwardian aristocratic gentleman. Sharp-featured, with deep-set, penetrating eyes, he
belonged to one of England's oldest 'landlord families'.[1] Winchester
and Oxford-educated – where he got a third – his temperament was
authentic 'Old Whig'. If Grey could be said to have enthusiasms,
they were for fly fishing and bird watching (he would publish, in
1927, *The Charm of Birds*). He spent his weekends in the woods and
by the streams, where 'Wordsworth came more readily to his lips

than Parliamentary speeches'.[2]

To the extent that he knew his own mind, Grey acted within the forms and constraints of the rigidly prescribed rites of his class. Displays of emotion, or candour, rather alarmed him. To express a firm position, to commit oneself, he considered naive, undiplomatic and vaguely un-English. It dangerously anchored one's actions to a principle. Far better, in Grey's mind, to play the long game, to hedge one's bets and play either side for all they were worth. He made a virtue of imperturbable inaction. He reacted to events; he rarely initiated them. Class alone cannot explain Grey's famous reserve. He had experienced great personal tragedy, with the deaths of his first wife and brother, and seems to have internalised his grief to the point of self-excision. Sometimes, he seemed not to be there.

A closer look reveals a thoughtful man, of greater ability than he was credited with, who often seemed deeply preoccupied: perhaps with his beloved birds? No, he was too serious to allow his pastimes to intrude on duty. Yet his mind did seem, disarmingly, elsewhere – on a different agenda. Nobody knew exactly how he felt or what he believed. Nobody outside the closed circle of the Foreign Office – and the secretary's mental gymnastics perplexed even his colleagues – knew how far Grey supported the Entente. As such, France and Russia detected a slightly sinister note beneath his cheerfulness.

And yet, his reform-mindedness confounded any attempt to portray him as stuffy and fogeyish. He was a man of great contradictions. In political terms, Grey was a true liberal. He helped reform the House of Lords, supported the suffragettes and strongly backed the National Insurance Bill. He was closely attuned to the demands of the new industrial working class, even as he looked down on their troubles from the great height of the English aristocracy. Therein lay the extraordinary *range* of his character. Socially at ease among the upper classes, he stretched his mind to comprehend the needs of the people.

No doubt, Grey and his Foreign Office colleagues were sincere in trying to avoid war. In Grey's mind, Britain was the wise old imperialist who had a duty, a *noblesse oblige*, to preserve the European peace. Yet his handling of the coming July crisis was 'so inept and dilatory', noted Albertini, over-harshly, 'that it failed to avert the catastrophe'.[3] To expect one man to avert the march to war was asking too much. None was able to grasp the reins of destiny and pull the world to its senses in July 1914 – the crisis month. Only a concerted effort could have done so, and that was distinctly lacking.

Yet Grey's diplomatic qualities were utterly inadequate to the challenge of 1914. He refused to make promises or commitments, and seemed to assume his sheer niceness would please everyone. Times such as these, however, called for sterner stuff. Grey's 'wait and see' style, his glad-handing of friend and foe, had the effect of raising suspicions and ratcheting up the tension. The more he strove for conciliation, to befriend all comers, the less he conciliated any of them. When Europe needed an assertive British bulldog, they got a vacillating fly fisherman.

All this seemed the product of a crushing fatalism, common to the mentality of Grey's class and to the lessons of his experience. One could merely try to influence events, not halt or fundamentally alter them, what happens will happen, and there's nothing new under the sun except British interests. Such seemed to sum up his mature outlook. In his younger days, however, Grey had been a passionate believer in principles, in the possibility of politics to effect change.

—

It was an older, not necessarily wiser, Edward Grey who guided British foreign policy in 1914. In the art of diplomacy, Grey's only constant was his inconsistency. If he had always seen Germany as the true enemy, as he often suggested, he never showed the courage of that conviction. He refused to stamp British military support on the Entente, a show of power that may have deterred German aggression and placed him in a position of strength from which to mediate.

By the spring, it seemed too late to play that hand. Grey had simply taken too long to impose British power. He drip-fed his conflicting loyalties to his European 'friends', which maximised their confusion. Until the last moment, he tantalised the Entente and the Germans with offers of friendship. 'In seeking friendship with both European power blocs,' writes Michael Ekstein, 'Grey was putting himself in a position where he was reluctant to fall out with either; and so in July 1914 he lacked a capacity for decisive action. It was left to other more committed nations to take the lead.'[4] Wittingly or not, right up to the outbreak of war, Grey let Berlin believe in the possibility of British neutrality. As we shall see, his vacillations and diplomatic feints added a potent ingredient to the recipe for a European war. Nowhere was this policy more dangerous than in his fresh attempt to charm the Germans.

———

In Berlin's eyes, a war with Russia drew nearer. The aim would be to *prevent* Russia from growing too powerful to defeat, to cut it down now before it was too late. In early 1914, senior German and Austro-Hungarian officials believed the time had come to strike. Moltke and Conrad, chiefs of their respective General Staffs, were the most vocal in expressing this belief.

The reasons were clear to Edward Grey, among other close observers of Germany in the British Foreign Office. Germany, despite its domestic economic success, had failed in ways that made the country a serious menace: it had failed to build a navy large enough to rival Britain's; it had failed to build a colonial empire; it had failed to fulfil the hopes of *Weltpolitik*. Psychologically, Germany felt cornered. Militarily, Berlin was ready to seize through force what she claimed to have been denied. The German people looked out on a hostile world that curbed their global aspirations.

Russian economic and military success rubbed salt into these wounds. In a few years, the Tsar's army would be at least twice the size of the Kaiser's. 'Russia's expanding military might was the major development in international relations in the year or so before the war,' writes Ekstein.[5] Social Darwinism lent weight to the argument that Germany should strike now, to stifle Russia's runaway strength.

In early 1914, Edward Grey tried to understand the world from Berlin's point of view. He believed Germany probably would launch a preventive war, lashing out, as it were, from her fortress. George Buchanan, the British ambassador in St Petersburg, had sent him a stream of reports on Russia's military strength, warning that 'unless Germany is prepared to make still further financial sacrifices for military purposes, the days of her hegemony in Europe will be numbered'.[6] Moreover, Russia's French-financed strategic railways would soon reach the German frontier. Both of these developments greatly disturbed the German leadership.

Russia's resurgent power transformed relations within the Triple Entente. The Franco-Russian Alliance, the core of the pact and the central deterrent to Germany, was stronger in 1914 than ever before. French spirits had revived. Its armed forces had returned to full strength and the French people were rampantly patriotic. Joined at the hip, France and Russia had grown arrogant, disconsolate, and demanded a higher price from London for their friendship. They pressed the British Government to declare its hand: were the British people with them in a war against Germany or not?

The Asquith government's vacillations especially worried Russia, which began to demand Britain's open support as the price of Entente membership. Thus far, no official treaty or alliance bound Britain to her Entente partners, merely self-interest and vague goodwill. This uncertainty prompted constant speculation in Paris and St Petersburg. Would Britain fight, if it came to blows? Or abstain? British fence sitting had become intolerable.

'The peace of the world,' Sergei Sazonov, the Russian foreign minister, wrote to his London ambassador Count Benckendorff on 19 February, 'will only be secure on the day when the Triple Entente, whose real existence is not better authenticated than the existence of the sea serpent, shall transform itself into a defensive alliance without secret clauses and publicly announced in all the world's press.'[7]

—

The likelihood of this plummeted when, in early 1914, relations between Berlin and London strangely improved. Indeed, they enjoyed a rare détente. There were even rumours of an Anglo-German alliance, eliciting the deepest anxiety in Paris and St Petersburg. The Anglo-German thaw related, as always, to the preservation of the British Empire and the delicate balancing act London constantly performed to protect it. This time, Franco-Russian colonial rivalries threatened British assets in the Middle East and Asia, and Germany offered a useful wedge in the great game.

It helped that Berlin seemed more approachable, in Grey's eyes, and somehow more mature. Hadn't the German leadership behaved constructively in disputes over the Balkans, Portuguese colonies and the Berlin to Baghdad Railway? The latter was especially sensitive, because it would give Germany a port in the Persian Gulf, threatening British trade in the region. The hopes of a deal augured well at the beginning of the year (one would be signed on 15 June 1914, removing Anglo-German tensions over the railway, and removing it as a cause of the war). In this light, Grey looked on Germany anew, as a potential friend.

Thus began a period of extraordinary British brinkmanship. It flirted with Germany while professing loyalty to the Entente, and immeasurably exacerbated tensions in Europe. London's dalliance with Germany was intolerable to Britain's Entente partners. Grey's strange notion that he could play off France and Russia against Germany may have seemed a clever gambit, but such tactics were unsustainable. Not even the elasticity of the Foreign Office's interpretation of loyalty stretched this far, as Buchanan made clear in a dispatch to Grey in April 1914:

> the great question [is] whether our understanding with Russia should be solidified into a defensive alliance or not . . . whether the advantages of being intimate friends of Russia is greater . . . than the disadvantage of being on our former cold terms with Germany. I doubt, no! I am sure we cannot have it both ways:

i.e. form a defensive alliance with France and Russia and at the
same time be on cordial terms with Germany.[8]

Buchanan chose Russia and France. He supported stronger relationships within the Triple Entente, possibly a British alliance with its
de facto partners. So, too, in varying degrees, did Crowe, Nicolson,
Bertie (in Paris), Goschen (in Berlin) and other senior British
ambassadors and diplomats. The country's military leaders strongly
favoured the Entente. It incensed Sir Henry Wilson, for example,
that Britain had so far refused openly to side with France. Younger
English diplomats, however, were friendlier towards Berlin and
appreciated the danger of antagonising the isolated German regime.
For them, Russia represented a cold, reactionary dictatorship with
no claim on British friendship. The Cabinet and government were
deeply divided on the issue. At one stage, more than half of the
Liberal MPs were either pro-German, neutralist or anti-war.

The choice sat at Grey's door. True to form, he refused to decide
either way. He continued to walk the tightrope between reassuring his Entente partners and appeasing his new German friends.
When either side pressed him to choose, he did nothing. He cheered
them all along, or spoke in warm platitudes, or simply vacillated.
Grey pursued this 'policy', or chronic state of indecision, until early
August.

—

In early 1914, St Petersburg, with French backing, moved to cement
relations with London once and for all. A strong motive was the
worst reverse in Russo-German relations in a decade. The catalyst
was the so-called Liman von Sanders Crisis in the winter of 1913–
14. This was the last straw for Sazonov, Russia's panic-prone foreign
minister.

The details seem innocuous, but the repercussions were immense
in this closed diplomatic world. Berlin provocatively named General
Otto Liman von Sanders, son of a wealthy family from Pomerania,

to head a 42-man military mission to Constantinople to retrain the Turkish Army, then vanquished and humiliated after the Balkan Wars. The five-year appointment effectively placed a German in command of the Turkish forces. Liman von Sanders would enjoy unusual influence: a seat on the Turkish War Council, from where he had the power to promote Turkish senior officers.

The announcement infuriated Sazonov. The German mission to Turkey amounted to 'a mortal blow'[9] to Russia's aspirations in the Black Sea and the Dardanelles. By commanding the Turks, von Sanders effectively took control of Constantinople, 'the nodal point', Sazonov later wrote, 'which stood at the junction of Europe and Asia' and 'the most important point on the famous Hamburg-Baghdad line'.[10] In Sazonov's mind, Berlin had entrusted the German mission with 'the task of firmly establishing German influence in the Turkish Empire'.[11] (Events would prove him right. In 1915, Liman von Sanders commanded the Turkish forces in the Dardanelles and made the inspired decision to promote Mustafa Kemal to lead the Turkish 19th Division, which would win a great victory over the British and ANZAC forces at Gallipoli, thus saving the Ottoman peninsula and denying the Allies a 'third front' against Germany.)

Sazonov acted at once. He meant to use the crisis to shoehorn London into a full military alliance with St Petersburg and Paris. His campaign began with an offer to talk. In March 1914, Sazonov proposed that Britain and Russia engage in joint naval and military discussions, with a view to shared operations. The Russophiles in Whitehall welcomed the offer, but Grey found himself in an extremely awkward position: how could he befriend Berlin while holding naval talks with Russia? St Petersburg and Berlin, like rival partners at a ball, wanted London to sign the top of their dance cards. 'Each power,' wrote Ekstein, 'now tried to wrest Great Britain from the sway of the other, but Grey's hope was to maintain good relations with both.'[12]

The tenth anniversary of the Entente Cordiale, celebrated by King George's state visit to Paris in April 1914, intensified Grey's dilemma: Anglo-Russian military talks would be on the Paris agenda. In Paris, Grey did his best to diminish their importance. As usual, he obfuscated and dithered, and sought refuge in talks about talks and the definition of the nature of the Triple Entente. On his return to London, the Cabinet met and agreed to hold naval talks with Russia, but in complete secrecy. But this served only to sharpen London's duplicity: to embrace Berlin while holding *secret* talks about battleships with Russia. Should the secret leak, the damage would be immense. The British foreign minister thought he could have it both ways: feathering the nest of the Triple Entente while reassuring the Germans that they had nothing to fear. The consequences of his diplomatic deceit were severe.

—

A case of espionage blew Grey's balancing act out of the water. In early 1914, a spy called Benno de Siebert, working for Germany in the Russian Embassy in London, sent to Berlin highly sensitive information on the proposed naval talks between London and St Petersburg. The fact that the 'talks' never amounted to much (and were stalled by the outbreak of war) is not the point. The point is Bethmann-Hollweg read the intelligence alongside Britain's public disavowals of any such talks with Russia. And he felt a deep sense of betrayal. De Siebert sent extracts of correspondence between Count Alexander Benckendorf, the Russian ambassador in London, and Sazonov, between April and May 1914. Their contents devastated Grey's hopes of maintaining better relations with Germany. Here is a brief selection.

On joint naval operations (in a letter from Benckendorf to Sazonov on 3 May 1914):

> Just as the agreements entered into with France, provide . . . for
> the cooperation of the armies, so, according to Sir Edward Grey,
> the nature of things demands that the eventual agreements with
> Russia should relate to the navy.

On Prime Minister Asquith's support for joint Anglo-Russian operations (in letters from 5–18 May):

> Asquith . . . is very favourably disposed to . . . eventual military conventions between Russia and England analogous to those which exist between France and England.[13]

A letter from Sazonov to the Russian ambassador, 15–28 May, contained a series of extremely undiplomatic revelations: the possible extent of Anglo-Russian operations in the North Sea, and the sharing of signals, cables and cyphers – which horrified German intelligence when it arrived. Sazonov wrote:

> On May 13–26, 1914, a consultation took place in the office of the Chief of Naval Staff . . . as to a convention between Russia and England, which concerns the active co-operations of their naval fighting forces, should warlike operations, agreed upon by Russia and England, take place with the participation of France
> . . .

Demanding Britain to send more ships to the Mediterranean and to permit Russian vessels to use British ports, Sazonov concluded his extraordinary shopping list:

> the conference recognised that it was desirable that all details of the relations, between the Russian and the British navies . . . should be established. For this purpose, it will be necessary to come to an understanding as to signals and special ciphers, wireless messages, and the relations between the British and the Russian naval staffs . . .[14]

———

On receiving this intelligence, Berlin fell into a state of profound despondency. Grey's juggling act had been blown wide open, and the usually restrained Bethmann-Hollweg was on the warpath. Whitehall's treachery was unconscionable, but he needed conclusive proof that Anglo-Russian naval talks were serious and hostile.

Bethmann-Hollweg decided to tease an answer out of London by placing an 'exclusive' story in the German newspaper *Berliner Tageblatt*, 'sourced' to Paris. The article, which first reported the 'naval talks' between Russia and Britain, provoked a heated debate in the House of Commons, as Bethmann-Hollweg hoped. Would Grey please explain the rumoured naval talks with Russia, an MP asked the foreign secretary. Grey gave an unconvincing reply, which did nothing to warm London's cooling relations with Berlin. The German Government, Grey later wrote, 'are now genuinely alarmed at the military preparation in Russia . . .'[15] His own actions had been instrumental in alarming them.

The Anglo-German détente thus fizzled out as quickly as it had come to life. Grey refused to accept its failure. He made a diplomatic art of self-deception. Alone in Europe, he imagined he could indulge in a ménage à quatre: befriend the German eagle, calm the Russian bear and pacify the French cock – all in British interests. He would fail to satisfy any of them. Meanwhile, the true shape of European power lay exposed for all to see: if the Triple Entente and Triple Alliance were not hostile blocs deeply willing the world to war, then they were nothing. That was how the Kaiser, Bethmann-Hollweg, Moltke, Berchtold and Conrad viewed the Entente in early 1914. And that was the forbidding psychological state in which Berlin and Vienna received news of the assassination in Sarajevo.

24

THE USES OF FRANZ
FERDINAND, DEAD

*[Germany] would be choked to death by a ring of enemies
. . . by Slav race hatred against Teutons, and by lowering
ill-will against the victor of 1870. And that is the
reason why German policy thought it proper to approve
Austria's decision to take action against Serbia.*

Chancellor Bethmann-Hollweg

RECKLESSNESS, PRIDE OR PIG-HEADEDNESS explained the
Austrian Archduke Franz Ferdinand's decision to persevere with a
state visit to Sarajevo, the capital of Bosnia-Herzegovina, on St Vitus'
Day, 28 June 1914, when Bosnian Serbs were celebrating the anniversary of the sacred Battle of Kosovo. Probably, it was a combination
of all three. Ferdinand, heir to the Austro-Hungarian throne, was a
vain, impulsive man, of limited intelligence, given to unrealistic ideas
about the future of the empire. In 1914, he was 50 years old, and he
believed the lie that his popularity exceeded the confines of his small
circle of nodding courtiers, anxious for placement when he ascended
the throne, many of whom he dismissed as 'toadies'.

In fact, he was widely disliked, at court and among the Austrian elite. He had a tendency to fly at his detractors, in bursts of violent rage. He had more than a touch of the Kaiser's spoilt-brattishness (the two were friends). 'When I am Commander-in-Chief,' he once told Conrad, 'I shall do as I will; if anyone does anything else I shall have them all shot.'[1] And yet, for a Habsburg, he was unusually reform-minded: he encouraged the self-determination of the non-Serbian Slavs, and the Hungarian minorities, to the fury of the Magyar elite. His strengths were probably administrative: he made sensible changes to the Austrian military. And there was another, personal side. His tenderness to those he loved redeemed him. A happily married man – in a world in which happy marriages were rare – he doted on his wife, whom the Austrian court contemptuously dismissed as 'common', and their children, and his family responded by providing him with a warm and loving refuge from the coldness of the Viennese court.

It was a brilliant summer's day in Sarajevo. The archduke and duchess had completed their duties over the previous two days – he had inspected military manoeuvres, she had visited schools and orphanages – and they were now heading into town for a welcoming ceremony and formal celebration of their 14th wedding anniversary. The Bosnian capital put on a strained show of loyalty to the visiting Habsburg heir. The dynasty's black and yellow standard with the red eagle in the centre flew on the streets and draped the archduke's motorcade. The representatives of a dozen different minorities obediently turned out in their religious and military attire. 'The very headgear,' writes Adam Hochschild, 'reflected the crazy quilt of this ungainly empire that threatened to come apart at the seams: homburgs, yarmulkes, mitres, fezzes, turbans, plus cavalry helmets and brimmed military caps . . .'[2]

Yet the mood in the city was tense, and the authorities were nervous. The timing of the visit gravely offended the Bosnian Serb minority. Over the previous days, the governor of Bosnia, General Oskar Potiorek, had ignored clear warnings about violent groups of Bosnian Serbs. The Bosnian chief of police, Dr Edmund Gerde, alone seemed to realise the provocation of a state visit on St Vitus' Day, and appealed to the town's military committee to take extra precautions. 'Don't worry, these lesser breeds would not dare to do anything,' replied the committee chairman, a highly bred Austrian. As he minuted Gerde's concerns, he added, scornfully, 'You see phantoms everywhere.'[3] Security was extremely lax. Gerde's requests for an additional cordon of soldiers to reinforce the police (he had only 120 men) had been ignored. The archduke's itinerary was even published in the papers the day before.

—

Phantoms *were* everywhere. A seven-man Bosnian-Serb death squad had been assigned to assassinate Franz Ferdinand. Trained in Serbia, they had been smuggled across the border a few weeks earlier. They answered to the Serbian 'revolutionary' network formed in 1911 called *Ujedinjenje ili Smrt* (Unification or Death), or 'The Black Hand' by its enemies. The Black Hand dignified itself as a 'nationalist movement' with close connections to the Serbian revolutionary group *Narodna Odbrana* (National Defence), formed after the annexation of Bosnia-Herzegovina (see Chapter 13). *Narodna Odbrana*'s initial purpose 'was to recruit and train partisans for a possible war between Serbia and Austria', writes Michael Shackelford. It evolved into a pan-Slavic cultural movement and lost authority to the powerful inner circle of The Black Hand, who took over the dirty work of terrorising and assassinating Serbia's enemies.[4] New members of The Black Hand were obliged to swear 'before God, on my honor and my life, that I will execute all missions and commands without question. I swear before God, on my honor and on my life, that I will take all the secrets of this organization into my grave with me'.[5]

The Black Hand's commander, to whom the district committees and cells ultimately answered, was Colonel Dragutin Dimitrijević (code-named 'Apis'), who presided over a ten-member Executive

Committee based in Belgrade. Despite their links with the Serbian Government, neither the committee nor the government approved the plot to kill the archduke. It was Dimitrijević's personal project. He planned the assassination and selected the assassins, without the backing of the Serb authorities, who saw that it might lead to war with Austria.

In this light, Dimitrijević and the members of The Black Hand were not as 'secret' as they liked to portray themselves. Well known to the Serbian Government, Dimitrijević had served as head of the Serbian General Staff's Intelligence Service and was closely connected with senior politicians. He frequented fashionable Belgrade coffee shops, where he liked to hint at his secretive work. Other Black Hand members held important army and political posts and influenced government policy. 'The Serbian government was fairly well informed of Black Hand activities,' writes Shackelford. 'Crown Prince Alexander was an enthusiastic and financial supporter.'[6] Yet their friendly relations had cooled by 1914. Serb prime minister Nikola Pašić had displeased the organisation, it seems – and especially Dimitrijević – by not acting aggressively enough in fostering the pan-Serb cause. Even so, there is little doubt that the Serbian Government knew in advance of a murder plot to kill Franz Ferdinand. The question is whether the Belgrade government actively supported The Black Hand in carrying out the assassination (see Chapter 26).

——

In this light, Dimitrijević deserves closer examination. By June 1914, he was something of a legend in the grisly business of assassination, with a long history of violence on behalf of the Serbian state. Cunning, cultured and articulate, he was a gentleman killer quite unlike the rougher breed of Serbia's past heroes. 'He had the characteristics which cast a spell on men,' his enemy Stanojević wrote admiringly.[7] He was a brilliant organiser, utterly ruthless and scrupulously loyal. His chief flaw was that he laboured under the illusion that he had none. 'Dimitriević was convinced that his own ideas were the right ones on all matters, events and circumstances,' wrote Stanojević. 'He believed that his opinions and activities enjoyed the monopoly of patriotism. Hence anyone who did not agree with him could not in his eyes be either honourable or wise or a patriot.'[8]

In other words, Apis was not very politically astute. If he possessed a sharp military brain, his political ideas were 'dim and confused', actuated by little more than hatred of Austria-Hungary and the Ottoman Empire. He recurs with Flashman-like frequency at earlier scenes of gore and bloodshed, spilt in the name of Serbia. In 1903, on behalf of the government, who disapproved of the dynastic plans of the then royal family, Dimitrijević led the assassination of King Alexander I and his wife, Queen Draga, the last of the Obrenović dynasty. They were dispatched with customary Serbian overkill. Wrenched from their hiding place – the bedroom cupboard, or, some claim, a 'panic room' – the 26-year-old king and his young wife were shot, mutilated, disembowelled and, lest any signs of life remained, thrown from a second-floor window of the palace onto piles of garden manure.[9] For his role in the assassinations, the parliament proclaimed Dimitrijević 'the saviour of the Fatherland'.

Promoted to professor of Tactics at the Military Academy, Dimitrijević excelled at war games and planned several victories in the Balkan Wars of 1912–13. From 1911, he doubled as leader of The Black Hand and drew up a list of assassination targets. He had planned to start at the top, with the murder of Emperor Franz Joseph – the grandeur of the target flattered Apis's ambitions. This came to nothing, and in early 1914 Dimitrijević turned his attention to the heir to the throne.

—

Franz Ferdinand had made himself a prime target by promising concessions to the southern Balkan states still under Austro-Hungarian rule, such as Bosnia-Herzegovina and Croatia, which contained many Serbs. This received little support at court, where Ferdinand

incurred the wrath of the emperor, his uncle, and the anti-Slav movement. Nor did it appease the Serbs. Had it succeeded, Ferdinand's
plan would have frustrated Serbia's hopes of unifying the Slavs into a
single state, with its capital in Belgrade. Franz Ferdinand thus found
himself caught between the Slav haters in Vienna and the Habsburg
haters in Belgrade. The Balkans were no place for moderates and
appeasers. Nor did he endear himself to the Hungarians: his anti-
Magyar views enraged the Magyar elite. The heir to the throne was a
marked man – on all sides of politics.

In 1914, Dimitrijević and his henchmen selected the assassination squad: seven impoverished Bosnian youths, bound by their
wretched provenance, revolutionary zeal and hatred of Austria-
Hungary. Three – Gavrilo Princip, Nedeljko Čabrinović and Trifko
Grabež – were trained in bomb throwing and marksmanship, and
were smuggled back into Bosnia a few weeks before St Vitus' Day.
There followed a confusing period, during which The Black Hand's
top committee, acting without Apis's support, ordered the cancellation of the assassination and the recall of the mission. The order was
too late, or ignored. The latter seems most likely, given the network
of Black Hand agents who could have got word to the assassins, who
'idled around in Sarajevo for a month. Nothing more was done to
stop them.'[10]

Of the seven assassins, Gavrilo ('Gavro') Princip was the leader
and driving force – a quiet lad with a ruthless determination that
echoed Apis's. Born in 1894 into the impoverished Bosnian village
of Obljaj, his unforgiving, unsanitary upbringing was depressingly
typical of the Bosnian peasantry. He was raised in a little hut with
an earthen floor, furnished with chests, a stone bench and an open
hearth, above which hung a few metal cauldrons. He was one of
nine children, six of whom died at birth or in infancy.[11] His father, a
farmer and postman, was an austere man of devout Orthodox inclinations. His mother, a chronically hard-working woman of more
pragmatic leanings, seemed to endure the wrath of God as stoically
as she did another baby and the weather. To young Gavro, the great

world appeared to him through legends and stories. The Princip men had a long and honourable tradition of resistance to the Ottomans – a rebellious spirit they now directed at the Austro-Hungarians. They shared memories and legends of great Serb victories at *selos*, village gatherings of entertainment and poetry readings, which gave vent to a litany of grievances.

Gavro was a keen student, who read quietly, absorbed a great deal and developed a keen sense of classroom justice. '[E]very blow he received he would return twofold,' his mother was quoted as saying.[12] With the help of his 20-year-old brother, he enrolled in a commercial school in Sarajevo, but his interests strayed to student politics. He later attended Sarajevo High School, a seedbed of student radicalism. He wrote poems and lyrical vignettes, romantic and solipsistic. A brief love affair bloomed and faltered. His general hatred for Bosnia's Austrian overlords sharpened into a yearning for action. This 'emotional, solitary' youth, Dr Martin Pappenheim, his prison medical officer, would later write, dreamt of the 'union of the southern Slavs outside the framework of Austria', to be achieved by revolution and assassination.[13] Expelled from school for laziness and student activism, Gavro left home and walked 300 kilometres to Belgrade, kissing the soil, he later claimed, at the Serbian border.[14] There, he joined the company of self-exiled Bosnian Serbs, keen to avenge their little country. Like other young Bosnians, this slight, insecure, sharp-minded young man, acutely focused on his political enemies, was a gift to The Black Hand, who secretly recruited and trained him.

—

The motorcade made its way along Appel Quay. Franz Ferdinand and his wife sat in the third vehicle, a gleaming Graf and Stift open sports car, facing General Potiorek, the governor of Bosnia. The leading automobile carried the mayor and chief of police; further dignitaries rode in the two other vehicles. The archduke sported a blue serge tunic, black trousers, white gloves, a brace of medals and peaked hat adorned with green peacock feathers, the ceremonial uniform of a general of the Hussars; the duchess wore a wide white hat, with an ostrich-feather veil, a dress of white silk, tied with a red sash, and an ermine stole.

The motorcade advanced towards the junction of three bridges, where the seven assassins were waiting: five (Danilo Ilić, Vijetko Popović, Mohamed Mehmedbašić, Nedeljko Čabrinović and Vaso Čubrilović) at the Cumuria Bridge, armed with a bomb and revolvers; Gavrilo Princip at the Latin Bridge, armed with a pistol; and Trifko Grabež at the third bridge. A 'regular avenue of assassins', the archbishop of Sarajevo later described it.[15]

The archduke survived the first bridge. A bomb thrown by Nedeljko Čabrinović rolled off the hood and exploded against a back wheel of the oncoming car, slightly wounding Potiorek's aide-de-camp, who was taken to hospital. The other assassins lost their nerve and failed to shoot. Čabrinović tried to escape along the riverbed but was soon caught and arrested. He swallowed a cyanide pill, but it was old and merely induced vomiting. Shaken, but determined to look unfazed, Ferdinand ordered the motorcade to continue. No precautions were taken, and the car's hood remained down. The vehicle sped off, too fast for the two remaining assassins to target it.

Only on arriving at the Town Hall did Ferdinand notice the slight graze on the duchess's neck, where the bomb's detonator had struck her. This elicited a strange response in her husband: selfish indignation and bravado, rather than caution or protectiveness for his wife. He dismissed a rushed exit under a security cordon, as advised, as a sign of weakness. Ferdinand made his hurt feelings known by interrupting, in high-blown tones, the mayor's welcoming speech: 'Mr Mayor, I came here on a state visit and I get bombs thrown at me. It is outrageous. Now you may speak.'[16] Dismayed silence met this bizarre interruption, and the official proceedings resumed.

Their Highnesses had displayed 'the greatest coolness', remarked Count Franz von Harrach, who travelled in the front seat of the archduke's vehicle. After the bomb attack, Ferdinand told him (he recalled), 'Today we shall get a few more bullets still . . .'[17] General Potiorek played down the risk of a second attack – yet, at the same time, he advised amending the program. They would not visit the museum, as planned, he suggested, but return at speed along another route. Ferdinand objected: he must first visit the slightly wounded man (Colonel Merizzi) in hospital – a perverse decision in the circumstances. That involved returning along the Appel Quay, the same route as published in the itinerary.

As they approached the Latin Bridge, where Princip lurked near Moritz Schiller's delicatessen, the chauffeur of the lead car seemed to lose his head. He took a sharp right into the narrow Francis Joseph Street, the original route. The archduke's car followed but had to stop when the driver of the leading car, realising his error, and with Potiorek shouting for them to return to the altered route, began reversing.

At this point, Princip lunged forward to the right-hand side of the open vehicle, where the archduke and the duchess sat exposed. The first bullet struck Ferdinand in the jugular; the second hit his wife in the stomach. Count Harrach witnessed the couple's last moments alive:

> Her Highness cried, 'For God's sake! What has happened to you?' Then she sank down from her seat with her face between the archduke's knees . . . Then his Royal Highness said: 'Soferl, Soferl! Don't die. Live for my children!' Thereupon I seized the Archduke by the coat-collar to prevent his head from sinking forwards and asked him, 'Is Your Royal Highness in great pain?' To which he clearly replied: 'It is nothing.' Now his expression changed and he repeated six or seven times: 'It is nothing', more and more losing consciousness.[18]

The royal couple were dead on arrival at the hospital. Princip was beaten to the ground before he could shoot himself or swallow his cyanide capsule. He was carted off to the police station. Judge Pfeffer later observed, after interrogating Princip:

The young assassin, exhausted by beating, was unable to utter a word. He was undersized, emaciated, sallow, sharp-featured . . . his clear blue eyes, burning and piercing but serene, had nothing criminal or cruel in their expression. They spoke of innate intelligence . . . he regarded the Heir Apparent as the embodiment of the supreme power which exercised its terrible pressure on the Yugoslavs.[19]

Princip told the judge:

From the footboard, I aimed at the Archduke . . . I do not remember what I thought . . . I know only that I fired twice or perhaps several times, without knowing whether I had hit or missed, because at that moment the crowd began to beat me.[20]

Borijove Jevtic, a leader of *Narodna Odbrana* who was arrested with Princip, shared a prison cell with the assassin. He recalls that, when Princip was awoken at night and told he would be taken to another prison, he appealed to the prison governor:

There is no need to carry me to another prison. My life is already ebbing away. I suggest that you nail me to a cross and burn me alive. My flaming body will be a torch to light my people on their path to freedom.[21]

At his trial, Princip showed no remorse. He maintained his silence about The Black Hand, saying only:

In trying to insinuate that someone else has instigated the assassination, one strays from the truth. The idea arose in our own minds, and we ourselves executed it. We have loved the people. I have nothing to say in my defence.

Confused over whether he turned 20 before or after the crime, the court gave him the benefit of the doubt and he escaped the death penalty. He was sentenced to life imprisonment and would die in the hospital of Theresienstadt Prison in April 1918, of tuberculosis of the bone, a few months before the end of the war.

—

For a few days, European governments were unmoved. Nobody then imagined that the murder would trigger events leading to the outbreak of a world war. No head of state acted with any urgency. The assassination was a regrettable tragedy, which would exacerbate Austro-Serbian tensions, no more. The outpourings of anger in the press and on the streets – with the unleashing of lynch mobs against Serbs – flared up and died down. The event had none of the extreme tension of Agadir or the Balkan Wars. Not until four days later did Vienna start to fume at this outrageous attack on the dignity of the monarchy.

The likely repercussions for Serb-Austrian relations were not high in Poincaré's mind, for example. The French president was at Longchamp when he heard the news, and he saw no reason to abandon the joy of witnessing the Baron de Rothschild's horse win the Grand Prix.[22] Other matters of state and a sensational murder trial, of the wife of the former prime minister Joseph Caillaux, occupied his mind. In London, Edward Grey's government was similarly unmoved: a Bosnian Serb had committed a heinous crime, and commiserations were sent to Vienna. In Berlin, most senior officials were away and did not see fit to return to address the matter. The Kaiser was at the Kiel Regatta, the chancellor at his country estate, and Moltke, the chief of staff, and Tirpitz were on holiday. Even the German press, after its initial huffing and puffing, expressed the hope that Austria would exercise restraint and the crime should not trigger a new Balkan war.

In Vienna and Budapest, the murders carried darker consequences. At first, nobody cared beyond the enactment of the usual rituals; some were disgracefully relieved. The emperor Franz Joseph showed extraordinarily little remorse at the death of his nephew and heir to his throne. On hearing the news, he was heard to sigh, 'It is God's will!'[23] God, he meant, had intervened to preserve the crown from his nephew, whom he loathed. A less credible account has the emperor falling, thunderstruck, into a chair, mumbling, 'Horrible . . . Horrible!' and then exclaiming suddenly, as if to himself, 'The Almighty is not mocked! . . . Order which I, alas, had not the strength to maintain, has been restored by a higher will.'[24] In public, he made no effort even to seem upset by the couple's death. Four days after the murders, he met the German ambassador and regaled him with talk of hunting, the death of the Italian chief of staff, and other chatter, but said nothing about the assassinations. On 5 July, he told Conrad merely that he regretted not advising Ferdinand against the trip to Bosnia.

The sources of the emperor's callous reaction were well known in Vienna. Franz Joseph had little feeling for the archduke and less for his wife, Sophia. The emperor had dreaded the thought of the empire passing to the couple. The death by suicide of his only son, Crown Prince Rudolph, fated the crown to his nephew, the next in line, and, if that sequence was not distressing enough for the old man, Franz Ferdinand further infuriated him by marrying a 'low-born' woman. Though the product of a prominent aristocratic family from the Kingdom of Bohemia (now the Czech Republic), Sophia Chotek had been treated in Vienna as if she had no royal lineage, making her ineligible to serve as empress-consort (in fact, she had been a distant descendant of the sister of King Rudolph I of Germany).

The emperor had refused to permit the union, but hotheaded Franz had gone ahead regardless, disgracing himself at court and rendering the marriage morganatic. The court had grudgingly bestowed upon his new wife the title of 'Duchess of Hohenberg' but refused to let her perform the normal 'affairs of state' – such as appearing by her husband's side at the right balls. Further alienating the emperor had been Franz Ferdinand's curiously subversive ideas, which the Viennese court and Hungary's Magyar elite regarded as wrong-headed and dangerous. They particularly hated his plan to 'liberate' the Hungarian minorities, which might have provoked a civil war and broken up the empire. Nor had Vienna warmed to his moderate policies towards the Southern Slavs. He offered concessions to Bosnia, Herzegovina, Macedonia and Bulgaria in exchange for their loyalty.

And so, at news of his death, a sigh of relief settled over the royal courts in Vienna and Budapest. Heinrich Kanner, a leading Viennese journalist, dared to write, 'the death of Archduke Francis Ferdinand, leaving aside the group of his special adherents, came as a relief in wide political circles even to the highest official circles'.[25] The emperor's anti-Slav courtiers were quietly satisfied, and the Magyar nobles visibly relieved at this turn of events. Their power would remain intact. The assassinations were the hand of providence, concluded the Hungarian Count László Szőgyény-Marich.

The couple's posthumous humiliation accompanied them to the grave. No European royals were invited to the funeral – the Kaiser was pointedly discouraged from going. Nor were the couple's distraught children allowed to attend. Only the emperor and senior court figures were present. The ceremonies were swift and graceless. The duchess's coffin was cheap and small, and bore only her gloves and fan, with no insignia denoting her rank.

Sophia's family and Ferdinand's friends were outraged. 'It caused a real scandal,' writes Albertini, 'to see how the antipathy felt for the Heir Apparent in the highest circles of the Monarchy stifled all sense of compassion in the presence of so great a tragedy, and gave rise to disgraceful funeral arrangements.'[26] Infuriated by this lack of respect, about 150 of the couple's close friends, led by the duchess's brother, 'forced their way into the procession'.[27] A terrible thunderstorm broke over the cortège as the remains were conveyed to their final resting place, as Seton-Watson relates, 'borne across the Danube and up the hilly road to Artstetten where Francis Ferdinand had built the memorial chapel because the wife of his choice was too low-born to rest in the stifling Hapsburg vaults of the Capucine Church in Vienna'.[28]

—

So much, then, for Habsburg 'outrage' at the assassination. If Vienna was privately satisfied at this providential solution to the accession – the sound Archduke Charles, Ferdinand's nephew, would now inherit the crown – the government was publicly furious at Serbia. The archduke's murder wrung few tears at court, yet at diplomatic level it was considered an unforgivable assault by 'Serbia' – not a lone assassin – on the dignity of the empire. The murder in Sarajevo had Belgrade's fingerprints all over it – of that, no one in power in Vienna had any doubt.

The question was how should Austria-Hungary make Serbia pay? Surely, the world could not deny Austria-Hungary the right to expect, at the very least, answers from Serbia and the harshest punishment of those involved. To that end, Belgrade must be forced to conduct a thorough investigation. Yet the desire for justice went only a fraction along the spectrum of reprisals that Vienna had in mind. Austria thirsted for military action against Serbia; the Viennese government's bloated pride would settle for nothing less. A great clamour for harsh military reprisals went up, and a note of jubilation infected the Austrian armed forces. At last, here was a true *casus belli*.

Conrad was, as usual, at his most belligerent. 'The outrage,' he told colleagues in Vienna on 29 June, 'was a Serbian machination.' It would 'lead to war with Serbia' and 'brought with it the danger that Russia and Roumania would have to be counted as enemies'.[29] Conrad believed Austria was defending itself against wanton state aggression. To him, this was a national provocation, to be met with vengeance and vast armies on the march. It never occurred to him to listen to Serbia's explanation, attempt to localise the damage or curb the rippling effect of aggression. On the contrary, mobilisation against Serbia was 'inevitable'.[30] Nor would Conrad, this 'architect of apocalypse',[31] resist dusting down and championing his long-standing policy against Serbia and Russia:

The favourable occasions for combating this inexorable menace were missed years ago. In vain did I at that time exhort to action. How easy would it be for me now to play the part of unheeded warner, standing aside and saying, 'You would not listen to me, now pull your cart-wheels out of the quagmire'. But this is not the time for such reproaches . . . The Sarajevo outrage has toppled over the house of cards built up with diplomatic documents, in which Austro-Hungarian policy thought it dwelt secure, the Monarchy has been seized by the throat and forced to choose between letting itself be strangled and making a last effort to defend itself against attack.[32]

Conrad was nothing if not consistent. Since 1909, his faction had been hungering for war with Serbia: over the annexation, over Serbian expansion and during the Balkan Wars. To cast Austria-Hungary's position as one of 'self-defence' or 'vengeance' was merely to add a new expedient to an existing policy of aggression. This went a lot further than revenge. The archduke's death offered Vienna not only a pretext for military intervention but also an opportunity to crush Serbian ambitions to create an enlarged Slavic state in the Balkans. Here was a chance to absorb the peninsula into the Austro-Hungarian Empire once and for all.

The French ambassador in Vienna, M. Dumaine, cabled Paris on 2 July:

The crime of Sarajevo arouses the most acute resentment in Austrian military circles and among all those who are not content to allow Servia [Serbia] to maintain in the Balkans the position which she has acquired. The investigation into the origin of the crime which it is desired to exact from the Government at Belgrade under conditions intolerable to their dignity would, in case of a refusal, furnish grounds of complaint which would admit of resort to military measures.[33]

—

Count Leopold Berchtold grasped the occasion like a man who, having been found sleeping at his post the night before, snaps to attention at the dawn bugle. The bumbling Austrian foreign minister's golden moment had arrived: a chance to draw the sword against Serbia and all who befriended it – including, conceivably, the kingdom of Roumania, which seemed to have gone over to the Russian camp – and rehabilitate his standing in the government. The senior Austrian and Hungarian noblemen and statesmen, the emperor, Conrad and Count János Forgách – all bitter enemies of the Serbs – stiffened Berchtold's resolve.

The only dissenting voice of any influence was that of István Tisza, the Hungarian premier. Tisza, a hardbitten political operator of pacifist inclinations forged out of a stiff Calvinist upbringing, opposed war 'even if victorious'. He wrote to his niece on 26 August 1914, 'war means misery, anguish, devastation, the shedding of innocent blood, the suffering of innocent women and children'.[34] For a while, Tisza adhered to the spirit of this sentimental letter to a young lady. He alerted the emperor on 1 July that there were insufficient grounds for provoking a war with Serbia, that the Serbian Government may yet produce a satisfactory explanation, and that Austro-Hungarian military action would provide the kindling for a major war.

This was inconvenient. Without Hungarian backing, Berchtold had little room to move. He could hardly contemplate mobilising Austro-Hungarian forces without Hungary's approval. Nor would Vienna contemplate war with Serbia without the backing of the mother ship, Germany. So Berchtold turned to Austria's powerful ally for the backing needed to launch a war: if Berlin could be cemented to the Austrian war faction, then Hungary would be forced to follow.

This was tricky, in diplomatic terms. For one thing, the Triple Alliance did not technically oblige Germany to defend Austria-Hungary if, for example, Austria attacked Serbia and Russia in reply attacked Austria. So Berchtold and his collaborators needed a new statement of support from Berlin – an open commitment to support Austrian actions in a highly fluid situation. Here lay the genesis of Germany's 'blank cheque',

—

On 4 July, Vienna received a sign of Germany's initial feelings, which urged restraint. The Austrian ambassador in Berlin, Count László Szőgyény-Marich, cabled to report that Arthur Zimmermann, German undersecretary of foreign affairs, thought 'a strong line of action' by the dual monarchy against Serbia 'entirely understandable' but recommended 'great prudence' and advised 'against making any humiliating demands on Serbia'.[35] That would not do: harsh, warlike action depended on Berlin's support, reasoned Berchtold. Szőgyény-Marich's telegram was consigned to a drawer and would not see the light of day until after the war.

Austria then sought to extract a much firmer line from Germany: a definitive commitment to military action. The next day, the Austrian emperor granted Conrad an audience. Their discussion set the tone for the coming events. 'If the answer runs that Germany will take her stand at our side, do we then make war on Serbia?' Conrad asked Franz Joseph. Both men were deeply reluctant to contemplate war without Berlin's backing. The emperor replied, 'In that case, yes.'[36]

And so, on 4 July, determined to wrest a firmer line from Germany, Berchtold sent Count Alexander Graf von Hoyos, his chef du cabinet in the Austria-Hungary Foreign Ministry, to Berlin. Hoyos, an Austrian nobleman of Spanish extraction, was a protégé of Aehrenthal's and a hard-line anti-Slav. He also happened to be the grandson of British engineer Robert Whitehead, inventor of the torpedo. He arrived in Berlin bearing two documents. One made a strong case for diplomatic action against Serbia. Written before the Sarajevo outrage, it had been updated to account for feelings since the 'revolting murder' and now urged a firm military solution to the Serbian problem, inviting Bulgaria and the wobbling Roumania to join the Triple Alliance. The second was a letter to the Kaiser from Emperor Franz Joseph, drafted by Berchtold. It stated with crystalline clarity the Austrian case for war:

> The attack directed against my poor nephew is the direct consequence of the agitation carried on by the Russian and Serbian Pan-Slavists whose sole aim is the weakening of the Triple Alliance and the destruction of my Empire.
>
> . . . it is no longer an affair at Sarajevo of the single bloody deed of an individual but of a well-organized conspiracy, of which the threads reach to Belgrade and if, as is probable, it be impossible to prove the complicity of the Serbian Government, nevertheless it cannot be doubted that the policies leading to the reunion of all the Southern Slavs under the Serbian flag is favourable to crimes of this character and that the continuance of this state of things constitutes a constant danger to my house and to my realm.

'Serbia', Franz Joseph concluded, 'which is at present the pivot of Pan-Slavist policy', should be 'eliminated as a political factor in the Balkans'.[37]

Here, then, was Austria's highest policy response to the Sarajevo assassination. Vienna aimed not only to punish Serbia but also to terminate Serbia's polity and crush pan-Slavism in the Balkans – the fulfilment of which depended on Berlin's reply.

—

In Berlin, the Hoyos Mission fell like a spark in a tinderbox. The Kaiser's fury at the assassination of his old friend had already curdled into a desire for action: a Slav maniac had murdered his royal ally. One of Wilhelm's outbursts with which he customarily daubed official correspondence had the eerie authority of a command. 'Now or never' he scribbled beside the words 'at last a final and fundamental reckoning should be had with the Serbs' (in a letter from Tschirschky to Bethmann-Hollweg of 2 July).[38]

Yet the spark did not trigger an immediate explosion. The Kaiser hesitated, as he often would, when confronted with stark reality. He mumbled about having to consult the chancellor before committing himself to an answer. After a solid lunch, however, the Kaiser's feelings hardened. With his impetuosity in full flight, Wilhelm offered Germany's 'full support' to whatever action Austria chose in the Balkans. It was the Kaiser's opinion that 'this action must not be delayed', the Austrian ambassador in Berlin cabled Berchtold. Wilhelm warned that 'Russia's attitude will no doubt be hostile' but assured Vienna that, 'should a war between Austria-Hungary and Russia be unavoidable', Germany would stand by Austria's side.[39]

Hoyos thus fulfilled a personal as well as a diplomatic mission. He, like others in the Austrian regime, wanted war with Serbia. 'We shall wipe Serbia out,' Hoyos had confided to German officials.[40] Bethmann-Hollweg and Zimmermann confirmed Hoyos' hopes in a meeting that day: Germany would stand firm with Austria whatever action Vienna chose. That did not mean they wanted a European or world war. At this point, they expected to localise it.

The next day, the Kaiser met Chancellor Bethmann-Hollweg and reprised his commitment to harsh Austrian military action. Bethmann-Hollweg concurred. An immediate strike against Serbia was 'the best solution' to their difficulties in the Balkans, he told the Kaiser. Bethmann-Hollweg saw German open-ended support as the self-interested defence of its only ally. He later wrote:

> If this ally had collapsed . . . from the failure of its friends to protect its vital interests, then Germany would be completely isolated. [Germany] would be choked to death by a ring of enemies, banded together in a common campaign for World dominion . . . by Slav race hatred against Teutons, and by lowering ill-will against the victor of 1870. And that is the reason why German policy thought it proper to approve Austria's decision to take action against Serbia . . .[41]

Here, then, was the chancellor's defence of Germany's famous blank cheque to Austria-Hungary, which he sent to Vienna later that day. Germany would support *any* action against Serbia that Vienna chose to unleash. And Berlin urged its ally to strike with the greatest possible severity (see Appendix 1 for the full text):

> Telegram from the Imperial Chancellor, von Bethmann-Hollweg, to the German Ambassador at Vienna, Tschirschky, July 6, 1914
>
> Berlin, July 6, 1914. Confidential. For Your Excellency's personal information and guidance
>
> ... His Majesty desires to say that he is not blind to the danger which threatens Austria-Hungary and thus the Triple Alliance as a result of the Russian and Serbian Pan-Slavic agitation ... as far as concerns Serbia, His Majesty, of course, cannot interfere in the dispute now going on between Austria-Hungary and that country, as it is a matter not within his competence. The Emperor Francis Joseph may, however, rest assured that His Majesty will faithfully stand by Austria-Hungary, as is required by the obligations of his alliance and of his ancient friendship.
>
> BETHMANN-HOLLWEG[42]

The Austro-Hungarians were thus free to act as they wished, confident in the knowledge of having mother Germany at their rear. The striking thing about the blank cheque, as Hew Strachan shows, 'is not that it was issued, but that it was indeed blank'.[43] Nobody then knew when, and for how much, Vienna would cash the cheque.

25

AUSTRIA-HUNGARY: DESPERATE FOR WAR

All present except the Royal Hungarian Premier hold the belief that a purely diplomatic success, even if it ended with a glaring humiliation of Serbia, would be worthless and that therefore such stringent demands must be addressed to Serbia, that will make a refusal almost certain, so that the road to a radical solution by means of a military action should be opened.

Austro-Hungarian Council of Ministers[1]

PROTOCOL of the Council of Ministers for Common Affairs, with Berchtold in the chair.

7 July 1914

PRESENT: The Imp. and Roy. President of the Council of Ministers Count Stürgkh; the Roy. Hungarian Premier Count Tisza; the Imp. and Roy. Joint Minister for Finances Ritter von Bilinski; the Imp. and Roy. Minister of War F. Z. M. Ritter von Krobatin; the Imp. and Roy. Chief of the General Staff G. d. I. Baron von Conrad; the Deputy Chief of the Naval Staff, Rear-Admiral von Kailer

Keeper of the Protocol: Secretary of legation, Count Hoyos

Subject of Council: Bosnian concerns. The diplomatic action against Serbia.

Eight men, representing four nationalities, sat at the long table in Vienna's Ballplatz, the seat of government, to decide what to do with Serbia. Berchtold had convened the meeting on the assumption that military action was inevitable and desirable. Seizing his moment in the sun, the Austrian foreign minister had 'allotted the places with careful ceremony, as at a great dinner party'.[2] Here was Prime Minister Stürgkh, tall and weather-beaten, sporting a long, grey, pointy beard, an ineffectual, rather stuffy nobleman, who seemed to be as surprised as the world at his ascent to high office. Beside him sat Bilinski, a 'pale foxy faced Pole' and sharp-minded operator, who knew the empire's secrets and was 'perhaps the most dangerous man in the room'.[3] The most influential in the room was Conrad von Hötzendorf, aloof and silent, content to let the conversation run its course, enjoying the moment of *Schadenfreude* at having forewarned everyone that it would come to this. Supporting him were Conrad's military colleagues, General von Krobatin, representing the army, and Admiral Karl von Kailer, resplendent in the green, white and gold of their imperial offices. With the secret encouragement of Moltke, Conrad's dream of war with Serbia was now to be fulfilled. Yet, in coming weeks, even Conrad would pale at Moltke's assertion that Sarajevo presented 'the perfect opportunity for a different war, the great war of reckoning with Russia'.[4]

As the discussion progressed, it emerged that all except Count Tisza, the Hungarian premier, believed Austria-Hungary must avenge the Sarajevo outrage with a military strike. Tisza was one of those rare politicians who were unafraid to articulate the prodding of their conscience. He sat quietly among them and seemed intent on trying to protect them from the consequences of their actions.

He failed. In the following hours, seven Austrian politicians would effectively declare war on Serbia, aware that by doing so they risked plunging Europe into a conflagration. Their chief motives were an obsessive concern with the preservation of Austro-Hungarian prestige, a desire to punish the Serbian nation and the deeper aim of destroying pan-Slavism.

'When we crush Serbia,' wrote the official Berthold Molden in an internal memo before the meeting, sent on 6 July 1914, 'Serbian imperialism within and beyond our border will be defeated for a long time to come.' It would also send a powerful lesson to Russia, he urged, if Vienna struck now: 'Today we still have our fate in our hands, tomorrow, perhaps, we will not.'[5]

And there were deep internal pressures driving Vienna to war. The empire was on the verge of disintegration. '[T]he Dual Monarchy,' writes F. Roy Bridge, 'was by 1914 in a critical state bordering on decomposition, which rendered some foreign action imperative as a diversion or a solution.'[6] In the more exacting words of Baron Leopold von Andrian-Werburg, the admired Austro-Hungarian consul general in Warsaw, 'We are heading for collapse and partition and do not defend ourselves . . . After Turkey comes Austria, that is the catchword in Eastern Europe.'[7]

The Council thus concentrated almost exclusively on the restoration of the honour of the Austro-Hungarian Empire. To this end, they meant to extract a war with Serbia out of the opportunity presented by Franz Ferdinand's death. '[I]n order to erase the impression of decline and disintegration,' Molden urged, 'a striking deed, a knock-out punch would be necessary . . . It is incontestable that the moral effect of an action would be extremely favourable. Austria-Hungary . . . would again believe in itself. It would mean: I have the will, therefore I am.'[8]

The likely consequences of the war, in terms of the destruction and loss of life, received little attention. The Council's only question was should Austria-Hungary strike now or fashion a diplomatic action against Serbia that would lead to war anyway? Everyone at the table except Tisza wanted war with Serbia. How they went about getting one would forever redound to the dual empire's disgrace.

———

The meeting began, redolent with the tortured logic that equated the continued honour and existence of the Habsburg Empire with the crushing of Serbia.[9] Berchtold, the reconstituted warrior, opened the discussion by confronting Tisza, the peace-seeker. The Hungarian premier represented the other 'half' of the dual empire, and Berchtold needed Tisza's firm support before he could act. To sway him, Berchtold came armed with Germany's blank cheque. Its provenance and resolution persuaded Tisza. He wearily accepted – even if he resisted – the likelihood of 'warlike action' against Serbia, but he would never consent to a surprise attack on the nation. Without offering the Serbs a prior diplomatic warning, Austria-Hungary would 'draw upon ourselves the enmity of the Balkan states' (with the exception of Bulgaria, which contemplated joining the Triple Alliance after her defeat in the Second Balkan War).

Tisza urged restraint on his colleagues. He suggested they send a list of strong demands to Serbia. If these were rejected, 'we must make out an ultimatum'. Its terms should be harsh, he advised, but 'not such that they cannot be complied with'. He added, 'If Serbia accepted them, we should have a splendid diplomatic success and our *prestige* in the Balkans would gain immensely.'[10] If rejected, they could vote for war; but Serbia, with Russian aid, he warned, could not be annihilated: 'Russia would fight to the death before allowing this.' Nor would Tisza consent to the annexing of any part of Serbia. He summed up: war was neither for Germany to decide nor necessary or desirable at this point – for a range of reasons. Roumania's position was uncertain, and she may enter the war against the Triple Alliance. On the other hand, he said, the likelihood of Bulgaria and Turkey joining the Alliance would strengthen Vienna's diplomatic position.

Berchtold, confident of the Council's backing, rejected this course. Only 'the exertion of main force' could put an end to the pretensions and propaganda of 'Greater Serbia', he said. He dismissed the threat of Roumania, and rather petulantly added that Austria-Hungary did not need a war to gain prestige. Austria-Hungary already enjoyed great diplomatic prestige. Tisza then sidetracked the meeting with a point about France's falling birth rate, which would allow Germany to muster more men against Russia. But Russia's birth rate, Berchtold countered, had also accelerated.

To which Stürgkh drew the Council's wavering attention back to the key point: the question of their response to the assassination and 'whether we might not solve the Bosnian difficulty by exercising force against Serbia'.[11] The whole situation had changed, he warned: 'It now shows a psychological character and is decidedly more than ever pointing to a solution at the point of the sword.' He cited a memorandum from General Potiorek, the Bosnian governor, who blamed Serbia for the violence in Bosnia. Only a blow against Belgrade would stop the insurgency.

Stürgkh reminded the Council of the persuasive power of Germany's blank cheque and made a pointed riposte to Tisza: yes, it was for Austria-Hungary to decide whether to go to war, but Germany strongly influenced the decision. Berlin had promised 'unreserved loyalty' and advised Vienna 'to act without delay'. He, with Bilinski's support, warned Tisza to remember that 'by a weak and hesitating policy we might risk not being so certain of German support at some future time. This is surely of the highest importance.'[12] A diplomatic success was valueless, he declared.

—

The discussion then degenerated into bathos. All except Tisza wanted war but could not decide how to get one. Somehow, a diplomatic provocation had to force war on Serbia. The point was to avoid an international outcry over taking up arms against the Balkan state 'without warning' (*sans crier gare*). Perceptions were critical. The Austro-Hungarian leaders must appear reasonable; they must seem to be offering Serbia terms, not a dagger at the throat. Prime Minister Stürgkh sounded comfortable with this poisonous line of thought: 'If a foregoing diplomatic action [e.g. an ultimatum to Serbia] is . . . resorted to it should be taken with the firm resolve that this action can only end in war . . .' In other words, the 'diplomatic action' must be so formulated as to *guarantee* war against Serbia.

At this point, War Minister Krobatin dusted down the old Darwinian argument, that a failure to act would be seen as unworthy and weak: 'a diplomatic success would be of no use at all. A success of this kind would be interpreted as weakness.' Austria-Hungary must avenge its honour with an act of force and strength. He directed his remarks at the person, not the policies, of Tisza, and implicitly questioned the courage and strength of anyone who supported the Hungarian leader. Nobody did; nobody in the room wished to seem weak.

'From a military point of view,' Krobatin declared – with the lethal finality implicit in the phrase – 'it is desirable that the mobilization be carried through as immediately and as secretly as possible, and that an ultimatum should be addressed to Serbia when the mobilization is complete'. Tisza opposed this.

The minutes thus recorded the abhorrent tactic:

> All present except the Royal Hungarian Premier hold the belief that a purely diplomatic success, even if it ended with a glaring humiliation of Serbia, would be worthless and that therefore such stringent demands must be addressed to Serbia, that will make a refusal almost certain, so that the road to a radical solution by means of a military action should be opened.[13]

They turned then to the question of how Serbia should be punished. It was agreed that, upon crushing Serbia, a reliable European prince should replace its royal family (the Karageorgevich dynasty), who would be dethroned. The defeated Serbs should then be made vassals of the empire. All this proceeded on the high authority of men presumptuous of victory. None anticipated the strength of Serbian resistance; none countenanced the possibility that their actions would lead to the destruction of their own Crown and Empire.

Tisza interjected again. The terms of an ultimatum, he said, should not be so harsh 'as to make our intention of raising unacceptable demands clear to everybody'. Otherwise, 'we would not have a lawful basis for our declaration of war'.[14] Tisza's protests were effectively ignored, or misrepresented.

A long debate ensued over the nature of the coming war. Could the war be localised to the Balkans? Russia's entry was expected, necessitating the involvement of Germany. France would then surely follow its ally. A European war would result. Tisza had peered into the abyss. A small voice of sanity, he 'appealed again to all present to consider carefully what they were about to decide'.[15]

They decided to proceed with the drafting of the unacceptable ultimatum. The meeting closed; the delegates packed up. Berchtold advised them to take their summer vacation, to maintain a semblance of normality.

—

Pause to reflect on what had been decided that day. Seven officials, newly empowered by the German promise of support, had agreed to force war on Serbia through a diplomatic con, without delay, and without the findings of the investigation into the assassination of Franz Ferdinand. They would do so by drafting an ultimatum deliberately worded as to be unacceptable. They refused to consider moderate alternatives, such as diplomatic demands or economic sanctions. The assassination had little actual bearing on these discussions, other than as a catalyst, barely mentioned. These men wanted war – were desperate for it – for deeper reasons: the destruction of pan-Slavism and the preservation of the empire. Sarajevo merely served as a public justification. In sum, they had embarked on an exercise in diplomatic deception that, they knew, could bring total war to Europe. They proceeded safe in the knowledge that Germany would always be at their side, especially in the event of Russia's intervention.

An important distinction: these were Austria-Hungary's war aims; it did not follow that Germany shared them. Germany hoped and expected, at this point, that the war would be confined to the Balkans. Neither Bethmann-Hollweg nor the Kaiser wanted a pan-European war. They did not, in early July, plan to destroy Europe to gain an empire. 'I do not believe in any serious warlike development,' the Kaiser told Eduard von Capelle, the admiral of the fleet, before departing on his Baltic cruise on 6 July. 'The Tsar,' he added, 'will not place himself on the side of regicides. Besides, neither Russia nor France is prepared for war.'[16] Bethmann-Hollweg and Foreign Minister Jagow felt the same, as did other civilian leaders.

Germany failed to transmit these concerns to Vienna. It fatefully gave the Austro-Hungarians the freedom to do as they wished in the Balkans. The blank cheque, being blank, imposed no limits or conditions, and sent no sign that Berlin hoped to 'localise' the war. Szőgyény-Marich's telegram, as we've seen, urged lenience but sat ignored in a drawer. The German 'curse' of the blank cheque drove Austria-Hungary to ignore the counsel of restraint and act with extreme prejudice in all its dealings with Belgrade.

26

EXCEPTIONAL TRANQUILLITY

[Berchtold, the Austrian foreign minister] was still
considering what demands could be put that would
be wholly impossible for the Serbs to accept.
Baron Heinrich von Tschirschky, German ambassador to Vienna,
10 July 1914

IF THE GERMANS WANTED AUSTRIA to avenge Serbia by
going to war in the Balkans, they had a relaxed way of showing it.
Vienna would act firmly, but not precipitately, the Germans reassured themselves, and any hostilities would be localised. Russia
would stay out of it, the Kaiser felt sure. With these sanguine
thoughts, all the key ministers went on holiday. On 6 July – the day
Germany handed the blank cheque to Austria – the Kaiser embarked
on his summer cruise; Chancellor Bethmann-Hollweg prepared to
leave for his country estate (from where he would run the country by
telephone); Secretary of State Jagow was honeymooning in Lucerne;
Moltke and Tirpitz, the commanders of the army and navy, were
already by the spa or sea; and the quarter-master general, essential to
any mobilisation plan, was attending a relative's funeral in Hanover.

The Kaiser had offered to stay in Berlin but Bethmann-Hollweg dissuaded him, to avoid creating alarm abroad. This was, after all, Wilhelm's traditional summer holiday. And so the royal yacht *Hohenzollern* put to sea, bound for Scandinavian waters, contactable only by wireless, for three long weeks. One can hear Bethmann-Hollweg's sigh of relief. Back on German soil, Moltke, then at the spa town of Karlsbad, in Baden, was similarly advised to stay away. The Austrians and Hungarians, too, rather ostentatiously left for their summer holidays. Conrad and Krobatin were advised to stay away until 22 July. 'It would be a good thing,' Berchtold told Conrad, 'if you and the Minister of War would go on leave for a while, so as to keep up an appearance that nothing is going on.'[1] No doubt, Gina, his Italian mistress, was delighted.

And so this high political pantomime began. It was not a smokescreen to cover a sinister German plan to declare war on the Entente, as is often supposed; at this stage, the German Government – if not Moltke and the military leaders – hoped to confine a war, if it should come, to the Balkans. The semblance of business as usual was a contrivance to cover Austria's actions, in which Germany had an intimate role. Behind the sangfroid, however, everyone realised the risks of a wider conflict. Berlin knew that Russia would feel compelled to intervene. If so, that would make a European war most likely. The German General Staff were on alert and 'ready to jump' if circumstances turned awry, according to General von Waldersee, who left for his holiday on 8 July. They were all expected back in Berlin on or before 23 July, the date set for the ultimatum to Serbia.

The procession of holidaymakers stayed in close touch with their offices in Berlin, Vienna and Budapest, where a strange calm replaced the street protests in the days after the assassination. The cities were, in effect, being tranquillised. Austrian officials moved to restrain the violent press, then in a war of words with the Serbian media. Berlin muzzled the pan-Germans, whose bellicose utterances about world domination were felt to be inopportune. The Kaiser even prevailed upon his son, Crown Prince Friedrich Wilhelm, to curb his 'wilful war-baiting'.[2] The usual court formalities were extended, with cold-blooded pretence, to Serbia. King Peter I of Serbia even received his customary birthday telegram from Wilhelm. The prospect of war was no reason to relax royal protocol.

—

Thus began the 'July Crisis', the month in which most of the world, without realising it, stood on the abyss. It was indeed, for a time, a period of 'exceptional tranquillity', as Churchill noticed: all the key players were taking in the sun.[3] The machinery of state had drained the body of Franz Ferdinand of its diplomatic usefulness, and Austria-Hungary, encouraged by Germany, carefully determined the next stage in the tragedy of what many would later describe as 'inevitable' and 'unstoppable' events. On the contrary, the leaders of the Austrian and German Governments, careless of the risks, determined the stations of the Third Balkan War every step of the way.

Nobody wanted a *European* war, they later claimed. Yet their outlook and policies made a continental war likely, and varied according to hidden agendas, flaring up and dying down with terrific and unexpected force. Germany's civilian leaders expected Vienna, at this stage, to confine the conflict to a local stoush with Serbia. The Prussian generals paid lip-service to this policy. 'Austria must beat the Serbs,' Moltke, the chief of the General Staff, told the German military attaché in Vienna on 13 July, 'and then make peace quickly, demanding an Austro-Serbian alliance as the sole condition.'[4] At other times, however, Moltke spoke by turns zealously or resignedly of a European catastrophe, a chance to take the war to Russia, enact the Schlieffen Plan and settle Germany's great reckoning with the world.

Germany did not wish to seem the belligerent, however. Berlin delicately removed itself from Vienna's deliberations – refusing to help draft the ultimatum, for example – and stood back to watch the process it had started. Ministers were instructed to affect surprise at the harshness of the document, when made public. Hans von Schoen, Bavarian counsellor in Berlin, advised:

The administration will immediately upon the presentation of the Austrian note at Belgrade, initiate diplomatic action with the Powers in the interests of the localization of the war. It will claim that the Austrian action has been just as much of a surprise to it as to the other Powers, pointing out the fact that the Kaiser is on his northern journey and that the Chief of the General Staff and the Prussian Minister for War are away on leave of absence.[5]

Reckless cynicism had not actuated this policy; Germans and Austrians genuinely believed in it as a valid and legitimate course of action. The manufacture of a *casus belli* seemed to them eminently proper, in the circumstances. Behind the smokescreen, Vienna continued diligently to work on the Serbian ultimatum. Berlin was kept closely informed: Jagow had returned early from his honeymoon and Bethmann-Hollweg made occasional sneak visits to Berlin. The ambassadors remained at their posts.

The key elements of the ultimatum were in place by 10 July. The draft prefigured the harshness of the final tract. Vienna should demand, for example, an Austro-Hungarian agency in Belgrade to 'keep an eye . . . on Greater Serbia machinations';[6] Serbia should have no more than 48 hours to respond; and key Serbian officials should be sacked. Thus, Baron Heinrich von Tschirschky, German ambassador to Vienna, reported to the foreign minister Jagow.

Much of this amounted to a humiliating intrusion on Serbian sovereignty, which was the point, of course. Berchtold nonetheless feared the Serbs might actually accept the demands and obviate war. If so, wrote Tschirschky, 'it would prove a solution which would be "very disagreeable" to him, and he was still considering what *demands* could *be put* that would be *wholly impossible for the Serbs to accept*' (Tschirschky's emphasis).[7]

The Kaiser inserted in these top-secret communiqués his usual infantile margin notes, full of chest-thumping derision. Beside a reference, for example, to Count Tisza, who made the mistake of suggesting that they try to behave 'like gentlemen', the Kaiser had scrawled,

'To act like "gentlemen" to murderers, after what has happened! Idiocy!'[8] The Kaiser even proposed, 'Evacuate the Sanjak!' as an additional demand on Serbia. 'Then the row would be on at once! Austria must absolutely get that [the Sanjak] back at once, in order to prevent the union of Serbia and Montenegro and the gaining of the seacoast by the Serbians.'[9] Nobody acted on these royal suggestions, but they added a frantic, vexatious dimension to the process.

—

And so the ultimatum continued its grim migration from the drafters' desk to the official sphere, absorbing comments and amendments, and slowly taking shape. The process paused over a report by the chief legal counsel at the Ballplatz, Dr Friedrich von Wiesner, who had been sent to Sarajevo to monitor the investigation and assess whether Belgrade bore any responsibility for the assassination. Wiesner had bad news for Berchtold. According to the judicial inquiry in Bosnia:

> there is nothing to prove or even to suppose that the Serbian Government is accessory to the inducement for the crime, its preparation or the furnishing of weapons. On the contrary, there are reasons to believe that this is altogether out of the question.[10]

That was not what Berchtold wanted to hear. Wiesner, however, gave the Austrian foreign minister some straws: the anti-Austrian 'movement' had probably originated in Serbia, he advised; Serbian state officials (Ciganović and Major Tankosić) jointly provided bombs, Brownings, ammunition and prussic acid; and the assassins Princip, Čabrinović and Grabež were secretly brought across the Serb-Bosnian frontier 'by Serbian organs'. Wiesner cited the *Narodna Odbrana*, and not The Black Hand and its leader, Apis, neither of whom had yet been implicated.[11]

Berchtold had what he needed: the discovery of loose links between some junior Belgrade officials and the assassination. He hastened the completion of the ultimatum, scheduled for delivery to Serbia on 23 July. The date had been carefully chosen: at the end of the harvest – 'lightening the difficulties of mobilisation' and 'preventing great economic losses'[12] – and on the day Poincaré would wind up his state visit to St Petersburg. The Austrians wondered whether perhaps to delay the note, to avoid the possibility of the Tsar, Poincaré's entourage and assorted grand dukes ganging up over champagne in an unofficial war room. The final delivery date was fixed for 5 pm on Thursday 23 July. Serbia would have 48 hours to reply, by 5 pm Saturday 25 July.

The Austro-Hungarian charade disguised the mobilisation of arms and men. Vienna started mobilising Austria's forces in the *second week* of July – a fortnight before they sent the ultimatum to Serbia. Even Tisza gave up his objections to war. Germany's unconditional support and the firmness of Franz Joseph had changed his mind. 'Well, a real man at last,' noted the Kaiser when he heard of Tisza's change of heart.[13] His apostasy left nobody to restrain the beast: all now wanted and expected war. Tisza even adopted, at times, a 'sharper tone' than the hawks. None was helplessly swept along by events, as they later claimed.

Vienna's lies should not surprise the twenty-first-century reader, hardened to a century of deceit by governments wishing to wage war. Their staggering irresponsibility is sadly familiar to us, in an age when governments manufacture *casus belli* and then lie about their true provenance – for example, by 'sexing up' intelligence dossiers (to make the British case for going to war in Iraq), inventing a naval strike in the Gulf of Tonkin (to justify American entry in the Vietnam War) and claiming weapons of mass destruction existed when none did (the Allied case for war against Iraq). And those were merely the lies of democratic, supposedly accountable governments. Totalitarian states, of course, openly, routinely lie to their people and the world to create pretexts for wars – such as the Soviet Union (in Eastern Europe in 1945), North Korea (against South Korea in 1950), Nazi Germany (against Czechoslovakia and Poland in 1939), and Japan (in Manchuria and China in the 1930s).

—

Britain, Russia and France watched and waited. They were initially optimistic that the Balkan troubles could be resolved or contained. They had no knowledge, of course, of the ultimatum and the proceedings in Vienna and Berlin. Their ambassadors in those cities went on holiday. Utterly deceived, Russia's ambassador to Austria actually departed for a vacation on 21 July, having persuaded himself that Austria would make no demands on Serbia that might lead to 'international complications' – i.e. dragging Russia into war.[14]

Ever the attentive intermediary, Edward Grey offered to play the role of peacemaker, between St Petersburg and Berlin. On 9 July, he told the German ambassador Count Lichnowsky that he would try to persuade the Russians to adopt 'a more peaceful view' and 'conciliatory attitude' towards Austria. He also reassured the German diplomat that England was not obliged to saddle up with France or Russia in the event of a European war. 'England wished to preserve an absolutely free hand,' Grey said (as Lichnowsky reported to Berlin).[15]

Yet, typically, Grey blurred the picture, to maintain the 'balance'. To whom had Britain pledged allegiance if war came, Lichnowsky wanted to know. Would Britain remain neutral? Grey refused to give a straight answer. Having assured the German ambassador that England had no formal *military* relationship with the Entente powers, Grey undermined that assurance. On the other hand, he cautioned, he did not wish to 'mislead' his German friends. England's relations with France and Russia had lost none of their intimacy. In fact, there had been 'conversations' with French and Russian military authorities, but these 'had absolutely no aggressive intent'. In other words, English policy, Grey told the exasperated German diplomat, 'was aimed towards the maintenance of peace'.[16] Lichnowsky, by now, had no idea what 'English policy' stood for. Grey, however, seemed thoroughly pleased with himself and concluded their meeting by declaring 'in cheerful tones' that he saw no reason for pessimism.[17]

Another event drew darker rings round the British Cabinet's eyes. The Ulster Rebellion was far more distracting than another flare-up in the Balkans. A new Home Rule Bill sparked bitter resentment in Ulster, which threatened to revolt. The crisis dominated political debate in Westminster and threatened to tear apart Asquith's Liberal Party. So serious were the Irish problems that Churchill wondered whether 'our parliamentary institutions were strong enough to survive the passions by which they were convulsed'.[18] It was even feared the British Expeditionary Force would be needed in Ulster, to the consternation of Sir Henry Wilson, who, ever-mindful of the threat to France, recorded in his diary his disgust with Asquith's 'pestilent government' and cabinet of 'Cowards, Blackguards and Fools'.[19]

—

Poincaré and his government were similarly immured in domestic crises to worry too much about another Balkan fracas. The murder trial of Henriette Caillaux, the second wife of former prime minister Joseph Caillaux, would proceed on 20 July. The case obsessed the nation. Gaston Calmette, the editor of *Le Figaro*, had been running a ferocious press campaign against Caillaux, who, as prime minister, had tried to introduce an income tax and held a moderate position during the Agadir Crisis. *Le Figaro* had threatened to publish love letters that Caillaux had sent to Henriette when he was still married to his first wife. On 16 March, Henriette presented herself at *Le Figaro*'s office with a pistol concealed in her black muffs. On admission to the editor's office, she fired six bullets into Calmette's body. He died six hours later. She made no attempt to escape and insisted on being taken to the police station by her chauffeur.

The drama had a serious political dimension. The trial was a political embarrassment for Poincaré, who was struggling after his poor performance at the April–May general elections. It was further rumoured that Calmette possessed two deciphered German telegrams, which revealed Caillaux's secret talks with the Germans during the Agadir Crisis.[20] Hearing the rumours, the German ambassador in Paris protested against the interception of German communications and warned that, if the documents were revealed, 'a bomb would explode'.[21] Caillaux's supporters even threatened to blackmail Poincaré, by producing witnesses ready to say that the president had backed Calmette's campaign against the former prime minister. Until 24 July, the Caillaux trial completely dominated the French media; the French people were mesmerised. The newspapers gave little attention to the repercussions of Franz Ferdinand's murder. The 'July Crisis' did not exist for the French people or the government, and the prospect of a European war seemed remote. The nation, delighting in the details of the Caillaux case, settled into a summer of relaxed voyeurism. In the event, Henriette was acquitted of murder. She had committed a 'crime of passion', the court heard.

With some relief, President Poincaré, his new prime minister, the grossly inexperienced René Viviani, and their entourage left Paris on 15 July for a long-planned state cruise to Russia and Scandinavia. They were due to return on 31 July and would be at sea for most of the trip, with limited radio communication. Those left in charge at the Foreign Ministry were 'either inexperienced or completely ignorant of foreign affairs', writes Keiger. 'On the eve of war, French leaders were literally and metaphorically at sea.'[22]

27

THE ULTIMATUM TO SERBIA

It is clear from the . . . confessions of the criminal
authors of the assassination on the 28th June that the
murder at Sarajevo was conceived at Belgrade.
The Austro-Hungarian Ultimatum to Serbia, delivered
to Belgrade on 23 July 1914 at 6 pm

THROUGHOUT JULY, the Belgrade government did nothing
to help itself. It failed to restrain hard-line Serbs from celebrating
– hugging and dancing in the streets – the assassination of Franz
Ferdinand. It encouraged through inaction the bovine press, which
enjoyed unusual freedom in Europe. Serb papers hailed the assassins
as national heroes and 'martyrs' (as *Piemont*, the organ of The Black
Hand, described Princip), and accused the Austrians of wanton
provocation by staging a state visit on Serbia's most sacred day. Some
papers, such as the *Balkan*, even demanded that Austria 'be put
under international control'.[1] These reports, fully aired in Austria
and Germany, reflected a popular Serb feeling that the assassination
of Franz Ferdinand was a blow for pan-Slav freedom.

Serbia's incendiary press inflamed feelings in Vienna and Berlin,
and cemented the view that Belgrade had planned the Sarajevo

attack. A violent press war ensued. The Vienna papers, which were more or less government-controlled, openly accused the Serbian Government of direct responsibility for the Sarajevo outrage: 'the whole conspiracy in its wider issues was organised at Belgrade among youth inspired with the Great Serbian idea.'[2] This press war had grave consequences. In 1914, Europe's leading newspapers enjoyed great power over political and public opinion. Serbia's distempered editorials were driving the countries to war, according to Belgrade's ambassador in Vienna. 'The excitement in military and Government circles against Serbia is steadily growing owing to the tone of our press,' Jovan Jovanović, Serb minister at Vienna, wrote to Nikola Pašić, prime minister and minister for foreign affairs, on 6 July.[3]

After the gale of pan-Slavism subsided, a cold calm settled over the country amid a heightened awareness of the probability of military consequences arising from the murder. The Serbian Government adopted a posture of sincere regret. While 'horrified' at the murder, Belgrade indignantly rejected any suggestion of Serbian responsibility. Pašić quickly moved to distance his administration from the crime. His stance never deviated from the line he gave the Austrians two days after the assassination. His ambassador in Vienna relayed his views thus:

> The Royal Serbian Government condemn most energetically the Sarajevo outrage and on their part will certainly most loyally do everything to prove that they will not tolerate within their territory the fostering of any agitation or illegal proceedings calculated to disturb our already delicate relations with Austria-Hungary. . . . the Government are prepared also to submit to trial any persons implicated in the plot, in the event of its being proved that there are any in Serbia.[4]

Evidence still could not be found linking the Serbian Government directly to the assassination – nothing to connect Prime Minister Pašić or his ministers to the plot to kill the archduke. Yet Pašić and his ministers were well aware in advance of the plan. They had an intimate knowledge of *Ujedinjenje ili Smrt*, or The Black Hand, and its leader Dragutin Dimitrijević (aka Apis). In fact, Pašić had been kept closely informed of Apis's plans to assassinate Franz Ferdinand, through Major Vojislav Tankosić and Milan Ciganović, who had liaised between the terrorist group and the three Bosnian assassins.

Under Austrian interrogation, Black Hand members later revealed that Apis, Tankosić and Ciganović had organised the assassination. Indeed, Apis had masterminded it, as everyone in power in Belgrade knew. It later emerged that he had originally trained his young assassins to kill Bosnian governor Potiorek, but, when he heard of the archduke's visit, he saw a great chance to eliminate the heir to the hated Austro-Hungarian throne.

—

All this put the Serb government in a very awkward position. Pašić's government had severed links with The Black Hand well before the assassination and ordered the arrest of the three Bosnian Serb assassins when they crossed the border (the order failed to get through, or was ignored). But the prime minister could hardly cite this in Serbia's defence, because it would have revealed the existence of the secret organisation and persuaded Austria of Serbia's involvement in the crime at the highest levels. 'If it became known,' Apis's nephew Milan Živanović said after the war, 'that Apis was the instigator of the Sarajevo outrage, the impression would be created that the whole Serbian General Staff and probably the Belgrade Government itself was involved in the crime.'[5] And there was fear: everyone feared The Black Hand, which had often demonstrated its cold-blooded willingness to kill its opponents.

So Prime Minister Pašić did what most politicians do when they find themselves in a corner: nothing. He sat on his hands. He refused to initiate any investigation of Serbian accomplices to the assassination. He argued that agreeing to investigate a murder committed outside Serbia was in itself an admission of complicity. Instead,

Belgrade placed the onus on Austria to produce evidence of any connection between Sarajevo and the Serbian Government. And then he pumped out press releases denying Serbia's involvement.

Pašić stuck to this position throughout the crisis. On 8 July, for example, he told the new German military attaché that Serbia 'could not possibly be held responsible for the excesses of callow and overwrought lads' and promised to 'exercise strict control over the nationalistic organisations and expel all elements seeking a hiding place here' (undertakings which the Kaiser dismissed as 'Bunkum' and 'Blah').[6]

Yet Serbia was closely attuned to the military consequences of its actions. A few days later, Pašić heard the ominous news that Austria meant to serve a list of demands on Serbia. 'Austria-Hungary,' his Berlin ambassador Jovanović wrote, 'will draw up in the form of a memorandum an accusation against Serbia . . . At the same time Austria-Hungary will also hand us a note containing her demands, which we shall be requested to accept unconditionally.'[7]

—

The sudden death on 10 July of Nicholas Hartwig, the portly Russian ambassador whose hard-line pro-Slav position had made him a cult figure in Belgrade, came at the worst possible time for the Belgrade government. Serbia had lost a diplomat who unhesitatingly pressed the Serb cause in Moscow. Hartwig's generous, well-attended funeral made a lavish comparison beside the nasty little burial of the archduke and duchess. Pašić felt keenly the loss of this powerful representative of Russia, Serbia's most faithful ally and a man who, for all his pan-Slav bluster, knew the game and would have counselled caution in the crisis. On 15 July, for example, Pašić unwisely left Belgrade to campaign around the country for the forthcoming Serbian elections. He intended to use the spiralling threat to Serbia as a vote-winner, a chance to rally the Serbian people in defiance of Vienna – a move that Hartwig would surely have advised against.

Pašić grew bolder. On 20 July, in dismay at the growing

impression in Europe of Belgrade's hand in the murder, he authorised the dispatch of a telegram to the major European powers, disavowing any Serb involvement in the Sarajevo outrage. Pašić wanted it known that Vienna had failed to request any information from Serbia in relation to the judicial hearings in Sarajevo. He promised, too, that:

> we will meet the wishes of the Austro-Hungarian Empire in the event of our being requested to subject to trial in our independent Courts any accomplices in the outrage who are in Serbia . . . But we can never comply with demands which may be directed against the dignity of Serbia, and which would be inacceptable to any country which respects and maintains its independence.[8]

Three days before Austria dispatched the ultimatum, Pašić received a fresh warning from Jovanović. It amounted to a call to arms:

> Sir,
> . . . Austria is preparing for war against Serbia. The general conviction that prevails here is that it would be nothing short of suicide for Austria-Hungary once more to fail to take advantage of the opportunity to act against Serbia. It is believed that the two opportunities previously missed – the annexation of Bosnia and the Balkan War – have been extremely injurious to Austria-Hungary. In addition, the conviction is steadily growing that Serbia, after her two wars, is completely exhausted, and that a war against Serbia would in fact merely mean a military expedition to be concluded by a speedy occupation . . . The seriousness of Austrian intentions is further emphasised by the military preparations which are being made, especially in the vicinity of the Serbian frontier.[9]

In this state of fraught anticipation, Serbia prepared to receive the Austrian ultimatum. At 4.30 pm on 23 July, Baron Giesl von

Gieslingen, Austro-Hungarian minister at Belgrade, telephoned the Serbian Foreign Ministry to say that he had an 'important communication' for the premier. In Pašić's absence, Giesl informed Dr Laza Paču, acting prime minister and minister for foreign affairs, that he had 'a note' to deliver on behalf of the Austro-Hungarian Government to the Royal Serbian Government.[10]

—

If we strip away the diplomatic noise and examine the true provenance of Vienna's ultimatum, the last stages of the march to war become clearer. Throughout July, Berlin posed as innocent peacemaker to Vienna's stark aggressor. On the contrary, Berlin was intimately involved in the Austrian action, every step of the way, and spun a web of lies to cover its actual role. The story is intricate, yet vital.

A circular sent by Berlin on 21 July to its embassies in London, Paris and St Petersburg gave the appearance that Germany had no knowledge of the Austrian ultimatum. The circular stated, with contrived innocence, that Austria-Hungary's demands on Serbia 'can only be regarded as fair and moderate'. Germany's ambassadors were therefore instructed 'to give emphatic expression' to the view that the conflict between Austria-Hungary and Serbia must be limited 'to those directly concerned. We anxiously desire the localization of the conflict because any intervention by another Power might . . . bring incalculable consequences in its train.'[11]

Berlin's ambassadors, then, were expected to portray an effective declaration of war on Serbia as a 'fair and moderate' action. They were to pat the head of a gorgon. Bethmann-Hollweg, Jagow, Zimmermann and other senior German Government officials, if not their ambassadors, knew the wording of the ultimatum yet wished to give the impression they knew nothing, so they could later claim they were innocent of Austria's extremely harsh terms – in other words, so they could help to provoke a war and then abjure responsibility for it.

The truth is, of course, that the German Government knew everything in Vienna's box of tricks. Berlin had been pulling the strings throughout. '[A]ll the acts and all the roles in the tragedy were settled in advance in Berlin,' concludes Albertini. The key evidence of German complicity was a telegram sent by Hans Schoen, the Bavarian League counsellor in Berlin, to the league's Munich office on 18 July.

Zimmermann, the undersecretary of state, had told him the contents of Vienna's ultimatum to Serbia. It would demand, for example, that the King of Serbia be compelled publicly to dissociate his government from the pan-Serb movements, and that an Austrian official be permitted to participate in the judicial proceedings against the 'accomplices' in the Sarajevo murder. Such demands, Zimmermann concluded, were 'incompatible with Serbia's dignity', and self-evidently Belgrade would not comply: 'The consequence therefore is no doubt war.'[12] Zimmermann enlarged upon Germany's true role, in what could even turn into a European war. Berlin, Schoen quoted him as saying, 'absolutely agreed that Austria is to use the favourable moment [to declare war] even at the risk of further complications [i.e. a European war] . . .'.[13]

If this happened, Zimmermann said, Germany would take 'diplomatic steps' to give the impression of being innocent of Austria's actions. For example, the German Government would try to 'localise' the war immediately after the delivery of the Austrian note to Belgrade (by pointing out that the Kaiser, chief of the General Staff and the Prussian war minister were absent on leave, 'proof of the fact that Germany has been no less taken by surprise by the Austrian action than the other powers . . .').[14] In other words, Germany's protestations of innocence at the contents of the note to Serbia were, as the Kaiser might have put it, 'Bunkum'.

—

The Entente powers also got wind of the Austrian note a few days in advance of its delivery. Russia's reaction was the most violent and portentous. 'A whole country could not be held responsible for the acts of individuals,' Sazonov, the Russian foreign minister, shouted at Count Heinrich von Pourtalès, German ambassador at St Petersburg, when he heard the news.[15] Vienna wanted 'the annihilation of Serbia',[16] Sazonov exclaimed. ('And the best thing, too,' the Kaiser noted on the transcript of this discussion.)

Russia would not permit Austria-Hungary to make any threats against Serbia 'or to take any military measures', Sazonov later remarked to the Italian ambassador. '*La politique de la Russe*,' he said, '*est pacifique, mais pas passive.*'[17]

Paris first heard of the Austrian note on 20 July, when a spy in Vienna – 'a person specially well informed as to official news', according to the French Yellow Book, the colour-coded digest published by various countries after the war that contained all diplomatic correspondence – sent an assessment of Austria's demands and the likely repercussions. The Consular Report reached Paris a day before Poincaré met the Tsar, on 21 July, in St Petersburg:

> much will be demanded of Servia [Serbia]; . . . The tenor of the note and its imperious tone almost certainly ensure that Belgrade will refuse. Then military operations will begin. There is here, and equally at Berlin, a party which accepts the idea of a conflict of widespread dimensions, in other words a conflagration.[18]

Austria would 'probably' have to declare war on Serbia before Russia had completed its railways, the memo said. That left a few weeks at most. Yet Vienna had not reached any consensus on the scale of the likely conflict: 'Count Berchtold and the diplomatists desire at the most localised operations against [Serbia]. But everything must be regarded as possible.'[19] In other words, both Germany and Austria now contemplated the risk of a European war.

Poincaré does not appear to have received the full text of this nerve-shaking letter before he met the Tsar. But he had already reached more or less the same conclusion. He arrived at St Petersburg on 20 July and received a fittingly lavish reception aboard the Tsar's yacht, the *Alexandria*. The two allies sat in the stern and talked long and deep. The French president soon dominated the slightly addled Nicholas. The next day, their talks focused on the Austro-Serbian dispute. The two allies would do everything to support Serbia, a relationship Poincaré brazenly underlined at a diplomatic reception that afternoon.

'Have you news of Serbia?' the French president asked the rather sheepish Austrian ambassador to Russia, Count Frigyes Szapáry.

'The judicial inquiry is proceeding,' Szapáry mutely replied.

To which Poincaré warned Szapáry that every government in Europe should be twice as vigilant in the present climate:

> With a little goodwill this Serbian business is easy to settle. But it can just as easily become acute. Serbia has some very warm friends in the Russian people. And Russia has an ally in France. There are plenty of complications to be feared![20]

This hardly appeased Szapáry, who interpreted it as a Franco-Russian threat, not a plea for calm. Later, Poincaré, alone with the Tsar and Maurice Paléologue, the new French ambassador to St Petersburg, laid bare his concerns about the chat with the Austrian ambassador. 'I'm not satisfied with this conversation,' he said. 'The Ambassador had obviously been instructed to say nothing.' He concluded that 'Austria has a *coup de théâtre* in store for us'.[21]

—

When the Wilhelmstrasse received an official copy of the ultimatum, a day early, on 22 July, the senior ministers acted in character. They publicly affected great surprise at its harshness. Jagow had in fact seen a version on the previous day. 'Its content seemed to me to be pretty stiff and going beyond its purpose,' Jagow lied to Count László Szőgyény, Austro-Hungarian ambassador to Berlin. Bethmann-Hollweg, Zimmermann and other German ministers also feigned surprise at the 'tough' terms. The note was 'in every respect too sharp'.[22]

It is easy to prove that they feigned surprise and incredulity. If they thought the ultimatum so harsh, and likely to lead to war, why did none of them seek to ease its terms, or send their concerns to Vienna, or amend the note before it reached Serbia? Why did they not issue fresh instructions to their ambassadors, who had been told to regard the note as 'fair and moderate'?

Jagow later claimed that he had had no time to amend the ultimatum: Szőgyény had told him it had already gone to Belgrade.[23] This was a bald-faced lie: it was not due for delivery until two days later, on 23 July. In truth, the German Government had ample time to ask Vienna to amend their harsh terms but did nothing. Their inaction chimed with Berlin's general deceit, which sought to persuade the world that it had neither knowledge of nor involvement in Austria's determination to wage war on Serbia.

—

And so the world slid further towards a general catastrophe. The Austro-Hungarian Government, goaded by Germany, continued mobilising. A war council met in Vienna on 19 July and decided unanimously that Austro-Hungarian forces should strike soon, as Serbian forces were amassing along the border. And, once victorious, the imperial army would depose the Serbian royal line and redraw the frontiers.[24]

On 22 July, eight Austro-Hungarian army corps – more than 300,000 men – approached the Serbian border. Vienna intended to attack Serbia with 'the greatest severity', M. Dumaine, the French ambassador, cabled Paris that day.[25] At the same time, the official Austro-Hungarian news agency reprinted the most inflammatory passages of the Serbian press, to arouse public feeling for war.

Through these precipitate actions, Berlin and Vienna sent the wrong message to St Petersburg and France. They were acutely aware of the likelihood of a wider war in an extremely tense situation: one doesn't secure a wasp's nest by shaking the tree. Yet that is exactly what they did. Berlin's lies about the German position, its deceitful role in the production of a completely unacceptable ultimatum to Serbia, and its refusal to press Vienna to moderate the terms, all pointed to a determination to wage war, even at the risk of sparking a Europe-wide conflict. They still talked of a 'local', Balkan war but knew the likely, terrible repercussions. And, when the world discovered that Berlin 'held all the threads', noted Albertini, 'such an avalanche of general indignation and mistrust' would descend on the German rulers that they would be 'totally discredited and all attempts to save the peace . . . in vain'.[26]

—

Giesl arrived at the Serb Foreign Ministry in Belgrade an hour late, at 6 pm. In Prime Minister Pašić's absence, Dr Paču, acting prime minister, had been delegated to receive him. Paču refused to receive the note; the prime minister had that responsibility. Giesl dismissed this excuse: in the age of railways and telegraph, the premier's return 'could be only a matter of a few hours'.[27] Paču continued to refuse to accept the ultimatum, so Giesl left the sealed envelope on the table and told him to do as he wished with it. If the Serbian officials, he declared, refused to send an unconditional acceptance of Vienna's demands within the 48-hour deadline, he was commissioned to pack up the Austro-Hungarian Embassy and leave Belgrade together with his staff and passports. He turned and left.

On Giesl's departure, Paču and his colleagues tore open the letter and scoured its contents. Austria-Hungary's principal demands were as follows (see Appendix 2 for the full text):

The Austro-Hungarian Ultimatum to Serbia
Vienna 22nd July 1914
        . . . It is clear from the statements and confessions of the
criminal authors of the assassination on the 28th June that the
murder . . . was conceived at Belgrade . . .

The Royal Serbian Government will [as a result] pledge itself:

1. to suppress every publication which shall incite to hatred and contempt of the Monarchy, and the general tendency of which shall be directed against the territorial integrity of the latter;

2. to proceed at once to the dissolution of the *Narodna Odbrana*, to confiscate all of its means of propaganda, and in the same manner to proceed against the other unions and associations in Serbia which occupy themselves with propaganda against Austria-Hungary; . . .

4. to remove from the military and administrative service in general all officers and officials who have been guilty of carrying on the propaganda against Austria-Hungary, whose names the Imperial and Royal Government reserves the right to make known to the Royal Government when communicating the material evidence now in its possession;

5. to agree to the cooperation in Serbia of the organs of the Imperial and Royal Government in the suppression of the subversive movement directed against the integrity of the Monarchy;

6. to institute a judicial inquiry against every participant in the conspiracy of the twenty-eighth of June who may be found in Serbian territory; the organs of the [Austro-Hungarian] Government delegated for this purpose will take part in the proceedings . . .

7. to undertake with all haste the arrest of Major Vojislav Tankosić and of one Milan Ciganovitch, a Serbian official, who have been compromised by the results of the inquiry . . .[28]

Austria-Hungary expected Serbia's reply no later than Saturday 25th at 6 pm. The ultimatum maximised Serbian humiliation and trod all over its sovereignty. Of its time, and expressed in such terms, it was utterly unacceptable and amounted to a declaration of war.

28

YOU ARE SETTING FIRE TO EUROPE

If Austria-Hungary devours Serbia we will go to war with her.
Sergei Sazonov, Russian foreign minister, on
learning of the Austrian ultimatum

Well, go to it!
The Kaiser's response

SERBIA HAD 48 HOURS TO ACT. Prime Minister Pašić decided
to do nothing and continued his election tour. At the time, he was
en route to Salonika. His Cabinet finally persuaded him to return
to Belgrade, but he would not be back until 5 am on the 24th. In
Pašić's absence, the ministers sat down to study the terms. Austria's
severe tone surprised them. Vienna clearly wanted more than their
acquiescence; they wanted war. Paču, the acting prime minister,
alerted Serbia's legations in Europe.

All through the day they pored over the document and were
unable to decide what to do. 'It is said to be impossible to carry out

the demands set forth within forty-eight hours,' Germany's man in Belgrade, Baron von Griesinger, reported to Berlin. He kept a close ear to the huddle of Serbian officials. Several points (2, 4, 5 and 6) amounted to 'a direct attack upon Serbian sovereignty' and appeared to be clearly unacceptable, he telegrammed Berlin.[1] In the margins to this cable, the Kaiser noted, 'How hollow the whole so-called Serbian power is proving itself to be; thus it is seen to be with all the Slav nations! Just tread hard on the heels of that rabble!'[2]

When Pašić returned to Belgrade, he immediately decided that Serbia must have more time: the document was impossible either to accept or reject. Until then, they would try to meet the deadline. 'But,' Pašić warned, 'if war is unavoidable – we shall fight.'[3] In that event, Belgrade would have to be abandoned, and the government started preparing to leave for a southern location.

———

European embassies received the note early in the morning of the 24th, cutting the time available for mediation by 15 hours. '*C'est la guerre européenne!*', exclaimed the stupefied Russian foreign minister Sazonov when he read the telegram.[4] His worst fears had been realised. He summoned Austrian ambassador Frigyes Szapáry, who appeared in his office at 10 am and solemnly read out the terms of the note. Austria had taken this step, Szapáry added, to 'preserve its territory from the insurrectional miasma' spreading across Serbia.[5]

Dismissing this, Sazonov almost shouted, 'What you want is war with Serbia, and you have burnt your bridges behind you!'

'Austria was the most pacific dynasty in the world,' Szapáry abruptly countered. '[W]hat we wanted was to preserve our territory from revolution and our dynasty from bombs.'

'One can see how pacific you are,' Sazonov snorted, 'since you are setting fire to Europe!'[6]

The meeting lasted an hour and a half. Sazonov alighted on certain clauses that especially offended him. He protested 'most vividly' at the dissolution of *Narodna Odbrana*. That was 'a condition Serbia would never accept', he warned. Nor would it accept Austria's insistence in sending royal functionaries to suppress 'subversive elements' in Serbia.

'From first to last,' Szapáry reported back to Vienna, Sazonov was 'non-compliant and hostile'. Szapáry left the room with the Russian's warning of the likely impact of the note on 'England, France and Europe' ringing in his ears. Not once had Sazonov mentioned Russia's intentions in the meeting, because this was not just a 'Slav' issue. Sazonov was determined to make it a European one, to persuade his European partners to join in condemning Austria.[7]

—

Sazonov zealously pursued the course of widening the issue and dragging the European powers into the Balkan cauldron. That day, 24 July, a meeting of the Russian Council of Ministers accepted his recommendation to enlist his Entente partners in pressing Austria to give Serbia longer to reply. At the same time, Sazonov took the exceedingly reckless step of initiating a partial mobilisation against Austria. He gave the Russian war and navy ministers leave to appeal to the Tsar, if circumstances required, to order the mobilisation of forces then stationed at Kiev, Odessa, Moscow and Kazan – 13 army corps or more than 1,100,000 men – and to prepare the Baltic and Black Sea fleets.[8] This extremely unwise and provocative act represented a huge stride towards a European war, because any sign of Russian mobilisation would immediately activate German mobilisation – and technically pull Italy into a war against Russia (as a *casus foederis* under the Triple Alliance). Partial mobilisation only made sense as a prelude to full mobilisation of Russia's vast forces – a point not lost on Germany's commanders as they gazed into the eastern haze.

The next day, Sazonov angrily denounced the Austrian note before the German ambassador Count Pourtalès. Sazonov was 'very much excited', Pourtalès reported to Berlin, 'and gave vent to boundless reproaches against Austria-Hungary'. The Austro-Serbian quarrel could not be settled between the two parties, he quoted the Russian as saying. It 'was a European affair', Sazonov cried, 'and it was for Europe to investigate [whether Serbia had met its obligations]'. Sazonov even called for a European tribunal to sit in judgment on Austria-Hungary.[9]

'Rot!' screamed the Kaiser from the margins. Pourtalès argued more diplomatically against this idea. Vienna would never consent to European arbitration, no more than would any power. The German ambassador infuriated Sazonov by suggesting that Russia was defending 'the cause of regicide', and 'expressed the fear that he was under the sway of his blind, relentless hatred against Austria'.

To which Sazonov replied that he felt 'not hatred but contempt'. 'If Austria-Hungary,' he said, 'devours Serbia we will go to war with her.' ('Well, go to it!' the Kaiser childishly noted.)[10]

Pourtalès retorted that Austria had no territorial claims on Serbia, to which an incredulous Sazonov exploded that Bulgaria would be next, and 'then we shall have [Austria-Hungary] at the Black Sea'.[11] Pourtalès dismissed this as unworthy of serious discussion and left Sazonov's office deeply agitated, his face purple and his eyes flashing.[12]

The French ambassador Maurice Paléologue, waiting outside, later claimed to have warned Sazonov, 'If conversations between St Petersburg and Berlin are to continue in this strain they won't last long. Very soon we shall see the Emperor Wilhelm rise in his "shining armour". Please be calm. Exhaust every possibility of compromise!'[13] The Frenchman's plea for restraint, recorded in his memoir, must be treated with suspicion: Paléologue was anything but 'calm' or willing to compromise. A flamboyant character, he tended to make defiant shows of unity with Russia that went beyond his diplomatic remit from Paris.

—

Russia continued to act on its darkest suspicion that Berlin and Vienna were conspiring to provoke a European war. At this stage, however – despite the Kaiser's and Moltke's sabre rattling – wiser heads in Berlin and Vienna genuinely hoped to limit it to the Balkans, as a punishment to Serbia. Yet Sazonov's agitation helped to escalate what might have been limited to a local conflict to a pan-European war. Later that day (24 July), he wrote to his diplomatic missions throughout Europe, demanding their host countries' support and urging an extension of the deadline to Belgrade.

The next day, he urged Britain to declare its hand for the Entente, through the rarely used tactic of appealing to the Russian Tsar, whose family ties with the English king offered an entry point. He alerted Nicholas II to the pressing political questions in the Balkans, 'on the chance that Your Imperial Majesty might deign to refer them in your most exalted reply to the King of England'. He told the Tsar:

> The clear aim [of Austria], which is apparently supported by
> Germany – is the total annihilation of Serbia . . . There can be
> no doubt that deceitful and provocative actions of this kind will
> meet with no sympathy in England from either the Government
> or public opinion. If Austria persists any longer with this line
> of policy, Russia will not be able to remain indifferent . . . It
> is to be hoped that in this event Russia and England will both
> find themselves on the side of right and justice and that the
> disinterested policies of Russia, whose sole aim is to prevent the
> establishment of Austrian hegemony in the Balkans will find
> active support [in] England.[14]

Sazonov telegrammed the same message to his ambassador in London that day and instructed him to press England to stand by its Entente partners: 'we count upon it that England will at once side with Russia and France, in order to maintain the European balance of power . . .'[15]

—

In receipt, the British Government exuded its usual imperturbable calm. As so often in crises, the English were determined not to appear ruffled. The worst thing was to panic. This was not merely an aristocratic affectation but rather a sort of bolted-on insouciance, which, as the temperature rose throughout July, failed to disguise a tic of anxiety on Edward Grey's face. Events would soon overwhelm the studied calm of Whitehall, and British leaders would join their European partners with their heads in their hands and hopes to the wind.

For now, the foreign minister refused to be dragged into a row between Vienna and Belgrade. Grey continued to think he could have it both ways, to indulge his Janus-faced friendship with both Germany and his Entente partners. Yet the landing of the ultimatum on his desk brought London closer to the day of reckoning. 'The most formidable document that was ever addressed from one State to another,' Grey famously concluded.[16] (Not so by today's standards of diplomatic bullying: rejection of NATO's ultimatums, for example, to modern Serbia in the 1990s, led to immediate aerial bombardment.)

In general, Grey cared little for Austria's ultimatum and less for Serbia, so long as they avoided war. He saw merit in some of Austria's demands, but he strongly questioned several. How could 'Organs' of Austria-Hungary be placed in Serbia without terminating Serbia's independence, he asked Count Mensdorff, the Austrian ambassador in London. 'The collaboration of police-organs,' Mensdorff answered, stupidly, 'does not touch a State's sovereignty.'[17] Yet what most troubled the British foreign secretary was the sharp deadline and the fact that 'the Note, so to speak, dictates its own answer'.[18]

In marked contrast to Sazonov, Grey was careful not to apportion blame, and set out on a policy of compromise and mediation. If war should come to the Balkans, he decided, it must be confined to the Balkans. On the 24th, Grey addressed himself to the Serbian ambassador in London, Mateja Bošković, and firmly advised the Serbs 'to express concern and regret that any officials, however subordinate, should have been accomplices in the murder of the Archduke, and promise, if this is proved, to give fullest satisfaction'. He urged

Belgrade furthermore to 'give a favourable reply on as many points as possible within the limit of time, and not to meet Austrian demands with a blank negative'.[19] This advice completely misread Belgrade's pride, rather like politely asking a Scordisci tribesman to shine the boots of a Visigoth. Serbia would do as it chose.

—

That night, Paris and St Petersburg used the crisis to press London for a firm statement of trilateral support. At 8 pm, Grey received a telegram from Buchanan, British ambassador in St Petersburg, warning that France and Russia 'were determined to make a strong stand even if we declined to join them'. France and Russia insisted that London declare 'complete solidarity with them'.[20] Yet Buchanan had been perilously misled. A firm stand, at that juncture, was not in fact French policy. Buchanan, unknown to him, had stumbled on a dangerous misreading of the truth. France had not yet responded at presidential level. Poincaré was at sea. The source of France's 'strong stand' with Russia was Maurice Paléologue, the unruly French ambassador, who had of his own accord, without any instructions from Paris, given Russia 'a pledge of France's unconditional solidarity'.[21]

The episode showed how easily a single, reckless statement by an errant official could crank up the tension, to an explosive degree. The British ambassador assumed Paléologue had spoken with the full authority of the French president. In other words, he believed France and Russia had already closed ranks and anticipated a European war – and now, as a bloc, they demanded to know where Britain stood. Paléologue had also dismissed, without authority from Paris, any effort to extend the deadline, to mediate, and reiterated to Buchanan that 'a firm and united attitude was our only chance of averting war'.[22] Paléologue may have been accurate about the deterrent effect of a united stand, yet the peaceful arts of mediation and negotiation did not accompany the bellicose Franco-Russian position. They were issuing threats of war, not appeals for peace.

The Buchanan telegram inspired that warrior-like civil servant Eyre Crowe to take up his pen. With his familiar warlike phrases – 'the moment has passed', 'we shall gain nothing', 'we should decide *now*', etc. – Crowe urged the government to mobilise the British fleet, in order to deter Germany and show that Britain stood firm with France and Russia. 'The point that matters is whether Germany is or is not absolutely determined to have this war,' Crowe wrote (in a minute to Buchanan's telegram). Crowe suggested flushing the Germans out, by 'putting our whole fleet on an immediate war footing' the moment either Austria or Russia began to mobilise. This 'may conceivably make Germany realize the seriousness of the danger to which she would be exposed if England took part in the war'.[23]

He may have been right. We cannot know the effect of Crowe's advice, if acted on. Perhaps Austria-Hungary would have shrunk from the sight of a British dreadnought on the high seas and packed up its arsenals. Crowe rather had in mind the symbolism of the ships, which would prove Britain had no intention of remaining neutral and would stand firm with the Entente. Whether this would have deterred Germany at this late stage is hypothetical. On the contrary, it may have so enraged them as to accelerate the coming of a European war. What nobody in London then knew was that the German and Russian generals were already preparing for a wider war.

The Crowe proposal ascended the rungs of power and 'merited serious consideration' in Cabinet.[24] Churchill advised that the mobilisation of the fleet would take 24 hours. (We ought to remind ourselves that this escalation stemmed from a French diplomat's wilful misrepresentation of French policy towards Russia.) Grey did nothing. He refused to clarify the British position to France or Russia. Nobody in fact knew the true British position. Perhaps Grey should have committed Britain firmly to the Entente at that moment, as Crowe urged – the most tantalising 'what if' of the July weeks. It was probably too late. The deterrent power of Entente unity may have passed. And to use the stick without a carrot risked a terrible escalation: Grey had offered no clear proposals (yet) to mediate. The great powers' rush to arms, without any pacifying alternatives, was a gross overreaction and escalated the crisis way beyond the confines of the Balkans.

The next day, Grey's mood soured, and his hopes that the war may be confined to the Balkans receded. 'If war does take place,' he replied to Buchanan, 'we may be drawn into it by the development of other issues, and I am therefore anxious to prevent war.'[25] In particular, he feared the entry of Russia, looming on the sidelines like a great black bear. 'The brusque, sudden and peremptory character [of the Austrian note] makes it almost inevitable that in very short time Austria and Russia will both have mobilised against each other,' he wrote.[26] Sincere in his efforts to preserve peace, but understandably confused about how to avoid war, he resolved merely to advise Russia and Austria not to breach their borders, and to press Vienna to extend the deadline. 'He could only hope that a mild and pacific view of the situation would gain ground,' the German ambassador informed Berlin – an apt summary of Grey's disposition throughout the crisis.[27]

Albertini offers a much harsher verdict: faced with an Austro-German fait accompli, Grey did nothing. His inert response showed 'a complete failure to understand what was at issue'. He should have given Austria and Germany 'a severe warning', advises Albertini (exchanging his historian's hat for a policy adviser's). Grey should have urged Germany to restrain Austria, and he should have advised St Petersburg to 'refrain from all measures of mobilisation'.[28] Yet Grey stood aside and watched the catastrophe unfold as though he was observing a terrible accident in slow motion. If Britain had any power in European affairs, now was the time to wield it.

—

In Paris, reactions were muted, because Poincaré and Viviani were somewhere in the Baltic, returning from their Russian visit. The inexperienced finance minister Bienvenu-Martin was in charge in Paris. He proved unable to control France's man in St Petersburg, Paléologue, whose unwise intervention had dramatically escalated events. No doubt, Poincaré supported a firm line against Serbia too, but he would not have made it so provocatively.

France's moderate ambassadors rejected the provocative stand of Paléologue and Sazonov. Jules Cambon, French ambassador to Berlin, shared British hopes of mediation. He believed that Austria should be told to extend the deadline. He favoured a European conference. Neither tactic won support in Paris. And his ideas were impracticable now, with the deadline fast approaching.

—

All this was mere diplomatic badinage, because Berlin and Vienna had already rejected any extension of the deadline and any form of mediation. 'We cannot concede a prolongation of the term,' Berchtold declared. He deigned not to announce this to the wider world; instead, he made it known in a telegram to a minor Austrian diplomat then on holiday in the tiny Austrian town of Lambach. It arrived on Saturday 25 July at 4 pm, two hours before the deadline.[29] Clearly, Berchtold had no interest in the counsel of the British or French.

Germany sat poker-faced throughout, caught in the web of lies in which it had enmeshed itself. In character, Berlin's ministers feigned complete ignorance of the note and shared the Entente's incredulity at the Austrian action. Within hours of the ultimatum's appearance, the German Government dispatched telegrams to its embassies, claiming that Germany had no prior knowledge of the note or its stiff terms – and yet, having launched it, Austria must stick to its threat and 'could not pull back'.

Secretary of State Jagow proved a most emphatic liar, repeating again and again – 'very earnestly' to the British ambassador in Berlin – that 'he had had no previous knowledge of the Austro-Hungarian note . . .'.[30] Jules Cambon scorned this obvious lie, and made a diplomatic point of the man's shameless deceit. 'It is not less strik-ing,' he informed Paris, 'to notice the pains with which Herr von Jagow, and all the officials placed under his orders, pretend to every one that they were ignorant of the scope of the note sent by Austria to Servia.'[31]

The Kaiser scowled down from his palace. One early piece of intelligence elicited his furious reaction. Edward Grey, according to a cable from Jagow, had dared to suggest that Austria should not compromise Serbian sovereignty:

> Right! Grey must be told this plainly and seriously! So that he will see that I'm not fooling. Grey is committing the error of setting Serbia on the same plane with Austria and other Great Powers! That is unheard of! Serbia is nothing but a band of robbers that must be seized for its crimes![32]

29

THE SERBS REPLY

[Austria-Hungary] wished to crush a small state. Then a war would follow in which other Powers would be led to take a part.

Edward Grey, British foreign secretary, 26 July 1914

RUSSIAN SUPPORT STIFFENED Serbia's spine. Around noon on 25 July – five hours before the deadline – Serbia received a telegram from Sazonov. He promised Russia's full support and advised Serbia to accept all points on the ultimatum that did not conflict with Serbia's sovereign rights.[1] Russia's open-ended support echoed the blank cheque that Germany had given Austria a few weeks earlier.

The Serbian Government would do exactly as Russia advised. That afternoon, Pašić informed the French and Russian Embassies of the likely contents of Serbia's reply. It seemed to M. Boppe, the French official, that Serbia had indeed fallen on its sword and accepted just about every clause.[2] This included dissolving all associations that might agitate against Austria-Hungary, modifying the press law, and dismissing from service in the army, and the government offices, any officials proved to have taken part in anti-Austro-Hungarian agitation.

But not every clause would be adhered to. Serbia would, it seemed, refuse to accept the demand that Austrian officials be allowed to join the investigation of Serb 'accessories' to the assassination (the critical Point 6), because it trampled on Serbia's sovereign rights. The murder, we should remember, was committed in Bosnia, outside Serb territory. But sovereignty was not the real reason Serbia refused: Belgrade feared that Austrian investigators would expose the role of The Black Hand, which had had close relations with the Belgrade government.

As the deadline approached, the word spread that Serbia had submitted to most of Austria's clauses but rejected some. Did that still mean war? Would Austria accept Serbia's partial prostration? Truculent Germans and Austrians feared that Serbia might actually accept *all* their demands – thus denying them the war they so dearly sought. Indeed, a prominent German confessed to Jules Cambon, French ambassador in Berlin, that Germans greatly feared Serbia would accept *every point*.

So it was with indecent relief that Berliners read in the local press that General Giesl, Austro-Hungarian minister at Belgrade, was preparing to leave Serbia. At the news, large crowds queued at newspaper offices in Berlin shouting 'Hurrah!' for Germany and singing patriotic songs. An alarmed Cambon advised Paris:

> I, for my part, see in Great Britain the only Power which might be listened to at Berlin. Whatever happens, Paris, St Petersburg and London will not succeed in maintaining peace with dignity unless they show a firm and absolutely united front.[3]

———

Little Serbia proved a resilient participant in the great game of European power. The Serb Government sensed, no matter how conciliatory its reply, that Vienna and Berlin *wanted* war in the Balkans – a fact that eluded Grey and outraged Sazonov. Belgrade started officially mobilising its army at 3 pm on the 25th, two hours before the deadline. At the same time, the government officers and the garrison began to evacuate Belgrade for the southern city of Niš.

Confident of Russia's backing, the Serbs planned to use their reply to Austria to achieve three vital diplomatic aims: to win the support of the Serbian armed forces and extreme nationalists, by showing them that the country would not capitulate to Vienna; to win the sympathy of European governments and public opinion; and to cast Austria-Hungary as the aggressor.

So they took extreme care over the draft. The final version, sent for translation at midday on the 25th, was whisked away several times during the afternoon and 'so full of crossings out and additions as to be almost incomprehensible'.[4] At 4 pm, it was ready for typing, and, after some dithering over who should deliver it, Pašić personally took it to the Austrian Legation in Belgrade, at 5.45 pm. There, he addressed General Giesl, the Austrian ambassador, in broken German: 'Part of your demands we have accepted . . . for the rest we place our hopes on your loyalty and chivalry as an Austrian general.'[5]

Pašić returned to his office and wrote to the Serb embassies in Europe. 'Austria-Hungary,' he warned, 'unless they are determined to make war at all costs, will see their way to accept the full satisfaction offered in the Serb reply.'[6] The government then boarded trains for Niš, Serbia's third-largest city and new wartime capital, leaving the near-deserted city of Belgrade at the mercy of the Austrian forces then massing on the border.

—

General Giesl knew exactly what was expected of him. On receiving Serbia's reply from Pašić, he glanced at it, saw it was inadequate and signed a previously prepared letter, which was immediately handed back to the Serbian Government. The letter severed diplomatic relations with Serbia and announced the departure of the Austro-Hungarian Legation. Giesl, his bags packed, ordered the destruction of the Embassy's code books and, with his wife and staff, caught the 6.30 train to the Austrian frontier. 'I found the streets,' he later wrote to Albertini, 'leading to the station and the station itself occupied by the Serbian military.'[7] He would attribute Belgrade's sudden self-confidence to Sazonov's earlier telegram, pledging Russian backing for Serbian actions.

The Serbs well knew their reply had no chance of acceptance. Yet their answer grovelled less than many later supposed (see Appendix 3). With Russia fast at their shoulder, they took a harder line than they would have done. Of the ten points, Belgrade partially or fully rejected Points 4, 5, 6 and 9, and had reservations about the rest. There was more than a hint of mockery, even derision, running through some their answers, whose curious circular sentences began with apparent offers to cooperate ('The Royal Serbian Government regret that . . .', 'The Royal Serbian Government undertake to eliminate . . .') and ended by pulling the rug from under Austria's feet. Serbia's tone of mock innocence ('Who? Us?'), their semblance of hurt pride and sly references to the harm done to their 'good neighbourly relations' with Vienna (relations were anything but!) were calculated to irritate and provoke.

Consider, for example, Serbia's replies to Austria-Hungary's three key demands, Points 4, 5, 6:[8]

> 4. [Serbia] agree to remove from the military service all such persons as the judicial inquiry [then underway in Bosnia] may have proved to be guilty of such acts directed against the integrity of the territory of the Austro-Hungarian Monarchy, and they expect [Austria-Hungary] to communicate to them at a later date the names and the acts of these officers and functionaries . . .

Here, Serbia had agreed to sack the guilty parties, but only after Vienna sent them the names, rendering the whole exercise futile, because Serbia refused to allow Austrian investigation of its officials (see 6, below).

5. [Serbia] must confess that they do not clearly grasp the meaning of the scope of the demand made by [Austria-Hungary] that Serbia shall undertake to accept the collaboration of the representatives of [Austria-Hungary] upon their territory, but they declare that they will admit such collaboration as agrees with the principle of international law, with criminal procedure and with good neighbourly relations.

If this meant anything, it meant that Serbia had no idea what Austria was on about, but would act according to Austria's wishes at such time as they became clear, in accordance with 'international law', etc.

6. . . . . As regards the participation of Austro-Hungarian agents in [Serbia's inquiry into the assassination] . . . [Serbia] cannot accept [those agents on its soil], as it would be a violation of the Constitution and of the law of criminal procedure . . .

In other words, shove off. Was Austria-Hungary actually going to declare war on Serbia because Belgrade had refused to accept Viennese policemen on its soil?

The Austro-Hungarians responded with all the puffed-up indignation of an ailing and desperate empire. They attacked Serbia's answers in turn, in order to win the propaganda battle and justify the real war. They circulated their reply to the European embassies on 28 July. Most cities did not receive it. In any case, it persuaded nobody of Austria's cause. Austria-Hungary also demanded that Serbia muzzle its anti-Austrian press, confiscate any propaganda deemed to incite hatred and contempt for Austria-Hungary and punish the perpetrators. In response, Serbia merely proposed a new press law, with a vague commitment to control it.[9]

The rest of Austria's objections amounted to legalese, phony indignation and diplomatic pedantry. The whole exercise, of course, was a grotesque charade, on both sides. Take Serbia's sly reservation

– 'we possess no proof that the *Narodna Odbrana* and other similar societies have committed any criminal act' – while in the next breath agreeing to 'dissolve the *Narodna Odbrana* Society and every other society that may be directing its efforts against Austria-Hungary'.[10] In other words, Serbia had agreed to dissolve its most important cultural organisation for no reason whatsoever, making the gesture worthless.

Reading these documents cold, one is left staggering at the callousness and cynicism of the individuals involved. In the light of the Austro-German war plans, they are intelligible as a set of malicious diplomatic contrivances. Austria's demands were merely the devious machinations of a sclerotic empire desperate to extract a *casus belli* in order to destroy its hated neighbour and restore its 'prestige'. Serbia knew this. Its answers had nothing to do with satisfying Austria, but everything to do with appealing to European opinion and unifying the Serbian people in advance of likely hostilities.

—

Vienna was in a quandary at the Serbian reply. Serbia had refused to give Vienna a firm case for war. Why had Serbia not rejected everything as anticipated, the government wondered. Were they not men of honour? How dare they actually submit to so much! Serbia's reply made war difficult to declare. And, worse, by going further to meet Austria's demands than many expected, Serbia had enlisted European sympathy and stolen the wind from Vienna's sails.

For a moment, Berchtold was oddly relieved: here was a chance to avoid conflict. Perhaps Belgrade had grovelled enough? Berchtold, back to his old leisurely, aristocratic self, briefly entertained the idea that a diplomatic victory may be enough. The Austrian armed forces, too, faltered in their resolve. The General Staff, warned Conrad, 'like a horse three times taken up to an obstacle and each time reined back, will refuse to jump it'.[11] The Austrians, fearing actually to commit the deed now it was upon them, dreaded the consequences. Berchtold appeared to flirt with the idea of waging a phony war, which would retrieve Austrian honour without risking a European conflict. Quick to don his armour in a show of political defiance, he was equally quick to discard it when the battle stared him in the face. He seemed to have lost his nerve at the critical moment.

—

Events energised Sir Edward Grey. From London, on the same day (25 July) – though he had not yet read Serbia's reply – he telegrammed Paris to propose a mediated solution to the crisis. Grey suggested that Britain, France, Germany and Italy, acting in concert, should 'press on both Russia and Austria that their armies should not cross the frontier' – and give mediation a chance.[12] It was a radical proposal for a ménage à quatre that bridged the divide between the Triple Entente and Triple Alliance. It had little chance of success.

That day, Grey met Count Lichnowsky, the German ambassador in London. Lichnowsky was by all accounts a 'good German', who later incurred his country's wrath for disavowing his government's behaviour during the crisis. Grey warned the Count that, if Austria invaded Serbia, it demonstrated that Vienna aimed not merely at satisfaction of the questions in the ultimatum, 'but that she wished to crush a small state'. 'Then,' he added, 'a war would follow in which other Powers would be led to take a part.' This time, Grey backed up his concerns with firm actions. He decided to make public an order to postpone the decision to demobilise the fleet, taken by Churchill, the first lord of the Admiralty, the previous week.[13] The Royal Navy remained on alert.

The order did not reach Bethmann-Hollweg, who told the Kaiser the next day that the English fleet was proceeding to demobilise and giving crews leave according to schedule. In appreciation, the chancellor suggested that Germany's High Seas Fleet 'remain in Norway for the present' – as this would 'lighten the burden' of England's proposed mediation action at St Petersburg, which 'is evidently beginning to get shaky'.[14] The Kaiser angrily rejected this and ordered the German fleet to sail for Kiel, because, 'there is a Russian fleet! In the

Baltic there are now five Russian torpedo boat flotillas engaged in practice cruises . . .'

Grey's mediation attempts with Russia were indeed shaky. His telegram to St Petersburg warned of the danger of a general European war unless mediation was given a chance. He said the same to the Germans, to the chagrin of the Russians. According to Grey, the Russian ambassador in London warned St Petersburg, 'Austrian mobilisation must lead to Russian mobilisation, [and] that grave danger of a general war will thereupon arise.'[15] Only if Germany, France, Italy and Great Britain abstained from immediate mobilisation could war be avoided, Grey believed. The essential point was to persuade Germany *not* to mobilise.

—

The 26th July was a Saturday, and the great cities went about their business blissfully unaware of the frenzied diplomatic activity down the telegraph lines, which continued all day. Elegantly composed letters flew among the embassies of Europe, attuning their governments to changing positions, new appeals, old lies. Events seemed to acquire a momentum all of their own. Serbia and Austria-Hungary continued to mobilise. The Serbian forces were under orders to await Austria's initiation of hostilities. The Belgrade government re-established itself in Niš. St Petersburg repeatedly made clear it would not stand aside if Austria attacked Serbia. And Berlin continued to speak in dilatory tongues: Secretary of State Herr von Jagow pretended to believe that the Austrian action would remain localised and would not lead to general military consequences.

An explosion of chauvinism erupted on the streets of Berlin, Hamburg, Munich and other German cities. Passionate crowds demanded war. Photographs of the time suggest that Adolf Hitler was among them. Jules Cambon wrote ominously – and accurately – to Paris that Germany would 'immediately reply to the first military steps taken by Russia' and 'not wait for a pretext before attacking us'. Bienvenu-Martin sent this directly to Poincaré, then still at sea.[16]

—

Amid the dwindling hopes of peace, Germany moved to cast all responsibility for a European war on Russia. In executing this plan, Bethmann-Hollweg repeatedly protested to Paris and London that Austria-Hungary had no desire for territorial gain in Serbia, only to punish the Serbs for Sarajevo.

And yet, if Russia mobilised, he warned, 'we shall be forced to countermeasures very much against our own wishes. Our desire to localize the conflict and to preserve the peace of Europe remains unchanged.'[17] He went further: 'the decision whether there is to be a European war rests solely with Russia which has to bear the entire responsibility. We depend upon France [to] exercise its influence at St. Petersburg in favour of peace.'[18]

Russia, as Germany knew, had already started to prepare for war. On the 25th, the government ordered 'preliminary preparations for mobilization' and the drafting of an imperial *ukase* – the Tsar's authorisation for the execution of war plans. The *ukase* could be enacted whenever the Foreign Ministry chose. It authorised the mobilisation of 1,100,000 men.[19]

30

EVERY CAUSE FOR WAR HAS VANISHED

A brilliant achievement in a time limit of only forty-eight hours!
It is more than one could have expected!
A great moral success for Vienna; but with it all reason for war
is gone and Giesl ought to have quietly stayed on in Belgrade!
After that I should never have ordered mobilization.
Kaiser Wilhelm II, on reading the Serbian reply to the Austrian ultimatum

---

EUROPE, BY THAT STRANGE INABILITY OF NATIONS – like individuals – to see themselves as others see them, by the clash of flawed men elevated far beyond their abilities, by a superstitious belief in the false gods of might, manifest destiny and the survival of the fittest, moved closer to a general war.

Yet the ease with which war could have been avoided cries out from several events and telegrams in the last week of July. Consider the cheerful cable of 26 July, sent by Count Pourtalès, German ambassador in St Petersburg, to Berlin, in which he recounts a 'pleasant' meeting with the Russian foreign minister Sazonov and the Austrian ambassador Count Szapáry. A day earlier, Szapáry had been the recipient of Sazonov's wrath. Now, it seems, all was forgiven, in a haze of bonhomie. The Austrian ultimatum did not wholly bother the Russians after all, according to this fleeting exchange. Suddenly, the Russian and the Austrian parties were constructive. They spoke with goodwill, a willingness to mediate, where a day earlier they were passing through the gates of hell. Indeed, Sazonov 'might be able to come to an agreement as a result of alterations . . . perhaps it was only a matter of words'.[1] Only a matter of words?

In Vienna, too, the prospect of war briefly receded. Between 25 and 27 July, the government sat and pondered on how to postpone or perhaps avoid the military action it once so zealously pursued. Berchtold, rather like a turtle pulling in its head, withdrew into his irresolute character. For two days, the Austrians were poised between war and peace. The agreeable, even prostrate, tone of the Serb reply gave them pause for thought: are we going to declare war over this? How would it look in the eyes of the world? *Le Matin*, for example, reflected the mood of the world toward the Serbian reply: 'Never in history has a nation made so many concessions,' it reported on 27 July, '. . . never in history has a nation been so humiliated in order to preserve peace. Most of the Austrian conditions were unacceptable. However, Serbia has agreed to all the conditions.'[2]

Even Conrad had his doubts about attacking Serbia over this. For the Austrians, only the *declaration* of war now meant war. The severing of diplomatic relations, the departure of Giesl from Belgrade, the closure of the legation: none of this technically meant war. If the wildest enthusiasm for battle filled the streets of Vienna, the government wavered in a kind of limbo, as if awaiting the hand of destiny.

———

The hand of destiny came – from Berlin, where ministers had presumed Austria-Hungary would declare war automatically on receipt of Serbia's inadequate reply. When Vienna hesitated, Gottlieb von Jagow, the German foreign minister, pressed Austria to attack Serbia. Berlin made its position clear, in a note to Berchtold on the 25th:

here the general belief is [after receiving the Serb reply] your declaration of war and war operations will follow immediately. Here every delay . . . is regarded as signifying the danger that foreign powers might interfere. We are urgently advised to proceed without delay and to place before the world a *fait accompli*.[3]

Austria continued mobilising but would not yet attack.

Meanwhile, Bethmann-Hollweg, Jagow, Moltke and the Prussian commanders noted with alarm the rumours issuing from St Petersburg of Russia's mobilisation. In this atmosphere, the vehemence with which Germany urged Austria to punish the Serbs risked a catastrophic war. Russia and Germany were now preparing for this danger, and, by doing so, hastened that very outcome. The Russian partial mobilisation had clearly begun. The German General Staff brought forward the planned invasion of Belgium.

—

Back in England, a relaxed Sir Edward Grey had taken himself off to his weekend fishing retreat, at Itchen Abbas in Hampshire. It was the 26th, a Sunday, and in London the Foreign Ministry, alarmed at the news coming in of Russia's partial mobilisation, felt obliged to interrupt Grey's relaxations with a telegram proposing that he renew his efforts at mediation. To be precise, would he immediately reiterate his proposal for a four-power conference, of Britain, France, Italy and Germany?

Grey acted. He dispatched a message to the British embassies in Paris, Vienna, St Petersburg, Niš, Berlin and Rome, asking them to prevail upon their host nations to attend a conference to be held in London at once to deal with the gathering crisis. The conference, Nicolson grimly advised Grey, 'seems to me the only chance of avoiding a conflict – it is, I admit, a very poor chance – but in any case we shall have done our utmost.'[4] Their utmost? If an invitation to a few leaders to attend a peace conference was England's 'utmost', heaven help Europe. In fairness, though, this was the only serious attempt to bring the European powers together to avert war.

Germany knocked the idea on the head at once. 'We could not take part in such a conference,' Bethmann-Hollweg telegrammed Lichnowsky in London the next day, 'as we would not be able to summon Austria before a European court of justice in her case with Serbia.'[5] He missed the point: the conference was not a court of arbitration; nor did it propose one. It simply aimed to bring the powers together in the hope that *talking* would prevent the downward spiral to war. The truth is, Germany feared that it would be isolated and railroaded, that Berlin's delegate would be in a minority of one at a meeting with Britain, France and Italy. (Italy had made clear it would not join a war against Serbia with its Alliance partners.) Moreover, a conference might expose Germany's true role as the hand behind the Austrian ultimatum.

So Berlin bluntly rejected Grey's conference proposal. 'The German government,' it told Vienna, 'assures in the most decided way that it does not identify itself with [Grey's proposals], that on the contrary it advises to disregard them, but that it must pass them on, to satisfy the English Government.'[6] The Germans were, as Nicolson pointed out at the time, simply 'playing with the English' – going through the motions, nodding, passing on London's ideas – and in the meantime preparing for war.

—

In this spirit of earnest belligerence, deaf to the entreaties of mediation, Germany accelerated the lurch to a European war. Consider German foreign minister Jagow, who rejected the *form* of 'a real conference' to deal with the affairs of Austria and Russia. Jagow, a weak, put-upon man, refused even to discuss the contents of such a meeting. During Jagow's extraordinary talks with Jules Cambon, the French ambassador (and tireless voice of reason), on 27 July, the feelings of the German's true masters – Bethmann-Hollweg, Moltke and the generals – shine through.

'The great object,' Cambon reminded Jagow, 'which Sir Edward Grey had in view went beyond any question of form . . . what was important was the co-operation of Great Britain and France with Germany and Italy in a work of peace.'[7] This cooperation could take effect only through common *démarches* at St Petersburg and at Vienna, and offered an opportunity to demonstrate a European spirit of conciliation.

Jagow evaded the point. He insisted that he could not intervene in the Balkan troubles; Austria must be free to determine its fate. To which Cambon asked whether Jagow was 'bound to follow [Vienna] everywhere with his eyes blindfolded'. Jagow ignored this provocation. Cambon warily asked whether Jagow had actually read Serbia's reply.

'I have not yet had time,' Jagow said.

It was a deadening admission. The Serbian reply had been delivered to his office that morning, 27 July, and sat on his desk. Yet the German foreign minister had failed even to read the document that had prompted the threat of war, revealing his astonishing neglect of a basic diplomatic duty at a time of extreme tension.

'I regret it,' Cambon said. 'You would see that except on some points of detail Servia has yielded entirely. It appears then that, since Austria has obtained the satisfaction which your support has procured for her, you might today advise her to be content . . .'

To this impetuous but entirely valid assertion, Jagow made no clear answer. So Cambon tossed aside diplomatic niceties and bluntly asked, 'Does Germany wish for war?'

Jagow 'protested energetically' that Germany did not, saying that he knew what was in Cambon's mind, 'but it is wholly incorrect'.

'You must then,' Cambon replied, 'act consistently. When you read the Serbian reply, I entreat you in the name of humanity to weigh the terms in your conscience, and do not personally assume a part of the responsibility for the catastrophe which you are allowing to be prepared.'

Jagow protested afresh. He was ready to join England and

France, he said, in a common mediation effort, but only if there was a form of intervention 'which he could accept'. 'For the rest,' he added, 'direct conversations between Vienna and St. Petersburg have been entered upon and are in progress. I expect very good results from them . . .'

Utterly dismayed, Cambon passingly remarked, as he left Jagow's office, that 'this morning I had had the impression that the hour of *détente* had struck, but I now saw clearly that there was nothing in it'.

Recounting this depressing discussion, Cambon suggested in his telegram to Paris that Grey reissue his mediation proposal in another form, 'so that Germany . . . would have to assume the responsibilities that belong to her in the eyes of England'.[8]

—

At about noon on the 27th, Edward Grey underwent a marked change. He turned from being everyone's friend, apparently relaxed and cheerful, into a highly wrought participant in the July crisis. That morning, he had read the full text of Serbia's reply to the Austrian ultimatum and glimpsed, for the first time, the likely role of Vienna and Germany, and the consequences. No longer would he treat the Austro-Serbian issue as of no consequence to British interests. He seemed to have stumbled on a yawning chasm that had hitherto passed unnoticed.

Amazed by the extent of Serbia's prostration, and moved to deep seriousness by the implications, Grey immediately summoned Lichnowsky, the ever-reliable German ambassador, and instructed him at once to communicate a message to Berlin. Serbia, Grey said, had virtually agreed to 'everything demanded of her' – a level of compliance he correctly attributed to Russian pressure. If Austria then proceeded to occupy Belgrade, and Russia answered that challenge with the sword, 'the result would be the most frightful war that Europe had ever seen, and no one could tell to what such a war might lead'. Grey appealed to Berlin to influence Vienna to accept the Serbian reply, or at the very least submit to mediation. He told the German ambassador most seriously that it 'lay in our [German and British] hands to bring the matter to a settlement'.[9]

The estimable Lichnowsky offered Berlin, in the same telegram, his assessment of the marked change in Grey, the first clear sign to the Germans of where this inscrutable Englishman would cast Britain's destiny:

> I found the Minister irritated for the first time. He spoke with great seriousness and seemed absolutely to expect that we should successfully make use of our influence to settle the matter. He is also going to make a statement in the House of Commons today in which he is to express his point of view. In any event, I am convinced that in case it should come to war after all, we should no longer be able to count on British sympathy or British support . . . Also, everybody here is convinced, and I hear it in the mouths of my colleagues, that the key to the situation is to be found in Berlin, and that, if peace is seriously desired there, Austria can be restrained from prosecuting, as Sir E. Grey expresses it, a foolhardy policy.[10]

Here, then, was the first sign to Berlin of the way Britain would most likely jump in the event of a European war. And it was backed up by action. The British First Fleet then concentrated at Portland had received orders not to disperse, as reported in the British press. The Admiralty remained on full alert. 'At no time in all these last three years were we more completely ready,' Churchill later wrote. 'The test mobilization had been completed . . . the whole of the 1st and 2nd Fleets were complete in every way for battle.'[11]

That night, Lichnowsky sent an even stronger message to Berlin, which warned of the serious rift between Germany and Britain that would follow an Austrian move to 'crush Serbia':

> I would like to point out that our entire future relations with England depend on the success of this move of Sir Edward Grey

[i.e. in asking Germany to restrain Austria] . . . The impression is constantly gaining force here – and I noticed it plainly in my interview with Sir Edward Grey – that the whole Serbian question has devolved into a test of strength between the Triple Alliance and the Triple Entente. Therefore, should Austria's intention of using the present opportunity to overthrow Serbia ('to crush Serbia', as Sir E. Grey expressed it) become more and more apparent, England, I am certain, would place herself unconditionally by the side of France and of Russia, in order to show that she is not willing to permit a moral, or perhaps a military, defeat of her group. If it comes to war under these circumstances, we shall have England against us . . .[12]

———

Edward Grey had belatedly come around to the opinion that the best way of preventing a general war was to stop a local one. Germany, however, did not share that view. On no account could Germany comply with Grey's advice, replied Bethmann-Hollweg at 2 am on 28 July. Grey had previously shown little interest in the *Austro-Serbian* conflict, he wrote. Instead, Grey had sought only to mediate in the event of an *Austro-Russian* conflict. Bethmann-Hollweg continued:

> Now, Sir Edward has deserted this ground and asks us to mediate to persuade Austria to accept the Serbian reply . . . [This] cannot be acceded to. It is impossible for us to counsel Vienna to give a belated sanction to the Serbian reply, which they had immediately refused as unsatisfactory.

Clearly, the risk of Britain openly siding with France and Russia had little purchase on Bethmann-Hollweg at this time.

Bethmann-Hollweg and Jagow still believed that war could be confined to the Balkans. In Berlin's eyes, it was not only Austria's right 'but her duty' to punish Serbia. They persisted with the refrain that the Habsburgs sought no Serbian territory and did not deny the Serbian kingdom's right to exist (the latter a false assumption). All Austria wanted, Bethmann-Hollweg telegrammed London – in his role of agent provocateur – was to 'secure herself against the continuation of the undermining of her own existence through Greater Serbia propaganda'.[13]

Stripped of euphemism and bluster, Bethmann-Hollweg's words can be boiled down to this: Austria had a 'duty' to attack Serbia because Belgrade had given Austria a bad press. It was an absurd reason to go to war, as Grey knew. By this rationale, every nation had a 'duty' to attack another nation that published damaging propaganda about it. Obviously, Germany had other, unstated motives in rejecting mediation. And they lay with the machinations of Moltke and the Prussian generals, for whom war had become a certainty if Russia, as the evidence suggested, had mobilised.

—

Grey's mediation attempt had been rebuffed. Now, his vexations rose. France and Russia continued to press him to declare his hand for the Entente. A solid three-way bloc, Sazonov said on the 27th, was the only way of 'winning over Germany to the cause of peace'.[14] Grey did nothing, at first. Then, a hair-raising minute that Eyre Crowe added to the latest dispatch from Russia had the effect of pushing the foreign secretary off the fence. The civilians in the British Government were about to have a lesson in the meaning of 'mobilisation'.

With his inimitable sense of the worst-case scenario, Crowe reprised the definition:

I am afraid that the real difficulty to be overcome will be found in the question of mobilization . . . If Russia mobilises we have been warned Germany will do the same, and as German mobilization is directed almost entirely against France, the latter cannot possibly delay her own mobilization for even the fraction of a day . . . This however means that within 24 hours His Majesty's Government will be faced with the question whether, in a quarrel so imposed by Austria on an unwilling France, Great Britain will stand idly aside, or take sides. The question is a momentous one, which it is not for a departmental note to elaborate.[15]

Elsewhere, Crowe made another revealing comment, aimed at the head, if not the heart, of his foreign secretary. The German Government, he warned, had not said a single word of restraint or moderation in the direction of Vienna: 'If a word had been said, we may be certain that the German Government would claim credit for having spoken at all. The inference is not reassuring . . .' A general sense of having been deceived gripped the British leadership, as Germany's true role in Austria's ultimatum came to light.

—

That night, Bethmann-Hollweg put flesh on the skeleton of Crowe's frighteningly imminent vision. If Russia mobilised, yes, Germany would have to follow suit. But what did Germany mean by 'mobilisation', asked Sir Edward Goschen, the Rugby and Oxford-educated British ambassador at Berlin (whose father was German). Bethmann-Hollweg explained that 'if Russia only mobilised in [the] south Germany would not mobilise, but if she mobilised in [the] north Germany would have to do so too'. Russia's system of mobilisation was so complicated that Germany would have trouble locating it, and 'would therefore have to be very careful not to be taken by surprise'.[16]

Yet Grey still failed to act. He did nothing to restrain Russia from mobilising, which, once in full flood, would obviously bounce the Germans into the war. He failed to declare Britain's hand for Russia and France, which may have given Berlin and Vienna pause for thought (although that window was rapidly closing). And he perilously allowed Berlin to continue to think that Britain may, when it came to blows, remain neutral: '. . . as long as the dispute was one between

Austria-Hungary and Servia alone,' he told the House of Commons on the 27th, in phrases that warmed the ears of the central powers, 'I felt that we had no title to interfere, but that, if the relations between Austria-Hungary and Russia became threatening, the question would then be one of the peace of Europe: a matter that concerned us all.'[17] He shortened this in his memoirs to, 'It was better that Serbia should give way than that European peace should be broken.'[18] Both statements misrepresent his new position in July 1914: he now realised that a local Balkan war would almost certainly lead to a general European war. And so he pressed Germany to restrain Austria and Serbia, to no avail. In Grey's defence, he was the only leading politician who sincerely tried, for a few days, to promote peace.

—

Into these highly charged affairs sailed the dreamlike opinions of the Kaiser, fresh back from his summer voyage. He had returned prematurely early, on the 26th, on hearing of the Serbian reply. Meeting him at Potsdam station was the pale figure of his fraught chancellor, Bethmann-Hollweg, who feared the Kaiser would react violently on learning the extent of Berlin's deceptions.

'How did it all happen?' Wilhelm asked later, bemused to return to a world utterly changed since his departure. He had left Europe in peace; he returned to find Austria and Serbia mobilising against each other, and Germany on the brink of war with Russia. The chancellor offered to resign, rather than explain the complex series of events. Wilhelm refused to accept it. 'You've made this stew,' he growled. 'Now you're going to eat it!'[19]

At about 10 am on 28 July, Wilhelm read the Serbian reply. He took up his pen and footnoted it:

A brilliant achievement in a time limit of only forty-eight hours!
It is more than one could have expected!
A great moral success for Vienna; but with it all reason for war
is gone and Giesl ought to have quietly stayed on in Belgrade!

After that I should never have ordered mobilization.[20]

Few statements better reveal the distance between the Kaiser's understanding and the chain of events. He then wrote a long, peace-mongering missive to Jagow, as divorced from reality as it was hopeful of peace:

> Having read over the Serbian reply, I am convinced that on the whole the wishes of the Danube Monarchy have been acceded to. The few reservations that Serbia makes . . . could, according to my opinion, be settled by negotiation. But it contains the announcement . . . of a capitulation of a most humiliating kind, and as a result every cause for war falls to the ground.

The Kaiser's words seemed to descend from another realm, detached from the one he inhabited. He proposed, as a sop to Austria's demands – and to give her mobilised armies something to do – that Belgrade be taken 'hostage' and parts of the country occupied until Serbia acted on its promises: 'I propose that we say to Austria: "Serbia has been forced to retreat in a very humiliating manner and we offer our congratulations. Naturally, as a result, every cause for war has vanished".' He then offered himself as a 'mediator for peace'.[21]

Peace was the furthest thing from the minds of Moltke, Conrad and the generals. An hour later, Vienna informed Berlin of Russia's 'extensive military preparations' in St Petersburg, Kiev, Warsaw, Moscow and Odessa. If true, Conrad, the Austrian chief of staff, wondered whether Austria should march against Serbia with all its forces at once, or 'whether we must use our chief army against Russia'. In the telegram, Berchtold warned that, if Russia was really mobilising, 'the time it is gaining, makes it absolutely imperative that Austria-Hungary, and . . . Germany also, should immediately take comprehensive counter-measures'.[22]

31

AUSTRIA-HUNGARY DECLARES WAR ON SERBIA

[T]here is a sense of horror in the air, of the dreadful and
unforeseeable consequences of the world war; a horror though that
doesn't just make our blood run cold, but also sweeps us upward,
ready to make the highest sacrifices of both blood and possessions.

Editorial in *Daheim*, a German military journal, in response to
news of Austria-Hungary's declaration of war on Serbia

AT 11.10 AM ON 28 JULY 1914, Count Leopold von
Berchtold, the Austro-Hungarian foreign minister, sent a telegram
to 'M. N. Pašić, Serbian Prime Minister'. It arrived at the Serbian
Government's wartime location at Niš at 12.30 pm:

[Telegraphic] Vienna

The Royal Serbian Government not having answered in
a satisfactory manner the note of 23 July 1914, presented by
the Austro-Hungarian Minister at Belgrade, the Imperial and
Royal Government are themselves compelled to see to the
safeguarding of their rights and interests, and, with this object,

to have recourse to force of arms. Austria-Hungary consequently considers herself henceforward in state of war with Serbia.
COUNT BERCHTOLD[1]

Under pressure from Berlin, Austria-Hungary thus declared war on Serbia – the first time it had been declared by telegram – despite continuing mediation attempts and in the teeth of fierce Russian opposition. Berchtold had received permission to issue the declaration from Emperor Franz Joseph that morning. He did so in two ways, both of which redounded to the foreign minister's disgrace: first, by hastening war in order to kill off the chances of peace talks. 'The Triple Entente,' Berchtold wrote to His Majesty, 'might make another attempt to achieve a peaceful settlement of the conflict unless a clear situation is created by the declaration of war.'[2] Second, by informing the emperor that Serbian forces had fired on Austro-Hungarian troops at Temes-Kubin – a claim that proved utterly false and was deleted from the final declaration.

Berchtold later denied he had deliberately deceived the emperor. 'The view,' he wrote to the Italian historian Albertini in 1932, 'that the Emperor was "pushed into war" is totally false. His Majesty was in full possession of a clear mind and unimpaired judgment and convinced of his lofty mission . . .'[3] If true, why did he delete the claim that Serb forces had fired on Austrian troops from the declaration? Berchtold had misled his emperor in order to extract a stronger case for war than the Serbian ultimatum, then corrected the lie by deleting it.

—

At Niš, Serbia's leaders were at first confused. Was Austria's declaration of war real or a hoax, they wondered. Their legations in St Petersburg, London and Paris soon persuaded Pašić of the declaration's authenticity. Europe bridled at the news; all talks, and talks about talks, ceased or hovered aimlessly as the prospect of a general war displaced the fragile hope of peace.

'The declaration of war will make very difficult the initiation of *pourparlers* by the four Powers,' Alfred Dumaine, the French ambassador at Vienna, told Paris.[4] Vienna's sudden resolution to go to war aroused the most disquieting suspicions 'that Germany should have pushed her on to aggressive action against Servia', he wrote, 'in order to be able herself to enter into war with Russia and France, in circumstances which she supposes ought to be most favourable to herself'. Certainly, Grey's four-power conference was now doomed.

The Russians sent messages of warm support to Niš, eliciting tearful words of gratitude from their Slavic allies. 'Deeply touched by the telegram which your Majesty was pleased to address to me yesterday,' Prince Alexander, the Serb heir apparent, wrote to the Tsar on 29 July. 'Your Majesty may rest assured that the cordial sympathy which your Majesty feels towards my country . . . fills our hearts with the belief that the future of Servia is secure . . .'[5] On reading the Tsar's encouraging words, Pašić crossed himself and exclaimed, 'The Tsar is great and merciful!' He then embraced the Russian chargé d'affaires, overcome with emotion.[6]

—

Austrian newspapers published the emperor's declaration the following morning. Once the bombast and plain lies are removed, Austria's true motives for going to war emerge. Avenging the death of the archduke (whose name was not even mentioned) and punishing the Serbs for their inadequate reply had little to do with the declaration of war. These were mere triggers. Austria-Hungary went to war to protect the imperial system and its power – in short, to preserve the divine right of kings.

'To My Peoples!' began the declaration, bearing Emperor Franz Joseph's name. 'To protect the honour of our monarchy, to protect its reputation and its position of power, and to protect its vested interests, the activities of a hate-filled enemy force Me, after many long years of peace, to reach for My sword.'[7]

Many Austro-Hungarians rejoiced. The press reacted with extreme prejudice. The Slavs were a kind of vermin to be exterminated, according to the organ of the Lower Austria's Farmers' Union, *Der Bauernbündler* (circulation 74,000), on 1 August 1914. Describing the Serbs as 'devious and hateful people', it thundered:

RISE AGAINST THOSE SERBIAN CUTTHROATS!

. . . After the murder in Sarajevo . . . our patience is at an end. Austria finally wants to be left alone by those regicides! It is not a war to conquer Serbia, as we truly don't desire any union with regicides! . . . Our allies, Germany and Italy, are standing by us, too, and so we join into the words of the poet: 'Old Austria awake! Dawdle no longer! Grab these scoundrels by the throat and use unmerciful force to impose respect of your good sword on them! . . . Oh don't delay, and avenge the murder with iron on their fathers! – Don't hesitate and put them to the sword . . .! Action is the password of world history.'[8]

'Never before have you seen Vienna so full of people than this evening,' reported the German military newspaper *Daheim* (Home), published in Heidelberg. The people:

didn't know what else to do with their emotions but to crowd towards the War Office and sing patriotic songs there. There was no window unlit in that gigantic new building, there was feverish activity, the orderly officers were leaving into all directions, messengers came and went, high-ranking military officers were met with an enthusiastic welcome and rushed into the hallway, and outside in front of the gates, a sea of people was surging, all tram traffic having to cease.

The army commandeered the postal and telegraphic service (telephones were only available for local calls), and took charge of the railways. The stock exchange closed, and newspaper sales soared. 'Special editions! Special editions anyone?' rang out the cries of newspaper boys.

Speakers on the pedestal of the Radetzky monument hailed the German emperor and the king of Italy. Every officer received applause. Austria-Hungary went to war in a state of ecstasy, according to the press. Outpourings of joy touched every house and every family, mother and wife. 'Our Count Berchtold played like a virtuoso on the instrument of the people's soul,' *Daheim* continued. 'Austria has another face now. It can act again, it is raising itself upwards in a manly fashion, carrying all its peoples along: none of them refuses to follow the Emperor who has now finally mounted his horse.'[9]

In Germany, *Daheim* warned of a world war and issued a furious call to arms, accompanied by photos of the Austrian and German leaders. 'They are forcing us to take up the sword,' reported the paper on 31 July. It went on:

> The thundering of Serbian canons conjured up a world war. From border to border, Germany will echo with rage. The time of our trial has come. Europe is trembling, but we are not afraid
> . . .
>
> If Russia thinks it can try and overrun Germany and the Ostmark with the help of France and England and so open up the way to the Mediterranean sea, it will – God willing – bash its head in on Germany and Austria's military walls . . .
>
> [T]here is a sense of horror in the air, of the dreadful and unforeseeable consequences of the world war; a horror though that doesn't just make our blood run cold, but also sweeps us upward, ready to make the highest sacrifices of both blood and possessions . . .[10]

The papers published military songs to rally the soldiers, such as 'The Emperor is Calling!':

> . . . Germany, take a grip with a strong fist
> to scare enemies both left and right

rise up in angry flames!

Now it's enough of those feisty taunts

of those insulting tones from East and West . . .

All of Germany stands united!

Now the day of redress is finally come!

May God send what He deems fit to send!

Let it be worthwhile, worthwhile all those flames!

The Emperor is calling! Would anyone not come immediately?!

It's for our homeland! Emperor and Reich!

All of Germany stands united![11]

—

One blot on Austria's new-found confidence was the untested quality of the Austro-Hungarian troops, who were being sent to fight experienced Serbs. *Daheim* reported:

> By the time this issue reaches our readers, some larger operations will probably already have taken place in the Serbian theatre of war. The Austrian army will not have any easy work of it, and the war won't be a walk in the park. Even if the Serbian army is outnumbered . . . it still has an advantage not to be underestimated: its experience in the Balkan wars.[12]

In July 1914, Austria-Hungary fielded 378,000 combatants, from a total standing army of 36,000 officers, 410,000 non-commissioned officers and men, about 87,000 horses and 1200 artillery pieces.[13] After full mobilisation, Austro-Hungarian forces would grow to more than three million men, most of them unfit for combat.[14]

Units/weapons	Austro-Hungarian	Serbian
battalions	329	209
batteries	143	122
squadrons	51	44
engineer companies	45	22

field guns	756	558
machine guns	490	210
total combatants	378,000	250,000

The Serbian Army was much better prepared. It contained a ruthless core of warriors, battle-hardened in the worst of the Balkan Wars. Though it had recently doubled in size, adding five new divisions of well-trained men, the force totalled just 250,000 combatants. They were poorly equipped, with fewer modern rifles – 180,000 – than men. Up to a third of its front-line units relied upon clapped-out old pieces until Russian replacements arrived halfway through August.

Fierce Serb nationalism and hatred of the Habsburgs compensated for these deficiencies and unified them into a force that would prove more than a match for the Austro-Hungarians – a confused, multinational army of Austrians, Hungarians, Croats, Italians, Czechs, Ukrainians, Poles, Slovenes, Slovaks and others. The half-witted enthusiasm of the Good Soldier Švejk more accurately reflected their calibre than the bluster of the emperor and the press.

—

The Serbian Army mobilised more quickly than the Austrians. On 30 July, the Prince Regent published a manifesto, signed by the Serbian ministers, which urged the people to 'Defend your homes and Servia with all your might'.[15] At the solemn opening of the *Skupchtina* (parliament) that day, Serbia's Prince Regent read the speech in his own name. The Prince emphasised 'the gracious communication' of the Tsar, that Russia would never abandon Serbia. At each mention of the Tsar and Russia, 'the hall resounded with loud bursts of wild cheering'. France and England also 'called forth approving plaudits'.[16]

Throughout that night, Austrian guns pounded the emptying city of Belgrade, provoking fury in Russia. Yet Sazonov's earlier rage had retreated. He now saw the true dimensions of the unfolding catastrophe and offered, at this late stage, to conciliate, 'in order to prove his sincere desire to safeguard peace'. He hurriedly devised a 'formula for peace', as requested by the British ambassador, which stated:

> If Austria consents to stay the march of her troops on Servian territory, and . . . admits that the great Powers may examine the satisfaction which Servia can accord to the Austro-Hungarian Government, without injury to her sovereign rights . . ., Russia undertakes to preserve her waiting attitude.[17]

As peace feelers went, this did not go far. Laden with conditions, it offered no hope of negotiation or compromise. It promised merely a pause in Russia's obvious war preparations. Serbia waited and held back, as the Austrians pounded their near-empty capital. None realised they were about to embark on a four-year campaign that would kill or wound 1.1 million Serbian people: 60 per cent of the total male population and 27 per cent of the overall population – the worst casualty rate of the Great War.

32

WILLY, NICKY AND GEORGIE

The military measures [Russia's partial mobilisation]
which have now come into force were decided
five days ago for reasons of defence.
Tsar Nicholas II – 'Nicky' – to the Kaiser

The whole weight of the decision lies solely on you[r] shoulders
now, who have to bear the responsibility for Peace or War.
Kaiser Wilhelm II – 'Willy' – to the Tsar

We shall try all we can to keep out of this and remain neutral.
King George V – 'Georgie' – to the Kaiser's brother

HOPES OF MEDIATION MELTED AWAY, and the mediocrities in charge floundered in the grip of a crisis the scale of which they failed to apprehend. The great alliances on which European peace and deterrence had depended for 20 years were turning into dynamos of aggression, and the generals and admirals were seizing the reins of state. And then, all of a sudden, came a twinkle of hope from a most unlikely source: the three emperors – King, Kaiser and Tsar.

Tsar Nicholas II and Kaiser Wilhelm II were not only emperors, they were also relations, and this blend of familiarity, power and prestige lent a little oxygen to diplomacy. The Tsar and Kaiser had been corresponding regularly for years. Their 'Willy–Nicky' telegrams flew to and fro between Berlin and St Petersburg in a sort of light, schoolboy prattle that belied the gravity of the machinations in the commoners' realm below.

The telegrams of critical interest begin on 29 July and end on 1 August. The context is intriguing. Both monarchs were horrified by the thought of the Balkan War widening to engulf Europe. Yet they were by now, to a large extent, stooges for their generals and ministers. Neither emperor had a firm grip on the affairs of state. Wilhelm's offer to 'mediate' was an illusion; his attempts were ignored or 'accommodated'. On his return from holiday, the Kaiser had re-entered a changed world over which he had limited control. He knew little of his chancellor's role as conductor of the Austrian war on Serbia. Nor was he aware that Moltke, chief of the German General Staff, had warned his Austrian counterpart, Conrad von Hötzendorf, to prepare for the likelihood that the 'local war' in the Balkans would lead to a general war with Russia. Meanwhile, the German Parliament had grown chaotic and divided, with the generals in the ascendant over the civilian politicians in determining what Germany should do next. In this situation, Bethmann-Hollweg fell back on the Kaiser as a last resort, in the hope of influencing the Tsar to stop Russia mobilising – or, if not, and Germany was forced to mobilise, as Moltke wished, to blame the Russians for starting the war.

Would Your Majesty 'have the goodness to send a telegram to the Tsar?' Bethmann-Hollweg asked Wilhelm. 'Such a telegram, should a war prove to be inevitable, would throw the clearest light on Russia's responsibility. I most humbly take the liberty of appending a draft of such a telegram.'[1] Wilhelm obliged and sent the following:

Kaiser to Tsar, July 28th, 10:45 P.M.

I have heard with the greatest anxiety of the impression which is caused by the action of Austria-Hungary against Servia. The unscrupulous agitation which has been going on for years in Servia, has led to the revolting crime of which Archduke Franz Ferdinand has become a victim . . . On the other hand I by no means overlook the difficulty encountered by You and Your Government to stem the tide of public opinion . . . I shall use my entire influence to induce Austria-Hungary to obtain a frank and satisfactory understanding with Russia. I hope confidently that You will support me in my efforts to overcome all difficulties which may yet arise. Your most sincere and devoted friend and cousin.

Willy

In Russia, the generals advised the Tsar on how to reply. The most influential were General Sukhomlinov, the minister for war, Grand Duke Nikolay Nikolaevich, the Russian commander-in-chief, and the quartermaster general, Yury Danilov, who had been quickly recalled to St Petersburg:

Tsar to Kaiser, July 29, 1:00 A.M.
Peter's Court Palais

Am glad you are back. In this serious moment, I appeal to you to help me. An ignoble war has been declared to a weak country. The indignation in Russia shared fully by me is enormous. I foresee that very soon I shall be overwhelmed by the pressure forced upon me and be forced to take extreme measures which will lead to war. To try and avoid such a calamity as a European war I beg you in the name of our old friendship to do what you can to stop your allies from going too far.

Nicky

The Willy–Nicky letters, far from exerting restraint, had the perverse effect of making matters worse. With relations like these . . .

Kaiser to Tsar, July 29, 6:30 P.M.
Berlin

. . . as I told you in my first telegram, I cannot consider
Austria's action against Servia an 'ignoble' war. Austria knows by
experience that Servian promises on paper are wholly unreliable
. . . Austria does not want to make any territorial conquests at
the expense of Servia. I therefore suggest that it would be quite
possible for Russia to remain a spectator of the austro-servian
conflict without involving Europe in the most horrible war she
ever witnessed . . . Of course military measures on the part of
Russia would be looked upon by Austria as a calamity we both
wish to avoid and jeopardize my position as mediator which I
readily accepted on your appeal to my friendship and my help.

Willy

Tsar to Kaiser, July 29, 8:20 P.M.
Peter's Court Palais

Thanks for your telegram conciliatory and friendly.
Whereas official message presented today by your ambassador
to my minister was conveyed in a very different tone [this was
Pourtalès' cable to Jagow]. Beg you to explain this divergency!
It would be right to give over the Austro-servian problem to the
Hague conference. Trust in your wisdom and friendship.

Your loving Nicky

Kaiser to Tsar, July 30, 1:20 A.M.
Berlin

Best thanks for telegram. It is quite out of the question that
my ambassador's language could have been in contradiction
with the tenor of my telegram. Count Pourtalès was instructed
to draw the attention of your government to the danger & grave
consequences involved by a mobilisation; I said the same in my

telegram to you. Austria has only mobilised against Servia & only a part of her army. If, as it is now the case, according to the communication by you & your Government, Russia mobilises against Austria, my rôle as mediator . . . will be endangered if not ruined. The whole weight of the decision lies solely on you[r] shoulders now, who have to bear the responsibility for Peace or War.

   Willy[2]

Tsar to Kaiser, July 30, 1:20 A.M.
Peter's Court Palais

   Thank you heartily for your quick answer . . . The military measures [Russia's partial mobilisation] which have now come into force were decided five days ago for reasons of defence on account of Austria's preparations. I hope from all my heart that these measures won't in any way interfere with your part as mediator which I greatly value. We need your strong pressure on Austria to come to an understanding with us.

   Nicky

As their telegrams show, neither the Tsar nor the Kaiser really wanted war. Willy and Nicky were put up to writing and doing what their generals and ministers required. They were the 'hand that signed the paper'. Their signatures were essential to any act of war. The striking thing is that both Tsar and Kaiser thought peace was in their gift. Technically, they had the power to order, restrain or halt mobilisation; in practice, neither would. The Tsar briefly tried to downscale Russian mobilisation but was largely disobeyed and then compelled to change his mind (see Chapter 34). Yet both monarchs exerted residual influence, as symbols of power and the nodding amanuenses for the decisions of others.

   Their people had not yet fully realised the dismal truth about their rulers. Had the Kaiser and Tsar been stronger characters, responsible with the uses of power, had they been able to influence their ministers and generals, it is tempting to believe a European war might have been averted.

—

What of their relation 'Georgie' – King George V of England? George had cordial relations with the Tsar but loathed his nephew the Kaiser. His diary reveals his personal views on the war. Like them, he opposed it but was helpless to act. He was not an autocrat, of course, like his cousins; his powers were circumscribed by parliament. Yet he still exerted great influence, as a figurehead and adviser. Indeed, George's off-hand remarks to the Kaiser's brother unwittingly made the situation worse, with grave repercussions.

On 27 July, King George referred to the possibility of war, for the first time, in his diary. It was a 'very serious state of affairs', he concluded. 'It looks as if we were on the verge of a general European war.'[3] Prime Minister Asquith reassured the King that Britain would remain a spectator to war in the Balkans. Few in Britain had heard of Serbia; why go to war over a little peasant kingdom?

King George shared the prime minister's view in a discussion the day before with the Kaiser's brother, Heinrich, then returning home after a visit to England. 'We shall try,' George said, 'all we can to keep out of this and remain neutral.'[4] Heinrich misunderstood him, thinking he meant Britain would remain neutral in a European war.

The next day, King George received a telegram from the Tsar – prompted by Sazonov – which openly pressed Britain to declare her hand for the Entente:

Austria has gone off upon a reckless war, which can easily end in a general conflagration. It is awful! . . . If a general war broke out I know that we shall have France's and England's full support. As a last resort I have written to William to ask him to bear a strong pressure upon Austria so as to enable us to discuss matters with her.[5]

The three monarchs were under the sway of the same delusion: that is, Georgie thought Nicky was encouraging Willy to mediate, while neither Willy nor Nicky were doing any such thing. In this instance, King George was left at three removes from reality.

Alas, the would-be royal peacemakers were persuaded to stand aside. They did their generals' bidding. The Willy–Nicky dialogue fizzled like a spent firecracker. Their telegrams were wishful thought bubbles, which their governments and commanders would soon pop. The cogs of mobilisation continued on their dreadful path. The tone of King George's diary, written on the brink of war, captures the pathos of helpless royalty. 'Where will it all end?' he wrote. 'Winston Churchill came to see me, the Navy is all ready for War, but please God it will not come. These are very anxious days for me to live in.'[6]

33

THE END OF BRITISH 'NEUTRALITY'

You must inform the German Chancellor that his proposal that we should bind ourselves to neutrality on such terms cannot for a moment be entertained.
Edward Grey, British foreign secretary, to Edward Goschen, British ambassador in Berlin

---

Edward VII is stronger after his death than I who am alive!
Kaiser Wilhelm II, on hearing of Grey's decision

ON 29 JULY, Heinrich presented his brother the Kaiser with King George's passing opinion that Britain would remain 'neutral' in a future war. Emboldened by this royal intelligence, Wilhelm called a snap meeting of his military chiefs, who were anxious to move Germany to a state of *Kriegsgefahrzustand*, the 'state of danger of war' that preceded full mobilisation. The Kaiser announced what Heinrich had heard from George the day before: Britain would remain neutral, after all! Disbelief greeted the announcement.

Tirpitz dared to suggest the remark had been misinterpreted or exaggerated. 'I have the word of a King, and that is enough for me,' the
Kaiser smiled.[1]

Yet the King (and Asquith and Grey) had meant that Britain
would 'remain neutral' in a local war over Serbia; not that Britain
would stand aside and watch Germany tear France apart. Disabusing
the Germans of this glaring misconception would be a most painful
process.

———

It began in London that afternoon, when Edward Grey sent for
Lichnowsky and asked, once again, 'in a friendly and private communication', whether Germany would take part in mediation *à
quatre*. Grey, almost alone in Europe, gallantly clung to his mediation hopes. Only four-way talks could avoid 'a European catastrophe', he said. He reassured Lichnowsky that the British Government
desired, as before, 'to cultivate our previous friendship, and would
stand aside *as long as the conflict remained confined to Austria and
Russia*' (my emphasis).[2]

The British foreign secretary then revealed a hard truth, in his
usual soft, felicitous way. Grey warned that, if Germany and France
went to war, then 'the British government would, under the circumstances, find itself forced to make up its mind quickly'. To go to war?
With whom? Grey left the awful words hanging. He meant, of course,
that Britain would be compelled to join France and Russia in a war
against Germany and Austria-Hungary. 'If war breaks out,' Grey said,
'it will be the greatest catastrophe that the world has ever seen.'[3]

Kindly disposed to the German diplomat, Grey added that 'it
was far from his desire to express any kind of threat'; he wished only
to protect himself 'from the reproach of bad faith' and Lichnowsky
from disappointment. Until now, he concluded, the British
Government had recognised that Austria deserved 'a certain satisfaction'; but British feelings were now 'beginning to turn completely to
the other side'.[4]

With such velvet diplomacy, Grey had quietly destroyed German hopes that Britain would stay out of the war. Lichnowsky, utterly shaken, had the unenviable task of transmitting the shattering news to Berlin. His telegram, however, would not reach Bethmann-Hollweg in time to stop the chancellor from making a last, brazen bid for British neutrality.

—

That evening, on his return from a meeting in Potsdam with the Kaiser and Tirpitz, Bethmann-Hollweg summoned Edward Goschen, the British ambassador. The chancellor intended, as it were, to lay all his cards on the table: to make the strongest bid yet to keep Britain out of the war.

If Russia attacked Austria, Bethmann-Hollweg warned, it might render 'a European conflagration inevitable'. In that event, the German chancellor 'hoped Great Britain would remain neutral'. He knew that Britain would never allow Germany to crush France, but that would not happen, he insisted. Occupying France was never Germany's intention. Germany 'was ready to give every assurance to the British Government *provided that Great Britain remained neutral* that, in the event of a victorious war, Germany aimed at no territorial acquisitions at the expense of France' (my emphasis).[5] His pledge pointedly did not include France's colonies.

These were amazing revelations, and they told the British Government all it needed to know about the perversity of the chancellor's statesmanship. That Bethmann-Hollweg thought he could bribe Britain to remain neutral by offering *not to occupy* France revealed the extent to which he had utterly misread the British Government and the will of the people. He was incapable of seeing German actions from any perspective but his own.

The chancellor then proposed, to Goschen's astonishment, that 'these assurances' might form the basis of 'a general neutrality agreement between the two countries', which had been the object of his policy, he said, ever since he became chancellor. He asked Goschen how the British Government might react. Goschen calmly replied that he thought Edward Grey 'would like to retain full liberty of action'.[6]

When Goschen's telegram recounting this extraordinary meeting reached London, Eyre Crowe promptly got to work. Bethmann-Hollweg's 'astounding proposals' reflected discredit on the statesman, he advised. 'It is clear that Germany is practically determined to go to war, and that the one restraining influence so far has been the fear of England joining in the defence of France and Belgium.'[7] Crowe's fears about Germany resonated more credibly now, with Europe on the brink of war.

—

Later that night, after Bethmann-Hollweg's great gamble, Grey's clarification of the British position arrived. Clearly, Britain would join the war on the French and Russian side, if hostilities widened to Europe. Grey had confirmed Germany's worst nightmare.

The Kaiser read the telegram (from Lichnowsky) with rising, apoplectic rage. Not for the first time had he been made to look a fool before his ministers. Had the King lied to him about British neutrality? Howls of disgust filled the margins of the cable as Wilhelm vented his humiliation. Grey was 'a common cheat', he raged, whose actions were 'mean and Mephistophelian' and therefore 'thoroughly English'. 'He has shown bad faith all these years.'[8]

The Kaiser concluded with a burst of wrath:

> England reveals herself in her true colours the moment when she thinks we are . . . so to speak, disposed of! That mean crew of shopkeepers has tried to trick us with dinners and speeches. The boldest deception, the words of the King to [the Kaiser's brother Heinrich] for me: 'We shall remain neutral and try to keep out of this as long as possible.' Grey proves the King a liar . . . Common cur! England *alone* bears the responsibility for peace and war, not we any longer! That must be made clear to

the world. [The Kaiser's emphasis.][9]

It was completely lost on Wilhelm that his brother Heinrich had simply misunderstood King George.

While the Kaiser was reduced to blustering incoherence, Bethmann-Hollweg was close to collapse. Lichnowsky's telegram confirmed for the first time that Britain would almost certainly join the Entente in a European war. Only last night, the chancellor had played Germany's keenest hand, to secure exactly what Grey now so abruptly snatched away. He sent the devastating news to Baron Heinrich von Tschirschky, German ambassador in Vienna, that afternoon. The British decision to stand by the Triple Entente, Bethmann-Hollweg warned, meant that Germany and Austria faced:

> a conflagration in which England will be against us; Italy and Roumania to all appearances will not go with us, and we two shall be opposed to four Great Powers. On Germany, thanks to England's opposition, the principal burden of the fight would fall.[10]

Bethmann-Hollweg bitterly regretted his earlier plea for British neutrality; from a diplomatic point of view, he had been thoroughly snookered. In the face of this dramatic reversal, Austria-Hungary, now at war, demanded reassurances of Berlin's resolve. The chancellor hesitated, then wired his ambassador in Vienna: 'We are of course ready to fulfil [our] obligation . . . but must decline to be drawn wantonly into a world conflagration . . .'[11] With Russia preparing to mobilise, however, Germany would now rely on Austria-Hungary to help hold the enemy in the east, as Bismarck had foreseen. In his weakness, Bethmann-Hollweg had failed to insist on this.

———

The Kaiser's distempered mind, meanwhile, rampaged Lear-like across these and later telegrams in bursts of empurpled incoherence, daft even by Wilhelm's standards. One long screed unwittingly prophesied the fate of the Reich and cursed the British Empire to destruction:

> For I have no doubt left about it, England, Russia and France have agreed among themselves . . . to take the Austro-Serbian conflict for an excuse for waging a war of extermination against us . . . either we are shamefully to betray our allies, sacrifice them to Russia – thereby breaking up the Triple Alliance, or we are to be attacked in common by the Triple Entente for our fidelity to our allies and punished, whereby they will satisfy their jealousy by totally ruining us. That is the real, naked situation *in nuce*, which, slowly and cleverly set going, certainly by Edward VII . . . and finally brought to a conclusion by George V and set to work . . .
>
> So the famous 'encirclement' of Germany has finally become a complete fact. The net has been suddenly thrown over our head, and England sneeringly reaps the most brilliant success of her persistently prosecuted purely anti-German world policy . . . A great achievement which arouses the admiration even of him who is to be destroyed as its result. Edward VII is stronger after his death than I who am alive! And there have been people who believed that England could be won over or pacific, by this or that puny measure!!! All my warnings, all my pleas, were voiced for nothing . . .
>
> . . . we are brought into a situation which offers England the desired pretext for annihilating us under the hypocritical cloak of justice, namely, of helping France . . . This whole business must now be ruthlessly uncovered and the mask of Christian peaceableness publicly and brusquely torn from its face . . . and the pharisaical hypocrisy exposed on the pillory!! And our consuls in Turkey and India, agents, etc. must fire the whole Muhammedan world to fierce rebellion against this hated, lying,

conscienceless nation of shopkeepers; for if we are to be bled to death, England shall at least lose India.[12]

The Kaiser's outburst has provoked much discussion. Albertini's was the pithiest. 'It reveals the whole man,' he wrote. The bankruptcy of Germany's *Weltpolitik* plunged him into 'towering rages from which all sense of truth was banned'. It was not true, however, that the Kaiser 'more than any other man' had made a European war imminent, as Albertini claims.[13] Truth is not amenable to apportioning blame so easily. The roles of the Tsar, Bethmann-Hollweg, Moltke, Sazonov, Grey, Berchtold, Conrad and lesser officials, and their joint inability or unwillingness to respond to what was happening to them, brought the world closer to war.

—

Then, on 30 July, Grey received Bethmann-Hollweg's witless bribe for British neutrality. Flabbergasted, he replied at once through Goschen. His cable is unusually strong-worded and decisive, and expressed precisely the British Government's position up to the declaration of war. Note his sly refusal to accept German claims on French colonies:

> You must inform the German Chancellor that his proposal that we should bind ourselves to neutrality on such terms cannot for a moment be entertained.
>
> He asks us in effect . . . to stand by while French colonies are taken and France is beaten so long as Germany does not take French territory . . . [S]uch a proposal is unacceptable, for France could be so crushed as to lose her position as a Great Power and become subordinate to German policy . . .
>
> But apart from that, for us to make this bargain with Germany at the expense of France would be a disgrace from which the good name of this country would never recover.

> The Chancellor also in effect asks us to bargain away whatever obligation or interest we have as regards the neutrality of Belgium. We could not entertain that bargain either.

Grey went on to reject Germany's 'neutrality pact' and suggested instead that a mutual accommodation between the two power blocs be agreed, if and when the crisis passed. That idea had hitherto been too 'Utopian' to form the subject of a definite proposal, he said.[14]

Thus spoke Grey's heart and mind, with a firm and authentic eloquence with which – had he deployed it earlier – he might have slashed through the bracken of confusion, paranoia and distrust that enmeshed his hopes of peace. For once, he had awoken from his policy of 'rigid passivity';[15] for once, he had articulated a clear British direction and not merely reacted to events; for once, he had decided to *decide*.[16] His new-found conviction, however, took shape too late to exert any restraining influence on the world.

—

And then it faltered. Grey still refused to commit Britain to any position in defence of France, even though he knew that everything tended in that direction. The French quietly fumed at perfidious Albion. Jules Cambon, French ambassador to Berlin, claimed that Grey's uncertainty had given hope to the war party in Germany. If he would only declare on the side of France, 'it would decide the German attitude in favour of peace'. The extremity of Cambon's charge stung Grey to explain himself.

'[I]t was quite wrong to suppose that we had left Germany under the impression that we would not intervene,' he explained (via the British ambassador in Paris, Sir Francis Bertie, on 31 July). 'I had refused overtures to promise that we should remain neutral.' Grey admitted, however, that Britain *still* could not give any pledge to the Entente at that time. His reason? He feared a stockmarket collapse. 'The commercial and financial situation was exceedingly serious,' he warned; 'there was danger of a complete collapse that would involve us and everyone else in ruin; and it was possible that our standing aside might be the only means of preventing a complete collapse of European credit.'[17] This reeked of disingenuousness: were the French expected to believe that Grey placed a higher priority on calming the London stockmarket than on the freedom of France? Grey's whole position was looking increasingly worn and dishevelled. He fell back on Belgium, whose freedom served as a sort of talisman to the British Cabinet. Violation of Belgian neutrality might decide the issue for the government, he added. But the 'only answer' Grey could give France at that moment 'was that we could not undertake any definite engagement'.[18]

—

At a Cabinet meeting the next day (1 August), Grey shared the events of the past two days. The British Government remained masters of their actions, he insisted, as though that was a virtue, in the circumstances, and were determined to defend Belgian neutrality.[19] France had agreed to respect Belgium's freedom, in response to British inquiries on the matter; Germany had so far not answered. And the British position? Grey asked the Cabinet for authority to make a statement to the House of Commons on Monday 3 August, in which he would clarify the matter once and for all.

In transmitting these commitments to Lichnowsky that day, Grey's words lost all potency. He reverted to mealy-mouthed half-measures. Should Germany, he meekly advised, violate Belgian neutrality in a war with France, 'a reversal of [British] public opinion would take place' that would 'make it difficult for the government here to adopt an attitude of friendly neutrality'. Surely, an attitude of 'unfriendly neutrality' was not what he had in mind. Surely, he meant a commitment to the Entente. Grey dragged all Europe by creeping increments to the truth.

The Kaiser appended his usual expletives to Grey's statement: 'Rot!' 'Humbug!' 'The rascal is crazy or an idiot!' etc. Yet Wilhelm also made a coherent point that seriously raised Berlin's hackles.

Britain, he wrote, had 'cut the cable to Emden – a war measure, then! While she is still negotiating.'[20] It seems he was right. In the early hours of 1 August (the exact date is disputed), a British cable ship in the waters near Emden, in the North Sea, dragging a grappling hook behind her, had dredged up five underwater cables and cut them. These were some of Germany's secure links with her overseas embassies. Berlin would now have to rely solely on wireless, and heavily coded messages, to prevent the enemy from listening in.[21] The sabotage was technically an act of terrorism.

—

The direction of events was music to the ears of Eyre Crowe, whose great anti-German project must have seemed like a prophecy come true. He capitalised on the mood, with a series of minutes to Grey. 'If and when it is certain,' he wrote, 'that France and Russia cannot avoid the war, and are going into it, my opinion, for what it is worth, is that British interests require us to take our place beside them as allies, and in that case our intervention should be immediate and decided.'

In a forceful memo, sent directly to Grey, he wrote that Britain had no 'contractual obligation' to France, admittedly, but that 'the Entente has been made, strengthened, put to the test and celebrated in a manner justifying the belief that a moral bond was being forged'. That bond should now compel Britain to stand by France in her hour of need, he declared: 'France has not sought the quarrel. It has been forced upon her.'[22] Grey sat and waited.

34

SMASH YOUR TELEPHONE: RUSSIA MOBILISES

I will not become responsible for a monstrous slaughter.
Tsar Nicholas II, under pressure to order full Russian mobilisation

---

Mobilization is not a mechanical process which one can arrest at will, as one can a wagon, and then set in motion again.
General Vladimir Sukhomlinov, Russian war minister

'A CHAIN OF RECKLESSNESS AND ERROR' brought a catastrophic war to Europe, concludes Albertini.[1] Nowhere is his verdict more apt than in the fraught process of 'mobilisation' – moving men and supplies to concentration points in readiness for war. For Germany, it would take a matter of days; for Russia, facing huge distances, over a fortnight. The crucial thing is that, in 1914, Germany interpreted the order to mobilise as a *declaration of war*, because full mobilisation was virtually impossible to stop. The Russian military more or less shared this understanding; yet Sazonov and the civilian leaders seemed blind to it. In this light, the first nation to order

Revulsion at Nijinsky's 'disgusting faun' added to the conservative backlash against La Belle Époque, the artistic and social gossamer on a rigid, autocratic world. (© Bettmann/CORBIS)

Modern nostalgia-seekers typically evoke the poet Rupert Brooke, the 'most handsome man in England', and other English writers to romanticise the war. Brooke died of an infected mosquito bite near Gallipoli. (© Michael Nicholson/Corbis)

British inventor Sir Hiram Stevens Maxim in 1884, with his Maxim machine gun, the weapon that drove British colonial conquest and the predecessor of those that would kill on such a huge scale on the Western Front. (© Bettmann/CORBIS)

Count Otto von Bismarck, the 'Iron Chancellor', whose towering achievement was the unification of Germany, forging a new racial consciousness in Europe. (© Underwood & Underwood/Corbis)

Kaiser Wilhelm II: of unsound mind, his outrageous remarks unsettled European leaders. His generals would later sideline him. His 'world policy' (*Weltpolitik*) would prove illusory.

(© Sammlung Sauer/dpa/Corbis)

The Balkan pressure cooker reached boiling point in 1912, when the first of two Balkan wars showed all Europe that a clash in the peninsula could easily inflame the continent.

(© Bettmann/CORBIS)

Turkish-armed troops prepare to confront Serbian and Bulgarian forces in 1912, the last stand by the Turks after centuries of occupying the Balkan peninsula. (© Bettmann/CORBIS)

Queen Victoria, with the Prince of Wales, Edward (later Edward VII), Prince George (later George V) and Prince Edward (later Edward VIII), of the House of Saxe-Coburg and Gotha. In 1917, the British royal family would change its name to Windsor.

(State Library of Victoria H2002.196/62)

Count Alfred von Schlieffen, the Prussian general who devised the Schlieffen Plan (1905) for a two-front war against France and Russia. It would damn Europe to years of carnage. (© Bettmann/CORBIS)

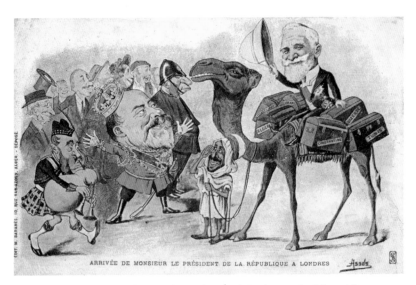

ARRIVÉE DE MONSIEUR LE PRÉSIDENT DE LA RÉPUBLIQUE A LONDRES

King Edward VII meets the then French President Émile Loubet, just back from Africa, on 6 July 1903. Edward's historic visit to Paris smoothed the signing of the Entente Cordiale. (© Michael Nicholson/Corbis)

FIVE YEARS HEAD OF THE FOREIGN OFFICE : THE LATE SIR EYRE CROWE.

Eyre Crowe, a German-born British civil servant, whose anti-German tirades were, for a time, influential in the Foreign Office. (National Library of Australia, Illustrated London News 9 May 1925)

Count Franz Conrad von Hötzendorf, Austrian chief-of-staff. A virulent Serb-hater, his intense love affair with a married woman warped his judgement. (Library of Congress LC-B2- 3289-10)

Chancellor Theo von Bethmann-Hollweg appealed, on the eve of battle, for the British to remain neutral. The coming war, he said, would 'uproot everything that exists'. (© CORBIS)

GENERAL VON BERNHARDI.

He has been called " a lesser Treitschke," whose doctrines he has popularised and applied to the conditions of to-day. Unlike Treitschke he is not a " learned " man, although on military matters he is an authority. He therefore justifies and advocates warlike operations of the most ruthless character and asserts its inevitability from the point of view of Germany's needs and rights.

Like many senior Prussians, General Friedrich Adolf Julius von Bernhardi, an influential writer, believed war a noble, Darwinian enterprise that would determine the racially fittest.
(Mary Evans Picture Library/PHILI/AAP IMAGE)

General Sir Henry Wilson drew up the British war plan and tirelessly pressed the government to declare its military support for France.
(Mary Evans Picture Library/AAP IMAGE)

Raymond Poincaré, French president in 1914, deeply distrusted Germany and silenced his diplomats' efforts to seek a rapprochement with Berlin. (© CORBIS)

Admiral Alfred von Tirpitz masterminded the Tirpitz Plan, to build a German navy powerful enough to rival Britain's command of the sea. (Mary Evans Picture Library/AAP IMAGE)

Abrasive French politician Georges Clemenceau accused his political opponents, who failed to press for the return of Alsace and Lorraine, of treason. (© Hulton-Deutsch Collection/CORBIS)

Britain's great fleet assembled off Portsmouth, three weeks before the declaration of war. Germany would never match British sea supremacy. (Mary Evans Picture Library/AAP IMAGE)

Sir Edward Grey (right), foreign secretary, and Lord Haldane, then lord chancellor, during the July crisis. Grey would refuse to commit Britain to France's defence until the last moment. (Mary Evans Picture Library/AAP IMAGE)

Archduke Franz Ferdinand and his wife, Sophie, set off on their motorcade through Sarajevo hours before a Bosnian Serb assassin murdered them. (Mary Evans Picture Library/AAP IMAGE)

Police capture Bosnian Serb Gavrilo Princip, murderer of Franz Ferdinand, in Sarajevo, 28 June 1914. He escaped the death penalty due to his youth. (AP/AAP IMAGE)

Princip (left) and accomplices Milan Ciganovic and Nedeljko Čabrinović. The Black Hand, a Serb terrorist organisation, had recruited them to kill the archduke.

(Roger Viollet Collection/Getty Images)

Winston Churchill, first lord of the Admiralty, ordered the mobilisation of the British fleet in readiness for the outbreak of war. He would later play a central role in the Gallipoli campaign. (Mary Evans Picture Library/AAP IMAGE)

King George V inspects his German regiment, of which he was honorary colonel, in Berlin with his cousin, Kaiser Wilhelm II, in 1913 – just 18 months before Britain declared war on Germany. (Mary Evans Picture Library/AAP IMAGE)

'Nicky', Tsar Nicholas II of Russia and his cousin, 'Georgie', George V of England. Telegrams flew between the two monarchs, and their cousin, 'Willy', the Kaiser, in doomed attempts to avert hostilities. (© Bettmann/CORBIS)

Adolf Hitler cheering among the crowd in the Odeonplatz, Munich, after war was declared, on 2 August 1914. Hitler eagerly volunteered and participated in the First Battle of Ypres.
(Mary Evans Picture Library/AAP IMAGE)

One of many British recruitment posters featuring Lord Kitchener, which would compel more than a million men to volunteer for the armed forces by 1915.
(Mary Evans Picture Library/AAP IMAGE)

The Massacre of Dinant, Belgium, 23 August 1914, in which 410 inhabitants were slaughtered. German troops were under orders to kill civilians and burn villages to crush the Belgian resistance. (© Lebrecht Music & Arts/Corbis)

A crowd of joyful Belgians kissing the Union Jack outside the British consulate in Ostend, on news that the British Expeditionary Force were being sent to defend Belgian neutrality. (Mary Evans Picture Library/AAP IMAGE)

The 11th Hussars, a British cavalry unit formed in 1715, arrive at Le Havre on 16 August 1914. They would fight at Mons and the Marne where, like other cavalry, they would join the infantry in the trenches. (Mary Evans Picture Library/AAP IMAGE)

Field Marshal Sir John French (left), commander of the British Expeditionary Force in 1914. He failed to cooperate with his allies, and was forced to resign in 1915.

(Library of Congress LC-B2-3209-10)

General Joseph Gallieni, the much-loved French commander and strategic expert, who came out of retirement at the last moment to organise the fortification and defence of Paris before the German onslaught.

(Library of Congress LC-B2- 3253-6)

French military authorities dispatched some 600 taxi cabs to ferry almost 6000 reserve infantry troops to the front before the First Battle of the Marne, freeing France's choked rail system.

(© Bettmann/CORBIS)

Marshal Joseph Joffre, President Raymond Poincaré, King George V, General Ferdinand Foch and British commander Sir Douglas Haig, at Beauquesne, France, in January 1918. By then, the war had claimed millions of lives, for no gain to either side.

(© Hulton-Deutsch Collection/CORBIS)

A convoy of German prisoners being led away after the crucial Allied victory at the battle of the Marne, which saved France from the humiliation of another Sedan. (Mary Evans Picture Library/AAP IMAGE)

No Man's Land, seen from the trenches of the 2nd Royal Scots Fusiliers, during the first battle of Ypres, in winter 1914. On four further occasions the two sides would fight over the strategically important Belgian city. (Mary Evans Picture Library/AAP IMAGE)

Flanders, three years later. Four Australian troops walk over duckboards in the cratered and waterlogged fields near Ypres, October 1917. (National Library of Australia, an23998557)

Over the top: a composite shot of combat near Ypres, in 1917, showing the deadly openness of the battlefield and the early use of aircraft. (National Library of Australia, an23478249)

German machine gunners near Rheims. The Germans were forced back to entrenched positions on the Aisne, from where they would not be dislodged until 1918, after horrific bloodshed. (© Bettmann/CORBIS)

Women in London's East End hoist the 'White Feather' flag, deriding those not enlisting with the message, 'Serve your country or wear this.' Thousands of men would endure the humiliation of a white feather. (Hulton Archive/Getty Images)

The morning after the first battle of Passchendaele: Allied wounded around a blockhouse near the site of Zonnebeke railway station, 12 October 1917. Passchendaele would be one of the worst of the war, killing or wounding an estimated 400,000 German and 250,000 Commonwealth troops, fighting in a sea of mud. (National Library of Australia, an24574133)

...ould be branded the aggressor and responsible for

...ed to be blamed for starting it. Thus began the
... of provoking the other to strike first, of feinting
and dancing around each other, daring one's opponent to jump.
Mediation, compromise, patience . . . the diplomatic arts had little
purchase on this game of bluff and counter-bluff. Austria-Hungary,
Russia and Germany all recklessly ordered more or less 'partial' or
preparatory mobilisation in mid-to-late July, which hijacked the
possibility of peaceful mediation. *Kriegsgefahrzustand*, for example,
meant the 'state of danger of war': the German military preparation
of key railway points, the marshalling of supplies, but not necessarily the recall of troops to their colours. Russia's 'preparations for war'
meant the same. In practice, these euphemisms meant what the generals and admirals wanted them to mean. Britain, meanwhile, kept
the fleet on high alert. France, in Poincaré's absence, expressed solidarity with Russia.

—

In German eyes, everything hinged on Russia. The full mobilisation
of the Russian Army guaranteed a European war. If Russia mobilised, Germany must follow. It was Moltke, after all, who famously
wrote in a letter to Conrad on 21 January 1909, 'The moment
Russia mobilises, Germany . . . will unquestionably mobilise her
whole army.'[2] Little had changed in the intervening years, except
that Moltke's resolve had momentarily frayed. Near the end of July,
'the situation continues to be extremely obscure', he wrote wearily
to his wife. 'It will be about another fortnight before anything definite can be known . . .'[3] Moltke wavered between extreme bellicosity
and utter dread. At one moment, he seemed to be trying to imitate
Frederick the Great or his father, Moltke the Elder, victor of France
in 1871. At another, he would shun the awful consequences of his
actions: the annihilation 'for decades to come of the civilisation of
almost the whole of Europe'.[4]

Moltke and the German General Staff had glimpsed the 1.
of hell, according to the following sequence: 1) Russia mobilises to
defend Serbia; 2) Austria-Hungary and Russia at war; 3) Germany
mobilises to defend Austria-Hungary; 4) Russia orders full mobilisation, signalling war with Germany; 5) Germany ignites the (revised)
Schlieffen Plan and declares war on Russia and France.

They watched the railway lines. Sudden, concentrated activity on
the railways, the avenues of death for millions of young men, would
mark the start of mobilisation. By July 1914, Germany's tracks were
not as advanced as everyone thought. French railways were superior to Germany's, with more double-tracked and transverse lines,
according to Moltke and Wilhelm Groener, head of the railway section of the General Staff. Berlin feared that France could mobilise 'as
much as five times faster if both sides mobilised at the same time'.[5] In
the east, the picture looked worse: Germany had only four double-
tracked lines to the Vistula, and only two running beyond the river
to East Prussia. 'No trunk lines at all ran into Posen, and Germany
was poorly equipped to fight alongside its Austrian ally,' writes
David Stevenson.[6] In other words, Germany's very weakness, its *ill-
preparedness* for war – in terms of fewer railway lines, allies, colonies
and naval strength – made the case for a preventive war, of 'striking'
now, seem imperative to the German generals. 'In 1914,' Stevenson
concludes, 'the Central Powers snatched at what they thought to be
a fast-receding opportunity to escape from their security dilemmas
. . .'[7]

—

By provoking Russian mobilisation, Bethmann-Hollweg and
Jagow – who now thought war inevitable – would be able to say
'Russia *started it*'. They set about trying to engineer that outcome,
to 'bounce' Russia into ordering full mobilisation. Yet Russia well
knew that mobilising its vast armies would be more complex and
time-consuming than for any other European nation, which is why
it felt compelled to start sooner. In any case, German 'restraint' had

no claim on virtue: Berlin was poised to mobilise within moments of Russia's announcement.

The key events leading to Russia's full mobilisation are intricate and interwoven. By placing them in a simple timeline, we can see why a 'local' war between Austria and Serbia spread into a European war, and how mobilisation was the crucial lubricant.

Timeline of Russian mobilisation in 1914

St Petersburg, 25 July: Russia secretly decides to order 'preparatory' mobilisation, in response to Austria's ultimatum to Serbia.[8]

Berlin, 27 July: German foreign minister Jagow assures the Entente powers that Germany would not mobilise if Russia's partial deployment were directed only at Austria.[9]

Vienna/Belgrade, 28 July: Austria-Hungary declares war on Serbia.

Berlin, 28 July, morning: Bethmann-Hollweg advises the Kaiser to write to the Tsar, initiating the Willy–Nicky telegrams, a diplomatic strategy designed to brand Russia the aggressor. German war minister Erich von Falkenhayn, with the Kaiser's support, orders troops on manoeuvres to return to their garrisons. German 'partial' mobilisation secretly begins.

St Petersburg, 28 July, afternoon: The Russian Government, in response to the Austrian declaration of war, informs Berlin that it intends to mobilise the military districts of Odessa, Kiev, Moscow and Kazan. It promises its partial mobilisation will pose no threat to Germany.[10] Russian military experts object to 'partial mobilisation' because it threatens to derail their plans for full mobilisation.

London, 29 July, morning: Britain sends an official 'warning telegram' authorising the secret, partial mobilisation of the fleet. The First Squadron continues to Scapa Flow, and the Second and Third Squadrons are held at their bases.[11]

Berlin, 29 July: In a long, hair-raising memorandum to Bethmann-Hollweg, Moltke presses for German war readiness in response to *any* Russian move, disavowing Jagow's earlier assurances of restraint. Russia, he writes, has 'cunningly contrived' to provoke Germany to instigate hostilities, by gradually mobilising. If Germany fully mobilised, Russia and her French ally could then claim Germany started it, 'and the mutual butchery of the civilised nations of Europe will begin'. He concludes, 'The military situation is becoming from day to day more unfavourable for us, and can, if our prospective opponents prepare themselves further, unmolested, lead to fateful consequences for us.'[12]

Paris, 29 July: Poincaré and Viviani arrive back in Paris, and immediately urge Russia not to give Germany any pretext for general mobilisation.

Berlin, 4 pm, 29 July: The German General Staff receives the disquieting news that Belgium means to resist invasion. Brussels calls up reserves, doubling its effective strength to 100,000, and reinforces fortifications and border defences.

St Petersburg, 29 July, day–evening: Russia receives news of Austria's bombing of Belgrade. Sazonov angrily informs the Austrian ambassador, 'You are only wanting to gain time by negotiations and are meanwhile advancing and bombarding an unprotected city.'[13] That night, Sazonov, the minister for war Vladimir Sukhomlinov and the chief of the General Staff Lieutenant General Yanushkevich order full mobilisation: 'in view of the small probability of avoiding a war with Germany [we must] prepare for it in every way . . . the risk could not be accepted of delaying a general mobilisation later by effecting a partial mobilisation now'.[14] Sazonov telephones the result to the Tsar. Nicholas, with extreme reluctance, signs two mobilisation *ukases*, one for partial, the other for general, to be used as events dictate. He thus gives the military a free hand to act as they see fit.

St Petersburg, nearing midnight, 29 July (the timing is disputed)[15]: Sazonov makes a perfunctory offer to Berlin to suspend all 'military preparations' if Austria halts at Belgrade and withdraws the harshest terms of its ultimatum to Serbia.[16] Germany refuses.

St Petersburg, before midnight, 29 July: The Tsar, extremely agitated, telephones the war minister to downgrade the general mobilisation order to 'partial'. The reason, he says, is that he has received an offer from the Kaiser to mediate between Vienna and Belgrade (see Chapter 32). Wilhelm's closing words – 'of course, military measures on the part of Russia . . . would precipitate a calamity we both wish to avoid and jeopardise my position as mediator'[17] – persuade the Tsar to reverse the general mobilisation order. 'I will not become responsible for a monstrous slaughter,' Nicholas exclaims. The Russian Army is furious. '[M]obilization,' Sukhomlinov argues, 'is not a mechanical process which one can arrest at will, as one can a wagon, and then set in motion again.'[18] But the Tsar insists, and the partial mobilisation order is enacted at midnight (though it is questionable whether the general obeys).

Berlin, 1.45 am, 30 July: The Tsar unwisely informs the Kaiser that 'the military measures [partial mobilisation in four cities] which have now come into force were decided five days ago for reasons of defence on account of Austria's preparations' and were in no sense meant to interfere with the Kaiser's role as 'mediator'.[19] Wilhelm interprets this as 'full mobilisation' and writes angrily in the margin that the Russians were now:

> a week ahead of us . . . I cannot agree to any more mediation since the Tsar . . . has secretly mobilised behind my back. It is only a manoeuvre, in order to hold us back and increase the start they have already got. My work is at an end![20]

Berlin, nearing dawn, 30 July: A cable arrives of a half-hearted effort by Sazonov to persuade Berlin to join a four-power peace conference, which the German ambassador Pourtalès dismisses as 'a very difficult if not an impossible matter now that Russia had decided to take the fateful step of mobilization'. To which Sazonov replies that the cancellation of the mobilisation order was no longer possible and that 'Austrian mobilization was responsible for it'.[21]

Berlin, morning, 30 July: Moltke telephones Conrad to warn him that German mobilisation would 'unquestionably lead to war', meaning a European war.[22]

St Petersburg, 30 July: Russia's army commanders implore Sazonov to get permission from the Tsar to reinstate full mobilisation. General Nikolai Yanushkevich, chief of the General Staff, asks Sazonov to telephone him immediately, if successful. 'After that,' Yanushkevich said, 'I shall go away, smash my telephone and generally adopt measures which will prevent anyone from finding me for the purpose of giving contrary orders which would again stop our general mobilisation.'[23]

The Tsar's Palace, Peterhof, from 2 pm, 30 July: Sazonov spends an hour trying to persuade Nicholas to reinstate full mobilisation and that war with Germany is inevitable. Germany has refused to respond to Russia's 'peaceful proposals', he says. Russia must therefore meet the risk fully armed, 'to put away any fears that our warlike preparations would bring about a war'. Conscious of his terrible responsibility, the Tsar refuses to act. (Earlier, the Tsarina had tried to influence him to stay his hand; she had received a telegram from Rasputin predicting that war would destroy the Russian Empire.) General Tatistchev, an envoy, dares to break the silence – 'Yes, it is hard to decide' – to which the Tsar brusquely interjects, 'I will decide!'[24] Nicholas finally agrees to sign the order to restore full mobilisation. '[I]t would be dangerous', he resignedly explains, 'not to make timely preparations for what was apparently an inevitable war.'

The Tsar's Palace, Peterhof, late afternoon, 30 July: Sazonov immediately informs General Yanushkevich, chief of the General Staff, 'Now you can smash your telephone.'[25] Full Russian mobilisation resumes.

Berlin, evening, 30 July: Moltke and Falkenhayn, anxious about news of Russian 'military measures' – which they now presume to mean full mobilisation – press the German Government to mobilise. Bethmann-Hollweg seeks more time. They agree a deadline for the decision: noon the next day, 31 July.

St Petersburg, dawn, 31 July: The secret of Russian mobilisation is out. Red placards with a call to arms hang from the walls and plaster windows.

Berlin, 31 July, 11.55 am: The delay pays off for Germany. Five minutes before its own deadline (to decide to mobilise), the Berlin Government receives a telegram from Count Pourtalès, German ambassador in St Petersburg, confirming that Russia has ordered the full mobilisation of her army and fleet.

Berlin/St Petersburg, 31 July, between 2 and 3 pm: The Kaiser and Tsar send their last telegrams. The Kaiser touchingly imagines he is 'mediating' at a time when his own government is preparing to go to war with Russia. Wilhelm writes:

> On your appeal to my friendship and your call for assistance [I] began to mediate between you and the Austro-Hungarian Government. While this action was proceeding your troops were mobilised against Austria-Hungary, my ally . . . I now receive authentic news of serious preparations for war on my Eastern frontier. Responsibility for the safety of my empire forces preventive measures of defence upon me . . . The responsibility for the disaster which is now threatening the whole civilized world will not be laid at my door. In this moment it still lies in your power to avert it . . . The peace of Europe may still be maintained by you, if Russia will agree to stop the milit[ary] measures which must threaten Germany and Austria-Hungary. – Willy[26]

Berlin/St Petersburg, 31 July, between 2 and 3 pm: In a reply of astonishing candour, the Tsar admits that he is powerless to overrule his military commanders:

> I thank you heartily for your mediation which begins to give one hope that all may yet end peacefully. It is *technically* impossible to stop our military preparations which were obligatory owing to Austria's mobilisation. We are far from wishing war. As long as the negociations [*sic*] with

Austria on Servia's account are taking place my troops shall not make any *provocative* action. I give you my solemn word for this. I put all my trust in God's mercy and hope in your successful mediation in Vienna for the welfare of our countries and for the peace of Europe. Your affectionate – Nicky[27]

Paris, 31 July, afternoon: The French Government learns of Russia's general mobilisation. 'Russia,' writes Maurice Paléologue from St Petersburg, 'knowing that Germany was arming, could no longer delay the conversion of her partial mobilisation into a general mobilisation.'[28]

Berlin, 31 July, evening: The Kaiser, under pressure from Bethmann-Hollweg and the generals, proclaims *Kriegsgefahrzustand*, and tells Russia to revoke its decision to mobilise or face war.[29] The German General Staff assumes that war is now certain, having observed an 'accumulation of [Russian] troops on the East Prussian frontier', and the 'declaration of the state of war over all important parts of the Russian west frontier'. The Russian mobilisation 'was in full swing against us'.[30]

So it came. Bethmann-Hollweg's government had succeeded in engineering a situation that, on the face of it, cleared Germany of blame for starting a European war. He could now tell the German people that Russia had, by mobilising first, forced Germany to defend itself. Jules Cambon wrote:

The whole theory of German blamelessness rests on the fact that it was Russia who first ordered mobilization, thus forcing her adversaries' hands. The one thing overlooked is that no comparison could be drawn between Russian and German Mobilization; that while one took several weeks to complete, the other required only a few days; that there existed in Germany a formidable institution in the 'Imminent Danger of War', tantamount to mobilization in advance.[31]

Indeed, for Germany to pose as a passive innocent was unconscionable. The Germans had refused every appeal for mediation, talks, pauses and conferences. They had orchestrated the Austro-Serbian war. Even so, Russia had acted with reckless precipitation – from partial to full to partial to full military deployment – and handed Germany a trump card. Russia's decision to mobilise was a 'gift' to the Prussian generals, who received it five minutes before they were poised to do the same.[32] The German people, even the socialists, were immediately won over and rallied to fight Germany's 'defensive' war. It was on.

35

GERMANY DECLARES WAR ON RUSSIA

[T]he Kaiser will have the Russian Government informed that he must regard himself as in a state of war with Russia brought on by Russia herself . . . and that, as France does not guarantee her neutrality, we must assume that we are also in a state of war with France . . . We have not willed the war, it has been thrust upon us.

Theobald von Bethmann-Hollweg, German chancellor,
to the Bundesrat, 1 August 1914

ON 31 JULY, Germany proclaimed *Kriegsgefahrzustand*. The government held back from announcing full mobilisation. That would mean, in Germany's case, 'war on two fronts', as Bethmann-Hollweg warned his Cabinet that day.[1] The Schlieffen Plan may have been almost a decade old, but it still prescribed, in a revised form, a lightning encirclement of northern France and *then* a massed attack on Russia.

That prospect horrified the civilian leadership and the Kaiser, whose disquiet deepened with every passing hour. Even now, they clung to the hope of a peaceful solution. Yet the generals were taking control. Moltke and the German General Staff were champing at the bit to mobilise as soon as possible, now that Russia had done so. 'The [German] military authorities,' the French ambassador Jules Cambon cabled Paris, 'are very anxious that mobilization should be ordered, because every delay makes Germany lose some of her advantages.'[2]

The weakening of civilian resolve virtually handed the General Staff the reins of power. Moltke had recovered from his earlier docility and sent the first of many instructions to Vienna, pressing them to join Germany in the fight against Russia (the Serbs were fading in importance, and the archduke's murder an irrelevance). 'That is good!' Conrad shouted on receipt of the message, adding, 'Who is in command, Moltke or Bethmann-Hollweg? . . . I had the impression that Germany was wavering. Now, however, I have satisfactory explanations . . .'[3]

It seemed that Moltke was. In asking Vienna to order full mobilisation, he had usurped the chancellor and acted without the government's authority. Germany's civilian leaders were seen as increasingly redundant and inept, in the eyes of Moltke, Tirpitz, War Minister Falkenhayn and the Prussian commanders. If war had come, as they all believed, only the armed forces could save Germany. Hour by hour, news arrived of the Russian threat. 'Hence it was [Moltke's] duty,' wrote Wilhelm years later, from his exile in Holland, '. . . to warn his Viennese colleagues of the absolute necessity of the most speedy Austro-Hungarian countermeasures.'[4]

Haggard, exhausted, horrified at the course of events, Bethmann-Hollweg tried to impose a semblance of authority. Soon after Russia mobilised, he and Moltke agreed to send an ultimatum to St Petersburg, offering Russia a stark choice: stop mobilising or face war. But they didn't use the word 'war'; they warned only that Germany would order 'full mobilisation'. Misunderstanding the distinction would have terrible consequences for Russia. Russia had 12 hours to reply. At the same time, the Cabinet activated the *Kriegsgefahrzustand*: all railway lines and depots were commandeered; the press controlled; martial law proclaimed; troops ordered to return to their garrisons and reserves called up – every measure executed short of actually moving the troops to the border.

At 5 pm on the 30th, Bethmann-Hollweg admitted to the Cabinet that he had lost control of the nation. Speaking in thin, slow, aggrieved tones, the chancellor warned that Russia had mobilised; England was sure to fight with the Entente; Italy's position was uncertain; and neither Roumania nor Bulgaria could be relied on. He knew not what to do, he said; events had overtaken him. His painful candour was that of a desperate man anxious to share a great load, to spread his responsibility. He cried out from a place of terrible isolation. He snatched at 'might have beens' and lost opportunities. He bemoaned the failure by England and Germany to mediate (he seemed to have forgotten that he had helped to kill that possibility). He even openly admitted – now – that Serbia, 'except on small points', had satisfied the Austrian ultimatum!

—

Meanwhile, all four monarchs – the Kaiser, the Tsar, the King and the Austro-Hungarian Emperor – shrank from war. Wilhelm's bluster disguised an essentially frightened man who panicked now that hostilities were upon him and the survival of his regime was at stake. The Tsar, appalled at his complicity in the coming slaughter, endured nerve-wracking regret. King George issued antique sentiments of dismay, and mild hopes of preserving the peace, even as events sped far beyond his influence or understanding. Old Franz Joseph in Vienna bustled about his palace, out of sight and mind.

The civilian ministers responsible – Bethmann-Hollweg, Grey, Poincaré, Jagow and even the wavering Berchtold – more or less hoped that war could be avoided yet were at a loss to know how, now the world was on the brink. France had never wanted war. Only Sazonov and Conrad openly urged general mobilisation (and both wavered once the decision had been taken).

If so many leaders claimed to be working against war, why could it not be stopped? Why were governments and kings helpless to stall the machinery of mobilisation? Albertini asks, in a rhetorical departure from his usual composure:

> If nobody wanted war, and if, should it break out . . . why was it not being avoided at all cost and the civil government again put in the position of control which it ought never to have let slip? But not one of the men in power in Germany, whether civilian or soldier, rose that day in Berlin to save Prussia and the Empire, just as on the morrow in Vienna no one rose to save the Monarchy.[5]

One answer is that the monarchs and government officials had, to a greater or lesser degree, surrendered their authority. They had lost the influence they once enjoyed and, in Central and Eastern Europe, ceded authority to the military. Bethmann-Hollweg had 'lost all control',[6] and was a creature of the generals. The Kaiser had been reduced to sending dictated telegrams. The other monarchs were similarly helpless and merely sealed or signed the documents with which they were presented. The civilians in government in Russia, Austria-Hungary and Germany were losing executive power to the armed forces. Grey and Asquith were under siege by British conservatives to make a firm stand against Germany. Grey had lost any credibility he once enjoyed in Europe. Only Poincaré seemed to be the master of his house.

Just when they were needed most to exert a restraining hand, the civilian leaders, and their monarchs, yielded to the diktat of blood and iron. The gigantic forces of mobilisation converged on Europe like a nuclear missile in slow motion – unstoppable once they pushed the button, or set the trains rolling – and Schlieffen's terrifying vision of a war on two enormous fronts was about to become real.

—

The German people awoke on 31 July to the fact of Russian war drums. At noon, the Kaiser served his only useful remaining function: to rally the people, in whose eyes he retained a measure of affection. Sword in his good hand, he stood resplendent on the balcony of the royal palace in Berlin:

> A momentous hour has struck for Germany . . . The sword has been forced into our hands . . . War will demand enormous sacrifices by the German people, but we shall show the enemy what it means to attack Germany. And so I commend you to God. Go forth into the churches, kneel down before God, and implore his help for our brave army.[7]

They went forth and prayed. In coming days, Orthodox, Catholic and Anglican Christians similarly knelt in their churches, and enlisted Russian, French and British gods to their cause. All were persuaded that He was on their side, that He would serve them all.

—

Berlin sent its ultimatum to Russia later that day. In the meantime, Bethmann-Hollweg, pumped up by the General Staff, moved to lock Vienna into the coming fight with Russia. Austria-Hungary had not yet assured Berlin of its support in a general war against the Tsar's regime, compared to which its action against Serbia seemed a skirmish. Conrad and Berchtold assumed until now that they would be fighting a local war in the Balkans, *not* a major offensive against the Russians. Most of their troops, they now learnt, were needed to hold Russia in the east, while the rump German Army dealt with France in the west. Schlieffen's ghost would not be denied.

And so, on 30 July, Bethmann-Hollweg asked Conrad to order Vienna's general mobilisation against Russia. For this, Conrad needed Emperor Franz Joseph's permission. The news affrighted the House of Habsburg. Had they partially mobilised against Serbia, to punish regicide, only to take on the might of Russia? On the 31st, Bethmann-Hollweg made this brutally clear to Vienna, and so hammered a further nail into the Habsburg coffin: 'we have pro-claimed imminent danger of war, which will probably be followed within forty-eight hours by mobilization. This inevitably means war. We expect from Austria-Hungary immediate active participa-tion in the war against Russia.'[8] The demand stunned the Austro-Hungarian Government and created 'an entirely new situation', Conrad wrote on 1 August.[9] To meet it, Vienna had to redirect most of its army – which was then heading south to fight Serbia – north-east to face Russia.

———

At 3.25 pm on 31 July – five minutes before Bethmann-Hollweg sent his ultimatum to Russia – a fresh offer to mediate sailed in from Sir Edward Grey. The British foreign secretary stubbornly persisted with these grand gestures. That he acted in earnest made them all the more engaging and somewhat eccentric. Would the European powers kindly drop everything and come and share a peace pipe with Britain? This, at a time when all Europe was steeling itself for Armageddon. But nobody appeared to listen to Grey any more. Never had he seemed so out of touch. In his latest telegram, he suggested, with his familiar, studied vagueness, that he would 'not immediately take the part of France' if Germany showed 'some evi-dence of a conciliatory spirit'. Grey repeatedly stressed that 'England was bound by no treaties'.[10]

Was this a golden, last-minute chance to resume mediation talks with Britain? To pull back from mobilising against Russia and save Europe? Alas, the moment passed. (The Grey offer, in any case, seems to have been miscommunicated.) Five minutes later, Bethmann-Hollweg resumed his grisly task. The progress of events, like a raging current, quite overwhelmed him. With Moltke breath-ing down his neck, he dispatched the German ultimatum to St Petersburg and sentenced Europe to death:

Russia has mobilised her *entire* army and navy against us. On account of these Russian measures, we have been forced, for the safety of the country, to proclaim the threatening state of war, which does not yet imply mobilisation. Mobilization, however, is bound to follow if Russia does not stop every measure of war against us and against Austria-Hungary within 12 hours, and notifies us definitely to this effect. Please to communicate this at once to M. Sazonov and wire hour of communication.[11]

Russia had until 12 noon on Saturday 1 August to respond. For Germany, 'mobilisation' meant war, but the ultimatum did not make that clear.

Moments later, Bethmann-Hollweg sent another ultimatum to Paris, via Ambassador Wilhelm von Schoen. Berlin demanded an answer, within 18 hours, to the question of 'whether, in a war between Germany and Russia, France would remain neutral'. The French note did define the German meaning of mobilisation: 'war'. It also carried a 'secret' note, which demanded the impossible: if France agreed to remain neutral, 'we shall have to demand the turning over of the fortresses of Toul and Verdun as a pledge of neutrality; these we could occupy and return after the completion of the war with Russia'.[12] The French had until 4 pm on 1 August to reply.

The full face of German arrogance and ambition had finally revealed itself. In sending impossible demands to Russia and France, which each country knew neither would accept, Germany had irrevocably committed itself to a two-front war.

—

In St Petersburg that evening, Sazonov read the German ultimatum with mild composure, entirely unsuited to the gravity of the occasion. Sazonov still thought peace salvageable because Germany hadn't threatened war; it had simply threatened to mobilise. He had plainly not understood the meaning Germany placed on the word. Blind to his error, he tried to reassure Ambassador Pourtalès that Russian mobilisation 'did not at all imply . . . going to war'.[13] After all, the Tsar had given his solemn word not to order hostilities.

Pourtalès was not reassured. The Count understood the true meaning of mobilisation, in the Prussian mind. The German Supreme Command, he argued, could hardly be expected to wait 'until Russia had assembled her mighty army masses on our frontier'.[14] Sazonov still failed to comprehend the nature of what confronted him. He had that night and half a day to find out.

Night passed. Day dawned. Birds sang. Animal life carried on, oblivious to the deadly schemes of men. Pourtalès's first act, at 7 am, was to write to Count Fredericks, the minister at the court of the Tsar, who had offered to help avert war:

> The situation has become extremely grave, and I seek everywhere means to avert a misfortune . . . but that if by noon today Russia does not positively state to us that she is stopping her war preparations . . . the order for mobilization will be given today. You no doubt know what that means with us. . . . in that case we are only a finger's breadth from war . . .[15]

He would not receive a reply until 2 pm that day.

Meanwhile, in Berlin that morning, Bethmann-Hollweg rose to address the Bundesrat, to inform parliament of the situation. His speech was a tissue of half-truths and self-justifications, but a single terrible sentence, which grotesquely cast Germany as a victim, lay at its core:

> If the Russian reply is unsatisfactory and there is no absolute unambiguous declaration of neutrality from France . . . the Kaiser will have the Russian Government informed that he must regard himself as in a state of war with Russia brought on by Russia herself . . . and that, as France does not guarantee her neutrality, we must assume that we are also in a state of war with France . . . We have not willed the war, it has been thrust upon us . . .[16]

———

In Peterhof that afternoon, Count Fredericks replied to Pourtalès's letter. Their last hope of rescinding the decision to mobilise lay, ironically, in the Willy–Nicky letters. Fredericks read out the Tsar's latest telegram, which reached the Kaiser at around 2.05 pm Berlin time. It failed to answer Germany's demands:

> Tsar to Kaiser, August 1
> St Petersburg
> I received your telegram. Understand you are obliged to mobilise but wish to have the same guarantee from you as I gave you, that these measures do not mean war and that we shall continue negotiating . . . Our long proved friendship must succeed, with God's help, in avoiding bloodshed. Anxiously, full of confidence await your answer.
> Nicky[17]

Clearly, the Tsar and Sazonov seemed to think war could still be averted, as *both* countries mobilised. Either that, or the Russians were merely buying time, in order to mass their armies on the German border. Bethmann-Hollweg and Moltke believed the latter interpretation, and urged Willy to reply at once:

> Kaiser to Tsar, August 1
> Berlin
> Thanks for your telegram. I yesterday pointed out to your government the way by which alone war may be avoided. Although I requested an answer for noon today, no telegram from my ambassador conveying an answer from your Government has reached me as yet. I therefore have been obliged to mobilise my army. Immediate affirmative clear and unmistakable answer from your government is the only way to avoid endless misery . . . I must request you to immediatly [*sic*] order your troops on

no account to commit the slightest act of trespassing over our frontiers.

Willy

Between the lines breathed the voice of the Prussian General Staff. Time ticked away. No reply came. At 4 pm, the Germans stopped waiting. War Minister Falkenhayn drove to the chancellor's office to request him to accompany him to the Kaiser's palace and 'ask for the promulgation of the mobilization order'. Falkenhayn records the moment in his diary:

After considerable resistance [Bethmann-Hollweg] consented and we rang up Moltke and Tirpitz. Meanwhile, His Majesty himself rang and asked us to bring along the mobilization order. At 5 o'clock in the afternoon the signing of the order by His Majesty on the table made from timbers of Nelson's 'Victory'. As he signed I said: 'God bless Your Majesty and your arms, God protect the beloved Fatherland.' The Kaiser gave me a long hand shake and we both had tears in our eyes.[18]

At 7.10 that night, St Petersburg time, Count Pourtalès presented Sazonov with Germany's declaration of war on Russia:

The Imperial German Government have used every effort since the beginning of the crisis to bring about a peaceful settlement . . . but Russia, without waiting for any result, proceeded to a general mobilisation of her forces both on land and sea. In consequence of this threatening step, which was not justified by any military proceedings on the part of Germany, the German Empire was faced by a grave and imminent danger. If the German Government had failed to guard against this peril, they would have compromised the safety and the very existence of Germany. The German Government were, therefore, obliged . . . to insist upon a cessation of the aforesaid military acts. Russia .

[refused] to answer this demand. I therefore have the honour, on the instructions of my Government, to inform your Excellency as follows: His Majesty the Emperor, my august Sovereign, in the name of the German Empire, accepts the challenge, and considers himself at war with Russia.[19]

36

GERMANY DECLARES WAR ON FRANCE

*Unfortunately, the telegram was so mutilated that . . . only
fragments of it could be deciphered . . . I had to make up my
mind to fall back on the little that could be clearly understood
from the telegram to justify the declaration of war.*
Baron von Schoen, German ambassador in Paris, on receipt of
his instructions to declare war on France, 4 August 1914

---

*And now to arms, all of us! I have seen weeping among
those who cannot go first. Everyone's turn will come.
There will not be a child of our land who will not have
a part in the enormous struggle. To die is nothing.*
Georges Clemenceau to the French Parliament, 4 August 1914

THE STEADY SOUND of Germany's war drums, the mobilisation of France's close ally Russia and the persistent refusal of British help conspired against restraint at the Quai D'Orsay. In France, everything hastened action, lest the Germans reached the border first

– so thought generals Joseph Joffre and Ferdinand Foch. The hope of mediation had passed, despite the persistence of Edward Grey. On 31 July, France heard further ominous news: Downing Street again refused to commit to the Entente. Exasperated, Poincaré appealed directly to George V later that day: 'the more England, France and Russia at the present moment give a strong impression of unity in their diplomatic action, the more it will still be legitimate to count on peace being preserved'.[1] Still, Grey refused to act. The British Government and Parliament were deeply split over whether to commit to a war with Germany. The deterrent power, if any, of British intervention had in any case disappeared: Germany and Russia were at war, and France was pleading for help.

Like Germany and Russia, France began 'mobilising' without using the word. On 31 July, the nation had had no choice. German forces had closed the bridges over the Moselle, at Schengen and Rennich, according to dispatches from the French legation in Luxembourg.[2] The Grand Duchy asked Germany and France to respect its neutrality in the event of war. The German ambassador in Paris, Baron von Schoen, put a lethal interpretation on the border tension when he visited the French prime minister Viviani that day, to press the ultimatum on France: 'If we mobilise there will inevitably be war.'[3]

The threat spurred the French commanders, who pressed their civilian leaders to act. On hearing of Baron von Schoen's mission, Joffre, the French commander, requested the war minister, Adolphe Messimy, to 'give orders for our general mobilization without an instant's delay, for I consider it imperative'. Messimy, who sported a large, walrus-like set of whiskers, promised to address the issue at a Cabinet meeting that evening. The ministers delayed the order but gave Joffre permission to send all army corps a preparatory warning the next day. '[M]ost likely,' Joffre wrote to his commanders, 'orders for mobilization will be issued today, 1 August, during the evening. Proceed at once to make all preparations which would facilitate mobilization.'[4]

From the moment Germany proclaimed a state of war danger, French rail workers were readied for 'instant action'.[5] The mobilisation of France's *troupes de couverture* – the troops dispatched to the frontier to meet the enemy's first attack – began at 9 pm on 31 July and was completed by noon on 3 August (without any suspension of ordinary railway traffic). This initial operation involved nearly 600 trains. French forces moved into positions ten kilometres from the Luxembourg–Vosges border, with firm instructions not to go nearer to avoid clashing with German patrols and giving Berlin a pretext to declare war.

Meanwhile, the French fleet was on alert in the Mediterranean, to guard the country's southern ports. The Royal Navy would protect France's northern and western ports, as agreed under the 1912 naval protocol. That role, however, placed Britain under no obligation to fight on land, Grey reminded the French. If technically correct, his lack of goodwill, inconsistent with the spirit of the Cordiale, made Cambon wonder whether 'the word "honour" should not be struck out of the English vocabulary'.[6] Grey would, however, undertake to call his divided Cabinet in urgent session on Sunday 2 August, to address the subject.

—

On 1 August, events impinged fast and hard on the French Government. A decision had to be made at once for full mobilisation, Joffre insisted. Again, he pressed the government to give the order, at a Cabinet meeting that morning. He appeared 'with the placid face of a calm, resolute man whose only fear is lest France, outstripped by German mobilisation, the most rapid of them all, might speedily find herself in an irreparable state of inferiority'.[7] Outside in the streets of the cities, the air was thundery with rumour. 'Paris,' wrote Edith Wharton, 'went on steadily about her midsummer business of feeding, dressing, and amusing the great army of tourists who were the only invader she had seen for nearly half a century.'[8]

At 11 am on 1 August, as arranged, the French prime minister

René Viviani – soon to be relieved of his duty as foreign minister – met Baron von Schoen at the Quai d'Orsay. The German ambassador wanted a reply to the German ultimatum he had sent the day before: would France remain neutral in a Russo-German war? Would it relinquish its forts to Germany? The answer was obvious to both men: no. (There are various versions of the conversation.) France would protect its own interests, which implicitly meant those of its chief ally, Russia.

The noon deadline passed. The French treated the German ultimatum with the contempt it deserved. The very suggestion that they abandon the great forts of Verdun and Toul to German occupation – the price of 'neutrality' – grossly offended French pride. To Joffre's relief, the French Cabinet ordered full mobilisation at 4 pm that day, at about the same time as Germany. It would proceed just after midnight, on 2 August.

All France read the order the next morning. A white sign saying 'General Mobilisation' appeared on the wall of the Ministere de la Marine. Little blue mobilisation orders appeared outside newspaper offices, records Recouly.[9] Edith Wharton, the American author who was in Paris at the time, witnessed the moment:

> Passers by read the notice and went on. There were no cheers, no gesticulations: the dramatic sense of the race had already told them that the event was too great to be dramatized. Like a monstrous landslide it had fallen across the path of an orderly laborious nation . . .[10]

The full mobilisation of the French Army began with a rush to the railways. On 2 August, every railhead, depot and carriage was clogged with men, supplies and ammunition. Over the next three weeks, some 4750 trains would speed to the Franco-German border, including 250 special trains carrying siege supplies to the great French forts stretching from Verdun to Belfort. At its completion, the French Government would thank the railway workers for the 'patriotic zeal and admirable devotion' with which they had toiled day and night.[11] Later in the war, the *Journal des Transports* would declare, 'One can justly say that the first victory in this great conflict has been won by the railwaymen.'[12]

That day, demonstrations, for and against the war, filled the city streets. '[P]rocessions on the boulevard, on the Place de la Concorde, where an innumerable crowd surged to and fro,' wrote Recouly. 'Mobilisation is not war,' Poincaré told the people.[13] By their actions, few people seemed to believe him. The prospect of war transformed the nation. Yesterday, the French people 'had been leading a thousand different lives', wrote Edith Wharton, '. . . as alien as enemies across a frontier'. Today 'workers and idlers, thieves, beggars, saints, poets, drabs and sharpers, genuine people and showy shams, were all bumping up against each other in an instinctive community of emotion'.[14] Every ounce of human energy fed the war effort; normal routines were abandoned. 'There was something strangely moving,' Wharton recalled, 'in this new Paris of the August evenings, so exposed yet so serene, as though her very beauty shielded her.'[15]

—

How the French people found themselves mobilising for a third war with Germany in a hundred years is painful to comprehend. France had not provoked war. Its leaders were silent for most of July. President Poincaré had been at sea. Of any nation, the French were the least to blame for the crisis. Nobody in power in France had openly pressed for war.

And yet, French officials were not entirely blameless. Their errant ambassador in St Petersburg, Maurice Paléologue, had urged Sazonov to take a strong stand against Germany, without Paris's approval. Paléologue's personal zeal had driven his 'diplomacy' – which did much to encourage Russia's monumental blunder of mobilising early. Yet Poincaré added ballast to Paléologue's position: on his return to Paris on 29 July, the French president did nothing to restrain St Petersburg. He turned instead to London. He sought *allies*, not mediators.

Russia's mobilisation was a delicate issue for France. Technically, it did not compel Poincaré to go to war. The Franco-Russian Alliance obliged the signatories to *defend* each other if attacked. In mobilising first, however, Russia had made the initial aggressive move. France should have acted to pull her ally back from the brink, in keeping with Poincaré's promise in 1912. France, he said, would 'never take the responsibility of letting [war] be declared'.[16] Yet, tragically, that is exactly what the French Government did do: it 'let' war be declared, first on Russia and then on France itself, by doing nothing to resist it.

That's not to say that Poincaré handed St Petersburg a blank cheque to wage war. Perhaps the president believed in his policy towards Russia: 'to do what lay in our power to induce our ally to exercise moderation in matters in which we are much less directly concerned . . . [e.g. Serbia].'[17] Why, then, did Paris do so little? The French Government merely sent a rather confusing telegram, on 31 July, which urged Russia 'in the overruling interests of peace . . . to avoid anything which might render inevitable or precipitate the crisis'.[18] By then, it was too late: the Russians had already mobilised. That same day, Poincaré had said he thought war 'inevitable', according to Francis Bertie, British ambassador in Paris.[19] The French Government seemed resigned to the fatalism that infected everyone in those last, desperate days; they *accepted* war.

—

Contradicting this picture of French innocence is another, darker narrative, which goes like this: the French Government may not have wanted war but did nothing to avert it and, once war looked likely, welcomed and even relished the prospect. War presented Paris with a golden opportunity. Never had France seemed better equipped to take the offensive to Germany, to exact revenge for 1815, 1870 and 1911, and reclaim Alsace-Lorraine. Her railways were more advanced, her armies swelling under the terms of the three-year national-service law. She enjoyed a robust alliance with Russia, possessor of Europe's largest army, and the tentative support of Britain. 'For the third time within a century,' writes Keiger, 'France was faced with a German invasion. But whereas in 1815 and 1870 she had been alone, she was now supported by two powerful allies.'[20]

In this light, war presented France with an opportunity, not a threat. An article in the respectable *Le Matin* on 1 August ran:

> We well know that never has war offered itself under aspects more favourable to us . . . [W]hen Germany will have to bear almost alone the brunt of the attack from the Entente armies and navies, in truth . . . would we not feel the strong temptation of war? Nevertheless it is not for this war that we shall be held responsible by posterity. If it comes, we shall meet it with high hopes. We are convinced that it will bring us the reparations which are our due.[21]

Poincaré expressed similar sentiments, according to media reports. If true, his claims about France not wanting war sound hollow. The alignment of events in France's favour gave the government the perfect opportunity to remove the German threat forever.

Nor was the coming of war 'inevitable' or a 'shock' to the French people. Politicians on all sides were acutely aware of the slide to war but did little to resist it, with the exception of a few vocal dissenters, such as the fiery socialist Jean Jaurès, who warned that a war with Germany would leave all of France a smouldering ruin. Great crowds, fired up by the jingoist press, were impatient for war. Yet large anti-war protests gave the lie to the claim that most people were overwhelmingly in favour.[22] Throughout July, the French opposition furiously debated whether to oppose or support the war. In the event, the socialists rallied behind the government, abandoning Jaurès's principled stand.

Jaurès's assassination on the night of 31 July – shot by a young fanatic as he sat dining in a Paris cafe – was the most shocking expression of French war fever. Posthumously hailed for his courage in opposing the war, Jaurès, in his last weeks alive, was vilified for his outspoken belief in Franco-German rapprochement and subjected to violent tirades in the press, who branded him a 'pro-German socialist traitor' and 'sinister agent of negation and corruption' who 'vowed to give Paris to the Prussians'.[23] On 23 July, the journalist Charles Maurras wrote, with shocking irresponsibility, 'We have no wish to incite anyone to political assassination, but M. Jean Jaurès may well shake in his shoes!'[24] On 29 July, Jaurès bravely spoke out against a war with Germany for the last time and urged the government to work towards peace. Two days later, he was dead.

—

The German regime was yet to sup on the dregs of its debasement. The absurd ultimatum was not enough. Somehow, it needed to manufacture a *casus belli* to attack France; or, better still, to goad France into declaring war first. To this end, the German and Austrian press proved useful. Complicit pawns in the government's hands, they published a series of outrageous lies about French border violations. Reportedly, 80 French officers dressed in Prussian uniforms had tried to cross the border near Walbeck, in motor vehicles. 'The attempt did not succeed,' lied a German press service. Elsewhere, 'companies' of French troops had crossed the German border on 3 August and occupied the towns of Gottestal, Metzer, Markirch and Schluchtpass, according to the Wolff Bureau, a press agency. This too was a shameless fiction: French troops had been ordered to remain ten kilometres from the German border, to avoid any such risk.

The German inventions grew more fantastic. 'Two French air force officers flew across Nuremberg in a plane, dropping bombs on the town,' claimed Vienna and Budapest papers on 2 and 3 August.[25] A similar story appeared in the Wolff Agency, claiming French planes had flown over the Rhineland. 'Yesterday night, an enemy airship has been observed flying from Kerprich to Andernach,' it stated. 'Enemy planes were observed flying from Düren to Cologne. A

French plane was shot down near Wesel.'[26] In fact, a civilian French aviator had simply lost his way, landed at Mulhouse and flown off. The most shocking provocation appeared in the German newspaper *Die Neue Zeitung* on 4 August, which claimed that French doctors in Metz had tried to poison the wells with cholera bacillus.[27] The alleged perpetrator of this 'hideous deed' had been shot by firing squad, claimed a separate report. In sum, Germany accused France of 20 frontier violations, all of which were groundless calumnies.

Sentient men in Berlin imagined the world would believe these inventions, which were clearly designed to justify an invasion of France. But Paris refused to play Berlin's insidious game. Its embassies firmly protested and demanded that Germany correct the lies.[28] Viviani counter-claimed that German troops had fired on a French customs post, and entered the villages of Joncherey and Baron, killing a French soldier. The Germans initially dismissed these claims as fabrications. Yet, on 4 August, an embarrassed Moltke was forced to concede that a patrol of German troops had illegally entered French territory, 'against express order[s]'. Two soldiers were shot.[29]

On 3 August, the German Government's perfidy plumbed new depths. At 1.05, Schoen, the German ambassador in Paris, received a coded telegram from Bethmann-Hollweg. Schoen later claimed it had been garbled. The first paragraph, which was partly illegible, stated that a French airman had been 'shot down while attempting to destroy railroad near Wesel'; that French airmen had dropped anti-German fliers at Nuremburg and Karlsruhe; and that French troops had violated the German borders. The second, legible, half of the message read, 'By these acts France has placed us in a state of war. Will Your Excellency please communicate the above to the French Government today at 6 p.m., ask for passports, and take your leave, handing affairs to the American Embassy.'[30] (An earlier draft had accused French troops of violating Belgian neutrality, but not even the German Government seemed able to wear so malicious a fabrication, the tragic irony of which appears to have been lost on them, and Bethmann-Hollweg had it excised.)

Schoen, equipped with his unreadable instructions, went ahead and delivered the German declaration of war *blind to the reasons for Germany going to war*. All he could say later in his defence was that the coded telegram bore the chancellor's signature and was 'a matter of special importance'. He claimed to be able to discern words alleging that French airmen had attacked 'Nuremberg, Wesel and Karlsruhe'. Germany thus justified its invasion of France with a lie as malicious as it was indecipherable, as Schoen later unwittingly acknowledged. In an astonishingly cavalier explanation, he wrote:

> Unfortunately, the telegram was so mutilated that . . . only fragments of it could be deciphered . . . There was no time to make an inquiry as to the illegible part. As I knew from other sources that we felt bound to declare war in consequence of a French air attack on Nuremberg, I had to make up my mind to fall back on the little that could be clearly understood from the telegram to justify the declaration of war.[31]

Ambassador Schoen appears to have excelled in the cameo role allotted to him, of the dull, dutiful messenger down the ages, whose task – to deliver threats of blood and destruction – he accomplishes without a tic of anxiety, deaf to the remonstrances of conscience, concerned only to do as he is told. The truth of his mission remains a mystery. Did the French cipher-readers deliberately garble the cable? Did Schoen himself desecrate the message? If he felt self-disgust at his mission, why did he not wait until a readable telegram arrived? The controversy continued after the war but boils down to this: the Germans were merely arguing over *which lie* in the telegram – French air attacks (legible) or French border violations (illegible) – best fitted their purpose, to justify going to war.

The wretched man thus bore the dreadful document to Foreign Minister Viviani's office at the Quai d'Orsay. On the way, French protesters leapt on the running board of Schoen's vehicle, shouting and threatening him with wild gestures, as if already aware of his shameful mission. Ushered into the minister's presence, he bowed low and read aloud the German declaration of war (see Appendix 5 for the full text):

> The German . . . authorities have established a certain number of flagrantly hostile acts committed on German territory by French military aviators. Several of these have openly violated the neutrality of Belgium by flying over the territory of that country; one has attempted to destroy buildings near Wesel; others have been seen in the district of the Eifel, one has thrown bombs on the railway near Karlsruhe and Nuremberg. I am instructed . . . that in the presence of these acts of aggression the German Empire considers itself in a state of war with France . . . My diplomatic mission having thus come to an end it only remains for me to request your Excellency to be good enough to furnish me with my passports . . . (Signed) SCHOEN.[32]

Viviani listened in silence, and then rose to protest against 'the injustice and insanity' of the German thesis. There was nothing more to say. Schoen received a safe passage back to Germany, in stark contrast to poor Jules Cambon, the French ambassador in Berlin, who had to bribe his way out of Germany in gold, 'travel in locked carriages like a sort of prisoner' and suffer the indignation of being held at gunpoint by German troops at the Danish border and extorted out of his remaining funds.[33]

—

That day, 4 August 1914, Raymond Poincaré, the president of the French Republic, stood to address an Extraordinary Session of the French Parliament. The deputies remained standing during his speech (for the full text, see Appendix 6):

Gentlemen,
France has just been the object of a violent and premeditated

attack, which is an insolent defiance of the law of nations. Before any declaration of war had been sent to us, even before the German Ambassador had asked for his passports, our territory has been violated. The German Empire has waited till yesterday evening to give at this late stage the true name to a state of things which it had already created . . .

In the war which is beginning France will have Right on her side, the eternal power of which cannot with impunity be disregarded by nations any more than by individuals *(loud and unanimous applause).* She will be heroically defended by all her sons; nothing will break their sacred union before the enemy; today they are joined together as brothers in a common indignation against the aggressor, and in a common patriotic faith *(loud and prolonged applause and cries of 'Vive la France').*

She is faithfully-helped by Russia, her ally; she is supported by the loyal friendship of Great Britain . . . For today once again she stands before the universe for Liberty, Justice and Reason. *Haut les coeurs et vive la France! (unanimous and prolonged applause).*[34]

Clemenceau later delivered a rousing call to arms. The coming struggle would pitch the glory of Latinate Europe against the barbarity of the Goths, he said. France, he declared, would fight 'for the independence of nationalities in Europe . . . for the greatest ideas that have honoured the thought of mankind, ideas that have come to us from Athens and Rome . . .' The Germans were 'like those barbarians who melted into ingots the marvels of ancient art after the pillaging of Rome in order to make savage ornaments . . .' France and Russia were about to fight 'a Teutonism delirious in megalomania, ambitious to realize what Alexander, Caesar, Napoleon could not accomplish: to impose upon a world that desires to be free the supremacy of steel . . .' He concluded:

And now to arms, all of us! I have seen weeping among those who cannot go first. Everyone's turn will come. There will not be a child of our land who will not have a part in the enormous struggle. To die is nothing. We must win. And for that we need all men's power. The weakest will have his share of glory. There come times, in the lives of peoples, when there passes over them a tempest of heroic action.[35]

37

NECESSITY KNOWS NO LAW

If die we must, better death with honour. We have no
other choice. Our submission would serve no end.
Charles de Broqueville, prime minister of Belgium,
rejecting Germany's ultimatum

Thus we were forced to ignore the rightful protests of the
Governments of Luxembourg and Belgium. The wrong – I
speak openly – the wrong we thereby commit we will try to
make good as soon as our military aims have been attained.
He who is menaced as we are and is fighting for his highest
possession can only consider how he is to hack his way through.
Chancellor Theobald von Bethmann-Hollweg to the Reichstag, 4 August 1914

BELGIUM HAD NOT BEEN IDLE. A week earlier, on 24 July, the
Belgian minister for foreign affairs, M. Davignon, told his ambassadors in Paris, Berlin, London, Vienna and St Petersburg to hand a
signed letter to the governments of their host countries the moment
the Belgian Army mobilised, if that should happen. Until then, they
were to keep the letter, undated, in their safes.

The Belgian letter affirmed the nation's determination to fight to defend its neutrality, bestowed by the Treaty of London of 19 April 1839. Under the Treaty, Prussia, Britain and France recognised the independence of Belgium (from the Netherlands, of which it had been a de facto part until 1830) and guaranteed Belgian neutrality *in perpetuity* (according to the critical Article VII). This committed the signatories to guard Belgium's neutrality in the event of an invasion.[1] Like Switzerland, Belgium existed in a state of 'armed neutrality', under which 'belligerents may not invade'[2] and Belgium's right to resist invaders would 'not compromise its neutrality'.[3]

For most of the nineteenth century, the great powers gave the matter little thought. None seemed inclined to defend Belgium if it came to blows, with the signal exception of Britain, who, in 1870 and 1887, intervened on behalf of Belgian neutrality. To cheers in the House of Commons, Prime Minister Gladstone had declared in 1870 that England would never 'quietly stand by and witness the perpetration of the direct crime that ever stained the pages of history in the darkest of ages, and thus became participators in the sin'. Grey would soon quote his words in defending Belgian neutrality in more perilous circumstances.[4] Brussels thus came to see Britain as its default protector.

In the intervening years, the possibility of another war between France and Germany threatened Belgium. The Kaiser made this embarrassingly clear to King Leopold, during his visit to Berlin in 1904. To Leopold's horror, Wilhelm insisted that Belgium choose sides in the great struggle with France: 'In the event of Belgium's not being on my side, I shall be actuated by strategic considerations only.'[5]

Wilhelm had carelessly revealed to the Belgian king the central plank of the Schlieffen Plan, the success of which depended on the free movement of German forces through Belgium. Leopold alerted his government to this astonishing revelation, but little was done. In the ensuing years, the German threat to Belgium became part of common military and political discourse, throughout

Europe. '[T]o take the offensive against France it will be necessary to violate Belgian neutrality,' Moltke told Bethmann-Hollweg on 21 December 1912. He went on:

> Only an advance through Belgian territory gives us the hope of attacking and beating the French Army in the open field. In this way we shall find facing us the English Expeditionary Force and – unless we achieve a treaty with Belgium – the Belgian army. Nevertheless, this operation offers better prospects of success than a frontal attack against the fortified French eastern front [i.e. around the forts of Verdun and Toul].[6]

For a moment, in 1911, some thought *France* might be the first to violate Belgian territory, as a pre-emptive strike on Germany. Paris, too, saw Belgium as a free northern corridor for the easy movement of troops, avoiding the heavily fortified central border region. But on 20 October 1911 the French Foreign Ministry decided against any first violation of Belgian neutrality. 'It is our duty,' it said in a letter to General Joseph Joffre, commander of the French forces, 'to take no initiative which might be regarded as a violation of Belgian neutrality. But it seems certain that Germany will march her troops across Belgian territory.'[7] In which case, France would take whatever steps necessary to defend itself – including, if need be, entering Belgian territory *after* Germany had violated it. 'At the first news,' Joffre asked a meeting of the Council of National Defence on 9 January 1912, 'of the violation of Belgian territory by the Germans, may our armies penetrate Belgian territory?'[8] The council handed him complete authority to do so.

—

The clouds darkened further over Belgium's future. In 1913, the German opposition raised the question of Belgian neutrality in the Reichstag. On 29 April, the Social Democrats pressed Gottlieb von Jagow, the German foreign minister – a quiet, clinical diplomat and reputed to be the worst speaker in the house – to clarify Germany's position. 'Belgian neutrality,' he glibly replied, 'is provided for by International conventions and Germany is determined to respect those Conventions.'[9] His answer did not satisfy the socialists, who kept haranguing the government. The then war minister, General August von Heeringen, declared, 'Germany will not lose sight of the fact that the neutrality of Belgium is guaranteed by international treaty.'[10]

Neither answer had guaranteed Belgium's neutrality. Jagow (who privately opposed the invasion of Belgium) had merely offered to respect a convention; Heeringen had said he would keep sight of it. Henceforth, Brussels had every reason to feel very worried. Its concerns deepened when the Belgian ambassador in Berlin, Baron Eugène Beyens, asked Jagow for a direct answer. Jagow, irritated, replied that he could add nothing to what had been said in the Reichstag.

Germany soon revealed what was in store for Belgium. On a visit to Berlin in November 1913, the new king Albert – a bold, intelligent and much-admired monarch – listened in astonishment as the Kaiser and Moltke disburdened themselves of Germany's plans. The Kaiser ranted about a coming war with France, but Moltke delivered the *coup de grâce*, disdainfully advising Albert that 'small countries, such as Belgium, would be well advised to rally to the side of the strong if they wished to retain their independence'.[11]

—

By 1914, Belgian politicians were awake to the German threat but vainly hoped that Berlin's steamroller would spare 'small countries'. A strange spirit of denial permeated the Belgian media and many statesmen. The Belgian armed forces, however, were made of sterner stuff and were determined to resist an invasion, should it come. The construction of the great forts at Namur and Liège were clear symbols of defiance – to *any* foreign invader. On 29 July, Belgium called up three classes of militia and placed its regular forces on a 'strengthened peace footing' – one of the more colourful euphemisms for 'not mobilising'. 'This step should in no way be confused with mobilization,' the foreign minister assured his ambassadors.[12]

Two days later, on 1 August 1914, Belgium's ambassadors in Paris, Berlin, London, Vienna and St Petersburg were instructed to present the letter sitting in their safes to their host governments. It declared:

> Belgium confidently expects that her territory will remain free from any attack, should hostilities break out upon her frontiers. All necessary steps to ensure respect of Belgian neutrality have nevertheless been taken by the Government. The Belgian army has been mobilised and is taking up such strategic positions as have been chosen to secure the defence of the country and the respect of its neutrality. The forts of Antwerp and on the Meuse have been put in a state of defence . . .[13]

That day, as German forces gathered on the Luxembourg border, London sent a pointed question to France and Germany: did they intend to respect Belgium's neutrality?[14] Paris immediately said it would, adding that, 'In the event of this neutrality not being respected by another Power, the French Government . . . might find it necessary to modify their attitude.'[15] In other words, France reserved the right to fight Germany on Belgian soil. Berlin refused to answer the question, ominously explaining that 'she was not in a position to reply'.[16]

On Sunday 2 August, German soldiers entered the Grand Duchy of Luxembourg, by the bridges of Wasserbillig and Remich, and headed south, in the direction of the capital. Armoured trains packed with troops and ammunition followed, violating the country's neutrality as guaranteed by the Treaty of London of 1867.[17] Luxembourg's prime minister Paul Eyschen reported an 'invasion'.[18] The country's token army of 400 soldiers sensibly laid down their weapons and let the Germans pass. The next day, tens of thousands of German soldiers occupied Luxembourg; they would stay for another four years. This brazen precedent warned Belgium of its own, more dreadful, destiny: the execution of the Schlieffen-Moltke Plan had begun.

—

The Luxembourg example failed to disabuse Belgium of its hopes. Even then, many Belgians clung to the belief that their nation would be spared. Their expectations were about to be crushed altogether. At 7 pm on 2 August, the German ambassador in the Belgian capital, Klaus von Below-Saleske, requested an urgent meeting with Davignon.

'What is the matter?' Davignon asked the breathless German diplomat.

'I came up the stairs too quickly, it is nothing,' Below-Saleske replied. 'I have a most confidential communication to make to you on behalf of my government.'

Davignon opened the envelope, read it, then re-read it, and visibly paled as he comprehended its meaning. 'No surely?' he muttered, trembling. 'No surely it is not possible?'

He let the paper fall to the floor between them. Below-Saleske had recovered his composure sufficiently to declare that Germany meant no harm to Belgium, to which Davignon reacted with extreme indignation. The German threat to violate Belgian neutrality was unacceptable. Below-Saleske turned and departed, leaving the terrible document, one of the most chilling of the war, at Davignon's feet.[19] It said:

Kaiserlich Deutsche Gesandschaft in Belgien-Brüssel, August 2, 1914 (Very Confidential). RELIABLE information has been received by the German Government to the effect that French forces intend to march on the line of the Meuse by Givet and Namur. This information leaves no doubt as to the intention of France to march through Belgian territory against Germany. The

German Government cannot but fear that Belgium . . . will be unable . . . to repel so considerable a French invasion with sufficient prospect of success to afford an adequate guarantee against danger to Germany. It is essential for the self-defence of Germany that she should anticipate any such hostile attack . . .

In order to exclude any possibility of misunderstanding, the German Government make the following declaration:

1. Germany has in view no act of hostility against Belgium. In the event of Belgium being prepared in the coming war to maintain an attitude of friendly neutrality towards Germany, the German Government bind themselves, at the conclusion of peace, to guarantee the possessions and independence of the Belgian Kingdom in full.
2. Germany undertakes, under the above-mentioned condition, to evacuate Belgian territory on the conclusion of peace.
3. If Belgium adopts a friendly attitude, Germany is prepared, in cooperation with the Belgian authorities, to purchase all necessaries for her troops against a cash payment, and to pay an indemnity for any damage that may have been caused by German troops.
4. Should Belgium oppose the German troops, and in particular should she throw difficulties in the way of their march by a resistance of the fortresses on the Meuse, or by destroying railways, roads, tunnels, or other similar works, Germany will, to her regret, be compelled to consider Belgium as an enemy. In this event . . . the eventual adjustment of the relations between the two States must be left to the decision of arms . . .[20]

Written by Moltke, the German ultimatum to Belgium was an implicit declaration of war on France and, if she resisted, Belgium – without actually declaring it. Germany would later insult the world's intelligence by describing the document as nothing more than a precaution. Brussels had 12 hours to reply, by 8 am the next morning, 3 August.

—

They had to work overnight. The Belgian Foreign Ministry translated the ultimatum. Cabinet ministers were summoned to the palace. The despicable request would be rejected, all agreed. But how should the consequences be communicated to the people, King Albert wondered. German 'hostilities', he warned, would 'assume a character of violence undreamt of by them'.[21] Their beloved monarch's words swept up the ministers in a fervour of patriotism, recalled Prime Minister Charles de Broqueville:

> If die we must, better death with honour. We have no other choice. Our submission would serve no end. The stake for which Germany has begun this war is the freedom of Europe. Let us make no mistake about it, if Germany is victorious, Belgium . . . will be annexed to the Reich.[22]

Their answer, then, would be 'no', the meeting unanimously concluded. The German ultimatum must be firmly rejected. The discussion turned to the readiness of the Belgian forces to withstand the coming blow. Where should the army be concentrated? Where was the best line of defence? Could they depend on France and Britain? For how long could the fortifications at Liège, Namur and Antwerp withstand the shock? A month? For hours, the King, his Cabinet and generals debated how Belgium might confront the most powerful army on earth. Belgium, it transpired, had no plan.

Near midnight, three members of the Belgian Crown Council sat around a huge wooden table in the palace to draft the reply to Germany. They soon repaired to the Foreign Ministry, to escape the would-be editors who milled around. At 1.30 am, the German ambassador Below-Saleske appeared, and repeated the lies about French border violations and air attacks. French bad faith, he claimed – to the Belgians' disgust – was a direct threat both to Belgium and to Germany.

The Belgian ministers completed their reply at 2 am on 3 August. As they prepared to leave, King Albert rose. 'Gentlemen,' he said, 'this is the dawn of a dark day. But it promises to be a brilliant one.' Seemingly to himself, he added, 'If we had been weak enough to yield, tomorrow in the streets of Brussels the people would have hanged us.'[23]

———

At 7 am, Davignon delivered the Belgian reply to Germany's ambassador. The measured tone and restrained language framed a nobility of mind that would forever redound to the bravery and spirit of Belgium (see Appendix 7 for full text):

> This note has made a deep and painful impression upon the Belgian Government. The intentions attributed to France by Germany are in contradiction to the formal declarations made to us on August 1, in the name of the French Government. Moreover, if, contrary to our expectation, Belgian neutrality should be violated by France . . . the Belgian army would offer the most vigorous resistance . . .
>
> The attack upon her independence with which the German Government threaten her constitutes a flagrant violation of international law. No strategic interest justifies such a violation of law. The Belgian Government, if they were to accept the proposals submitted to them, would sacrifice the honour of the nation and betray their duty towards Europe . . . [T]he Belgian Government are firmly resolved to repel, by all the means in their power, every attack upon their rights.[24]

Moltke, surprised and faintly troubled, brusquely replied that afternoon: 'our troops will be entering Belgian territory tomorrow morning'. He drew the line at declaring war on Belgium, still hoping that

Brussels would be made to 'realize the seriousness of the situation'. Nobody in the German Government took seriously the idea that Belgium would resist the German Army's march on France.

The next morning, Brussels telegrammed the British, French and Russian Foreign Ministries to appeal for concerted action against 'the forcible measures taken by Germany against Belgium . . .' It repeated, to the admiration of all, the golden commitment of the Belgian people. They would 'firmly . . . resist by all the means in their power' the German Army.[25] At the same time, the Belgian Government broke off relations with the German ambassador, handed his legation their passports and ejected them from the country.[26]

—

The first German troops crossed the Belgian border that morning. A moment later, Chancellor Theobald von Bethmann-Hollweg addressed the Reichstag (see Appendix 8 for full text):

> A stupendous fate is breaking over Europe . . . We wished to continue our work of peace, and, like a silent vow, the feeling that animated everyone from the Emperor down to the youngest soldier was this: Only in defence of a just cause shall our sword fly from its scabbard. The day has now come when we must draw it, against our wish, and in spite of our sincere endeavours. Russia has set fire to the building. We are at war with Russia and France − a war that has been forced upon us . . .[27]

Bethmann-Hollweg proceeded to give a truncated version of history, distorted by untruths and omissions, and redounding always to Germany's honourable intent amid the perfidy of its neighbours. He unwittingly laid bare the psychology of a nation chronically under siege, a people always wronged, never the wrongdoers. He ignored Russia's warnings that it would not stand by to watch Austria crush Serbia; ignored the fact that everyone knew the Third Balkan War, which Germany had provoked, could not be confined to the peninsula. He said nothing, obviously, of Germany's role in orchestrating it, and of pressing Vienna to fight, first against Serbia and then against Russia. He excised Berlin's refusal to engage constructively in mediation attempts. He understandably made much of Russia's reckless decision to order partial mobilisation, which was admittedly the Entente's greatest error. But his claim that Germany had made clear to Russia 'what mobilization on our frontiers meant' was untrue. Sazonov plainly had *not* understood what it meant, because the German ultimatum failed to clarify the threat (unlike the one Berlin sent to France, which did do so, in very strong terms). He then reissued the worthless lies about French aviators and French border violations. 'Though war had not been declared,' he said, 'France thus broke the peace and actually attacked us . . . Our troops, in accordance with their orders, have remained strictly on the defensive.'

At this point, Bethmann-Hollweg issued the notorious sentence, 'Gentlemen, we are now in a state of necessity, and necessity knows no law.' From there, the German Government tossed the law to the winds. Henceforth, Germany would behave as if thousands of years of evolving human restraint were mythology, and would proceed to act outside all internationally accepted rules. The remark horrified the embassies of Europe. Belgium quaked at the realisation that she was about to feel the full force of German lawlessness. Bethmann-Hollweg later sourced his words to Moltke, who believed that fighting a war on two fronts made the Belgian invasion a case of 'absolute military necessity': 'I had to accommodate my view to his.'[28]

Bethmann-Hollweg then admitted that Germany had already committed two 'necessary' lawless acts – the invasions of Luxembourg and Belgium – in phrases that heaped shame upon ignominy:

> Our troops have occupied Luxembourg and perhaps have already entered Belgian territory. Gentlemen, that is a breach of international law. It is true that the French Government declared

at Brussels that France would respect Belgian neutrality as long as her adversary respected it. We knew, however, that France stood ready for an invasion. France could wait, we could not. A French attack on our flank on the lower Rhine might have been disastrous. Thus we were forced to ignore the rightful protests of the Governments of Luxembourg and Belgium. The wrong – I speak openly – the wrong we thereby commit we will try to make good as soon as our military aims have been attained. He who is menaced as we are and is fighting for his highest possession can only consider how he is to hack his way through (*durchhauen*).

His words drew 'great and repeated applause'.

Astonishingly, Bethmann-Hollweg seemed to think British neutrality still negotiable:

We have informed the British Government that, as long as Great Britain remains neutral, our fleet will not attack the northern coast of France, and that we will not violate the territorial integrity and independence of Belgium. These assurances I now repeat before the world, and I may add that, as long as Great Britain remains neutral, we would also be willing, upon reciprocity being assured, to take no warlike measures against French commercial shipping . . .

Gentlemen, so much for the facts. I repeat the words of the Emperor: 'With a clear conscience we enter the lists.' We are fighting for the fruits of our works of peace, for the inheritance of a great past and for our future. The fifty years are not yet past during which Count Moltke [the elder] said we should have to remain armed to defend the inheritance that we won in 1870. Now the great hour of trial has struck for our people. But with clear confidence we go forward to meet it. Our army is in the field, our navy is ready for battle – behind them stands the entire German nation – the entire German nation united to the last man . . .[29]

They said it, but they did not feel it. No signs of clear confidence that day animated the appearance of the chancellor, who reminded Tirpitz of a 'drowning man'. Never had the Kaiser shown 'such a tragic and disturbed face' as he did in those August days, remarked an old friend.[30] Germany knew it had lost the diplomatic war. It knew it clung to the vestiges of a failed and lawless enterprise. Its civilian leaders had dismally failed to avoid war and done much to start it. The destiny of the country now lay in the sights of the generals.

38

THE LAST LAMP

*[I]f we are engaged in war, we shall suffer but little
more than we shall suffer even if we stand aside.*
Sir Edward Grey, British foreign secretary, to the
House of Commons, 3 August 1914

---

*[J]ust for a scrap of paper, Great Britain was
going to make war on a kindred nation.*
Chancellor Bethmann-Hollweg, describing the
British commitment to Belgian neutrality

THE TERRIBLE CHOICE that confronted Britain had split the
Cabinet and left several ministers reeling from what they were
being asked to do. A strange unreality permeated their deliberations in these last days of peace, as though H. G. Wells's creations
had landed on earth and the government had to respond to the
threat within hours.[1] Some ministers seemed helpless, incapable of
facing the great question of the day: whether or not to join France
in a war against Germany. One Cabinet member, John Burns, had
already resigned, refusing to be a party to a decision for a war of

catastrophic dimensions; John Morley would soon join him. Several 'neutralist' Cabinet members – Lloyd George, Lewis Harcourt, Earl Beauchamp, Jack Pease, John Simon and Walter Runciman – were undecided. They refused to countenance British intervention in a war with Germany, and feared the terrible repercussions for British lives and the economy. Their votes were critical to any British decision to go to war, as they held the balance of power in the Cabinet. Somehow, they had to be persuaded. Grey did so, step by step.

At the epic Cabinet meeting of 2 August, Grey managed to weld together a semblance of unity on the critical question of defending France's northern ports, which had been left naked to the storm (as the French fleet was then in the Mediterranean). It was Britain's responsibility to protect its waters and the French ports, Grey said. After a marathon debate, a majority agreed. That did not yet mean war. On one point the neutralists were rent with self-doubt: the invasion of Belgium. It piqued their consciences, the threatened wholesale mauling of a neutral country. All agreed to reconsider their position if Germany violated Belgian neutrality. The Conservative opposition preyed on the Liberals' indecisiveness, and a letter pledging to support the government 'in going in with France' gave Grey an ace against the minority who opposed the war.

The meeting broke for lunch. Grey drove to London Zoo 'and spent an hour communing with the birds'.[2] Asquith sat in his office. The ministers continued the debate over lunch at Beauchamp's house, without reaching a resolution. Later that day, they met again, and decided their position in time for the resumption of the Cabinet meeting at 6 pm: any threat to Belgium was intolerable. A majority now agreed that a German invasion of France was a threat to British interests. But the *casus belli*, the moral issue that decided the British neutralists for war, was the breach of Belgian neutrality. 'The issue of Belgium was all important,' concluded Steiner and Neilson, 'because the radical conscience needed a *raison d'être*.'[3]

On 3 August, the British Cabinet received news of the German ultimatum to Belgium. Ministers had been aware of it for three days, but official confirmation played directly into Grey's hand at a crucial moment. On the same day, Bethmann-Hollweg and Jagow, ever needful of British neutrality, sent a telegram to Grey trying to justify their terms to Belgium. They hoped that 'England will regard the German action as only self-defence against [the] French menace'.[4] Inherent in his words were two gigantic lies: first, that France was threatening to invade Germany through Belgium (it wasn't); and second, that in consequence Germany had been forced to *defend itself* by violating Belgian neutrality (Germany had launched an offensive war on a neutral country).

At the same time, Bethmann-Hollweg instructed Lichnowsky to tell Grey 'that if we have taken the step of infringing Belgian neutrality we have been forced thereto by the duty of self-preservation. We were in a military impasse.'[5] The German chancellor actually believed that Grey would not only understand but also *sympathise* with Germany's predicament. Even now, they clung like drowning men to their one hope: that Britain would stay neutral. Their banal exercises in diplomatic deceit had the opposite effect, of firming British resolve to confront the Prussian menace, now spreading like an oil slick across the Belgian frontier.

Bethmann-Hollweg's whole chancellorship had been directed at keeping Britain out of the war. Now, he stared in disbelief at the unravelling of his life's work. The German ministers were desperate men, snatching at chimeras and hurling utter falsehoods down the telegraph lines. Moltke was 'literally on the brink of nervous breakdown' as the offensive began.[6]

———

News of the German ultimatum to Belgium set British public opinion 'on fire from sea to sea' (according to David Lloyd George). The public clamoured to defend Belgium, to support the war, where days earlier there had been widespread opposition to British intervention.[7] The surge of support rescued the Cabinet from its last-minute vacillations. Untainted by the cynicism of high politics, the British people genuinely rose to defend little Belgium's right to exist. The strength of public feeling eased the Cabinet's decision to act – not out of any strict legal or even moral obligation to Belgium, convenient as these were as public justifications for the war, but rather in the national interest: to defend France, Europe and beyond from German aggression.

In such circumstances, the Cabinet met again on 3 August to approve the contents of Grey's speech to the House of Commons that afternoon. The great issues had been thrashed out the day before; today's meeting was more emotional than analytical. Yet Simon and Beauchamp had serious misgivings, hesitated about whether to lend their support and contemplated resigning. The loss of their votes would tilt the Cabinet vote to staying out. The government, in order to take the country to war, would have to rely on the support of Bonar Law's Conservative opposition – an unappealing option. It was hoped that the evidence of Germany's threat to Belgium would secure the dissenters' support. 'We had a rather moving scene,' Asquith later wrote, 'Lloyd George making a strong appeal to them not to go, or at least to delay it.'[8] The fate of the country, the lives of millions, lay in the gift of a slender Cabinet majority.

—

At 3 pm, Grey rose to address parliament. He would say only what Cabinet had agreed to let him say. By turns oddly personal and obtuse, with flourishes of eloquence, his speech did not declare war or rouse the nation. But it drove the British people to the brink of that decision. Close students saw that Grey had, in essence, taken Britain to war (see Appendix 9):

> [I]t is clear that the peace of Europe cannot be preserved. Russia and Germany, at any rate, have declared war upon each other . . . [France] are involved in it because of their obligation of honour under a definite alliance with Russia. Well, it is only fair to say to the House that that obligation of honour cannot apply

in the same way to us. We are not parties to the Franco-Russian alliance. We do not even know the terms of the alliance . . . But how far that friendship entails . . . an obligation, let every man look into his own heart, and his own feelings, and construe the extent of the obligation for himself. I construe it myself as I feel it, but I do not wish to urge upon any one else more than their feelings dictate as to what they should feel about the obligation. The House, individually and collectively, may judge for itself. I speak my personal view . . .

My own feeling is that if a foreign fleet, engaged in a war which France had not sought, and in which she had not been the aggressor, came down the English Channel and bombarded and battered the undefended coasts of France, we could not stand aside . . . *(Cheers)* with our arms folded, looking on dispassionately, doing nothing . . .

But I also want to look at the matter without sentiment, and from the point of view of British interests . . . We are in the presence of a European conflagration; can anybody set limits to the consequences that may arise out of it? . . . We feel strongly that France was entitled to know – and to know at once! – whether or not in the event of attack upon her unprotected northern and western coast she could depend upon British support. In that emergency . . . yesterday afternoon I gave to the French Ambassador the following statement:

'I am authorised to give an assurance that if the German fleet comes into the Channel or through the North Sea to undertake hostile operations against the French coasts or shipping, the British fleet will give all the protection in its power . . .'

I read that to the House, not as a declaration of war on our part . . . but as binding us to take aggressive action should that contingency arise . . .

It now appears . . . that an ultimatum has been given to Belgium by Germany, the object of which was to offer Belgium friendly relations with Germany on condition that she would facilitate the passage of German troops through Belgium. *(Ironical laughter)* . . . We were sounded in the course of last week as to whether, if a guarantee were given that, after the war, Belgian integrity would be preserved, that would content us. We replied that we could not bargain away whatever interests or obligations we had in Belgian neutrality . . . *(Cheers)*

If, in a crisis like this, we run away *(Loud cheers)* from those obligations of honour and interest as regards the Belgian treaty, I doubt whether, whatever material force we might have at the end, it would be of very much value in face of the respect that we should have lost . . . For us, with a powerful fleet, which we believe able to protect our commerce, to protect our shores, and to protect our interests, if we are engaged in war, we shall suffer but little more than we shall suffer even if we stand aside.

We are going to suffer, I am afraid, terribly in this war, whether we are in it or whether we stand aside . . . There is but one way in which the Government could make certain at the present moment of keeping outside this war, and that would be that it should immediately issue a proclamation of unconditional neutrality. We cannot do that. *(Cheers)* We have made the commitment to France that I have read to the House which prevents us doing that. We have got the consideration of Belgium which prevents us also from any unconditional neutrality . . .

If we did take that line by saying, 'We will have nothing whatever to do with this matter' . . . we should, I believe, sacrifice our respect and good name and reputation before the world, and should not escape the most serious and grave economic consequences. *(Cheers and a voice, 'No')* . . . We know, if the facts all be as I have stated them . . . that the use of [aggressive action] may be forced upon us. As far as the forces of the Crown are concerned, we are ready . . . *(Loud cheers, etc.)*[9]

Grey sat. The applause of parliament excused the lameness and ambivalence of much of the language – for example, 'I construe it myself as I feel it, but I do not wish to urge upon any one else more than their feelings dictate.' No sign, there, of a foreign secretary trying to persuade his country to go to war. And indeed Grey, the calm ornithologist and fly fisherman, privately hated war. Yet his speech succeeded. He won the support of Liberals and Conservatives. His core point rose above his interminable subclauses: the German threat to France, and British interests in Europe, had ultimately forced Britain's hand. The smaller crime (the violation of Belgian neutrality) that led to the larger crime (the invasion of France) snared the consciences of the neutralists and non-interventionists. London would not stand by and watch a single power, Germany, dominate all of Europe. Whatever happened, Belgium was never going to be a 'local' war.

—

At a Cabinet meeting that evening, under Asquith's pressure, Simon and Beauchamp withdrew their threats to resign. The risks to Belgium had finally won over the Cabinet radicals. 'The small anti-war group had been routed,' write Steiner and Neilson, 'shattered by the course of events and the determination to enter the war as a united government.'[10] Burns and Morley were the only ministers to resign in protest at the decision to go to war.

The German threat to violate Belgium, then, resulted in the one thing Berlin most feared: it sealed Britain's decision for war, by unifying the Liberal government. 'By requiring,' Ferguson writes, 'a German advance through the whole of Belgium, the Schlieffen Plan helped save the Liberal Government.'[11] It also killed off any last-minute chance of British neutrality. The Cabinet no longer relied on the united support of the Conservatives and Ulster Unionist opposition.

Britain had arrived, circuitously, at the same place as France and Russia: a commitment to the defence of the Entente. Grey had done so for arch political reasons: in British self-interest, with public support. Had he committed to France weeks earlier, British intervention might have checked German aggression and prevented a European war. But the timing would have split the Cabinet and, without the Belgian card, failed to carry the neutralists and the British public. The politician in Grey failed to act when his words would have had their greatest deterrent effect. By delaying his hand, he triumphed politically – and condemned the country to a world war.

Words of helplessness were all the civilian leaders had left to express. Tears breached the dam of English reserve that evening. The calm of the Foreign Office and the punctiliousness of public servants yielded to the open sobbing of men conscious of their role in the tragedy of the world. Asquith's wife, Margot, joined the prime minister in his office in the Commons. 'So it's all up?' she asked. 'Yes it's all up,' he answered, without looking at her. He sat at his desk, with pen in hand. She got up and leant her head against his. She wrote, 'we could not speak for the tears'.[12]

That evening, Grey stood with a friend at a window in Whitehall, watching the sun set over St James's Park and the street lamps being lit on the Mall. Grey said, 'The lamps are going out all over Europe, we shall not see them lit again in our lifetime.'[13]

—

In Berlin, a brief glow of happiness passed over Bethmann-Hollweg's face when he heard Lichnowsky's rose-tinted account of Grey's great speech. The German ambassador had read only a parliamentary report of it that night and misunderstood the British foreign secretary's words. Grey's inability to speak plainly – a trait of Foreign Office mandarins – had confused Lichnowsky, whose usual perspicacity deserted him. '[T]he English government', he cheerfully reported to Berlin at 10 pm that night, 'for the time being does not contemplate intervening in the conflict and abandoning its neutrality . . . we can receive the speech with satisfaction and regard it as a big success that England is not immediately joining her Entente associates'.[14]

The next morning, Lichnowsky read the full speech. Realising his error, he immediately wrote to the chancellor, crushing Bethmann-Hollweg's hopes of the previous night. 'I must correct my impressions of yesterday,' he wrote, 'by saying that I do not believe that we shall be able to count much longer on England's neutrality.' He added, witheringly:

> I do not anticipate that . . . the British government will keep out, unless we are in a position to evacuate Belgian territory in the very shortest possible time. Hence we shall probably have to reckon on England's early hostility . . . the [British] Government will have behind it the overwhelming majority of Parliament in any active policy the purpose of which is the protection of France and Belgium. The news that reached here yesterday concerning the invasion of Belgium by German troops brought about a complete reversal of public opinion, to our disadvantage.[15]

—

Outside the Commons after Grey's speech, Churchill had approached the foreign secretary. 'What happens now?' he asked. 'Now,' Grey replied, 'we shall send them an ultimatum to stop the invasion of Belgium within 24 hours.'[16] Grey later told Cambon, 'If they refuse, it will be war.'[17] Grey's tough talk lost potency in the execution. He delayed sending the ultimatum until 2 pm on 4 August – that is, *after* the invasion of Belgium had begun. Germany was given five hours to reply, by 11 pm British time, midnight in Berlin. The moderate language and slightly ingratiating tone muted the ultimatum's impact. Would Germany, Grey inquired, respect Belgium's neutrality, refrain from invading the country and kindly reply at once? It was all done with consummate British courtesy. There was no 'or else, war!', no punitive measures, no language the Prussians understood. In any case, it was all too late.

In Berlin, Sir Edward Goschen, Britain's ambassador, served the ultimatum in person. Asquith, Grey, Lloyd George and other senior government members gathered in the Cabinet room that night to await the reply. They already knew the answer, but protocol was essential.

Goschen informed Jagow that:

> unless the Imperial Government could give the assurance by 12
> o'clock that night that they would proceed no further with their
> violation of the Belgian frontier and stop their advance, I had
> been instructed to demand my passports and inform [Germany]
> that His Majesty's Government would have to take all steps in
> their power to uphold the neutrality of Belgium . . .[18]

Jagow replied that he was 'sorry to say that his answer must be "No"
as, in consequence of the German troops having crossed the frontier that morning, Belgian neutrality had been already violated'. He
explained that Germany:

> had to advance into France by the quickest and easiest way so as
> to be able to . . . strike some decisive blow as early as possible. It
> was a matter of life and death for . . . Rapidity of action was the
> great German asset while that of Russia was an inexhaustible
> supply of troops.[19]

Goschen persisted: were there any circumstances under which
Germany would withdraw? Even if he had 24 hours to consider the
question, Jagow replied, his answer must be the same. To which
Goschen demanded his passports and requested a meeting with
Chancellor Bethmann-Hollweg.

—

'I found the Chancellor very agitated,' Goschen recalled. Bethmann-
Hollweg, aware that all was lost and Britain had all but declared
war on Germany, started violently haranguing the British emissary.
'[J]ust for a word "neutrality"', the chancellor shouted, 'a word
which in war time had so often been disregarded, *just for a scrap of
paper*, Great Britain was going to make war on a kindred nation who
desired nothing better than to be friends with her!' What Britain

had done, Bethmann-Hollweg raved, was 'unthinkable, it was like striking a man from behind while he was fighting for his life against two assailants'. In consequence, Britain must be held responsible 'for all the terrible events that might happen!'.

Goschen strongly protested. But the chancellor wished him to understand 'that for strategical reasons it was a matter of life and death to Germany to advance through Belgium and violate her neutrality'. Goschen replied that it was 'a matter of "life and death" for the honour of Great Britain that she should keep her solemn engagement to do her utmost to defend Belgium's neutrality if attacked . . . or what confidence could anyone have in engagements given by Great Britain in the future?'

'But at what price . . .?' Bethmann-Hollweg almost pleaded. 'Has the British Government thought of that?'

The chancellor was so fraught, so 'little disposed to hear reason', that he refused to listen. As the British diplomat prepared to leave, Bethmann-Hollweg said that the blow – of England joining Germany's enemies – 'was all the greater' given the two nations' efforts to maintain peace between Austria and Russia. Goschen agreed: the tragedy was that Britain and Germany should fall apart 'just at the moment when the relations between them had been more friendly and cordial than they had been for years'.[20]

Goschen then burst into tears, according to Bethmann-Hollweg's account, and 'asked to be allowed to remain awhile in my anteroom because he could not let himself be seen in such a state . . .'[21] The chancellor was no less fraught. Yet his dismissal of the Treaty of London (guaranteeing Belgian neutrality) as 'a scrap of paper' said all one needed to know about his respect for the rights of smaller nations and Germany's lawlessness. He had gravely underestimated genuine British feeling for the freedom of Belgium. And he misread the artfulness of British diplomacy, according to which the defence of Belgian neutrality was part of an overall impetus driving Britain to war. And, yes, that included, as Grey made clear, British self-interest in the wider sphere.

The grey areas had eluded Bethmann-Hollweg. In his hunt for 'sound' motives, for black and white clarity, he condemned what he saw as staggering British cynicism over Belgium. Even if that was partly true, it was as nothing compared to the outrage of the German crime, for which the chancellor actually expected British understanding! He later revealed the depths of his personal crisis:

> England drew the sword only because she believed her own interests demanded it. Just for Belgian neutrality one would never have entered the war. That is what I meant when I told Sir E Goschen that . . . the Belgian neutrality treaty had for her only the value of a scrap of paper. I may have been a bit excited and aroused. Who would not have been at seeing the hopes and work of the whole period of my Chancellorship going for naught?[22]

The chancellor's policies, Goschen later reflected, 'had tumbled down like a house of cards'.

Grey, too, experienced a tumbling sensation. At 3 pm on 4 August, a few hours before Asquith declared war on Germany, the foreign secretary received a call from W. H. Page, the United States ambassador. 'It will not end with Belgium,' Grey told him. 'Next will come Holland, and after Holland, Denmark . . . England would be forever contemptible if it should sit by and see this treaty violated.' The German war party, Grey warned, had now got the upper hand. 'Thus the efforts of a lifetime go for nothing,' he said tearfully. 'I feel like a man who has wasted his life.' The American ambassador came away 'with a sort of stunned sense of the impending ruin of half the world'.[23]

—

At 7 pm that night, the prime minister told a packed House that Germany had failed 'in any sense' to send 'a satisfactory communication' to the British request for assurances of Belgian neutrality:

Nothing of the sort was received, and the Foreign Office released this statement [which he read out]: 'Owing to the summary rejection by the German Government of the request made by His Majesty's Government for assurances that the neutrality of Belgium would be respected, His Majesty's Ambassador in Berlin has received his passport, and His Majesty's Government has declared to the German Government that a state of war exists between Great Britain and Germany as from 11 pm on August 4th.'[24]

As Big Ben struck 11 pm, Britain mobilised. 'Midnight came,' Grey wrote. 'We were at war.'[25] In the streets and outside Buckingham Palace, great crowds sang 'God Save the King'. Admiral Sir John Jellicoe assumed command of the Royal Navy; Field Marshal Sir John French would lead the British Expeditionary Force. Churchill dispatched his war telegrams to the fleet throughout the world: 'Commence hostilities against Germany.' The generals sent their orders to the commanders of the army. The government took control of the railways. The Commons voted £100,000 in war finance in five minutes.[26]

In Berlin that night, Goschen received Herr von Zimmermann, the undersecretary of state for foreign affairs. Zimmermann casually asked whether a demand for passports was a declaration of war. Goschen diverted his attention to the ultimatum, which expired at midnight and was already redundant. *That*, the two men agreed, was a declaration of war.

Outside the embassy, an angry crowd had gathered. They had read in *Berliner Tageblatt* that Great Britain had declared war on Germany. They overpowered the small police force sent to guard the embassy, and, 'when the crash of glass and the landing of cobble stones into the drawing-room where we were all sitting warned us that the situation was getting unpleasant', Goschen telephoned for more police.

On the 5th, the British War Council met and agreed, under

pressure from Sir Henry Wilson, whose great plan relied on it, to send the British Expeditionary Force to northern France, and not Antwerp, as proposed by Sir John French. They argued over whether to concentrate the troops at Amiens or Maubeuge. Maubeuge was agreed. A few, confused by continental geography, thought Liège was in Holland.

In Berlin, the British ambassador and his staff received their passports, burnt the cyphers and confidential papers, and sealed the archives. They were 'smuggled away in taxi-cabs to the station by side streets' to avoid the violent attention the crowds had directed at the departing Russian and French legations, and travelled to the border in a private restaurant car attached to the train to protect them.[27]

On the 6th, the British Cabinet met to approve the dispatch of troops. Only four infantry divisions and one cavalry would be sent, to Wilson's dismay. He had wanted all six. Earl Kitchener shocked the meeting by declaring that the war would take years, not months, to win.

39

SWEET AND RIGHT TO DIE FOR YOUR COUNTRY . . .

You have no quarrel with Germany! German workmen
have no quarrel with their French comrades . . .
Keir Hardie, Scottish socialist and founder of the British Labour Party,
3 August 1914, the day before Britain declared war on Germany

---

IN AUGUST 1914, many young men of combat age were willing to die for their country. Boys of the privileged classes were particularly receptive to exhortations to fight for the holy triumvirate of God, King (or Emperor) and Country. Their birthright and education had instilled such values in them. The extent to which they believed in this varied according to the individual and would change as the war deteriorated. The point is, at the outbreak of war, most 'right-thinking' young men regarded self-sacrifice for God, King and Country as just and honourable, and not the monstrous lie later recorded in war poems and post-war literature.

The poet Rupert Brooke articulated the message for his generation in '1914', the most popular poem of the period:

Now, God be thanked Who has matched us with His hour,
And caught our youth, and wakened us from sleeping . . .
Glad from a world grown old and cold and weary,
Leave the sick hearts that honour could not move,
And half-men, and their dirty songs and dreary,
And all the little emptiness of love!

. . .

Honour has come back, as a king, to earth . . .
And Nobleness walks in our ways again;
And we have come into our heritage.[1]

The holy triumvirate was alive and well. God was not dead, contrary to Nietzsche's announcement of His passing; the workers of the world rallied to King and Kaiser, and had not united (nor would they, in Britain, Germany and France), contrary to Marx's predictions; and patriotism and the nation state were flexing their chauvinistic muscles, contrary to the dreams of socialists and internationalists.

By 1914, Europe had not fought a general war for a hundred years. Since the Napoleonic Wars, Darwin had intervened, and the 'fittest' nation would be the victor in the next war, according to the bastardised doctrine that most military commanders more or less believed in because, explained Walter Bagehot, 'In every particular state of the world, those nations which are strongest tend to prevail over the others; and in certain marked peculiarities the strongest tend to be the best.'[2] The cult of manifest destiny, of the triumph of the fittest race to rule the world, acquired a pseudo-scientific foundation. And nowhere was this more fervently believed than in the Prussian officers' mess and in the thoughts and work of men such as General Bernhardi, Conrad von Hötzendorf and Field Marshal Colmar von der Goltz. Yet belief in the supremacy of race infected all classes and opinions, rich and poor, left and right, from the London literary set of H. G. Wells and Beatrice and Sidney Webb to the German and Italian 'decadent' authors, Thomas Mann and

Gabriele d'Annunzio, 'father' of Italian fascism. Mann hailed the fate of Germany as the supreme race and bringer of *Kultur* to the world. He longed for war as 'a purification, a liberation, an enormous hope'. 'The victory of Germany,' he wrote, 'will be a victory of the soul over numbers. The German soul is opposed to the pacifist ideal of civilisation for is not peace an element of civil corruption?'[3]

Young men were receptive to all this. 'If the youth of the rival countries howled for war in 1914,' argues the historian Michael Howard, 'it was because for a generation or more they had been taught to howl.'[4] The horrors that haunted French and German veterans of 1870–71, the nightmares of Russian troops who survived the disastrous war with Japan in 1904–05, barely impinged on the minds of the new generation. They glorified the ideal of youthful self-sacrifice, which the old establishment – politicians, editors and the church – ennobled with their traditional, unthinking reflex.

The 'new' Frenchman, for example, was a 'patriot' in that he was willing and 'even eager to give up his life, if that sacrifice would lead to the revival of his country and the throwing off of the unbearable German yoke', according to a major survey of young Frenchmen (see below).[5] Germany similarly rehabilitated the old slogan 'For throne and altar' to rally German youth to the cause of war.[6] In England, 'there was a new interest in war and the tools of war', revived by the Boer conflict and the naval rivalry with Germany.[7]

—

To understand why so many privileged young men were willing to risk their lives, briefly imagine the world through their eyes. They lived in the sway of words such as 'heroism', 'patriotism' and 'gamesmanship'. It is no exaggeration to say that the wealthy young Englishman of 1914 breathed the lines of Sir Henry Newbolt's poem 'Vitaï Lampada' (1898), in which the rugby public-school spirit won a distant colonial bloodbath:

. . . The sand of the desert is sodden red –

Red with the wreck of a square that broke;
The Gatling's jammed and the Colonel's dead,
And the regiment blind with dust and smoke;
The river of death has brimmed his banks,
And England's far, and Honour a name,
But the voice of a schoolboy rallies the ranks:
'Play up! play up! and play the game!'

Wars were literally to be led, and won, on the playing fields of Eton, or some other cloistered public school. Upper-class youth craved the glory of Gordon or Kitchener, or other imperial heroes. Most were willing to lay down their lives for the honour. Of 5588 Etonians who would serve on the Western Front between 1914 and 1918, 1159 would be killed and 1469 wounded – a 47 per cent casualty rate. Other British public schools would send, and lose, similar proportions, prompting Robert Wohl to speak not of a 'lost generation' but of a 'lost elite' of Englishmen.[8] One should keep this in perspective, he warns: of 700,000 British men who would die in the coming war, 37,452 would be officers.

Government-run schools and civic boys' clubs appealed to the less privileged to join the war effort. The Boy Scouts, the Boys' Brigade and the Church Lads' Brigades imbued in young men the idea that the nation's survival depended on patriotism, manly virtue and self-sacrifice. School prize-givings, officer cadets, and speech-day war heroes such as Lord Roberts and Baden Powell all enshrined in the young male the idea that fighting for one's country was the highest virtue. There was no shortage of pedagogues and propagandists ready to press the message home. Newbolt – a milder, English version of the demonic German teacher in the opening scenes of *All Quiet on the Western Front* – was a founding member of the War Propaganda Unit, set up in September 1914. Its committee included H. G. Wells, Rudyard Kipling, Arthur Conan Doyle, G. K. Chesterton and 20 other prominent British authors, who helped the government sell the war as a great and noble enterprise.

They reached their target. The captain of a rugby team wrote soon after hostilities began (he would die at Ypres in 1917):

[D]espite the horrors of war, it is at least a big thing. I mean to say that in it one is brought face to face with realities. The follies, luxury, selfishness, and general pettiness of the vile, commercial sort of existence led by nine-tenths of the people of the world in peacetime is replaced in war by a savagery that is at least more honest and outspoken.[9]

That captured the mood for many English lads in 1914: war was romantic and *real*.

By the time the famous posters appeared of Kitchener exhorting Britons to enlist – 'Your King and Country Need You' – English boys were literally climbing over themselves to sign up. The Territorial Army – set up expressly to defend Britain from invasion – was virtually ordered to volunteer, and it willingly did so, despite the resistance of many parents.[10] The enlisters were not all dreaming of glory and honour, as Ferguson shows. Other motives were: self-defence – most volunteered at the height of the Battle of Mons (see Chapter 41); the great adventure of war – perhaps the biggest magnet to young men; susceptibility to propaganda – the Parliamentary Recruiting Committee, formed on 27 August, enticed many lads through public meetings and some 54 million posters; the fear of seeming a coward, heightened by legions of women handing white feathers to men not in uniform and crude pamphlets to parents such as 'Is your best boy wearing khaki?'; peer-group pressure, chiefly through the creation of Pals Battalions, raised in local areas or industries (for example, the Stockbrokers' Battalion of the Royal Fusiliers, the Liverpool clerks' battalions, or companies of sportsmen such as boxers and footballers), exploiting an impulsive urge to go with your mates; and economic pressure – the recruitment height, in August 1914, coincided with high unemployment.[11] By the end of 1914, more than a million British men would volunteer to fight, producing the largest non-conscript army the world has ever seen.

—

An unusual number of young Frenchmen in 1914 similarly expressed a determination to fight and die for France. Unlike their English peers, however, they would rush to the recruiting stations in *defiance* of their parents' generation. That was the remarkable conclusion of a study conducted in 1912 for the Parisian daily *L'Opinion* by two young French intellectuals, Henri Massis and Alfred de Tarde. Entitled *The Young Men of Today* (*Les Jeunes Gens d'aujourd'hui*), the survey sparked a revolution in French attitudes to the young. Working under the pseudonym Agathon (Socrates' disciple, whose name meant 'good, brave in war'), Massis and de Tarde profiled the thoughts of men then studying at the universities and *grandes écoles*. Their findings (rather decidedly) confirmed what they had reported a few years earlier: French professors at the Sorbonne were slavishly adhering to a bland German teaching model and 'Germanising' French culture with 'Teutonic' ideas.[12]

Young Frenchmen, Agathon concluded, longed to feel proud of France. One disaffected youth wrote to the survey:

> At the age when one is anxious for notions that have some application to life, at a time when we looked to our teachers for the prestige of a spiritual authority, asking them to help us find ourselves, what did we discover? An empty science that failed to take into account the needs of the intelligence, a pedantic materialism, a skeptical mode of inquiry that degrades and diminishes. Everything in their teaching forced us to serve as inert slaves or to exasperate ourselves in rebellion.[13]

French students had undergone a 'transformation of character', Agathon concluded. They represented 'a new kind of human being', no less, differentiated not simply by age and appearance but by a new way of thinking. This reinterpretation extended to all the institutions of the past, including war:

> The word 'War!' has attained a sudden prestige. It is a young, entirely new word, tricked out with the seductive fascination which the eternal warrior instinct in the heart of man keeps reviving. These young people invest it with all the beauty for which they long and which their daily life does not give them. War, in their eyes, is above all the opportunity for the display of virtues which they feel to be supreme, energy, leadership, devotion to a cause that matters more than themselves.[14]

It is tempting to dismiss them as another solipsistic young generation, earnestly believing in their originality. Yet, by 1914, these French lads *did* seem different from their parents' tribe, in several ways. The older generation had grown up in the French society of the 1870s–1890s, cynical, decadent and humiliated by the Prussian war. They were 'self-doubting, morally flabby' individuals, Agathon claimed, 'incapable of energetic action, lacking faith, obsessed with decadence, and ready to accept the defeat and eclipse of their country'.[15] A flaccid dilettantism had depleted their energies and reduced their concentration.

The confident young French men of 1914, by contrast, had 'exiled self doubt'. They were men of action and élan, drawn to aircraft, motor cars and sport rather than books and art. They yearned for the absolute over the relative, loathed the decadence of the Belle Époque, and upheld, like their role model, the soldier of fortune Ernest Psichari, the army, family and church. If Massis and de Tarde were right – and most contemporaries, including Émile Faguet, France's Gallup of his day, grudgingly conceded the validity of their findings – France had come full circle, from the fag ends of the *fin de siècle* back to the conservative, patriotic society that existed before the Franco-Prussian War. It was as if the bohemian époque had never existed. 'The militarization of minds' is how the historian

Robert Wohl describes the process. Indeed, these young men longed for war; it was their 'secret hope', concluded Agathon.[16]

The idea of youth as the nation's saviour provoked a fierce national debate. A stream of articles and novels appeared: all of France, it seemed, wanted to understand the new Frenchman. His 'prototype' had a limited provenance, of course. Agathon's samples were privileged students at the universities and *grandes écoles*, and not the young men from the provinces and working classes, millions of whom would volunteer, and become the famous moustachioed poilu. Yet both groups shared certain attributes. They saw themselves as part of a '*Union sacrée*',[17] dedicated to the renewal of France. They longed for war as a great adventure, which would define their manhood. They sought to expunge the German threat and reclaim the nation's lost honour. Action, not words or thoughts, motivated them. They rejected the stale cynicism and decadence of the older generation. Courage, manhood and old-fashioned French élan would be their gifts to the nation.

—

In Germany, privileged young men were consciously programmed as warriors and leaders, whose first duty was to defend the Fatherland. German teachers, academics and politicians set out to create a generation of bold and confident soldiers, actuated by the virtues of patriotism and self-sacrifice. This took a radical form in 1914. Progressive educators encouraged the young to rebel against dispassionate conservatism and cold materialism, and rediscover the manly virtues of honour and self-sacrifice.

On the eve of war, 3100 German professors signed a declaration allying education and militarism:

> We instructors at Germany's universities and institutes of higher learning serve scholarship and carry forth a work of peace. But it fills us with dismay that the enemies of Germany, England at the head, wishes . . . to polarize the spirit of German scholarship

from what they call Prussian militarism. In the German army, there is no other spirit than in the German people, for both are one . . . Service in the army also makes our youth effective for all the works of peace including scholarship. For the army educates them to sacrificial faithfulness to duty and lends them the self-confidence and sense of honour of the truly free man who submits himself willingly to the whole . . . Now our army stands in battle for Germany's freedom . . . Our belief is that salvation for the very culture of Europe depends on the victory that German 'militarism' will gain: manly virtue, faithfulness, the will to sacrifice found in the united, free German people.[18]

Those virtues could be taught, of course. The German Youth Movement was an unofficial 'boot camp' for German officers. Formed in 1913, it had more than 25,000 members in 1914. On retreats in the countryside, young Germans were shown how to discover their spiritual affinity with the Fatherland, to believe in themselves as future leaders, to commit acts that marked them down as men of substance.

German boys responded to a gallery of romantic role models in German history and literature. But their 1914 character seemed closer to selfish young Hans Castorp, knight errant of Thomas Mann's epic novel *The Magic Mountain*,[19] who leaves his mountain resort where he was confined for seven years, exposing himself to radical politics, 'humanism' and love, and, exhausted by his search for 'truth', flings himself on the frontier of experience, the battlefield.

In October 1913, a year after Mann completed his novel, the Youth Movement held a retreat on Meissner Mountain. Thousands were drilled in self-reliance, resourcefulness and other solid Teutonic qualities. Through this 'change of blood', Germany could hope for a national revival, 'an insurrection of the sons against the fathers', observed Arthur Moeller van den Bruck, a cultural critic (who would later influence the rise of Nazism).[20] The rustic camp aimed to turn frail young men from the cities into the torchbearers of a spiritual rejuvenation of Germany, no less. They were the tools with which to 'revolutionise' German minds and shake off their 'sleeping sickness', argued Franz Pfemfert, publisher of the weekly journal *Die Aktion*.[21]

Pre-war examples of this mentality proliferated in diaries, songs and novels. George Heym confided in his diary in 1911, 'I suffer in the superficial enthusiasm of this banal age. For I need tremendous emotions to be happy.'[22] Fritz von Unruh, son of a Prussian general, who volunteered in 1914, glorified self-sacrifice in his pre-war plays.

These teenage Teutonic knights eagerly volunteered for the German Army. Most were from the middle classes. Their blonde exuberance may be seen in the opening scenes of *All Quiet on the Western Front*, to the delight of elderly militarists who played out their fantasy of German domination of the world through these dreamy, defiant young men. In the opening battles, hundreds of thousands of similar German boys would hurl themselves at the French, British and Russian lines singing patriotic songs, shouting slogans and dying in huge numbers. At first, it was at Ypres, where several regiments of German volunteer students marched into lines of British riflemen, singing *Die Wacht am Rhein* and other patriotic songs; 40,000 were killed or wounded in what the Germans called the *Kindermord* (see Chapter 45). Of 1.6 million German men who died in the war, 40 per cent were aged between 20 and 25.[23]

—

While English public schools, French *grandes écoles* and Prussian military colleges yielded the officers, the factories of northern England, the German mines, the Russian steppe and Europe's sprawling slums produced the millions of young men needed to fill the ranks. The political interest in these working-class lads amounted to this: would they fight for their country or for their class? Were they prepared to lay down their lives for King and Kaiser, or for Marx? Had socialism claimed them for a war against their employers? Were their loyalties with Keir Hardie, the British Labour leader, Jean Jaurès, the fiery French socialist, and August Bebel, founder of the German social democrats – or with the conservative/liberal mainstream? Class war was not some dreary student ideal. Until mid-1914, socialist leaders were hailing the end of the capitalist system and its replacement with a command economy along Marxist lines.

Huge anti-war rallies were held in London and Paris on the eve of war. The biggest in years descended on Trafalgar Square on 3 August. To wild applause, Keir Hardie called for a general strike if Britain declared war. 'You have no quarrel with Germany!' he shouted. 'German workmen have no quarrel with their French comrades . . .' The People, he roared, had no say in the treaties that compelled Britain to go to war.[24] In this light, 'the central conflict on the agenda of 1911–1914 was the potential for class war, not the gigantic clash of European arms', writes Jay Winter.[25] That is stretching the revolutionary zeal of the British worker a bit far. Nor was malnutrition in Europe as rife as in mediaeval times, as two prominent English sociologists observed,[26] yet certainly extreme poverty and extreme wealth had accentuated a deep divide in European society. This was regardless of the fact that (rather like in the late twentieth century), the great bourgeois midriff and the German junkers had rapidly expanded and never had it so good.

The war provided a great distraction from all this, a force for unity from the enemy *within*. On the eve of war, conservative politicians feared and rejected the masses' demands for more representative unions, universal suffrage, proper healthcare, welfare and education. Workhouses, sweatshops, child labour and a high infant mortality were not the residue of a Dickensian world, according to Charles Masterman's best-selling *The Condition of England*, published in 1909; the 'broken poor' were widely visible at a time when the 'super-wealthy' luxuriated in riches.[27]

Fear and hatred divided the classes, Masterman mused; revolution was in the air:

> The rich despise the Working People; the Middle Classes fear them . . . The Middle Class elector is becoming irritated and

indignant against working-class legislation. He is growing tired of the plaint of the unemployed and the insistent crying of the poor.[28]

—

By 1914, the European voices calling for social reform had won the political argument, as historian and former British Labour politician Roy Hattersley rightly concludes. The question was how to introduce it. No party could deny the need for reform. They could, however, delay it, and the outbreak of war served that purpose. Asquith's Liberal government was the most progressive in Europe, but the Conservative-controlled House of Lords voted down many bills. Churchill, when at the Board of Trade, managed to pass measures against sweatshops and child labour. And the Lords passed the Trade Disputes Act, the Workmen's Compensation Act and Eight Hours Act, as well as national insurance for the unemployed, old-age pensions and free school meals. But their Lordships rejected the most far-reaching reforms (such as the Education Bill of 1906), and few countenanced votes for women.

Nonetheless, the British reforms represented an age of enlightenment alongside the stern reactionary regimes of Germany, Austria-Hungary and Russia, who chose to suppress dissent (thus building their own coffins). The Tsarist regime, after the agrarian reforms of 1905–06, shut the door on social justice, giving oxygen to Bolshevism; the Kaiser disowned much of Bismarck's pioneering efforts; and the Austrian emperor simply refused to listen to any proposal that curbed the powers of his sclerotic regime.

Attempts at reform halted as war approached, and virtually all the anti-war crusaders laid aside their principles and backed their governments. The guns of August throttled their political ideals. Opposing a war never won an election, they well knew. In Britain, the Labour Party and trade unions urged their members to postpone the 'revolution' until they had defeated the new enemy. The supporters of a free Ireland set aside their demands for Home Rule to support the war.[29] Even the suffragettes put their fight for women's rights on ice – believing the defeat of the chauvinistic Germans more important than the struggle at home. Some even joined the white-feather brigades.

In Germany, the left-winger August Bebel came around to the view that patriotism and socialism were compatible. When war came, socialists would pick up a gun and fight like any man for the Fatherland.[30] The metamorphosis was swift. On 25 July 1914, Germany's Social Democratic Party had appealed to its members to oppose the coming war; then, on 4 August, it voted for the government's war credits. So, too, in France, where, on 31 July 1914, the French socialist party organised huge rallies against the war after the assassination of Jean Jaurès. A few days later, at the declaration of war, a majority of French socialists voted for war credits, leaving Jaurès's dream in shreds.

Only religious groups (such as the Quakers), pacifists and minority parties maintained their firm opposition to the war after its declaration, plus a few individuals, such as Bertrand Russell, Rosa Luxemburg and Karl Liebknecht. Lenin's Bolsheviks, a little mob of violent revolutionaries, self-interestedly supported the war as a means of destroying Russia's ruling class.

—

Left-wingers defended the abandonment of their principles by claiming that they had no choice other than to support the government once war was declared. The sharp contrast between their old values and new pragmatism sent a strong message to working-class youth: fight first and win freedom second. But had the left-wingers surrendered their principles to populism? Were there darker forces at work?

True social reform could wait, the governments decided. In 1914, patriotism proved a far stronger social glue than class loyalty. Governments in league with the press were adept at manipulating this, of course, igniting spasms of extreme nationalism on the slightest pretext. The German Government, and its press poodles, had

overtly 'managed' the people's expectations, as von Müller advised
Bethmann-Hollweg in 1912:

> The people must not be in a position of asking themselves only
> at the outbreak of a great European war what are the interests
> that Germany would be fighting for. The people ought rather to
> be accustomed to the idea of such a war beforehand.

'Attack from the Slavs' was the slogan they initially adopted.[31]

The French and Russian Governments, with more or less subtlety, similarly massaged the people's minds, attuning them to expect
war.[32] Unusually, the British Foreign Office did not adopt a concerted campaign of public 'education'. The British press did it for
them.

By the eve of war, the mystical allure of the 'motherland' or
'fatherland' embalmed the majority of European people in a patriotic illusion, the defence of which delayed tangible progress and
social reform. That is not to say that everyone wanted war (most
didn't); simply, that they placed the defeat of their perceived enemies as a higher priority than social justice and were swept along
in the national enthusiasm. The declarations of war brought people
together in a 'sacred pact' that transcended class barriers and social
divisions. Few inquired too deeply into the *actual* threat Germany
posed to Britain or France, or Russia to Germany. The fact is that a
great swathe of citizens were willing to give their lives for the homeland in its hour of need, regardless of whether they were rich or poor,
young or old – or knew the reasons why.

—

And off they went. In the first week of August, everyone flocked to
the railways. All over Europe, thousands of loved ones gathered to
farewell the soldiers at the great train stations: the Gare du Nord
and Gare de L'Est in Paris; Waterloo and Victoria in London; the
Bahnhofs in Potsdam, Bremen, Metz and dozens of German cities;

and Russia's vast termini in St Petersburg and Moscow. In Germany alone, 11,000 trains had been timetabled between 2 and 18 August for the movement of the troops.

Rolling stock of every kind was commandeered for the war effort. Bewildered civilian passengers were turned out of their carriages. In France, as elsewhere, 'trains were formed out of cattle trucks, goods vans, passenger coaches, anything would do', wrote the then liaison officer (and future major general) Edward Spears, 'and all were sent on, oh so slowly, to strange destinations, carrying nothing but men, always men, packed tightly together, not knowing whither they were being sent'.[33] The spirit of war spread over Europe like a gigantic hand, transforming France (and other nations) 'from a land of commerce and art into an immense armed camp'. At a moment's notice, men left peaceful preoccupations, spent a day farewelling their families and went 'quietly each to his appointed place, shouldering the heavy pack and rifle and putting on the ill-fitting uniform made shabby by many previous wearers'.[34]

The race to the front excited tremendous bursts of music and song: 'La Marseillaise', 'Das Lied der Deutschen (Deutschland über Alles)', military tunes and the beat of martial bands. Years of patriotic anticipation converged on this single moment. With 'Ausflug nach Paris' or 'À Berlin' scrawled in chalk on their sides, the trains shunted out of the stations packed with young men waving and singing at the windows. 'Vive la France! Vive l'Armée!' the French people shouted along the lines. Keegan writes:

> Departure had everywhere been holidaylike, with wives and sweethearts, hobble-skirted, high-waisted, marching down the road to the terminus arm-in-arm with the men in the outside ranks. The Germans marched to war with flowers in the muzzles of their rifles or stuck between the top buttons of their tunics; the French marched in close-pressed ranks, bowed under the weight of enormous packs . . . Russian soldiers paraded before their regimental icons for a blessing by the chaplain, Austrians

to shouts of loyalty to Franz Joseph . . . In whichever country, mobilization entailed enormous upheaval, the translation of civil society into the nation in arms. The British Army, all-regular as it was, stood the readiest for war . . .[35]

Herman Baumann, 37, of Halle in Westphalia, head baker in the Reserve Baker Column No. 9, 7th Reserve Corps, departed for Belgium in the first week of August, via Hamm and Düsseldorf:

we saw thousands and thousands of soldiers in coaches, on foot, on horses, and long, long military trains, everything pressing towards the west . . . the coaches were decorated with oak and birch branches and colourful ribbons. On every coach, you could read: 'Let's go to Paris!' 'Everyone stab a Frenchman dead!'[36]

Thus Herman began his diary, a vivid record of an army cook's journey into France and his efforts to keep the soldiers fed. At the time, Herman's wife, Pauline, was pregnant with their fourth daughter. 'In case anyone should find this little book,' he wrote on the front page, 'I would urgently entreat him to send it to my wife. Thanks very much in advance.'[37]

At the border depots and railheads, the German troops detrained and began the long march to the front. They were expected to cover up to 32 kilometres a day (almost double Schlieffen's prescribed daily quota) in stiff leather boots that left the feet a mass of blisters until forced to conform to the shape of the boot. They marched laden with packs, rifles, trenching tools, rations, field dressings and ammunition pouches, weighing 27 kilograms; they marched through the sweltering heat of midsummer, over fields, across rivers, down valleys, all of which were familiar sites to their ancestors. Many of their fathers had fought here in 1870, their grandfathers in 1812, and so on back through time. The euphoria had repeated itself in each generation, of this being *their* war, the test of *their* courage, the defence of *their* nation. Like their French, British and Russian counterparts, they looked into the distance as their fathers and grandfathers had done, as though they had been waiting an eternity for this moment. Their eyes were the same.

Herman Baumann wrote on 16 August:

> Roll call at 9 am ready for a field march. Then everything is ready: First Lieutenant: 'We are now decamping to enemy territory. I hope that everyone will do their duty with a Hurrah on their lips', then we are walking to the station post-haste, singing and waving our scarves – accompanied by cheers all around. We move via Aachen. Had a repast for the last time here, then to Herbestal. At Welkenrat – Belgium – we see the first signs of destruction, burnt-out houses, shattered windows, whole villages in ruins.[38]

No precedent prepared the new generation for the coming war. None had yet experienced the scything machine guns, the whistling shells, the 'green sea'[39] of mustard gas. The new weapons existed on paper, in arsenals or in scientists' heads. The new methods of mass slaughter were yet to disabuse the young soldiers of their excitement, 'ardent for some desperate glory'[40] on a foreign field. Horace's edict, *'Dulce et decorum est pro patria mori'*,[41] answered the prayers of millions, of all social classes, young and old, men and women, for whom it was indeed sweet and right to die for one's country. A job, a vote, healthcare, a better standard of living could all wait.

Part 4

1914 – ON THE GROUND

40

THE RAPE OF BELGIUM

*In the future, villages in the vicinity of places where railway
and telegraph lines are destroyed will be punished without
pity (whether they are guilty or not of the acts in question).
With this in view hostages have been taken in all villages
near the railway lines, which are threatened by such
attacks. Upon the first attempt to destroy lines of railway,
telegraph or telephone, they will immediately be shot.*
Field Marshal Colmar Frieherr von der Goltz,
German military governor of Belgium

NOBODY EXPECTED LITTLE BELGIUM to put up any resistance, least of all the Germans. The 'rage of dreaming sheep' was how a Prussian statesman described the Belgians' determinations to defend their neutrality. 'I will go through Belgium like *that*!' the Kaiser, with a chop of his hand, had indiscreetly confided in a British officer before the war.[1] At 8.02 on the morning of 4 August, the first grey lines of German infantry crossed the Belgian border at Gemmerich. Belgian sentries promptly opened fire, not realising they had shot the spearhead of three German armies – nearly 800,000 troops – the vanguard of whom were now bristling to invade Belgian and French territory. The German reconnaissance patrol briefly dispersed; the Germans soon returned, in force.

Belgium still had a chance to save itself, Berlin warned. When Baron Beyens, the Belgian ambassador in Berlin, requested his passports that day, Jagow repeated the German offer to spare Belgium and repair any damage if Brussels would kindly stand aside, refrain from destroying roads, railways, bridges, etc., and allow the safe passage of hundreds of thousands of German troops through Belgian territory. While they were at it, would they mind abandoning their huge forts at Liège and Namur, the first big obstacles to the German advance? Within an hour, the answer came back: no. To the astonishment of the world, Belgium would stick to its resolution and fight. As King Albert rode to parliament in Brussels that morning to commit his nation to war against the mightiest land army ever assembled, the German infantry prepared to enter the French-speaking region of Wallonia, whose main town is Liège.

In Brussels, meanwhile, crowds, flags and euphoria greeted the King's open carriage. He walked briskly into the hall, his little sailor-suited 12-year-old son and heir beside him, with the Queen and courtiers in the audience, and delivered the speech that will forever redound to Belgium's glory: 'Never since 1830 [when Belgium won independence] has a more grave moment come to Belgium: the integrity of our territory is threatened!' To great cheers of 'Long live the King! Long live Belgium!', Albert warned:

> if we must resist the invasion of our soil and must defend our threatened homes, this duty, hard though it be, will find us ordered and prepared for the greatest sacrifices. From this moment . . . the valiant youth of our nation stand ready, firmly resolved with the traditional tenacity and calmness of the Belgians to defend their fatherland at a moment of danger . . .[2]

Then he turned to the members of the Legislative Chamber: 'Gentlemen, are you determined unswervingly to maintain intact the sacred gift of our ancestors?' The hall resounded with cries of 'Yes! Yes! Yes!'. 'If the foreigner,' the King concluded, '. . . should violate our territory, he will find all Belgians grouped around their sovereign . . . and around a Government possessing the absolute confidence of the entire nation.' A great roar went up: 'Long live the King, long live Belgium!' The King paused. 'God will be with us in this just cause,' he reassured them, and departed.

The streets swam with delirious crowds, crying 'Down with the Germans!', 'Death to the assassins!'[3] Soldiers were mobbed as heroes. Inside the Chamber, tearful and shaken, the prime minister Baron Charles de Broqueville solemnly addressed his fellow deputies: 'I declare in the name of the whole nation, united heart and soul, that this people, even if they are conquered, will never be subdued.'[4] He would disagree with his sovereign, however, over the deployment of the Belgian forces, scattering them around the country in the spirit of non-confrontational neutrality rather than aligning them on the German border.

—

Soon after the King's speech, the question of where to place the Belgian Army was redundant. Within an hour, the brunt of the German invasion – the cavalry – had made short work of the border resistance and entered Belgian territory proper, hoisting the black eagle in every village and issuing proclamations that the destruction of roads and bridges would be considered hostile acts. As they barged into each community, the Germans were, at first, almost apologetic: they had violated Belgian territory 'with regret' and meant no harm, so long as the Belgians stood aside.

Advancing across Belgium that morning were General Alexander von Kluck's First Army, on the right wing; General Karl von Bülow's Second Army, in the centre; and General Max von Hausen's Third Army, on the left wing: more than 700,000 troops. Line after line of grey-uniformed soldiers crammed every road and lane, in col- umns 50–60 kilometres long, accompanied by reconnaissance motorcyclists, officers in automobiles, field kitchens, medical units, engineers, horses with carts of supplies, ammunition trucks and piece after piece of horse-drawn artillery. Not yet visible were the huge Krupp and Skoda guns – including the 16.5-inch (42-centi-metre) Big Bertha super-heavyweight howitzers, the largest of their kind, specially designed to destroy modern fortresses with their con-crete-smashing shells.

Their destination was the French border. That meant pass-ing through the heavily fortified mediaeval city of Liège, which stands 150 metres above the northern bank of the River Meuse. Surrounding the city in 1914 were 12 forts, linked along a 50-kilo-metre defensive circumference that guarded the gateway to Belgium. Built in the 1880s, the forts at Liège, like those at Namur and Antwerp, tended to be badly maintained, undersupplied and garri-soned by elderly reservists. Yet they were very sturdily built, situated largely underground, and enclosed in dry moats ten metres deep – designed, in short, to resist the most crushing blow. The 12 forts at Liège possessed a total of 400 protruding guns. The Belgian Army inspired less confidence: it persisted 'in a chaos of improvisation',[5] fielding 117,000 inexperienced, poorly trained volunteers, who were ill-supplied, with no entrenching tools or proper equipment, and only half the number of machine guns per unit as the Germans. Another 200,000 manned the forts, of whom about 25,000–30,000, under the robust command of General Gerard Leman, garrisoned Liège. They had little idea of the scale of what they were about to confront, yet they were determined to resist the onslaught.

—

One after another, the Belgian villagers stirred and murmured 'Uhlan' or 'Hun' at the German approach, then stood silently aside as thousands of grey-uniformed troops passed through bearing a forest of flags. All that could be heard were the great crump of boots on the cobblestones and the rising chorus of the German anthem or patriotic songs. A verse from a favourite ran:

So a whole world is threatening us
– so what? We are of good cheer
And if someone should try to get in our way
give us our rifles! We are good shots.
Brothers, move on! To the Vistula, to the Rhine!
Dear Fatherland, no need to fear!
Just and good, that is our war!
Now lead us, Emperor, into battle and to victory![6]

Sixty-eight-year-old Alexander von Kluck, a bald, severe-looking general whom the English troops would call 'old one o'clock' (because he would start shelling them at 1 am), had the most exacting task of the German generals. Von Kluck, a veteran of the Franco-Prussian War, led the 'hammer' – Schlieffen's critical right wing – comprising 18,000 men per mile of front (ten men per metre), 6000 more than Bülow's army, and probably the densest force ever fielded. Their job was to smash a path to Paris and take the city. To this end, the critical thing was 'the full employment of all available *time*', Kluck wrote.[7] The troops' marching capacity must be kept 'at the highest pitch', he insisted; every man must be on guard against sore feet, ill-fitting boots, exhaustion and injury.[8] Kluck had good reason: his men were ordered to march over 30 kilometres a day through hostile country, subjected to sniper and guerrilla attack, at the end of which they were expected to square up to the shock of battle, conquer France and return to fight in the east – a near-impossible task, by any reckoning. But first they had to crush the Belgian resistance, which threatened to delay Schlieffen's cherished timetable.

Liège was the first major obstacle to Kluck's progress. He ordered an 'Army of the Meuse' of six brigades, commanded by General Otto von Emmich, to subdue the fortified city. Emmich's forces, 60,000 strong – more than double the Belgian garrison – pulled up at the edge of town on 4 and 5 August. The liaison officer between the general's headquarters and the attacking forces was a bull-necked major general called Erich Ludendorff, a protégé of Schlieffen's, who knew that every day lost weakened his master's victory plan. War by timetable would tolerate no delay.

And so, on a clear day in August (the 7th), the 'hacking through' of Belgium began. Ludendorff, the most forceful commander in the German Army, a man 'devoid of moral or physical fear, indifferent to the opinion even of superiors',[9] who 'within two years was to exercise greater power over the people and fate of Germany than anyone since Frederick the Great'[10], surveyed with irritated surprise the Belgian resistance at Liège. He noted two bridges still standing; the rest destroyed. He examined the fortifications and the sporadic rifle fire issuing from the pathetic Belgian force stationed around the city's perimeter. Persuaded that Belgium seriously intended to defy German power – the prospect of which he had earlier dismissed as unthinkable – Ludendorff took a pivotal role in organising the city's destruction.

Barbara Tuchman's and John Keegan's masterful accounts of the end of Liège bear little improvement, and I defer to them and other sources in briefly sketching the story. In essence, it tells of the awesome defiance of General Leman's men during almost two weeks of constant shelling, infantry attacks and even a zeppelin raid – a stand that infuriated the Germans, drew stunned admiration around the world and conferred the Grand Cross of the Legion of Honour on the city's inhabitants for defending, as Poincaré said, 'the independence of Europe' from Germany's wrath. Ludendorff was the architect of the city's destruction. Seeing that infantry assaults merely wasted lives, he cut off the city and ordered up the big guns.

On 9 August, the first of the Krupp monsters arrived. '[T]heir squat barrels', Tuchman writes, 'doubled by the recoil cylinders that grew on their backs like tumours, pointed cavernous mouths upward at the sky'.[11] At 6.30 pm on 12 August, the first shell began its 4000-metre trajectory, taking 60 seconds to reach Fort Pontisse. It fell short. The following shells were 'walked' towards the target, through the eyes of forward observers. Over the next four days, hundreds of shells weighing 2000 pounds (907 kilograms) – the heaviest ever shot – split and then smashed open the concrete ceilings of the forts, mangled bodies within, fragmented walls, scattered offices and released deadly brown fumes through the subterranean chambers in which the huddled remnant of the Belgian resistance 'became hysterical, even mad in the awful apprehension of the next shot'.[12]

'The third phase of the bombardment,' wrote General Leman later, 'began at 5 o'clock in the morning of the 15th, firing being kept up without a break until two in the afternoon.' The shelling wrecked the offices of the General Staff at Fort Loncin:

> All light was extinguished by the force of the explosion, and the officers ran the risk of asphyxiation by the horrible gases emitted from the shell . . . Nobody will ever be able to form any adequate idea of what the reality was like. I have only learned since that when the big siege mortars entered into action they hurled against us shells weighing 1,000 kilos, the explosive force of which surpasses anything known hitherto. Their approach was to be heard in an acute buzzing; and they burst with a thunderous roar, raising clouds of missiles, stones and dust . . .[13]

By 14 August, the eastern and northern forts had fallen. By the 16th, all except one had ceased to exist. 'The forts that still held out,' wrote Kluck, with summary bluntness, 'were quickly taken with the help of the 42 cm howitzers.'[14] Entering Fort Loncin, the Germans found Leman's body wedged under a block of masonry, surely dead. In fact, he was unconscious, after being blown off his feet and inhaling the poisonous gas that issued from the spent shells. German troops carried him to Emmich, to whom he surrendered his sword. (Emmich handed it back at once, Leman recalled, 'in recognition of our courage'.[15]) Because he had been taken unconscious, 'I have not surrendered either the fortress or the forts,' Leman wrote to King Albert. He went on:

> Deign, Sire, to pardon my defects in this letter. I am physically

shattered by the explosion of Loncin. In Germany, whither I am proceeding, my thoughts will be, as they have ever been, of Belgium and the King. I would willingly have given my life the better to serve them, but death was denied me.[16]

The fall of Liège heralded the intensification of 'punitive measures' against the Belgian people, known to the Entente powers as the first atrocities of the war. The French newspaper *Le Matin* reported an early example, headlined 'AFTER THE PASSAGE OF THE HORDE'. In mid-August, as the advance German units destroyed Liège, the people of the village of Mouland, on the Dutch–Belgian border, stood aside as the Germans poured into their country. Their restraint did not help them. '[I]n Mouland,' *Le Matin* reported, 'people were peaceful and defenceless, but the Germans . . . have destroyed and bombed this pretty village without hesitation.'[17]

On 19 August, the German Army baker Herman Baumann was billeted in a village near Liège. He witnessed what became of Belgian villages whose inhabitants dared to shoot on the German forces:

Machine guns were deployed. [Our troops] kept shooting for hours until they had shot all the houses to pieces . . . whole streets and easily 50 houses were destroyed. In the morning, about 50 dead covered the square . . . Hundreds of people were arrested, they were all taken to the museum yard, where a summary court martial was held. You could see young lads as well as old people, also priests. The result was that in the afternoon, 30 people were shot by firing squad. Heartbreaking scenes.

On the 22nd, Baumann 'wanted to take a leak' and went behind an old brickworks. 'Hardly had I sat down, and a bullet came whistling towards me from the old huts, passing close to my ear . . . Now everything was searched and a man with a shotgun found, then questioned and shot.'[18] Some German soldiers were disgusted; others were blind to these excesses, or still believed they were fighting a holy crusade. One soldier, who had been in the field for 31 days, replied to a German cleric called Pastor Meyersiek (first name unavailable in German archives), who was in the habit of writing to young men from their village of Oestinghausen, 'Dear Pastor, I had my baptism of fire at Liège . . . I thank my God daily for the protection he has afforded me . . .'[19]

—

The destruction of Liège freed General von Kluck's progress through Belgium, via Louvain and Brussels, to the region around Mons on the French border (see Map 4). His troops were two days behind Schlieffen's schedule. At the same time, Bülow's Second Army advanced through the centre, via Huy and Andenne towards Namur, where, between 21 and 25 August, the city succumbed to the same hellish pounding. The Germans gave no warning to the civilians caught inside. 'Shells fell upon the prison, the hospital, the Burgomaster's house and the railway station, causing conflagration,' noted an official inquiry.[20] The Belgian 4th Division were driven out. The massacre of civilians and the burning of homes followed.

From Namur, Bülow's forces resumed in a south-westerly direction towards Charleroi, on the Sambre River. Von Hausen's Third Army moved along the most southerly line, towards Dinant, beyond which the French forces were massing. This outline scarcely portrays the sheer scale and ferocity of the Germans' advance, and the crushing weight of their impact on Belgian civilian life (of which more below).

The great question on King Albert's mind was whether to withdraw the Belgian troops to Antwerp or to keep them in the lines in the hope that French reinforcements would arrive to save them from complete annihilation. He decided to withdraw – to the fury of the French colonel Adelbert, Poincaré's representative on the Belgian General Staff. To do otherwise risked the complete destruction of the Belgian Army. In the event, the King had the decision made for him, when French reinforcements failed to arrive at the expected location, leaving the Belgian Army exposed. They withdrew on the 18th, eluding Kluck's jaws and leaving Brussels naked to the storm.

'They always managed to escape our grasp,' Kluck later conceded, 'so that their army has not been decisively beaten . . . It has, nevertheless, been so severely handled that a comparatively small force will be able to contain it in Antwerp.'[21] On the contrary, the brave Belgian Army lived on to menace the German rear, destroy railroads and bridges, cut telegraph and telephone wires, and generally make extreme nuisances of themselves, the punishment for which would be vengeance on the civilian population. Belgian civilians, 'assisted by soldiers in plain clothes', similarly waged 'extremely aggressive guerrilla warfare' on the German lines, Kluck later complained, personally affronted that the Belgian people would dare to defend their country.[22]

—

Brussels fell to the vanguard of Kluck's army on 20 August. It had entered the city a few days earlier. Three soldiers on bicycles rode into the Boulevard du Régent and asked the way to the Gare du Nord. News of their arrival hit the citizens 'like a thunderclap', according to a German press report.[23] Many people fled; others dismantled the barricades and barbed wire, fearing retribution. The mayor went out to meet the first troops, bearing a white flag. A German officer at the head of the lines assured him that 'nothing would happen to the people if they would give up all acts of violence towards the Germans'.[24] Thousands of citizens crowded into the Gare du Nord, hoping to escape via Ostend to England. Soon, the railway services were terminated.

There followed 'not men marching, but a force of nature like a tidal wave . . . rolling through Brussels', wrote the American correspondent Richard Harding Davis. 'The infantry came in in files of five, two hundred men to each company; the lancers in columns of four, with not a pennant missing.'[25] They passed in one unbroken steel-grey column, 55–65 kilometres long: 'You returned to watch it, fascinated. It held the mystery and menace of fog rolling toward you across the sea.' The passing Germans sang 'Fatherland, My Fatherland' in perfect rhythm. Then came the 'rumble of siege guns, the creaking of wheels and of chains clanking against the cobblestones and the sharp bell-like voices of the bugles'.[26]

Still they came, well into the afternoon, a deep, sombre mass of men in grey. Brightly dressed French dragoons and cuirassiers were easily distinguishable 'against the green gorse' at half a mile, Harding Davis recalled; so, too, 'the yellow khaki of our own American Army' which was 'about as invisible as the flag of Spain'. But not the grey German ranks, who, by now, in Harding Davis's imaginative account, seemed to have merged with the paving stones.[27]

The German Army meant to spend as little time as possible in Belgium. They moved into Brussels 'as smoothly and as compactly as an Empire State Express. There were no halts, no open place, no stragglers.'[28] Not a chin-strap or a horseshoe was missing. Everything was minutely organised, choreographed for war. Smoke poured from wheeled stoves. Mounted messengers from post-office wagons galloped along the columns, distributing letters. Past sunset, the grey columns continued: thousands of hooves and steel-capped boots struck tiny sparks from the flagstones. Horse-drawn wagons and siege guns were still rumbling through Brussels at midnight.

—

The 'martyrdom of Belgium'[29] proceeded in the villages and farms, up against walls and in the flames of people's homes. For General von Kluck, the 'shooting of individuals and the burning of houses' were 'punishments under martial law', which, he later wrote, were 'slow in remedying the evil'.[30] It strains comprehension how Kluck imagined his defence of German behaviour in Belgium would reach credulous ears. Yet other generals shared his view that whole villages of innocents should be massacred for the actions of the '*franc-tireurs*', the civilian resistance. In so doing, they offered a model for the blind, mass destruction of civilian life in the Second World War and the Vietnam War. Ludendorff described the Belgian resistance as 'disgusting'. Hausen, who presided over the massacre at Dinant, found the Belgians' implacable hostility and 'ungentlemanly behaviour' affronting: it seemed his hosts had refused to shake his hand. Firing on the German lines, sabotaging the roads, destroying bridges and railway lines were violations of international law, the Germans claimed. They failed or refused to see that the Belgians were engaged in legitimate acts of self-defence against an unlawful invader. And their guerrilla tactics hit their mark, critically delaying the German advance. 'These evil practices,' Kluck conceded, 'ate into the very vitals of the Army until the southern frontier of Belgium had been reached.'[31]

German retribution was merciless and bloody. It expressed a policy that blamed Belgium for any disruption of the German Army, part of a 'general system of terror' often directed at innocent communities who had not lifted a finger against the invader. Revelations of the slaughter of Belgian men, women and children and the rape of women would soon astonish the world. Whole towns were selected for destruction without any evidence that the inhabitants had resisted the occupying force.

The people of Namur dared not attack the German lines, yet they were to be terrorised *pour encourager les autres*. The shooting of civilians and the burning of homes began at 9 pm on 24 August. 'Six dwellers in the Rue Rogier, who were [fleeing] their burning houses, were shot on their own doorsteps,' noted the Official Belgian Commission of Inquiry, based on the evidence of hundreds of witnesses (and the source for the testimonials that follow, unless otherwise stated).[32] The city erupted in panic. People streamed from their homes, many in their nightgowns. Seventy-five were shot or burnt to death. The Germans burnt the Town Hall, the Place d'Armes and a whole civilian quarter. On passing through Namur on 29 August, Herman Baumann observed 'ruined houses, several are still burning, corpses are being pulled out, half-burnt. The most beautiful building in the town, the museum, is also in ruins.'[33]

At Andenne, on 20 August, a single shot and an explosion were heard as the German troops marched through town, on their way to Charleroi on the French border. Nobody was hit. The Germans halted and fired back in disorder. They brought up a machine gun. The people fled, hiding in their cellars, bolting their doors and shutters. The destruction of the bridge and a nearby tunnel may also have provoked German fury. The pillage began: every window and shutter smashed, houses burnt. The next day, the residents were herded through the streets at gunpoint, their hands in the air. A man who aided his 80-year-old father, who couldn't put up his arms, was struck in the neck with an axe. Any who resisted were shot; 40–50 people were selected at random and shot. Some were axed to death. More than 300 civilians were murdered at Andenne: 'no other Belgian town was the theatre of so many scenes of ferocity and cruelty'. The survivors later told the inquiry that 'Andenne was sacrificed merely to establish a reign of terror'.[34]

At Tamines, on the River Sambre, on 22 August, the Germans herded 400–450 men in front of the local church and opened fire – punishment for their defying the occupation and shouting '*Vive la France*'. The official inquiry stated, 'as the shooting was a slow business the officers ordered up a machine gun, which swept off all the unhappy peasants still standing'.[35] The wounded hobbled to their feet and were shot down again. The next day, a Sunday, the people were ordered to bury a pile of corpses in the town square: 'fathers buried the bodies of their sons and sons the bodies of their fathers', while the German officers watched, 'drinking champagne'.[36] A gravedigger testified to burying 350–400 corpses. On leaving Tamines, the Germans burnt 264 houses. The Belgian inquiry estimates 650 dead; later research puts the figure at 385.

Similar atrocities were inflicted on many other Belgian communities, at Dinant, in the district of Philippeville, and the villages of Hastière and Surice, according to the official Belgian inquiry. In these and other places, the populations were terrorised or killed, and the towns utterly destroyed. At Dinant, hundreds of bodies,

including that of a three-week-old baby, were identified as the victims of two firing squads. The official Belgian inquiry lists 700 dead.
Later research finds evidence of duplication and puts the figure at
410. In these communities, parish priests were routinely shot, and
massacres of the menfolk usually followed. Women were hunted
down and raped, by crazed, drunken soldiers whose officers were
unable or unwilling to restrain them. A German infantry regiment
broke up a church service in one village, drove them onto the street
and shot 50 of the men. During another massacre, women and
children were forced to watch the execution of their husbands and
fathers. At the village of Surice, a crowd of tearful women shouted,
'Shoot me too; shoot me with my husband!' German soldiers plun-
dered the corpses, taking 'watches, rings, purses and pocketbooks'.[37]

Eyewitnesses to these events were plentiful. Many German soldiers unwittingly produced evidence of their army's appalling behaviour, of which they wrote approvingly in their diaries. 'Many an
officer marching at the head of his company,' wrote Walter Delius,
for example, on 16 August, 'had been cut down from behind by a
sniper with his hunting rifle . . . This explains the nameless anger
by our soldiers, who had strict orders to proceed ruthlessly if they
encountered any armed resistance.'

At Namur on 25 August:

We passed by smoking ruins of villages completely shot to pieces.
No stone was left on top of the other. Corpses both human and
horse were still lying around in huge numbers, you could see
the wounded through the shot-out windows – friend and foe all
a-jumble – lying on the straw, moaning.

And at Maubeuge on 28 August:

The few monks and scholars left behind are scarily friendly. It is
well known that the catholic clergy organised the Francs-Tireur
war by the Belgian population. There were quite a few of this

Jesuit riff-raff which were put against a wall and shot.[38]

By the end of August, Belgium had been subjected to the horror of 'a mediaeval war': massacres, rapes and the sacking of whole towns. These were not arbitrary acts of vengeance. They were organised. The 1902 German Military Code, which laid down the *Kriegsbrauch*, or 'custom of war', explicitly states that 'an energetically conducted war' should extend to 'the destruction of material and moral resources' (i.e. property, civilian lives, including women and children). 'Humanitarian' acts were in conflict with the rules of war.[39] In other words, German atrocities in Belgium were *prescribed*, the corollary being the suspension of conscience and compassion.

The man responsible for enforcing the *Kriegsbrauch* was Field Marshal Colmar Freiherr von der Goltz, appointed military governor of Belgium at the start of the occupation (he would later die of typhus or, some believe, poisoning by Turkish assassins). He was a dour, pitiless individual, who adhered grimly to his rule book, however barbaric; his ruthless example would later impress Hitler. 'It is the stern necessity of war,' von der Goltz ordered in early September, 'that the punishment for hostile acts falls not only on the guilty, but on the innocent as well.' He clarified this on 5 October:

> In the future, villages in the vicinity of places where railway and telegraph lines are destroyed will be punished without pity (whether they are guilty or not of the acts in question). With this in view hostages have been taken in all villages near the railway lines, which are threatened by such attacks. Upon the first attempt to destroy lines of railway, telegraph or telephone, they will immediately be shot.[40]

The result was virtual lawlessness, as German officers lost control of their men. By the end of August 1914, the Belgian civilian dead outnumbered the military casualties. For these acts, Germany revealed to the world 'a monstrous and disconcerting moral phenomenon', concluded the official report on the Martyrdom of Belgium.[41]

—

The truth of the allegations of German atrocities has been a source of constant heated debate. Doubts arose after the publication of the Bryce Report of the Committee on Alleged German Outrages, conducted in December 1914 by Viscount James Bryce, a respected scholar who had always sought accommodation with Germany and was initially sceptical of the allegations he was asked to investigate. Yet his committee's report drew severe censure after it emerged that it had relied on rumour, hearsay and depositions given without oaths. Bryce had not interviewed a single witness, yet claimed to have drawn on 500 witness statements and 37 German diary entries. The Bryce Report was roundly condemned as an example of mendacious British war propaganda – appearing five days after the sinking of the *Lusitania* in 1915 – designed to draw the Americans into the war.

Bryce claimed that the German Army subjected Belgium to a 'systematic terror campaign against civilians'.[42] He cited 'evidence' of the cutting off of hands; the mass rape and mutilation of women; the slaughter of whole families, 'including not infrequently . . . quite small children'; and the British War Propaganda Unit's most-peddled atrocity, the bayoneting of a baby, based on the testimony of a 'Belgian witness' in a village near Louvain.[43] Historians have since discredited some of these stories, destroying the Bryce Committee's credibility. And yet research since the war has shown that Bryce actually understated the truth in several important ways. The Germans massacred more civilians than Bryce estimated, at Aarschot (169 dead; Bryce estimated 10), Dinant (410) and Tamines (385). In the latter two cases, Bryce gave no estimate of deaths. In sum, while the Bryce Committee's motive (propaganda) and methods have discredited his conclusions, the Belgian official inquiry and subsequent research has corroborated many of his findings.

—

An act of barbarity that would forever redound to German disgrace was visited upon the Belgian town of Louvain on 25 August. For the next six days, the German Army burnt Louvain's cathedral and university to the ground, murdered many of its residents and destroyed one of the world's finest cultural centrepieces: Louvain's peerless library, the cherished receptacle of 230,000 ancient volumes, including 750 mediaeval manuscripts. All were reduced to ashes. The sack of Louvain, reported in the world's press, provoked universal disgust. 'Are you descendants of Goethe or Attila the Hun?' wondered the writer Romain Rolland in a letter of protest.[44]

Judicial inquiries ran for months and years, and tended to hinge on who provoked the atrocity. Did Belgian civilians or snipers first open fire on Germans? Did the German troops in a skirmish at nearby Malines seek retribution? Was drunkenness responsible? When they arrived at Louvain, the Germans had shown exemplary restraint, with troops queuing in shops, and buying postcards and souvenirs.[45] The people had obediently placed any weapons they owned in the Church of St Pierre, as ordered.

Yet this whole line of inquiry missed the point. Who fired on whom is ultimately irrelevant. The question of blame lay in the general crime of Germany's unlawful occupation of a neutral country and the imposition of *Kriegsbrauch* on the Belgian people. These were not common acts of barbarity, as King Albert argued; they were ordained according to the German code book.

—

Reports of German outrages in Belgium elicited worldwide revulsion. Arthur Benson, the English poet, initially refused to believe the stories, for which the English papers flogged him as 'pro-German'. On the contrary, his better angels had simply blocked his ears at what he thought was hearsay. His mind, then attuned to the task of composing the lyrics to Elgar's 'Land of Hope and Glory', simply could not admit the ghastly stories of German cruelty, as he recorded in his diary:

Saturday 22nd August:

I begin to realise what an awful affair this is, whatever happens.
I . . . wrote two more stanzas for Elgar of *Land of Hope And Glory*
– I don't know if they'll do. Very evil dreams of the deaths of
friends by some unknown natural unmentionable calamity.

Friday 28th August:

The Archbishop arrived for dinner. The Abp looked well, but
worn. He cast a very lurid light upon many things . . . – ie that
the report of the fall of Namur was circulated by the French to
permit them to withdraw their troops.

Wednesday 2nd September:

[Hears from a friend that] I was attacked as pro-German in
the *Daily Express* for one of my . . . articles about not trusting to
hearsay about atrocities. This rather upset me . . . I wrote to the
editor asking him to explain that my article was written before
reliable news arrived.

Thursday 8th October:

[After meeting Belgian refugee children, he heard] . . . horrid
tales of two little Belgian girls whose hands had been cut off at
the wrist by German soldiers.[46]

—

In answer, the German Government attempted to exonerate its army.
In doing so, it merely aggravated the guilt. Its 300-page White Book,
published on 17 May 1915, five days after the Bryce Report, claimed
that German soldiers had been the targets of an 'unorganised people's war' against which they had acted with 'humanity, restraint
and Christian forbearance'.[47] The evidence demonstrated precisely
the opposite, concluded Sir Edward Grimwood Mears, appointed to
head the British inquiry into 'The Destruction of Belgium' in 1915.
No doubt, Sir Edward, working in wartime, was subject to the same

criticism as Bryce, of producing propaganda. Yet his demolition of the White Book (drawn up by an all-German panel appointed in Berlin) certainly points to a web of lies, inconsistencies and falsehoods. For example, the German deposition made not a single mention of alcohol or drunkenness, rendering it utterly inconsistent with virtually every eyewitness. It neither asked nor answered the question, 'In what state were the German troops during the occupation?' It consulted very few German soldiers' diaries, which do reveal a pattern of plunder and violence lubricated by copious amounts of alcohol. Nor did the German White Book even address widespread allegations of rape, pillage and desecration of property, which were referred to in the German soldiers' diaries.[48] It acknowledged responsibility for massacres but refused to call them 'war crimes'; they were punishments. At Dinant, for example, 'wives and children who clustered around the men . . . simply got in the way . . .'[49]

Indeed, the 'evidence' that the German Government produced to support its case was so flimsy as to 'sufficiently condemn itself', Sir Edward concluded.[50] At Andenne, for example, the White Book claimed, on the evidence of three unreliable witnesses, that the German forces were virtually decimated and that Belgian civilians had used hand grenades and machine guns. No such weapons were later found or produced as evidence. The only machine gun in operation at Andenne was the German one, 'engaged in piling up the list of 234 dead'.[51]

More egregiously, the Germans claimed that their soldiers' sack of Louvain was 'devoid of truth'. Apparently, German troops had behaved with exemplary restraint, according to Major von Klewitz's evidence. At Louvain, they accused Belgians of firing on them first; and, indeed, some isolated sharpshooters fired 'pellets from sporting weapons'.[52] Yet the Germans discredited their own case, again, by drawing on self-incriminating witnesses. One soldier, Private Richard Gruner, admitted that only two German soldiers were required as 'eyewitnesses' to condemn a Belgian to death, and 80–100 were killed in this way in Louvain, he recalled, including 'some 10 or 15 priests'. Twenty-six priests were herded into a field near Louvain and forced to watch the execution of 23-year-old Father Eugene Dupiereux, a philosophy student, found to have possessed a document that accused the Germans of burning Louvain's cathedral and university, for which 'the barbarians can no longer have a word to say against Khalif Omar for burning the library at Alexandria. And all in the name of German culture!'[53] Eugene was shot through the head as he clasped a crucifix. Among the witnesses were his twin brother, Robert, and 16 fellow students.

In their 'defence' of their behaviour at Louvain, German troops casuistically claimed that 'only' one-sixth of the town was burnt, and that the burning of the cathedral was an unavoidable accident, which German troops 'in a self-sacrificing manner' tried to extinguish.[54] In fact, the cathedral was deliberately torched, according to an eyewitness.[55]

In the end, the Germans performed Sir Edward's job for him: they indicted themselves. The publication of the White Book amounted to an astonishing official blunder, by actually naming many German officers responsible for the massacres. For example, soldiers referred to routine hostage-taking in unthreatening towns, to 'heaps of bodies' at Dinant and to other self-incriminating details, such as a wounded eight-year-old girl, 'an elderly woman who had been shot in the upper part of the thigh', and the shooting of 'young lads'.[56] Grimwood Mears concluded that German soldiers, in whose minds the teachings of *Kriegsbrauch* had 'inculcated savagery', were ordered to use terror 'as a legitimate weapon' against Belgian civilians.[57] Their purpose was to crush the Belgian people, whose acts of resistance were clogging up the German war plan. Most atrocities took place in the third week of August, when a speedy passage through Belgium was vital if they were to meet the Motlke–Schlieffen deadline: 'The need for hacking a way through had been imperative from the outset.'[58]

The Bishop of Namur, in a letter to the Governor-General in Belgium, later described the German defence as without mercy in its logic. He found in the White Book not a word concerning the tragedy at Surice, Spontin, Namur, Fehe, Gommeries, Latour, or some 65 other places where the Germans pillaged, massacred and set communities alight.[59] In short, the Berlin government's attempt to exonerate its troops merely added an overlay of lies to a litany of war crimes.

The Belgian resistance, on the other hand, had heroically held up the German advance, which had fallen two to three days behind schedule. The Schlieffen timetable had not accounted for the Belgians' disobliging destruction of bridges, roads and railway lines. The human factor had intruded upon the great plan like a strange and unruly visitation, aberrant and perverse, in Prussian eyes. Belgian sabotage was a gift to the French and British, whose divisions were approaching the frontier with Belgium ahead of Kluck, thus thwarting Germany's dream of the quick defeat of France. Not until 24 August, writes the rail expert Edwin Pratt, were the German forces in a position to attack the French Army, 'which by that time had been joined by the first arrivals of the British Expeditionary Force'.[60]

41

ON THE FRENCH FRONTIERS

[T]he War was decided in the first twenty days of fighting,
and all that happened afterwards consisted in battles
which, however formidable and devastating, were but
desperate and vain appeals against the decision of Fate.
Winston Churchill

An address by Field-Marshal Kitchener to the British Troops:

(This paper is to be considered by each soldier as confidential, and to be kept in his Active Service Pay Book.)

You are ordered abroad as a soldier of the King to help our French comrades against the invasion of a common enemy. You have to perform a task which will need your courage, your energy, your patience . . . The operations in which you are engaged will, for the most part, take place in a friendly country, and you can do your own country no better service than in showing yourself in France and Belgium in the true character of a British soldier. Be invariably courteous, considerate and kind. Never do anything likely to injure or destroy property, and always look upon looting as a disgraceful act . . . In this new experience you may find temptations both in wine and women. You must entirely resist both temptations, and, while treating all women with perfect courtesy, you should avoid any intimacy.

Do your duty bravely.

Fear God.

Honour the King.

KITCHENER, Field-Marshal.[1]

With Kitchener's words in their pockets, if not always in their heads – the advice to resist wine and women would be cheerfully ignored – the British Expeditionary Force (BEF) embarked for France and a war that many, such as Gunner Captain A. Corbett-Smith, looked forward to as 'the most gorgeous adventure' of their lives.[2] Not for 99 years had Britain fought a battle on the European mainland. Now, they came by train and sea, joyful, laughing, eager to get to France. 'Veeve France,' the lads shouted as they set off for the Channel. Some even sang the 'Marseillaise'.[3] Their 'contemptible little army', as the Kaiser had dismissed it,[4] comprised five divisions (four infantry and one cavalry – one division short of Henry Wilson's requirements), a mere 100,000 soldiers. They were heading to a battlefield where, from the west, 70 German divisions were advancing on about 70 French divisions – a total of 2.5 million men – stretched across more than 500 kilometres from Flanders to Belfort. Of these men, the Germans fielded 1.5 million and the French more than a million, with an additional three million reservists on call. On the Eastern Front, the Russian commanders similarly dealt in the deployment of millions of combat-ready troops and reservists. Accompanying these huge armies were similar numbers of horses: Russia's 24 cavalry divisions required the entrainment of more than a million; Germany's army carried 715,000.[5] The world had never witnessed the mobilisation of men on this scale. Napoleon's Grande Armée, at its height in 1812, in preparation for the invasion of Russia, numbered 685,000 troops, the largest then recorded.

Alone among British politicians and commanders, Field Marshal Horatio Herbert Kitchener, 1st Earl Kitchener, had foreseen the kind of war that awaited the BEF: a long campaign of at least three years, he told the astonished British War Council. Tapped by Asquith in 1914 to serve as the new war secretary, Kitchener brought long and intimidating experience to the Cabinet. He was a man of imperious moral passion, rare intelligence and utter dedication to public duty. His 'almost cloistral notion of discipline', concluded his biographer Sir George Arthur, 'fed a reputation for extreme abstemiousness and colossal self-control': 'I have no home,' Kitchener would say.[6] Work was his home. Childless, he took a close interest in the children of friends. The only time anyone saw him break down during the extremities of war was on hearing of the death of the second of two brothers he had watched grow up.[7] Contemptuous of those who undermined the war effort, or endangered the soldiers' lives, he told a nosy war correspondent, 'If you wish to sell your country, you should raise the price of your newspaper – a penny is too cheap.'[8]

Kitchener was one of those rare individuals whose record justi-fied his reputation. The actuality of his achievements outdid the legend. With every promotion, the stories of his Olympian exploits flowed home to Britain: at 24, a captain in the Royal Engineers in Africa (when he mapped the Holy Land); an intelligence officer in the Nile Campaign; conqueror of the Sudanese at the battle of Omdurman; an inspiring leader in the victory over the Boers; an enlightened imperial master of Sudan (ordering the reconstruction of the mosques of Khartoum and guaranteeing freedom of religion); and commander-in-chief in India, where he reorganised the Indian Army. Fluent in Arabic and French, more at home in a kasbah, the Raj or a Bedouin tent than in Whitehall, Kitchener returned to London in 1914 in the wake of a legend: the hero and feared leader upon whom the British would take the war to Germany on a scale unprecedented in the history of the empire.

Kitchener swiftly disabused the War Council of their hopes that he would be more amenable than his uncompromising reputation led them to fear. At their first meeting, on 5 August, Kitchener, then at the height of his powers, proceeded to condemn the British war plan as utterly inadequate to the demands of the coming campaign, and to demolish their expectations of a short war. 'We must be pre-pared,' he told his shocked colleagues, 'to put armies of millions in the field and maintain them for several years.' To defeat Germany, Britain must raise an army of 70 divisions, more than a million men, he advised; they would take years to train and deploy. He condemned the dispatch of the small Regular Army to France, where it would serve no useful purpose, as a mere bolted-on gesture of near-criminal neglect. It denuded Britain of a properly trained force, and of the officers who knew how to raise one. It was too late, however, to change the existing plan, which had been in place for years under Sir Henry Wilson's guiding hand.

Outwardly compelled to accept it, privately Kitchener believed it risked the complete destruction of Britain's only standing army. The one consoling thought was that the Old Contemptibles, as they would soon call themselves, in a mock-echo of the Kaiser, were the best-trained soldiers in Europe. At once, Kitchener set himself the task of reinforcing them, of raising a 'New Army'. By the end of the year, a million British lads would respond to the most urgent recruitment campaign in British history, featuring the famous poster: 'BRITONS' – then an illustration of Kitchener – 'WANTS YOU'. For now, however, the BEF would go into battle as little more than a symbolic show of support for the French, a political 'gesture' that would lead to their virtual annihilation, as Kitchener had feared, along with hundreds of thousands of Frenchmen.

—

'No part of the Great War compares with its opening,' wrote Churchill. 'The measured, silent drawing together of gigantic forces, the uncertainty of their movements and positions, the number of unknown and unknowable facts made the first collision a drama never surpassed. Nor was there any other period in the War when . . . the slaughter was so swift or the stakes so high.' He added, with a note of crushing resignation, 'the War was decided in the first twenty days of fighting, and all that happened afterwards consisted in battles which, however formidable and devastating, were but desperate and vain appeals against the decision of Fate'.[9]

Only from a great height may we comprehend the nature of the Western theatre: a sprawling panorama of millions of men, horses, carts, vehicles and wheeled guns, strung out like ant trails over tens of miles, the troops weighed down by heavy packs, forced to follow and, where possible, exploit the natural contours of the earth, streaming together like the tributaries of a river, branching out like a delta, congregating on the high ground, disappearing into forests and valleys, or stationed in fixed lines along canals and riverbanks, soon to charge into battle at the sound of a whistle in blinding flashes of steel and powder, or to wait, entrenched, for the coming shriek of artillery, and then the dreaded charge of the enemy, thousands of whom would disappear in puffs of shellfire, the scatter of balls of shrapnel and the roving sights of rifles and machine guns.

The great French offensive opened on the frontiers with Alsace and Lorraine. A burst of energised aggression, a sudden, withering blow, drawing on the best of the French cavalry, would reclaim the lost provinces and throw the German troops off the French border. That was the essence of Plan XVII, developed by General Foch and modified by General Joseph Joffre. One reads between the lines Foch's memory of Prussian humiliation; the hour of French vengeance had come. It would rely on the qualities that France cherished most in its troops: speed, courage, imagination and that great intangible factor, élan, thought to have repeatedly given Napoleon the edge over numerically superior forces. But where France lost in 1870 as a result of 'an attachment to the defensive', it would come close to losing in 1914 'as a consequence of its exclusive passion for the offensive', as Foch later observed.[10]

Plan XVII had undergone several variations under the eye of the supreme French commander, General Joseph Joffre, who looked as physically ill suited as he was determined to execute it. Joffre was a 'bulky, slow-moving loosely-built man', Edward Spears, the British liaison officer in Joffre's HQ, observed, 'in clothes that would have been the despair of Savile Row, yet unmistakably a soldier'.[11] Joffre sported a great white moustache that seemed vaguely stuck on and moved in unison with his bluff, mutton-chopped face, crowned with white hair, upon which he wore his red and gold general's cap well forward, tilting his head back to examine his interlocutors. He was a big, portly figure, his black tunic sloping outwards from the third button down, over a pair of baggy red breeches. If he spoke at all, he spoke slowly, gruffly and always pertinently. Yet his mind was racing. The effect was to convey a sense of huge potential energy bound up in a great, slow-moving tortoise.

Hugely popular with the troops, 'Papa Joffre', as they called him, made the war his own personal project. He oversaw the French campaign with the insouciance of a rather lazy Zeus, deigning rarely to miss his long lunches and heavy naps, even in the worst of the coming crises. His famous imperturbability was reassuring, but his utter sangfroid in the face of real emergencies would exasperate his staff. Sometimes, he would appear at meetings, listen to reports and depart without having said a word, leaving his staff mystified as to his wishes.[12] But he was decisive in crises and ruthless in sacking incompetent generals. During the summer of 1914, he would dismiss three army commanders, ten corps commanders and 38 divisional commanders, replacing them with young, combative and highly intelligent men such as Foch and Franchet d'Espèrey (whom the English would call 'Desperate Frankie').[13] Joffre's greatest strength was a peerless mastery of logistics, supply and the direction of troop movement, qualities that would save the French Army in the coming emergency, thanks in no small degree to the patient attention to detail of his chief of staff, General Henri Mathias Berthelot.

In mid-August, Joffre launched his revised conception of the land offensive. He ordered the First and Second Armies, led by Generals Auguste Dubail and Édouard de Castelnau, to march into Alsace and Lorraine at points where he believed the enemy to be weakest. An 'army' comprised about five corps; each corps contained some 40,000 men, of whom about 30,000 were combatants. So, on the 14th, Dubail and de Castelnau unfurled their colours at the head of almost half a million men and advanced into the lost provinces with the panache of liberators. Here at last was the great unleashing of French verve the nation had dreamt of, and which the late socialist Jean Jaurès feared would lead to the 'submersion' of all France in defeat. The French cavalry officers were dressed for the show, in brass helmets with long horsehair plumes, scarlet trousers and frogged jackets not worn in battle since 1870. The French cuirassiers outdid them for sartorial antiquity, sporting the bright armoured breastplates little changed since Waterloo.

French confidence flew forward, on a wing and a prayer, to the battles ahead, buoyed along by their unbreakable faith in the strategy of Papa Joffre. Yet sheer dash could not overcome certain irreducible facts. The French plan had a deep strategic flaw. It lacked the support of the Fifth Army, commanded by General Charles Lanrezac, a superb theoretician (and military academic) with an irritating habit of letting his superiors know it. Accepting Lanrezac's concerns of a German build-up on the Belgian border, Joffre had been compelled to authorise the Fifth Army to stay on the Meuse in defensive positions. So Dubail and de Castelnau advanced into German-occupied Lorraine without the density and depth the French plan had anticipated. There were many other weaknesses too: the French guns were at that point inferior to the German. At a tactical level, poor communications and weak intelligence endangered the attack. The two French armies lost touch soon after their departure, due to bad telephone lines, and advanced into the Vosges as separate, uncoordinated units. At the same time, French intelligence had gravely underestimated German strength. All this conspired against the success of Plan XVII, but surely good old French élan would still win the day.

Waiting in the foothills were eight, not six, corps of the German Sixth and Seventh Armies, commanded respectively by the irrepressible Rupprecht, Crown Prince of Bavaria, regarded as the best of the royal commanders, and the bullet-headed General Josias von Heeringen. The German generals had no intention of fighting a frontal battle at this juncture. They fell back, as planned, drawing the French lines deeper into the eagle's talons. For four days, the French

First and Second Armies advanced into German territory, across the River Meurthe, over fields of alfalfa and grain, past neatly arranged haystacks, towards Saarburg and Morhange. The Germans fought fierce rearguard actions, and their heavy guns tore apart the forward French lines. Carts of bloody, mangled bodies came down the roads, a ghastly notice to the oncoming troops. Still they came, until, on the 18th, Dubail celebrated the taking of Saarburg.

Then the front 'lost its sponginess', in Keegan's vivid phrase.[14] Anxious to take the war to the French, Prince Rupprecht soon got his chance to counter-offend. On 20 August, the two German armies, under the joint authority of General Konrad Dellmensingen, coordinated by a single telephone system and armed with heavier guns and greater numbers, threw everything at Dubail's advance corps. Those not annihilated fell back in disarray, with the exception of several sturdy units who managed a miraculous counter-offensive. It proved short-lived. The French had won a brief tactical success, and then succumbed to Germany's superior numbers and artillery. In Foch's abrupt summary, the French continued the offensive 'in violation of the principles which modern weapons have now imposed'.[15]

—

The Second Army fared worse. On the 21st, de Castelnau received news that his son had been killed in battle. After a moment's silence, he said softly to his staff, 'We will continue, gentlemen.' His words, when reported, summoned a quiet defiance in the French people, who would continue for four more years with the loss of millions of sons. The next day, German heavy artillery pounded de Castelnau's men – four thousand shells fell on the French lines at St Geneviève, in a rain of steel that lasted 75 hours. These French men were the first in history to be subjected to massed modern artillery, and the experience left them utterly devastated, staggering around in bewilderment and terror. The French guns replied with a similar, sustained pounding of the German front. When the firing subsided, Lieutenant Ernst von Rohm raised his field glasses to survey the French lines. He saw none, just a plain strewn with the dead and the dying. Then he stood up and urged his comrades to join him. None except three were able to stand. One, his bugler, said, 'Herr Lieutenant, there is nobody there anymore.'[16]

The French were soundly defeated at Lorraine, driven back whence they came by superior German tactics, guns and numbers. Thousands of numbed, humiliated, maddened French soldiers retreated en masse beyond the Meurthe. Only Ferdinand Foch's unyielding XX Corps, part of de Castelnau's Second Army, had held the line, on the high ground on the extreme left flank near Nancy.

The Alsace campaign to the south offered the only good news for the French that day. There, General Paul Pau's Armée d'Alsace had succeeded in capturing Mulhouse and the surrounding region. He was soon compelled, however, to abandon it and join General Lanrezac's embattled lines on the Belgian frontier. Pau's command lasted barely two months, a casualty of Joffre's periodic purges of elderly or incompetent commanders, of whom he would sack 58 by the end of the year. After Pau lost his foothold in Mulhouse, Alsace fell back into German hands, where it remained for another four years.

Many soldiers maintained their high spirits, despite these reversals, but many conscripts, too, adopted an ironic, put-upon frame of mind, sceptical of the enterprise and motivated chiefly by a determination to survive. Here, for example, is Raymond Clément, a French stretcher-bearer, trudging into Alsace with his medical kit, never short of amazement at what he is being asked to do and always with an eye on relief. In many ways, he typifies the ordinary soldier, in all armies. On the road to Gincrey, near Metz, he wrote:

17th August: My feet are better. I can carry my bag again . . . With three of my comrades, we look for food. We find vegetables, milk, wine, and apples picked up under the trees . . . We conceive the following menu: vegetable soup, fried beef and onions, and apple with milk . . . Since this morning we clearly heard the cannons. The weather is still grey, with the same thick rain as yesterday . . . Today we officially know the staff's plan: attacking the enemy along a 400 km front. This great battle could begin in a few days.

18th–20th August: We read a poster in a town hall: The challenge of Clemenceau to Germany and Viviani's proclamation to the soldiers. Two pages of vibrating patriotism. We spend the 19th here, and we do a training exercise of transportation of the wounded in a field. This afternoon we receive the first issues of the 'Bulletin des Armées'. The commander asked me to read it to the whole company. It is a moving moment, and the reading takes at least an hour. The morning of the 20th I can wash my clothes. Unfortunately the water from the washer is quite dirty.

21st August: Departure! This time the march is terrible. The hours go by, the sun rises, the afternoon comes, and we are still marching. When we arrive at Longuyon we are cheered. The people give us beer, lemonade that quench our terrible thirst. A solar eclipse darkens the sky, but the heat doesn't decrease. Suddenly the thunder rumbles and we have to walk under heavy rain. The night falls when we arrive in the village of Cons la Grand Ville, after having walked 50 kilometres. Are we still men? Will we even have the strength to eat? Anyway, why should we stop since they are slowly turning us into robots?[17]

—

Meanwhile, the French Third and Fourth Armies, commanded respectively by Generals Pierre Ruffey and Fernand de Langle de Cary, prepared to enact the next stage of Joffre's great offensive: a huge attack into the Ardennes – a rough, wild region bounded by France, Germany and Belgium, and covered in dense forest, boggy moors and mountains. Persuaded of German weakness in this forbidding terrain, Joffre ordered his generals to attack along a 40-kilometre front into the forested hills towards the towns of Arlon and

Neufchâteau. The idea was to force the Germans back through the Ardennes, link up with Lanrezac's Fifth Army and drive the Germans out of Belgium. Joffre's headquarters reassured his commanders of no serious opposition. Again, French intelligence was mistaken: eight German corps were then bearing down on the area, at least equal to the French in strength. Some belonged to the Fifth Army, commanded by Kaiser Wilhelm's son, the Crown Prince, 'a narrow chested willowy creature', writes Tuchman, '. . . a partisan of the most aggressive militarist opinion', whose photograph sold in Berlin shops inscribed with 'Only by relying on the sword can we gain the place in the sun that is our due . . .'.[18]

De Langle, a wiry, highly energised man, impatient for battle, and Ruffey, a more reflective commander with a passion for big guns, soon felt the full brunt of German might. On 22 August, the vanguard of the two armies, blinded in the misty, primordial conditions, literally crashed into each other, on an incline that favoured the Germans. Hostile units would stumble together and suddenly engage in point-blank combat. The Germans immediately entrenched themselves. The French, lacking entrenching tools, charged the German lines with bayonets drawn, straight into machine guns. Thousands fell. Mounds of bodies propped corpses upright, as though alive and still standing. 'Rain is falling,' wrote a French sergeant during the terrible night, 'shells are screaming and bursting . . . Whenever it stops we hear the wounded crying from all over the woods. Two or three men go mad every day.'[19]

The French infantry panicked and fled. Only the hardened Colonial Corps, which had garrisoned French colonies in Africa and Indochina, 'pressed forward with a determination the unblooded conscripts of the metropolitan army could not match'.[20] That was their undoing. Enveloped by overwhelming German numbers, they were cut to pieces. The 3rd Colonial Division was virtually annihilated: 11,000 of its 15,000 men were killed or wounded. The French survivors limped back. In recognition of the German victory, 'Papa William' duly awarded the Crown Prince the Iron Cross, First and

Second Class. The Germans regrouped and prepared to take the war into the heart of France.

Joffre later admitted his strategic errors in the Ardennes but refused at the time to accept the outcome and urged the exhausted French forces to resume the offensive. This they attempted on the 23rd, but they could not. Ruffey had a fair excuse for yielding: Joffre had denuded him of 50,000 reserves at the last moment. The next day, the French armies retired behind the protection of the Meuse and prepared for the hitherto unthinkable: to *defend* France.

Joffre's great plan had failed. Those who survived it lived to remember the humiliating psychological adjustment, from the offender to the besieged. He had disastrously misapplied Plan XVII.[21] Ferdinand Foch, the Catholic general who had inspired the plan, alone among the French generals had refused to yield. 'They won't walk over the XXth without protest!' he later wrote. But Foch's last hope of reclaiming Alsace and Lorraine – where he'd witnessed the Prussian humiliation of his countrymen 40 years earlier – had vanished. The French offensive was over. The defensive war began on the Belgian border, where French and British troops somehow had to stop the incessant waves of German grey.

The French press were reduced to hailing the doomed courage of the colonial troops. *L'Humanité* reported on 26 August:

> Despite the soldiers' enormous fatigue after three consecutive days of combat, and despite the incurred losses, the morale of the troops is excellent . . . The day before yesterday, the major fact was the great clash between the Algerian and Senegalese troops, versus the renowned Prussian Guard. Our African soldiers fought . . . with an inexpressible fury. The Guard has suffered in this battle that ended in violent hand-to-hand combat . . . Our calm and determined army will continue its wonderful effort. Our army knows the price of this effort. Our army fights for civilization.[22]

The newspaper failed to state that the French colonials were all but wiped out.

The Teutonic press were ecstatic. The Austrian paper *Die Neue Zeitung* reported under the headline 'The Beaten Frenchmen' that the Germans:

> eventually got even with the invading French for good. Eight French army corps had invaded the Lorraine between Metz and the Vosges. They suffered a devastating defeat, with the Germans under the command of the Crown Prince of Bavaria giving them a good whack on the head . . . The defeat of the French, who so far have lost more than 15,000 prisoners and 150 guns, was unparalleled. The battle at Metz also was the largest battle ever seen in a European theatre of war: there were some 700,000 to 800,000 soldiers facing each other.[23]

Raymond Clément was one of them, staggering along in a world of horrors the scale of which he scarcely comprehended.

—

General Charles Lanrezac had a brief, unhappy war. The commander of the French Fifth Army had the unfortunate duty of warning Joffre of the massive German build-up on the Belgian border. He cabled Joffre but was ignored; French headquarters were absorbed with Alsace and Lorraine, and this news did not fit in with Joffre's plans. Lanrezac's mistake was to speak the truth, to give the lie to French preconceptions of the kind of war they *should* be fighting. He irritated Joffre with his persistent and unhelpful revelations, regardless of whether they were true. It did not occur to French headquarters 'that the Germans would gamble on Russia's slowness to the extent of leaving only 250,000 men on the eastern front'.[24] This initial error led Joffre to assume that Germany had not committed enough men to the Western theatre. Surely they were not intending to invade France across the Meuse River?

This attitude followed a pattern of France and Britain routinely underestimating German strength. When Henry Wilson heard that 17 or 18 German divisions were approaching the Meuse River, he wrote, 'The more the better, as it will weaken their centre.'[25] In fact, there were more than *30 divisions* on the Meuse River: the toughest elements of the German right wing. If the German forces outnumbered the French and British forces by 1.5 to 1 over the whole theatre, they fielded almost twice as many troops as their adversaries on the right wing pouring through Belgium.

It fell to Lanrezac to mount the first attempt to resist this diabolical onslaught. In the coming weeks, Edward Spears, who moved to Fifth Army Headquarters at Rethel on 14 August in anticipation of the arrival of the British, witnessed the unedifying spectacle of Lanrezac's psychological demise. When they first met, Spears had thought of Lanrezac as a 'veritable lion'. Yet he found the French general in a disconsolate state. As early as 31 July, Lanrezac had warned Joffre of the German sweep through Belgium. Joffre had persistently ignored his advice, and, on 9 August, he ordered Lanrezac to join the coming attack on the Ardennes, in a north-easterly direction. On the 14th, Lanrezac again warned Joffre, in person, that the Fifth Army would be left utterly exposed if it joined the Ardennes attack. At that moment, he rightly feared that Kluck's forces were about to attack across the Meuse (see Map 4). Lanrezac's worst fears were confirmed on his return to his office, where he found an intelligence summary warning of eight German Army corps and four cavalry divisions between Luxembourg and Liège. The intelligence was accurate, confirming 'the threat of an enveloping movement carried out by very considerable forces on both banks of the Meuse'.[26]

The following day, Joffre accepted the danger and authorised Lanrezac – in the famous Instruction Particulere No. 10 – to divert part of his army to the north, in the direction of Mariembourg and Philippeville, directly in the path of the German downward thrust. In technical military terms, the instruction 'marked the surrender of the initiative to the Germans'.[27] But Joffre clung to the hope of relaunching the offensive on the ground of his choice, denuding Lanrezac of some of his reserves to bolster the Ardennes offensive. In sum, Lanrezac now faced one of the hardest jobs of any general in the war: to resist the most powerful German offensive with a weakened army and no sign yet of the British.

—

The BEF landed at the French ports of Calais, Le Havre, Rouen and Boulogne on or around 13 August, and entrained for Amiens, the concentration point before setting off on the long march towards the Belgian border. As professional soldiers, they were the best trained and most experienced in the field. On active service, they knew what was expected of them, and they knew the punishment if they failed, as outlined in the officers' guidelines: DEATH, 'when a sentry, sleeping at his post'; DEATH, 'leaving his CO to go in search of plunder'; DEATH, 'quitting his guard without leave' (i.e. desertion).[28] During the war, 346 British soldiers would be executed, most for desertion, and most in the later years of the war. Only four were shot in 1914, compared with some 600 Frenchmen executed, the majority of whom were shot in the first year.[29] Many British troops were veterans of the Boer War and skilled marksmen – certainly the best in the field – and they carried a rifle, the famous Lee-Enfield .303, that had a faster firing rate than the German Gewehr 98. Their destination was the drab Belgian industrial town of Mons, where the .303 would demonstrate its firepower in the most exacting of conditions.

Lieutenant Aubrey Herbert wrote in his diary:

We arrived very early at Le Havre in a blazing sun. As we came in, the French soldiers tumbled out of their barracks and came to cheer us. Our men had never seen foreign uniforms before, and roared with laughter at their colours. Stephen Burton of the Coldstream Guards rebuked his men. He said: 'These French troops are our Allies; they are going to fight with us against the Germans.' Whereupon one man said: 'Poor chaps, they deserve to be encouraged,' and took off his cap and waved it, and shouted 'Vive l'Empereur!' He was a bit behind the times . . .[30]

At every station, 'enormous crowds' met the British Army. They 'cheered and would have kissed our hands if we had let them. They made speeches and piled wreaths of flowers upon the Colonel, who was at first very shy, but driven to make a speech, liked it, and became almost garrulous.'[31] As the British troops travelled through the countryside, the French villagers 'pelt us with fruit, cigarettes, chocolate, bread, anything', one officer wrote to *The Times* (one of the few who was fluent in French). 'One village had stretched across the road a big banner, "Honour to the British Army".'[32] Endless cries of '*Vivent Les Anglais!*' accompanied people making signs of hanging, or cutting their throats, and pointing up the road towards the front.

On 21 August, the BEF appeared where they were supposed to be, somewhere south of Le Cateau, marching up the road to the delight of French villagers, who welcomed them with flowers and kisses. En route, they passed a monument to Marlborough's defeat of the armies of Louis XIV; further ahead, beyond their destination, was Waterloo. They reached the Belgian border on the 21st. 'As we crossed the frontier,' Herbert noted, 'the men wanted to cheer, but they were ordered to be quiet, "so as not to let the Germans hear them". This order gave an unpleasant impression of the proximity of the Germans.'[33] The Belgians, he observed, 'were honest and pathetic. There were no signs of panic, but there was a ghastly silence in the towns . . . [W]e were halted on a plain near a big town which we did not then know was Mons. We were . . . told that the Germans were close to us and that we had to drive them back.'[34]

By the next day (22 August), they had converted every cottage 'into a little fortress',[35] and entrenched themselves along the banks of the canal. Rifles and machine guns sprouted from windows and ditches. And there they awaited Kluck's First Army.

At home, meanwhile, thousands of British reinforcements were preparing to depart. Cambridge was 'simply crammed with troops', wrote Arthur Benson in his diary on 19 August. 'They have tents in Coe Fen and Parkers Piece. They walk about everywhere. They play little games on Midsummer Common, and seem to be good-natured and robust.' In the following days, he encountered columns of men in 'honey-coloured uniforms, little red-faced tramping men – what a small race we are! . . . I was made uncomfortable by passing all these men and felt both ostentatious and luxurious in my nice car.'[36]

Public enthusiasm for war seemed endemic, now it had been declared. Benson saw examples everywhere, such as C. C. Perry, 'an extraordinarily heavy, egotistical, boring, dreary teacher of German, formerly and wholly unofficial Eton master, goes about the street waving a little Union Jack, and saying to any soldiers he meets "Splendid fellows, splendid fellows – God bless you!"'[37]

—

At the same time, the BEF's commander, Field Marshal Sir John French, was establishing his headquarters at Bavai. One approached Sir John with caution. He was a thickset, ruddy-faced, imperious little bulldog of a man, with the requisite white moustache drooping over the corners of his unimpressed mouth. The soldiers liked him; his peers always seemed to have excuses for him. He had served in the colonies – India, South Africa – and in every senior role, including aide-de-camp general to the King in 1911. A cavalry man, a hero of the Boer War, he was made chief of the Imperial General Staff in 1912 and promoted to the supreme rank of field marshal in 1913, notwithstanding rumours of an adulterous affair in India. In 1914, then, this knighted baton-wielding commander stood at the pinnacle of the British military hierarchy. He arrived in France at the head of a small army, with little to gain and everything to lose.

Sir John's war started badly. He made no effort to get along with Lanrezac, with whom he would have to cooperate and whose far bigger forces were strung out to the east, protecting Sir John's right flank. That fact did little to moderate Sir John's disapproval of Lanrezac, whose intellectual renown elicited the put-down 'Staff College pedant'. Sir John took an instant dislike to his French counterpart, for whom the feeling was intensely mutual.[38] The language barrier had not helped. In a famous exchange on 17 August, Sir John, who had little French, asked Lanrezac, who had less English, whether the Germans would cross the River Meuse at the town of Huy. 'À Huy' came out of Sir John's mouth as something vaguely naval, like 'ahoy'. 'Tell the Marshal,' Lanrezac scornfully replied, after Henry Wilson had translated the question, 'I think the Germans have come to the Meuse to fish.' Sir John picked up the sneering tone, if not the meaning. Wilson calmly rescued the moment: 'He says they are going to cross the river, sir.'[39] But the meeting, for both generals, had been a fiasco.

The serious misunderstandings between French and Lanrezac would have seemed comical in any other business. In a state of war, they threatened a tragedy. The two men barely spoke, did not confer and even failed, at times, to return the other's calls. They would not meet again until 26 August, after the battles of Charleroi and Mons had been desperately fought and lost. 'It was of course the armies that paid the penalty,' wrote Spears, of this clash of wills.[40]

—

The survival of the British Army depended on what happened to the much bigger French forces, strung out for 40 kilometres along the Meuse and Sambre. If they fell back, the British would be forced to retire too (to avoid exposing their right flank to encirclement). The beginning of the end came on the 21st–22nd, when Lanrezac's Fifth Army suffered severe losses to devastating German attacks at the industrial town of Charleroi and on the Sambre. The shock confirmed Lanrezac's worst fears of a wide German envelopment. German forces had surged over an undefended bridge and ruptured the French lines.

The German offensive at the battle of the Sambre – the inspiration, again, of Ludendorff, who personally approved the attack

– soundly defeated Lanrezac's forward units, with terrible casualties. Several regiments lost almost half their men. Despite ferocious street fighting, the French failed to dislodge the Germans from Charleroi. In an amazing innovation, German spotter planes identified the French positions and guided the German artillery to their targets, shredding Lanrezac's lines. His men fell back, but not without a few defiant counterblows. One colonial battalion charged a German gun battery with bayonets, after which just two soldiers returned unwounded out of the battalion's 1030 men.[41] In sum, about 30,000 Frenchmen and 11,000 Germans were killed or wounded at the battles of Charleroi and on the Sambre.

Throughout these terrific clashes, loving correspondence somehow continued between the soldiers and their families. Wives and husbands struggled to stay in contact during a maelstrom beyond their comprehension, which wrenched their little lives apart like an earthquake. Many letters were the simple statements of young men unwilling, or unable, to articulate what they had just endured. Hence, young Maurice Leroi, to his mother, on 23 August: 'Dear Mother, Yesterday we had a big battle. I am still in good health. Your loving son.'[42]

Marie Dubois implored her husband, Andre, for news, any news. Most of the time, she received an impenetrable silence, and her tone despaired, to the point of hectoring him. She simply had no idea of the hell into which he had disappeared. The young Parisian couple had a little girl, Madeleine, whom they called Mado. Marie wrote on 26 August:

> My dear André . . . Write to me and tell me if you received my letters. This one is the 16th letter I have sent, all of them to the military barracks of Pélissier . . . Tell me if you have a table to eat from, or if you eat with your fingers? Is the military barracks in the open, or is it under shelter? I guess you mustn't get much sleep, but still, do you get any? In short, give me some details . . . Has your beard grown? Do you shave it? How big is it? Are

your shoes still comfortable? Does your neck still hurt? Are you often wet? Did you buy a belt? Did you get the chance to bring your socks and tissues to the laundry? Haven't you had too much trouble? Please forgive me for asking so many questions. Answer only what you want to . . .

Strong kisses,

Marie[43]

Another young couple, Henri and Marie Michel, wrote lovingly to each other. Originally from the village of Précigné in the *département* of the Sarthe, in the west of France, the couple had a baby girl called Nano. During the war, Marie and Nano lived in Le Mans. Her husband was an infantry officer. Marie wrote to him on 21 August:

My dear little friend [*petit ami*],

. . . I wish your letters arrived quicker, and were longer, but I shouldn't be so difficult in times of war. Nano sleeps next to me in her small bed. She just woke up and said: 'I wish my papa could come now'. She's beginning to feel that it has been a long time since you left. Yet this time may be nothing compared to what we still have to wait. But once again my darling, I assure you that we are both brave, and I'll do everything I can to remain reasonable.

Tuesday, August 25th:

My dear little Henri,

. . . We know that since Saturday a huge battle is engaged all along the Eastern border, and that this is going to last a little while . . . My poor darling! I am so sad to be far away from you, and without any news from you, but yet I can swear that I have never been so brave. It is my way to pay my tribute to the country. I hope . . . that you will come back, maybe sick, but I hope. However, if somehow something bad happens to you, be sure that I will do my best to raise Nano and take care of your beloved father. I will stay at Précigné to live surrounded by your memory.[44]

The letters never ceased, from hundreds of thousands of women anxious for news and receiving little, until either their boyfriend or husband staggered home on leave or they heard that he was wounded and in hospital, a prisoner of war or killed in action.

The war would overwhelm not only families but also the commanders, who groaned beneath the tragedy. The losses on the Sambre – to which many of these letters referred – deepened the mood of hesitancy and indecision that now gripped Lanrezac. The forceful commander Franchet d'Espèrey virtually pleaded to be allowed to counter-attack. Lanrezac refused, to his staff's disgust. On the afternoon of 21 August, the French commander sank beneath the weight of his responsibilities and seemed paralysed. He expounded on the reasons for not attacking to his incredulous staff. Every military historian has 'pronounced his own version of what went on in the soul of General Lanrezac that afternoon', observes Tuchman.[45] Spears witnessed it, with deep consternation, chiefly for the fate of the British, digging in at Mons.[46] The truth seems simply that, overwhelmed by German strength and disheartened by his appalling casualties, Lanrezac was desperate to save the remnants of his army. He knew that Joffre would deny him that decision, so he acted alone. If he refused to allow his men the chance of defeat with honour, in retrospect, given German numbers and subsequent events, he made the correct decision. Few would credit Lanrezac with the foresight and moral courage he showed at that moment.

—

In similar circumstances, Sir John French was about to experience his own severe setback, in the form of a threefold blow: a personal tragedy, a political humiliation and a military reversal. Against French's wishes, Kitchener had appointed the combative Sir Horace Smith-Dorrien as commander of II Corps, to replace Sir John's friend General Sir James Grierson, who had suddenly collapsed and died on the 17th. Sir John could tolerate his personal grief, and the undermining of his authority. But he could not tolerate the silence issuing from Lanrezac, of whose battle plans, then in disarray, Sir John was basically ignorant – a problem he himself had largely created.

All along the Sambre and the Meuse, Lanrezac's forces were now forced to withdraw. To save his army from another Sedan, Lanrezac had waved on what was already happening: he ordered the retreat. Of this, he failed initially to inform Joffre, who would never forgive him; yet Lanrezac's unauthorised withdrawal would serve Joffre well, as a scapegoat for the larger failure of the offensive, for which he himself bore most responsibility. Lanrezac reassured his devastated staff that the Fifth Army would regroup and live to fight another day. And so they fell back.

Lanrezac's action, however, imperilled the British forces. What most worried Sir John, in his headquarters at Bavai, was the gap opening up between the British, who were digging in at Mons, and the French forces, who were withdrawing. It offered the Germans an opportunity to surge through in order to outflank and destroy his army. The further Lanrezac's army retreated, the more that outcome loomed. If they stayed put, the British would be left like an island in swirling grey flood waters, without any flanking embankment to cling to.

Just before midnight on 22 August, before Lanrezac gave the order to retreat, Sir John received a message from the French general's headquarters. It requested help and asked the British to attack Kluck's flank. The request revealed the extent of French ignorance: the outer limit of the German right flank extended miles away to the west of Sir John's narrow front. To attack and outflank was impossible. Sir John focused instead on how to save his army. He replied only that he would defend the Mons canal for 24 hours.

—

The BEF stuck to Mons – even as the French prepared to retire – like a peculiarly stubborn barnacle. Here they were, the only career soldiers in the field, 80,000 young men of the British Expeditionary Force, deployed along a 30-kilometre front that broadly followed the Mons-Conde Canal. To the west was Smith-Dorrien's II Corps; to the east General Douglas Haig's I Corps. There had already been contacts. On the 21st, British reconnaissance bicyclists had bumped into a German unit near Obourg; in the skirmish, Private John Parr was shot dead, the first British casualty of the war. On the 22nd, when the Germans detected an ambush near Casteau laid by Captain Hornby's 4th Dragoon Guards, and fell back, Hornby's men pursued them with sabres drawn, inflicting the first German casualties of the British war in hand-to-hand combat.

In the last week of August, the full brunt of Kluck's right wing closed on Mons, where the British waited, aligned along the canal or peering out of every house, their Lee-Enfields poised, surveying the Belgian fields. 'Old one o'clock' arrived on the 23rd. His advance units were stunned to find the entire BEF dug in ahead of them. 'Kluck's troops simply blundered into BEF and then tried to steam-roller it out of the way,' wrote John Paul Harris.[47] 'The British,' wrote Keegan, 'if only for a moment, were to be cast into the role of opposing both the concept and the substance of the Schlieffen Plan.'[48]

Herbert wrote:

> We were told that a tremendous German attack was to take place in the morning, we disliked the idea, as . . . it was obvious that there was hardly any means of defence. To stay was to be destroyed, as the Colonel said casually . . . We wrote farewell letters which were never sent. I kept mine in my pocket, as I thought it would do for a future occasion. They began to shell us heavily.[49]

That morning, German guns began shelling the town and probing the British positions. Then, on the horizon, bearing down from the north in a great dark line, came the first of six divisions of the German First Army, Schlieffen's famous right wing, which opened fire. 'It was as if a scythe of bullets passed directly over our heads about a foot above the earthworks,' wrote Herbert. 'It came in gusts, whistling and sighing. The men behaved very well. A good many of them were praying and crossing themselves. A man next to me said: "It's hell fire we're going into." It seemed inevitable that any man who went over the bank must be cut neatly in two.'[50]

The Germans were inexperienced in the use of their weapons, as many British accounts testify. Colonel T. S. Wollocombe MC, of the Middlesex Regiment, recalled:

> As I walked along the brick wall, bullets were hitting it like hail on a window, but most of them high above my head. It was no use running and I am glad I did not, as when I got to about the centre of the wall, just in front of me I heard a regular hail of bullets hit the wall in rapid succession – they all hit in practically the same place, though I didn't stop to look, I expect they drilled a hole in the wall pretty well. They were about level with my chest and I thought it was funny that the gun – for it was a machine gun – had not been traversed along the wall to make certain of me . . .[51]

(Wollocombe, one of four sons of the Rev. J. H. B. Wollocombe, rector of Stowford in Devon, all of whom served in the war, was mentioned three times in dispatches and awarded the Military Cross. His younger brother, Frank, a lieutenant in the 9th Devons, died on the Somme in 1916.)

Densely packed, advancing in parade-ground formation, the Germans offered easy targets to the British riflemen, who kept firing their '15 rounds a minute' as long as German soldiers appeared in their sights. So intense was the long-range rifle fire that at least one German diarist likened it to raking machine guns.[52] The German Private Hinrich Oetjen, 22, experienced it. Having decamped to

Waterloo on the 21st, where his unit paid their respects at the monument to the battle against Napoleon, they prepared to attack their former ally of a century ago. On the 23rd, they arrived at the village of St Symphorien, to the west of Mons, and occupied a barn. Soon after midnight, on the 24th, they awoke to a hail of British fire: 'the English were shooting like mad, keeping it up about a quarter of an hour . . . the tiles of the barn were shot to pieces'.[53]

The British kept it up all day, inflicting as many as 5000 German casualties, Keegan calculates, for 1600 British killed and wounded. Kluck later conceded that the 'severe opposition' of the British had delayed his advance.[54] The first attacks fell mostly on Smith-Dorrien's men – about five German divisions attacking his two. The German waves literally overran the British positions. The Royal Fusiliers and Gordon Highlanders faced the worst of it. All day, the German infantry ran at them. Lieutenant Maurice Dease, 'though two or three times badly wounded', controlled the fire of his machine guns until, wounded for the fifth time, he finally evacuated to the battalion aid station. Virtually all his men were either wounded or dead.[55] Similarly, Private Sidney Godley, though badly wounded, continued firing his machine gun for two hours to cover the British retreat.[56] Among the last at Mons, he then dismantled his gun and threw it into the canal, to avoid its capture. The two men bracketed the British class hierarchy. Dease, Irish-born, England raised, went to Stonyhurst College and Sandhurst, and died of his wounds at Mons. Godley, a London ironmonger, though taken prisoner, survived the war to become a school caretaker in the East End. Both were awarded the Victoria Cross; courage recognised no social distinctions. Theirs were among the last acts of resistance before the British abandoned Mons and joined the French retreat.

42

THE RETREAT

Kaiser Bill is feeling ill,
The Crown Prince, he's gone barmy.
We don't give a fuck for old von Kluck
And all his bleedin' army
Sung by British soldiers during the retreat

SIR JOHN FRENCH heard of Lanrezac's decision to retreat with deep dismay. A nervous Lieutenant Edward Spears, the British liaison officer, sped to Sir John's headquarters on the night of 23 August expressly to inform him. Lanrezac, Spears said, had warned Joffre that German victories on the Sambre had forced a general withdrawal. It would start the following day. Sir John struggled to digest the news. Only a few hours earlier, he had declared that he would stand 'on the ground now occupied' and reinforce his positions with new units expected overnight.[1] The British commander had no choice other than to follow his French allies and order the British forces to pull back. Without Lanrezac's army to protect their right flank, and with signs of a vast German envelopment to the west, the BEF risked being surrounded and annihilated. The generals – on both sides – fumed and argued and sought scapegoats for these reversals, and historians have made endless pronouncements on who was to blame. The fact is, Sir John and Lanrezac – and their fellow commanders – cared deeply for their soldiers. Theirs was a crushing responsibility, for the lives of their men, for the survival of their armies, for the expected victory of their nations. Their actions must be judged according to that scale, rather than some sterile military doctrine or 'blame game'.

News of the unauthorised retreat unsettled even Joffre's titanic repose. And yet, while angered at Lanrezac's peremptory decision, Joffre understood its rationale and notified the war minister Adolphe Messimy, in a now-famous minute, on the morning of the 24th. The German victories – 'checks', Joffre called them – in the Ardennes and all along the Sambre had forced the French to abandon the offensive, at least for now. The French armies had 'not shown on the battlefield those offensive qualities for which we had hoped', Joffre explained. In fact, several French commanders – the outstanding examples being d'Espèrey and Foch – and their troops had shown precisely that mettle, but their over-exuberant offensive had failed to penetrate far superior German numbers.

Joffre continued:

> We are therefore compelled to resort to the defensive, using our fortresses [Verdun, Toul and others] and great topographical obstacles [the Vosges mountains, the Rivers Seine, Somme and their tributaries] to enable us to yield as little ground as possible. Our object must be to last out, trying to wear the enemy down, and to resume the offensive when the time comes.[2]

The grandeur of his stoicism, when all seemed lost, astonished all who witnessed it. 'The Commander-in-Chief,' Foch later recalled, 'never for a moment lost his wonderful calm.'[3] Beneath his unflappable countenance, Joffre's mind sped ahead. When all around him lay the wreckage of his plans, in the shattered villages and denuded forests, in the bloated corpses that nobody had the time to bury, in the vast confusion of the battlefield and the stumbling, bloody ranks of his vanquished armies, Joffre conceived, with rhino-like fortitude, a plan for a new offensive. Yet still he had no clear news from the Eastern Front: what were the Russians doing?

—

And so the orders went out. All along the line, from the BEF's extreme left flank at Condé to the French extreme right on the River Meuse, the two armies fell back. In the predawn hours of 24 August, the British Army packed up and headed off down the road. After only two days of action, they were retreating. The dead word had no place in the vocabulary of the British soldier. It countermanded the whole mentality of these men, whose gut instincts were to stay and fight, to do what they were sent to do: drive the Germans out of Belgium. Nobody used the word. None spoke openly of retreat. They were engaged in a 'fighting withdrawal', they told themselves, until such time as they could turn and renew the attack.

Trooper Alfred Tilney, of the 4th (Royal Irish) Dragoon Guards, wrote:

> Retreat!!! . . . hateful enough to soldiers at any time . . . What seemed to hurt our fellows most was the sight of the refugees; the roads were full of them, all with their few belongings, and carrying babies in many cases, hopelessly hurrying out of the invader's path. The fate of many of those who were too late needs no repeating. Only a few hours before, these same people had been cheering us on to victory, and now we were retiring, it seemed as if we had let them down; they didn't understand. Could we blame them? We did not understand ourselves.[4]

They rose and staggered off, marching back whence they'd come, guided by French locals through the residue of night. Further back were the French soldiers, similarly aghast at what had become of the offensive, yet determined to hope for another chance.

At 8 am, the Germans smashed through Mons, crossed the canal and came 'in hot pursuit in overwhelming numbers'.[5] Their approaching lines resembled 'a dense, overpowering cloud rolling down', like a fog that penetrated every gap, recalled Major Corbett-Smith.[6] That day, the British unleashed one of their 'splendid but hopeless' cavalry charges, when the 9th Lancers galloped 365 metres back towards the German lines to save a battery of Royal Field Artillery, which was still in action minus most of its men. Captain Francis Grenfell earned one of several British Victoria Crosses awarded during the retreat that day, when, though hit twice, he succeeded in removing the guns from German range. 'For gallantry in action against unbroken infantry at Andregnies, Belgium, on 24 August 1914, and for gallant conduct in assisting to save the guns of the 119th Battery, Royal Field Artillery, near Doubon the same day', Grenfell earned the highest Commonwealth military honour.[7] He would be killed in action in 1915.

—

The retreat proved more terrible than anyone had conceived. The British troops were supposed to fall back in an orderly 'echelon formation': one half pulled back to set up a new position in the rear; the other half kept forward to stall and frustrate the enemy's advance. The forward half would then fall back, in a leapfrogging action, to establish a new rear, while the rear units would hold their position to confront the enemy. Every so often, a sudden counter-offensive would be thrown at the oncoming German forces. The retreat started well, but, after a few days, Germany's 'thunderbolt movements' smashed apart the British retirement plan. Relentless German night attacks, more guns, and 'spotter' aircraft wreaked havoc in the British lines. The Germans hoped to drive the British into the fortress of Maubeuge and destroy them. They underestimated the British soldier, who kept his head and refused to 'bunch up', far less hide in a fort.

The British had to 'fight backwards' without a moment's rest. The guns would be rolled into place, blasted at the approaching German lines, then pulled back. When the enemy got nearer, up jumped a line of infantry, which raced at the Germans with fixed bayonets. Those who survived the onslaught would stagger back to rejoin the retreat. Over and over, the British and French troops repeated this terrifying procedure, with huge casualties – now a confused rabble, now a disciplined, fighting withdrawal, sometimes in panic, usually with angry defiance. The people who had once showered them with flowers and kissed their cheeks now observed long lines of despond-ent men, bandaged and exhausted, stumbling back whence they came. And their presence brought terror with it: shellfire and the approach of the Germans, prompting the people to panic and flee too. 'Of what use was it to tell them that this was only a strategical retirement?' Corbett-Smith recalled thinking.[8]

As at Mons, Smith-Dorrien's II Corps bore the worst of it. His men received the order to retreat at 3 am. They were utterly exhausted, after two days of near-constant battle. Every one of his regiments had lost heavily the day before. Most of his officers were dead or wounded. Some units had no commanders and were bereft of direction. Now, Smith-Dorrien's men again stood in the path of the German maelstrom. It was pitch black and drizzling with rain. Men were 'foolish with fatigue' and 'just dropped off to sleep in the middle of whatever they were doing'.[9]

General Haig's troops, who saw little fighting at Mons, had been ordered to cover Smith-Dorrien's withdrawal. Haig decided he could not carry out the order, ignored it, and hastened his own corps' retreat. His disobedience was partly personal: the relationship between Haig and Smith-Dorrien and their staffs had broken down. Haig claimed that he simply could not fulfil the order to help Smith-Dorrien, according to a withering critique by Dr John Paul Harris, a senior lecturer at Sandhurst: 'At noon Smith-Dorrien came in person to see Haig to plead for [his] help . . . By that time, however, virtu-ally all of Haig's troops were in full retreat. II Corps was left to its own devices. It suffered another 2500 casualties on 24 August.'[10]

—

On the afternoon of 25 August, General Smith-Dorrien decided he would stand and fight. He was stuck in Le Cateau, a town in the Cambrésis region. The roads to the south were clogged and unpassable; the Germans were on their heels; the telephone lines to GHQ were down; the troops were exhausted. The invader pressed heavily on the town, and once again Smith-Dorrien's II Corps were caught in the line of fire. The British commander summoned his divisional leaders. Unless they moved off at once, they would be forced into battle before daybreak. There was silence, then a desire to act.

'Very well, gentlemen, we will fight,' Smith-Dorrien said calmly. The message went by motor car to GHQ, where Sir John received it with characteristic gloom; he would later criticise Smith-Dorrien. Few were more despondent than Henry Wilson, the architect of the British plan, which lay in ruins. Fearing the destruction of the British Army, he sent a motorcyclist to get Smith-Dorrien to the phone. 'If you stand there and fight, there will be another Sedan,' Wilson said. But Smith-Dorrien had no choice, he replied. The guns could be heard in the background, he shouted. The battle had begun. 'Good luck to you,' Wilson replied, 'yours is the first cheerful voice I have heard in three days.'[11]

Tuesday 25 August brought a terrible night. Around 9.30 pm, Smith-Dorrien's men, shallowly entrenched in the line running from Bavai to the west of Le Cateau, had collapsed, hoping for a moment's respite. They got none. Through the darkness came the scream of shellfire, and the blaze of rifle and machine-gun fire. The Germans were upon the town. A battalion of Coldstream Guards, part of Brigadier Robert Scott-Kerr's Fourth (Guards) Brigade, who had just arrived, threw themselves at the enemy with fixed bayonets and clubbed rifles. Elsewhere, British machine gunners and riflemen, freshly awake, swept the German lines pouring into Le Cateau. Soon, hundreds of Germans lay dead on the edge of town. The British briefly prevailed and held the attack. Yet the night battle was a prelude to the true onslaught that day (26 August), at a time when a great gap had opened up between Smith-Dorrien's and Haig's men.

In the early hours of 26 August, the British forces – reinforced by the arrival of elements of the 14,500-strong 4th Division – absorbed massed German attacks, which drew on seemingly limitless supplies of men. For the next 11 hours the British fought like demons – just as the French troops were doing, on a larger and more deadly scale, to the east.

At Le Cateau, Kluck had in fact deployed three infantry divisions – about the same as the British. But the British were defending. The Germans had been ordered to 'punch through' resistance at any cost. Wave upon wave bore down on the British divisions. As one line fell, another immediately appeared, such was the extreme pressure on *time*. 'In front of us,' wrote one German soldier, 'there still swarmed a number of scattered English troops, who . . . again and again forced us to waste time in deployment, as we could not tell what their strength might be.'[12]

Of the many acts of courage on both sides that day, one received the highest validation. Fred Holmes, 24, a lance corporal in the King's Own Yorkshire Light Infantry, carried a badly wounded man on his back for over three kilometres until he found stretcher-bearers, then returned to the front line to help remove the guns, where he was himself badly wounded. Holmes's action received the Victoria Cross for bravery.[13]

The British lines began to break, chewed up by heavy artillery strikes, which demonstrated for the first time the terrible effects of air-bursting shrapnel shells on entrenched lines of men. Smith-Dorrien ordered a withdrawal at 5 pm, but it did not reach everyone. The Gordon Highlanders never received it. The worst single disaster for the BEF in that first month was the virtual destruction of the 1st Gordon Highland regiment, who lost their way in the dark and found themselves marching into the German lines, thinking they were French. On recognising the enemy, the Germans opened fire and wiped out the stray soldiers within minutes.

The British escape from Le Cateau was extremely tricky. It would never have succeeded without the aid of the French Cavalry Corps, commanded by General André Sordet, who covered the British left flank as they withdrew. Of the 40,000 British and Germans who fought at Le Cateau, Smith-Dorrien lost about 5000 killed, wounded or taken prisoner, and 38 guns.[14] Yet his decision to stand and fight seriously delayed the German advance and is now seen as one of the most critical holding actions of the war.

During the withdrawal from Le Cateau some British troops came upon the hideous handiwork of the invaders on the civilian population: a hospital, clearly marked with a Red Cross flag, fiercely burnt. It had contained 400 wounded (an unknown number escaped the furnace). Strewn about the main street lay 'horrible evidence that *they* had been at work'. 'Mingled with dead or wounded combatants,' wrote Major Corbett-Smith, 'were bodies of women and children many terribly mutilated, while other women knelt beside them, with stone-set faces or gasping through hysterical weeping. From behind shutters or half-closed doors others looked out, blinded with terror.' One image never left his mind, he later wrote:

> Hanging up in the open window of a shop, strung from a hook in the cross-beam, like a joint in a butcher's shop, was the body of a little girl, five years old, perhaps. Its poor little hands had been hacked off, and through the slender body were vicious bayonet stabs.[15]

At the sight, Corbett-Smith's brigade 'saw red': 'There was no more talk of taking prisoners.' They streamed out of Le Cateau, their trucks, carts and horses laden with French civilians, mostly women, who had pleaded to be taken away.

—

The British headed south through Péronne, St Quentin and Noyon, Compiègne and Soissons, passing Villers-Cotterêts, Verberie and

Néry, and other towns whose names were scorched into the memories of the men who fought there, or tried to rest there, or simply
wished to stop there, exhausted, hungry and ever anxious to know
when they would regroup and *fight back*.

Reversals on the battlefield had not crushed the soldiers' spirits.
At several points down the long route south, they would stop and
fight further short delaying actions. They longed to enact Joffre's
words, 'to resume the offensive', to turn, regroup and take the war
back to the Germans. 'Everybody got very sick of [the retreat],' wrote
the British officer Aubrey Herbert, 'and all day long one was hearing
officers and men saying how they wanted to turn and fight.'[16] Victory
depended on the right moment. Joffre initially planned to launch
the counter-offensive at the line of the Somme River, 120 kilometres south-west of Mons. That swiftly proved optimistic. In fact, the
retreat would take the Allied armies to the very edge of Paris.

A few miles north of St Quentin, the enemy again fell upon the
Allied heels. Shells burst ever closer. 'The Germans are just behind!'
shouted an orderly, running through the terrified crowds of civilians towards the weary soldiers. A staff officer ordered the columns
to retire in St Quentin, 'and then there was one mad rush', recalls
Corbett-Smith.[17] Soon, St Quentin, too, fell to the *teutonicus furioso*.

One town, wrote Aubrey Herbert, 'was pitch-black except where
the torches glowed on the faces and on the bayonets of the men, or
where shells flashed and burst.' Soissons was 'a sunlit town of the
dead. Four out of five houses were shut. Most of the well-to-do
people had gone. It was silent streets and blind houses. The clatter-
ing which Moonshine [his horse] made on the cobbles was almost
creepy.'[18]

On 28 August, near Noyon, 19-year-old Rupert William Cave-
Orme, an officer in the Lincolnshire Regiment, volunteered to get
rations from the last train in town: 'Raised a van from Army S.C.
drove to station through double columns of dead beat men, horses
and guns and arrived just in time to stop the supply train, talk with
General of Staff. Rations to men at 1am . . .'[19] The medical officer

who witnessed Cave-Orme's courage promised to recommend him for a decoration but was killed before he could do so. Rations were rushed to the hungry troops.

The grim procession continued south for another week: motor cars, lorries, ammunition carts, wheeled artillery, cavalry patrols and long columns of dirty, ragged, bearded men, their losses unknown, bandaged wounded lying on medical trucks, crying out, or trudging along as best they could, knowing that to fall meant death or captivity. ('It is impossible now to rescue wounded men,' Aubrey Herbert's commanding officer told him.[20]) These were interspersed with ordinary French villagers, terrified women and children, borne down by what they could carry, strung out for miles in flight from the distant rumble, which shrouded the northern horizon like a dust storm. Nobody knew where or when the retreat would end.

Bridges were blown behind them, most spectacularly the beautiful arch over the River Oise, near Compiègne. It was 'one long ghastly nightmare', wrote Corbett-Smith. Much staff work at retreating corps and division headquarters fell to pieces – not that any men lost their heads, he said, but military order could not keep pace with the frenzied momentum of the German attack. Men got lost, cut adrift from the lines through sheer exhaustion or their wounds. Horses, too hungry to drag the artillery or supply carts, collapsed and were shot: 'push the poor beast out of the road. An old pal, was he? Aye, he was a fine "wheeler", that dark bay! . . . Nothing matters now but keeping on the move. Yes, better shoot him. He deserves a clean end.'[21]

One of the youngest soldiers in the BEF was 16-year-old trumpeter Jim Naylor, of the 30th Brigade Ammunition Column (3rd Division), whose parents were in India. He wrote in late August:

Dear Dad, Mother and Eileen [his sister],
I am still keeping quite well . . . We get very good food . . . sometimes a loaf between 3 or 4 men. We also get a piece of bacon and cheeses and some jam. We get plenty of tobacco and

cigarettes but I always give mine away. We get an issue of rum about two or three times a week, but I don't have any of that. I have not seen any of our Indian troops out here yet but I have seen a lot of French Indians or Africans . . . It is just beginning to get cold now, so do you mind sending me a pair of gloves. Put them in a box and make them very secure please will you. I won't be sorry when this is all over. Yes we were at Mons right enough and I hope we won't have anymore retiring like that. No I don't do much sleeping in barns, etc. It is a lot healthier outside in the open. The barns generally have plenty of insects about don't they? Well I think I had better dry up, I hope you get this letter safely . . .

Your loving, Jim[22]

At the opposite end of the hierarchy was Brigadier Robert Scott-Kerr, one of the most highly ranked British casualties of the retreat. Educated at Eton and Trinity College, Cambridge, Scott-Kerr was commissioned with the 24th Regiment of the South Wales Borderers in 1879, after they had been cut to pieces during the Zulu Wars. He subsequently fought in the Sudan Campaign (1885) and the Boer War (1900–02), where he received a Distinguished Service Order. In France, he commanded the 4th (Guards) Brigade, 2nd Division. Severely wounded in the thigh at Villers-Cotterêts on 1 September, he was sent home, where he would lead a unit of the Home Guard for the rest of the war. He retired in 1919 with the honorary rank of brigadier general.

—

An hour's clash that morning, in an orchard on the west side of the Oise River, near the village of Néry, produced one of the bravest actions of the war. Captain Edward Bradbury's L Battery, of the Royal Horse Artillery, were groping their way through thick fog when suddenly a whole column of German cavalry loomed out of the white soup. A British officer galloped away to warn the brigade;

the battery took cover. Soon, the fog cleared to reveal, on the crest of a hill not 550 metres away, six German regiments, dismounted and standing beside their 12 guns. Bradbury's men had time to swing three guns into action, but the storm of German shot and shell swiftly demobilised two, leaving one British gun functioning. 'Captain Bradbury went to get ammunition from a wagon,' witnessed the Irishman, Sergeant David Nelson, 'but he only got about 4 yards . . . when a shell from the enemy completely cut both his legs off midway between knees and body.'[23] With phenomenal strength, Bradbury then 'propped himself up and continued to direct the fire until he fell dead'.[24] Nelson and Sergeant Major Thomas Dorrell stayed with the gun – the only one in operation against eight German guns – and, despite both being badly wounded, kept firing until they expended their ammunition. Nelson refused orders to retire.

Most of L Battery were annihilated in that hour. Nelson wrote:

> During the awful carnage, the moaning of dying men and horses were audible amidst the terrific thundering of cannon; the scenes in most cases beyond description. One man in full view of me had his head cut clean off his body. Another was literally blown to pieces, another was practically severed at the breast, loins, knees and ankles. One horse had its head and neck completely severed from the shoulders.[25]

In the breech of his rifle, Nelson found a mass of flesh and blood torn from a man's head; the body lay nearby. He later found nine bullet holes in his jacket, which he had taken off and left on the ground beside him. British reinforcements arrived and poured steady fire onto the German flank, driving them back. Eight of the German guns were captured.

The surviving British units marched all night, until 10 am on 2 September. '[The infantry] threw away everything just carried their ammunition and rifles', wrote the stretcher-bearer Sergeant David

Lloyd-Burch, of No. 10 Field Ambulance, 4th Division (*sic* all that follows). 'I think this was the worst march we had. men were beginning to get broken down, you would see men walk out of the ranks exhausted. all those what fell out were either killed or taken prisoners. the Germans made our English troops suffer.'[26]

Lloyd-Burch was ordered to find more stretcher squads in Néry:

> my first case was a poor Dragoon. a part of his back had been blown away. he died before I could remove him . . . Capt Bradbury RHA was among the dead, he had both legs blown off. we got two more carts filled with dead but had to leave them as the Germans were advancing again. before leaving we found six more wounded men. These we placed in a country cart . . . we walked with these poor wounded men. how they screamed. their wounds were bad and the jolt of the carts on the rough roads. I was thankful when we got to our field ambulance . . .[27]

That night, the Germans found Nelson in the hospital in Néry, when they overran the town. A bullet had punctured his lung, and he couldn't breathe when lying down. They took him away. Later, he managed to escape, reached the French lines, 'and was found by the sister of Lord Kitchener in a dazed condition at Dinant'.[28] Bradbury, Nelson and Dorrell were each awarded the Victoria Cross, Bradbury posthumously. Nelson managed a near-miracle: he survived his wounds, escaped German captivity and rejoined the British lines, only to be killed in action on 8 April 1918. Dorrell lived until 1971.

Around this time, Aubrey Herbert was badly wounded in the side. His experience typifies what happened to many of the immobile: they were left behind. 'The Red Cross men gave a loud whistle when they saw my wound, and said the bullet had gone through me.' As the Germans approached, Herbert urged the medical officers to leave: 'they . . . would only get killed or taken themselves'. So they gave him morphia, placed him in a stretcher and left. He then lost consciousness. He woke to see 'a German with a red beard, with the sun shining on his helmet and bayonet . . . looking like an angel of death'. He prodded near Herbert with his bayonet: 'it seemed to me that there was going to be another atrocity'. Instead, the German soldier was 'extraordinarily kind and polite. He put something under my head; offered me wine, water, and cigarettes.' The German forces then passed in great crowds. 'They seemed like steel locusts.' Some were 'very unpleasant'. One waved his bayonet under Nelson's nose and said, 'I would like to put this in your throat and turn it round and round.' The German medical staff later removed the bullet and dressed his wound. Herbert survived, and was sent into German captivity.[29]

—

Along the retreating French lines to the east, the dread of 'another Sedan' wrung anxiety from every regiment. The Germans were 'advancing on Paris, the heart of the country, at furious speed', Foch had warned.[30] The order went out to 'Fight in retreat'. The French troops did so with suicidal determination, blowing up roads and bridges as they went, rounding on the Germans when topographic advantages or landscapes familiar to French commanders presented themselves.

On hundreds of occasions, as they fell back through town after town – Sedan, Maissin, Signy L'Abbaye, Rethel, Guise-St Quentin – they turned and confronted the German flanking movements that swirled around them. Often, they were forced to charge with fixed bayonets the German troops who had got around to the rear, in order to cut through. At Guise-St Quentin (28–29 August), the ever-reluctant Lanrezac rekindled something of his old self-confidence. In a stunning German reversal, with echoes of Smith-Dorrien at Le Cateau, Lanrezac turned his forces on Guise and retook the town. It was but a soupçon of hope. Bülow's unstoppable counter-offensive soon prised the French off, and Joffre dismally authorised Lanrezac to resume the retreat. On the 30th, the Fifth Army abandoned Guise to the invader, blowing up the bridges over the Oise as they went.

The delay at least gave Joffre breathing space to establish the new Sixth Army on the north-east periphery of Paris.

—

Meanwhile, at Lexy, a village in the Meurthe-et-Moselle, in deepest Lorraine, the hesitant stretcher-bearer Raymond Clément's unit:

> suddenly receives the order to leave . . . We jump in a ditch, and run away in a single file, while the bullets whistle all around us. Behind us, Lexy is bombed with incendiary shells. The village is burning. We left just in time! . . . [N]o one informs us of the fact [of the retreat]. The commanders lie to us to make us walk day and night. They talk about strategic issues. We finally learned the truth many months later! . . . A day ago they were talking about victory![31]

Further south, on 30 August, 'hundreds of men are falling' in a battle at Fosses, Clément wrote. He went on:

> For the first time we can do our stretcher-bearing job. Guided by the doctor, we search the battlefront with our flashlights [for] a lieutenant's body, killed during the action. Our team finds him under a hedge, close to a hole made by a '210' [shell]. The soil still smells of sulphur . . . I will never forget this horrible sight. The lieutenant is here, lying on the ground, without convulsing, still wearing his handsome black and red uniform. One of his gloved hands still carry the whistle that hangs from his neck. But his head is cracked open. The right side of his skull has been completely scalped by shrapnel, and half of his head is gone. Blood and brain spread around him . . . We have to load him in the stretcher to bring him into the village. I am so horrified that I can't help my friends do it. We finally carry the stretcher on our shoulders. His head and his wound are just beside me. Despite the darkness of the night, I can sometimes see the hole

in his head, and I have the feeling that the viscous mixture that goes out of it will reach through the stretcher to touch me. Our mournful procession joins the ambulances in the middle of the night.

The next day, Clément recorded:

we care for the wounded . . . The poor mutilated men scream and laugh at the same time because of the fever. They talk and talk about their wounds, their transportation, their future. The doctor's hands, reddened with blood, pour the iodine solution into these horrible wounds. The doctor talks slowly: 'my poor man'. But we receive news: the Germans are back . . . We quickly load as many wounded as we can in the trucks, the carts and every other vehicle we can find in the village . . . But we managed to evacuate everybody. But when it is our turn to leave, we have to abandon some poor men in the barn.

In early September, Clément and his fellow stretcher-bearers survived another fire fight:

it is a real miracle that we are all alive . . . We hardly had any time to recover, before we were ordered to leave again, but a French Dragoon rides by with a gun in his hand. He yells: 'Where are you going? Are you running away? Go back and fight the enemy!' We struggle to explain that we can't fight with instruments and stretchers.[32]

Elsewhere in the carnage, young Maurice Leroi had thoughts only for his mother. He wrote on 1 September:

I won't tell you what we are actually doing or where we actually are, I'd rather tell you about it when I come back home, because

I do believe I will survive the war, my lucky star protects me.
And what about you? Are you still doing fine? You bet we will
have a party when we meet again! I can't think of anything else
to tell you for the moment. With all my love,

Your loving son, Maurice[33]

Other French diarists limited themselves to the brutal facts. 'Starting
the 20th of August,' wrote Private Emile Fossey, 34, of Le Lorey,
'begins the retreat while fighting around Charleroi; back to France at
Rocroi, retreat through Guise, Marle, until Provins, always on foot
(50 to 60 Km per day) and still fighting, under a scorching heat and
without supply.'[34]

—

At the end of August, Ferdinand Foch was appointed commander
of the mobile 9th Army – the 'Foch Detachment' – formed on the
29th. On arriving at his Vitry HQ, he received 'a rude awakening': 'The front of the invasion now reaches from the Somme to the
Vosges.' In those few words, Foch realised that Belgium and all of
northern France to the River Somme were in German hands.

Yet Joffre's steadiness and the fact that the retreat, further south,
was becoming orderly and no longer forced gave Foch comfort.
The French and British were now *deciding to retire*, just as Joffre
had originally planned (see Map 5): the French Third Army would
pull back behind Verdun; the Fourth Army beyond the Aisne, from
Vouziers to Guignicourt; the Fifth Army to Laon; and the British
Army behind the Somme, from Ham to Bray. At the same time,
Joffre deployed the newly raised Sixth Army well out to the west, in
the area around Amiens, to contend with Kluck's far right wing. The
sense of an organised containment of the enemy was taking shape,
funnelling Kluck away from Paris, towards the valley of the Marne.

Foch's new division would cover the Fourth Army's right flank,
from the direction of Rocroi, and block the widening gap between
the Fourth and Fifth Armies. This meant that his men were to

fling themselves in the path of the German steamroller wherever it tried to gouge a hole in the French defences. 'You have been sent by Providence,' was how General de Langle de Cary, the exhausted Fourth Army commander, greeted Foch's arrival.

Foch moved quickly to reassign officers to units who had lost their commanders. Thousands of French officers were dead or wounded, and their men had no leaders: 'Some of the bravest of these troops, such as the Bretons of the XI Corps, were wandering about, incapable of accomplishing any useful result from lack of proper direction.'[35] Getting to know his men, Foch found great reserves of élan: the Moroccan Division were 'full of spirit' but in need of reinforcements; those who had suffered most, the XI Corps, at Maissin, 'were constantly asking for officers to be sent to lead them against the enemy once more'.[36]

But for how long? How much further? A cool exchange between Joffre and Foch, at around 7.30 pm on 31 August, at Fourth Army HQ in Monthois, answered the question. Foch replied that his men 'will have trouble holding on for two, let alone three days, in the face of hostile forces already identified as two corps . . .'. He gave three reasons. First, the Champagne area favoured the enemy: 'There are no strong positions for the defence, the woods are easily penetrated and no important streams afford us lines of resistance.' Second, the IX Corps' artillery was weak (a perennial problem). And, third, the men were fatigued.[37] The detachment had no choice other than to fall back further, in tandem with the Fourth Army, to seal up the gaps.

And so, bitterly authorising the retreat to continue, Joffre sent one of his abrupt rallying calls: 'All ranks must be made to understand that this retirement is being effected with a view to future operations, that it is not being forced upon us by the enemy.'[38]

If any moment defined the indomitable will of the French commander, surely this was it. Joffre had gilded the truth: in many places, the Germans were still, in fact, forcing the retreat. But it was a statement that envisaged a different future, with a powerful, implicit, morale-boosting truth: the French general could not contemplate defeat. His overriding priority was to restore the French *esprit de corps*, and, when the moment came, turn and resume the offensive.

———

The euphoria of victory sustained the exhausted German ranks, who had earlier seemed to be on a rampage. The 'very superior force' of the German Army had a 'tendency . . . to envelop me', Sir John French later conceded. 'I determined to make a great effort to continue the retreat till I could put some substantial object, such as the Somme or the Oise, between my troops and the enemy.'[39]

Sir John found neither. The scent of victory, of Paris, drove the Germans on. Yet, by the end of August, the German pace had slowed. Smith-Dorrien's brave stand at Le Cateau and Lanrezac's similar feat at Guise-St Quentin (28–29 August) had checked the enemy's advance. North of the Somme, Kluck still imagined the British were retreating westwards, to fall back on Calais. He was wrong: the *entire* French and British forces were withdrawing to the Marne Valley, due east of Paris, in a line between the capital and Verdun. But Kluck's perception of a divided enemy encouraged him to pursue the remaining French forces by swinging east inside Paris. His error of judgement played into the Allies' hands.

Though badly damaged, the British were far from destroyed, Kluck knew. Where were the prisoners, wondered Moltke's headquarters. The soldiers at the front wondered the same thing: where were the enemy? 'For two days now,' wrote the young German lieutenant Walter Delius (fighting near Maubeuge on 28 August), 'we have been hunting down the English, unfortunately they always managed to slip through our fingers time and again.'[40]

Kluck was unconcerned. The advance was close to schedule. 'During its fourteen days' offensive,' he later wrote, self-reverentially, 'the First Army had now completed two-thirds of the wheel through Brussels on Paris. The requirements of the strategic situation [i.e. the Schlieffen timetable] made it impossible to give any rest days in the true sense of the word. Marches and fights, battles and marches, followed one another without interval.[41] The result was the dissipation of German strength. The three German armies had lost more than five corps in that fortnight: two of Kluck's had been sent to invest Antwerp; and Bülow and Hausen had each lost a corps to the Eastern Front (despite Ludendorff's protesting that they weren't needed there). The rest, approaching 200,000 casualties, were dead or wounded. Can't be helped, the weakened right wing would continue the pursuit, Kluck decided. '[B]oth man and horse are capable of amazing achievements in war,' he assured himself, and pressed on. His communication lines, which stretched all the way back to Belgium, were his main concern.[42]

On 28 August, a telegram from the Kaiser congratulated the German Army on its 'brilliant successes' after winning 'rapid and decisive victories against the Belgian, the British and the French'.[43] Good news from Wilhelm tended to be the kiss of death – witness his delight at the Serbian reply and his misplaced faith in King George's 'neutrality'. The pattern persisted that day, with a decision that would mark the beginning of the end of Kluck's steamroller. Independent of Moltke and the German Supreme Headquarters (OHL), the field commander decided to act on his hunch of enemy weakness: he would pursue the flank of the French Army, 'force it away from Paris' (i.e. towards the east) and destroy it.[44]

Thus began Kluck's great 'wheel inwards', east of the capital, at a time when he and his staff were at their most confident. He presumed the British were incapacitated and fleeing west (they were withdrawing, in good order, south); the French were in a state of 'extreme depression' (they were aching to resume the attack – many were reported to be singing as they retired); and his forces in every battle had defeated the enemy 'in detail' (they had not). That night, by the light of campfires, the German officers sang patriotic songs 'taken up by thousands of voices'. The next morning, 'we resumed our march', wrote one of Kluck's officers, 'in the hope of celebrating the anniversary of Sedan before Paris'.[45]

Word of the 'rout' of France and Britain delighted the Austro-German press. 'The French defeated', headlined the Austrian paper *Die Neue Zeitung* on 24 August. 'Germans break through French fortification lines . . . The English cavalry tried to confront the German's victorious advance at Maubeuge. The German soldiers however didn't see the joke with those English mercenaries, so that the English cavalry brigade was miserably routed.'[46]

—

What did the German advance look like on the ground? It presented the horrific spectacle of an army of barbarians bleeding the country white, slaughtering everything in its path. Kluck's timetable coupled ignorance with callous disregard for his men. They were in a wretched state, yet he flogged his soldiers like pack horses until they dropped. The German soldier used his mind merely to coax his body forward, to prepare to fight, to plug holes in the gaps of the advance, to send his men to die in great numbers. The living rushed up to replace the dead or dying, in a seemingly endless supply of manpower. The wounded were carried back to hastily contrived field hospitals in the conquered terrain. Villages were commandeered and homes occupied, cellars and food stores ransacked, medical supplies pilfered, civilians threatened or shot if they refused to cooperate. Anything that fed the ravenous beast was gnawed to the bone.

Lieutenant Walter Delius participated in the ravages of France. He wrote in his diary on 30 August:

To handle the men with all the bad food and the red wine flowing . . . is often terribly difficult. Yesterday evening, one of my men . . . was so drunk that I had him tied to the wheel as a punishment. A horribly brutal measure, but we are at war. I no longer find it difficult to kick in a stranger's door and break all his windows. Some days ago, due to a lack of stables, I quartered part of my horses on linoleum and parquet flooring!! . . .

Next day, near the fortress of Maubeuge, Delius experienced

> another large-scale raid into the villages all around . . . We unceremoniously drove out all the inhabitants, cutting all telephone lines, searching all the houses, in particular of course all vicarages. We didn't find anything suspicious, except for several hundreds of carrier pigeons. I will never forget those scenes with all those poor displaced inhabitants.[47]

After the capture of Maubeuge – 'Hurrah, hurrah, hurrah,' he wrote, 'the fortress is in our hands, having surrendered all 40,000 men and 400 cannons' (and 15,000 bottles of wine) – his unit

> bombarded the villages around and set them alight. Ha, the way that crackled and burned! . . . Mothers and old people, surrounded by hordes of children, wander around the remains of their old homes, crying and helpless. Hundreds of beautiful cattle are lying in the meadows, killed by shrapnel. . . . When I marched through the ruined villages the other day, I kept asking myself, was that really necessary, did we have to cause that much destruction? . . . it is only once you have seen your own losses with your own eyes that you are gripped by a seething rage.[48]

A sense of compassion had not deserted every German. Herman Baumann, the army baker, wrote:

> Everywhere you see . . . houses shot to pieces and starving people. I was lying on my satchel in front of a shabby house, hunger was staring out of the eyes of a woman with her five children, I give the woman my sandwich, she is sharing it out amongst her children, crying.[49]

———

Further south, tremulous French villages awaited the invader.

Bernardine Dazin, a well-educated young woman, lived with her family in Équancourt, a village in the *département* of the Somme. Her father, Diogene Dazin, assisted the mayor (and would become mayor himself after the war). The family chose to stay as the Germans swept through and gave their house to the occupying forces (which later drew unjustified accusations of collaboration).

'This morning, it's a revolution in the village,' Bernardine wrote in her diary on the 27th. She continued:

> It is said 'the Germans are here'. A horrible day, fear is in every heart. People begin to panic. Ah! How close to God we are in these moments. He is our only source of strength and comfort. Every night the church is full for salvation. [But] the parishioners are running away in total disorder, some of them by cars, other by cart or just walking, with almost nothing. But we stay and we wait. We are resigned to be the witnesses of atrocities. Around noon, some English troops walk on the pavement. They are going to Étricourt.[50]

The next day:

> some Uhlans came to requisition our flour, our bread, our butter, our eggs . . . Lots of infantrymen are crowding [the village]. The cannons are aimed all around the houses on the uplands. We fear a battle. We put a mattress in the verandah in front of the glass door of the kitchen, and the cellar is ready for us . . .

Later that day, 'three pointed helmets pass in full gallop. At 8 o'clock at night, some German soldiers are singing, they say they are going to Paris.' The day after, 'we are astounded to learn that the Germans are close to Ham and are still advancing. We live in total ignorance without seeing anything else than the military cars rolling on the pavement.'[51]

As the retreat ground on, the horses' legs buckled and the animals fell forward, 'taking the skin off their knees'. For the men, 'the greatest strain', recalled Ben Clouting of the 4th Dragoon Guards, '. . . worse than any physical discomfort or even hunger was . . . fatigue. Pain could be endured, food scrounged, but the desire for rest was never-ending.' He fell off his horse 'more than once, and watched others do the same, slowly slumping forward, grabbing for their horse's neck . . . At any halt men fell asleep instantaneously.'[52] Many of the foot soldiers, or infantry, lost touch with the regiments and struggled along in ones and twos, cramming food in their mouths when it appeared – just biscuits and bully beef for the British.[53] Yet the Allied retreat grew less punishing the further south they went. Men's spirits rallied as the German pursuit petered out. In the British ranks, the old song resumed:

> Kaiser Bill is feeling ill,
> The Crown Prince, he's gone barmy.
> We don't give a fuck for old von Kluck
> And all his bleedin' army.

On the 4–5 September, the French and British armies reached the valley of the Marne. They had fallen back some 290 kilometres. The Allied armies had together lost more than 200,000 – the bulk of them French. That statistic reflected the French determination to redeem themselves and save their country. Behind them to the north, like a giant tendrilous organism, parasitic and irremovable, the German forces had attached themselves to their country, drawing sustenance from French villages and supply lines that stretched all the way back to the German railheads.

At the Marne, Joffre ordered a general halt. Here he would begin the preparations for the counter-offensive. In his mind there would be no further retreat. Every soldier would be primed to fight to the death. His immediate task was to communicate these momentous thoughts to his exhausted men.

—

The British public, meanwhile, woke up to news of the disaster. It seemed the Germans had crushed the BEF and the French forces, and advanced to within 50 kilometres of Paris. People despaired. The Americans offered no help and scorned the war: they had declared their neutrality on 4 August. Whitehall felt the Americans had misrepresented the case for and against it. Something had to be done. On 2 September, Arthur Benson, still grappling with the lyrics to 'Land of Hope and Glory', and still accused of near-traitorous sympathies with the Germans, attended the first meeting of the War Propaganda Unit, chaired by Charles Masterman. A dozen of Britain's finest writers and thinkers assembled at Wellington House at Buckingham Gate to find ways of 'selling' the war to the Americans and Italians, who, the British Government felt, had undermined it. Some began with the midday prayer, 'O God, guard and bless our sailors and soldiers, and give us victory and peace. Amen.'[54]

Benson wrote in his diary:

It was an extraordinary gathering. Galsworthy [the novelist John Galsworthy] cool bald and solemn, Conan Doyle [crime writer Arthur Conan Doyle] strong solid and good humoured, R Bridges [the Poet Laureate Robert Bridges] a glorious sight, wavy hair, black coat . . . Hall Caine [novelist Sir Thomas Henry Hall Caine] with long hair, high white collars, dressed [like] a Victorian statesman, Wells [science-fiction writer H. G. Wells] fat brown and . . . very smart, Chesterton [poet and critic G. K. Chesterton] enormous, steaming with sweat, his hair dripping . . . Hardy [novelist Thomas Hardy] very old and faded, Trevelyan [historian G. M. Trevelyan] very dark and gloomy, Murry [novelist and publisher John Middleton Murry] very bald and mild, Barrie [Scottish writer J. M. Barrie] small and insignificant, Arnold Bennett [novelist and critic] very pert and looking ever much a cad, Newbolt [poet and novelist Sir Henry Newbolt] cool and anxious . . . and many others who I didn't know.[55]

Little was decided. Trevelyan 'very unwillingly' read a manifesto, to polite applause. Everyone made a speech. Chesterton humorously declared that he was ready to write pamphlets that 'would appeal even to Americans'. Bennett said a few words 'in an incredibly cockney accent, Barrie in quite as incredible a Scotch accent said he would do a lecture in America . . .'. Benson 'could offer no suggestion myself', concluding, 'I don't think our strength lies in propaganda.'[56]

A few days later, Benson read the British commander's denigrating account of the extraordinary stand at the battle of Le Cateau: 'Sir John French's great despatch shows that our force was very nearly annihilated on Aug 26. The story of that awful retreat thrills me through and through.'[57] Benson, like most British people, had no idea of the total casualties inflicted thus far. French dead and wounded, in the month of August, totalled 206,515, out of a total field army of 1,600,000. The true figure, with the addition of officers and support divisions, approached 300,000.[58] The British were yet to experience casualties on this scale.

43

THE MIRACLE OF THE MARNE

Troops . . . must die where they stand rather than give way.
Under present conditions no weakness can be tolerated.
General Joseph Joffre's orders before the battle of the Marne

---

IN PARIS, the politicians could have used a piece of Joffre's Olympian calm. At news of French losses, they fought and bickered and stormed about like a gaggle of panicked geese. Furious rows, copious tears, stubborn gallic pride and, in Poincaré's presence, a numbing pretence of calm all climaxed in War Minister Adolphe Messimy's great tantrum of 29 August. He slammed the table with terrific force and ridiculed the government as 'an undignified farce', flinging in their faces the prophecy of the revered General Joseph Gallieni, who quietly had said in retirement what nobody would say in public: the Germans would be at the gates of Paris by 5 September. All their prodigious intellects and affectations of sangfroid were of little consequence in the face of the coming storm. Terrible rumours flew around the city of the rout of the French Army, of another Sedan, of the occupation of Paris. Lanrezac's stand at Guise-St Quentin lent a little relief, and then sank in the general swim of defeat, firing fears that Joffre and GHQ were misleading the politicians.

Poincaré stood by his supreme commander. Joffre, the president insisted, would resume the offensive when he and the Sixth Army were ready. Adolphe Messimy would not be consoled and foresaw 'a great defeat'. He thus became the political price of the failure of Plan XVII and was sacked.[1] (He later served bravely as an infantry officer. Twice wounded, he rose to divisional commander and liberated Colmar, proving himself more useful at the front than in the rear.) More truculently, General Victor Michel lost his job as military governor of Paris, for the same reasons that he'd lost his earlier command to Joffre: a want of offensive spirit. The apparent winner – or collector of the hospital pass – was General Gallieni, who came out of retirement like a French Cincinnatus to serve as the new military governor of Paris, tasked with defending the city without adequate resources or, yet, an army.

Few accolades have been denied this extraordinary figure. A tall, slender man 'with piercing eyes behind his glasses', Gallieni 'appeared to us as an imposing example of powerful humanity', observed Poincaré.[2] Formidably intelligent, multilingual, limitlessly resourceful, a veteran of Sedan, the conqueror of Madagascar, a colonial administrator and the only man to whom Joffre deferred (and who passed over the offer of supreme commander to the latter, his protégé, on account of ill health), Gallieni was, on his appointment as saviour of Paris, turning 66, ill with prostatitis and a grieving widower of a few weeks. He set to work with every last ounce of energy he could summon. Destined to play a critical role in the execution of the great battle of the Marne, his first priority was the fortification of the city. He took the pent-up disillusionment of his ailing years, and his disgust at the political arrivistes and mediocrities who surrounded him, and projected them with furious intensity on this last noble task before he died: to defend and preserve from the German hordes the most beautiful city in the world.

On his first day, he set to turning Paris into a vast entrenched camp. It would be a base for offensive action, not a closed fortress awaiting German besiegement.[3] To this end, Gallieni pleaded for troops: Paris had none. By 29 August, he had received a single naval brigade. In desperation, he turned to the people, and pressed into service every man, woman and child capable of using a trenching tool. Within a day, Gallieni had organised the delivery of 10,000 spades and, despite legal objections, 10,000 bowie knives, to complete the earthworks. Together, the citizens and soldiers ringed the city in a vast system of trenches and earthen barriers, pocked with 'wolf pits' – deep holes, embedded with spikes, flanked by barbed wire and guarded with nests of machine guns. Gallieni requisitioned all available means of transport, including the city's taxicabs, henceforth destined for immortality in their coming role in the battle. He overrode all petty legal objections and, like Joffre, purged his staff of the incompetent, the weak or the rule-bound. He shook Paris from its summer daze and vestigial romance, and cloaked its green parks and golden stone in the cold steel and grey hue of war.

Frustrated by the bureaucracy that required written permission to demolish buildings, Gallieni extended the Zone of the Armies to encompass the suburbs and the hinterland, to a radius of 32 kilometres north and east to Dammartin and Lagny. Demolition commenced. Peripheral buildings and bridges were blown, and valuable works of art retrieved and sent to Bordeaux. Gallieni issued orders, to be fulfilled if the Germans reached the city, to destroy the beautiful bridges, the Eiffel Tower (the radio transmission station) and other architectural jewels now reduced to the status of infrastructure useful to the enemy. Demolition squads were to raze whatever necessary to clear fields of fire.

The politicians were persuaded to leave Paris and move the seat of government to Bordeaux. They could not risk a repeat of Sedan and the humiliation of being imprisoned in the city. Gallieni made up their minds, telling them they were 'no longer safe in the capital'. On 3 September, a relay of trains carried the president, his ministers, secretaries, officials and the important State papers out of the city, as well as the most precious works of art from the Paris museums.[4]

After German planes dropped a few primitive bombs on the city in early September, the people needed no further warnings. Thousands of Parisians evacuated to the south. That day, Gallieni issued a proclamation to those who remained:

> CITIZENS OF PARIS, the members of the government of the Republic have left Paris to give a new impetus to national defence. I have been mandated to defend Paris against the invader. I will fulfil this mandate until the bitter end.[5]

But the city's future looked bleak. Without an army to defend it, Paris stood at the mercy of the enemy's siege guns and massed ranks. In Bordeaux, Poincaré clung to the hope that the Russians were then besieging Berlin. In fact, the Muscovites were being cut to pieces.

—

In early September 1914, everyone's attention turned to a gentle valley along the Marne River, due east of Paris, soon to be the scene of 'the most decisive land battle since Waterloo'.[6] As at Waterloo, a century before, the Marne would determine the fate of Europe and the world. This is not hindsight. Commanders and soldiers were palpably aware of it.

Such thoughts were furthest from the mind of Lieutenant Edward Spears in early August, as he lay floating in the Marne River, near Vitry, 'just a charming cool stream that none of us in our wildest dreams connected directly with the war'. Surely this 'lovely valley', he mused, was the last place on earth likely to see the French and British Armies, who had headed north and east with such confidence, straggle in with 'despair and rage gnawing at their hearts, footsore, weary, exhausted'. No prophet swam with him that day,

> to tell us that in years to come the name of the Marne would evoke, not a picture of a broad and sleepy stream, but of a gigantic battlefield, to be quoted for ever not only as one of the

great turning points in human history, but as one of the sixteen decisive battles of the world.[7]

The mind of Kluck offers a starting point to the mystery behind the Miracle of the Marne, as it was destined to be called. Until now, Kluck appeared to be the driver of events, at the head of Schlieffen's hammer blow, on which the whole German strategy relied. Yet, by the end of August, the French retreat had turned Kluck into the creature of Joffre's design. The retreat had dragged out the German supply lines and lured the Germans to the battlefield of Joffre's choice. 'The truth is [Kluck] was being led by the nose' was Keegan's pithy summary. 'Every mile he marched in pursuit of the Fifth Army, once he had crossed the Oise and headed towards the Marne, served Joffre's purpose.'[8]

The German armies had lost much of their strength, through attrition and the transfer of two reserve corps to the siege of Antwerp and two more to the eastern theatre. Their supply lines periodically buckled. 'The further course of the campaign,' Kluck later wrote, 'was to make the greatest possible demands on the capacity of the transport and supply columns, the life-blood of the Army.'[9] Fields of oats fed the horses, but the men had to live off the plunder of villages, or irregular deliveries coming down the great supply loop, delayed by Belgian and French sabotage, smashed bridges, roads and railheads, and reliant on 'wholly inadequate' cadres in the German Supply Service.[10]

If Ludendorff was among the few still listening to the whisper of Schlieffen's ghost – 'Keep the right wing strong!' – by the first week of September, nearing the 30th day of the war, Kluck's 'right wing' was weak and weakening. They were men, after all. They were exhausted, hungry and drank heavily: drunkenness seemed to enliven their spirits. Their uniforms were in rags. Only the prospect of a triumphal entry into Paris kept them going.

Kluck's original strategy – the vast encirclement of Paris from the west, which Moltke had pressed on him on 27 August – now yielded to the demands of expedience. On the morning of 29 August, Kluck made a now-famous decision, loaded with portent for the fate of Europe. The capital could wait; he would instead turn inside Paris and pursue the French forces in a south-easterly direction away from it, and there crush them between his, Bülow's and Hausen's armies. Bülow approved the 'inward wheel' – it would help him defeat the Fifth Army, which had escaped his forces at Guise. Both generals dismissed any further threat from the British, 'seemingly incapacitated at Le Cateau', and turned their sights on Lanrezac's flank (see Map 6).

The German headquarters (OHL), now located in Luxembourg, agreed to the change. To encircle Paris would have forced Kluck on a long, fruitless march west. Moltke's hasty approval of the new strategy reflected deep anxieties: time was running out. While assured that Germany had won a succession of victories, Moltke had not yet heard the magic words declaring a complete breakthrough or encirclement. His concerns deepened; the setback at Guise was a worrying omen. And there were large gaps opening up between the three German armies, an invitation to the French and British to stretch them wider. Nor were the retreating armies spent. Kluck got a taste of the enemy's strength when, on 1 September, the British forces turned and inflicted a ferocious counter-attack on his lines near Compiègne, then slipped away into the night. Once more, the German jaws snapped on the wisp of a phantom. Once again, 'old one o'clock' was left holding the vestiges of British kit, dumped by the roadside in their haste to escape.

On the night of 2 September, Kluck received a new General Order from OHL. It confirmed the decision to wheel inwards but added a humiliating instruction. 'The intention,' the message stated, 'is to drive the French back in a south-easterly direction, cutting them off from Paris.' Kluck was to follow Bülow's Second Army in echelon formation and protect the flanks of both. In other words, he was to 'exploit the success of the Second Army'. To a man of Kluck's ego, this was monstrous: his men had not marched more than 370 kilometres, through Belgium and France, merely to mop up after a rival general. He ignored the instruction and ordered his men to march on the existing line, leaving only a reserve corps behind to protect his right flank. The decision would later infuriate Bülow and fatally widen the gaps between the armies.

On 2 September, Kluck again displayed cavalier disregard for OHL. He dismissed fresh orders to outflank and destroy the British as 'fruitless' because 'the British Army had escaped from the enveloping movement just in time' and retired across the Marne in the direction of Coulommiers. 'A chance of dealing a decisive blow against the British Army was now no longer to be hoped for . . .'[11] He claimed to have encountered a British cavalry division east of Senlis, just north-east of the Paris defence line, but this was false: there were no British troops near Senlis. Kluck had encountered instead elements of Gallieni's Sixth Army, who were now limbering up to enact their contribution to the Allied counterblow.

—

In the French camp, the great white-haired commander did not panic. Joffre lumbered incongruously around his new GHQ, a converted girls' school at Bar-sur-Aube, monitoring the retreat, calmly examining his new plan and ever confident of something that eluded the importunate mortals who bustled about him in the twilight. Joffre possessed, to a rare degree, the Clausewitzian ingredient critical to military success: an unusual greatness of soul. The calamities that visited him would have crushed the strongest of men, but Joffre seemed to absorb adversity and transform it into opportunity. With every disaster, he grew in stature. Consider what he faced in those first few days of September:

- Sir John French had as good as broken under the pressure and lost Joffre's confidence. The British commander had threatened to retire so far south of the Seine that he appeared to be abandoning his French allies. That was how it seemed to Joffre. That was how it seemed to Kitchener, in London, when Sir John's report arrived on 31 August. The Cabinet listened in alarm as Kitchener gravely read out the letters of Sir John's handling of the retreat. 'You will,' Kitchener instructed his field commander in response, 'as far as possible conform with the plans of General Joffre for the conduct of the campaign.' Sir John failed to do as ordered. In fact, Sir John and Joffre 'had never yet been within a mile of the heart of each other', in the devastating verdict of Sir William Roberston, the British quartermaster general.[12] Sir John seemed not to understand Joffre's design, which Henry Wilson had clearly translated for him. Losing patience with the unruly field marshal, Kitchener deemed it necessary to go to Paris personally to order Sir John to act as instructed. The size of Sir John's rank and reputation stayed the hand of his executioner, for now. (Largely the architect of his own demise, Sir John would later dare to undermine the author- ity of Kitchener, leading to the termination of his command in December 1915. General Haig, who had intrigued against him, would replace him.)

– By early September, nobody knew precisely where the French and British should stop, turn and fight. Line after line, from Charleroi to the Somme to Guise-St Quentin, had failed to hold the German invasion. Joffre had earlier intended to launch the counter-offensive as far back as the Seine.[13] However, aerial reconnaissance and the near-mirac- ulous discovery of maps and vital intelligence on a dead German officer's body confirmed Kluck's redirection to the south-east. So Joffre resolved on a separate plan: to continue the withdrawal away from Paris, giving him time to bring up reinforcements (including two corps from the First and Second Armies on the Moselle), to extricate his forces from the constant threat of envelopment, and to replenish them.

– On 1 September, the anniversary of Sedan, Joffre
received news of the German victory over the Russians
at Tannenberg. Their great ally had not reached Berlin,
as hoped. Darkness spread over France at the news. The
grimmest portents affrighted the politicians and staff
officers.

Oblivious to the counsel of despair, Joffre devoted the first few days
of September to reinforcing and reorganising the French armies, and
developing a plan for the counter-offensive. He did so with exceptional gusto and versatility, despite the initial objections of Gallieni
and his staff. They questioned the instruction that the newly formed
Sixth Army, under General Maunory, should attack Kluck's right
flank, because it denied Paris its only defensive army. Yet, on seeing
the evidence of Kluck's swing to the south-east, Gallieni immediately fell into line with Joffre's plan. 'They offer us their flank! They
offer us their flank!' shouted Gallieni's two most senior staff officers
(see Map 6). Gallieni himself now acted with the gazelle-like agility
of a man half his age: the Sixth Army would attack Kluck's flanks as
soon as Joffre gave the order.

The only act that strained Joffre was his painful decision to
relieve General Lanrezac. The Fifth Army (and *not* the British
Army, as the English press liked to think) had borne the brunt of
the German invasion. They had fought Kluck and Bülow all the
way from Belgium to the Marne Valley. If Lanrezac had technically
disobeyed orders, his actions had saved the Fifth Army and delivered what Joffre needed: troops. On the Sambre, he had failed; at
Guise, he excelled. 'But the constant factor, the trait that emerges
constantly in the story of the retreat of the Fifth Army, is the reluctance of its Commander to fight,' concluded Spears.[14] True enough,
yet, had he fought, Lanrezac may have bled his army to death and
fallen on the Marne with nothing but an empty kitbag to show
Joffre. But failure, or the perception of failure, demanded heads,
and Joffre had lost confidence in his general. Lanrezac also seemed

profoundly depressed. On 3 September, Joffre replaced him with General Franchet d'Espèrey, the mercurial little veteran of Indochina and Africa, whom the English dubbed Desperate Frankie. Lanrezac seemed relieved, according to Joffre's memoir; not so, according to Lanrezac's.

—

On 3 and 4 September, the great armies drew up on the Marne. Bend your mind to comprehend the scene on the ground: hundreds of thousands of troops straddling a broad river valley, on a front that stretched 240 kilometres west to east, from the outskirts of Paris to the city of Verdun, beyond which lay the north–south front, on the Moselle, where Generals Edouard de Castelnau and Fernand de Langle de Cary had hitherto held back the massed ranks of Prince Rupprecht, then itching to break through and deliver Paris to Berlin. For four bloody weeks, the French had held the German lines bristling on the Moselle, with a casualty rate that knew few precedents in military history. Even at this critical hour, Castelnau warned Joffre that Nancy may fall at any time. Joffre asked him to hold on for 24 hours. Their resilience would prove critical. If the Germans broke through from the east, Joffre's planned counter-offensive would collapse.

From the north, mile after mile of German troops, hundreds of thousands of men, approached the Marne Valley, virtually sleep-walking, bedraggled, unfed. Kluck, Bülow and Hausen thought nothing of force-marching these lads 40 kilometres on 3 September, at the end of which they literally fell into their billets. Their glittering prize seemed within reach and sustained them: Paris. Here was their Cannae, their Sedan, the moment they dispatched the enemy once and for all. The Marne would be a mop-up, not a battle, they were told: the French and British were decimated. Disinformation such as this kept them going. Wasn't the enemy suing for peace? Hadn't the French offered terms? So ran the rumours.

In OHL's Luxembourg chateau, Moltke lurked in a state of

fitful depression, curiously resilient to the harbingers of good news. He brooded on the scene like a vulture witnessing a distant carcass spring to life. No news of a victory for days, yet the Germans were supposed to be 'advancing triumphantly in all directions', he wondered. Their horses were now dying, and there were very few equine vets. Little bread was getting through, and a serious shortage of shells loomed. 'Logistically, Schlieffen's plan was a nonsense,' Hew Strachan concluded of the supply failure.[15] And where were the prisoners? There were none. The French were said to be singing – singing! – in retreat. Something strange was going on, Moltke ruminated, in the far hills of the Marne Valley.

On the morning of the 4th, Moltke acted on his doubts. He sent an operational order that admitted, for the first time, the failure of the Schlieffen Plan: the right wing had not achieved its goal, 30 days after the invasion of Belgium. The enemy had evaded the enveloping attacks of Kluck and Bülow, and had 'joined up with the forces of Paris'. The German armies would halt north of the Marne Valley, rest and await reinforcements before the final attack. Halt? If Schlieffen could turn in his grave, he would have done so then. Had Moltke lost his mind, senior Prussians in Berlin, such as von Falkenhayn, wondered. Why halt so near the prey? Why stall on the threshold of victory? Moltke, on the contrary, decided to consolidate and rest his armies for he had sensed the danger developing on the far right flank, signs of activity emanating from an unexpected source: the French capital. Premonitions of disaster rippled through Moltke's castle.

—

The mood in the French camp sprang forward that day. Gallieni energised his men for the attack. He needed Joffre's nod and the British support. At 9.45 am, he phoned Joffre. Joffre would not, or could not, come to the phone. Gallieni's staff officer pressed upon the French GHQ the urgency. Hours passed. Lunch arrived. Gallieni's man phoned again. When the call came, Joffre and his staff were arguing over a map: should they wait a day, pull back to the Seine, regroup and attack fresh? Or seize the moment offered by Kluck's error and launch the attack almost immediately? Could the French soldiers summon the strength, unrested, to take the battle straight back to their tormentors? Gallieni finally got Joffre on the line. If the fresh Sixth 'Mobile' Army were going to attack, they should do so as soon as possible, he advised, to break Kluck's right flank. If so, that meant the whole of the French force should attack at the same time, to concentrate the blow.

When? Were they ready? Joffre dispatched the questions to his commanders, Foch, d'Espèrey and de Langle, and waited under a tree in the playground of the girls' school for their replies. 'For most of the afternoon,' Tuchman writes, 'the ponderous figure in his black tunic, baggy red pants, and army-issue boots from which, to the despair of his aides, he had banished the affectation of spurs, remained silent and motionless.'[16]

Elsewhere that afternoon, Sir John French absented himself from two critical meetings, convened by Gallieni and d'Espèrey. Both French generals were determined to persuade the British to join the attack, which they hoped would start the next day. Sir John had, as expected, refused. So Gallieni himself drove to the British headquarters to persuade Sir John that the British forces were essential, in plugging the gap between the Fifth and Sixth Armies. Sir John wasn't there, and Gallieni received only the refusals of Sir Archibald Murray, the British chief of staff: the men needed rest and reinforcements (Murray himself had suffered a near-physical breakdown during the retreat from Mons, and would be relieved from his post in 1915). All true, and yet the hour had come to act, Gallieni insisted. Murray promised to pass on his message to Sir John, nothing more.

Then, at Bray, at 3 pm, Sir John failed to appear at a second meeting, prearranged with Franchet d'Espèrey, who had hoped to establish a workable relationship with the British field marshal, or salvage something from the wreckage of the latter's relations with Lanrezac.

The ubiquitous Henry Wilson showed up instead and struck a chord with d'Espèrey, as Wilson tended to with lively, aggressive French generals.

'You are our ally,' d'Espèrey told Wilson, 'I shall keep no secrets from you.' He then read out Joffre's letter, which asked the French generals if they were ready to attack. 'I am going to answer that my army is prepared,' d'Espèrey said. 'I hope you will not oblige us to do it alone.'[17] Pleased to find an aggressive, kindred spirit, Wilson agreed at once that Britain must join the offensive – pending Sir John's approval. (Elsewhere, Foch simply sent word back to Joffre: 'Ready to attack.')

Joffre had reached the same decision and issued General Order No. 6 at 10 that night, 4 September: 'The time has come to profit by the adventurous position of the German First Army and concentrate against that army all efforts of the Allied Armies of the extreme left.'[18] All the Allied forces would rejoin the battle. Separate orders were sent to the French Third and Fourth Armies on the Moselle front. The counterblow would commence on 7 September. A great flurry of messages and phone calls rallied the commanders to their posts.

The next day dawned on frenzied activity in the French camp. The night before, Joffre had conceded Gallieni's point: the attack must start at dawn on 6 September, a day earlier than planned. A lightning attack by the Sixth Army from the east of Paris offered a far better chance of snapping the stem of Kluck's army. Yet nothing was assured. That day, the Germans showed why they were still so dangerous, when General von Gronau, on Kluck's far right wing, attacked the Sixth Army's probing forces with astonishing force and speed. This fierce prelude ran well into the night, alerting Kluck to French strength on his right flank, which at the time was dangerously exposed because he had unwisely crossed the Marne River, leaving only one reserve corps to guard his flank and rear north of the river. Thus, the battle of the Marne 'opened a day earlier . . . and on terms dictated by the enemy'.[19]

—

But what of Sir John French, who seemed to be disappearing south, and of whom nobody had heard a word? He was last in touch on the 4th, when he had insisted on continuing his retreat, 15–25 kilometres beyond the Seine. The British commander had thoroughly lost his nerve, thought Joffre, who took the precaution of sending Order No. 6 by special courier to the British HQ, in the village of Melun. In response, Sir John simply dallied further and did nothing. All the entreaties of Gallieni, d'Espèrey, Joffre and Wilson had failed to budge the baton-wielding Briton.

To a man, it seemed, the BEF were eager to resume battle and restore their self-esteem. Yet never before had the cliché 'lions led by donkeys' (or one donkey) seemed so apt. Their actual destiny existed in the state of curious limbo in Sir John's head. At 9.15 am, according to Spears, whose memoir is understandably charitable to his commander, Sir John seemed to accede to Joffre's request to join the French offensive. Yet his actual position remained unclear. '[T]he details of the marches', Sir John wrote, were 'being studied'.[20] This was not good enough, Joffre insisted, in a long telegram to Adolphe Messimy, the French minister of war, imploring him to intervene. 'To obtain victory,' Joffre wrote, 'I shall drive the blow home with all our forces, holding absolutely nothing back. It is essential that the British Army should act likewise . . .' In a measure of Joffre's unrelenting determination, he asked the minister to renew the pressure on Sir John, adding, 'If I could give orders to the British Army as I would give them to a French Army holding the [same] position, I would attack immediately.'[21]

To no avail. So Joffre personally resolved to fix the problem. If Sir John would not come to France, France would go to Sir John. Joffre drove 185 kilometres to the British headquarters (the French commander tended to be driven everywhere, at great speed, packing hundreds of kilometres into his weekly peregrinations up and down the lines). The historians Tyng, Tuchman, Spears and Keegan have tenderly rendered this famous meeting. Into Sir John's chateau strode Joffre, followed by his staff. They found the British field marshal 'looking as usual as if he had lost his last friend', flanked by Archibald Murray, Henry Wilson and Victor Huguet, the prickly French liaison officer who always seemed to linger over crises. Unusually, Joffre was the first to speak. He spoke as he had never done, in war or peace, with a passion that astonished his British audience. His outstretched arms 'seemed to throw his heart on the table'. '[T]he lives of all French people,' Joffre declared – to 'appeal' or 'plead' was not his style – 'the soil of France, the future of Europe' depended on Britain joining the battle. The supreme moment had arrived: 'I cannot believe the British Army will refuse to do its share in this supreme crisis . . . history would severely judge your absence.' He concluded with a clenched fist, brought down hard on the table, 'Monsieur le Marechal, the honour of England is at stake!'[22]

There followed the strangest sight. Sir John 'suddenly reddened . . . slowly tears came into [his] eyes . . . and rolled down his cheeks'. He struggled to say in French, 'We will do all we possibly can.' Wilson translated this, for Joffre's uncomprehending ears, 'The Field Marshal says "Yes".'[23] The British retreat would halt; the men would about-face and join the attack. At our great distance, Joffre's sigh of relief is almost audible.

Tea followed. And then, with 'the Field Marshal's word' in his pocket, Joffre returned to his new HQ, a converted monk's cell at Châttilon-sur-Seine, where he gathered his generals and staff: 'Gentlemen, we will fight on the Marne.' The orders cascaded through the ranks and stiffened every sinew. That evening, all through the French and British camps, the troops prepared for battle. Joffre's last orders of the day resounded in every soldier's mind: 'Troops who can no longer advance must at any cost keep the ground that has been won, and must die where they stand rather than give way. Under present conditions no weakness can be tolerated.'[24]

—

In Paris that afternoon, General Maunory, commander of the Sixth Army, asked Gallieni where his line of retreat should be, in the event that he should be overwhelmed. 'Nowhere,' Gallieni replied.[25] Every French soldier must fight to the death. Thus spoke the voice of vengeance for Sedan and the humiliation of the retreat, which reso-nated with the poilu, who seethed to get back in the fight.

So too did the BEF. That evening, a British major, briefed for the attack, approached his men with a spring in his step. They jumped up. 'Paris?' they asked. 'Not – not – is it advance, sir?' The major nodded: 'We are going to advance.' A cheer went up, 'which must have startled the French government in Bordeaux', recalls Corbett-Smith. The drivers rushed to their horses; the gunners rushed to the limbers to help hook in. 'The major stood up in his stirrups with a splendid laugh in his eyes: "Sub-sections right-about-wheel! Walk, march!"'[26] The great retreat had ended. 'What a glorious day,' wrote Sergeant Bradlaugh Sanderson, of the 2nd King's Royal Rifle Corps. 'Instead of going to Paris, we are to take the offensive . . . There wasn't half a cheer.' The Tommies struck up renditions of 'It's a Long Way to Tipperary' and 'Rule Britannia' as they marched off.[27]

On the eve of battle, many Frenchmen similarly believed they were being forced back on the capital. Maurice Leroi wrote on 5 September:

> Dear mother, . . . we are constantly retreating, we are even talking about withdrawing to Paris, but you shouldn't be frightened about this, because there must be some underlying reasons for this decision . . . which makes me think that we are trying to lure them into a trap? Anyway, trying to understand the regiment is just a waste of time . . . Tell me how you are doing. Your loving son etc.[28]

The troops had little time to write to loved ones, driving the passion-ate Marie Dubois to despair of 'my André'. Recollecting their honey-moon, she wrote:

You were my husband for a few hours and . . . even if the future frightened me (not from a physical point of view), I was happy. But I was much more happier in February . . . because you weren't just the ordinary husband that I desired, you were my André, the André who hadn't left my thoughts at any moment . . . the André whom I wanted to live for, to passionately love him with all my soul and body. This is what this road makes me think about, and I restrain my tears . . . With love, Marie

A week later, she glumly appealed to him:

If the card that I received yesterday from you was short, I think it's because you're a little upset about not having received any news from me. However I have already written you 22 letters with this one. Last night I dreamed that you wrote me a very long letter. I wish it was true, I really do!

In late September, she would despair, 'It's becoming harder and harder to wait for your news. The last letter I received was from last Monday, and you didn't say much . . . I really would like to live your life a little . . .'[29]

The army chaplains and padres tried to ease the soldiers' nerves, by talking to the nervous and hearing confessions (if Catholic). Fearful young men found spiritual solace in their gentle admonishments. Other troops were less inclined to see the possibility of divine intervention in the horror and bloodshed of war, and ignored the clerics. Pastor Meyersiek continued to correspond with German soldiers from his village of Oetinghausen. His first letter to arrive on the Marne read:

My dear comrades . . . we are praying for you . . . Every Wednesday we congregate at 8.30pm before God to shine God's light on the war, and to remember all of you before the Lord. . . . my greetings from home [are] born of the realisation of the great perils your body and soul are facing out there, in morally depraved France and Belgium . . . Beware the absinthe, a noxious alcoholic drink of the French, but also beware alcohol generally. It endangers you both morally and physically. . . . How did our Emperor put it: 'The one nation imbibing the least alcohol will win!' And this is to be you. And you know 'we must win!' . . . And now a heartfelt, 'God be with you from victory to victory!' . . . May God keep Germany free! Your hometown pastor.[30]

———

All night, the armies prepared themselves. The French were psychologically, if not physically, ready, attuned to the single, unequivocal choice: victory or death. The existence of their very country was at stake. At dawn on the 6th, the shelling began, tremendous and relentless, all along the French and German lines. At the sound of the bugles, the French lines advanced with the exhilaration of soldiers on the offensive.

Battle broke out along this immense front like a rippling storm, from the eastern edge of Paris to the Aisne River (see Map 6). Foch's Ninth Army – charged with filling the gap between d'Espèrey's Fifth and de Langle's Fourth Armies – advanced swiftly and took the village of Toulon-la-Montagne. They were soon exposed to Bülow's forces, though, and withdrew to Bannes, just north of Fère-Champenoise. 'It is imperative,' Foch told his men, 'that [we] take up by evening defensive positions of such indisputable strength as to prevent the enemy . . . from advancing further south.'[31] Desperate fighting continued all day around the Bois de la Branle, where the village of Villeneuve was taken and retaken three times. It fell to Foch that night.

These were just two clashes in a cascade all along the opposing lines, of surging infantry, amid bursts of cannon, machine-gun and rifle fire. The historians Tyng, Keegan and Strachan, and the memoirs of Foch and Kluck, give the precise military positions and orders. We aim simply to give a sense of the battle, and what it meant. Bear in mind that, when we speak of an army or mention a general, we refer to a force of some 150,000–200,000 men (with the exception of Sir John French's BEF, at around 100,000, and Maunory's Sixth Army, of 80,000–90,000), each organised into corps, divisions, brigades, regiments, battalions, companies and platoons with their distinctive colours, names and identities.

The critical decision of the Marne, from which all else followed, was Kluck's. The realisation of French strength (Maunory) on the periphery of Paris made up his mind to reinforce his attack in that direction. Against Moltke's wishes, he swung back to the west, fatally extending the gap between his troops and Bülow's Second Army to an unbridgeable 50 kilometres. That handed the initiative to the French and British. D'Espèrey attacked the German left flank from the east; Maunory's Sixth Army stung von Kluck's right flank from the west; and the British, who were late starters, inflicted a sharp reminder of their existence at Rozoy, in the centre. The triple blow widened the gap with Bülow's army, whose exposed flank soon came under an explosive surprise attack from d'Espèrey's energised men.

Maunory's great anticipated flanking attack on the Paris front almost failed. Kluck and his troops showed immense agility in anticipating the strike, and initially crushed the hopes of the Sixth Army. But, gradually, Maunory prevailed, aided at a critical moment by the arrival of reinforcements from Paris – delivered by taxi. To the delight of the country, Gallieni had commandeered some 600 cabs to take reinforcements to the front, in two shuttles. The drivers were honoured to be ordered to 'go to the battle', as they proudly told their passengers. 'What about the fare?' one driver asked. The government later compensated the drivers at 27 per cent of the meter price.[32] Their comical, high-bodied vehicles carried some 6000 troops, many travelling on the roofs and running boards, to the lines beyond Dammartin, from where the soldiers were thrown into combat at Nanteuil. The railways, of course, were the main deployers of men and materiel, and ran around the clock. Yet the taxis could travel beyond the railheads, saving marching time. Whether they were decisive or not has done nothing to dim the legend of the 'taxi drivers who saved Paris'.

—

The whole German line now found itself under attack on both flanks – on the Ourcq to the west and the Moselle in the east, with d'Espèrey, Foch, de Langle and the BEF attacking up the centre. Hemmed in, the Germans threw all their weight at the centre, in an attempt to ram through the French and British resistance. 'For this final effort,' wrote Foch, '[the enemy] intended to put every man he had left . . .' to throw the French forces 'out of action' or 'force them apart and dash through the resulting breach'.[33] In so doing, Kluck seemed to apply Caesar's maxim (as he later wrote): 'in great and dangerous operations one must act, not think'.[34]

In response, the French generals hurled everything they had at the invader. 'Attack, whatever happens!' Foch urged every Frenchman. 'The Germans are at the extreme limit of their efforts . . . Victory will come to the side that outlasts the other!'[35]

Kluck's eastern flank was the first to give. At 1.30 pm on the 6th, d'Espèrey reported cracks in the German lines. Later that day, clear evidence arrived that elements of the German First Army, the famous 'right wing', were withdrawing to Montmirail. For the first time in the war, the Germans were falling back. That afternoon came better news: the French were 'pushing forward with success' all along the lines. Foch's Ninth Army 'had been violently attacked on the whole of its front', he later wrote. 'The day's fighting had been severe, but the Ninth Army had fulfilled its mission. It had withstood the . . . greater portion of the German Second Army.'[36]

In coming days, the Germans fought back. The fighting on the 7th, 8th and 9th was 'furious on both sides'.[37] Foch experienced the toughest battles of the year. Always interpreting his orders offensively, on the 7th and 8th he confronted Hausen's Third Army on the western edge of the Marshes of St Gond, the source of the Petit

Moran River. The two sides fought themselves to a virtual stalemate, broken by a ferocious German bayonet charge out of the marsh-land in the predawn mist on the 8th – a display of aggression wholly unexpected from Hausen, which rattled even Foch's robust spirits. It was short-lived. The French commander then drafted his famous signal: 'My centre is giving way, my right is in retreat, situation excellent. I attack.'[38] And he did. He held the German attack on the 8th, and the next day. As d'Espèrey flung reinforcements behind his busted lines, Foch appealed to his exhausted men for the last time, 'to put into this offensive all the strength they had left in them'.[39]

And so, after terrific artillery fire all along the front, the French troops threw themselves into the breach like men possessed, driven by some unearthly force, a self-overcoming power. The Germans fell back. The French drove forward 'in marvellous spirits', capturing village after village. All about lay the Prussian dead and wounded. The coherence of thought and action between Foch and d'Espèrey, and the astonishing resilience of the troops – notably the Moroccan Division at Mondemont – delivered a decisive French victory in the St Gond marshes. By the 10th, Foch's men were marching north, amid abounding signs of the Germans' 'precipitate retreat'.[40]

Meanwhile, the British were surging up the centre almost unop-posed, driving a wedge between Kluck and Bülow, and sealing off one from the other. The links between the German First and Second Armies were now completely severed. They fought as independent organisms, rendering them perilously vulnerable to outflanking and encirclement. Yet the Germans continued to bludgeon the French on the western flank, where, on the 7th–8th, General von Quast's IX Corps made a furious bid for Paris. Putting a division of French reservists to flight, he came within 50 kilometres of the capital.

Parisians could hear the artillery but were blissfully unaware that an entire German corps lay on their doorstep. A couple wrote to *Le Matin* on 7 September:

Yesterday afternoon, we were walking through the garden of

the Palais Royal, one of the loveliest places in Paris, when we suddenly stopped, both surprised and delighted, to ask: 'Is it true that we are now under siege?' Indeed, in the soft atmosphere of the Palais Royal, this beautiful Sunday in Paris looked completely normal and pacific. Under the arches, the happy and unconscious kids play like they always do, their mothers quietly converse near the flowerbeds . . . However, lots of Parisians left the capital . . . yesterday the cannons were heard in the East.[41]

The gutsy Parisian women who stayed behind would be the city's saviours, announced Paul Strauss, senator of the Seine. He wrote in *Le Figaro* on 8 September:

This noble Paris, which the foreigner imagined frivolous but always misunderstood what it really was, is now ready to endure every ordeal for the salvation of the country . . . Parisian women as well as the women from the suburbs have the same strong soul . . . They have . . . taken the place of those who left the capital, and never said a word that would dishearten the men. This heroic Paris, we must defend with all our energy . . . for what it represents in the heritage of the civilization and the glory of France.[42]

Von Quast's advance on Paris amounted to an isolated breakthrough in the broader theatre. The Allies then threatened the complete encirclement and annihilation of the German armies (which, had they succeeded, might have spared the world four years of misery) – unless something gave. Something did. On the afternoon of 8 September, Kluck received the order to retreat. It arrived by the hand of Lieutenant Colonel Richard Hentsch, liaison officer between OHL and the German forces, whose brains predestined him for greater things than the role of messenger. He was authorised to order a retreat of the right wing if that was the only way to close the gap between Kluck and Bülow.[43]

If one of the greatest Prussian soldiers in the history of the Reich had devised the Schlieffen Plan, it took a Saxon intelligence officer called Hentsch to kill it. Having driven from Luxembourg to the headquarters of successive German generals, Hentsch found Bülow's description of their 'catastrophic' predicament persuasive and agreed to recommend a general retreat to Kluck – his next stop. Kluck bitterly obliged, 'fully conscious of the tremendous consequences of his decision'.[44] At the sight of the German front dissolving, d'Espèrey hailed the victorious moment in his Order of the Day on the 9th: 'Held on both flanks, his centre broken, the enemy is now retreating towards the east and north by forced marches.'[45]

Kluck's retreat heralded the end of the Schlieffen Plan. The Prussian dream lay trampled in the mud of Belgium and France. 'The German army is seriously defeated,' blared *Le Matin*; 'the German army are in full retreat,' headlined *Le Petit Parisien*.[46] The German papers were silent, or lied. But the Germans had lost a battle, not the war. Over the next ten days, they retreated in order, to merge and reform as a single reinforced entity, on the hills above the north bank of the River Aisne.

—

The troops marched back through the villages whence they'd come. Their failure provoked a punitive frame of mind in some German soldiers. Appalling incidents were reported. One pitiable French woman told the British troops that her little boy had died after the Uhlans cut off one of his legs. She also claimed they had molested every girl in the village.[47]

The British engineer E. S. Butcher, entering a village evacuated by the Germans, found 'all the water poisoned and everywhere looted'. In Flagny and Hondevilliers:

> about 800 Germans lay killed, our artillery caught them in massed columns. These villages were pitiful sights: every single house looted and a few burnt to the ground, the names of the

German officers were chalked on the houses, where they slept in them the night before.[48]

On the 12th, German troops fell back through the village of Équancourt, in the Somme, home of the young woman Bernardine Dazin and her family, whose house had been used as a billet. She wrote:

> A German patrol passes in front of our house. A German comes in and asks for some wine and eggs . . . He looks sad and depressed. It looks totally different from their liveliness in the days of August! In the afternoon the Germans come again to take some wine, butter and eggs for their wounded in Moislains.

The next morning, a German patrol passed through the village and stopped. 'They say, "we are winning",' Bernardine wrote. 'So what are they doing here? Why do we see the patrols again? I think that Joffre finally tricked them.' On the 15th, events confirmed her thoughts: 'Nine German cars go rolling through the street. Two hours later, we see two French machine guns racing after them. 1830: We hear shots.'[49]

French and German soldiers also wrote of their return to this familiar, battered landscape. 'We learn that the enemy is retreating,' wrote Raymond Clément, the French stretcher-bearer, on 7 September. 'It's all we know about the battle of the Marne, we were just part of it without knowing it.' Later, as his unit advanced:

> we can clearly see the horrors of the war. We are going through shelled and burned-out villages, where we can still see and smell the smoke: Villers-aux-Vents, Sommeilles, Rembercourt-aux-Pots and Laheycourt, where the church is full of French and German wounded. Their retreat seems to have been a real disarray . . . They have really behaved like highway robbers. We can see all kinds of objects in the fields: here, a chair, a piano,

a pedestal, there a pillow, a pendulum, a vase, some statues, further a table still set with a lot of empty Champagne bottles. We can imagine what kind of parties they organised here to celebrate their success.[50]

Between 5 and 9 October, Clément passed through the town of Clermont-en-Argonne: 'We saw this town one month ago; it was a nice place. Now we can see only empty walls instead of houses and the streets are full of rubble. The Germans burned the houses down before they left. Everything burned.'[51]

German supply units fell back as far as the Belgian border. Herman Baumann, the sharp-eyed army baker, withdrew to the vicinity of Maubeuge:

Along the streets, tons of rifles, ammunition, equipment. We are working our way through this chaos, houses shot to pieces everywhere, sometimes still burning. Large columns of prisoners are passing us by, a picture of utter misery. Blown-up horse carcasses are still lying in the fortress ditches. The ovens are still warm. The enemy has just stopped . . .[52]

—

The Miracle of the Marne reverberates today, if we may be permitted an audacious retrospective. The battle marked the beginning of the end of the German military adventure in the Great War and heralded four more years of attrition, culminating in the German defeat and the humiliation of Versailles, which in turn would condemn Germany to beggary, hyperinflation and Nazism. How the confluence of thought, character and action in this gentle riverine valley led to the reversal of German military power has vexed historians ever since. Dozens of books on the Marne (the finest single account being Sewell Tyng's *The Campaign of the Marne*) offer as many reasons for the German defeat: Kluck's misjudged swivel, which opened a great gap in the German forces; the astonishing mettle of the poilu on the

Moselle; the declaration of Italian neutrality freeing French troops on the Italian frontier; the faster firing rate of the French 75-milli-metre guns; the brilliance of the French generals (Gallieni's decisive-ness, Joffre's stoic resolve and the guts of Foch); the complete failure of German intelligence;[53] and the speed of the French railway system in concentrating so many men, so quickly, in one place. Doubts linger over the British: was their performance critical or negligible? The closest answer seems to be that, while Sir John French's forces joined the battle late in 'a tentative, hesitant manner' (Haig's corps did not apparently cross the start line until 3 pm, after the Germans had sounded the retreat),[54] the BEF served the vital job of closing the gap between France's Fifth and Sixth Armies. For that, they were certainly vital. The true paean to British courage was to come, in the appalling siege of Ypres.

The reason for Germany's defeat 'that transcends all others' was 'the extraordinary and peculiar aptitude of the French soldier to recover quickly', concluded Kluck, with decent magnanim-ity. '[T]hat men who have retreated for ten days, sleeping on the ground and half dead with fatigue, should be able to take up their rifles and attack when the bugle sounds, is a thing upon which we never counted. It was a possibility not studied in our war academy.'[55] Spears similarly hailed French resourcefulness: the battle 'proved the genius of the French race for instantaneous comprehension and adaptability', he wrote. 'No people but the French . . . having started so badly could in so short a time have learned so much.'[56] Perhaps, yet he ought to have added the bane of all armies: the utter exhaus-tion of the Germans, now dependent on long and unreliable supply lines.

After the war, Erich Ludendorff would perversely blame the defeat on an unholy alliance of freemasonry, world Jewry and the sinister influence of Rudolf Steiner's 'occult' theosophy on Moltke's wife.[57] This strain of paranoia emerged later in Ludendorff's career. For now, Germany's most formidable general was called on to apply his extraor-dinary powers of command to the eastern struggle with Russia.

44

SERBIAN SHOCK, RUSSIAN ROUT, AUSTRIAN ANNIHILATION

The Tsar trusted me. How can I face him after such a disaster?
Russian general Alexander Samsonov, on the day he shot himself

---

NO ACTS MORE FULLY REVEAL a man's character than love and war. On the battlefield, Lanrezac and Sir John French had felt the hard truth of that judgement, as had Joffre, in the disastrous opening stages of the French offensive. So, too, had dozens of sacked generals and thousands of unknown young men, in their private struggle with the demons of cowardice and self-doubt. Now, this unsparing measure of self-worth would be applied on the plains and river valleys, and around the great lakes of Prussia, Poland and Russia.

Napoleon's and Hitler's disastrous attempts to subdue Muscovy offer no guiding rationale for such an adventure, unless brute ambition or megalomania may be construed as valid 'strategic imperatives'. Napoleon's Grand Armée drew up at the smouldering ruins of Moscow, which had been abandoned by the Tsar and virtually everyone, to face his worst enemy: winter. He had left France with 685,000 men, representing almost every European nation; he returned to Paris with 120,000 survivors trudging along after him. Hitler ordered the Sixth Army to bleed in the cauldron of Stalingrad rather than allow General Friedrich Paulus to retreat, after the bloodiest battle in the history of warfare left 850,000 German and 1,150,000 Russian dead, wounded or missing and marked the beginning of the destruction of the Third Reich.

In 1914, a century after Napoleon, Germany's decision to declare war on Russia at least had a comprehensible aim: strike now, and prevent the beast from growing so powerful that Germany would never be rid of the Slavic threat. From August to mid-September, Germany had no intention of attacking or invading Russia. The Schlieffen Plan dictated that the Muscovites should be 'held' until Germany had defeated France, after which the Reich's combined army would be entrained to the Eastern Front. By late August – before the Marne blew the incredible scenario away – Schlieffen's posthumous demands were starting to oppress rather than guide Moltke and OHL. The notion that 22 German divisions would be moving east by the 27th day of mobilisation, as Schlieffen had envisaged, was absurdly optimistic.

Everything hinged on a quick victory in the west. But the Germans needed to win much more than a few battles against France: they needed a *war of annihilation*, a victory so complete that France would surrender to German occupation, or self-administration, in defeat, rather like 1871 – and all in 42 days. The astonishing thing is not only the baffling scale of German ambition but also how close the nation actually came to realising it.

Until Moltke received a clear answer of victory from the west, a single German Army – the Eighth – would defend East Prussia. Their orders were not to attack. They were to hold and delay Russia's massed forces for as long as possible. Above all, they were not to waste German lives in the eastern meat grinder – the loss of entire armies in the east was a very real fear.

—

It is beyond our scope – and the reader's patience – to narrate the full story of the vast battles in the east. A solid, witheringly dense single volume exists on the main confrontation: Walter Showalter's *Tannenberg: Clash of Empires 1914*. Norman Stone's *The Eastern Front: 1914–1917* covers the full story on the Eastern Front from 1914 to 1918. Tuchman, Keegan, Strachan and Gilbert offer mercifully clear outlines of the key struggles. We aim simply to continue that tradition, and to assess the battles' impact in the context and direction of the war.

While Germany and Russia prepared for their great test, a savage little struggle proceeded in the south, between Austria-Hungary and Serbia. Dismissed in retrospect as a sideshow, the Third Balkan War deserves our passing notice. It was Austria-Hungary's irrational determination to 'punish' Serbia that was the chief, immediate cause of the European conflict. Its outcome realised the worst fears of Moltke and the General Staff about the reliability of the Austro-Hungarian Army.

From the start, the Habsburgs' polyglot army – an ethnic and religious gaggle speaking some 15 languages – was to be split in three. Count Conrad von Hötzendorf reckoned he needed 20 divisions to defeat Serbia. But that left only 28 to go to the far more exacting Galician front in Poland, to assist Germany against Russia. He decided to create three armies. Eight divisions would go to Serbia, 28 to the Russian front, and 12 would serve as a floating force, the 'Strafexpedition' – to go to Serbia as a 'demonstration' and/or to Galicia when required. Austria-Hungary had initially expected to mobilise against Serbia and then, possibly, Russia. Now, it faced the prospect of fighting Serbia and Russia at the same time – a nightmare for which Vienna was unprepared.

Conrad's calculations gravely underestimated Serbia's determination. A military 'demonstration' would never deter a people whose history showed they would fight to the death rather than tolerate invasion. They had not thrown Turkey out of the Balkans only to be enslaved by Austria. By early August, the Serbs were more thoroughly blooded than any army in Europe. The Serbian commander, Radomir Putnik, had won a spectacular victory over the Turks in 1912, earning him the title *voivoide* or war leader. His troops had then fought and defeated the Bulgarians. Putnik's army had a ferocious reputation, not least for the practice of mutilating corpses, among other unprintable atrocities. Vienna, however, rationalised away the Serbian Army as a barbarian horde, a 'peasant mob', who would cower at the sight of the imperial Austro-Hungarian armies and their allies, the Croats, Czechs, Slovenes, etc.[1] Instead, in one of the year's most sensational upsets, Serbia's 180,000 troops soundly defeated the Austro-Hungarian forces (of 190,000), in a series of battles between August and December. By December, the Serbs had evicted the Austrians from their country and thoroughly humiliated Conrad, whose beloved Gina would not see her conqueror's laurels that year.

The Serbs delivered the first blow, between 12 and 24 August, on the plain enclosed by the Rivers Drina and Sava. Instead of being lured into the enemy's arched front line, the wily Putnik withheld his forces on the hills above the River Vardar. The Austro-Hungarians arrived on the plain below on the night of 14 August, after completing a 105-kilometre march in the previous 48 hours. From his commanding heights, Putnik poured fire down onto the advancing Austrians, exacting terrific casualties at close range and forcing General Potiorek, the Austrian commander – who had chaperoned Franz Ferdinand around Sarajevo six weeks earlier – to demand reinforcements, i.e. the 'demonstration' forces of the floating Strafexpedition. On his third request, Conrad granted them. That merely prolonged the Austrian failure. The battles – back and forth across the plain – raged until 24 August, when, unable to break Serbia's infuriating resistance, Potiorek's forces fell back over the Sava.

The Serbs recklessly chased victory by invading Austrian territory but were forced back in early September, with 5000 casualties. A few weeks later, they attacked the Austrian forces in Bosnia, forcing Gavrilo Princip's jailers to transfer him to Theresienstadt fortress in Bohemia. Reinforcements enabled Potiorek to launch a fresh attack, resulting in Austria-Hungary capturing Belgrade, only to be evicted from Serbian territory in December 1914 after 12 days of ferocious fighting, during which King Peter himself took up a rifle in the Serbian front lines. In total, Austria-Hungary suffered 38,000 casualties to Serbia's 18,000. Not until late 1915 would the central powers return to deal with Serbia, with German forces and thousands of guns. The Serbian people would be literally driven off their land and into the sea, the prelude to the more ghastly revenge of Hitler, who would invade and occupy the entire Balkan region.

—

Meanwhile, Germany and Russia, the patrons of Austria and Serbia, met on the plains of Eastern Prussia and Poland. The great 'cauldron wars' of the Tannenberg campaign – so-named not because they fought at Tannenberg, which was 30 kilometres to the west of the battlefield, but because the Germans hoped to efface the memory of the defeat of the Teutonic Knights to an army of Poles, Lithuanians and Tatars at Tannenberg in 1410 – were a terrifying mixture of Napoleonic élan and modern weaponry, where the fabled 'offensive' met the early-twentieth-century howitzer; where new technology, such as telephones and radio, often broke down and were discarded in favour of the old certainties – bugles, flags and 'spirit'; where densely packed units marched headlong into their opponents' guns, with appalling casualties. Old tactical doctrines often collapsed. Whole units broke up and fled the horror of vast battlefields smashed apart under modern shellfire.

The Russians fielded two armies: the First Army, of 200,000 men in more than 20 divisions, including seven of cavalry, under General Paul von Rennenkampf, who was thought to be daring and aggressive; and the Second Army, of 150,000 men, under General Alexander Samsonov, a noble-minded commander of the 'old school', beloved of his men, in whose lives he took a close interest. Both fell under the overall command of Russian Army Group General Yakov Zhilinsky, severe, doctrinaire and generally unloved. They led some of the most feared and exotic regiments – Cossacks, Hussars, Grenadiers, Siberians and the Tsar's Imperial Guards – drawn from all over the empire.

Confronting the Russians from the west were four corps of the German Eighth Army, under the command of the weak-minded, immensely fat General Maximilian von Prittwitz, the bluest of blue-blooded Prussians, which accounted for his over-promotion. A 'German version of Falstaff' was Tuchman's verdict. Mocked as 'Fatty' (der Dicke) by his detractors, Prittwitz seems to have been a lazy, coarse and self-indulgent man, puffed up by unmerited pride, who 'never moved if he could help it'.[2] Under him were four hard-driving German generals, determined to make their mark in the annals of Prussian military glory: Hermann von Francois, August von Mackensen, Otto von Below and Friedrich von Scholtz. They rode at the head of a few fine Prussian regiments, yet most of the German units were reservists and conscripts.

On paper, Russia seemed assured of victory. The Russians fielded twice as many troops as the Germans (the exact ratio was 29 Russians to 16 Germans) and twice as many cavalry. In practice, deep, unaddressed flaws hobbled Russia's chances. Lingering enmity divided the two generals, both of whom were blooded as cavalry commanders in the Russo-Japanese War. There, Samsonov had accused Rennenkampf of failing to assist him in the (lost) Battle of Mukden in 1905. That failure rankled, and turned into a grudge. The two generals were even (wrongly) reputed to have come to blows. Old enmities die hard – and they died very hard at Tannenberg.

Worse, Russian soldiers were no match for the Germans, in experience, education or application. They lacked initiative and were ignorant, observed Major General Sir Alfred Knox, the British military attaché to Russia in 1914. He wrote in his diary:

It was impossible to hope for individuality in recruits, 75 per cent of whom were drawn from the peasant class. The Tartar domination and serfdom seem to have robbed them of all natural initiative, leaving only a wonderful capacity for patient endurance... They were lazy and happy-go-lucky, doing nothing thoroughly unless driven to it. The bulk of them went willingly to the war ... because they had little idea what war meant. They lacked the . . . thinking patriotism to make their morale proof against the effects of heavy loss and heavy loss resulted from unintelligent leadership and lack of proper equipment.[3]

Later assessments of the Russian Army bear out his view. Though brave in the right circumstances, the Russian soldier 'was easily disheartened by setback', wrote Keegan, '. . . and would surrender easily and without shame, en masse, if he felt abandoned or betrayed. The trinity of Tsar, Church and country still had power to evoke unthinking courage; but defeat, and drink, could rapidly rot devotion to the regiment's colours . . .'[4]

Yet the Russian commanders expected the men to compensate for these inadequacies through sheer grit and blind faith. Knox wrote:

Owing to the rigour of the climate and the lower general civilisation, the Russian soldier was more fitted to stand privation and should have been more fitted to stand nerve strain than the men of Central Europe . . . The simple faith of the Russian soldier in God and the Emperor seemed to provide an overwhelming asset to the leader with sufficient imagination to realise its value.[5]

Showalter concurred: 'the Russian soldiers were appreciably better than their officers. In attack they overran positions by weight of numbers; in defence they were likely to die before they ran. But they tended, for good or ill, to stay where they were placed.'[6]

Yet they were woefully supplied. The men lacked proper food, warm clothes and adequate boots. They were short of ammunition, shells and proper supply lines. Russia's seven divisions of heavy field artillery had just 1000 shells per field gun – a fraction of the German tally. Peacetime deterioration and Russia's poor factory output explained the shortage: the General Staff did not expect a long war. Russia had 320 planes and no dirigibles equal to the German Zeppelins. Her troops relied on a mere 418 transport vehicles and two motorised ambulances. Beyond the railheads, horse and cart were the chief form of transport to the front – slow and prone to breakdown. In spite of all this, Russian verve would somehow win through. 'For a long war,' Sir Alfred Knox concluded, 'Russia was outclassed in every factor of success except in the number of her fighting men and in their mollusc-like quality of recovery after severe defeat.'[7]

—

The German and Russian Armies first clashed in East Prussia, in what would be called the Battle of Gumbinnen, the prelude to the broader Tannenberg campaign. The Russians started badly: a great gap opened up between the two armies, a result of geography and strategic error, exacerbated by Sazonov and Rennenkampf's failure to cooperate. The two generals reached the East Prussian front five days apart (Rennenkampf arrived first, on 15 August). This ever-widening gap, which German intelligence picked up, exposed the two Russian forces to the risk of defeat in detail: that is, it gave the Germans a chance to attack one, and then the other, rather than face the full Russian strength at once (see Map 7).

Persuaded that the Russians were weaker than hitherto thought, and yet a persistent threat to Prussian towns, Prittwitz sent his finest three and a half corps to attack Rennenkampf's First Army north of the Masurian Lakes. To attack was technically against Moltke's orders, which had prescribed a delaying action. So Prittwitz insisted that his corps hold off for as long as possible.

The aggressive, jumpy, insubordinate von Francois was having none of that – and defied orders by driving deep into the Russian lines and advancing as far as the town of Gumbinnen and beyond. Von Mackensen's and von Below's corps were compelled to keep up, to protect Francois from isolation and encirclement. The Russians repulsed this initial success with devastating fire from entrenched positions and the use of artillery at close range, which landed chiefly on Mackensen's and Below's men. Those who were not slaughtered or wounded fell back in confusion. Many were too rattled to rejoin the lines – such was the effect, diagnosed for the first time in the east, of modern artillery on the toughest military constitution.

The whole of the Eighth Army seemed momentarily threatened with destruction. Prittwitz acted in character: he panicked, and insisted that the German forces must retreat, as far back as the Vistula, if necessary. If so, that meant abandoning all East Prussia to the enemy. Prittwitz's proposal stunned Moltke at OHL. The Eighth Army seemed to have failed in their sole task of holding the Russians and were now imperilled. It was the 20th day of the French invasion and Prittwitz – largely due to Francois's precipitate action – appeared to have flirted with collapse.

The Germans were amazed to see, however, that Rennenkampf failed to follow up his success. No Russian units pursued the German retreat. In fact, on 20 August, the Russian general ordered a halt and famously advised a staff officer, who had been permitted to rest so long as he kept his uniform on, 'You can take off your clothes now; the Germans are retiring.'[8] The remark has provoked controversy, because a triumphant commander would never rest. He would pursue and destroy his broken enemy. Rennenkampf's enemies even used the incident as evidence of their unfounded charge that he was a traitor, stemming from his German Baltic descent. In truth, it seems the Russians were simply human, all too human, and too exhausted to give chase.

———

Moltke soon realised the opportunity the failure presented. At last, he had the ammunition to relieve Prittwitz, whose powerful connections had hitherto protected him. His orders to retreat, and to abandon East Prussian villages and towns to the Russian idea of mercy, were unconscionable. Clearly, Prittwitz had lost his nerve, and Moltke immediately sought a forceful new chief of staff whom he could trust to reinvigorate the German forces.

Moltke settled on the figure of General Erich Ludendorff, the conqueror of the Belgians at Liège, the victor of the French on the Sambre, and reputed to be the most intelligent, aggressive and decisive of German generals. Ludendorff lived and breathed the idea, practice and necessity of war. He had personally tested and approved the Schlieffen Plan. Striding about in his greatcoat and spiked helmet, he sent tremors into the hearts of his underlings wherever he went. Applying Darwin's theories to the racial and social lot of mankind (as did most Prussian officers), Ludendorff regarded peace as an aberration, a mere interval between the natural and inevitable condition of the human race: forever to be at each other's throats.

Of Ludendorff's private character, not even the great anecdote hunter Barbara Tuchman was able to find one with which to humanise him: 'he moved without attendant anecdotes, a man without a shadow', she wrote (no disrespect meant to Tuchman: fine anecdotes are the delicacies of great popular history).[9] Even Ludendorff's friends and family had little to add to the stern military profile of a man who literally lived for war. On 23 August, this forbidding character promptly left the French lines to travel to the eastern theatre. In the letter of transfer, Moltke's staff officer nervously apologised for whisking Ludendorff away from the French action, adding, 'of course you will not be held responsible for what has already happened in the East but with your energy you can prevent the worst from happening'.[10]

To complete the eclipse of Prittwitz, Moltke appointed a new commander-in-chief in the east. It took no persuading to bring out of retirement that great, lumbering veteran Paul von Beneckendorf und Hindenburg, the *éminence grise* of the Prussian Army, his breast heavy with decorations and old wisdom. A direct descendant of Martin Luther and the heir, on his father's side, to one of the most prestigious Prussian families, Hindenburg had fought with distinction as a young officer in the Austro-Prussian (1866) and Franco-Prussian (1870–71) wars, and risen rapidly to the rank of general of the infantry (equivalent to a British or US lieutenant general) in 1903. He retired in 1911. His appointment in 1914 as commander of the Eighth Army drew more on his symbolic power than his intellect. 'I am ready,' he said simply, on receiving the phone call at his home in Hanover.

Hindenburg shrewdly delegated most critical tasks to Ludendorff, in whom he recognised the sharper military mind and with whom he developed a close rapport that would become the most successful partnership of the war. Indeed, Hindenburg's knack of deferring critical questions to Ludendorff's ruthless intuition raised the relationship to something beyond a 'happy marriage', as Hindenburg called it, to a kind of military symbiosis.

—

Prittwitz and his staff officers had not failed as completely as Moltke feared; they had left something of value before they departed. On arriving at their eastern HQ at Rastenburg (Hitler's future HQ, the Wolf's Lair), Hindenburg and Ludendorff had no need of a new plan: their predecessor's revised strategy was straight out of the Prussian textbook and redounded to the credit of the disgraced commander – or, more likely, to the wise counsel of Max Hoffmann, his scheming, highly intelligent chief of staff, on whom Ludendorff and Hindenburg would heavily rely in the coming clash.

Prittwitz had ordered the movement of the I and XVII Corps from the northern to the southern theatre, to join the other two German corps in confronting Samsonov's divisions (see Map 7). They had packed up quickly, leaving a film of cavalry and Landwehr reservists in front of Rennenkampf. Everything depended on Rennenkampf staying where he was – and the Russian general conveniently acted according to the German script. In fact, Rennenkampf assumed his enemy had been badly mauled and was retreating to the Prussian fortress at Königsberg. He thus devoted his time to preparing for siege warfare.

Ludendorff endorsed the plan he inherited and compelled all units – including Mackensen's exhausted and battered corps – to press south, to attack and destroy Samsonov's flanks, in a classic encirclement. There would be no further retreat. But how could the Germans be sure Rennenkampf would not resume his offensive? The German trump card was their superior intelligence, in the form of radio intercepts. Both sides were listening to each other's radio signals, but the Russians had fewer resources, decoders and interpreters. The German Eighth Army fielded several light, mobile radio sets, two heavy receiver/transmitters at Riesenburg, with ranges of 240 kilometres, as well as two permanent heavy receiver/transmitters at Thorn and Posen, with cypher experts attached. Together, these picked up critical messages issuing between Rennenkampf's headquarters in Vilna and Samsonov's headquarters in Ostrołęka. In fact, German headquarters had intercepted and interpreted radio signals sent *en clair* between the Russian generals, and gleaned an accurate idea of the enemy's movements, including Rennenkampf's plan to head for Königsberg and his widening gap with Samsonov. Such intelligence was the military equivalent of divine intervention.

—

On 25 August, Ludendorff ordered Francois to attack Samsonov's left wing at Usdau. Francois replied with the same insubordination he had got away with under Prittwitz. His men were not ready, he claimed; they were still arriving by train from the north. Nor was his heavy artillery in place. At once, Ludendorff and Hindenburg, with Hoffmann following, went down to Francois's HQ and gave him a taste of the new regime: he would attack, he would obey orders, regardless. In that case, Francois impertinently replied, 'I . . . will be obliged to fight by bayonet.' Ludendorff waved aside his protestations and drove off. Francois, irked, would drag his feet for two days. The delay would prove fortuitous.

At the same time, a German signalman handed Chief of Staff Hoffmann a gift from the airwaves. German intelligence had intercepted Russian movements, revealing that Rennenkampf could not hope to reach the German Army in time – and that Samsonov was to continue his advance in a north-westerly direction – in other words, to advance *further* into the German trap.

Samsonov had earlier resisted these instructions to advance, pleading a lack of bread for his exhausted troops and oats for the famished horses. There were no beds for the wounded, who 'were lying anywhere, on the straw or on the floor . . .' wrote the British military attaché.[11] 'I don't know how the men bear it any longer,' a staff officer reported to Zhilinsky, who ignored it. Regardless of the terrible state of the men, Zhilinsky ordered Samsonov to press an 'energetic offensive' with the aim of cutting off the German retreat to the Vistula. Zhilinsky invited the grand duke and Sir Alfred Knox, the British attaché, to dine with him that night. As they ate, he complained that 'Samsonov was moving too slowly'. Samsonov had taken Neidenburg, Knox wrote, 'but Jilinski [sic] thinks he should be by now at Allenstein. He repeated that he was dissatisfied with Samsonov for moving too slowly.'[12] Zhilinsky little knew that his orders were driving Samsonov into the German vice. Rennenkampf continued to do nothing, thinking he was holding the German units in the north, where few German units remained. They were all heading south. When Rennenkampf actually moved, he headed north towards Königsberg, not south to assist Samsonov.

Ludendorff and Hindenburg digested all this and planned accordingly. Mackensen's and Below's corps, streaming down from Gumbinnen, would attack Samsonov's right wing, while Francois and von Scholtz would be in position to devastate Samsonov's left wing. The Russian ranks – some 200,000–230,000 men – were at that time advancing directly into the pincers of this classic 'Cannae', the almost complete encirclement of Samsonov's men.

Ludendorff suffered an initial fit of nerves, which Hoffman delighted in recording. Yet the Battle of Tannenberg went almost precisely as the Germans planned, with a few unexpected shocks. Ludendorff, for example, was astonished to hear that Moltke had decided to transfer three corps and a cavalry division from the west to the eastern theatre. Ludendorff, who knew the exact troop density that Schlieffen prescribed to defeat the French, protested that he did not need them. They were coming anyway. Moltke's alarm over the reversals in the east and misplaced confidence in the victory in the west made up his mind. (The reinforcements would not arrive until the first week of September, just before the Marne victory.) Moltke's sudden decision, Ludendorff later argued, had denuded the German forces of the strength they needed to tip the scales in France. That outcome was hypothetical, but the decision would serve to indict Moltke. On 14 September, Erich von Falkenhayn replaced him as chief of the German General Staff.

—

Samsonov looked deeply troubled when Sir Alfred Knox visited him at his Neidenburg headquarters on 25 August: 'he had not yet received a letter from his wife'. A dramatic telegram interrupted their meal, at which Samsonov and his generals 'buckled on their swords, said good-bye'. The interruption seems to have been the opening German shelling of the Russian lines. Indeed, a horrifying vision of the coming slaughter descended on Samsonov on 26 and 27 August, when the fleeing survivors of German massed artillery came staggering into Neidenburg. They were hungry, exhausted and terrified. Knox witnessed this 'long convoy of wounded' entering town: 'Losses, according to all accounts, have been dreadful, and chiefly from artillery fire, the number of German guns exceeding the Russian.' He encountered a nun driving a cartload of wounded men, abandoned on the road when the drivers ran away. The town's police chief guided her to a field hospital.[13]

On the 27th, Francois bombarded the Russian positions at

Usdau. The targets were General Artamanov's legendary I Corps, none of whom had eaten in two days. All were dead, wounded or in retreat by 11 am. Rennenkampf remained in the north, as ignorant as Zhilinsky of their fellow commander's predicament. False reports crowded the phone lines. Chaos ensued in the Russian ranks. The Germans were within eight kilometres of Neidenburg. Knox wrote:

> We ran out [of the railway station] to see an enormous Zeppelin hovering at a height of about 900 to 1000 metres in the sun. It looked so extraordinarily peaceful! Suddenly it threw four bombs, one after the other, in quick succession. The loss was six killed and fourteen wounded, but it might have been far greater, for the station was crowded . . . The Zeppelin hovered round and finally sailed away.[14]

On the 28th, Samsonov got news that three corps had been driven back in disorder. In the face of disaster, the Russian general returned his automobiles and wireless equipment to headquarters and, in a mad moment, cut his communication lines with Zhilinsky (from whom he dreaded further orders). He then set off for the front line on horseback, determined to see the battle with his own eyes and join the fight as a divisional commander. Knox witnessed his departure:

> We found Samsonov sitting on the ground poring over maps and surrounded with his staff . . . Suddenly he stood up and ordered eight [Cossacks] to dismount and give up their animals . . . He concluded that he did not know what was going to happen . . . I said goodbye and Samsonov, with his seven staff officers, mounted the Cossack horses and rode north-west, followed by the remainder of the squadron. Both he and his staff were as calm as possible. They said: 'The enemy has luck one day, we will have luck another.'[15]

Over the next two days, the two armies of 350,000 men tried to smash each other apart. German artillery easily outgunned the Russians: great volleys of shellfire hurtled to the earth, dismembering the Russian lines. Units raced forward and were thrown back; others disappeared 'behind a curtain of smoke and mist to some unknown fate'.[16] Villagers and refugees clogged the roads and tracks. Who knew precisely the state of the battle? Who could say who was winning? Ludendorff positioned himself as close as possible, on a hill above Usdau, to direct his generals. Samsonov was somewhere at the front, cut off from Zhilinsky, as good as missing. All his guns and transports were lost.

The fog of war lifted on desperate scenes. On 29–30 August, in flight from Francois's forces, which had blocked his southern escape route, Samsonov and his men suddenly encountered new German divisions bearing down on them from the north. These were Mackensen's forces, survivors of the worst of Gumbinnen. Their arrival spelt the end for Samsonov's army, who were now completely cut off (see Map 7).

There followed total panic, slaughter and the complete capitulation of Russia's Second Army. Samsonov and his staff rode out of the furnace, barely escaping with their lives. 'The Tsar trusted me. How can I face him after such a disaster?' the distraught Samsonov confided in his staff.[17] A day later, in a wood near Willenberg, feeling sick and depressed, he shot himself. His officers staggered 64 kilometres back to Russian soil, travelling through the woods at night. The Germans rounded up 92,000 Russian prisoners, and counted 50,000 Russians killed and wounded. To put this in perspective, by the end of August more than half a million French, German and British troops had been killed or wounded in the western theatre.

One of Samsonov's generals, Nikolaj Martos, a small man with a grey beard, was wounded when shrapnel hit his car. His travelling companion, an officer's wife – dressed as a man in order to be an interpreter – jumped out and fled into the forest, where she was killed. The Germans captured Martos and took him to headquarters, where Ludendorff crudely taunted him. The magnanimous

Hindenburg clasped the Russian's quivering hands and promised to return his sword. No wonder he shook: Martos had lost virtually his entire XV Corps, of which only a single officer would return to Russia.

The whole Russian machine had failed, Knox wrote. He ascribed the annihilation of Samsonov's army to the power of German artillery and the corps commanders' inability to communicate. 'On the other hand,' he added, 'many Russians fought with determination till the end.' As late as the 30th, the Russians were 'fighting with immense obstinacy', Hindenburg reported. They kept fighting until virtually all were dead or captured. 'The Russians were just great big-hearted children,' Knox concluded, 'who had thought out nothing and had stumbled half-asleep into a wasp's nest.'[18] (His verdict was premature. Russian stubbornness would receive ferocious direction during the Brusilov offensive and crush the Austro-Hungarian Army – see below.)

Meanwhile, Rennenkampf's First Army had done nothing, oblivious to the slaughter in the south. Alerted to the fate of Samsonov, he activated his corps commanders and prepared to face the combined enemy. On 7 September, the entire German Eighth Army, reinforced by the IX Corps and a corps of Guard Reserves, which had arrived from the west, returned north to attack the Russian forces in the battle of the Masurian Lakes: to defeat the Russians in detail. They swiftly broke the Russians' left flank, which forced Rennenkampf into a long and tortuous fighting withdrawal. All through September, his forces fell back beyond the lakes and then, on the 25th, turned to inflict a counter-offensive on the over-stretched Germans, reclaiming much of the territory lost. It was a brief respite. Rennenkampf was the next Russian commander to lose his nerve, and he gave up. Zhilinsky later accused him of deserting his army. Yet Zhilinsky shared the blame for the collapse – a textbook example of 'defeat in detail' – and both commanders lost their jobs. Rennenkampf was discharged in disgrace.

—

The humiliation of Tannenberg did not inhibit spirited Russian offensives elsewhere – most spectacularly on the Galician front, against their old foe, Austria-Hungary. In a series of battles fought between 16 August and 10 September in the shadow of the Carpathians, Conrad von Hötzendorf faced his own, personal Waterloo. His 37 resplendently turned-out imperial divisions, 900,000 men representing Austro-German, Magyar, Czech, Slovak, Croat, Slovene, Ukrainian, Pole, Bosnian Muslim and other ethnicities, prepared for battle confident of victory along a 400-kilometre front bounded by the Vistula and Dneister Rivers – a natural funnel that would largely determine the outcome. They faced Russia's southwestern imperial forces (the Third, Fourth, Fifth and Eighth armies), 1,200,000 men under the command of General Nikolay Ivanov, a highly decorated artillery expert with whom Sir Alfred Knox dined the night before battle: 'He is . . . beloved by his men, with whom he continually converses. He is simple and unpretentious in his manner . . . Ivanov allows no wine at his table till the war is over. It was interesting to see [his dinner guests] imbibing lemonade.'[19]

Conrad's forces won an initial success, driving the Russians deep into the Bug Valley. But, soon, adverse terrain, poor intelligence and confused ranks (Conrad's orders had to be issued in 15 languages) handed Russia's General Ivanov the chance to counter-attack. He did so with unremitting energy. The slaughter began at Zlotchow and continued for days. This, however, failed to disabuse Conrad of the belief that he was winning a great victory, the evidence for which seemed to be small successes that he mistook for larger ones. We need not delve into the grisly details of the awful Battle of Lemberg, except to say that it crushed Austria-Hungary's military pride. By 10 September, Russia had inflicted 100,000 casualties and taken 300,000 prisoners, according to Keegan.[20] Other sources claim the figures respectively were 250,000 casualties and 100,000 prisoners.[21] The rampaging Russian Army gave chase, forcing Conrad's troops on a 240-kilometre retreat, during which many of the finest Austrian units and their commanders were annihilated.

By any measure, it was a catastrophic result for Vienna (a mere prelude to a far worse defeat to Russia's General Brusilov in 1916), the memory of which the Austro-Hungarian Empire would never efface. Emperor Franz Joseph's finest units, the XIV Tyrolean Corps and the 6th Mounted Rifle Regiment, virtually ceased to exist. The resistance of the Austro-Hungarian troops in the fortress of Przemyśl offered the only consoling heroic stand in a sea of defeat. Some six Russian divisions had swirled around this great fortress and proceeded to break the will of the 127,000 soldiers and 18,000 civilians caught inside. They held out for 133 days, the longest siege of the war, ending with the surrender of 110,000. The battle for Warsaw would also prove a Russian victory, the first defeat for Hindenburg and Ludendorff. In the final months of 1914, these exhausting confrontations bore hundreds of thousands of men back and forth over the plains of Eastern Europe, in a desperate bid for supremacy, which ended, as at the battle for Łódź, in stalemate, with no clear victor.

—

Tannenberg, the central struggle in the east, did not kill men on the scale of the war in France, yet the German victory held a deep significance. The Germans had held and driven back the Russian offensive, and initiated the long, miserable process of breaking the Muscovite spirit. It was the first clear victory of the First World War. It saved Eastern Prussia. And it showed the Germans that the Russians were not, as hitherto thought, inviolable. Samsonov's Second Army had been comprehensively annihilated, with just a few thousand stragglers from the XIII and XV Corps escaping the German noose. Yet those losses were a fraction of the total Russian manpower, and in terms of sheer body count Russia was far from a spent force: millions of recruits and reservists were then in training.

The battle's significance is better understood 'in the realm of will', as Showalter writes: it temporarily broke Russia's. Germany's Eighth Army, mostly 'ill-equipped reserve and fortress troops', had defeated a Russian force twice its size. 'The stage seemed set for an overwhelming [Russian] victory and the effect of Tannenberg was therefore even more crushing.'[22] Testifying before the post-revolutionary provisional government's commission of inquiry, A. J. Guchkov, the Russian war minister, said that he believed the war was lost 'as early as August 1914' after Samsonov's defeat.[23]

In Germany, the victory gathered the mystique of legend. A clutch of Iron Crosses went to a roll call of Tannenberg heroes. The generals bickered over who 'won' the battle. Francois and Hoffmann later claimed most of the credit, dismissing the legend that grew around Hindenburg. Prittwitz even bagged his share, as the initiator of the encirclement. But the victory redounded to the effectiveness of the Hindenburg–Ludendorff partnership. Both, too, would later dispute the other's influence. Hindenburg seemed to do little – Hoffmann later joked that the commander slept through the battles – yet his granite presence fortified the German Army and buttressed Ludendorff, who drew strength from the tough old veteran beside him. But the quiet accolades went to Ludendorff, who is consistently recognised as the true victor of Tannenberg, the 'brains and driving force' behind Hindenburg, and a commander 'destined by intellect, character and personality . . . as the real wielder of power'.[24] Indeed, 25 years later, Hitler's preening generals would vainly aspire to a similar stature in the eyes of posterity. Hitler himself, despite his loathing for the Prussian aristocracy, seized on the Tannenberg legend and associated himself where possible with the ageing Hindenburg.

In Austria-Hungary's case, the eastern war heralded the end of the Habsburg Empire. It would take two more years to destroy the empire's offensive capacity, but the writing was on the wall after the Galician collapse. Conrad continued to lead Austria-Hungary's motley armies to devastating defeats, culminating in his loss to Russia's General Brusilov in 1916, one of the deadliest battles of all time, which resulted in more than 1.3 million Austro-Hungarian, German and Turkish casualties. Conrad died in 1925 a bitter, broken man. In 2012, Austria decided, after long debate, to remove the 'grave of honour' designation from the Hötzendorf tomb. A few

Viennese streets and a German comic book still bear his name. One or two historians continue to believe he was the greatest military strategist of the war; if so, the death rate of the men under his command, and his failure to deploy a winning strategy, tell a different story. Churchill had the last word: Conrad broke his armies' heart, he wrote, and used it up in less than a month.[25]

The Tsar's armies stayed in the war until 1917, when the Bolsheviks seized the chance to exploit their failure and turned the troops against the government. The Russian officers, most of whom refused to join the Red Army, found themselves vilified, exiled, imprisoned or doomed to fight in the White Army, the losing side in the ensuing civil war against Lenin. But that was all in the future. In 1914, the most important result of the stalemate in the east was the concentration of the war in France, in the trenches and 'mincing machines' of the Western Front, where the fate of millions and the future of Europe would now be decided.

45

THE CREATION OF THE WESTERN FRONT

[L]ike scanning the death roll after Agincourt or Flodden.
British novelist John Buchan on reading the
casualty list of the First Battle of Ypres

And from the distance the strains of a song reached our ears, coming
closer and closer, leaping from company to company, and just as
Death plunged a busy hand into our ranks, the song reached us too
and we passed it along: Deutschland, Deutschland über Alles.
Corporal Adolf Hitler, of the 6th Bavarian ÜBER Reserve Division
(XIV Reserve Corps), during the *Kindermord* at Ypres

'I THINK A CURSE SHOULD REST ON ME,' Winston
Churchill told Violet Asquith in 1915, 'because I *love* this war.
I know it's smashing & shattering the lives of thousands every
moment – & yet – I *can't* help it – I enjoy every second of it.'[1] For
Churchill, the war was not an avoidable tragedy or grotesque mani-
festation of political failure but a source of excitement. In delighting

551

in the sheer thrill of war, the first lord of the Admiralty said what few dared admit: many people, careless or ignorant of the horror at the front lines, shared Churchill's revelry, if for different reasons (the abandonment of peacetime restraint, life may end tomorrow, so let's dance in the streets tonight, etc.). No doubt, many people loathed the war. Families who had lost or dreaded the loss of sons, brothers and husbands wished it would end. Yet, undoubtedly, the war, once it had begun, was popular. The nation rallied as one, delighting in news of victory and stories of heroism. For many, it was indeed a lovely war.

Severe censorship served as handmaiden to the illusion. Anyone caught taking unauthorised photographs of front lines or battles faced the death penalty. David Lloyd George's literary propagandists, the fine writers appointed to the War Propaganda Unit, were reliably on hand to spread good news and educate the nation in the rightness of the war. At least Churchill had the honesty to acknowledge the cost of his enjoyment, in 'thousands of shattered lives'. In September 1914, those lives were about to descend into a darker circle of hell, which would reduce men to living and fighting in the troglodyte world of the trenches.

The first trenches were dug in the valley of the Aisne, the river flowing through the *départements* of Oise and Aisne, to which the Germans had retreated by 12 September. To the south lay the wreckage of their recent conquest, the most terrible symbol of which was the bombed-out ruin of Reims Cathedral, eight centuries of gothic architectural perfection destroyed in a moment of German shellfire. *Le Figaro* responded:

> Death to the barbarians. They burned down the Library of Louvain! Yesterday they bombed the Cathedral of Reims! . . . This useless act of miserable barbarity increases even more our feeling of hatred against this country. And more than ever, we will join the cold and wonderful will of England: to ask for peace only when the crushed, exhausted, and dying imperial Germany

would have disappeared. We must kill the beast.[2]

A fortnight later, after it had digested the end of Reims and other towns, *Le Matin* led: 'The arrogant German will soon be forced to kneel down and ask for forgiveness . . . The Teuton will crawl in front of the Allies, just like he crawled in front of Napoleon . . .'[3]

The higher ground on the northern bank of the Aisne, between Compiègne and Berry-au-Bac, where the river is about 30 metres wide, offered a solid defensive position. The Germans started digging. All along the lines, the infantry took up their trenching tools and dug, and dug, as if hurriedly preparing a mass grave. The Germans knew what they were doing: they had practised trench warfare on operations since 1904. Their trenches were models of Teutonic strength and efficiency, and would continue to be for the duration, unlike the first French and British trenches, which were mere scrapes. The digging responded to a terminal order: 'The lines so reached will be fortified and defended,' Moltke instructed.[4] There would be no further retreat. It was Moltke's last instruction before Erich von Falkenhayn replaced him, on 14 September. Never again would snipers see riflemen in their sights, lying prostrate in the open; the Germans, French, British and their allies would not stop digging until the armistice in 1918.

—

Most British and French infantrymen still hoped for a short war. 'Over by Christmas' did the rounds in September–October 1914. Entrenching themselves suggested a mole-like suspension of time, in this dreadful place. Hell, they weren't even moving. While some of the BEF had experienced trench warfare in the Boer campaign, and knew what to do, the Tommies were prone to hope. They dug accordingly. Their first trenches were waterlogged ditches, muddy and rat-infested, barely deep enough to shelter a man's body, the desultory expression of wishful thinking. (Compare these with the labyrinths of 1916–18, as deep as two metres, laid with boards, framed in solid wood or, in some German trenches, concrete, packed with sandbags, fitted with firing holes, officers' quarters, field hospitals, etc., and connected to the rear through zigzagging support and flanking trenches. Barbed wire, taut between stakes, blocked the approaches and completed the trench system.)

The trench-shy French soldiers were even less inclined to dig – at first. They shunned the subterranean war as an affront to their die-hard dreams of the offensive. To sit and wait under the crust of the earth was psychologically and literally beneath them. 'Sometimes the Germans are just 200 metres in front of us,' Brigadier Jérémie Trichereau, a French artillery officer, wrote scornfully to his brother in October. 'They bury themselves as much as they can to stay sheltered.'[5] The French cavalry tended to share the infantry's resistance to trenches: it was hard to bury one's horse. So the poilu continued to fight more or less exposed, until the battle of the Aisne finally rid their commanders of their blind faith in the efficacy of the charge, and they started digging in.

The young officer Henri Michel wrote to his wife, Marie, that September:

For 3 days and 2 nights now, we have been buried in a 1m 50 trench that we dug 50m to the East of the village of Amy, at the border of the Somme . . . We are on the first line. 600 metres from us some Uhlans are getting shot. This little village received more than 1000 shells the last three days, and it is almost destroyed. The villagers are hiding in the cellars . . . You have all my love, I never stop thinking about you and how happy I will be to see you again, Henri.[6]

A few weeks later, he added:

We are living like moles, you have no idea, my darling. When the shells fall, they throw everything 10 metres away, they make holes that can bury a rider with his horse. We call them the

'marmites' [craters] . . . And always the scream 'let's go!', and
we go over the top with our bayonets to charge the Fritz trench.[7]

At the end of November, he wrote, 'Marie, I am getting tired, I feel
sad, I want to see you again, and to be far from all these horrors of
fire and blood, from all the dead bodies rotting in the plain.'[8]

The early trench lines ran from Noyon to Reims, then west to
Verdun, before twisting south to Switzerland. Their existence signalled the end of open warfare, the war of movement, and the start of
underground attrition, in which the defenders always had the advantage, because the attackers had to go 'over the top' of the parapet
and charge the enemy's lines across the full gaze of no-man's-land.
The tactical challenge of the war, from the Aisne on, came down to a
simple question: how do we destroy and break through the enemy's
trench lines? Charge them? Outflank them? Bayonet them? Bomb
them? Plant explosives beneath them? Gas them? In coming years,
they would try, and fail, at every attempt. And a single forlorn fact
attests to the grim constancy of that failure: there were three battles
of the Aisne – in 1914, 1917 and 1918. All were fought to a standstill.
All killed or wounded thousands.

Charges on trench lines plainly resulted in countless, pointless
casualties, for the gaining of little or no ground, as any half-witted
observer could see. Yet, despite the evidence of their eyes, the commanders would continue to order frontal attack on trenches for the
duration of the war, in the belief that sustained artillery would kill,
wound or so addle the defenders they would be incapable of resist-
ing the infantry. Locked into their underground redoubts, each side
relied on heavy artillery to break holes in the opponents' lines and to
pound the enemy into submission.

At the Aisne, the German 8-inch (200-millimetre) howitzers
proved far deadlier than the 6-inch (150-millimetre) British guns
that were raced over the Channel. Under such fire, no rank was
immune; death came suddenly, almost casually. 'Took cover behind
hay stack,' the engineer E. S. Butcher recalled, 'shells continued to

drop just in front of us.' He was standing near General Edmund Allenby, who commanded the cavalry division of the BEF, which had so distinguished itself at Mons: 'one shell exploded not five yards [4.5 metres] in front of us, and bits flew into the hay just above our heads . . . as I left a shell exploded where we had been standing killing my chum who I had been speaking to just previously'.[9]

It was a terrifying experience to sit in a trench beneath exploding shells, some of which burst underground and others scattered thousands of fragments of shrapnel over them (and others, later, would release poison gas). Those who survived were prone to a severe form of shock, which, at its worst, caused complete nervous breakdown (and the symptoms of 'post-traumatic stress disorder' in later life). Yet no soldier could escape the terror of it: to flee the trench was desertion, punishable by death. They simply had to sit and bear it. Some soldiers surrendered rather than endure it any longer. The Germans sometimes 'surrender themselves', wrote Trichereau to his brother, 'because they don't have the right to step back; if they do they risk the death penalty'.[10]

Yet the men in the trenches found a source of solace – in mateship. The most intimate relationships were formed, and the division between officer and private underwent a levelling effect: they were all in this hole together. Even the rigid Prussian hierarchy could not resist the levelling effect of such intimate proximity, as Walter Delius, the German officer, wrote later that year:

At this time, the relationship between men and officers did attain a different face. Despite the best of discipline and order, the men became much closer to the officers from a human point of view . . . Even if our upbringing was not based on the principles of a master race mentality, Father's strong reticence towards democracy, of which he could only see the darkest sides, still had left their impression on me. Now finally I recognised that people who were not brought up according to conservative principles, were not automatically all notorious villains, but personalities whose attitude inside their circle of comrades and before the enemy wrought the highest of respect from everyone . . . Here, living together in the trenches in closest proximity, any hubris and silly conceit fell away, and you saw that the same thoughts and worries, the dangers you lived through together, united you with each other.[11]

At the front, the trenches were the place of greater safety. The space between the enemies' forward trench lines, called 'no-man's-land' – sometimes as narrow as 50–100 metres – soon turned into a bombed-out landscape of mud and stumps, rolls of wire and detritus, pocked with craters filled with water and bodies, from where the cries of the wounded rose through the long nights, unaided until they expired. In no-man's-land, the slightest sound or tremor drew immediate rifle or machine-gun fire. It was easy to see why the infantry would prefer night attacks, of crawling towards the enemy, over the mad daylight charges of 1916. But the constant, extreme stress of waiting for the shell that might kill you broke many young men – to the point where advancing seemed a relief. Those who suffered shell shock were jollied along, told to get on with it. At the time, the government, the hospitals and many people dismissed the condition as merely a case of 'nerves' or cowardice.

———

And so, on the night of 13 September, the Germans sat in their newly dug trenches along the Chemin des Dames, the road frequented by Louis XV's daughters (hence 'the path of the ladies') that follows the ridge above the northern bank of the Aisne, awaiting their pursuers in the mud and cold that would be the soldiers' companions for years to come. The British came across the river on pontoons or broken bridges and reached the shore between Bourg-et-Comin and Venizel in dense fog. They advanced up the slope and, emerging like ghosts from the clearing mist, met raking German rifle and machine-gun fire from unseen positions – the first time soldiers had tried to attack a trench line in the war. They were killed, wounded or stopped.

The French Fifth Army advanced to Berry-au-Bac by exploiting the gap between Kluck and Bülow. Their attacks were similarly short-lived. The British and French troops were helpless before the dug-in German lines. When a line buckled, under artillery or concentrated infantry attack, fresh troops poured into the gap and furiously dug back in. On 14 September, the first load of trenching stores arrived – a sign the Germans were there to stay. They dug deeper trenches, support trenches and connecting trenches. They laid wire between stakes . . . anything to slow down the enemy's charge. And there they sat, and watched, and waited.

The French and British had no choice other than to follow the German lead. They started digging. Orders went out for spades and pickaxes from local farms. The first Allied trench system took shape beyond the north bank of the Aisne. It was a shallow, shoddy effort, but it was a start – making the Aisne the first entrenched battlefield in the Western theatre. The advantage lay with the defenders, until infantry attacks were timed to coincide with artillery (as at the first battles of Passchendaele in 1917). After one Allied charge, the German lines slept in the trenches, 'between the cooling guns, and amidst the dead and wounded . . . with the wind whistling around the battlefield', wrote a German historian. The horses slept standing up. Hundreds of the severely wounded lay on straw bedding in their own blood. But the Germans held the position: '. . . the storm had been repelled'.[12]

—

By 20 September, the armies were locked in position in the Aisne valley. Neither side could advance. The trench lines, which were deepening vertically and horizontally, warned against frontal assaults. Inertia set in, and long periods of monotony, interspersed with shellfire, became the norm. The German officer Walter Delius wrote:

If we had hoped for a quick advance at first, we slowly came to understand that we were stuck and would be so for weeks to come. It cost us quite some effort to admit this to ourselves, because our hopes for victory . . . had to be buried. A depressed mood ensued. Orders from above led us to the conclusion that they no longer expected any further advance. The infantry barricaded themselves into the trenches . . .[13]

A fortnight later, he wrote of the trenches resembling 'a labyrinth, and it often happens that we get completely lost. You're not allowed to show your nose, as otherwise those English and their eagle eyes soon show you what's what.'[14]

The agony of slow attrition reached British drawing rooms. 'The war,' wrote Arthur Benson, on reading of the first trenches on 19 September, 'settles down into a sort of physical ache, at the thought of the hideous struggle going on hour after hour and all the lives lost *for so little* . . . It seems now a sort of statement in the Aisne. Neither side can [go] forward.'[15] A week later, 'the awful Aisne battle goes on, the Germans being entrenched strongly . . . the whole wretched waste of it is sickening to me'.[16]

Nor was there any hope of a breakthrough in the east, where the mighty alignments on the Moselle stood, immoveable. So the armies turned to the only open space, to the north and north-west, between Champagne and Flanders. The 'race to the sea' ensued, the scurry of troops and weapons from the Aisne to the Belgian coast in a 'frenzied search' for 'the open flank' (see Map 8).[17] Both sides were racing not to the sea but to find 'the northern wing of the opposing army', to punch a hole in the enemy's lines before they had a chance to dig in.[18]

The four nations had different strategic goals in the race. The Germans had the twin aim of breaking through the French and British lines to complete the march on Paris and occupying the channel ports to sever the supply link with England. The French aimed to protect Paris from the German wheel, and outflank and then drive the enemy back through Belgium. The British aimed to defend the Channel ports and coastal towns, especially Ypres, which were vital to reinforcing the BEF. And the Belgian Army, forced back from the relief of Antwerp, aimed to support their Anglo-French allies, chiefly by defending the Yser canal system between Ypres and the North Sea.

The great race began in mid-September and ended in November, running from the Aisne to the mouth of the Yser. It covered 250 kilometres and involved a series of pitched battles along a 'ribbon of death', at the Aisne (12–15 September), Picardy (22–26 September), Albert (25–29 September), Artois (27 September–10 October), La Bassée (10 October–2 November), Messines (12 October–2 November) and Armentières (13 October–2 November), climaxing in the appalling struggles of Yser and Ypres (late October–mid-November). Ypres was the most important strategic point. The ancient walled town – known to the Romans, rebuilt in mediaeval times – was the last defensive barrier before the Allied ports of Calais and Boulogne, the loss of which would have broken the shortest supply route between England and France.[19] For the German Army, the occupation of Ypres would enable them to block the Allied armies pouring across Flanders and protect the Ghent–Roeselare rail network axis, critical to German mobility in Belgium and the supply of their entire northern flank.[20]

That is the big picture. Up close, these battles involved hundreds of thousands of men locked in the deadliest sequence of armed violence in human history (soon to be outdone in the vast struggles on the Somme and Verdun in 1916). The battle for Ypres alone resulted in the near-annihilation of the BEF, which suffered a casualty rate of more than 30 per cent. A detailed narrative of this appalling campaign is beyond our scope (Ian Beckett's *Ypres: The First Battle 1914* is the most detailed single-volume study). We offer an outline of the battle that ended the race to the sea, killed, wounded or put out of action four-fifths of the BEF and is rightly remembered as one of the greatest testaments to British courage in history.

—

In early October, Erich von Falkenhayn, Motlke's successor, made up his mind to send the German Sixth Army to Flanders. He would soon reinforce it with the Fourth Army, rustled up from the survivors of the siege of Antwerp, and other units coming from the east. He meant to strike on the Flanders front 'as soon as possible and with forces as strong as possible'.[21] The German aim was to cut a path to the coastal ports of Dunkirk and Calais, and destroy them, thus severing the British lifeline to France. At the same time, the French sent the newly formed Tenth Army, under General Maunory, supported by British reinforcements, who landed in late September and early October. In early October, Foch was promoted to lead the French Northern Army Group, with technical responsibility for coordinating the Belgian and British forces (attached, as they necessarily were, to the vastly bigger French Army). In this role, Foch would reapply his guiding principle that had served him so well on the Marne. A commanding general, he later explained,

> must not let himself be influenced by the uncertainties and dangers of his own particular situation . . . On the contrary, it is his duty to search his mind and call upon his imagination for means which will enable his troops to hold out until the crisis is over.[22]

In this spirit, Foch knew how to play Sir John French. Sir John initially refused to cooperate with his Gallic allies, informing Hubert Gough, his commander of cavalry, 'not to accede to any request for help from the French'. He refused to be drawn into action on their behalf.[23] The French generals were in no mood for Sir John's petulance. Foch had already lost his son and son-in-law in battle. General Édouard de Castelnau, commanding the Second Army, had lost two sons in action and had lapsed into depression (he would later lose a third son). Joffre and Foch wanted decisions, action and results.

(Sir John's reluctance to cooperate accelerated the process already in motion that would end with his dismissal, in December 1915, and replacement by General Haig.)

Sir John went to see Foch on 8 October, with news of the imminent fall of Antwerp. The old fortresses that protected the city (and sheltered the King and his government) were collapsing under the power of the German guns. To reinforce Antwerp, Churchill had ordered on 3 October the dispatch of two marine battalions and two naval brigades – a gesture Asquith dismissed as 'idle butchery'.[24] The brigades were part of the specially formed Royal Naval Division, sailors who fought as infantry, and came to be known as Churchill's 'Sea Dogs'. Their illustrious members included the poet Rupert Brooke, the future politician and satirist A. P. Herbert, the future governor general of New Zealand Bernard Freyberg, who would receive the Victoria Cross and three Disinguished Service Orders in the war, and Sub Lieutenant Arthur Tisdall, 25, a brilliant classicist, recipient of a double first at Cambridge and the Chancellor's Gold Medal. Tisdall, who would die in 1915 in an act of transcendent courage, for which he received a posthumous Victoria Cross, wrote home, 'The burning city of Antwerp is a terrible but magnificent sight against the blackness of the night, and lights up the whole country round . . . It's horrid to feel so useless.'[25]

Despite their determined resistance, the Belgian and British forces proved unable to save the city. Antwerp fell on 9 October. The Sea Dogs who weren't killed or taken prisoner were evacuated, along with the King and key ministers. The end of the siege released the German Fourth Army for the assault on Ypres and Yser, the last great prizes in the race to the sea.

Reflecting on the loss, Sir John gloomily asked Foch how the Allies should counter the Germans now they were 'masters of all Belgium'.[26] Foch answered with his usual buoyant optimism – he tended to see victories (in Lorraine, on the Marne) where Sir John had seen, or anticipated, disaster. It worked. After the meeting, Foch wrote to Joffre of his pleasure at the great recovery in French and

British confidence. He proposed to advance to the Belgian coast. The French forces would take the southerly roads via La Bassée and Lille, and the British would take the roads north of these. Sir John, Foch added, had undertaken 'to support the operations of the French troops as fully and as promptly as possible'.[27]

—

The war devolved upon Flanders fields. Contrary to the popular impression of Flanders as a flattened moonscape, as it soon became, in autumn 1914 it looked as it had for centuries: a bleak, rain-drenched land of gentle hills and ridges, capped with woods of ash, chestnut and oak, set in heavy, blue 'Ypres clay'. It was a land of monotony and mist, 'with an air of melancholic sadness melting almost imperceptibly into the grey waters of the North Sea'.[28] When Foch arrived, he looked out from the tower of Ypres' Cloth Hall on a sprinkling of white villages and hamlets, set in fields of tobacco and beetroot, interspersed with hedgerows and barns and heaps of manure, spreading into dreary plains seasonally strewn with poppies, which tended to grow out of soil churned by plough – or shellfire: 'a sea of green, with little white islands marking the location of the rich villages with their fine churches and graceful steeples. To see open country in any direction was impossible.'[29] Now, this gentle, industrious region was to be pounded beneath the guns and the boots of four national armies, in almost incessant combat, over four weeks, to mid-November.

Between 10 and 19 October, the British and Germans concentrated their forces on Ypres. The city was no stranger to hostilities or besiegement. The Romans had attacked it. So had successive forces of French, Dutch and English, in the bloody play of power through time. In 1383, Henry le Despenser, the Bishop of Norwich, led an English army to occupy Ypres. He remarked upon 'a nice old town, with narrow, cobbled-stoned streets and some fine buildings' and then besieged it for four months until French relief arrived.[30] After a French Army captured the city in 1678, the engineer Vauban installed a series of ramparts to deter further invaders.

In mid-October 1914, the BEF's II Corps (commanded by the inexhaustible Smith-Dorrien) and III Corps (commanded by the unimpressive General William Pulteney), and a Cavalry Corps (commanded by the forceful General Edmund Allenby – later Field Marshal Allenby, supporter of Lawrence of Arabia) occupied a series of ridges about eight kilometres to the east of the town, named on military maps according to their nearby villages: Passchendaele, Broodseinde, Messines, Gheluvelt. In the early clashes, overwhelming German numbers forced the British off these positions and back to the city's ramparts. General Hubert Hamilton, commanding the Third Division, was killed – a great blow to Smith-Dorrien, who wrote to his wife that he had 'lost my right arm, for in my Army Corps he was that to me'.[31] On 20 October, General Haig's I Corps arrived and were stationed on the outskirts of the town. No further reinforcements would arrive until 26 October (when the Lahore Division of the Indian Corps, the first Commonwealth troops, were expected).

On the 20th, the Germans unleashed another offensive, all along the front from Nieuport to Armentières. Defending Yser, the Belgians had constructed a line of formidable defences and trenches running along the canal, which they called the Belgian Bulwark. Six Belgian divisions held off the Germans for four days until, on the verge of collapse and having suffered 18,000 casualties, they resorted to a marvel of last-minute ingenuity: they flooded the heavily irrigated region to the east of the canal. Belgian engineers struck on a plan to inundate the whole area, by opening the Nieuport sluices to the sea and blocking 22 culverts under the Nieuport–Dixmude railway embankments.

This miraculous reversal of King Canute's mock-attempt to hold back the ocean relied on the coordination of the North Sea tides, the wind direction and the opening of the huge sluice gates. The Belgians accomplished it successfully between 26 and 30 October, creating a lagoon 28–35 kilometres long, 3–3.5 kilometres wide and around a metre deep. The forward Belgian units soon found themselves fighting up to their knees in water. Initially, the Germans attributed the rising water to heavy rainfall, but the retreating units looked back on 'green meadows . . . covered with dirty yellow water'.[32] The flood waters blocked the German assault, ended the battle of the Yser, checked any hope of Germany claiming the channel ports and freed France's XXXII Corps to fight at Ypres. The state of the German troops at this time was abysmal. Short of food, especially bread, with nothing hot to eat and compelled to drink green, polluted water, they had been reduced, an officer wrote in a diary found on his body, 'to the state of beasts'.[33]

—

In the last ten days of October, the far fresher German Fourth and Sixth Armies, under generals Wurttemberg and Rupprecht respectively, turned their full attention on Ypres. Unknown to Sir John French, whose troops were responsible for holding the city, and who persisted in believing flawed intelligence, the BEF were hugely outnumbered: 14 German infantry divisions were ranged against seven British and French (three of which were cavalry fighting as infantry). The Germans had twice as many guns and, later, ten times as many heavy artillery pieces. Both sides fielded two machine guns per battalion. The British excelled the Germans in a critical area: their superb riflemen, trained to fire their famous '15 aimed rounds a minute'[34] – far quicker than their conscript opponents.

The Germans mounted successive attacks across Flanders in huge, densely packed masses – easy targets for British rifle fire, which spat round after round in a hail of bullets. Once more, German troops imagined they were advancing on machine guns. Tens of thousands fell. Yet German weight of numbers ensured that many reached the British lines and virtually wiped out the 2nd Sherwood Foresters of Brigadier General Walter Congreve VC's 18th Brigade (6th Division) at Ennetières. Most of the battalion were killed, wounded or captured. Allenby's 9000-strong Cavalry Corps came under the sustained attack of 24,000 German troops, who drove them back to the Messines ridge. The cavalry were not on horseback; they had been entrenched, like the infantry. Occasionally, they saddled up 'to move from one part of the battlefield to another'.[35] Their trenches were hastily dug, a metre deep and mud-filled – and not the 'well-planned maze' that the official history recorded.[36] The first consignment of sandbags would not arrive until 28 October.

The Germans persisted. They used their huge numerical advantage to enclose the city in a slow, grinding vice. Sir John French still refused to believe they outnumbered him. Thinking that only one German corps threatened Haig's position, Sir John ordered him to advance towards Courtrai, the ultimate objective being Passchendaele. In fact, Haig confronted five German corps, forcing the thin British lines to fight separate, concentrated actions, with the artillery plugging the gaps. The truth of the German offensive confirmed Haig's poor opinion of his superior officer and sealed his ambition to replace him.

—

On the night of the 22nd, several German reserve regiments charged the British lines near Langemarck, allegedly singing 'Deutschland, Deutschland über Alles' as they ran, according to the 'Legend of Langemarck'. In fact, they attacked near the less German-sounding Bixschoote and were more likely to be singing 'Die Wacht am Rhein', a regimental marching song often used to distinguish each other in the mist.[37] Adolf Hitler, who fought at Ypres with the 6th Bavarian Reserve Division (XIV Reserve Corps), recalled in *Mein Kampf*:

> And from the distance the strains of a song reached our ears, coming closer and closer, leaping from company to company, and just as Death plunged a busy hand into our ranks, the song reached us too and we passed it along: Deutschland, Deutschland über Alles.[38]

This attack was more unrelenting than anything the British had experienced. The Germans came at them with unthinking, suicidal courage. They smashed up villages, churches, farms – anything in their path. They raced at the British lines with scarcely a care for their own necks, as if embracing death, as if to prove that their lives were expendable in the service of the state. Captain Harry Dillon, of the 2nd Oxford and Bucks Light Infantry, witnessed 'a great grey mass of humanity . . . charging, running for all God would let them straight on to us not 50 yards [45 metres] off'. He had warned his men what to expect, but nobody expected this. He had 'never shot so much in such a short time'. The attackers fell, veered off course, staggered to the ground, until only 'a great moan' rose in the night, and men 'with their arms and legs off' tried to crawl away.[39] Private H. J. Milton saw masses of Germans 'simply running into death, they gave great yells after they started but very few got back. The screams were terrible.'[40] Some British companies fired an average of 500 rounds per man that night.

The Germans had simply hurled themselves at the enemy lines at Ypres, as one recalls: 'This storming, we will never forget as long as we live.' The survivors staggered or crawled back to their trenches. 'There is not one house which has not been shot to pieces all around. Everything is one big pile of rubble.' They ravaged the fields and gardens for food. One soldier wrote:

> All the belongings of the inhabitants now fled have been destroyed, and we are using quite a few lovely pieces of furniture for firewood or similar. Our trenches are reinforced with doors, wardrobes and all sorts of other items we considered useful for building our winter accommodation . . . We are using all the straw and crops we can find. It either serves as our bedding or is threshed and used in bread making. The French will only feel the full misery of their situation when they return home.[41]

Today, the bodies of 24,917 German troops who fought at the

First Battle of Ypres lie buried in a mass grave at Langemarck. The German losses included some 3000 student volunteers. Their deaths – about 15 per cent of the total – gave rise to the legend of the *Kindermord bei Ypern* (the Massacre of the Innocents at Ypres). They were not children, as the legend suggests, though many were as young as 17–19. They were romantic dreamers, young Hans Castorps, believers in the glory of the Fatherland and prey to war propaganda that proselytised the minds of the young. Their British opponents were professional soldiers, tough-as-nails Tommy Atkinses, as Keegan writes: 'working class, long-service regulars, shilling–day-men of no birth and scanty education'.[42] They cared nothing for the mystical German patriotism of their young attackers. They were trained to kill, win the war and go home.

—

By 25 October, the British had withdrawn inside the half-circumference linking the villages of Messines, Hollebeke, Zandvoorde, Zonnebeke and Langemarck. A shell shortage had reduced their firing capacity to a 'deplorable state', wrote Sir John. The British Army had planned for an average expenditure of ten rounds per gun per day. At Ypres, they spent at least 50 rounds per day, and, in crises, 80. Some hard-pressed batteries had fired 1200 shells in 24 hours. Had the gun batteries fired at the preferred rate of the gunners, of four rounds *per minute*, each gun at Ypres would have exhausted the entire stock envisaged for six months in under seven hours.[43]

This dire situation seemed to contradict Sir John French's telegram to Kitchener two days later, in which he confidently stated that the Germans were 'quite incapable of making any strong and sustained attack'.[44] Few statements more painfully revealed the distance between British intelligence and reality. That day, Falkenhayn issued orders for a renewed offensive at Ypres, to take place on 30 October, using a powerful new force – Army Group Fabeck, under the command of General Max von Fabeck. It included the XIII, XV and II Bavarian Corps, well-trained, fresh troops backed up by a hellish concentration of artillery: 257 heavy guns and howitzers were brought up to the line from Messines to Gheluvelt. Their addition gave the Germans a two-to-one superiority in troop numbers and ten-to-one in guns.[45] Army Group Fabeck meant to smash the British defences apart and take Kemmel Hill, to the south of Ypres – a commanding position from which to bomb the city. Preliminary to the main offensive, Fabeck launched an attack on Gheluvelt on the 29th, using the existing Fourth Army troops, who drove back the fewer British forces in a brutal struggle for control of the crossroads east of Gheluvelt (it little helped that two British machine guns jammed at the junction).

The seriousness of the situation forced General Haig to send in his main corps reserves (2nd Brigade). They just held the village. Night came, with torrential rain. The British were, at this point, fighting for their lives. Yet their condition somehow eluded Sir John French, who imagined his troops were set to pursue the Germans. '[I]f the success can be followed up,' he cabled Kitchener that day, 'it will lead to a decisive result.'[46] Haig ignored these orders, dug in and waited for the coming blow. It came at dawn on Friday 30 October, with an hour of thunderous bombardment. At 6.30 am, Fabeck's fresh infantry attacked. Haig's men initially held the line, but the British cavalry were forced back, yielding the village of Zandvoorde. After a day of intense fighting, the BEF still held on, amazing the Germans and probably many of themselves.

—

Yet nothing in the BEF's experience compared with the German attack the next day, when Fabeck decided that Ypres must fall to the Kaiser. 'Saturday 31 October,' Harris writes, 'was to be one of the most critical day's fighting not merely of 1914 but of the whole war.'[47] The British would bear the full brunt of it, as 'nothing of special importance' was happening on the French lines, Foch later wrote.[48] The day dawned warmly, with a clearing mist, revealing lines of 'tired, haggard and unshaven men, unwashed, plastered with mud, many in little more than rags'. They were all that stood 'between the British Empire and ruin'.[49] Opposing them were double their numbers, and ten times their cannon-power.

None who lived to remember the bombardment that morning ever forgot it. The German guns churned up the British trenches all over Haig's I Corps, leaving a quagmire of mud and bodies, and forced the survivors back in shocked disbelief. Gheluvelt fell to the Germans at noon. The British commander at the front, General Lomax, called for reinforcements, but only 350 men of the Second Battalion, Worcestershire Regiment, under Brigadier General FitzClarence were available. Thrown into battle, they charged the town of Gheluvelt and, in an astonishing reversal, retook it – with awful losses. 'It was just as if we had all been under sentence of death and most suddenly received a free pardon,' according to one of Haig's staff.[50] (The war sentenced Lomax's new headquarters to death that day. Five of his staff officers were killed instantly when the chateau sustained a direct hit; Lomax and two others were mortally wounded.)

At some point – when all was lost, runs the apocryphal version – Haig called for his horse and rode majestically to the front to lead his men to victory. The general's ride down the Menin Road did occur (after breakfast, at 0800), yet its purpose and efficacy remain unclear. It was certainly not the 'turning point' of the battle, as Haig's apologists later suggested: Haig set off knowing full well the British had already retaken Gheluvelt. An equal contender for the 'turning point' might have been Foch's scrawled instructions to Sir John French that day: 'It is absolutely essential *not to retreat*,' he urged Sir John, 'therefore the men must dig in . . . and hold on to the ground they now occupy.'[51]

That is exactly what the BEF were doing. Let us dispense with generals' claims to have won the day: the true victors of Ypres were the British infantry (and cavalry fighting as infantry). They never gave up; they held on, rattling bullets 'over every bush, hedge and fragment of wall'.[52] To the south, the cavalry were forced back almost to Kemmel Hill but regained the initiative and drove the Germans back. Wherever the German infantry broke through the British lines, a maze of trenches, barricades, wire and special 'strong points' (the work of Haig's chief engineer Brigadier General Rice and his men) stopped them, at which point Allied rifles poured fire onto the intruders. These battles raged on several fronts: at Gheluvelt, near Armentières, at Nun's Wood (Nonnesbosschen) and Polygon Wood. By 11 November, the British and French troops had stopped the German advance. The fighting flickered out in exhaustion and an acute shell shortage. By then, the British were reduced to firing just six shells a day.

—

The Allies had won the First Battle of Ypres and held the city. The most famous regiments in British military history fought here, and members of some of Britain's oldest families died here: Wyndham, FitzClarence, Dawnay, Wellesley, Cadogan, Bruce, Gordon-Lennox, Kinnaird, Cavendish and Hamilton. The novelist John Buchan likened reading the casualty list to 'scanning the death roll after Agincourt or Flodden'.[53] Whole units were almost wiped out – killed, wounded, missing or sick. By 4 November, the 18,000-strong First Division, I Corps fielded just 92 officers and 3491 men. By 11 November, only four officers and 300 men were left of the 1st Guards Brigade, normally 4000 strong.[54] The British lost 55,395 men, killed, wounded and missing (out of a total force of just 163,897 – a crippling 34 per cent casualty rate), of whom 7960 died. The French suffered total casualties of more than 50,000, the Belgians 21,562 and the Germans 134,315, of whom 19,530 were killed.[55]

Nurses recorded the reality of these statistics on the ground – in the field clinics and hospitals. Martha Withhall, née Aitken, 32, an English nurse, wrote on 30 November 1914: 'Last night I had 48 patients, so fairly quiet. One poor man who had his leg shot off some days ago died. He was quite conscious to the last and every now and again would ask 'Sister has peace been declared yet, oh my poor mates in the trenches'. Poor lad he never thought how soon peace would be declared for him!'[56] That month, another British nurse, Edith Cavell, began helping Allied soldiers escape German-occupied Belgium. She was later arrested, charged with treason and shot by a German firing squad, despite international protest and outrage.

The casualties at Ypres, though horrendous, were but a fraction of the losses thus far. Total French deaths exceeded 300,000 in the first four months of the war (in September alone, France had lost 200,000 men – killed, wounded and missing), German deaths totalled 241,000, and Belgium and Britain had each suffered fatalities of 30,000.[57] Total casualties in France and Belgium – dead, wounded and missing – in the first four months exceeded a million men, then the most concentrated death rate in military history.

The Allied success at Ypres demonstrated a grim lesson: that entrenched lines defended by skilled marksmen would defeat a much bigger foe attacking over open ground. The approach of winter and the shell shortage postponed combat, and the war petered out in stalemate. They spent November and December deepening their trench lines and rebuilding their forces. All along the Western Front, the armies dug in. At the Aisne, the Somme, Verdun, the Moselle, in river valleys and on ridges, the two sides locked up the subsoil in zigzagging trench lines, supported by inverse A-frame wooden blocks that supported duckboards running just above the mud. Sandbagged, built to last, these would be the soldiers' homes for four more years.

Reinforcements poured into the lines. Between August and December, millions of new recruits arrived, from France, Britain, Russia and Germany: Kitcheners' Pal Battalions, young French poilu, a seemingly limitless supply of German youth and countless Russians from the furthest reaches of Siberia. All were quickly trained, dropped into a uniform and flung into combat. The French soldier Emile Fossey's battalion reached Ypres in November (they had previously fought on the Sambre): '[O]nce again we are in Belgium, where we will stay the whole winter . . . The trenches in which we must stand day and night are filled with water, mud, corpses . . .' The winter frost came: 'I carry supplies every night, 20 km back and forth, walking in the mud. It is hard, but the walk prevents my feet from freezing like many of my mates.'[58]

The pause in battle drew attention to their discomforts: foot-rot, rats and the most hated torment (and carriers of trench fever), lice. Raymond Clément, the French stretcher-bearer, wrote:

> Without telling any body, I take my clothes off. And I see hundreds of lice and larva jumping out of me! They are everywhere: in my shirt, my pants, my underwear, etc. I shake my clothes as much as I can, and finally wear them again . . . The only choice we have is to wait for the next relief, and boil our clothes.[59]

Rats scuttled along the trench floors, over the exhausted men, in search of food. They fed on rotting flesh. 'Rats came up from the canal,' Robert Graves later wrote, 'fed on the plentiful corpses, and multiplied exceedingly.' A new British recruit 'found two rats on his blanket tussling for the possession of a severed hand'.[60] The story was a great joke, Graves added.

On Christmas Eve at Saint Yvon, where the trenches were barely 50 metres apart, the Germans shouted, 'Happy Christmas, Tommy!' The British shouted back, 'Merry Christmas, Jerry!' Above the German parapet, a figure then appeared, and another, and another, walking towards the British trenches, across no-man's-land. The British held their fire and went out to meet the enemy. They exchanged rum and schnapps, and looked at each other's photos of their loved ones. Thus began the famous Christmas truce, one of the most endearing legends of the Great War. Sergeant David Lloyd-Burch witnessed the German and English troops 'burying the dead between the trenches. Cigarettes and cigars were exchanged. It was so exciting . . . to be above the trenches in daylight. At ordinary times meant sudden death. This truce continued till New Year's day . . . It seems terrible to think that they were exchanging souvenirs one day and killing one another the next.'[61]

Indeed, they weren't all singing 'Silent Night' along the Ypres Salient. The battle raged on in many places. Most Allied and German generals disapproved of, and later banned, fraternising with the enemy. Adolf Hitler frowned on the truce.

And so the two sides returned to their trenches, and resumed gazing malignly across no-man's-land, wondering what the New Year would bring over the parapets of trench lines that zigzagged from the Belgian coast to the Swiss mountains. This great fissure, 765 kilometres long, visible from space, would remain more or less in the same position – with periodic, bloody ruptures and incursions, spilling the blood of millions for little territorial gain – until 1918 (see Map 9). They called it the Western Front.

EPILOGUE

THE YEAR THE WORLD ENDED

It seems that something inside me is torn, something that
rooted me to my native country . . . I feel empty, I feel alone.
Everything is going away and seems to abandon me.
Raymond Clément, French stretcher-bearer, in his diary at the end of 1914

I walked up and down the walls of St Johns. How the
war has smashed us! There were no undergraduates
about, and there are now very few bachelor dons . . .
Arthur Benson, poet and scholar, in his diary, 15 December 1914

'INCONNU . . . INCONNU . . . INCONNU . . .' On thousands of little white crosses, the single French word for 'Unknown'. Its repetition on row upon row of graves in hundreds of cemeteries in northern France conveys a sense of something beyond death. It suggests annihilation, as though a whole people had been wiped out, obliterated, made extinct. The word is a terminal judgement, a forlorn appeal to the void. If these soldiers are unknown, what became of them? Who were they? What unlived life had been taken from them? *'Inconnu'* has none of the consoling spirit of the

Commonwealth epitaph to the missing, 'Known Unto God'. Even an atheist standing among the white stones at Thiepville, Villers-Bretonneux or Tyne Cot Cemetery could not help but feel some consolation in Kipling's gently hopeful line.

By the end of the war, three million soldiers were listed as missing, their bodies never identified. They disappeared in no-man's-land, in the mud of the Somme and Flanders, the Aisne and the Sambre. They bled to death in a crater. They were entombed in a shelled trench, or an underground mine. They drowned in the shell-churned swamp of Passchendaele. They disappeared into the Verdun mincing machine. They were torn apart, mashed with the soil, atomised. Body parts were unrecognisable. Nobody knew to whom this hand or foot belonged, or whose head this once was. In time, nobody would have known they were there.

But the administration of the First World War was efficient in this respect: the listing of names. Any man not present at the 'last post' – the last inspection of the day – was registered as missing. A small number would have deserted. Most were wounded or dead. If their bodies were never found, their names were listed on the walls of memorials as among the missing: at Ypres, the Somme, Verdun, Le Chemin des Dames, and hundreds of cemeteries in France and Belgium. Of 11,956 burials at the Tyne Cot Cemetery in Passchendaele – the largest Commonwealth war grave – 3587 lie in unmarked graves. A further 54,900 Commonwealth names are listed as missing on the Menin Gate at Ypres. The French, Germans and Russians also lost innumerable soldiers in the fathomless tomb of the battlefield. At Langemarck, north-east of Ypres, lies the largest unmarked grave in western Europe: 24,917 German soldiers are buried there, of whom 7977 remain unknown, many of them student casualties of the *Kindermord*.

Not until recently have corpses received identities. The first DNA-identified body of the Great War belonged to Australian soldier Jack Hunter, who died in the arms of his brother Jim in 1917 at Polygon Wood, near Ypres. Jim buried him with dignity in a temporary war cemetery. After the war, he returned to give his brother a proper funeral but could not find Jack's remains. Not until 2006 would a team of Australian archaeologists identify several corpses in the area. A list of the likely names of the soldiers was published, and their families agreed to participate in DNA tests. Jack Hunter's niece provided a sample of her DNA, which duly matched her uncle's. His name was removed from the list on Menin Gate and his remains reinterred on Remembrance Day, 2007, at Buttes New British Cemetery in Polygon Wood. 'At rest after being lost for 90 years,' reads his epitaph.

—

Together, the war-grave epitaphs tell a short history of human feeling. The tone subtly changed through the war years. At first, most tended to express the normal, heartfelt grief of parents, wives and families who had lost their sons, husbands or brothers:

> They never die who lived in the hearts they loved (Passchendaele);
> He is not dead, for such a man as my husband was can never die (Villers-Bretonneux);
> Our dear daddy and our hero we miss you (Polygon Wood);
> To our beloved son (various)

Meanings were made of the loss. He died for a noble cause, for freedom. He sacrificed himself so that others may live. Only the greatest lines from the Bible would do. In this respect, some epitaphs seemed to say more about the wishes of the family than the actual feelings of the soldier:

> Their glory shall not be blotted out (Ecclesiasticus 44:13, Loos);
> Greater love hath no man than this (John 15:13, various);
> As a flower he was cut off (a paraphrasing of Job 14:2, Passchendaele);
> His sacrifice was not in vain, ever remembered by all (Passchendaele)

Then a darker note intruded. As the war ground on, and the killing fields claimed millions of lives, a desperate, even defiant tone found expression on the gravestones. Parents spoke of their boys as 'broken'; they were 'lost'. Or they were simply 'Sacrificed'. For what? By whom? The questions linger unanswered over the fields of France, Belgium, Prussia and Poland. Soon, mothers and wives expressed their grief with greater intensity: the loss of their sons had killed something in them, too:

> No mother near to close his eyes
> Far from his native land he lies
> The shell that stilled his true brave heart broke mine
> Mother

Individuals walk along the rows of the dead, in contemplative solitude. One feels a kind of helpless numbness at the enormity of the waste, of the loss of so many young men who had never known adult love, or the adoration a father feels for his child. They were, in so many cases, lads whose lives were barely formed and whose promise would never be fulfilled.

But nothing prepares you for a new voice, as you linger in these aisles of grass: the sudden, cheerful voice of the soldier himself, shouting out from gravestones on which his family had chosen to inscribe the last line of his last letter home:

> The French are a grand nation, worth fighting for! (Passchendaele)
> I'm alright mother, cheerio (Passchendaele)

—

Nineteen-fourteen was the year the world ended, for millions of men, women and families. It was the end of dreams. It was the end of certainty. It was the end of many soldiers' faith in the propaganda, of the holy triumvirate of God, King and Country, of lyrical paeans to heroism and self-sacrifice, and all the shibboleths of tired old regimes . . . which they and their families would soon tear down as monstrous lies. Many families were with Kipling, who wrote, on the death of his son in 1916: 'If any question why we died, / Tell them, because our fathers lied.'

'You will soon change your style,' Robert Graves warned fellow poet Siegfried Sassoon in 1915, upon reading Sassoon's chivalrous lines, 'Return to greet me, colours that were my joy / Not in the woeful crimson of men slain.' Sassoon, who frowned on the gritty disillusionment of Graves' poem, 'Over the Brazier', had not yet experienced the trenches, as Graves had.[1] Later, after returning from France, Sassoon would find a new voice: 'The rank stench of those bodies haunts me still . . .'; 'War's a joke for me and you . . .' And the desolate bitterness of, 'I were fierce, and bald, and short of breath / I'd live with scarlet majors at the Base, / And speed glum heroes up the line to death . . . And when the war is done and youth stone dead / I'd toddle safely home and die – in bed.'

But it was the officer Wilfred Owen who brought the reality of the war searing to light to a dim and ignorant world. He told a truth neither the governments nor the press would. The very title of his poem 'Anthem for Doomed Youth' said it all, conjuring the image of a generation marching to their death. But 'Dulce et Decorum Est' went further. By describing a mustard-gas attack on a group of soldiers, it brought home what dying for one's country actually meant. No war writer has since matched the power to shock of Owen's simple phrases. Let us remind ourselves why:

Dulce et Decorum Est
Bent double, like old beggars under sacks,
Knock-kneed, coughing like hags, we cursed through sludge,
Till on the haunting flares we turned our backs
And towards our distant rest began to trudge.
Men marched asleep. Many had lost their boots
But limped on, blood-shod. All went lame; all blind;
Drunk with fatigue; deaf even to the hoots

Of disappointed shells that dropped behind.
GAS! Gas! Quick, boys! — An ecstasy of fumbling,
Fitting the clumsy helmets just in time;
But someone still was yelling out and stumbling
And floundering like a man in fire or lime . . .
Dim, through the misty panes and thick green light
As under a green sea, I saw him drowning.
In all my dreams, before my helpless sight,
He plunges at me, guttering, choking, drowning.
If in some smothering dreams you too could pace
Behind the wagon that we flung him in,
And watch the white eyes writhing in his face,
His hanging face, like a devil's sick of sin;
If you could hear, at every jolt, the blood
Come gargling from the froth-corrupted lungs,
Obscene as cancer, bitter as the cud
Of vile, incurable sores on innocent tongues, —
My friend, you would not tell with such high zest
To children ardent for some desperate glory,
The old Lie: Dulce et decorum est
Pro patria mori.[2]

—

Nineteen-fourteen destroyed minds, as well as bodies. If a soldier wasn't dead or wounded by the end of it, his mind was probably undone. Nineteen-fourteen ended the delusion that the human brain could endure the terror of shellfire, the shock of going 'over the top' and the interminable tension of waiting. Few at home understood, or tried to understand, the effects of sustained artillery attack on the brain and central nervous system, of wondering when a shell would land on you. One who did try was the psychiatrist W. H. R. Rivers, medical officer of Craiglockhart War Hospital (and a key character in Pat Barker's trilogy). Rivers's job was to examine and cure – to the extent that he could – then send back to the front men whose brains had been severely damaged, perhaps irretrievably, by a war that society had judged as rational and just. In this bleak trade-off between health and duty, the soldier's situation transcends mere irony. By succumbing to shell shock, he had somehow failed an otherwise normal society, in which it was deemed perfectly sane to subject him to shellfire while sitting in rat-riddled trenches in the dead of winter. (Medical science has recently changed that line of thinking. Today, an *abnormal* mental reaction – shell shock, post-traumatic stress disorder – to abnormal events – shelling, mass slaughter – is deemed 'normal'.[3] The human mind was not designed to endure, intact, such experiences, the doctors now tell us.)

In an address in December 1917, Rivers revealed the thinking at the time.[4] He had noticed in many of his patients – all veterans of the Great War – a tendency to repress their war experiences, 'to thrust out of his memory some part of his mental content'. The harm, Rivers argued, was not the act of repression but 'repression under conditions in which it fails to adapt the individual to his environment'. One is tempted to turn this on its head and wonder why damaged young minds were expected to adapt to the source of the damage: a world war, in which they were shelled to the edge of sanity. Surely, it should have been the other way around: a civilised human 'environment' should adapt to the expectations of sane young minds.

The disturbing psychological symptoms of the lads in Rivers's care were not, the doctor claimed, due to the shelling they had experienced. On the contrary, the patients' struggle to repress the memory of the trenches had caused their horrifying dreams, headaches and terrible bouts of depression. In other words, their failure to assimilate their experiences was the source of their sickness, and not the experience itself. *They* had willed their sickness. One can almost hear the sigh of relief in Whitehall and the Quai d'Orsay at a conclusion that, in its effect, exonerated them from responsibility for the damage to the young. But the soldiers, he warned, who tried to banish their horrible experiences from their minds, had been misled, and he offered several case studies to prove the point.

A young English officer was sent home from France 'on account of a wound received just as he was extricating himself from a mass of earth in which he had been buried'. In other words, the young man had been hit by shrapnel after he had been virtually buried alive – not an experience one expects to encounter in the normal run of things. He tried to lie about his symptoms, to repress them, to seem happy, in order to get back to the front line, to do his duty. But his symptoms got worse, and he was sent to Craiglockhart War Hospital for 'further observation'. Every night, he had vivid dreams of warfare. 'He could not sleep without a light in his room because in the dark his attention was attracted by every sound.' Terrible memories crowded his mind. Doctors and experts had so far told him to forget about them. He couldn't. Rivers was the first doctor to urge him to open up: 'We talked about his war experiences and his anxieties, and following this he had the best night he had had for five months.' Whether he continued to enjoy restful nights, Rivers does not say. He was 'cured' for now, and was sent back to the front.

Another officer, suffering cerebral concussion from a shell burst, collapsed a few months later after finding the remains of his close friend on the battlefield. The body was blown to pieces, 'with head and limbs lying separated from the trunk'. From then, the officer suffered a recurring nightmare in which his friend appeared as a leprous, mutilated monster, 'drawing nearer and nearer until the patient suddenly awoke pouring with sweat and in a state of the utmost terror. He dreaded to go to sleep, and spent each day looking forward in painful anticipation of the night.'

Rivers again worked his magic. He drew the officer's attention to the obvious fact that his friend had been 'killed outright' – i.e. instantly – and had been spared a long and painful death: 'He brightened at once and said that this aspect of the case had never occurred to him . . .'

In irredeemably ghastly cases, the psychiatrist's methods failed. Such was the case of a third young officer:

who was flung down by the explosion of a shell so that his face struck the distended abdomen of a German several days dead, the impact of his fall rupturing the swollen corpse. Before he lost consciousness, the patient had clearly realised his situation and knew that the substance which filled his mouth and produced the most horrible sensations of taste and smell was derived from the decomposed entrails of an enemy.

This officer experienced bursts of unbearable depression. One is tempted at this point to wonder whether the patients' war experiences were the direct cause of their symptoms and not the officers' understandable tendency to try to block them out. The poor man's 'reasonless dread' had a very clear reason, and one which is now, mercifully (and rather obviously), recognisable. Rivers could do nothing for this man, who was medically discharged.

Rivers was not expected, or paid, to blame the war: that would have denied the legitimacy of the whole apparatus of the war effort. His job was to make these young men's brains function as soldiers' brains should: to obey orders, to fight, and to die, if necessary. Owen, Sassoon and Graves came under his care. Many of his patients willingly returned to the front, more often than not to be back with their friends – although 'friend' is not quite the right word for these relationships in the trenches, which were more likely experiences of intense love on the cusp of death.

Rivers judged his methods a partial success, which was true within his narrow remit. He had succeeded in making men fight again. 'Several of the officers I have described,' he concluded, 'were able to return to some form of military duty, with a degree of success very unlikely if they had persisted in the process of repression . . .'[5] In other words, he had 'healed' normal men of their sane reaction to the war, and sent them back to bedlam.

—

The world as they knew it ended for those who were conscripted. The

French three-year law pressed into uniform men with families, pacifists and men with religious or conscientious objections. The same went for Germans and Russians. In Britain, several forms of unofficial conscription existed. Squires, parsons, retired officers, employers, schoolmasters, leader-writers, politicians, cartoonists, poets, music-hall singers and women exhorted men to put on a uniform and get to the front lines. These recruits were not, strictly speaking, 'volunteers'. 'They are conscripts. They have gone in because it would have been so infernally unpleasant to have stayed out.'[6]

Harold Begbie's song 'Fall In', written in 1914, expressed the general sentiment that drove more than a million British men to 'volunteer'. Many did so unwillingly but were unable to resist the overwhelming social pressure:

> How will you fare, sonny, how will you fare
> In the far-off winter night
> When you sit by the fire in the old man's chair
> And your neighbours talk of the fight?
> Will you slink away, as it were from a blow,
> Your old head shamed and bent?
> Or say, 'I was not with the first to go,
> But I went, thank God, I went'?

The press were reliable bullies, constantly publishing notices, in league with the government, that sought to shame the reluctant to enlist. A typical British newspaper notice ran:

TO THE MEN OF ENGLAND
The country is in danger.
Already thousands of men belonging to all classes have
volunteered for service with the colours.
The Government now asks for another 500,000 men.
Every able-bodied unmarried man, under 35 years of age, must
now offer his services to the nation.

Those men who do not will properly be regarded as cowards,
and unworthy of the name of Englishmen.[7]

The Order of the White Feather, founded in August 1914 by Admiral
Charles Fitzgerald with the support of popular female writers such as
Mary Ward and Emma Orczy, set the most odious example of unofficial conscription. 'Women's War: White Feathers for Slackers' bellowed the *Daily Mail* on Monday 31 August 1914: 'Thirty Folkestone
women have banded themselves together, and today they will present
a white feather to every young "slacker", deaf or indifferent to their
country's need.'[8]

The Order unleashed a female press gang on any man found out
of uniform. They would hound him without any effort to appreciate his individual circumstances. Thousands of zealous, uneducated
young women were persuaded – though most needed no persuading
– to hunt down any nervous lad, or father, who had not volunteered.
Women would taunt, embarrass and humiliate such men into uniform by planting the symbol of cowardice on his chest: a small white
goose feather.

As with any social program of compulsion decreed by some
distant authority, cases of heartless abuse and misapplication were
common. In their zeal to enact Kitchener's recruitment policy,
fanatical women made serious errors of judgement, which drove to
war men who were otherwise unfit or had good reasons not to fight.
That did not make Robert Smith, 34, a coward, deserving of public
humiliation. Smith, married, with two young children, received a
feather on his way home from work. 'That night,' his daughter later
recalled, 'he came home and cried his heart out. My father was no
coward, but had been reluctant to leave his family. He . . . had been
suffering from a serious illness. Soon after this incident my father
joined the army.'[9]

Pacifists such as Fenner Brockway received so many white feathers he had enough to make a fan. The writer Compton Mackenzie, a
soldier, ridiculed the Order as a mob of 'idiotic young women' who

'were using white feathers to get rid of boyfriends of whom they were tired'.[10] Or they targeted the young. A group of girls surrounded James Lovegrove, just 16, in the street, and started shouting and calling him a coward. They stuck a white feather on his coat. 'Oh, I did feel dreadful, so ashamed,' he later said. 'I went to the recruiting office. The sergeant there couldn't stop laughing at me, saying things like, "Looking for your father, sonny?" and "Come back next year when the war's over!" Well, I must have looked so crestfallen that he said "Let's check your measurements again".' Lovegrove was just five foot six inches (168 centimetres) and eight and a half stone (54 kilograms), but the sergeant wrote down six feet (183 centimetres) tall and twelve stone (76 kilograms): 'All lies of course – but I was in!' Similarly, one 15-year-old boy lied about his age to get into the army in 1914, and served at Mons, the Battle of the Marne and the First Battle of Ypres, before illness brought him home. On Putney Bridge, four girls gave him white feathers. 'I explained to them that I had been in the army and been discharged, and I was still only 16. Several people had collected around the girls and there was giggling, and I felt most uncomfortable and . . . very humiliated.' The boy walked straight into the nearest recruiting office and rejoined the army.[11]

Members of the Order of the White Feather condemned innumerable fathers to a war from which they would never return. James Cutmore had three small daughters, which saved him from conscription. The army rejected his attempt to volunteer in 1914 on account of his myopia. In 1916, as he walked home from work, a woman gave him a white feather. He enlisted the next day. By then, so many had died that the army cared little for short-sightedness. 'They just wanted a body to stop a shell.' Rifleman James Cutmore died of his wounds on 28 March 1918.[12] The family never recovered. Years later, his grandson, the British journalist Francis Beckett, described how, long after his death, Cutmore's family 'could still remember his dreadful, lingering, useless death' and how, on his last leave, 'he was so shell-shocked he could hardly speak and my grandmother ironed his uniform every day in the vain hope of killing the lice'.

The Order of the White Feather left thousands of British men deeply and irreparably damaged, as Will Ellsworth-Jones shows in *We Will Not Fight*, a history of a group of conscientious objectors. His research gives the lie to Virginia Woolf's claim that there were only 50 or 60 white feathers handed out. In saying so, Woolf had merely demonstrated her ignorance of the thoughts of ordinary women on the streets of British cities, many of whom refused to date a 'coward'. Most young men went willingly to war, of course. Most believed in the reasons why, or wanted to believe them in 1914, the year Britain recruited a million men – the biggest army of volunteers who had ever marched to war.

—

Nothing held when the truth came home: certainties, faiths, slogans seemed to lose their solidity, to dissolve. The cubists were proven right, but not in the way they expected: human perception had not dismantled objective truth. The war had *literally* destroyed solid forms and expectations. The very structure of existence ceased to exist. Parents choked by grief would turn in anger on the regimes that had flung their sons into the abyss. Authoritarians lost all authority. Demagogues who had demanded the blood of the nation's youth were reviled. Yet a collective sense of responsibility dawned on the older generation and muted their rage. How could *we* have let this happen, wondered parents, politicians, teachers, public servants, pillars of the community. How could *we* have stood by and watched (or urged on) the slaughter of the flower of our manhood? Nobody had any answers to that terrible question, but everyone found someone to blame: the Kaiser, Germany, Austria-Hungary, Russia, capitalists, Jews, socialists, Freemasonry, Serbia, the naval race, colonial rivalry, and so on.

The shocking facts were unassimilable. Western Europe, the self-declared apotheosis of civilisation, the provenance of the gentlest of faiths, a religion uniquely distinguished by charity and compassion, had subjected the world to a war that had literally consumed the best part of the younger generation. For four years, European governments had compelled millions of young men to go to war, to die, to be terribly mutilated, gassed or psychologically ruined. They had used propaganda, plain lies, white feathers, threats and political expedience to goad, threaten, terrify and humiliate men into uniform. By the end of it, nobody could quite comprehend the enormity of what they had done: 37 million people were killed or wounded in the First World War.

Nineteen-fourteen was the beginning of the end of ancient regimes and monarchies that had ruled Europe for centuries. Their crepuscular, unsustainable realms began the slide to oblivion. European kings and queens, except in a purely symbolic role, would soon cease to exist. Never again would a European government dare to invoke a crowned head (or 'god', for that matter) to justify war. The war Europe's autocracies waged to preserve their regimes in the end destroyed them all. Revolution and reform swept Germany, Russia and Austria-Hungary. In 1918, the Kaiser's cherished navy mutinied, and he was forced to abdicate. Herr Wilhelm Hohenzollern – now a common citizen – fled into exile, to the neutral Netherlands, where he would spend his days hunting small animals and chopping down trees. Article 227 of the Treaty of Versailles in 1919 demanded his prosecution 'for a supreme offence against international morality and the sanctity of treaties', but President Woodrow Wilson declined to support his extradition. Wilhelm's ravings continued: he blamed Freemasonry and the Jews for the two world wars. He eventually saw through the Nazis as a bunch of gangsters who made him ashamed to be German. He died in 1941 aged 82.

The Romanovs and Habsburgs fell too, in ignominious and violent ways. The writer Victor Serge predicted that outcome, in Russia, as early as 1912: 'Revolutionaries knew quite well that the autocratic Empire, with its hangmen, its pogroms, its finery, its famines, its Siberian jails and ancient iniquity, could never survive the war.'[13] We need not dwell on the 1917 Russian Revolution, except to say that it not only destroyed Tsarism forever but also freed the new Bolshevik regime to agree an immediate armistice with Germany in December 1917 (which led to the signing of the Treaty of Brest-Litovsk on 3 March 1918). At a stroke, Germany's eastern forces were sent to the Western Front, where they would soon fight the British, Australians, Canadians and New Zealanders in the battle of Passchendaele, which really went beyond anything hitherto comprehensible as battle. If it started hopefully, as a result of the Canadian general Arthur Currie's innovative use of the creeping barrage (he would sweep the enemy lines with shells as the Allied troops advanced, a technique with which he defeated the Germans at Vimy Ridge), the double blow of heavy rain and Haig's decision not to give Currie time to bring up his artillery produced the following scene: nests of German machine guns mowing down thousands of (mostly Australian) troops in a sea of mud and wire, some drowning in shell craters, others blown apart, shot up several times, on a bloody, swamp-like field that was later found to contain a body per square metre – probably the densest killing field in history.

Back in Russia, the Communist regime consolidated its power, and bred the forces that would give rise to the first experiment in pure totalitarianism, which was the seedbed of Stalinism, the gulag and the origins of the Cold War with the West.

In November 1918, the last Habsburg ruler, Charles I (reigning as Charles IV of Hungary), issued a proclamation recognising Austria's and Hungary's right to determine the future of the state and renouncing any role in state affairs. The Habsburg monarchy, one of the oldest dynasties in Europe, had annulled itself. In 1919, Austria's new republican government passed a law banishing the Habsburgs from Austrian territory until they renounced all future rights to the throne and accepted the status of private citizens. It took the family a few years to accept their non-existence as hereditary monarchs. If the collapse of these regimes may be construed as a 'good' outcome of the war, the question instantly rushes to mind: at what cost?

—

A more terrible world arose out of the ashes of peace. In reducing Germany to penury and humiliation, the Treaty of Versailles effectively prescribed another war, as John Maynard Keynes had most persuasively argued at the time:

> In Germany the total expenditure of the Empire, the Federal States, and the Communes in 1919–20 is estimated at 25 milliards [billions] of marks, of which not above 10 milliards are covered by previously existing taxation. This is without allowing anything for the payment of the indemnity. In Russia, Poland, Hungary, or Austria such a thing as a budget cannot be seriously considered to exist at all . . . Thus the menace of inflationism . . . is not merely a product of the war, of which peace begins the cure. It is a continuing phenomenon of which the end is not yet in sight.[14]

Military commanders also realised that another war was inevitable: Foch and Ludendorff, in different ways, divined a second world war from the runes of Versailles. So, too, did the disgusted corporal Adolf Hitler, who saw Versailles as the harbinger of another war of annihilation. The German economic crisis precipitated by Versailles led directly to the rise of Nazism, tempting some historians to judge the two world wars as a continuum – a single long war, interrupted by a brief party (the Roaring '20s) and a doomed experiment in German social democracy (the decadent Weimar Republic).

Austria-Hungary, Russia and Germany entered the Great War in order to preserve their power structures. They achieved precisely the opposite, and the social upheaval that swept them away would usher in bloodier regimes. If this may be construed as a 'good', if unintended, result of the war, the method exacted a horrific price: 16.5 million dead – including 6.8 million civilians – and the immeasurable grief those statistics imply (see Appendix 1). Hitler's and Stalin's regimes would not have been possible were it not for the conditions created by the First World War: economic chaos, utter devastation and, in Germany's case, collapse and beggary.

—

And so we turn to the vexed question of responsibility. Let us scupper one popular assumption. The murder in Sarajevo did not 'cause' the war any more than the flutter of butterfly wings. To think so is to read history through a rear-vision mirror, where the effect precedes the cause and is easily explained by it, rather like the teleological argument for the existence of God: we were born with eyelids to protect our eyes, or hair to warm our heads, ergo an intelligent designer must exist. Or, in this case: war followed a series of events that may be traced to an assassination; therefore, the assassination was a major cause of the war. To believe that is to exclude the true causes – the *uses* to which men put the murder; to relegate the great forces in play at the time to 'noises off' the stage; and to position the shooting of the archduke at centre-stage, loaded with portent and prophetic power.

Any number of cliffhanger-seeking books and films read the war in this way. Along came the murder of royalty, and the world went to war. No doubt, Ferdinand's death triggered the July crisis that hastened the outbreak of war. But it was not a cause or even a determining factor. It accelerated forces that were already in motion, which would have culminated in war anyway – *unless* the men in power behaved differently, i.e. sought to mediate and understand one another, and tried the diplomatic arts of peace-keeping. At the time Princip pulled the trigger, all the forces that actually caused the war were already in place. The archduke's death had a catalytic effect on nations already primed for aggression. Any other spark might have ignited war: Anglo-Russian naval talks, another German gunboat, Russian mobilisation . . .

In this light, nobody in positions of power sleepwalked to war, as the title of Christopher Clark's book suggests. Slumber is the last word one would apply to their actions. The leaders, as we've seen, were wide awake, sentient decision-makers who knew what was happening and were aware of the repercussions of their actions. Some went willingly to war (Austria-Hungary, Germany and Russia); or, when war seemed inevitable, accepted it with complacent resignation (France, Britain). In this sense, European politicians and military commanders collectively *manufactured* a war in a year that began more peacefully than any in the previous decade. By early 1914, the naval race was over; Britain and Germany were talking again; the Balkan Wars had concluded to Serbia's satisfaction; the Balkans seemed more at peace than ever; the Russian and German economies were flourishing.

Yet European leaders later claimed that the war was 'inevitable', 'ordained by God or Darwin' and 'unavoidable' – as if the tragedy unfolded before their eyes like some terrible accident, which they were helpless to avert. They dared to blame the war on superstitious, invisible forces that they were unable to thwart. They spoke of it as beyond their control, as divinely inspired, or the result of some Olympian intervention in the affairs of mortals. The 'hammer of destiny' brought the world to war, claimed Lloyd George, for whom 'the nations slithered over the brink into the boiling cauldron of war'.[15] '[P]rofound magnetic reactions' drew nations together 'like planetary bodies', claimed Churchill.[16] '[N]o human individual could have prevented it', claimed Earl Grey, who used to 'torture' himself 'by questioning whether by foresight or wisdom I could have prevented the war'.[17] German and Russian leaders similarly persuaded themselves that destiny or providence or even the strange distempered atmosphere of July 1914 had caused the war – an earthquake, tornado, etc. tearing through Europe, orchestrated by some malign spirit, and nothing could have been done differently, or better, to stop it.

Or they were in the grip of war plans, timetables – helpless prisoners of their preparations. Schlieffen's great plan, like a sacred scroll, seemed to exert a mystical hold on the German military mind, as if some prophetic power lay embedded in its sheets that bound the Prussian commanders to enact it. People seem to forget that governments, not prophets or gods, inflicted the abomination of the Great

War on the world. And they made little concerted effort to prevent it: mediation was scarcely given a chance in the rush to arms. There were many other chances to pull back from the brink. Bethmann-Hollweg, Sazonov, Moltke and Berchtold might have softened their terms, or agreed to Grey's attempt to mediate. Instead, in the hands of these 'pygmies' (as Hew Strachan described the men in charge at the time), the planet hurtled towards war.[18]

In this light, every major European nation had a share of responsibility for the war. If we must apportion blame, a spectrum from the most to least blameworthy would pass from Germany to Austria-Hungary, Russia, Britain and France. Germany had orchestrated the Austrian war with Serbia and consciously precipitated the domino effect that drew in Russia, whose grossly irresponsible decision to mobilise ensured it would soon be at war with Germany. Germany, however, seems less blameworthy than Fritz Fischer's case for the prosecution, which has persuaded a post-war consensus of Berlin's complete war guilt. He blames the war on German ambitions to subdue and possess all of Europe, by force. That, however, was Germany's war aim *after* the declaration of war. Before it, Germany had rather different war aims, which did not include European hegemony, as Niall Ferguson has persuasively argued. 'Was the Kaiser really Napoleon?' His answer seems eminently fair, given the absence of evidence: no, or not before war was declared.[19]

Weltpolitik demanded the accommodation of Germany's colonial ambitions; it did not prescribe a world war to fulfil those ambitions. Nor were Germany's civilian politicians or most German people eager to engage in a European war. Schlieffen's plan no doubt satisfied the armed forces, as a preventive war, and no doubt many Prussian commanders bristled for combat, as did a few diehard pan-Germans (such as Bernhardi). Yet Fischer argued that Germany had sought a European war of conquest as early as the Kaiser's 'war council' of December 1912. This meeting's chief decision was to launch a press campaign to prepare the public for the likelihood of war. The September 1914 program, of which so much has been made, and in which Berlin did outline a plan of global conquest, took shape *after* war had been declared.[20] And by then, of course, the world had changed. The belligerents were fighting for all or nothing: to conquer the enemy or face destruction.

The Great War, in short, was an avoidable, unnecessary exercise in collective stupidity and callousness, launched by profoundly flawed and (if we may be permitted the phrase) emotionally unintelligent men, most of whom were neither fit nor trained but *bred* to rule, and who saw the world as a Darwinian jungle in which Teuton, Slav (and their Latin and Anglo-Saxon allies) were somehow predestined to bash each other's brains out until the 'fittest' won.

Perhaps there is a decent hypocrisy in the 'boo-hoo brigade' of militarists, chauvinists and warmongering politicians who tearfully look back on the war as a great tragedy. It is a curious phenomenon that the very people who were most responsible for driving the world to fight, who goaded young men into uniform and delighted in their 'lovely war', would later ostentatiously mourn the victims at ceremonies and anniversaries. If the tears and bowed heads of they 'who grow old' are sincere, they will reasonably protest the next time their government compels a new generation to fight an unjust war, rather than rallying their people to arms. The unthinking reflex of youth is forgivable: war is an adventure; war makes heroes. The exploitation of that reflex by politicians is grossly irresponsible and, in the broadest sense, criminal. Only a legal construction distinguished the Great War from the government-sponsored mass murder of European youth. At least Winston Churchill had the honesty to say he enjoyed it.

—

In the end, the war terminated lives, destroyed minds, crushed the happiness of families and set in train a century of further bloodshed. It ended a way of seeing the world: it ruptured hopes, dreams and feelings. Men and women were transformed by the callous, daily routine of slaughter. As the killing increased, and became a normative part of life, people adjusted to it and became brutalised by it. At first some were saddened and outraged at the waste and horror. Yet the appalling bloodshed and lists of casualties soon had a numbing effect. Many others, incapable of imagining the reality of the Marne or the Somme, were satisfied, indeed happy, during the war years. Women were earning more money than they had ever done; the media barons and press were drearily excited by the unfolding 'story'; and there was a strange thrill among the public at being so close to the danger.

—

The soldiers, the people who had lost loved ones and friends, did not share the vicarious pleasure of a world apparently in the thrall of the death instinct. The poet and scholar Arthur Benson wandered Oxford in dismay at the loss of so many students. His thoughts progressed from numbness to despair to helplessness:

Thursday 6 August 1914
The mind has a curious power of accommodating itself to conditions, and I have lost my dazed feeling – though there's a melancholy gulf at the bottom of all one's thoughts into which hopes and interests fall like a cataract.

Tuesday 25 August 1914
[W]hichever way one looks, there is disaster – financial, social, cultural, political. I fear a real outburst of the stupidest militarism. I read the papers with hollow dreariness and find myself oddly drowsy and unable to work at anything. In the afternoon I went out for a solitary walk, full of ominous shadows . . .

Wednesday 26 August 1914
I scribbled a little, and wrote some new and rather loud verses for *Land of Hope and Glory* – vulgar stuff, and not in my manner at all, but rather rhetorical and like a brazen trumpet.

By the end of the year, the war had consumed that year's intake of students and their tutors, conspicuous by their absence from the blank common rooms and empty quads, Benson observed:

Tuesday 15 December 1914
I walked up and down the walls of St Johns. How the war has smashed us! There were no undergraduates about, and there are now very few bachelor dons . . .[21]

The French stretcher bearer Raymond Clément wrote of a gut-wrenching pain, of something irretrievably lost that seemed universal: 'It seems that something inside me is torn,' he wrote in his diary (9–11 October 1914), 'something that rooted me to my native country, where Henri and I used to play when we were children and where we grew up together. I feel empty, I feel alone. Everything is going away and seems to abandon me.'[22]

Marie Dubois continued imploring – and harassing – her husband André to the end of the year: 'Nothing came from you today, once again . . . I imagine horrible things. You are everything for me my dear, I can't live so far from you, it causes me too much suffering . . . I kiss you my darling with all my strength. What about your beard? Did you buy warm clothes . . .? Some warm underpants? You could do with another pair of warm socks or even several pairs?' She received little response.[23]

Life went on, and the trenches became home to millions of men for another four years. Corporal Hodder tried to explain to his little sister, then at primary school: 'Do you remember the book you used to read about the cave boy? Well, I'm like a cave boy now, living in great holes in the earth . . . I could tell you what it's like to be a cave boy, only a gentleman called a Censor reads all my letters and crosses out what he doesn't like . . .'[24] In the new year Herman Baumann's wife, Pauline, gave birth to a little girl.

Few letters more poignantly illustrate the tragedy of war than the last one the mother of 21-year-old Maurice Leroi sent him, on 4 October 1914:

> My dear Maurice,
>
> Yesterday, I have sent you by the postal service 3 packages of linen and of fleece, which I think will be of use, some chocolate, tobacco paper, and a box of matches, as well as a pencil for fear that you lost yours. I wasn't able to add more, seeing that the packages must not weigh more than one kilogramme . . . It has been a month since I received news from you. I hope you are still alive, and that I will see you again. I have since sent you several letters and postcards but have you received them?
>
> *Je te quitte en t'embrassant de tout mon coeur* [I leave you, and kiss you with all my heart]
>
> Your loving mother

Unknown to Mrs Leroi, her son had been mortally wounded at the Marne on 6 September 1914 and found dead in no-man's-land on the 13th. She had not seen his 'Death Notification' of 19 September 1914:

> Maurice Leroi
>
> FRENCH REPUBLIC
>
> 'Liberté, Egalité, Fraternité'
>
> Mayor of the 17th Arrondissement, 18 rue des Batignolles
>
> M. Mayor, I have the honour to inform you that M. LEROI Maurice Emile, soldier of the 13th Regiment of Artillery, has been gloriously killed by the enemy . . . during the battle of Laimont. Please inform his family Mme LEROI who is in your Arrondissement, 19 rue Truffaut, in the most sensitive and appropriate way possible.
>
> Chief of the Special Office of Accounting[25]

The accountants, the rubber-stampers of the inventory of the dead, cannot be allowed the last word. The goodwill of ordinary soldiers transcended their experience and, in sharing it, helped to restore some sense of humanity at home, without which the last 'drawing down of blinds'[26] would blot out forever the sun on their story. An unusually articulate example is G. B. Manwaring, a young officer of Kitchener's Army, whose letters to his family replenished a sense of hope in hell: 'Here one takes life at its true value; wealth loses its significance and health becomes one's primary asset . . . Surely we who come back will do so with new standards and new ideals, and so the countless sacrifice will not have been in vain . . . Many of those who survive . . . mean to make this new land of France their home. Starting afresh . . . marrying French girls . . .'

Days before he went over the top, he reflected: 'We are not ashamed of being afraid, as we often are . . . just afraid of being afraid . . . In warfare only cowards are the really brave men, for they have to force themselves to do things that brave men do instinctively.' He rejoiced in the capacity of his men, 'facing death from bullet, shell and gas' to stay 'the same cheery, lively animal, wondering when it will all cease'.

A new spirit of unselfishness, he believed, had entered the human race, 'or perchance the old selfishness bred by years of peace has died . . .' The war had banished class hatred, he dared to hope: 'If danger lies in that direction it must surely come from those who stayed at home.' And bred a new 'Faith': 'We stand perhaps in the darkest hour in the history of this planet – the darkest hour, yet to some at any rate there comes already the promise of the dawn . . . A new Faith is coming to Mankind – I purposely say Faith and not Religion, for the two are as different as a wedding is from a marriage. A finer, fuller, freer Faith devoid of dogma and creed, of ritual and form . . . A Faith whose prophets are the poets – whose Godhead is nature – cruel, relentless, beautiful nature.'[27]

Manwaring believed he found this faith, this sublime pathos, in the families – mothers, sisters, wives and fiancées – to whom he wrote to inform them of the deaths of men in his company. The reply of a young woman who had lost both her husband and brother expresses, in the circumstances, the infinite sadness that no historian, novelist, correspondent or poet can: 'Please don't laugh at me,' she wrote to him, 'but I am a lonely woman now, and if there is in your Company a lonely soldier who would be glad of letters and cigarettes, do me a kindness and let me have his name.'[28] And he found this faith in the soldiers he met, such as the Australian violinist who had lost both arms, and who asked a nurse, 'Sister, if only I could play the violin once more?' She found the soldier a violin, they rigged it up somehow and he played – 'crudely of course' – but he played.[29]

APPENDIX 1

CASUALTIES

Allies of World War I	Population (millions)	Military deaths	Direct civilian deaths (due to military action)	Excess civilian deaths (due to famine, disease & accidents)	Total deaths	Deaths as % of population	Military wounded
Australia	4.5	61,966			61,966	1.38%	152,171
Canada	7.2	64,976		2,000	66,976	0.92%	149,732
Indian Empire	315.1	74,187			74,187	0.02%	69,214
New Zealand	1.1	18,052			18,052	1.64%	41,317
Newfoundland	0.2	1,570			1,570	0.65%	2,314
United Kingdom	45.4	886,939	2,000	107,000	995,939	2.19%	1,663,435
Sub-total for British Empire	-	1,115,597	2,000	109,000	1,226,597	-	2,090,212
East Africa				See source			
Belgium	7.4	58,637	7,000	55,000	120,637	1.63%	44,686
France	39.6	1,397,800	40,000	260,000	1,697,800	4.29%	4,266,000
Greece	4.8	26,000		150,000	176,000	3.67%	21,000
Italy	35.6	651,000	4,000	585,000	1,240,000	3.48%	953,886
Empire of Japan	53.6	415			415	0%	907
Luxembourg	0.3				See source		
Montenegro	0.5	3,000			3,000	0.6%	10,000
Portugal	6.0	7,222		82,000	89,222	1.49%	13,751
Romania	7.5	250,000	120,000	330,000	700,000	9.33%	120,000
Russian Empire	175.1	1,811,000 to 2,254,369	500,000 (1914 borders)	1,000,000 (1914 borders)	3,311,000 to 3,754,369	1.89% to 2.14%	3,749,000 to 4,950,000
Serbia	4.5	275,000	150,000	300,000	725,000	16.11%	133,148
United States	92.0	116,708	757		117,465	0.13%	205,690
Total (Entente Powers)	800.4	5,712,379	823,757	2,871,000	9,407,136	1.19%	12,809,280

Central Powers	Population (millions)	Military deaths	Direct civilian deaths (due to military action)	Excess civilian deaths (due to famine, disease & accidents)	Total deaths	Deaths as % of population	Military wounded
Austria-Hungary	51.4	1,100,000	120,000	347,000	1,567,000	3.05%	3,620,000
Bulgaria	5.5	87,500		100,000	187,500	3.41%	152,390
German Empire	64.9	2,050,897	1,000	425,000	2,476,897	3.82%	4,247,143
Ottoman Empire	21.3	771,844		2,150,000	2,921,844	13.72%	400,000
Total (Central Powers)	143.1	4,010,241	121,000	3,022,000	7,153,241	5%	8,419,533
Neutral nations							
Denmark	2.7		722		722	0.03%	–
Norway	2.4		1,892		1,892	0.08%	–
Sweden	5.6		877		877	0.02%	–
Grand total	**954.2**	**9,722,620**	**948,248**	**5,893,000**	**16,563,868**	**1.75%**	**21,228,813**

SOURCE: http://en.wikipedia.org/wiki/World_War_I_casualties#Classification_of_casualty_statistics

(all ultimate sources by country given on this web page)

APPENDIX 2

GERMANY'S BLANK CHEQUE TO AUSTRIA-HUNGARY

AFTER SARAJEVO, Count Leopold von Berchtold, the Austro-Hungarian Foreign Minister, drew up a letter for the Emperor Francis Joseph to sign and send to Wilhelm II to try and convince both of Serbia's responsibility. On 6 July, Wilhelm II and his Imperial Chancellor, Theobald von Bethmann-Hollweg, telegrammed Berchtold that Austria-Hungary could rely that Germany would support whatever action was necessary to deal with Serbia – in effect offering von Berchtold a 'blank cheque'.

> *Telegram from the Imperial Chancellor, von Bethmann-Hollweg, to the German Ambassador at Vienna.* Tschirschky, 6 July 1914
> Berlin, July 6, 1914
> *Confidential. For Your Excellency's personal information and guidance*
>   The Austro-Hungarian Ambassador yesterday delivered to the Emperor a confidential personal letter from the Emperor Francis Joseph, which depicts the present situation from the Austro-Hungarian point of view, and describes the measures which Vienna has in view. A copy is now being forwarded to

Your Excellency.

I replied to Count Szögyény today on behalf of His Majesty that His Majesty sends his thanks to the Emperor Francis Joseph for his letter and would soon answer it personally. In the meantime His Majesty desires to say that he is not blind to the danger which threatens Austria-Hungary and thus the Triple Alliance as a result of the Russian and Serbian Pan-Slavic agitation. Even though His Majesty is known to feel no unqualified confidence in Bulgaria and her ruler, and naturally inclines more to ward our old ally Rumania and her Hohenzollern prince, yet he quite understands that the Emperor Francis Joseph, in view of the attitude of Rumania and of the danger of a new Balkan alliance aimed directly at the Danube Monarchy, is anxious to bring about an understanding between Bulgaria and the Triple alliance [. . .]. His Majesty will, further more, make an effort at Bucharest, according to the wishes of the Emperor Francis Joseph, to influence King Carol to the fulfilment of the duties of his alliance, to the renunciation of Serbia, and to the suppression of the Rumanian agitations directed against Austria-Hungary.

Finally, as far as concerns Serbia, His Majesty, of course, cannot interfere in the dispute now going on between Austria-Hungary and that country, as it is a matter not within his competence. The Emperor Francis Joseph may, however, rest assured that His Majesty will faithfully stand by Austria-Hungary, as is required by the obligations of his alliance and of his ancient friendship.

BETHMANN-HOLLWEG

SOURCE: WWI Document Archive > 1914 Documents > The 'Blank Cheque'

APPENDIX 3

THE AUSTRO-HUNGARIAN ULTIMATUM TO SERBIA

Vienna, July 22, 1914

Your Excellency will present the following note to the Royal Government on the afternoon of Thursday, July 23: On the 31st of March, 1909, the Royal Serbian Minister at the Court of Vienna made, in the name of his Government, the following declaration to the Imperial and Royal Government:

Serbia recognizes that her rights were not affected by the state of affairs created in Bosnia, and states that she will accordingly accommodate herself to the decisions to be reached by the Powers in connection with Article 25 of the Treaty of Berlin. Serbia, in accepting the advice of the Great Powers, binds herself to desist from the attitude of protest and opposition which she has assumed with regard to the annexation since October last, and she furthermore binds herself to alter the tendency of her present policy toward Austria-Hungary, and to live on the footing of friendly and neighborly relations with the latter in the future.

Now the history of the past few years, and particularly the painful events of the 28th of June, have proved the existence of

604

a subversive movement in Serbia, whose object it is to separate certain portions of its territory from the Austro-Hungarian Monarchy. This movement, which came into being under the very eyes of the Serbian Government, subsequently found expression outside of the territory of the Kingdom in acts of terrorism, in a number of attempts at assassination, and in murders.

Far from fulfilling the formal obligations contained in its declaration of the 31st of March, 1909, the Royal Serbian Government has done nothing to suppress this movement. It has tolerated the criminal activities of the various unions and associations directed against the Monarchy, the unchecked utterances of the press, the glorification of the authors of assassinations, the participation of officers and officials in subversive intrigues; it has tolerated an unhealthy propaganda in its public instruction; and it has tolerated, finally, every manifestation which could betray the people of Serbia into hatred of the Monarchy and contempt for its institutions.

This toleration of which the Royal Serbian Government was guilty, was still in evidence at that moment when the events of the twenty-eighth of June exhibited to the whole world the dreadful consequences of such tolerance.

It is clear from the statements and confessions of the criminal authors of the assassination of the twenty-eighth of June, that the murder at Sarajevo was conceived at Belgrade, that the murderers received the weapons and the bombs with which they were equipped from Serbian officers and officials who belonged to the Narodna Odbrana, and, finally, that the dispatch of the criminals and of their weapons to Bosnia was arranged and effected under the conduct of Serbian frontier authorities.

The results brought out by the inquiry no longer permit the Imperial and Royal Government to maintain the attitude of patient tolerance which it has observed for years toward those agitations which center at Belgrade and are spread thence into the territories of the Monarchy. Instead, these results impose upon the Imperial and Royal Government the obligation to put an end to those intrigues, which constitute a standing menace to the peace of the Monarchy.

In order to attain this end, the Imperial and Royal Government finds itself compelled to demand that the Serbian Government give official assurance that it will condemn the propaganda directed against Austria-Hungary, that is to say, the whole body of the efforts whose ultimate object it is to separate from the Monarchy territories that belong to it; and that it will obligate itself to suppress with all the means at its command this criminal and terroristic propaganda. In order to give these assurances a character of solemnity, the Royal Serbian Government will publish on the first page of its official organ of July 26/13, the following declaration:

'The Royal Serbian Government condemns the propaganda directed against Austria-Hungary, that is to say, the whole body of the efforts whose ultimate object it is to separate from the Austro-Hungarian Monarchy territories that belong to it, and it most sincerely regrets the dreadful consequences of these criminal transactions.

'The Royal Serbian Government regrets that Serbian officers and officials should have taken part in the above-mentioned propaganda and thus have endangered the friendly and neighborly relations, to the cultivation of which the Royal Government had most solemnly pledged itself by its declarations of March 31, 1909.

'The Royal Government, which disapproves and repels every idea and every attempt to interfere in the destinies of the population of whatever portion of Austria-Hungary, regards it as its duty most expressly to call attention of the officers, officials, and the whole population of the kingdom to the fact that for the future it will proceed with the utmost rigor against any persons who shall become guilty of any such activities, activities to prevent and to suppress which, the Government will bend every effort.'

This declaration shall be brought to the attention of the Royal army simultaneously by an order of the day from His Majesty the King, and by publication in the official organ of the army.

The Royal Serbian Government will furthermore pledge itself:

1. to suppress every publication which shall incite to hatred and contempt of the Monarchy, and the general tendency of which shall be directed against the territorial integrity of the latter;

2. to proceed at once to the dissolution of the Narodna Odbrana to confiscate all of its means of propaganda, and in the same manner to proceed against the other unions and associations in Serbia which occupy themselves with propaganda against Austria-Hungary; the Royal Government will take such measures as are necessary to make sure that the dissolved associations may not continue their activities under other names or in other forms;

3. to eliminate without delay from public instruction in Serbia, everything, whether connected with the teaching corps or with the methods of teaching, that serves or may serve to nourish the propaganda against Austria-Hungary;

4. to remove from the military and administrative service in general all officers and officials who have been guilty of carrying on the propaganda against Austria-Hungary, whose names the Imperial and Royal Government reserves the right to make known to the Royal Government when communicating the material evidence now in its possession;

5. to agree to the cooperation in Serbia of the organs of the Imperial and Royal Government in the suppression of the subversive movement directed against the integrity of the Monarchy;

6. to institute a judicial inquiry against every participant in the conspiracy of the twenty-eighth of June who may be found in Serbian territory; the organs of the Imperial and Royal

Government delegated for this purpose will take part in the proceedings held for this purpose;

7. to undertake with all haste the arrest of Major Voislav Tankosic and of one Milan Ciganovitch, a Serbian official, who have been compromised by the results of the inquiry;

8. by efficient measures to prevent the participation of Serbian authorities in the smuggling of weapons and explosives across the frontier; to dismiss from the service and to punish severely those members of the Frontier Service at Schabats and Losnitza who assisted the authors of the crime of Sarajevo to cross the frontier;

9. to make explanations to the Imperial and Royal Government concerning the unjustifiable utterances of high Serbian functionaries in Serbia and abroad, who, without regard for their official position, have not hesitated to express themselves in a manner hostile toward Austria-Hungary since the assassination of the twenty-eighth of June;

10. to inform the Imperial and Royal Government without delay of the execution of the measures comprised in the foregoing points.

The Imperial and Royal Government awaits the reply of the Royal Government by Saturday, the twenty-fifth instant, at 6 p.m., at the latest.

A reminder of the results of the investigation about Sarajevo, to the extent they relate to the functionaries named in points 7 and 8 [above], is appended to this note.

Appendix to Ultimatum:

The crime investigation undertaken at court in Sarajevo against Gavrilo Princip and his comrades on account of the assassination committed on the 28th of June this year, along with the guilt of accomplices, has up until now led to the following conclusions:

1. The plan of murdering Archduke Franz Ferdinand during his stay in Sarajevo was concocted in Belgrade by Gavrilo Princip, Nedeljko Cabrinovic, a certain Milan Ciganovic, and Trifko Grabesch with the assistance of Major Voija Takosic.

2. The six bombs and four Browning pistols along with ammunition – used as tools by the criminals – were procured and given to Princip, Cabrinovic and Grabesch in Belgrade by a certain Milan Ciganovic and Major Voija Takosic.

3. The bombs are hand grenades originating from the weapons depot of the Serbian army in Kragujevatz.

4. To guarantee the success of the assassination, Ciganovic instructed Princip, Cabrinovic and Grabesch in the use of the grenades and gave lessons on shooting Browning pistols to Princip and Grabesch in a forest next to the shooting range at Topschider.

5. To make possible Princip, Cabrinovic and Grabesch's passage across the Bosnia-Herzegovina border and the smuggling of their weapons, an entire secretive transportation system was organized by Ciganovic. The entry of the criminals and their weapons into Bosnia and Herzegovina was carried out by the main border officials of Shabatz (Rade Popovic) and Losnitza as well as by the customs agent Budivoj Grbic of Losnitza, with the complicity of several others.

On the occasion of handing over this note, would Your Excellency please also add orally that – in the event that no unconditionally positive answer of the Royal government might be received in the meantime – after the course of the 48-hour deadline referred to in this note, as measured from the day and hour of your announcing it, you are commissioned to leave the I. and R. Embassy of Belgrade together with your personnel.

SOURCE: *WWI Document Archive > 1914 Documents > The Austro-Hungarian Ultimatum to Serbia (English Translation)*

APPENDIX 4

THE SERBIAN REPLY TO THE AUSTRO-HUNGARIAN ULTIMATUM

25 July 1914:

The Royal Government has received the communication of the Imperial and Royal Government of the 23rd inst. and is convinced that its reply will dissipate any misunderstanding which threatens to destroy the friendly and neighbourly relations between the Austrian monarchy and the kingdom of Serbia.

The Royal Government is conscious that nowhere there have been renewed protests against the great neighbourly monarchy like those which at one time were expressed in the Skuptschina, as well as in the declaration and actions of the responsible representatives of the state at that time, and which were terminated by the Serbian declaration of March 31st, 1909; furthermore that since that time neither the different corporations of the kingdom, nor the officials have made an attempt to alter the political and judicial condition created in Bosnia and the Heregovina. The Royal Government states that the I. and R. [Imperial and Royal] Government has made no protestation in this sense excepting in the case of a textbook, in regard to which the I. and R. Government has received an entirely satisfactory explanation. Serbia has given during the time of the Balkan crisis in numerous cases evidence of her pacific and moderate policy, and it is only owing to Serbia and the sacrifices which she has brought in the interest of the peace of Europe that this peace has been preserved.

The Royal Government cannot be made responsible for expressions of a private character, as for instance newspaper articles and the peaceable work of societies, expressions which are of very common appearance in other countries, and which ordinarily are not under the control of the state. This, all the less, as the Royal Government has shown great courtesy in the solution of a whole series of questions which have arisen between Serbia and Austria-Hungary, whereby it has succeeded to solve the greater number thereof, in favour of the progress of both countries.

The Royal Government was therefore painfully surprised by the assertions that citizens of Serbia had participated in the preparations of the outrage in Sarajevo. The Government expected to be invited to cooperate in the investigation of the crime, and it was ready, in order to prove its complete correctness, to proceed against all persons in regard to whom it would receive information.

According to the wishes of the I. and R. Government, the Royal Government is prepared to surrender to the court, without regard to position and rank, every Serbian citizen for whose participation in the crime of Sarajevo it should have received proof. It binds itself particularly on the first page of the official organ of the 26th of July to publish the following enunciation:

The Royal Serbian Government condemns every propaganda which should be directed against Austria-Hungary, i.e., the entirety of such activities as aim towards the separation of certain territories from the Austro-Hungarian monarchy, and it regrets sincerely the lamentable consequences of these criminal machinations . . .

The Royal Government regrets that according to a communication of the I. and R. Government certain Serbian officers and functionaries have participated in the propaganda just referred to, and that these have there fore endangered the amicable relations for the observation of which the Royal Government had solemnly obliged itself through the declaration of March 31st, 1909 . . .

The Royal Government binds itself further:

1. During the next regular meeting of the Skuptschina to embody in the press laws a clause, to wit, that the incitement to hatred of, and contempt for, the Monarchy is to be most severely punished, as well as every publication whose general tendency is directed against the territorial integrity of Austria-Hungary.

It binds itself in view of the coming revision of the constitution to embody an amendment into Art. 22 of the constitutional law which permits the confiscation of such publications as is at present impossible according to the clear definition of Art. 12 of the constitution.

2. The Government possesses no proofs and the note of the I. and R. Government does not submit them that the society Narodna Odbrana and other similar societies have committed, up to the present, any criminal actions of this manner through any one of their members. Notwithstanding this, the Royal Government will accept the demand of the I. and R. Government and dissolve the society Narodna Odbrana, as well as every society which should set against Austria-Hungary.

3. The Royal Serbian Government binds itself without delay to eliminate from the public instruction in Serbia anything which might further the propaganda directed against Austria-Hungary provided the I. and R. Government furnishes actual proofs of this propaganda.

4. The Royal Government is also ready to dismiss those officers and officials from the military and civil services in regard to whom it has been proved by judicial investigation that they have been guilty of actions against the territorial integrity of the Monarchy; it expects that the I. and R. Government communicate to it for the purpose of starting the investigation the names of these officers and officials, and the facts with which they have been charged.

5. The Royal Government confesses that it is not clear about the sense and the scope of that demand of the I. and R. Government which concerns the obligation on the part of the Royal Serbian Government to permit the cooperation of officials of the I. and R. Government on Serbian territory, but it declares that it is willing to accept every cooperation which does not run counter to international law and criminal law, as well as to the friendly and neighbourly relations.

6. The Royal Government considers it its duty as a matter of course to begin an investigation against all those persons who have participated in the outrage of June 28th and who are in its territory. As far as the cooperation in this investigation of specially delegated officials of the I. and R. Government is concerned, this cannot be accepted, as this is a violation of the constitution and of criminal procedure. Yet in some cases the result of the investigation might be communicated to the Austro-Hungarian officials.

7. The Royal Government has ordered on the evening of the day on which the note was received the arrest of Major Voislar Tankosic. However, as far as Milan Ciganovitch is concerned, who is a citizen of the Austro-Hungarian Monarchy and who has been employed till June 28th with the Railroad Department, it has as yet been impossible to locate him, wherefore a warrant has been issued against him.

The I. and R. Government is asked to make known, as soon as possible for the purpose of conducting the investigation, the existing grounds for suspicion and the proofs of guilt, obtained in the investigation at Sarajevo.

8. The Serbian Government will amplify and render more severe the existing measures against the suppression of smuggling of arms and explosives.

It is a matter of course that it will proceed at once against, and punish severely, those officials of the frontier service on the line Shabatz-Loznica who violated their duty and who have permitted the perpetrators of the crime to cross the frontier.

9. The Royal Government is ready to give explanations about the expressions which its officials in Serbia and abroad have made in interviews after the outrage and which, according to the assertion of the I. and R. Government, were hostile to the Monarchy. As soon as the I. and R. Government points out in detail where those expressions were made and succeeds in proving that those expressions have actually been made by the functionaries concerned, the Royal Government itself will take care that the necessary evidences and proofs are collected.

10. The Royal Government will notify the I. and R. Government, so far as this has not been already done by the present note, of the execution of the measures in question as soon as one of those measures has been ordered and put into execution.

The Royal Serbian Government believes it to be to the common interest not to rush the solution of this affair and it is therefore, in case the I. and R. Government should not consider itself satisfied with this answer, ready, as ever, to accept a peaceable solution, be it by referring the decision of this question to the International Court at The Hague or by leaving it to the decision of the Great Powers who have participated in the working out of the declaration given by the Serbian Government on March 18/31st, 1909.

SOURCE: WWI Document Archive > Official Papers > The Serbian Response to the Austro-Hungarian Ultimatum (English translation)

APPENDIX 5

THE GERMAN DECLARATION OF WAR AGAINST FRANCE

PRESENTED BY THE GERMAN AMBASSADOR TO PARIS

M. Le President,

The German administrative and military authorities have established a certain number of flagrantly hostile acts committed on German territory by French military aviators.

Several of these have openly violated the neutrality of Belgium by flying over the territory of that country; one has attempted to destroy buildings near Wesel; others have been seen in the district of the Eifel; one has thrown bombs on the railway near Carlsruhe and Nuremberg.

I am instructed, and I have the honour to inform your Excellency, that in the presence of these acts of aggression the German Empire considers itself in a state of war with France in consequence of the acts of this latter Power.

At the same time, I have the honour to bring to the knowledge of your Excellency that the German authorities will retain French mercantile vessels in German ports, but they will release them if, within forty-eight hours, they are assured of complete reciprocity.

My diplomatic mission having thus come to an end, it only remains for me to request your Excellency to be good enough to furnish me with my passports, and to take the steps you consider suitable to assure my return to Germany, with the staff of the Embassy, as well as, with the Staff of the Bavarian Legation and of the German Consulate General in Paris.

Be good enough, M. le President, to receive the assurances of my deepest respect.

(Signed) SCHOEN.

SOURCE: Source Records of the Great War, Vol. II, ed. Charles F. Horne, National Alumni 1923

APPENDIX 6

POINCARÉ'S SPEECH TO THE FRENCH PARLIAMENT

MESSAGE FROM M. POINCARÉ, President of the Republic, read at the Extraordinary Session of Parliament, 4 August 1914. (Journal Officiel, 5 August 1914.)

(The Chamber rises and remains standing during the reading of the message.)

Gentlemen,

France has just been the object of a violent and premeditated attack, which is an insolent defiance of the law of nations. Before any declaration of war had been sent to us, even before the German Ambassador had asked for his passports, our territory has been violated. The German Empire has waited till yesterday evening to give at this late stage the true name to a state of things which it had already created. For more than forty years the French, in sincere love of peace, have buried at the bottom of their heart the desire for legitimate reparation. They have given to the world the example of a great nation which, definitely raised from defeat by the exercise of will, patience and labour, has only used its renewed and rejuvenated strength in the interest of progress and for the good of humanity. Since the ultimatum of Austria opened a crisis, which threatened the whole of Europe, France has persisted in following and in recommending on all sides a policy of prudence, wisdom and moderation. To her there can be imputed no act, no movement, no word which has not been peaceful and conciliatory. At the hour when the struggle is beginning, she has the right, in justice to herself, of solemnly declaring that she has made, up to the last moment, supreme efforts to avert the war now about to break out, the crushing responsibility for which the German Empire will have to bear before history. *(Unanimous and repeated applause.)*

On the very morrow of the day when we and our allies were publicly expressing our hope of seeing negotiations which had been begun under the auspices of the London Cabinet carried to a peaceful conclusion, Germany suddenly declared war upon Russia, she has invaded the territory of Luxemburg, she has outrageously insulted the noble Belgian nation *(loud and unanimous applause)*, our neighbour and our friend, and attempted treacherously to fall upon us while we were in the midst of diplomatic conversation. *(Fresh and repeated unanimous applause.)*

But France was watching. As alert as she was peaceful, she was prepared; and our enemies will meet on their path our valiant covering troops, who are at their post and will provide the screen behind which the mobilization of our national forces will be methodically completed. Our fine and courageous army, which France to-day accompanies with her maternal thought *(loud applause)* has risen eager to defend the honour of the flag and the soil of the country. *(Unanimous and repeated applause.)*

The President of the Republic interpreting the unanimous feeling of the country, expresses to our troops by land and sea the admiration and confidence of every Frenchman *(loud and prolonged applause)*. Closely united in a common feeling, the nation will persevere with the cool self-restraint of which, since the beginning of the crisis, she has given daily proof. Now, as always, she will know how to harmonise the most noble daring and most ardent enthusiasm with that self-control which is the sign of enduring energy and is the best guarantee of victory *(applause)*.

In the war which is beginning France will have Right on her side, the eternal power of which cannot with impunity be disregarded by nations any more than by individuals *(loud and unanimous applause)*. She will be heroically defended by all her sons; nothing will break their sacred union before the enemy; today they are joined together as brothers in a common indignation against the aggressor, and in a common patriotic faith *(loud and prolonged applause and cries of 'Vive la France')*. She is faithfully helped by Russia, her ally *(loud and unanimous applause)*; she is supported by the loyal friendship of Great Britain *(loud and unanimous applause)* . . . And already from every part of the civilised world sympathy and good wishes are coming to her. For to day once again she stands before the universe for Liberty, Justice and Reason *(loud and repeated applause)* 'Haut les coeurs et vive la France!' *(Unanimous and prolonged applause.)*

Raymond Poincaré

SOURCE: WWI Document Archive > 1914 Documents > President Poincaré's War

APPENDIX 7

THE GERMAN ULTIMATUM TO BELGIUM

Brussels, 2 August 1914

Imperial German Embassy in Belgium

HIGHLY CONFIDENTIAL

The Imperial Government possesses reliable information of the intended deployment of French forces on the Givet-Namur stretch of the Meuse. This information leaves no doubt about France's intention to advance against Germany through Belgian territory.

The Imperial Government cannot help but be concerned that without assistance Belgium, in spite of its good intentions, will not be able to repel a French attack with sufficient prospects of success to provide an adequate guarantee in the face of the threat to Germany. It is essential for Germany's survival to pre-empt this enemy attack.

The German Government would therefore consider it with utmost regret if Belgium saw an unfriendly act in the fact that measures taken by its enemies force Germany for defence purposes likewise to enter Belgian territory.

To exclude the possibility of misinterpretation, the Imperial

Government makes the following declaration:

1. Germany has no hostile intentions towards Belgium whatsoever. If Belgium is willing to adopt a position of benevolent neutrality towards Germany in the imminent war, the German Government promises to fully guarantee the kingdom's possessions and independence at the conclusion of peace.

2. Subject to the conditions laid down above, Germany is committed to withdrawing from the kingdom's territory as soon as peace is made.

3. If Belgium co-operates, Germany is prepared, with the agreement of the Royal Belgian authorities, to pay for the requirements of its troops in cash and to compensate for any damage that might have been caused by German troops.

4. If Belgium should take a hostile stance against German troops, especially if she obstructs their advance by resistance from her forts on the Meuse or by destroying railways, roads, tunnels or other structures, Germany will regrettably be forced to consider the kingdom an enemy. In this case Germany would be unable to undertake any obligations towards the kingdom, but would have to leave the later resolution of relations between the two states to be decided by military force.

The Imperial German Government hopes that this eventuality will not occur, and that the Royal Belgian Government will take suitable measures to prevent the events mentioned from taking place. In which case, the friendly bonds between the two neighbouring states would undergo further and lasting consolidation.

SOURCE: UK Archives, Catalogue reference: FO 371/1910 no. 400; http://www.nationalarchives. gov.uk/pathways/firstworldwar/first_world_war/p_ultimatum.htm

APPENDIX 8

BETHMANN-HOLLWEG'S ADDRESS TO THE REICHSTAG

REPORT OF A SPEECH DELIVERED by Herr von Bethmann-Hollweg, German Imperial Chancellor, on 4 August 1914

A stupendous fate is breaking over Europe. For forty-four years since the time we fought for and won the German Empire and our position in the world, we have lived in peace and have protected the peace of Europe. In the works of peace we have become strong and powerful, and have thus aroused the envy of others. With patience we have faced the fact that, under the pretence that Germany was desirous of war, enmity has been awakened against us in the East and the West, and chains have been fashioned for us. The wind then sown has brought forth the whirlwind which has now broken loose. We wished to continue our work of peace, and, like a silent vow, the feeling that animated everyone from the Emperor down to the youngest soldier was this: Only in defence of a just cause shall our sword fly from its scabbard. The day has now come when we must draw it, against our wish, and in spite of our sincere endeavours. Russia has set fire to the building. We are at war with Russia and France – a war that has been forced upon us.

Gentlemen, a number of documents, composed during the pressure of these last eventful days, is before you. Allow me to emphasize the facts that determine our attitude. From the first moment of the Austro-Servian conflict we declared that this question must be limited to Austria-Hungary and Servia, and we worked with this end in view. All Governments, especially that of Great Britain, took the same attitude. Russia alone asserted that she had to be heard in the settlement of this matter. Thus the danger of a European crisis raised its threatening head. As soon as the first definite information regarding the military preparations in Russia reached us, we declared at St Petersburg in a friendly but emphatic manner that military measures against Austria would find us on the side of our ally, and that military preparations against ourselves would oblige us to take countermeasures; but that mobilization would come very near to actual war. Russia assured us in the most solemn manner of her desire for peace, and declared that she was making no military preparations against us. In the meantime, Great Britain, warmly supported by us, tried to mediate between Vienna and St Petersburg.

On July 28th the Emperor telegraphed to the Czar asking him to take into consideration the fact that it was both the duty and the right of Austria-Hungary to defend herself against the pan-Serb agitation, which threatened to undermine her existence. The Emperor drew the Czar's attention to the solidarity of the interests of all monarchs in face of the murder of Serajevo. He asked for the latter's personal assistance in smoothing over the difficulties existing between Vienna and St. Petersburg. About the same time, and before receipt of this telegram, the Czar asked the Emperor to come to his aid and to induce Vienna to moderate her demands. The Emperor accepted the role of mediator. But scarcely had active steps on these lines begun, when Russia mobilized all her forces directed against Austria, while Austria-Hungary had mobilized only those of her corps which were directed against Servia. To the north she had mobilized only two of her corps, far from the Russian frontier. The Emperor immediately informed the Czar that this mobilization of Russian forces against Austria rendered the role of mediator, which he had accepted at the Czar's request, difficult, if not impossible.

In spite of this we continued our task of mediation at Vienna and carried it to the utmost point which was compatible with our position as an ally. Meanwhile Russia of her own accord renewed her assurances that she was making no military preparations against us. We come now to July 31st. The decision was to be taken at Vienna. Through our representations we had already obtained the resumption of direct conversations between Vienna and St. Petersburg, after they had been for some time interrupted. But before the final decision was taken at Vienna, the news arrived that Russia had mobilized her entire forces and that her mobilization was therefore directed against us also. The Russian Government, who knew from our repeated statements what mobilization on our frontiers meant, did not notify us of this mobilization, nor did they even offer any explanation. It was not until the afternoon of July 31st that the Emperor received a telegram from the Czar in which he guaranteed that his army would not assume a provocative attitude towards us. But mobilization on our frontiers had been in full swing since the night of July 30th–31st. While we were mediating at Vienna in compliance with Russia's request, Russian forces were appearing all along our extended and almost entirely open frontier, and France, though indeed not actually mobilizing, was admittedly making military preparations.

What was our position? For the sake of the peace of Europe we had, up till then, deliberately refrained from calling up a single reservist. Were we now to wait further in patience until the nations on either side of us chose the moment for their attack? It would have been a crime to expose Germany to such peril. Therefore, on July 31st we called upon Russia to demobilize as the only measure which could still preserve the peace of Europe. The Imperial Ambassador at St. Petersburg was also instructed to inform the Russian Government that in case our demand met with a refusal, we should have to consider that a state of war (*Kriegszustand*) existed. The Imperial Ambassador has executed these instructions. We have not yet learnt what Russia answered to our demand for demobilization. Telegraphic reports on this question have not reached us even though the wires still transmitted much less important information. Therefore, the time limit having long since expired, the Emperor was obliged to mobilize our forces on the 1st August at 5 p.m. At the same time we had to make certain what attitude France would assume. To our direct question, whether she would remain neutral in the event of a Russo-German War, France replied that she would do what her interests demanded. That was an evasion, if not a refusal. In spite of this, the Emperor ordered that the French frontier was to be unconditionally respected. This order, with one single exception, was strictly obeyed.

France, who mobilized at the same time as we did, assured us that she would respect a zone of 10 kilometres on the frontier. What really happened? Aviators dropped bombs, and cavalry patrols and French infantry detachments appeared on the territory of the Empire! Though war had not been declared, France thus broke the peace and actually attacked us. Regarding the one exception on our side which I mentioned, the Chief of the General Staff reports as follows: 'Only one of the French complaints about the crossing of their frontier from our side is justified. Against express orders, a patrol of the 14th Army Corps, apparently led by an officer, crossed the frontier on August 2nd. They seem to have been shot down, only one man having returned. But long before this isolated instance of crossing the frontier had occurred, French aviators had penetrated into Southern Germany and had thrown bombs on our railway lines. French troops had attacked our frontier guards on the Schlucht Pass. Our troops, in accordance with their orders, have remained strictly on the defensive.' This is the report of the General Staff.

Gentlemen, we are now in a state of necessity (*Notwehr*), and necessity knows no law. Our troops have occupied Luxemburg and perhaps have already entered Belgian territory. Gentlemen, that is a breach of international law. It is true that the French Government declared at Brussels that France would respect Belgian neutrality as long as her adversary respected it. We knew, however, that France stood ready for an invasion. France could wait, we could not. A French attack on our flank on the lower Rhine might have been disastrous. Thus we were forced to ignore the rightful protests of the Governments of Luxemburg and Belgium. The wrong – I speak openly – the wrong we thereby commit we will try to make good as soon as our military aims have been attained. He who is menaced as we are and is fighting for his highest possession can only consider how he is to hack his way through (*durchhauen*).

Gentlemen, we stand shoulder to shoulder with Austria-Hungary. As for Great Britain's attitude, the statements made by Sir Edward Grey in the House of Commons yesterday show the standpoint assumed by the British Government. We have informed the British Government that, as long as Great Britain remains neutral, our fleet will not attack the northern coast of France, and that we will not violate the territorial integrity and independence of Belgium. These assurances I now repeat before the world, and I may add that, as long as Great Britain remains neutral, we would also be willing, upon reciprocity being assured, to take no warlike measures against French commercial shipping.

Gentlemen, so much for the facts. I repeat the words of the Emperor: 'With a clear conscience we enter the lists.' We are fighting for the fruits of our works of peace, for the inheritance of a great past and for our future. The fifty years are not yet past during which Count Moltke said we should have to remain armed to defend the inheritance that we won in 1870. Now the great hour of trial has struck for our people. But with clear confidence we go forward to meet it. Our army is in the field, our navy is ready for battle – behind them stands the entire German nation – the entire German nation united to the last man. Gentlemen, you know your duty and all that it means. The proposed laws need no further explanations. I ask you to pass them quickly.

SOURCE: *German White Book*

APPENDIX 9

EDWARD GREY'S ADDRESS TO THE BRITISH PARLIAMENT

3 August 1914

The following are excerpts only:

> Last week I stated that we were working for peace not only for this country, but to preserve the peace of Europe. To-day events move so rapidly that it is exceedingly difficult to state with technical accuracy the actual state of affairs, but it is clear that the peace of Europe cannot be preserved. Russia and Germany, at any rate, have declared war upon each other.
>
> Before I proceed to state the position of his Majesty's Government I would like to clear the ground so that, before I come to state to the House what our attitude is with regard to the present crisis, the House may know exactly under what obligations the government is, or the House can be said to be, in coming to a decision on the matter. First of all, let me say, very shortly, that we have consistently worked with a single mind,

628

with all the earnestness in our power, to preserve peace. The House may be satisfied on that point. We have always done it. During these last years, as far as his Majesty's Government are concerned, we would have no difficulty in proving that we have done so. Throughout the Balkan crisis, by general admission, we worked for peace. The cooperation of the great powers of Europe was successful in working for peace in the Balkan crisis. It is true that some of the powers had great difficulty in adjusting their points of view. It took much time and labour and discussion before they could settle their differences, but peace was secured, because peace was their main object, and they were willing to give time and trouble rather than accentuate differences rapidly.

In the present crisis it has not been possible to secure the peace of Europe: because there has been little time, and there has been a disposition – at any rate in some quarters on which I will not dwell – to force things rapidly to an issue, at any rate to the great risk of peace, and, as we now know, the result of that is that the policy of peace as far as the great powers generally are concerned is in danger. I do not want to dwell on that, and to comment on it, and to say where the blame seems to us lie, which powers were most in favour of peace, which were most disposed to risk war or endanger peace, because I would like the House to approach this crisis in which we are now from the point of view of British interests, British honour, and British obligations, free from all passion as to why peace has not yet been preserved . . .

The situation in the present crisis is not precisely the same as it was in the Morocco question . . . It has originated in a dispute between Austria and Servia. I can say this with the most absolute confidence – no government and no country has less desire to be involved in war over a dispute with Austria than the country of France. They are involved in it because of their obligation of honour under a definite alliance with Russia. Well, it is only fair to say to the House that that obligation of honour cannot apply in the same way to us. We are not parties to the

Franco-Russian alliance. We do not even know the terms of the alliance. So far I have, I think, faithfully and completely cleared the ground with regard to the question of obligation.

I now come to what we think the situation requires of us. For many years we have had a long-standing friendship with France *(an Honorary Member: 'And with Germany!')*. I remember well the feeling in the House and my own feeling – for I spoke on the subject, I think, when the late Government made their agreement with France – the warm and cordial feeling resulting from the fact that these two nations, who had had perpetual differences in the past, had cleared these differences away; I remember saying, I think, that it seemed to me that some benign influence had been at work to produce the cordial atmosphere that had made that possible. But how far that friendship entails obligation – it has been a friendship between the nations and ratified by the nations – how far that entails an obligation, let every man look into his own heart, and his own feelings, and construe the extent of the obligation for himself. I construe it myself as I feel it, but I do not wish to urge upon any one else more than their feelings dictate as to what they should feel about the obligation. The House, individually and collectively, may judge for itself. I speak my personal view, and I have given the House my own feeling in the matter.

The French fleet is now in the Mediterranean, and the northern and western coasts of France are absolutely undefended. The French fleet being concentrated in the Mediterranean, the situation is very different from what it used to be, because the friendship which has grown up between the two countries has given them a sense of security that there was nothing to be feared from us. My own feeling is that if a foreign fleet, engaged in a war which France had not sought, and in which she had not been the aggressor, came down the English Channel and bombarded and battered the undefended coasts of France, we could not stand aside *(cheers)* and see this going on practically within sight of our eyes, with our arms folded, looking on dispassionately, doing nothing. I believe that would be the feeling of this country. There are times when one feels that if these circumstances actually did arise, it would be a feeling which would spread with irresistible force throughout the land.

But I also want to look at the matter without sentiment, and from the point of view of British interests, and it is on that that I am going to base and justify what I am presently going to say to the House. If we say nothing at this moment, what is France to do with her fleet in the Mediterranean? If she leaves it there, with no statement from us as to what we will do, she leaves her northern and western coasts absolutely undefended, at the mercy of a German fleet coming down the Channel to do as it pleases in a war which is a war of life and death between them. If we say nothing, it may be that the French fleet is withdrawn from the Mediterranean. We are in the presence of a European conflagration; can anybody set limits to the consequences that may arise out of it? Let us assume that to-day we stand aside in an attitude of neutrality, saying, "No, we cannot undertake and engage to help either party in this conflict." Let us suppose the French fleet is withdrawn from the Mediterranean; and let us assume that the consequences – which are already tremendous in what has happened in Europe even to countries which are at peace – in fact, equally whether countries are at peace or at war – let us assume that out of that come consequences unforeseen, which make it necessary at a sudden moment that, in defence of vital British interests, we should go to war; and let us assume which is quite possible – that Italy, who is now neutral *(Honorary Members: 'Hear, hear!')* – because, as I understand, she considers that this war is an aggressive war, and the Triple Alliance being a defensive alliance her obligation did not arise – let us assume that consequences which are not yet foreseen and which, perfectly legitimately consulting her own interests – make Italy depart from her attitude of neutrality at a time when we are forced in defence of vital British interest ourselves to fight – what then will be the position in the Mediterranean? It might be that at some critical moment those consequences would be forced upon us because our trade routes in the Mediterranean might be vital to this country?

Nobody can say that in the course of the next few weeks there is any particular trade route the keeping open of which may not be vital to this country. What will be our position then? We have not kept a fleet in the Mediterranean which is equal to dealing alone with a combination of other fleets in the Mediterranean. It would be the very moment when we could not detach more ships to the Mediterranean, and we might have exposed this country from our negative attitude at the present moment to the most appalling risk. I say that from the point of view of British interest. We feel strongly that France was entitled to know – and to know at once! – whether or not in the event of attack upon her unprotected northern and western coast she could depend upon British support. In that emergency and in these compelling circumstances, yesterday afternoon I gave to the French Ambassador the following statement:

I am authorised to give an assurance that if the German fleet comes into the Channel or through the North Sea to undertake hostile operations against the French coasts or shipping, the British fleet will give all the protection in its power. This assurance is, of course, subject to the policy of his Majesty's Government receiving the support of Parliament, and must not be taken as binding his Majesty's Government to take any action until the above contingency of action by the German fleet takes place.

I read that to the House, not as a declaration of war on our part, not as entailing immediate aggressive action on our part, but as binding us to take aggressive action should that contingency arise. Things move very hurriedly from hour to hour. French news comes in, and I cannot give this in any very formal way; but I understand that the German Government would be prepared, if we would pledge ourselves to neutrality, to agree that its fleet would not attack the northern coast of France. I have only heard that shortly before I came to the House, but it is far too narrow an engagement for us. And, Sir, there is the more serious consideration – becoming more serious every hour – there is the question of the neutrality of Belgium . . .

I will read to the House what took place last week on this subject. When mobilisation was beginning, I knew that this question must be a most important element in our policy – a most important subject for the House of Commons. I telegraphed at the same time in similar terms to both Paris and Berlin to say that it was essential for us to know whether the French and German Governments, respectively, were prepared to undertake an engagement to respect the neutrality of Belgium. These are the replies. I got from the French Government this reply:

The French Government are resolved to respect the neutrality of Belgium, and it would only be in the event of some other power violating that neutrality that France might find herself under the necessity, in order to assure the defence of her security, to act otherwise. This assurance has been given several times. The President of the Republic spoke of it to the King of the Belgians, and the French Minister at Brussels has spontaneously renewed the assurance to the Belgian Minister of Foreign Affairs to-day.

From the German Government the reply was: 'The Secretary of State for Foreign Affairs could not possibly give an answer before consulting the Emperor and the Imperial Chancellor.'

Sir Edward Goschen, to whom I had said it was important to have an answer soon, said he hoped the answer would not be too long delayed. The German Minister for Foreign Affairs then gave Sir Edward Goschen to understand that he rather doubted whether they could answer at all, as any reply they might give could not fail, in the event of war, to have the undesirable effect of disclosing, to a certain extent, part of their plan of campaign. I telegraphed at the same time to Brussels to the Belgian Government, and I got the following reply from Sir Francis Villiers:

The Minister for Foreign Affairs thanks me for the communication and replies that Belgium will, to the utmost of her power, maintain neutrality, and Belgium expects and desires other powers to observe and uphold it. He begged me to add that the relations between Belgium and the neighbouring Powers were excellent, and there was no reason to suspect their intentions, but that the Belgian Government believe, in the case of violence, they were in a position to defend the neutrality of their country.

It now appears from the news I have received to-day – which has come quite recently, and I am not yet quite sure how far it has reached me in an accurate form – that an ultimatum has been given to Belgium by Germany, the object of which was to offer Belgium friendly relations with Germany on condition that she would facilitate the passage of German troops through Belgium. *(Ironical laughter.)* Well, Sir, until one has these things absolutely definite, up to the last moment I do not wish to say all that one would say if one were in a position to give the House full, complete and absolute information upon the point. We were sounded in the course of last week as to whether, if a guarantee were given that, after the war, Belgian integrity would be preserved, that would content us. We replied that we could not bargain away whatever interests or obligations we had in Belgian neutrality. *(Cheers.)*

Shortly before I reached the House I was informed that the following telegram had been received from the King of the Belgians by our King – King George:

Remembering the numerous proofs of your Majesty's friendship and that of your predecessors, and the friendly attitude of England in 1870, and the proof of friendship she has just given us again, I make a supreme appeal to the diplomatic intervention of your Majesty's Government to safeguard the integrity of Belgium.

Diplomatic intervention took place last week on our part. What can diplomatic intervention do now? We have great and vital interests in the independence – and integrity is the least part – of Belgium. *(Loud cheers.)* If Belgium is compelled to submit to allow her neutrality to be violated, of course the situation is clear. Even if by agreement she admitted the violation of her neutrality, it is clear she could only do so under duress. The smaller States in that region of Europe ask but one thing. Their one desire is that they should be left alone and independent. The one thing they fear is, I think, not so much that their integrity but that their independence should be interfered with. If in this war, which is before Europe, the neutrality of those countries is violated, if the troops of one of the combatants violate its neutrality and no action be taken to resent it, at the end of war, whatever the integrity may be, the independence will be gone *(cheers)* . . .

No, Sir, if it be the case that there has been anything in the nature of an ultimatum to Belgium, asking her to compromise or violate her neutrality, whatever may have been offered to her in return, her independence is gone if that holds. If her independence goes, the independence of Holland will follow. I ask the House from the point of view of British interests to consider what may be at stake. If France is beaten in a struggle of life and death, beaten to her knees, loses her position as a great power, becomes subordinate to the will and power of one greater than herself – consequences which I do not anticipate, because I am sure that France has the power to defend herself with all the energy and ability and patriotism which she has shown so often *(loud cheers)* – still, if that were to happen and if Belgium fell under the same dominating influence, and then Holland, and then Denmark, then would not Mr Gladstone's words come true, that just opposite to us there would be a common interest against the unmeasured aggrandisement of any power? *(Loud cheers.)*

It may be said, I suppose, that we might stand aside, husband our strength, and that, whatever happened in the course of this war, at the end of it intervene with effect to put things right, and to adjust them to our own point of view. If, in a crisis like this, we run away *(loud cheers)* from those obligations of honour and interest as regards the Belgian treaty, I doubt whether, whatever material force we might have at the end, it would be of very much value in face of the respect that we should have lost. And I do not believe, whether a great power stands outside this war or not, it is going to be in a position at the end of it to exert its superior strength. For us, with a powerful fleet, which we believe able to protect our commerce, to protect our shores, and to protect our interests, if we are engaged in war, we shall suffer but little more than we shall suffer even if we stand aside.

We are going to suffer, I am afraid, terribly in this war, whether we are in it or whether we stand aside. Foreign trade is going to stop, not because the trade routes are closed, but because there is no trade at the other end. Continental nations engaged in war all their populations, all their energies, all their wealth, engaged in a desperate struggle they cannot carry on the trade with us that they are carrying on in times of peace, whether we are parties to the war or whether we are not. I do not believe for a moment that at the end of this war, even if we stood aside and remained aside, we should be in a position, a material position, to use our force decisively to undo what had happened in the course of the war, to prevent the whole of the west of Europe opposite to us – if that had been the result of the war – falling under the domination of a single power, and I am quite sure that our moral position would be such as – *[the rest of the sentence – 'to have lost us all respect.' – was lost in a loud outburst of cheering]*. I can only say that I have put the question of Belgium somewhat hypothetically, because I am not yet sure of all the facts, but, if the facts turn out to be as they have reached us at present, it is quite clear that there is an obligation on this country to do its utmost to prevent the consequences to which those facts will lead if they are undisputed . . .

One thing I would say. The one bright spot in the whole of this terrible situation is Ireland. *(Prolonged cheers.)* The general feeling throughout Ireland, and I would like this to be clearly understood abroad, does not make that a consideration that we feel we have to take into account *(cheers)*. I have told the House how far we have at present gone in commitments, and the conditions which influence our policy; and I have put and dealt at length to the House upon how vital the condition of the neutrality of Belgium is.

What other policy is there before the House? There is but one way in which the Government could make certain at the present moment of keeping outside this war, and that would be that it should immediately issue a proclamation of unconditional neutrality. We cannot do that. *(Cheers.)* We have made the commitment to France that I have read to the House which prevents us doing that. We have got the consideration of Belgium which prevents us also from any unconditional neutrality, and, without these conditions absolutely satisfied and satisfactory, we are bound not to shrink from proceeding to the use of all the forces in our power. If we did take that line by saying, 'We will have nothing whatever to do with this matter' under no conditions – the Belgian treaty obligations, the possible position in the Mediterranean, with damage to British interests, and what may happen to France from our failure to support France – if we were to say that all those things matter nothing, were as nothing, and to say we would stand aside, we should, I believe, sacrifice our respect and good name and reputation before the world, and should not escape the most serious and grave economic consequences. *(Cheers and a voice, 'No.')*

My object has been to explain the view of the Government, and to place before the House the issue and the choice. I do not for a moment conceal, after what I have said, and after the information, incomplete as it is, that I have given to the House with regard to Belgium, that we must be prepared, and we are prepared, for the consequences of having to use all the strength we have at any moment – we know not how soon – to defend ourselves and to take our part. We know, if the facts all be as I have stated them, though I have announced no intending aggressive action on our part, no final decision to resort to force at a moment's notice, until we know the whole of the case, that the use of it may be forced upon us. As far as the forces of the Crown are concerned, we are ready. I believe the Prime Minister and my Rt Hon. friend, the First Lord of the Admiralty, have no doubt whatever that the readiness and the efficiency of those forces were never at a higher mark than they are to-day, and never was there a time when confidence was more justified in the power of the Navy to protect our commerce and to protect our shores. The thought is with us always of the suffering and misery entailed, from which no country in Europe will escape, and from which no abdication or neutrality will save us. The amount of harm that can be done by an enemy ship to our trade is infinitesimal, compared with the amount of harm that must be done by the economic condition that is caused on the Continent.

The most awful responsibility is resting upon the Government in deciding what to advise the House of Commons to do. We have disclosed our minds to the House of Commons. We have disclosed the issue, the information which we have, and made clear to the House, I trust, that we are prepared to face that situation, and that should it develop, as probably it may develop, we will face it. We worked for peace up to the last moment, and beyond the last moment. How hard, how persistently, and how earnestly we strove for peace last week the House will see from the papers that will be before it.

But that is over, as far as the peace of Europe is concerned. We are now face to face with a situation and all the consequences which it may yet have to unfold. We believe we shall have the support of the House at large in proceeding to whatever the consequences may be and whatever measures may be forced upon us by the development of facts or action taken by others. I believe the country, so quickly has the situation been forced upon it, has not had time to realise the issue. It perhaps is still thinking of the quarrel between Austria and Servia, and not the complications of this matter which have grown out of the quarrel between Austria and Servia. Russia and Germany we know are at war. We do not yet know officially that Austria, the ally whom Germany is to support, is yet at war with Russia. We know that a good deal has been happening on the French frontier. We do not know that the German Ambassador has left Paris.

The situation has developed so rapidly that technically, as regards the condition of the war, it is most difficult to describe what has actually happened. I wanted to bring out the underlying issues which would affect our own conduct, and our own policy, and to put them clearly. I have now put the vital facts before the House, and if, as seems not improbable, we are forced, and rapidly forced, to take our stand upon those issues, then I believe, when the country realises what is at stake, what the real issues are, the magnitude of the impending dangers in the west of Europe, which I have endeavored to describe to the House, we shall be supported throughout, not only by the House of Commons, but by the determination, the resolution, the courage, and the endurance of the whole country.

—

Later in the day Sir Edward added the following words:

I want to give the House some information which I have received, and which was not in my possession when I made my statement this afternoon. It is information I have received from the Belgian Legation in London, and is to the following effect:

Germany sent yesterday evening at seven o'clock a note proposing to Belgium friendly neutrality, covering free passage on Belgian territory, and promising maintenance of independence of the kingdom and possession at the conclusion of peace, and threatening, in case of refusal, to treat Belgium as an enemy. A time-limit of twelve hours was fixed for the reply. The Belgians have answered that an attack on their neutrality would be a flagrant violation of the rights of nations, and that to accept the German proposal would be to sacrifice the honour of a nation. Conscious of its duty, Belgium is finally resolved to repel aggression by all possible means.

Of course, I can only say that the Government are prepared to take into grave consideration the information which they have received. I make no further comment upon it.

SOURCE: WWI Document Archive > 1914 Documents > Sir Edward Grey's Speech Before Parliament. From: Great Britain, Parliamentary Debates, Commons, Fifth Series, Vol. LXV, 1914, columns 1809–1834.

ACKNOWLEDGEMENTS

My thanks and gratitude to …

Marie-Morgane Le Moël and Ollie Ham (dear wife and son) for appreciating the demands of 'another bloody epic';

Kevin O'Brien, brilliant editor – precise, imperturbable and a pleasure to work with;

Everyone involved at Random House, notably Alison Urquhart, the publisher every writer needs, and the beatific whip hand behind most of my books; and Patrick Mangan, who guided the book superbly, from draft to completion.

My wonderful agent, Jane Burridge, one of the few people who understands the concept of the working lunch.

Thanks to researchers Elizabeth Donnelly (Britain), Léo Bourcart (France) and Elena Vogt (Germany), for their research assistance, chiefly in unearthing stories of soldiers and civilians; similarly, François Ferrette (Paris), Shirley Ham (Sydney) and Glenda Lynch (Canberra).

1914 absorbed hundreds of documents and newspapers, many in German and French, which were expertly translated by Tea Dietterich and her colleagues at 2M Language Services, and Léo Bourcart. Thanks also to David at Xou.

Others too numerous to list, from battlefield guides to archivists, orbited this book. I'd like to single out the Australia Council for the Arts, not only for granting a six-month Literary Residency in Paris – where this book was partly written – but also for their quiet, persistent championing of literature. I can think of no better place to attempt to fulfil their faith than in an atelier on the right bank of the Seine, a stone's throw from the Île Saint-Louis. Santé!

NOTES AND REFERENCES

Prelude

1. Fussell, p.24.
2. Quoted by André Derval in his introduction to Céline, *Journey to the End of the Night*, p. x.
3. Fussell, p. 158.
4. Strachan, *To Arms*, p. 103.
5. Fussell, p. 90.
6. E. Blunden, *Cambridge Magazine*, quoted in Fussell, p. 91.
7. Jones, pp. 110, 304.
8. Nesbitt, p. 91.
9. Rupert Brooke, 'The Soldier'.
10. Eksteins, p. 306.
11. Ibid., p. 56.
12. Ferguson, pp. 28–30.
13. Source in Ferguson, p. 98.
14. Fussell, p. 24.

Part 1   The Tyranny of the Past

Chapter 1   Nijinsky's Faun

1. Quoted in Hughes, p. 9.
2. See Wohl, R., *The Generation of 1914.*
3. Orwell, p. 407.
4. Quoted in Hattersley, p. 17.
5. Orwell, p. 409.
6. Carr, p. 140.
7. Kapos, pp. 85–6.
8. Ibid., p. 35.
9. Danchev, p. 3.
10. Quoted in Peck, p. 27.
11. Joll, pp. 64–5.
12. Eksteins, p. 39.
13. *Le Figaro*, 30 May 1912.
14. Buckle, p. 244.
15. Quoted in Eksteins, p. 11.

Chapter 2   The Rise of the Machines

1. Hughes, p. 11.
2. Hattersley, p. 434.
3. Hughes, p. 11.
4. See Chandler, A., *Scale and Scope: The Dynamics of Industrial Capitalism.*
5. Hattersley, p. 67.
6. Quoted in Hattersley, p. 69.
7. Quoted in Steiner and Neilson, p. 202.

8. Ibid., p. 203.
9. See Bloch, *Is War Now Impossible?*.
10. See Strachan, *To Arms*, from p. 1005.
11. Ibid., p. 1006.
12. Bloch, *The Contemporary Review*, 1901.
13. Masterman, p. 289.

Chapter 3   A German Place in the Sun
1. Quoted in Kennedy, *The Rise of the Anglo-German Antagonism 1860–1914*, p. 467.
2. Meredith, p. 2.
3. Ferguson, p. 38.
4. Pakenham, p. xxi.
5. Fischer, p. 11.
6. Ibid.
7. http://germanhistorydocs.ghi-dc.org/sub_document.cfm?document_id=1867.
8. See Treitschke.
9. Olson, J. (ed.), *Historical Dictionary of European Imperialism*, pp. 348–9.
10. Quoted in Kennedy, *The Rise of the Anglo-German Antagonism*, p. 172.
11. Ibid.
12. See Ferguson, pp. 35–6.
13. Ferguson, p. 36.
14. Quoted in Kennedy, *The Rise of the Anglo-German Antagonism*, p. 181.
15. Kennedy, p. 175.
16. Kennedy, p. 181.

Chapter 4   Serbian Vendettas
1. Albertini, Vol. 1, p. 13.
2. Ćorović, p. 192.
3. Judah, p. 25.
4. 'Heavenly People', Serb epic poem.
5. Judah, p. 25.
6. According to Zarko Korac, professor of psychology at the University of Belgrade, quoted in Judah, p. 27.
7. Extracted from Ibragimbeili, *Soviet Military Encyclopedia*.
8. Marx and Engels, p. 32.
9. Albertini, Vol. 1, p. 9.
10. Ludwig, p. 73.

Chapter 5   Enter Austria-Hungary
1. Taylor, *Habsburg Monarchy*, p. 9.
2. Ibid., p. 10.
3. Ibid., p. 34.
4. Quoted in Albertini, Vol. 1, p. 32.
5. Ibid., p. 35.
6. The World War I Document Archive, http://wwi.lib.byu.edu/index.php/The_Triple_Alliance_%28The_English_Translation%29.
7. Ibid.

Chapter 6   *The Kaiser's World*
1.   Steinberg, p. 472.
2.   Francke, pp. 270–5.
3.   Lutz, pp. 39–40.
4.   Steinberg, p. 436.
5.   Putnam, p. 33.
6.   Lutz, pp. 39–40.
7.   Geiss, pp. 21–2.
8.   Quoted in Kennedy, *The Rise of the Anglo-German Antagonism*, p. 311.
9.   Ibid.
10. Tirpitz, *My Memoirs*, I, p. 162.
11. Kennedy, *The Rise of the Anglo-German Antagonism*, p. 205.
12. Van der Poel, p. 135.
13. Quoted in Kennedy, *The Rise of the Anglo-German Antagonism*, p. 221.
14. Quoted in Fischer, p. 8.
15. A. Kruck, quoted in Geiss, p. 21.
16. Quoted in Geiss, p. 23.
17. Fischer, p. 13.
18. Ibid., p. 15.
19. Ibid., p. 18.
20. Ferguson, pp. 52–3.

Chapter 7   *The Franco-Russian Vice*
1.   Kennedy, *The Rise of the Anglo-German Antagonism*, p. 23.
2.   Quoted in Kennedy, *The Rise of the Anglo-German Antagonism*, p. 23.
3.   Joll, p. 11.
4.   http://www.mtholyoke.edu/~jihazel/pol116/annexation.html
5.   La déclaration des députés d'Alsace et de Lorraine déposée le 1er mars 1871,
     http://www.assemblee-nationale.fr/histoire/deputes-protestataires.asp.
6.   Kennedy, p. 129.
7.   Quoted in Keiger, p. 9.
8.   Keiger, p. 15.
9.   Ibid., p. 8.
10. Keiger, p. 10.
11. Quoted in Keiger, p. 10.
12. Ibid., p. 15.
13. Ibid., p. 13.
14. 'The Franco-Russian Alliance Military Convention – August 18, 1892', Yale Law
     School, The Avalon Project: http://avalon.law.yale.edu/19th_century/frrumil.asp.
15. Ibid.

Chapter 8   *The Wild Card*
1.   Grey, Vol. I, p. 42.
2.   Ibid., p. 43.
3.   Quoted in Albertini, Vol. 1, pp. 112–13.
4.   Asquith, p. 25.
5.   Albertini, Vol. 1, pp. 113–14.

6. Ibid., p. 115.
7. Brandenburg, pp. 176–81.

Part 2   Wilful Blindness and Blinkered Vision, 1900–1914

Chapter 9   Runaway War
1. Keegan, p. 27.
2. Ibid., p. 31.
3. Ibid.
4. Stevenson, 'War by Timetable?', pp. 163–94.
5. See Taylor, *War by Timetable*.
6. Stevenson, 'War by Timetable?', pp. 163–94.
7. Kern, p. 269.
8. Stevenson, 'War by Timetable?', pp. 163–94.
9. Ibid, p. 175.
10. Taylor, *War by Timetable*, p. 21.
11. Helmuth von Moltke the Younger to Bethmann-Hollweg, 1 January–8 March 1914, quoted in Davidson, p. 186.

Chapter 10   Schlieffen's Apocalypse
1. Keegan, p. 34.
2. Quoted in Strachan, *The First World War*, p. 42.
3. See Curtis, V. J., 'Understanding Schlieffen', The Army Doctrine and Training Bulletin, Vol 6, No 3, Fall-Winter 2003 or: http://www.army.forces.gc.ca/caj/documents/vol_06/iss_3/CAJ_vol6.3_13_e.pdf.
4. Keegan, p. 31.
5. Ibid., p. 31.
6. Ritter, *The Schlieffen Plan*, p. 145.
7. Herwig, H., in Murray, Knox and Bernstein, p. 260.
8. Ritter, p. 139.
9. Quoted in Keegan, p. 33.
10. Taylor, p. 21.
11. Keegan, p. 34.
12. Ibid., p. 37.
13. Carroll, pp. 577–8.
14. Ritter, p. 100.
15. Geiss, p. 37.

Chapter 11   England Comes in from the Cold
1. Churchill, Vol. I, p. 18.
2. Von Waldersee diary, quoted in Clark, p. 151.
3. Quoted in Albertini, Vol. 1, p. 147.
4. Schmitt, B., 'Triple Alliance and Triple Entente 1902–1914', p. 139.
5. Clark, p. 139.
6. As Sazonov reported in 1912. See Schmitt, 'Triple Alliance and Triple Entente 1902–1914'.

7. Albertini, Vol. 1, p. 149.
8. Quoted in Albertini, Vol. 1, p. 150.
9. Ibid.
10. Ibid., pp. 150–1.
11. Albertini, Vol. 1, p. 160.
12. Clark, p. 156.
13. Quoted in Clark, p. 156.
14. Clark, p. 157.
15. Schmitt, B., 'Triple Alliance and Triple Entente 1902–1914'.
16. Wolpert, p. 80.
17. Quoted in Albertini, Vol. 1, p. 189.
18. Schmitt, B., 'Triple Alliance and Triple Entente 1902–1914'.
19. Quoted in Albertini, Vol. 1, p. 189.

Chapter 12   English Germanophobia

1. See Swallow, 'Transitions in British Editorial Germanophobia 1899–1914: A Case Study of J. L. Garvin, Leo Maxse and St. Loe Strachey', pp. 63–4.
2. Kennedy, *The Rise of the Anglo-German Antagonism*, p. 136.
3. Ibid., p. 137.
4. Crowe, E., http://tmh.floonet.net/pdf/eyre_crowe_memo.pdf.
5. Kennedy, *The Rise of the Anglo-German Antagonism*, p. 253.
6. See Steiner and Neilson, p. 190; and Neilson, 'My Beloved Russians', pp. 521–4.
7. Williamson, 'The Reign of Sir Edward Grey as British Foreign Secretary', pp. 426–38.
8. Steiner and Neilson, p. 47–8.
9. Ibid., p. 195.
10. Ibid., p. 185.
11. Kennedy, *The Rise of the Anglo-German Antagonism*, p. 254.
12. Clark, p. 162.
13. Albertini, Vol. 1, p. 185.
14. Crowe, E., http://tmh.floonet.net/pdf/eyre_crowe_memo.pdf.
15. Ibid.
16. Ibid.
17. Ibid.
18. Clark, p. 163.
19. Crowe, E., http://tmh.floonet.net/pdf/eyre_crowe_memo.pdf.
20. Ibid.
21. Ibid.
22. Ibid.
23. Ibid.
24. Steiner and Neilson, p. 47.
25. Geiss, pp. 28–33.
26. Albertini, Vol. 1, p. 184.
27. Kennedy, *The Rise of the Anglo-German Antagonism*, p. 402.
28. See Ferguson, *The Pity of War*, Chapter 3.
29. 'Our True Foreign Policy', *The Saturday Review*, 24 August 1895, p. 17.
30. 'A Biological View of our Foreign Policy', *The Saturday Review*, 1 February 1896, p. 15.

31. See Ferguson, Chapter 1.
32. Quoted in Ferguson, p. 11.
33. Ferguson, p. 13.
34. Quoted in Ferguson, p. 14.
35. Ibid.

Chapter 13   *Meanwhile, in Bosnia-Herzegovina*

1. Quoted in Albertini, Vol. 1, p. 222.
2. Albertini, Vol. 1, p. 14.
3. Quoted in Albertini, Vol. 1, p. 191.
4. Albertini, Vol. 1, p. 191.
5. Quoted in Albertini, Vol. 1, p. 188.
6. Alexander Kerensky, 'Izvolsky's Personal Diplomatic Correspondence', pp. 386–92.
7. According to one of the secret articles of the Three Emperors' Alliance of 1881; quoted in Clark, p. 83.
8. Wank, Solomon, 'Aehrenthal's Programme' (see note 60), quoted in Clark, p. 84.
9. Albertini, Vol. 1, p. 195.
10. Quoted in Albertini, Vol. 1, p. 195.
11. Albertini, Vol. 1, p. 209.
12. Quoted in Albertini, Vol. 1, p. 228.
13. Joll, p. 173.
14. Quoted in Joll, p. 173.
15. Quoted in Albertini, Vol. 1, p. 225.
16. Quoted in Albertini, Vol. 1, p. 222.
17. Ninčić, p. 509.
18. Shackelford, extract, see: http://net.lib.byu.edu/estu/wwi/comment/blk-hand.html.
19. Ibid.
20. Strachan, *To Arms*, p. 45.

Chapter 14   *Teutons – and an Italian – Under Siege*

1. Sondhaus, p. 82.
2. Quoted in Sondhaus, p. 84.
3. Quoted in ibid.
4. Conrad to Gina, Vienna, 26 December 1908 (never sent), quoted in ibid., p. 111.
5. Ibid., p. 109.
6. Quoted in Albertini, Vol. 1, pp. 264–5.
7. Ibid., p. 269.
8. Jarausch, 'Revising German History: Bethmann Hollweg Revisited'.
9. Jarausch, ibid.
10. Ludwig, p. 44.
11. Jarausch, 'Revising German History: Bethmann Hollweg Revisited'.
12. Bethmann-Hollweg, p. 18.
13. Ibid., p. 30.
14. Ibid., p. 43.
15. Ibid., p. 45.

16. Quoted in Clark, p. 178.
17. Ibid., p. 181.
18. Ibid., p. 182.
19. The World War One Document Archive, The Daily Telegraph Affair, http://wwi. lib.byu.edu/index.php/The_Daily_Telegraph_Affair.
20. Cecil, Vol. 2, pp. 138–41.
21. Bülow, Vol. II, pp. 347–8.
22. Clark, p. 182.
23. Bethmann-Hollweg, pp. 19–20.

Chapter 15   A Gunboat to Agadir

1. Steiner and Neilson, p. 75.
2. Bethmann-Hollweg, pp. 31–2.
3. Clark, p. 206.
4. Ibid.
5. Quoted in Steiner and Neilson, p. 76.
6. Bethmann-Hollweg, p. 33.
7. Cosgrove, 'A Note on Lloyd George's Speech at the Mansion House, 21 July 1911', pp. 698–701.
8. Churchill, *The World Crisis*, Vol. I, pp. 47–8.
9. Steiner and Neilson, p. 76.
10. Quoted in Steiner and Neilson, p. 77.
11. *The Times*, 22 July 1911.
12. Churchill, *The World Crisis*, Vol. I, pp. 47–8.
13. Bethmann-Hollweg, pp. 35–6.
14. Strachan, *The First World War*, p. 40.
15. Ibid.
16. Clark, p. 205.
17. Yeats, 'The Second Coming'.

Chapter 16   Friedrich von Bernhardi's Fittest

1. Introduction to Bernhardi, *Germany and the Next War*.
2. Introduction to Bernhardi, *Germany and the Next War*.
3. Bernhardi, *Germany and the Next War*, online edition: https://www.h-net. org/~german/gtext/kaiserreich/bernhardi.html#note3.
4. Bernhardi, *Germany and the Next War*.
5. 'The German View of "The Next War"', *The Literary Digest*, 4 May 1912: http:// www.oldmagazinearticles.com/pdf/bernhardi_0001.jpg.
6. Quoted in ibid.

Chapter 17   Brigadier General Sir Henry Wilson's Plan

1. Steiner and Neilson, p. 207.
2. Quoted in ibid., p. 209.
3. Quoted in Keiger, p. 102.
4. Keiger, p. 110.
5. Ibid.
6. Steiner and Neilson, p. 210.

7. Kennedy, *The Rise of the Anglo-German Antagonism*, p. 432.
8. Quoted in Steiner and Neilson, p. 214.
9. Steiner and Neilson, p. 211.
10. Quoted in ibid., p. 213.
11. Henry Wilson, Appendix to 'The Military Aspect of the Continental Problem', Memorandum by the General Staff, 12 August 1911, National Archives, CAB 38/19/47.
12. Quoted in Koss, pp. 144–5.
13. Scott Diary, 4 May 1914.
14. Henry Wilson, Appendix to 'The Military Aspect of the Continental Problem', Memorandum by the General Staff, 12 August 1911, National Archives, CAB 38/19/47.
15. For a lively discussion of troop numbers, see twcenter.net: http://www.twcenter.net/forums/showthread.php?t=357390.
16. Peden, p. 47.
17. Minutes of 114th Meeting (Action to be taken in the event of intervention in a European war; Appreciation of the military situation on the outbreak of a Franco-German war; Naval criticism of the General Staff proposals; Admiralty policy on the outbreak of war), National Archives, CAB 38/19/49, pp. i–18.
18. Strachan, *To Arms*, p. 380.
19. Minutes of 114th Meeting (Action to be taken in the event of intervention in a European war; Appreciation of the military situation on the outbreak of a Franco-German war; Naval criticism of the General Staff proposals; Admiralty policy on the outbreak of war), National Archives, CAB 38/19/49, pp. i–18.
20. Quoted in Steiner and Neilson, p. 213.
21. Steiner and Neilson, p. 213.
22. Henry Wilson, Appendix to 'The Military Aspect of the Continental Problem', Memorandum by the General Staff, 12 August 1911, National Archives, CAB 38/19/47.

Chapter 18   French Vengeance

1. Payen, p. 17.
2. Quoted in Keiger, p. 45.
3. Ibid.
4. Ibid.
5. Ibid., p. 70.
6. Ibid.
7. Ibid.
8. Bethmann-Hollweg, pp. 40–1.
9. Quoted in Bruun, pp. 6–7.
10. Bruun, p. 9.
11. Ibid., p. 51.
12. Quoted in ibid., p. 13.
13. *The Statesman's Yearbook, 1906–1910*, quoted in Bruun, p. 81.
14. Foch, p. xxvii.
15. Ibid.
16. Ibid., p. xxviii.

17. Ibid., p. xxx.
18. Ibid., p. xxxix.
19. Ibid., p. xli.
20. Ibid., p. xl.

Chapter 19   Sea Supremacy

1. Kennedy, *The Rise of the Anglo-German Antagonism*, p. 416.
2. Quoted in Ferguson, p. 86.
3. Ibid.
4. Quoted in Kennedy, *The Rise of the Anglo-German Antagonism*, p. 421.
5. Berghahn, *Der Tirpitz: Genesis und Verfall einer innenpolitischen Krisenstrategie unter Wilhelm II.*
6. Quoted in Herwig, 'Imperial Germany', p. 75.
7. Ibid.
8. Herwig, *'Luxury' Fleet*, pp. 36, 38; Berghahn, *Tirpitz-Plan*, pp. 74 ff.
9. Quoted in Kennedy, *The Rise of the Anglo-German Antagonism*, p. 417.
10. Massie, pp. 177–9.
11. Herwig, 'Imperial Germany', p. 74.
12. Bernhardi, *The Next War*, online edition: https://www.h-net.org/~german/gtext/kaiserreich/bernhardi.html#note3.
13. Quoted in Kennedy, *The Rise of the Anglo-German Antagonism*, p. 420.
14. Steiner and Neilson, p. 52.
15. The World War One Document Archive, The Daily Telegraph Affair, http://wwi.lib.byu.edu/index.php/The_Daily_Telegraph_Affair.
16. Quoted in Albertini, Vol. 1, p. 322.
17. Quoted in Ferguson, p. 85.
18. Bethmann-Hollweg, p. 51.
19. Ibid., p. 55.
20. Steiner and Neilson, p. 102.
21. Bethmann-Hollweg, p. 58.
22. Steiner and Neilson, p. 103.
23. Quoted in Steiner and Neilson, p. 103.
24. Kennedy, *The Rise of the Anglo-German Antagonism*, p. 419.

Chapter 20   Crises in the Balkans

1. Bethmann-Hollweg, p. 75.
2. Quoted in Bethmann-Hollweg, p. 72.
3. Bethmann-Hollweg, p. 72.
4. Taube, pp. 225–7.
5. Albertini, Vol. 1, p. 366.
6. Quoted in Albertini, Vol. 1, p. 372.
7. Albertini, p. 372.
8. Quoted in Albertini, p. 376.
9. Ibid., p. 375.
10. Serbian Blue Book.
11. Strachan, *To Arms*, p. 50.
12. Ibid.

13. Kanner, p. 87.
14. That reassurance came from Sazonov in October 1912, and related to the generally accepted principle by which European powers would not tolerate changes in the territorial status quo in the Balkans (surely a running joke in the embassies).
15. Strachan, *To Arms*, p. 51.
16. Hötzendorf, Vol. III, p. 155.
17. Ibid., p. 147.
18. Quoted in Albertini, Vol. 1, p. 408.
19. Quoted in Albertini, Vol. 1, p. 413.
20. Strachan, *To Arms*, p. 51.
21. Quoted in Herwig, 'Imperial Germany', p. 83.
22. In a margin note by the Kaiser on Lichnowsky's telegram to Bethmann-Hollweg, 3 December 1912, quoted in Herwig, 'Imperial Germany', p. 83.
23. Strachan, *To Arms*, p. 52.
24. Herwig, 'Imperial Germany', pp. 81–97.
25. Quoted in Herwig, 'Imperial Germany', p. 83.
26. Ibid., p. 84.
27. Quoted in Albertini, Vol. 1, p. 455.
28. Quoted in Steiner and Neilson, p. 121.

Chapter 21   Armed for 'Inevitable War'

1. Quoted in Herwig, 'Imperial Germany', p. 81.
2. Quoted in Ferguson, p. 97.
3. Ibid., p. 98.
4. Ibid.
5. Ferguson, p. 32.
6. Ibid.
7. See argument in Taylor, *War by Timetable*.
8. Quoted in Kennedy, *The Rise of the Anglo-German Antagonism*, p. 419.
9. Ferguson, pp. 91–2.
10. Ibid., pp. 92–3.
11. Fischer, p. 36.
12. Stevenson, 'War by Timetable?', p. 187.
13. Herwig, 'Imperial Germany', p. 67.
14. Ibid., p. 66.
15. Ibid., p. 67.
16. Ibid., p. 67.
17. Ibid., p. 69.
18. Kuhl, pp. 96–8, 104–5.
19. Keiger, p. 125.
20. See Herwig, 'Germany and the "Short-War" Illusion: Toward a New Interpretation?', pp. 681–93.
21. Keiger, pp. 125–7.
22. Stevenson, *Armaments*, p. 167.
23. Ferguson, p. 97.
24. Quoted in Steiner and Neilson, p. 98.
25. Fischer, p. 37.

26. Herwig, 'Imperial Germany', p. 95.
27. Strachan, *The First World War*, p. 45.
28. Curtis, 'Understanding Schlieffen,' p. 56.

Part 3   1914 – In the Salons of Power

Chapter 22   *A Better Year?*
1. Smith, 'The Monarchy versus the Nation: The "Festive Year" 1913 in Wilhelmine Germany', pp. 257–74.
2. OECD Development Centre, 'The World Economy: International Trade and Capital Movements': http://www.theworldeconomy.org/advances/advances2.html.
3. Smith, 'The Monarchy versus the Nation: The "Festive Year" 1913 in Wilhelmine Germany', pp. 257–74.
4. Ibid.
5. Quoted in ibid., p. 260.
6. Quoted in ibid., p. 262.
7. Quoted in Cowles, p. 98.
8. Cowles, p. 135.
9. Ibid., pp. 135–6.
10. Lenin, *Collected Works,* pp. 74–7.
11. Cowles, p. 136.
12. WWI: The World War I Document Archive, 'Colonel House's Report to President Wilson': http://wwi.lib.byu.edu/index.php/Colonel_House%27s_Report_to_President_Wilson.

Chapter 23   *Edward Grey's Ménage à Quatre*
1. Quoted in Steiner and Neilson, p. 159.
2. Ludwig, p. 89.
3. Albertini, Vol. 2, p. 199.
4. Ekstein, 'Great Britain and the Triple Entente on the eve of the Sarajevo Crisis' in Hinsley, (ed.), *British Foreign Policy under Sir Edward Grey*, p. 348.
5. Ibid., p. 342.
6. Quoted in ibid., p. 343.
7. Sazonov, p. 128.
8. Quoted in Ekstein, p. 344.
9. Albertini, Vol. 1, p. 541.
10. Sazonov, pp. 124–5.
11. Ibid.
12. Ekstein, 'Great Britain and the Triple Entente on the eve of the Sarajevo Crisis' in Hinsley, (ed.), *British Foreign Policy under Sir Edward Grey*, p. 344.
13. Benckendorf to Sazonov, letters, 5–18 May 1914, in Siebert, B. de, *Entente Diplomacy and the World*, London 1921.
14. Ibid.
15. Quoted in Ekstein, p. 347.

Chapter 24   The Uses of Franz Ferdinand, Dead

1. Hötzendorf, Vol. I, p. 158.
2. Hochschild, pp. 79–80.
3. Quoted in Smith, David James, p. 166.
4. See Shackelford, The Black Hand: The Secret Serbian Terrorist Society (extract), The World War I Document Archive, http://net.lib.byu.edu/~rdh7/wwi/comment/blk-hand.html.
5. Ibid.
6. Ibid.
7. Stanojević, pp. 50–1.
8. Ibid.
9. Sulzberger, p. 202.
10. Shackelford, The Black Hand: The Secret Serbian Terrorist Society (extract), The World War I Document Archive, http://net.lib.byu.edu/~rdh7/wwi/comment/blk-hand.html.
11. Smith, David James, p. 8.
12. Ibid., p. 9.
13. Quoted in Albertini, Vol. 2, p. 42.
14. Smith, David James, p. 17.
15. Quoted in Albertini, Vol. 2, p. 35.
16. Sosnosky, p. 206.
17. Harrach memoir in Sosnosky, pp. 205–21; and http://www.firstworldwar.com/source/harrachmemoir.htm.
18. Ibid.
19. Pfeffer, pp. 27–8, quoted in Albertini, Vol. 2, p. 43.
20. Ibid.
21. The World War I Document Archive, 'The Assassination of Archduke Franz Ferdinand': http://wwi.lib.byu.edu/index.php/The_Assassination_of_Archduke_Franz_Ferdinand.
22. Keiger, p. 146.
23. Margutti, pp. 81–2.
24. Ibid.
25. Kanner, p. 192.
26. Albertini, Vol. 2, p. 115.
27. Ibid., Vol. 2, p. 118.
28. Seton-Watson, p. 104.
29. Hötzendorf, Vol. IV, pp. 30–1.
30. Ibid., p. 33.
31. See Sondhaus, *Franz Conrad Von Hotzendorf: Architect of the Apocalypse*.
32. Ibid., pp. 30–1.
33. French Yellow Book, Chapter II, No. 8. M. Dumaine, French Ambassador at Vienna, to M. René Viviani, President of the Council, minister for foreign affairs, Vienna, 2 July 1914.
34. Tisza, *Briefe*, p. 62, quoted in Albertini, Vol. 2, p. 127.
35. Quoted in Albertini, Vol. 2, p. 133.
36. Hötzendorf, Vol. IV, p. 36.
37. The World War I Document Archive, 'Autograph Letter of

Franz Joseph to the Kaiser': http://wwi.lib.byu.edu/index.php/
Autograph_Letter_of_Franz_Joseph_to_the_Kaiser.

38. Tschirschky to Bethmann-Hollweg, received 2 July 1914, quoted in Geiss, p. 64.
39. Szőgyény to Berchtold, received 5 July 1914, quoted in Geiss, p. 76.
40. Quoted in Ludwig, p. 43.
41. Bethmann-Hollweg, p. 113.
42. The World War I Document Archive, 'The "Blank Check"': http://wwi.lib.byu.
edu/index.php/The_%27Blank_Check%27.
43. Strachan, *To Arms*, p. 72.

Chapter 25   Austria-Hungary: Desperate for War

1. Ludwig, *July 1914*, p. 47.
2. Ibid.
3. Ibid.
4. Carter, p. 424.
5. Molden, Prememoria, appended to Solomon Wank, 'Desperate Counsel
in Vienna in July 1914: Berthold Molden's Unpublished Memorandum',
pp. 281–310.
6. Quoted in ibid.
7. Andrian-Werburg, *Der Kriegsbeginn*, quoted in ibid.
8. Molden, quoted in ibid.
9. Ibid.
10. Protocol of the [Austro-Hungarian War] Council, quoted in Geiss, p. 81.
11. Ibid., p. 83.
12. Ibid., pp. 83–4.
13. Ibid., p. 86.
14. Ibid.
15. Ibid., p. 87.
16. Quoted in Ludwig, *July 1914*, p. 45.

Chapter 26   Exceptional Tranquillity

1. Hötzendorf, Vol. IV, p. 61.
2. Quoted in Geiss, p. 91.
3. Churchill, *The World Crisis*, Vol. 1, p. 178.
4. Quoted in Keiger, p. 149.
5. Schoen cable in Geiss, p. 127.
6. Tschirschky to Jagow, in Geiss, pp. 106–8.
7. Ibid.
8. Ibid.
9. Kaiser's margin notes, in ibid.
10. Wiesner to Berchtold, in ibid., pp. 111–12.
11. Ibid.
12. Tschirschky to Jagow, in ibid., pp. 108–10.
13. Tschirschsky to Bethmann-Hollweg, ibid., p. 114.
14. Quoted in ibid., p. 92.
15. Lichnowsky to Bethmann-Hollweg, in ibid., pp. 104–5.
16. Ibid.

17. Ibid.
18. Churchill, Vol. I, pp. 181–6.
19. Steiner and Neilson, pp. 228–9.
20. Keiger, p. 139.
21. Quoted in ibid.
22. Ibid., p. 147.

Chapter 27   The Ultimatum to Serbia

1. The Austro-Hungarian Red Book, No 19.
2. Serbian Blue Book, No. 1.
3. Serbian Blue Book, No. 15.
4. Serbian Blue Book, No. 5, M. Yovanovitch, Serbian Minister at Vienna to M. N. Pashitch, the prime minister and minister for foreign affairs, Vienna, 17/30 June 1914.
5. Živanović in discussion with Albertini, quoted in Albertini, Vol. 2, p. 81.
6. Quoted in Albertini, Vol. 2, pp. 274–5.
7. Serbian Blue Book, No. 25.
8. Serbian Blue Book, No. 30.
9. Serbian Blue Book, No. 31.
10. Serbian Blue Book, No. 32.
11. Bethmann-Hollweg to German ambassadors in St Petersburg, Paris and London, in Geiss, p 149–150.
12. Quoted in Albertini, Vol. 2, pp. 269–70.
13. Ibid.
14. Ibid.
15. Pourtalès to Bethmann-Hollweg, in Geiss, pp. 151–3.
16. Ibid.
17. Ibid.
18. French Yellow Book, Chapter II, Preliminaries, No. 14, Memorandum (Extract from a Consular Report on the Economic and Political Situation in Austria), Vienna, 20 July 1914.
19. Ibid.
20. Paléologue, Vol. I, p. 19.
21. Paléologue, Vol. I, pp. 18–19. See also Albertini, Vol. 2, pp. 193–4, 265.
22. Quoted in Ludwig, p. 60.
23. Gottlieb von Jagow, see Albertini, Vol. 2, p. 265.
24. Protocol of the Council of Ministers of Common Affairs, Vienna, 19 July 1914, in Geiss, p. 139.
25. French Yellow Book, No. 18, M. Dumaine, French Ambassador at Vienna, to M. Bienvenu-Martin, acting minister for foreign affairs, Vienna, 22 July 1914.
26. Albertini, Vol. 2, p. 270.
27. Ibid., Vol. 2, p. 285.
28. The World War I Document Archive, 'The Austro-Hungarian Ultimatum to Serbia' (English Translation): http://wwi.lib.byu.edu/index.php/ The_Austro-Hungarian_Ultimatum_to_Serbia_(English_Translation).

Chapter 28   *You Are Setting Fire to Europe*

1. Griesinger to Jagow, 24 July 1914, in Geiss, p. 182.
2. Ibid.
3. Quoted in Albertini, Vol. 2, p. 349.
4. Quoted in Albertini, Vol. 2, pp. 290–1.
5. Berchtold to Austro-Hungarian ambassadors in Berlin, Rome, Paris, London and St Petersburg, 20 July 1914, in Geiss, pp. 147–9.
6. Szapáry to Berchtold, 24 July 1914, in Geiss, pp. 177–8.
7. Ibid.
8. *Special Journal of the Russian Council of Ministers*, in Geiss, pp. 186–7.
9. Pourtalès to Jagow, 25 July 1914, in Geiss, pp. 185–6; a different version given in Albertini, Vol. 2, p. 301, and Paléologue, Vol. I, p. 33.
10. Ibid.
11. Quoted in Albertini, Vol. 2, p. 301.
12. According to Paléologue, Vol. I, p. 33.
13. Ibid.
14. Sazonov's draft of a report to Nicholas II, 25 July 1914, in Geiss, pp. 208–9.
15. Russian Orange Book, No. 17, Russian Minister for Foreign Affairs to Russian Ambassador at London, St Petersburg, 12 July 1914.
16. Mensdorff to Berchtold, 24 July 1914, in Geiss, p. 175.
17. Ibid.
18. Ibid.
19. Geiss, p. 162.
20. Buchanan to Grey, 24 July 1914, in Geiss, p. 196.
21. Geiss, p. 163.
22. Buchanan to Grey, 24 July 1914, in Geiss, p. 197.
23. Eyre Crowe, minute to telegram, Buchanan to Grey, 24 July 1914, in Geiss, pp. 198–9.
24. Minute to telegram, Buchanan to Grey, 24 July 1914, in Geiss, p. 199.
25. Grey to Buchanan, 25 July 1914, in Geiss, p. 211.
26. Ibid.
27. Lichnowsky to Jagow, 24 July 1914, in Geiss, p. 183.
28. Albertini, Vol. 2, p. 345.
29. Berchtold to Baron Macchip, 25 July 1914, in Geiss, p. 200.
30. Rumbold to Grey, 25 July 1914, in Geiss, p. 212.
31. French Yellow Book, No. 30, M. Jules Cambon, French ambassador at Berlin, to M. Bienvenu-Martin, acting minister for foreign affairs, Berlin, 24 July 1914.
32. Kaiser's margin note in cable from Jagow, 23 July 1914, in Geiss, p. 170.

Chapter 29   *The Serbs Reply*

1. Sazonov, p. 177.
2. French Yellow Book, No. 46, M. Boppe, French minister at Belgrade, to M. Bienvenu-Martin, acting minister for foreign affairs, Belgrade, 25 July 1914.
3. French Yellow Book, No. 47, M. Jules Cambon, French ambassador at Berlin, to M. Bienvenu-Martin, acting minister for foreign affairs, Berlin, 25 July 1914.
4. Albertini, Vol. 2, p. 363.
5. Quoted in ibid., p. 373.

6. Ibid., p. 358.
7. Ibid., p. 373.
8. German White Book (English Translation), 'The Servian Answer (With Austria's Commentaries [in italics]', 25 July 1914.
9. Ibid.
10. Ibid. Different translation quoted in Albertini, Vol. 2, pp. 364–71.
11. Quoted by Musulin, in Albertini, Vol. 2, p. 387.
12. French Yellow Book, No. 50, M. Bienvenu-Martin, acting minister for foreign affairs, to the president of the Council (on board the *La France*) and to the French ambassadors at London, St Petersburg, Berlin, Vienna, Rome, Paris, 26 July 1914.
13. French Yellow Book, No. 66. M. de Fleuriau, French chargé d'affaires at London, to M. Bienvenu-Martin, acting minister for foreign affairs, London, 27 July 1914.
14. The World War I Document Archive, 'Wilhelm II's Intransigence': http://wwi.lib.byu.edu/index.php/Wilhelm_II%27s_Intransigence.
15. Russian Orange Book, No. 22, Russian ambassador at London to the Russian minister for foreign affairs, telegram, London, 12 July 1914.
16. French Yellow Book, No. 50, M. Bienvenu-Martin, acting minister for foreign affairs, to the president of the Council (on board the *La France*) and to the French ambassadors at London, St Petersburg, Berlin, Vienna, Rome, Paris, 26 July 1914.
17. German White Book, Exhibit 10, Telegram of the chancellor to the imperial ambassador at London, Urgent, 26 July 1914.
18. German White Book, Exhibit 10a, Telegram of the imperial chancellor to the imperial ambassador at Paris, 26 July 1914.
19. Quoted in Albertini, Vol. 2, p. 390.

Chapter 30   Every Cause for War Has Vanished

1. Pourtalès to Jagow, in Geiss, p. 230.
2. *Le Matin*, 27 July 1914.
3. Szőgyény to Berchtold, 25 July 1914, in Geiss, p. 200.
4. Nicolson to Grey, 26 July 1914, in ibid., p. 235.
5. Bethmann-Hollweg to Lichnowsky, 27 July 1914, in ibid., p. 237.
6. Szőgyény to Berchtold, 27 July 1914, in ibid., p. 236.
7. French Yellow Book, No. 74, M. Jules Cambon, French ambassador at Berlin, to M. Bienvenu-Martin, acting minister for foreign affairs, Berlin, 27 July 1914.
8. Ibid.
9. Lichnowsky to Jagow, 27 July 1914, in Geiss, p. 238.
10. Ibid., p. 239.
11. Churchill, Vol. I, pp. 194–5.
12. Lichnowsky to Jagow, 27 July 1914, in Geiss, pp. 240–1.
13. Bethmann-Hollweg to Lichnowsky, 28 July 1914, in ibid., pp. 243–4.
14. Buchanan to Grey, 27 July 1914, in ibid., pp. 249–50.
15. EAC minute, Buchanan to Grey, 27 July 1914, in ibid.
16. Goschen to Grey, 27 July 1914, in ibid., p. 253.
17. Grey to House of Commons, *Hansard*, HC Deb 27 July 1914 vol 65 cc936-9.
18. Grey, Vol. I, p. 310.

19. Butler, *Burden of Guilt*, p. 103.
20. Quoted in Albertini, Vol. 2, p. 467.
21. Kaiser Wilhelm II to Jagow, in Geiss, p. 256.
22. Berchtold to Szögyény, in ibid., p. 254.

Chapter 31   Austria-Hungary Declares War on Serbia
1. Serbian Blue Book, No. 45.
2. Quoted in Albertini, Vol. 2, p. 460.
3. Berchtold to Albertini, letter, quoted in Albertini, Vol. 2, p. 462.
4. French Yellow Book, No. 83, M. Dumaine, French Ambassador at Vienna, to M. Bienvenu-Martin, acting minister for foreign affairs, Vienna, 28 July 1914.
5. Russian Orange Book, No. 56, Telegram from His Royal Highness, Alexander of Servia, to His Majesty the Emperor of Russia.
6. Russian Orange Book, No. 57, Russian Chargé d'Affaires in Servia Russian Minister for Foreign Affairs Niš, telegram, 16 July 1914.
7. *Wiener Zeitung*, No. 175, Wednesday 29 July 1914. See the Austrian National Library webpage: http://www.anno.onb.ac.at/cgi-content/anno?datum=1914&zoom=10.
8. *Der Bauernbündler*, Year VII, newspaper of the Lower Austria's Farmers' Union, No. 175, 1 August 1914.
9. *Daheim*, 31 July 1914.
10. Ibid.
11. Ibid.
12. Ibid.
13. See Rothenburg, *The Army of Francis Joseph*, for details.
14. Maximilian Ehnl Edwin Sacken (Freiherr von.), p. 68.
15. Russian Orange Book, No. 59, Russian Chargé d'Affaires in Servia to Russian Minister for Foreign Affairs, telegram, Niš, 17 July 1914.
16. Ibid.
17. French Yellow Book, M. Paléologue, French Ambassador at St Petersburg to M. René Viviani, president of the Council, minister on foreign affairs, St Petersburg, 31 July 1914.

Chapter 32   Willy, Nicky and Georgie
1. Bethmann-Hollweg to Kaiser Wilhelm II, in Geiss, p. 258.
2. The World War I Document Archive, 'The Willy-Nicky Telegrams': http://wwi.lib.byu.edu/index.php/The_Willy-Nicky_Telegrams.
3. Quoted in Carter, p. 426.
4. Nicolson, *King George*, p. 246, quoted in Carter, p. 427.
5. Quoted in Carter, p. 429.
6. Ibid.

Chapter 33   The End of British 'Neutrality'
1. LaMar, p. 204.
2. Lichnowsky to Jagow, 29 July 1914, in Geiss, pp. 288–90.
3. Ibid.
4. Ibid.

5. Goschen to Grey, 29 July 1914, in Geiss, p. 300.
6. Ibid.
7. Ibid.
8. Lichnowsky to Jagow, 29 July 1914, in Geiss, pp. 288–90.
9. Ibid.
10. Bethmann-Hollweg to Tschirschky, 30 July 1914, in Geiss, pp. 291–2.
11. Ludwig, p. 144.
12. Kaiser's note to telegram, Pourtalès to Jagow, 30 July 1914, in Geiss, pp. 293–5. See other translations: Albertini, Vol. 3, pp. 34–5: and The World War I Document Archive, 'June-July, 1914, German Dispatches and the Kaiser's Notes': http://net.lib.byu.edu/~rdh7/wwi/1914/wilnotes.html.
13. Albertini, Vol. 3, p. 35.
14. Grey to Goschen, 30 July 1914, in Geiss, p. 315.
15. Williamson, 'The Reign of Sir Edward Grey as British Foreign Secretary', pp. 426–38.
16. See Valone, '"There Must Be Some Misunderstanding": Sir Edward Grey's Diplomacy of August 1, 1914', pp. 405–24.
17. The World War I Document Archive, 'Sir Edward Grey's Indecisiveness': http://wwi.lib.byu.edu/index.php/Sir_Edward_Grey%27s_Indecisiveness.
18. Ibid.
19. French Yellow Book, No. 126, M. Paul Cambon, French ambassador at London, to M. René Viviani, president of the Council, minister for foreign affairs, Paris, 1 August 1914.
20. Lichnowsky to Jagow, in Geiss, pp. 345–7.
21. See Butler, *Distant Victory*.
22. Crowe to Grey, 31 July 1914, in Geiss, pp. 330–1.

Chapter 34   Smash Your Telephone: Russia Mobilises

1. Albertini, Vol. 2, p. 485.
2. Hötzendorf, Vol. I, pp. 380–1.
3. Moltke, p. 381.
4. Quoted in Albertini, Vol. 2, p. 490.
5. Stevenson, 'War by Timetable?', p. 187.
6. Ibid., p. 188.
7. Ibid., p. 194.
8. Nicholas II to Wilhelm II, in Geiss, p. 291.
9. Nicholas II to Wilhelm II, Telegrams 102, 103, 110 in Geiss.
10. Sazonov to Bronevski, quoted in Albertini, Vol. 2, p. 540.
11. Churchill, pp. 210–13.
12. Moltke to Bethmann-Hollweg, in Geiss, pp. 282–4.
13. Szapáry to Berchtold, in Geiss, pp. 277–8.
14. Telegram 137 in Geiss, p. 298.
15. See Albertini, Vol. 2, pp. 563–4, which offers an alternative version of these intricate events.
16. Pourtalès to Jagow, in Geiss, pp. 303–4.
17. The World War I Document Archive, 'The Willy-Nicky Telegrams': http://wwi.lib.byu.edu/index.php/The_Willy-Nicky_Telegrams.

18. Quoted in Albertini, Vol. 2, p. 558.
19. Nicholas II to Wilhelm II, in Geiss, p. 291.
20. Ibid.
21. Pourtalès to Jagow, in ibid., pp. 293–4.
22. Hötzendorf, Vol. IV, p. 152.
23. Schilling, pp. 63–4, in Albertini, Vol. 2, p. 572.
24. Ibid.
25. Ibid.
26. The World War I Document Archive, 'The Willy-Nicky Telegrams': http://wwi.lib.byu.edu/index.php/The_Willy-Nicky_Telegrams.
27. Ibid.
28. French Yellow Book, No. 118, M. Paléologue, French ambassador at St Petersburg, to M. René Viviani, president of council, minister for foreign affairs, St Petersburg, 31 July 1914.
29. In Geiss, Numbers 158, 159.
30. German White Book, Germany's reasons for war with Russia: How Russia and her ruler betrayed Germany's confidence and thereby made the European War.
31. Tabouis, pp. 279–80.
32. Carter, p. 432.

Chapter 35   Germany Declares War on Russia

1. Albertini, Vol. 3, p. 38.
2. French Yellow Book, M. Jules Cambon, French ambassador at Berlin, to M. René Viviani, president of the council, minister for foreign affairs, Berlin, 30 July 1914.
3. Ludwig, p. 144.
4. Kaiser Wilhelm II to Albertini, letter, 11 March 1936, quoted in Albertini, Vol. 3, p. 12.
5. Albertini, Vol. 3, p. 16.
6. Ibid., Vol. 3, p. 16.
7. The World War I Document Archive, 'Wilhelm II's War Speeches': http://wwi.lib.byu.edu/index.php/Wilhelm_II%27s_War_Speeches.
8. Quoted in Albertini, Vol. 3, p. 39.
9. Hötzendorf, Vol. IV, pp. 164–5.
10. Quoted in Albertini, Vol. 3, p. 53.
11. German White Book, Exhibit 24, Telegram of the chancellor to the imperial ambassador at St Petersburg on 31 July 1914.
12. Bethmann-Hollweg to Schoen, in Geiss, p. 325; see alternative translation, German White Book, Exhibit 24, Telegram of the chancellor to the imperial ambassador at Paris on 31 July 1914.
13. Quoted in Albertini, Vol. 3, p. 61.
14. Pourtalès, pp. 74–5, quoted in Albertini, Vol. 3, p. 62.
15. Quoted in Albertini, Vol. 3, p. 64.
16. Quoted in Albertini, Vol. 3, pp. 167–8.
17. The World War I Document Archive, 'The Willy-Nicky Telegrams': http://wwi.lib.byu.edu/index.php/The_Willy-Nicky_Telegrams.
18. Quoted in Albertini, Vol. 3, p. 169.
19. Russian Orange Book, No. 76; see alternative translation, Albertini, Vol. 3, pp. 168–9.

Chapter 36   *Germany Declares War on France*

1. Poincaré, Vol. IV, pp. 438–40.
2. French Yellow Book, No. 111, M. Mollard, French minister at Luxembourg, to M. René Viviani, president of the council, minister for foreign affairs, Luxembourg, 31 July 1914.
3. Quoted in Albertini, Vol. 3, p. 80.
4. Joffre, Vol. I, pp. 126–7.
5. The World War I Document Archive, 'The Role of Railways in the War (extract)', by Edwin A. Pratt: http://wwi.lib.byu.edu/index.php/The_Role_of_Railways_in_the_War.
6. Quoted in Keiger, p. 162.
7. Poincaré, Vol. IV, p. 479.
8. Wharton, p. 7.
9. Recouly, p. 116, quoted in Albertini, p. 107.
10. Wharton, p. 9.
11. The World War I Document Archive, 'The Role of Railways in the War (extract)', by Edwin A. Pratt: http://wwi.lib.byu.edu/index.php/The_Role_of_Railways_in_the_War.
12. *Journal des Transports*, 30 January 1915, quoted in ibid.
13. Recouly, p. 116.
14. Wharton, p. 16.
15. Ibid., p. 21.
16. Quoted in Gerin, p. 71; see Albertini, Vol. 3, p. 81.
17. Quoted in Keiger, p. 164.
18. French Yellow Book; see another translation in Albertini, Vol. 3, p. 77.
19. Albertini, Vol. 3, pp. 68–9.
20. Keiger, p. 162.
21. *Le Matin*, 1 August 1914.
22. See study by Becker, quoted in Keiger, pp. 162–3.
23. See *Le Temps, Paris-Midi, Action Française*, March 1913 to July 1914.
24. *Action Française*, 23 July 1914.
25. *Pester Lloyd*, Budapest, 3 August 1914, 'At the cusp of world war, French planes dropping bombs on Nuremberg'.
26. Wolff Bureau [a German press service].
27. *Die Neue Zeitung*, 8 April 1914.
28. French Yellow Book, No. 146, M. René Viviani, president of the council, minister for foreign affairs, to M. Paul Cambon, French ambassador at London, Paris, 3 August 1914.
29. Quoted in Albertini, Vol. 3, p. 206.
30. Quoted in ibid., p. 213.
31. Quoted in ibid., p. 200.
32. French Yellow Book, No. 147, Letter handed by the German ambassador to M. René Viviani, president of the council, minister for foreign affairs, during his farewell audience, 3 August 1914, at 6.45 p.m.
33. Poincaré, Vol. IV, pp. 521–3.
34. French Yellow Book, No. 158, Message from M. Poincaré, president of the Republic, read at the Extraordinary Session of Parliament, 4 August 1914, *Journal Officiel*, 5 August 1914.

35. The World War I Document Archive, 'Clemenceau Calls France to Arms': http://wwi.lib.byu.edu/index.php/Clemenceau_Calls_France_to_Arms.

Chapter 37   Necessity Knows No Law

1. Hooydonk, E., 'Chapter 15: The Belgian Experience', in Chircop and Lindén (eds), *Places of Refuge*, p. 417.
2. Article 1, Hague Convention 1907.
3. Article 10, Hague Convention 1907.
4. Beer, L., 'Gladstone and Neutrality of Belgium', *The New York Times*, 26 November 1914
5. Bülow, Vol. II, pp. 72–4.
6. Bredt, p. 55.
7. Joffre, Vol. I, pp. 42–3.
8. Ibid., pp. 47–8.
9. Belgian Grey Book, Enclosure in No. 12, Baron Beyens, Belgian minister at Berlin, to M. Davignon, Belgian minister for foreign affairs, Berlin, 2 May 1913.
10. Ibid.
11. Galet, p. 23, quoted in Albertini, Vol. 3, p. 441.
12. Belgian Grey Book, No. 8, M. Davignon, Belgian minister for foreign affairs, to the Belgian ministers at Berlin, Paris, London, Vienna, St Petersburg, Rome, The Hague and Luxemburg, Brussels, 29 July 1914.
13. Belgian Grey Book, No. 2, M. Davignon, Belgian minister for foreign affairs, to the Belgian ministers at Paris, Berlin, London, Vienna and St Petersburg, Brussels, 24 July 1914.
14. Belgian Grey Book, No. 13, Count de Lalaing, Belgian Minister at London, to M. Davignon, Belgian minister for foreign affairs, London, 1 August 1914.
15. Belgian Grey Book, No. 15, M. Davignon, Belgian minister for foreign affairs, to the Belgian ministers at Berlin, Paris and London, Brussels, 1 August 1914.
16. French Yellow Book, No. 126, M. Paul Cambon, French ambassador at London, to M. René Viviani, president of the council, minister for foreign affairs, Paris, 1 August 1914.
17. Belgian Grey Book, No. 18, M. Eyschen, president of the Luxembourg Government to M. Davignon, Belgian minister for foreign affairs, telegram, Luxembourg, 2 August 1914.
18. Ibid.
19. Reconstruction of the meeting based on Crockaert, Vol. I, pp. 309–10, quoted in Albertini, Vol. 3, p. 456.
20. The World War I Document Archive, 'The German Request for Free Passage Through Belgium': http://wwi.lib.byu.edu/index.php/The_German_Request_for_Free_Passage_Through_Belgium.
21. Quoted in Albertini, Vol. 3, p. 458.
22. Ibid.
23. Ibid., pp. 329–30.
24. Belgian Grey Book, No. 22, Note communicated by M. Davignon, Belgian minister for foreign affairs, to Herr von Below-Saleske, German minister, Brussels, 3 August 1914.
25. Belgian Grey Book, No. 40, M. Davignon, Belgian minister for foreign affairs, to

British, French and Russian ministers at Brussels, Brussels, 4 August 1914.

26. Belgian Grey Book, No. 31, M. Davignon, Belgian minister for foreign affairs, to Herr von Below-Saleske, German minister at Brussels, Brussels, 4 August 1914.

27. German White Book, Report of a speech delivered by Herr von Bethmann-Hollweg, German imperial chancellor, on 4 August 1914.

28. Bethmann-Hollweg, p. 147.

29. German White Book: Report of a speech delivered by Herr von Bethmann-Hollweg, German imperial chancellor, on 4 August 1914.

30. Tirpitz, Vol. I, pp. 279, 280.

Chapter 38 The Last Lamp

1. Steiner and Neilson, p. 250.

2. Ibid., p. 252.

3. Ibid.

4. Jagow to Lichnowsky, quoted in Albertini, Vol. 3, pp. 476–7.

5. Bethmann-Hollweg to Lichnowsky, quoted in ibid., p. 480.

6. Ferguson, p. 177.

7. Lloyd George, Vol. I, pp. 65–6.

8. Asquith, Vol. II, p. 20.

9. The World War I Document Archive, 'Sir Edward Grey's Speech Before Parliament': http://wwi.lib.byu.edu/index.php/ Sir_Edward_Grey%27s_Speech_Before_Parliament.

10. Steiner and Neilson, p. 253.

11. Ferguson, p. 163.

12. Asquith, Vol. II, p. 195.

13. Grey, p. 20.

14. Quoted in Albertini, Vol. 3, p. 489.

15. Quoted in ibid.

16. Churchill, Vol. I, p. 220.

17. Quoted in Albertini, Vol. 3, p. 490.

18. Quoted in Fernand Passelecq, 'The Sincere Chancellor' (online pamphlet); see another version in Halsey, p. 177.

19. Ibid.

20. Ibid.

21. Bethmann-Hollweg, Vol. I, p. 180.

22. British Blue Book, No. 160, see also Times Documentary History of the War: http://archive.org/details/timesdocumentary08londuoft.

23. Hendrick, pp. 313–14.

24. British Blue Book, No. 160; see also Times Documentary History of the War: http://archive.org/details/timesdocumentary08londuoft.

25. Grey, Vol. II, p. 18.

26. *Daily Mirror* headlines, 4 August 1914.

27. British Blue Book, No. 160; see also Times Documentary History of the War: http://archive.org/details/timesdocumentary08londuoft.

Chapter 39 Sweet and Right to Die for Your Country . . .

1. Rupert Brooke, from '1914'.

2. Bagehot, pp. 41–2.
3. Quoted in Tuchman, p. 311.
4. Quoted in Steiner and Neilson, p. 167.
5. Wohl, p. 8.
6. Fischer, p. 7.
7. Steiner and Neilson, p. 165.
8. Wohl, p. 115.
9. Quoted in Steiner and Neilson, p. 174.
10. See Simkins, pp. 43–5.
11. See Ferguson, pp. 205–7.
12. Wesseling, 'Commotion at the Sorbonne: The Debate on the French University, 1910–1914', pp. 89–96.
13. Wohl, p. 7.
14. Quoted in Cowles, p. 205.
15. Wohl, p. 8.
16. Ibid., pp. 16–17.
17. Becker, p. 4.
18. The World War I Document Archive, 'Declaration of Professors of the German Reich': http://wwi.lib.byu.edu/index.php/ Declaration_of_Professors_of_the_German_Reich.
19. Mann, Thomas, *The Magic Mountain*. Mann's novel was conceived in 1912 but published after the war, in 1924.
20. Quoted in Wohl, p. 43.
21. Ibid., p. 45.
22. Ibid., p. 52.
23. Wall and Winter, p. 27.
24. Quoted in Hochschild, pp. 90–1.
25. Winter, p. 158.
26. See Hattersley, p. 66.
27. Masterman, extract from his pamphlet.
28. Ibid.
29. See Hattersley, pp. 1–3.
30. Carter, p. 432.
31. Quoted in Keith Wilson, 'The Foreign Office and the "Education" of Public Opinion before the First World War', pp. 403–11.
32. Ibid.
33. Spears, p. 15.
34. Ibid.
35. Keegan, p. 84.
36. Baumann, Herman, *War diary*.
37. Ibid.
38. Ibid.
39. Owen, Wilfred, 'Dulce Et Decorum Est', *The War Poems*.
40. Ibid.
41. Horace, *Odes*, III.2.13.

Part 4   On the Ground

Chapter 40   The Rape of Belgium

1. Tuchman, p. 164.
2. The World War I Document Archive, 'King Albert I of the Belgians' Speech to the Belgian Parliament': http://wwi.lib.byu.edu/index.php/King_Albert_I_of_the_Belgians%27_Speech_to_the_Belgian_Parliament.
3. Ibid.
4. Davignon, p. 2.
5. Tuchman, p. 170.
6. 'Heidelberger historische Bestände', German soldiers' song, printed in *Daheim*, the army field newspaper, No. 50. August–September 1914, p. 442.
7. Von Kluck, p. 7.
8. Ibid.
9. Keegan, p. 95.
10. Tuchman, p. 168.
11. Ibid., p. 191.
12. Quoted in ibid., p. 192.
13. The World War I Document Archive, 'The Fall of Liège, by General Leman': http://wwi.lib.byu.edu/index.php/The_Fall_of_Li%C3%A8ge,.
14. Von Kluck, p. 20.
15. The World War I Document Archive, 'The Fall of Liège, by General Leman': http://wwi.lib.byu.edu/index.php/The_Fall_of_Li%C3%A8ge,.
16. Ibid.
17. *Le Matin*, 19 August 1914.
18. Baumann, Herman, *War diary*.
19. Meyersiek, Pastor, *Letters to the Soldiers*.
20. The World War I Document Archive, 'The Martyrdom of Belgium: Official Report of Massacres of Peaceable Citizens, Women and Children by the German Army', W. Stewart Brown Company, Inc.: http://digicoll.library.wisc.edu/cgi-bin/History/History-idx?id=History.Martyrdom.
21. Von Kluck, p. 32.
22. Ibid., p. 33.
23. The World War I Document Archive, 'The Fall of Brussels': http://wwi.lib.byu.edu/index.php/The_Fall_of_Brussels.
24. Ibid.
25. Ibid.
26. Ibid.
27. Ibid.
28. Ibid.
29. The World War I Document Archive, 'The Martyrdom of Belgium: Official Report of Massacres of Peaceable Citizens, Women and Children by the German Army', W. Stewart Brown Company, Inc.: http://digicoll.library.wisc.edu/cgi-bin/History/History-idx?id=History.Martyrdom.
30. Von Kluck, p. 26.
31. Ibid.
32. The World War I Document Archive, 'The Martyrdom of Belgium: Official

Report of Massacres of Peaceable Citizens, Women and Children by the German Army', W. Stewart Brown Company, Inc.: http://digicoll.library.wisc.edu/cgi-bin/History/History-idx?id=History.Martyrdom.

33. Baumann, Herman, *War diary*.
34. The World War I Document Archive, 'The Martyrdom of Belgium: Official Report of Massacres of Peaceable Citizens, Women and Children by the German Army', W. Stewart Brown Company, Inc.: http://digicoll.library.wisc.edu/cgi-bin/History/History-idx?id=History.Martyrdom.
35. Ibid.
36. Ibid.
37. Ibid.
38. Delius, Walter, letters and diary entries.
39. The World War I Document Archive, 'The Martyrdom of Belgium: Official Report of Massacres of Peaceable Citizens, Women and Children by the German Army', W. Stewart Brown Company, Inc., The German Military Code: http://digicoll.library.wisc.edu/cgi-bin/History/History-idx?id=History.Martyrdom.
40. Quoted in Gilbert, p. 88.
41. The World War I Document Archive, 'The Martyrdom of Belgium: Official Report of Massacres of Peaceable Citizens, Women and Children by the German Army', W. Stewart Brown Company, Inc.: http://digicoll.library.wisc.edu/cgi-bin/History/History-idx?id=History.Martyrdom.
42. The Bryce Report, The Avalon Project, Yale Law School, Lillian Goldman Law Library: http://avalon.law.yale.edu/20th_century/brycere.asp.
43. Ibid.
44. Quoted in Tuchman, p. 321.
45. Tuchman, pp. 318–19.
46. Benson, Arthur, *Diary*.
47. Grimwood Mears, p. 14.
48. The World War I Document Archive, 'German Barbarians: What They Say', French War Office: http://digicoll.library.wisc.edu/cgi-bin/History/History-idx?id=History.Barbarians.
49. The Bryce Report, Comment by Linda Robertson, quoted in German White Book.
50. Grimwood Mears, p. 19.
51. Ibid., p. 23.
52. Ibid., p. 32.
53. The World War I Document Archive, 'An Eye-Witness at Louvain', Eyre & Spotiswoode Ltd, 1914: http://digicoll.library.wisc.edu/cgi-bin/History/History-idx?id=History.Louvain.
54. Grimwood Mears, p. 36.
55. The World War I Document Archive, 'An Eye-Witness at Louvain', Eyre & Spotiswoode Ltd, 1914: http://digicoll.library.wisc.edu/cgi-bin/History/History-idx?id=History.Louvain.
56. Grimwood Mears, p. 27.
57. Ibid., p. 37.
58. Ibid.
59. Quoted in 'U.S. Report on German Atrocities in Belgium, 12 September 1917',

Horne (ed.), *Source Records of the Great War*.
60. The World War I Document Archive, 'The Role of Railways in the War (extract)', by Edwin A. Pratt: http://wwi.lib.byu.edu/index.php/ The_Role_of_Railways_in_the_War.

Chapter 41   On the French Frontiers

1. The World War I Document Archive, 'Kitchener's Address to the Troops': http:// wwi.lib.byu.edu/index.php/Kitchener%27s_Address_to_the_Troops.
2. Corbett-Smith, p. 23.
3. Ibid., p. 31.
4. Quoted in Emden, p. 17.
5. Keegan, p. 83.
6. Arthur, p. 368.
7. Ibid., p. 369.
8. Ibid., p. 371.
9. Churchill, Foreword to Spears, p. vii.
10. Foch, p. lii.
11. Spears, p. 19.
12. Terrain, pp. 44–5.
13. Neillands, p. 16.
14. Keegan, p. 101.
15. Foch, p. 43.
16. Strachan, *The First World War*, p. 52.
17. Clément, Raymond, *Journal*.
18. Tuchman, p. 238.
19. Quoted in Tuchman, p. 241.
20. Keegan, p. 103.
21. See Robert A. Doughty, 'French Strategy in 1914: Joffre's Own', pp. 427–54.
22. *L'Humanité*, 26 August 1914.
23. *Die Neue Zeitung*, No. 233, Vienna, 25 August 1914.
24. Spears, p. 42.
25. Quoted in Tuchman, p. 245.
26. Spears, p. 65.
27. Ibid.
28. Corbett-Smith, p. 37.
29. Strachan, *To Arms*, p. 53.
30. WWI: The World War I Document Archive, 'Mons, Anzac and Kut', Aubrey Herbert diary: http://net.lib.byu.edu/estu//wwi/memoir/Mons/mons.htm.
31. Ibid.
32. Quoted in Corbett-Smith, p. 47.
33. WWI: The World War I Document Archive, 'Mons, Anzac and Kut', Aubrey Herbert diary: http://net.lib.byu.edu/estu//wwi/memoir/Mons/mons.htm.
34. Ibid.
35. Captain Bloem, quoted in Keegan, p. 109.
36. Benson, Arthur, *Diary*.
37. Ibid.
38. Terraine, pp. 47–9.

39. Quoted in Tuchman, pp. 219–20.
40. Spears, p. 80.
41. Tuchman, p. 250.
42. Leroi, Maurice, *Letters*.
43. Dubois, Marie, *Letters*.
44. Michel, Marie and Henri, *Letters*.
45. Tuchman, p. 252.
46. Spears, pp. 126–7.
47. Harris, p. 70.
48. Keegan, p. 108.
49. WWI: The World War I Document Archive, 'Mons, Anzac and Kut', Aubrey Herbert diary: http://net.lib.byu.edu/estu//wwi/memoir/Mons/mons.htm.
50. Ibid.
51. Papers of T. S. Wollocombe MC.
52. Captain Bloem, quoted in Keegan, p. 109.
53. Oetjen, Hinrich, *War diary*.
54. Von Kluck, p. 52.
55. *The London Gazette*, No. 28976, 13 November 1914, pp. 9373–4.
56. *The London Gazette* (Supplement), No. 28985, 24 November 1914, p. 9957.

Chapter 42   The Retreat

1. Keegan, p. 110.
2. Quoted in ibid.
3. Foch, p. 48.
4. Quoted in Emden, p. 46.
5. Corbett-Smith, p. 115.
6. Ibid., p. 123.
7. *The London Gazette*, No. 28976, 13 November 1914, p. 9373.
8. Corbett-Smith, p. 133.
9. Quoted in Emden, p. 48.
10. Harris, p. 73. Haig's published diaries omit his references to the retreat because, his editor remarks, 'Haig's diary adds nothing new to that oft-told tale' (Haig, p. 73).
11. Quoted in Tuchman, p. 357.
12. Quoted in Cave and Sheldon, p. 56.
13. Ibid.
14. Figures vary: see Cave and Sheldon, p. 9. Less reliable sources cite more than 7800 British casualties.
15. Corbett-Smith, p 170.
16. WWI: The World War I Document Archive, 'Mons, Anzac and Kut', Aubrey Herbert diary: http://net.lib.byu.edu/estu//wwi/memoir/Mons/mons.htm.
17. Corbett-Smith, p. 177.
18. WWI: The World War I Document Archive, 'Mons, Anzac and Kut', Aubrey Herbert diary: http://net.lib.byu.edu/estu//wwi/memoir/Mons/mons.htm.
19. Private Papers of Colonel R. W. Cave-Orme.
20. WWI: The World War I Document Archive, 'Mons, Anzac and Kut', Aubrey Herbert diary: http://net.lib.byu.edu/estu//wwi/memoir/Mons/mons.htm.

21. Quoted in Corbett-Smith, p. 185.
22. Papers of J. W. Naylor.
23. 'Account of the practical annihilation of L Battery', Papers of David Nelson VC.
24. *The London Gazette*, 26 November 1914.
25. 'Account of the practical annihilation of L Battery', Papers of David Nelson VC.
26. Papers of D. Lloyd-Burch.
27. Ibid.
28. Private Papers of David Nelson, Imperial War Museum, London.
29. WWI: The World War I Document Archive, 'Mons, Anzac and Kut', Aubrey Herbert diary: http://net.lib.byu.edu/estu//wwi/memoir/Mons/mons.htm.
30. Foch, p. 47.
31. Clément, Raymond, *Journal*.
32. Ibid.
33. Leroi, Maurice, *Letters*.
34. Fossey, Emile, *Journal*.
35. Foch, p. 54.
36. Ibid., p. 59.
37. Ibid., pp. 56–7.
38. Quoted in ibid., p. 57.
39. Sir John French, quoted in von Kluck, pp. 54–5.
40. Delius, Walter, *Letters and diary entries*.
41. Von Kluck, p. 69.
42. Words of Field Marshal Count Haeseler, quoted in von Kluck, p. 78.
43. Quoted in ibid., p. 75.
44. Quoted in ibid.
45. Tuchman, p. 362.
46. *Die Neue Zeitung*, 'The Beaten Frenchmen', No. 233, 25 August 1914.
47. Delius, Walter, *Letters and diary entries*.
48. Ibid.
49. Baumann, Herman, *War diary*.
50. Dazin, Bernardine, *Journal*.
51. Ibid.
52. Quoted in Keegan, p. 118.
53. Ibid.
54. WWI: The World War I Document Archive, Smith and Taylor, *The War. Our Sailors and Soldiers: The Chaplain-General's Call for Mid-day Prayer*, Society for Propagating Christian Knowledge, 1914–18: http://digicoll.library.wisc.edu/cgi-bin/History/History-idx?id=History.ChapGenPray.
55. Benson, Arthur, *Diary*.
56. Ibid.
57. Ibid.
58. Les Armées Francaises, Tome I, Vols 1 and 2, Paris Imprimerie Nationale, 1922–25, I, II, p. 825.

Chapter 43   The Miracle of the Marne

1. Quoted in Tuchman, p. 351.
2. Ibid., p. 348.

3. See ibid., pp. 373–5.
4. WWI: The World War I Document Archive, 'The Role of Railways in the War (extract)', by Edwin A. Pratt: http://wwi.lib.byu.edu/index.php/The_Role_of_Railways_in_the_War.
5. Proclamation of the General Gallieni, *Le Figaro*, 4 September 1914.
6. Herwig, *Battle of the Marne*, p. xii.
7. Spears, pp. 42–3.
8. Keegan, p. 119.
9. Von Kluck, p. 84.
10. Ibid.
11. Von Kluck, pp. 90–1.
12. Quoted in Tuchman, p. 391.
13. Banks, pp. 53–5.
14. Spears, p. 370.
15. Strachan, *To Arms*, p. 240.
16. Tuchman, p. 424.
17. Quoted in ibid., p. 427.
18. Joffre's General Order No. 6, quoted in Tuchman, p. 430. For all Joffre's General Orders in 1914, see the French Official History, Les Armées Francaises dans la grand guerre, Tome I, Vols 1 and 2, Paris Imprimerie Nationale, 1922–25.
19. Keegan, p. 125.
20. Spears, p. 411.
21. Quoted in ibid., p. 413.
22. There are various accounts of this famous meeting. See Joffre, p. 254; Muller, p. 106; Wilson, p. 174; Spears, pp. 415–18; Terraine, pp. 212–13; and Tuchman, pp. 433–4.
23. Quoted in Tuchman, p. 434; see also Terraine's account, pp. 212–213.
24. Quoted in Spears, p. 427.
25. Quoted in Tuchman, p. 432.
26. Corbett-Smith, pp. 225–6.
27. Quoted in Emden, pp. 51–2.
28. Leroi, Maurice, *Letters*.
29. Dubois, Marie, *Letters*.
30. Meyersiek, Pastor, *Letters to the soldiers*.
31. Foch, p. 69.
32. Leon Loupy, 'The Marne Taxis', Legends and Traditions of the Great War: http://www.worldwar1.com/heritage/marnetaxis.htm.
33. Foch, p. 76.
34. Von Kluck, p. 121.
35. Quoted in Tuchman, pp. 435–6.
36. Foch, pp. 72–3.
37. Ibid., p. 76.
38. Quoted in Keegan, p. 130.
39. Foch, p. 95.
40. Ibid., p. 97.
41. 'Sunday in Paris in a Time of War', *Le Matin*, 7 September 1914.
42. 'Paul Strauss, Senator of the Seine', *Le Figaro*, 8 September 1914.

43. Strachan, *First World War*, p. 57.
44. Von Kluck, p. 140.
45. See footnote, ibid., p. 145.
46. *Le Matin*, 12 September 1914; *Le Petit Parisien*, 12 September 1914.
47. According to Sergeant William Peacock, 1st Wales Borderers, quoted in Emden, p. 53.
48. Papers of E. S. Butcher.
49. Dazin, Bernardine, *Journal*.
50. Clément, Raymond, *Journal*.
51. Ibid.
52. Baumann, Herman, *War diary*.
53. See footnote, von Kluck, p. 119.
54. Harris, pp. 84–5.
55. Quoted in Tuchman, p. 436. From an interview Von Kluck gave to a Swedish journalist in 1918.
56. Spears, p. 432.
57. Herwig, *Battle of the Marne*, p. xvii; see full argument in Ludendorff (ed), *Das Marne-Drama*

Chapter 44   Serbian Shock, Russian Rout, Austrian Annihilation

1. See Lyon, '"A Peasant Mob": The Serbian Army on the Eve of the Great War', pp. 481–502.
2. Tuchman, p. 270.
3. Knox, pp. xxxi–xxxii.
4. Keegan, p. 154.
5. Knox, p. xxxi.
6. Showalter, p. 328.
7. Knox, p. xxxiv.
8. Quoted in Tuchman, p. 276.
9. Tuchman, p. 168.
10. Quoted in Tuchman, p. 282.
11. Knox, p. 71.
12. Ibid., p. 58.
13. Ibid., p. 72.
14. Ibid., p. 73.
15. Ibid., pp. 73–4.
16. Tuchman, p. 302.
17. Knox, p. 82.
18. Ibid., p. 86.
19. Ibid., p. 49.
20. Keegan, p. 174.
21. See Tuchman, p. 308; Showalter, p. 327.
22. Showalter, p. 324.
23. Quoted in ibid., p. 324.
24. Ibid.
25. Quoted in Showalter, p. 327.

Chapter 45   The Creation of the Western Front
1. Letter to Violet Bonham Carter, 1916. See: www.winstonchurchill.org.
2. *Le Figaro*, 20 September 1914.
3. Ibid., 7 November 1914.
4. Quoted in Keegan, p. 122.
5. Trichereau, Jérémie, *Letters*.
6. Michel, Marie and Henri, *Letters*.
7. Ibid., 5 November 1914.
8. Ibid., end of November.
9. Papers of E. S. Butcher.
10. Trichereau, Jérémie, *Letters*.
11. Delius, Walter, *Letters and diary entries*.
12. Stegemann, Vol. 2, pp. 30–4.
13. Delius, Walter, *Letters and diary entries*.
14. Ibid., 7 November 1914.
15. Benson, Arthur, *Diary*.
16. Ibid., 25 September 1914.
17. Keegan, p. 138.
18. Foch, p. 131.
19. Beckett, p. 101.
20. Mead, p. 196.
21. Quoted in Beckett, p. 16.
22. Foch, p. 135.
23. Beckett, p. 18.
24. Beckett, p. 25.
25. Tisdall, Arthur, VC, 'RND Personality', extract from a report by Heald, David, in *The Gallipolian*, pp. 634-40; see also: Tisdall, Arthur, Private Papers'.
26. Foch, p. 141.
27. Ibid., p. 144.
28. Beckett, quoting General Palat, p. 60.
29. Foch, p. 169.
30. Quoted in Beckett, p. 58.
31. Quoted in ibid., p. 70.
32. Quoted in ibid., p. 112.
33. Quoted in ibid.
34. Keegan, p. 143.
35. Quoted in Beckett, p. 90.
36. Quoted in ibid., p. 97.
37. See full account of the German Legend of Langemarck in Beckett, pp. 98–100.
38. Hitler, p. 151.
39. Quoted in Beckett, p. 103.
40. Ibid.
41. Unknown soldier, *Field postcard home*.
42. Keegan, p. 144.
43. See Beckett's analysis of the shell shortage, pp. 113–15.
44. Quoted in Beckett, p. 124.
45. Harris, p. 99.

46. Quoted in Harris, p. 100.

47. Ibid.

48. Foch, p. 176.

49. Quoted in Beckett, p. 159.

50. Quoted in Harris, p. 103.

51. Foch, p. 178.

52. Quoted in Beckett, p. 169.

53. Quoted in ibid., p. 233.

54. Harris, p. 105.

55. See Beckett, p. 226; Keegan, p. 146.

56. Private Papers of Mrs Martha Withhall (née Aitken).

57. Keegan, p. 146.

58. Fossey, Emile, *Journal*.

59. Clément, Raymond, *Journal*.

60. Graves, p. 137.

61. Papers of D. Lloyd-Burch.

Epilogue

1. Graves, p. 146.

2. Owen, Wilfred, *The War Poems*.

3. See *Mental Disorders: Diagnostic and Statistical Manual*, American Psychiatric Association, 1952.

4. WWI: The World War I Document Archive, W. H. R. Rivers, 'An Address on the Repression of War Experience', delivered before the Section of Psychiatry, Royal Society of Medicine, on 4 December 1917: http://net.lib.byu.edu/~rdh7/wwi/comment/rivers.htm.

5. Ibid.

6. *Bystander*, September 1914.

7. *Daily Express*, Friday, 7 August 1914.

8. *Daily Mail*, 31 August 1914.

9. http://www.spartacus.schoolnet.co.uk/FWWfeather.htm.

10. Ibid.

11. Francis Beckett, *The Guardian*, 11 November 2008.

12. Ibid.

13. http://en.wikipedia.org/wiki/Victor_Serge.

14. Keynes, p. 126.

15. Lloyd George, Vol. 1, p. 49.

16. Churchill, p. 27.

17. 'Was World War I necessary?', http://www.thefreelibrary.com/Was+World+War+I+necessary%3F-a062214340.

18. Strachan, *To Arms*, pp. 101–2.

19. For the most cogent case against Fischer, see Ferguson, pp. 169–70.

20. Further reading on the September programme, see Fischer's book; Ferguson pp. 171–3; and Tuchman, pp. 322–3.

21. Benson, Arthur, *Diary*.

22. Clément, Raymond, *Journal*.

23. Dubois, Marie, *Letters*.

24. Corporal H. G. Hodder, *Letters*, Persean School Magazine.
25. Leroi, Maurice, *Letters*.
26. 'Aubade', by Philip Larkin.
27. Manwaring, pp. 19, 96, 135–6, 163–4.
28. Ibid., p. 69.
29. Ibid., p. 164.

SOURCES

SELECT BIBLIOGRAPHY

Albertini, Luigi, *The Origins of the War of 1914* (3 vols), Enigma Press, New York 2005

Andrew, Christopher, and Noakes, Jeremy (eds), *Intelligence And International Relations, 1900–1945*, Liverpool University Press, Liverpool 1987

Arthur, Sir George, *Life of Lord Kitchener* (3 vols), Cosimo Classics, New York 2011

Asquith, Herbert Henry, *Memories and Reflections 1852–1927*, Cassell, London 1928

Asquith, Margot, *Autobiography*, Hardpress Publishing 2010

Bagehot, Walter, *Physics and Politics*, Ivan R. Dee, New York 1999

Banks, *A Military Atlas of the First World War*, Pen & Sword, Barnsley, South Yorkshire 2001

Barnett, Corelli, *The Great War*, BBC Books, London 2007

Becker, Jean Jacques, *The Great War and the French People*, (transl. by Pomerans, Arnold), Berg Publishers, Oxford 1986

Beckett, Ian, *Ypres: The First Battle, 1914*, Pearson, London 2006

Berghahn, Volker R., *Der Tirpitz: Genesis und Verfall einer innenpolitischen Krisenstrategie unter Wilhelm II*, Droste, Düsseldorf, 1971

Bernhardi, Friedrich von, *Germany and the Next War*, BiblioLife, Charleston, South Carolina 2009

Bethmann Hollweg, Theobald von, *Reflections on the World War*, (transl. by Young, George), Cornell University Library, New York, 1920

Bloch, I. S., *Is War Now Impossible?: Being an Abridgment of: The War of the Future in Its Technical, Economic & Political Relations*, Richards, London 1899

Bloem, Walter, *The Advance from Mons 1914: The Experiences of a German Infantry Officer*, Helion & Company, Solihull, Britain 2011

Bredt, Johann Victor, *Die belgische Neutralität und der Schlieffensche Feldzugsplan*, Georg Stilke, Berlin 1929

Bruun, Geoffrey, *Clemenceau*, Archon Books, North Haven, Connecticut 1968

Buckle, Richard, *Nijinsky: A Life of Genius and Madness*, Pegasus, Oakland 2012

Bülow, Bernhard von, *Memoirs of Prince Von Bülow*, Little, Brown, London 1931

Butler, Daniel Allen, *Distant Victory: The Battle of Jutland and the Allied Triumph in the First World War*, Praeger, Westport, Connecticut 2006

Butler, Daniel Allen, *The Burden of Guilt: How Germany Shattered the Last Days of Peace, Summer 1914*, Casemate Publishers, Havertown, Pennsylvania 2010

Carr, Edward, H., *What is History?* Vintage, London 1967

Carroll, E. M., *Germany and the Great Powers 1866–1914: A Study of Public Opinion and Foreign Policy*, New York, Prentice Hall, 1938

Carter, Miranda, *The Three Emperors*, Fig Tree, London 2009

Cave, Nigel and Sheldon, Jack, *Le Cateau*, Pen & Sword, Barnsley, South Yorkshire 2008

Cecil, LaMar, *Wilhelm II: Prince and Emperor, 1859–1900*, University of North Carolina Press, Chapel Hill, North Carolina 1989

Céline, Louis-Ferdinand, *Journey to the End of the Night*, Alma Classics, London 2012

Chandler, Alfred D., *Scale and Scope: The Dynamics of Industrial Capitalism*, Belknap Press of Harvard University Press 1994

Charmley, John, *Splendid Isolation? Britain and the Balance of Power 1874–1914*, Hodder & Stoughton, London 1999

Chircorp, Aldo & Lindén, Olof, (eds), *Places of Refuge for Ships: Emerging Environmental Concerns of a Maritime Custom*, Martinus Nijhoff Publishers, The Hague 2006

Churchill, W., *The World Crisis*, Thornton Butterworth, London 1927

Clark, Christopher, *The Sleepwalkers: How Europe Went to War in 1914*, HarperCollins, London 2013

Clay, Catrine, *King, Kaiser, Tsar: Three Royal Cousins Who Led the World to War*, Walker Books 2007

Foreign Office, Great Britain, *Collected Documents Relating to the Outbreak of the European War*, Cornell University Library, New York 2009

Corbett-Smith, Arthur, *The Retreat from Mons, by One Who Shared It*, Nabu Press, Charleston, South Carolina 2012

Coppard, George, *With a machine gun to Cambrai : the tale of a young Tommy in Kitchener's army 1914–1918*, H.M.S.O. / Imperial War Museum, London 1969

Cowles, Virginia, *1913: The Defiant Swan Song*, Weidenfeld & Nicolson, London 1967

Cruttwell, Charles, *The Role of British Strategy in the Great War*, Cambridge University Press, Cambridge 1936

Danchev, Alex, *Cézanne: A Life*, Profile Books, London, 2012

Davignon, Henri, *Belgium*, National Home-Reading Union, London 1915

Dunn, James Churchill, *The War the Infantry Knew, 1914–1919*, P. S. King & Son, London 1938

Ekstein, Michael, 'Great Britain and the Triple Entente on the Eve of the Sarajevo Crisis', in Hinsley, F., *British Foreign Policy under Sir Edward Grey*, Cambridge University Press, Cambridge 1977

Eksteins, Modris, *Rites of Spring: The Great War and the Birth of the Modern Age*, Houghton Mifflin Harcourt, Boston 2000

Ellis, John, *Eye-Deep in Hell: Trench Warfare in World War I*, The Johns Hopkins University Press, Baltimore 1989

Ellsworth-Jones, Will, *We Will Not Fight*, Aurum Press, London 2008

Emden, Richard van, *The Soldier's War: The Great War Through Veterans' Eyes*, Bloomsbury, London 2008

Essen, Léon Van Der, *The Invasion and the War in Belgium from Liége to the*

Yser, T. Fisher Unwin, London 1917

Falls, Cyril, *The Great War 1914–1918*, Easton Press, Norwalk, Connecticut 1987

Ferguson, Niall, *The Pity of War*, Basic Books, New York 1999

Fischer, Fritz, *Germany's Aims in the First World War*, W. W. Norton & Company, New York 1968

Foch, Ferdinand, *The Memoirs of Marshal Foch*, Doubleday, Doran and Co., New York 1931

Foley, Robert, *Alfred von Schlieffen's Military Writings*. Frank Cass, London 2003

Fox, Edward Lyell, *Behind the Scenes in Warring Germany*, McBride, Nast & Company, New York 1915.

Francke, Kuno (ed.), *The German Classics of the Nineteenth and Twentieth Centuries*, German Publication Society, New York 1913–14

Fussell, Paul, *The Great War and Modern Memory*, Oxford University Press, USA 2000

Geiss, Imanuel, *July 1914 The Outbreak of the First World War: Selected Documents*, Charles Scribner's Sons, New York 1967

Gilbert, Martin, *The First World War*, Holt Paperbacks, New York 2004

Graves, Robert, *Goodbye to All That*, Penguin, London 2000

Grey, Sir Edward, *Twenty-Five Years 1892–1916*, Hodder & Stoughton, New York 1925

Grimwood Mears, E., *The Destruction of Belgium: Germany's Confession and Avoidance*, William Heinemann, London 1916

Haig, Douglas, *The Private Papers of Douglas Haig, 1914–1919: Being selections from the private diary and correspondence of Field-Marshal the Earl Haig of Bemersyde*, Eyre & Spottiswoode, London 1952

Halsey, Francis, *The Literary Digest History of the World War*, Cosimo, New York 2009

Hamilton, Richard F. & Herwig, Holger H., *Decisions for War, 1914–1917*, Cambridge University Press, Cambridge 2004

Harris, John P., *Douglas Haig and the First World War*, Cambridge University Press, Cambridge 2009

Hašek, Jaroslav, *The Good Soldier Švejk: And His Fortunes in the World War*, Penguin Classics, London 2005

Hattersley, Roy, *The Edwardians*, St Martin's Press, New York 2005

Hendrick, Burton Jesse & Wilson, Woodrow, *The Life and Letters of W. H. Page*, Doubleday, Page & Company, New York 1922

Herwig, Holger, 'Imperial Germany', in May, Ernest R., *Knowing One's Enemies: Intelligence Assessment Before the Two World Wars*, Princeton University Press, New Jersey 1986

Herwig, Holger, *Luxury Fleet: Imperial German Navy, 1888–1918*, Allen & Unwin, London 1980

Herwig, Holger, *The Marne, 1914: The Opening of World War I and the Battle That Changed the World*, Random House Trade Paperbacks, London 2011

Hitler, Adolf, *Mein Kampf*, (transl. by Manheim, Ralph) Houghton Mifflin Company, Boston 1998

Hochschild, Adam, *To End All Wars: A Story of Loyalty and Rebellion, 1914–1918*, Mariner Books, Boston 2012

Horne, Charles (ed.), *Source Records of the Great War*, Vol. II, National Alumni 1923

Hötzendorf, Conrad von, *Aus meiner dienstzeit, 1906–1918*, University of Michigan Library, Ann Arbor 1921

Hughes, Robert, *The Shock of the New*, Alfred A. Knopf, New York 1991

Huguet, Charles Julien, *Britain and the War: a French Indictment*, (transl. by Minchin, Captain H. Cotton), Cassell, London 1928

Ibragimbeili, Kh. M., *Soviet Military Encyclopedia*, Mark Conrad (trans.), 1985

Jarausch, Konrad Hugo, *Enigmatic Chancellor: Bethmann Hollweg and the Hubris of Imperial Germany*, Yale University Press, New Haven, Connecticut 1973

Jenkins, Roy, *Churchill*, Pan, London 2002

Joffre, Joseph, *The Memoirs of Marshal Joffre*, (transl. by Mott, Thomas Bentley), Harper & Brothers, New York 1932

Joll, James, *Europe Since 1870: An International History*, Penguin, London 1990

Joll, James and Martel, Gordon, *The Origins of the First World War*, Pearson, London 2006

Jones, Nigel, *Rupert Brooke: Life, Death and Myth*, Richard Cohen Books, London 1999

Kanner, H., Kaiserliche *Katastrophenpolitik*, Leipzig 1922

Kapos, Martha (ed.), *The Impressionists – A Retrospective*, Hugh Lauter Levin Associates, Inc., London 1991

Keegan, John, *The First World War*, Vintage, London 2000

Keiger, John, *France and the Origins of the First World War*, Palgrave Macmillan, London 1984

Keiger, John, *Raymond Poincaré*, Cambridge University Press, Cambridge 1997

Kennedy, Paul, *The Rise of the Anglo-German Antagonism 1860–1914*, Humanity Books, New York 1987

Kern, Stephen, *The Culture of Time and Space 1880–1918*, Harvard University Press, Cambridge, Massachusetts 2003

Keynes, John Maynard, *The Economic Consequences of the Peace*, Management Laboratory Press, Hamburg 2009

Kluck, Alexander von, *The March on Paris: The Memoirs of Alexander von Kluck, 1914–1918*, Frontline Books, Barnsley, South Yorkshire 2012

Knox, Sir Alfred, *With the Russian Army, 1914–1917: Being Chiefly Extracts from the Diary of a Military Attaché*, Vol. 1, Hutchinson, London 1921

Koss, Stephen, *Asquith*, Columbia University Press, New York 1984

Kuhl, Hermann Joseph von, *Der deutsche Generalstab in Vorbereitung und Durchführung des Weltkrieges*, Ulan Press, Red Lion, Pennsylvania 2012

Lenin, Vladimir Ilyich, *Collected Works*, Progress Publishers, Moscow 1976

Lichnowsky, Karl Max, *My Mission to London, 1912–1914* [the Lichnowsky Memorandum], Cassell & Co, London 1918)

Lichnowsky, Karl Max, *Heading for the Abyss: Reminiscences*, Payson and
    Clarke, New York, 1928
Lloyd George, David, *War Memoirs of David Lloyd George* (6 vols), Ivor
    Nicholson & Watson, London 1933
Lomas, David, *Mons 1914: The BEF's Tactical Triumph*, Osprey Publishing,
    Oxford 1997
Ludendorff, Erich (ed), *Das Marnedrama*, Ludendorffs-Verlag 1934
Ludwig, Emil, *July 1914*, Putnam, London 1929
Ludwig, Emil, *Wilhelm Hohenzollern: The Last of the Kaisers*, AMS Press Inc,
    New York 1978
Lutz, H., *Die europäische politik un der Julikrise 1914* [European Policy and
    the July Crisis], The Reichstag Commission investigating the causes of
    the war, Hermann Lutz Papers, Hoover Institution Archives, Stanford
    University 1930
McMeekin, Sean, *The Russian Origins of the First World War*, Harvard
    University Press, Cambridge, Massachusetts 2011
Mahan, Alfred Thayer, *The Influence of Sea Power Upon History*, 1660–1783,
    Dover Publications, Mineola, New York 1987
Manwaring, G. B., *If We Return: Letters of a Soldier of Kitchener's Army*, John
    Lane Company, London 1918
Margutti, Albert von, *La Tragédie des Habsbourg*, Bibl. Rhombus, Vienna
    1923
Marx, Karl and Engels, Friedrich, *Collected Works of Karl Marx and Friedrich
    Engels, 1845-4*, Vol. 9, International Publishers, New York 1976
Massie, Robert K., *Dreadnought*, Ballantine Books, London 1992
Masterman, Charles, *The Condition of England*, Ulan Press, Red Lion,
    Pennsylvania 2012
May, Ernest R., *Knowing One's Enemies: Intelligence Assessment Before the Two
    World Wars*, Princeton University Press, New Jersey 1986
Mead, Gary, *The Good Soldier: A Biography of Douglas Haig*, Atlantic Books,
    London
2007
Meredith, Martin, *The State of Africa: A History of Fifty Years of Independence*,
    Simon & Schuster, New York 2007
Miller, S., Lynn-Jones, S., and Van Evera, S., (eds), *Military Strategy and the
    Origins of the First World War*, Princeton University Press, New Jersey
    1991
Moltke, Helmuth von, Essays, Speeches, and Memoirs of Field Marshal
    Count Helmuth von Moltke, Vol. 1 of 2 (Classic Reprint), Forgotten
    Books, Hong Kong 2012
Mombauer, Annika, *Helmuth von Moltke and the Origins of the First World
    War*, Cambridge University Press, Cambridge 2005
Mombauer, Annika, *The Origins of the First World War: Controversies and
    Consensus*, Routledge, Oxford 2002
Murray, W., Knox, A., and Bernstein, M., *The Making of Strategy: Rulers,
    States and War*, Cambridge University Press, Cambridge 1996
Neillands, Robin, *The Death of Glory: The Western Front 1915*, John Murray,
    London 2006

Neilson, Keith, *Britain and the Last Tsar: British Policy and Russia, 1894–1917*, Oxford University Press, Oxford 1995

Nesbitt, Cathleen, *A Little Love and Good Company*, Faber & Faber, London 1975

Ninčić, Momčilo, *La Crise bosniaque (1908–1909) et les puissances européennes*, Impr. R. Bussière 1937

Olson, James, (ed.), *Historical Dictionary of European Imperialism*, Greenwood Publishing, Westport, Connecticut 1991

Orwell, George, 'Such, Such Were the Joys', in *The Collected Essays, Journalism and Letters*, Harcourt Trade Publishers, Boston 1971

Maximilian Ehnl Edwin Sacken (Freiherr von.), Bundesministerium für Landesverteidigung, *Österreich-Ungarns letzter Krieg 1914–1918*, vol. 1, Verlag der Militärwissenschaftlichen Mitteilungen, Vienna 1930

Pakenham, Thomas, *The Scramble for Africa: White Man's Conquest of the Dark Continent from 1876 to 1912*, Avon Books, New York 1992

Paléologue, Maurice, *An Ambassador's Memoirs*, (transl. by Holt, Frederic), George H. Doran Company, New York 2008

Payen, Fernand, *Raymond Poincaré: l'homme, le parlementaire, l'avocat*, Bernard Grasset, Paris 1936

Peck, James F., *The Studios of Paris: William Bourguereau and his American Students*, Yale University Press, New Haven, Connecticut 2006

Peden, George C., *Arms, Economics and British Strategy: From Dreadnoughts to Hydrogen Bombs*, Cambridge University Press, Cambridge 2009

Prete, Roy A., *Strategy and Command: The Anglo-French Coalition on the Western Front, 1914*, McGill-Queen's University Press, Montreal/Kingston, 2009

Putnam, William Lowell, *The Kaiser Merchant Ships in World War I*, McFarland & Co, Jefferson, North Carolina 2001

Remak, Joachim, *Sarajevo: the Story of a Political Murder*, BiblioBazaar, Charleston, South Carolina 2011

Remak, Joachim, *The First World War: Causes, conduct, consequences*, Wiley, Hoboken, New Jersey 1971

Ritter, Gerhard, *The Schlieffen Plan: Critique of a Myth*, Praeger, New York 1958

Rothenburg, Gunther, *The Army of Francis Joseph*, Purdue University Press, West Lafayette 1976

Rubin, William, *Picasso and Braque: Pioneering Cubism*, Museum of Modern Art, New York 1989

Sazonov, Sergei, *Fateful Years, 1909–1916; the Reminiscences of Serge Sazonov*, Jonathan Cape, London 1928

Schlieffen, Alfred von, *Military Writings* (transl. by Foley, Robert), Frank Cass, London 2003

Schmitt, Bernadotte Everly, *The Annexation of Bosnia, 1908–1909*, Howard Fertig, New York 1971

Schmitt, Bernadotte Everly, *The Coming of the War, 1914*, C. Scribner's sons, New York 1930

Scott, C. P., *The Political Diaries of C. P. Scott*, Wilson, Trevor (ed.), Collins, London 1970

Siebert, B. de, *Entente Diplomacy and the World: Matrix of the history of Europe, 1904–14*, Knickerbocker Press, London 1921

Seton-Watson, Robert, *Sarajevo: A Study in the Origins of the Great War*, Hutchinson, London 1925

Shackelford, Micheal [sic], *The Black Hand: The Secret Serbian Terrorist Society*, Brigham Young University, Provo, Utah

Sheldon, Jack, *The German Army at Ypres 1914*, Pen & Sword Military, Barnsley, South Yorkshire 2010

Showalter, Walter, *Tannenberg: Clash of Empires 1914*, Potomac Books, Dulles, Virginia 2004

Simkins, Peter, *Kitchener's Army: The Raising of the New Armies 1914–1916*, Pen & Sword, Barnsley, South Yorkshire, 2007

Sladen, Douglas Brooke Wheelton, *Germany's Great Lie: The official German justification of the war exposed and criticized*, Hutchinson, London 1914

Smith, David James, *One Morning in Sarajevo: 28 June 1914*, Phoenix Press, London 2009

Sondhaus, Lawrence, *Franz Conrad von Hötzendorf: Architect of the Apocalypse*, Brill Academic Publishers, Leiden, Netherlands 2000

Sosnosky, Theodor von, *Franz Ferdinand. Der Erzherzog-Thronfolger. Ein Lebensbild*, Verlag Von R. Oldenbourg, Munich 1929

Sparrow, Geoffrey, On Four Fronts with the Royal Naval Division, Hodder & Stoughton, London 1918

Spears, Edward, *Liaison 1914*, Cassell, London 2001

Stallworthy, Jon (ed.), *Wilfred Owen: The War Poems*, Chatto & Windus, London 1994

Stanojević, Stanoje, *History of Bosnia and Herzegovina*, Belgrade

Stegemann, Hermann, *Geschichte des Krieges*, Deutsche Verlags-Anstalt, Munich 1918

Steinberg, Jonathan, *Bismarck: A Life*, Oxford University Press, USA 2013

Steiner, Zara, *Britain and the Origins of the First World War*, Macmillan, London 1977

Steiner and Neilson, *Britain and Origins of the First World War*, Palgrave Macmillan, London 2003

Stevenson, David, *Armaments and the Coming of War: Europe, 1904–1914*, Oxford University Press, Oxford 2000

Stevenson, David, *1914–1918: The History of the First World War*, Penguin, London 2005

Stone, Norman, *The Eastern Front: 1914–1917*, Penguin Global, USA 2004

Strachan, Hew, *The First World War*, Penguin, London 2005

Strachan, Hew, *The First World War: Volume I: To Arms*, Oxford University Press, USA 2003

Sulzberger, Cyrus Leo, *The Fall of Eagles*, Crown Publishers, New York 1977

Tabouis, Geneviève, *The Life of Jules Cambon*, Jonathan Cape, London 1938

Taube, Mikhail, *Der grossen Katastrophe entgegen. Die russische Politik der Vorkriegszeit und das Ende des Zarenreiches (1904–1917)*, K. F. Koehler, Leipzig 1937

Taylor, A. J. P., *War by Timetable: How the First World War Began*, Endeavour

Press, London 2013

Taylor, A. J. P., *Habsburg Monarchy, 1809–1918: A History of the Austrian Empire and Austria-Hungary*, Penguin, London 1990

Terrain, John, *The Western Front – 1914–1918*, Pen & Sword, Barnsley, South Yorkshire 1960

Terraine, John, *Mons: The Retreat to Victory*, Pen & Sword, Barnsley, South Yorkshire 2010

Tirpitz, Alfred von, *My Memoirs*, Nabu Press, Charleston, South Carolina 2010

Treitschke, Heinrich von, (transl. by Gowans, Adam), *Selections from Treitschke's Lectures on Politics*, Cornell University Library, New York 2009

Trevelyan, G. M., *Grey of Fallodon*, Longmans, London 1937

Tuchman, Barbara, *The Guns of August*, Presidio Press, New York 2004

Tyng, Sewell, *The Campaign of the Marne 1914*, Humphrey Milford, London 1935

Unruh, Fritz von, *Way of Sacrifice*, (transl. by Macartney, Carlile Aylmer), Alfred A. Knopf, New York 1928

Van der Poel, John, *The Jameson Raid*, Oxford University Press, Oxford 1951

Wall, Richard and Winter, Jay, *The Upheaval of War: Family, Work and Welfare in Europe, 1914–1918*, Cambridge University Press, Cambridge 1988

Warner, Philip, *Kitchener: The Man Behind the Legend*, Hamish Hamilton, London 1985

Waterhouse, Michael, *Edwardian Requiem: A Life of Sir Edward Grey*, Biteback Publishing, London 2013

Wharton, Edith, *Fighting France: From Dunkerque to Belport*, Echo Library, Fairford, Gloucester 2006

Whitlock, Brand, *Belgium Under the German Occupation: A Personal Narrative*, William Heinemann, London 1919

Wilson, Keith, *Decision for War, 1914*, UCL Press, London 1995

Wilson, Keith, *The Policy of the Entente: Essays on the Determinants of British Foreign Policy 1904–1914*, Cambridge University Press, Cambridge 1985

Winter, Jay, *Sites of Memory, Sites of Mourning: The Great War in European Cultural History*, Cambridge University Press, Cambridge 1995

Winter, Jay, *The Great War and the British People*, Palgrave Macmillan, London 2003

Wohl, Robert, *The Generation of 1914*, Harvard University Press, Cambridge, Massachusetts 2009

Wolff, Theodor, *The Eve of 1914*, Alfred A. Knopf, New York 1936

Wolpert, S., *Morley and India, 1906–1910*, University of California Press, Berkeley 1967

Zuber, Terence, *Inventing the Schlieffen Plan: German War Planning 1871–1914*, Oxford University Press, Oxford 2010

MEMOIRS, DIARIES, LETTERS, PERSONAL PAPERS

Britain

Aitken, Martha, Diary, Private Papers of Mrs M. Withhall (née Aitken), Document 17423, Imperial War Museum, London

Benson, Arthur Christopher, Diary, Pepys Library, Magdalene College, Cambridge University

Bradbury, Edward, VC, Imperial War Museum, London

Butcher, E. S., Diary, Private Papers, Document 6344, Imperial War Museum, London

Buckle, Archibald Walter, DSO (and Three Bars), 'Pen Picture by his youngest son Lionel Buckle', biographical sketch, Imperial War Museum, London; and Service Records, National Archives, Kew

Cavell, Edith, various papers and documents, Imperial War Museum, London

Cave-Orme, R. W., Private Papers, Document 4271 83/43/1, Imperial War Museum, London

Hodder, H. G. 'Bim', Letters in *The Pelican* (1914), school magazine, The Perse School, Cambridge

Lloyd-Burch, David, Private Papers, Document 1423 87/26/1, Imperial War Museum, London

Naylor, Jim, Private Papers, Document 2352 86/21/1, Imperial War Museum, London

Nelson, David, VC, 'Account of the Practical Annihilation of 'L' Battery, Royal Horse Artillery, at Nery, Oise, on 1st Septr, 1914', personal recollection; and 'The Victoria Cross', in O'Moore, Creagh & Humphris, E. M., The Times History of the War – VC Supplement, Imperial War Museum

Owen, Rowland Hely, Private Papers, Document 748, Imperial War Museum, London

Tisdall, Arthur, VC, 'RND Personality', extract from a report by Heald, David, in *The Gallipolian*, No 71 (Spring 1973), pp. 634-40; see also: Tisdall, Arthur, Private Papers, Document 82/3049, Imperial War Museum, London

West, W. F., 'Experiences whilst Prisoner of War in Germany From August 1914 till December 1918', Private Papers, Document 1767 92/10/1, Imperial War Museum, London

Wollocombe, T. S., Private Papers, Document 130 89/7/1, Imperial War Museum, London

France

Benoit, Charles, Police Reports of Charles Benoit, an anti-militarist, File B-a 1694, Archive Centre of the Police Prefecture of Paris. See also: www.maitron.org

Clément, Raymond, 'Brancardiers, bras cassés!', Journal, Aug–Dec 1914, Service Historique de la Défense de Vincenne

Dazin, Bernardine, 'Récit d'une femme sous l'occupation allemande en Picardie', Journal, Aug–Dec 1914, 1 réference, inventaire physique 047829, Museum of the Great War, Péronne

Marie Dubois (née Delabre), Letters, Aug 1914–April 1915, 139 réferences, inventaire physique – une sélection de 043062 à 043470, Museum of the Great War, Péronne

Fossey, Emile, 'Souvenirs de guerre 1914-1918', Journal, Aug 1914 – April 1915, 1 réference, inventaire physique 033157, Service Historique de la Défense de Vincenne

Leroi, Maurice, Letters, Golden Book (extract) and Death Notification, Aug–Dec 1914, Service Historique de la Défense de Vincenne

Michel, Marie and Henri, Letters and Journal, Aug–Nov 1914, Museum of the Great War, Péronne

Trichereau, Jérémie, Letters, Aug–Dec 1914, 68 réferences, inventaire physique – une sélection de 068686 à 068763, Museum of the Great War, Péronne

Unknown Woman, 'Letter to Loup – A Letter for Louis Bally', Letter, 29 Aug 1914, Museum of the Great War, Péronne

Germany

Baumann, Hermann, 'War Diary, 1914-1916', (ed. Magdalena Huck; transl. by Grieswelle, Martha, née Baumann), Document 300,10/collection military history, number 177, Archive Bielefeld, North-Rhine Westphalia

Delius, Walter, 'Kriegserinnerungen [war memories] 1914–1918,' *Collated from letters and diary entries*, Document 300,5/HgB, number 8, Archive Bielefeld, North-Rhine Westphalia

Krause, Ludwig Johann Eduard, *Diary*, Document 161, City Archive, Rostock

Meyersiek, Pastor, *Letters to the soldiers*, Document 300,10/collection military history, number 339, Archive Bielefeld, North-Rhine Westphalia

Oetjen, Hinrich, *War Diary*, August 1914 – May 1915, Document 7500-291, State Archive, Bremen

Schulze Smidt, Arthur, *War Diaries*, Booklet I–V (1914–1915), State Archive, Bremen

Unknown soldier, extract, 'Battle of Ypres [1914]', *Diary*, Document 300,10/collection military history, number 231, Archive Bielefeld, North-Rhine Westphalia

Unknown soldiers, *Field postcards home*, Document 300,10/collection military history, numbers 88, 331, Archive Bielefeld, North-Rhine Westphalia

DIGITAL SOURCES

Academic journals/research papers digitised on:

The CEDIAS, Centre d'Etudes, de Documentation, d'Information et d'Action Sociale, Paris: http://www.cedias.org

JSTOR: http://www.jstor.org

Oxford University Press (Journals): http://www.oxfordjournals.org

Sage: http://www.sagepublications.com

Wiley Online: http://onlinelibrary.wiley.com

Autograph Letter Collection: Women's Suffrage, The National Archives, Britain: http://www.nationalarchives.gov.uk/a2a/records. aspx?cat=106-901&cid=1035#1035

Asquith, Herbert, 'The war, its causes and its messages': Five speeches by the Prime Minister, August-October 1914:

HANSARD 1803–2005

Summary information for Mr Herbert Asquith

People (A): http://hansard.millbanksystems.com/people/a

The Bryce Report: http://avalon.law.yale.edu/20th_century/brycere.asp

Crowe, E., Memorandum on the present state of relations with France and Germany, British Documents on the Origins of the War, Vol III, 'The Testing of the Entente': http://tmh.floonet.net/pdf/eyre_crowe_memo.p

The German Naval Programme, 1912-1913: http://www.manorhouse.clara. net/book3/chapter17.htm

Gooch, G. P. and Temperley, H., (eds), *British Official Documents on the Origins of the War*, His Majesty's Stationery Office, London 1928. See also: http://www.gwpda.org/

The Hague Convention 1907: http://www.icrc.org/applic/ihl/ihl.nsf/Treaty. xsp?documentId=4D47F92DF3966A7EC12563CD002D6788&action= openDocument

Hansard, British Parliamentary Debates: http://hansard.millbanksystems. com/sittings/1910s

Harrach, Count Franz von, 'Memoir of assassination of Archduke Franz Ferdinand', cited in: http://www.firstworldwar.com/source/harrachmem-oir.htm

Hemphill, Alexander J., *Belgium under the surface,* The Commission for Relief in Belgium [1914-1918]: http://digital.library.wisc.edu/1711.dl/History. BelSurface

Meurer, Christian & Mayence, Fernand, 'The Blame for the Sack of Louvain' *Current History*, Vol. 28, no. 4., (July 1928), pp. 556-571: http://net.lib.byu. edu/estu/wwi/PDFs/Sack%20of%20Louvain.pdf

Passelecq, Fernand, 'The Sincere Chancellor' (an analysis of the interview between the British Ambassador Sir Edward Goschen and the German Chancellor, Theobald von Bethmann-Hollweg on 4 August 1914), *Nineteenth Century and After*, 1917, University of North Carolina Press, Open Library: http://archive.org/details/sincerechancello00pass

Wils, Eric, *The (63rd) Royal Naval Division – Sailors in the First World War*

Trenches, (transl. by Blokland, Guido): http://www.wereldoorlog1418.nl/
RND-Royal-Naval-Division/index.html

Smith, J. Taylor, *The war. Our sailors and soldiers: the Chaplain-General's
call for mid-day prayer*, Society for Propagating Christian Knowledge,
1914–1918: http://digital.library.wisc.edu/1711.dl/History.ChapGenPray

Wadstein, Elis, *Joseph Bédier's 'crimes allemands'*, A. Kroch & Co., 1916: The
German testimonials about German atrocities: http://digital.library.wisc.
edu/1711.dl/History.Wadstein

WWI Document Archive: http://wwi.lib.byu.edu/index.php/Main_Page -
follow links to:

- The Haig Debate:

Phillips, Gervase, Haig: The Great Captain, 1998

Miller, George, Haig: *Was* He a Great Captain? 1996

- Herbert, Aubrey, Mons, ANZAC & Kut, Hutchinson & Co, London 1919,
extract published on WWI archive: http://net.lib.byu.edu/estu//wwi/
memoir/Mons/mons.htm

- Records of national diplomatic communication: *The Belgian Grey Book, The
French Yellow Book, The German White Book, The Russian Orange Book,
The Serbian Blue Book, The Austro-Hungarian Red Book*, see also: http://
www.gwpda.org/

- Pratt, Edwin A. *The Rise of Rail-Power in War and Conquest* [extract]

- Rawes, Edward, October 1999: A Chronology of the Mediation Attempts in
July 1914

- Timeline of Events Leading to War: http://wwi.lib.byu.edu/index.php/
Timeline_of_Events

- Wilhelm II's War Speeches – Speech from the Balcony of the Royal
Palace, Berlin, August 1, 1914: http://wwi.lib.byu.edu/index.php/
Wilhelm_II%27s_War_Speeches

- The Willy-Nicky Telegrams: http://wwi.lib.byu.edu/index.php/
The_Willy-Nicky_Telegrams

ESSAYS, ARTICLES AND RESEARCH PAPERS

Andrew, Christopher, 'France and the Making of the Entente Cordial', *The
Historical Journal*, 10 (1), (1967), pp. 89-105

Coogan, John W. & Coogan, Peter F., 'The British Cabinet and the Anglo-
French Staff Talks, 1905-1914: Who Knew What and When Did He
Know It?', *The Journal of British Studies*, 24 (1), (January 1985), pp.
110-131

Cosgrove, Richard A., 'A Note on Lloyd George's Speech at the
Mansion House, 21 July 1911', *The Historical Journal*, 12 (1969)

Crockaert, Jacques, 'L'Ultimatum allemand du 2 août 1914', *Le Flambeau* 5,
No. 3 (March 1922), pp. 307-330

Curtis, V.J., 'Understanding Schlieffen,' *The Army Doctrine and Training Bulletin* 6, no. 3 (2003)

Doughty, Robert A., 'French Strategy in 1914: Joffre's Own', *The Journal of Military History*, Vol. 67, No. 2 (April 2003), Society for Military History, pp. 427-454

Ekstein, Michael, 'Some Notes on Sir Edward Grey's Policy in July 1914', *The Historical Journal*, Vol. 15, No. 2 (June 1972), Cambridge University Press, pp. 321-324

Ekstein, Michael, 'Sir Edward Grey and Imperial Germany in 1914', *Journal of Contemporary History*, Vol. 6, No. 3 (1971), Sage Publication, pp. 121-131

Farrar, L. L., 'The Limits of Choice: July 1914 Reconsidered', *The Journal of Conflict Resolution*, Vol. 16, No. 1 (March 1972), Sage Publications, pp. 1-23

Fay, Sidney Bradshaw, 'New Light on the Origins of the World War I. Berlin and Vienna, to July 29', *The American Historical Review*, Vol. 25, No. 4 (July 1920), Oxford University Press on behalf of the American Historical Association, pp. 616-639

Ferguson, Niall, 'Germany and the Origins of the First World War: New Perspectives', *The Historical Journal*, Vol. 35, No. 3 (September 1992), Cambridge University Press, pp. 725-752

French, John Denton Pinkstone, *The Despatches of Sir John French*, Chapman & Hall, London 1914

Friedberg, Aaron L., 'Britain and the experience of relative decline, 1895-1905', *Journal of Strategic Studies*, 10 (3), (September 1987), pp. 331-362

Foley, Robert, 'Preparing the German Army for the First World War: The Operational Ideas of Alfred von Schlieffen and Helmuth von Moltke the Younger', *War & Society*, Vol. 22, No. 2 (Oct 2004), University of New South Wales

Foley, Robert, 'The Real Schlieffen Plan', *War in History*, Vol. 13, Issue 1 (2006), pp. 91–115.

Gilbert, Bentley B., 'Pacifist to Interventionist: David Lloyd George in 1911 and 1914. Was Belgium an Issue?' *The Historical Journal*, Vol. 28, No. 4 (December 1985), Cambridge University Press, pp. 863-885

Hale, Frederick A., 'Fritz Fischer and the Historiography of World War One', *The History Teacher*, Vol. 9, No. 2 (February 1976), Society for History Education, pp. 258-279

Hamilton, Keith A., 'The "Wild Talk" of Joseph Caillaux: A Sequel to the Agadir Crisis', *The International History Review*, Vol. 9, No. 2 (May 1987), Taylor & Francis, pp. 195-226

Herwig, Holger, 'From Tirpitz plan to Schlieffen plan: Some observations on German military planning', *Journal of Strategic Studies*, 9 (1), (March 1986), pp. 53-63

Herwig, Holger, 'Germany and the "Short-War" Illusion: Toward A New Interpretation?', *The Journal of Military History*, Vol. 66, No. 3, (July 2002)

Imlay, Talbot C., 'The Origins of the First World War', *The Historical Journal*, Vol. 49, No. 4 (December, 2006), Cambridge University Press, pp.

1253-1271

Jarausch, Konrad, 'Revising German History: Bethmann Hollweg Revisited', *Central European History*, Vol. 21, No. 3 (September 1988), Cambridge University Press, pp. 224-243

Jarausch, Konrad, 'The Illusion of Limited War: Chancellor Bethmann Hollweg's Calculated Risk, July 1914', *Central European History*, Vol. 2, No. 1 (March 1969), Cambridge University Press on behalf of Conference Group for Central European History of the American Historical Association, pp. 48-76

Judah, Tim, 'The Serbs: The Sweet and Rotten Smell of History', *Daedalus*, Vol. 126, No. 3, A New Europe for the Old? (Summer 1997), The MIT Press, pp. 23-45

Kaiser, David E., 'Germany and the Origins of the First World War', *The Journal of Modern History*, Vol. 55, No. 3 (September 1983), The University of Chicago Press, pp. 442-474

Kann, Robert, 'Emperor William II and Archduke Francis Ferdinand in Their Correspondence', *The American Historical Review*, Vol. 57, No. 2 (January 1952), Oxford University Press on behalf of the American Historical Association, pp. 323-351

Kennedy, Paul, 'Idealists and Realists: British Views of Germany, 1864-1939', *Transactions of the Royal Historical Society*, 5 (25), (1975), pp. 137-156

Kerensky, Alexander, 'Izvolsky's Personal Diplomatic Correspondence', *The Slavonic and East European Review*, Vol. 16, No. 47 (January 1938)

Langdon, John W., 'Emerging from Fischer's Shadow: Recent Examinations of the Crisis of July 1914', *The History Teacher*, Vol. 20, No. 1 (November 1986), Society for History Education, pp. 63-86

Lewis, John, 'Conrad in 1914', *The Polish Review*, Vol. 20, No. 2/3, Joseph Conrad: Commemorative Essays: The Selected Proceedings of the International Conference of Conrad Scholars, 1974 (1975), University of Illinois Press on behalf of the Polish Institute of Arts & Sciences of America , pp. 217-222

Lingelbach, William E., [Untitled], *The American Historical Review*, Vol. 39, No. 2 (January 1934), Oxford University Press on behalf of the American Historical Association, pp. 333-335

Lyon, James M.B., '"A Peasant Mob": The Serbian Army on the Eve of the Great War', *The Journal of Military History*, Vol. 61, No. 3 (July 1997), Society for Military History, pp. 481-502

Neilson, Keith, 'My Beloved Russians', *The International History Review*, Vol. 9, No. 4 (November 1987)

Röhl, J. C. G., 'Admiral von Müller and the Approach of War, 1911-1914', *The Historical Journal*, Vol. 12, No. 4 (December 1969), Cambridge University Press, pp. 651-673

Remak, Joachim, '1914 – The Third Balkan War: Origins Reconsidered', *The Journal of Modern History*, Vol. 43, No. 3 (September 1971), The University of Chicago Press, pp. 353-366

Schmitt, Bernadotte E., 'Triple Alliance and Triple Entente, 1902-1914', *The American Historical Review*, Vol. 29, No. 3 (April 1924), Oxford

University Press, pp. 449-473

Schmitt, Bernadotte E., 'The Origins of the War of 1914', *The Journal of Modern History*, Vol. 24, No. 1 (March, 1952), The University of Chicago Press, pp. 69-74

Schmitt, Bernadotte E., 'July 1914: Thirty Years After', *The Journal of Modern History*, Vol. 16, No. 3 (September 1944), The University of Chicago Press, pp. 169-204

Schmitt, Bernadotte E., 'July 1914 Once More', *The Journal of Modern History*, Vol. 13, No. 2 (June 1941), The University of Chicago Press, pp. 225-236

Schmitt, Bernadotte E., 'The First World War, 1914-1918', *Proceedings of the American Philosophical Society*, Vol. 103, No. 3 (June 15, 1959), American Philosophical Society, pp. 321-331

Smith, Jeffrey R., 'The Monarchy versus the Nation: The "Festive Year" 1913 in Wilhelmine Germany', *German Studies Review*, Vol. 23, No. 2 (May 2000)

Stevenson, David, 'War by Timetable? The Railway Race before 1914', *Past & Present*, No. 162 (February 1999), Oxford University Press on behalf of the Past and Present Society, Oxford, pp. 163-194

Stevenson, David, 'Battlefield or Barrier? Rearmament and Military Planning in Belgium, 1902-1914', *The International History Review*, Vol. 29, No. 3 (September 2007), Taylor & Francis, pp. 473-507

Stone, Norman, 'Hungary and the Crisis of July 1914', *Journal of Contemporary History*, Vol. 1, No. 3, 1914 (July 1966), Sage Publications, pp. 153-170

Stone, Norman, 'Moltke-Conrad: Relations between the Austro-Hungarian and German General Staffs, 1909-14', *The Historical Journal*, Vol. 9, No. 2 (1966), Cambridge University Press, pp. 201-228

Stowell, Ellery C., [Untitled], *The American Historical Review*, Vol. 21, No. 3 (April 1916), Oxford University Press on behalf of the American Historical Association, pp. 596-600

Swallow, Douglas Muir, 'Transitions in British Editorial Germanophobia 1899–1914: A Case Study of J. L. Garvin, Leo Maxse and St. Loe Strachey', *Open Access Dissertations and Theses*, Paper 619, 1980.

Taylor, A. J. P., 'Accident Prone, or What Happened Next', *The Journal of Modern History*, Vol. 49, No. 1 (March 1977), The University of Chicago Press, pp. 1-18

Taylor, A. J. P., [Untitled], *The English Historical Review*, Vol. 69, No. 270 (January 1954), Oxford University Press, pp. 122-125

Tomaszewski, Fiona, 'Pomp, Circumstance, and Realpolitik: The Evolution of the Triple Entente of Russia, Great Britain, and France', *Jahrbücher für Geschichte Osteuropas*, Neue Folge, Bd. 47, H. 3 (1999), Franz Steiner Verlag, pp. 362-380

Trumpener, Ulrich, 'War Premeditated? German Intelligence Operations in July 1914', *Central European History*, Vol. 9, No. 1 (March 1976), Cambridge University Press, pp. 58-85

Turner, L.C.F., 'The Russian Mobilization in 1914', *Journal of Contemporary History*, Vol. 3, No. 1 (Jan., 1968), Sage Publications, pp. 65-88

Valone, Stephen, 'There Must Be Some Misunderstanding: Sir Edward Grey's Diplomacy of August 1, 1914', *Journal of British Studies*, Vol. 27, No. 4 (October 1988), Cambridge University Press, pp. 405-424

Wank, Solomon, 'Desperate Counsel in Vienna in July 1914: Berthold Molden's Unpublished Memorandum', *Central European History*, Vol. 26, No. 3 (1993), Cambridge University Press on behalf of Conference Group for Central European History of the American Historical Association, pp. 281-310

Wegerer, Alfred von, 'The Russian Mobilization of 1914', *Political Science Quarterly*, Vol. 43, No. 2 (June 1928), The Academy of Political Science, pp. 201-228

Wesseling, H. L., 'Commotion at the Sorbonne: The Debate on the French University, 1910–1914', *European Review*, 9 (2001)

Williamson Jr, Samuel R., 'Influence, Power, and the Policy Process: The Case of Franz Ferdinand, 1906-1914', *The Historical Journal*, Vol. 17, No. 2 (June 1974), Cambridge University Press, pp. 417-434

Williamson Jr, Samuel R., 'German perceptions of the Triple Entente after 1911', *Foreign Policy Analysis*, Vol. 7, Issue 2 (April 2011), Wiley Online Library, pp. 205-214

Williamson Jr, Samuel R., 'The Reign of Sir Edward Grey as British Foreign Secretary', *The International History Review*, Vol. 1, No. 3 (July 1979), Taylor & Francis, pp. 426-438

Williamson Jr, Samuel R., 'The Origins of World War I', *The Journal of Interdisciplinary History*, Vol. 18, No. 4, (The Origin and Prevention of Major Wars, Spring 1988), The MIT Press, pp. 795-818

Williamson Jr, Samuel R. & May, Ernest R., 'An Identity of Opinion: Historians and July 1914', *The Journal of Modern History*, Vol. 79, No. 2 (June 2007), The University of Chicago Press, pp. 335-387

Wilson, Keith, 'The Foreign Office and the "Education" of Public Opinion before the First World War', *The Historical Journal*, Vol. 26, No. 2 (June 1983), Cambridge University Press, pp. 403-411

NEWSPAPERS, MAGAZINES

Action Française, March 1913 – July 1914 (French newspaper)
The Bystander, September 1914 (British magazine)
Czernowitz Allgemeine Zeitung, August 1914 (German newspaper in Chernivtsi, Ukraine)
Der Bauernbündler, 1 August 1914 (Farmers' Union newspaper, southern Austria)
Daheim, August-September 1914 (German newspaper)
Daily Express, 1914
Daily Mail, 1914
Daily Mirror, 1914
Die Neue Zeitung, July-August 1914 (German-Austrian newspaper)

Évolution, October 1933 (French journal)
Le Figaro, 1912-1914 (French newspaper)
L'Humanité, 1914 (French newspaper)
The Literary Digest, 1912 (British magazine)
The Manchester Guardian, 1912-14 (and *The Guardian*, various years)
Le Matin, 1914 (French newspaper)
Marburger Zeitung, August 1914 (city of Marburger's newspaper)
Oesterreichische Volkszeitung, July-August 1914 (Austrian newspaper)
Paris-Midi, March 1913 – July 1914 (French newspaper)
Pester Lloyd, 1914 (Budapest newspaper)
Le Petit Parisien, 1914 (French newspaper)
Le Temps, March 1913 – July 1914 (French newspaper)
The Times, 1912-1914 (and various years)
Wiener Zeitung, 1914 (Viennese newspaper)
Wolff Bureau, 1914 (German news agency)

INDEX

Gallieni, General Joseph, 504–7, 510, 512, 514–19, 522, 528
Gallipoli, 242
Galsworthy, John, 502
Geiss, Imanuel, 118
Gerde, Dr Edmund, 248
German Army, 17, 83, 184, 220–1, 238, 496, 500, 532
  Army Group Fabeck, 568–9
  atrocities in Belgium, 442–52
  Eastern front, 535–50
  Eighth Army, 531, 535, 538, 541, 546, 548
  First Army, 434, 468, 476, 496, 516, 523
  Fourth Army, 562, 565
  invasion of Belgium, 395–8, 432–4
  Iron Crosses, 549
  Marne campaign, 508–29, 531
  Second Army, 434, 440, 509
  Serbia, 532
  Sixth Army, 561, 565
  Tannenberg, 534–50
  Third Army, 434, 440, 523
  Ypres, 560, 562–74
Germanophobia, 108–21, 153, 170
Germany, 9, 10, 26–34, 50–62, 142–3
  acceleration towards war, 318–20
  Army see German Army
  'blank cheque' to Austria-Hungary, 262, 265, 266–74, 306, 602–3
  Britain declaring war on, 410–12
  casualties, 442, 549, 568, 571, 572, 601
  colonies, 27, 29–34, 56
  declaration of war on France, 360, 369, 373–85, 615–16
  declaration of war on Russia, 362–72, 531
  Dual Alliance, 46, 47, 51
  economy, 15, 230
  Entente Cordiale, reaction to, 101–3
  first Reich, 27–34
  foreign trade, 60
  formation of, 27–8
  German Youth Movement, 421
  ill-preparedness for war, 354
  Military Code, 446
  mood in 1914, 228, 230
  Navy, 61–2, 82, 110, 187–98, 220
  Navy League, 192

  neo-mercantilism, 59
  population, 59
  press lies about France, 380–1
  railways, 84, 85, 354
  Reinsurance Treaty with Russia, 55, 69
  relationship with Europe, 80
  Russia, view of, 51–2
  Triple Alliance, 47–9, 56, 68, 99, 104, 142, 201, 210, 220, 245, 261, 265, 347
  ultimatum to Belgium, 391–3, 620–1
  willingness to die for, 420–2
Gheluvelt, 569–71
Giesl von Gieslingen, General, 287–8, 293, 307, 308, 315, 316
Gilbert, Martin, 532
Gladstone, William, 22, 31, 56, 64, 110, 387, 636
Godley, Private Sidney, 477
Gordon Highlanders, 484
Gorky, Maxim, 228, 232
Goschen, Sir Edward, 241, 324, 342, 344–5, 348, 407–11, 633–4
Gough, Hubert, 561
Grabež, Trifko, 251, 253, 278, 609
Grand Duke Alexander, 231
Graves, Robert, 573, 579, 583
Grbic, Budivoj, 609
Great Britain see Britain
Greece, 205, 212, 213, 600
Grenfell, Captain Francis, 481
Grey, Edward, 74, 105, 109–12, 114, 120, 133, 155–60, 168–72, 174, 182, 196, 212, 213, 214, 217, 235–45, 256, 280, 300–2, 305, 306, 307, 312, 313, 317, 318, 320–5, 329, 342–5, 348–51, 364–5, 367, 374, 375, 387, 399–410, 592, 593, 626, 628
  address to parliament, 402–7, 628–40
  four-way talks, 235–45, 343–4
  last minute peace talks, 367, 593
Grierson, Sir James, 473
Griesinger, Baron von, 296
Grimwood Mears, Sir Edward, 449, 450, 451
Groener, Wilhelm, 354
Gruner, Private Richard, 450
Guchkov, A. J., 549
Guillaumin, Armand, 5